AutoCADLT
Fundamentals and Applications

by

Ted Saufley
AutoCAD Certified Instructor
Clackamas Community College
Oregon City, OR

Certified Instructor

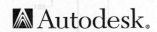
Registered Author/Publisher

Windows 3.1
(formerly Release 2)

Publisher
The Goodheart-Willcox Company, Inc.
Tinley Park, Illinois

Copyright 1997

by

THE GOODHEART-WILLCOX COMPANY, INC.

All rights reserved. No part of this book may be reproduced, stored in a retrieval system, or transmitted in any form or by any means, electronic, mechanical, photocopying, recording, or otherwise, without the prior written permission of The Goodheart-Willcox Company, Inc. Manufactured in the United States of America.

Library of Congress Catalog Card Number 96-14940
International Standard Book Number 1-56637-322-0

1 2 3 4 5 6 7 8 9 10   97   00 99 98 97 96

Library of Congress Cataloging-in-Publication Data
Saufley, Ted
    AutoCAD LT : fundamentals and applications : release 2 for Windows / by Ted Saufley.

        p. cm.
    ISBN 1-56637-322-0
    1. Computer graphics. 2. AutoCAD LT for Windows.

I. Title.
T385.S27 1996
604.2'0285'5369--dc20   96-14940
                                                                CIP

INTRODUCTION

AutoCAD LT—Fundamentals and Applications is a text and workbook combination that provides complete instruction in mastering AutoCAD LT™ commands and drawing techniques. Typical applications of AutoCAD LT are presented with basic and advanced concepts. The topics are covered in an easy-to-understand sequence, and progress in a way that allows you to become comfortable with the commands as your knowledge builds from one chapter to the next. In addition, *AutoCAD LT—Fundamentals and Applications,* offers the following features:

- Step-by-step use of AutoCAD LT commands.
- Easily understandable explanations of how and why the commands function as they do.
- Numerous illustrations to reinforce concepts.
- Professional tips explaining how to use AutoCAD LT effectively and efficiently.
- Exercises and tutorials involving tasks to reinforce chapter section topics.
- Chapter tests for reviewing commands and key AutoCAD LT concepts.
- Chapter problems to supplement each chapter.

Objectives

It is the goal of *AutoCAD LT—Fundamentals and Applications* to provide a step-by-step approach in mastering AutoCAD LT commands. Each topic is presented in a logical sequence that permits the user to progress from the most basic drawing commands to the more advanced editing and dimensioning functions. Additionally, the reader also becomes acquainted with:

- Quick and efficient drawing construction techniques.
- Dimensioning applications and practices, as interpreted through accepted standards.
- Drawing sectional views and creating custom hatch patterns.
- Creating special shapes and symbols for multiple use.
- Isometric drawing and dimensioning practices.
- Plotting and printing drawings.
- Using the Windows File Manager for drawing file management.
- Customizing the AutoCAD LT graphical user environment and menu system.
- Using clipboard graphics and Object Linking and Embedding (OLE).

Fonts used in this text

Different type faces are used throughout the chapters to define terms and identify AutoCAD LT commands. Important terms always appear in ***bold-italic face, serif*** type. AutoCAD LT menus, commands, variables, dialog box names, and button names are printed in **bold-face, sans serif** type. Filenames, directory names, paths, and keyboard-entry items appear in the text in Roman, sans serif type. Keyboard keys are shown inside brackets [ ] and appear in Roman, sans serif type. For example, [Enter] means to press the Enter (Return) key.

Prompt sequences are set apart from the body text with space above and below, and appear in Roman, sans serif type. Keyboard entry items in prompts appear in **bold-face, sans serif** type. In prompts, the [Enter] key is represented by the enter symbol (↵).

Checking the AutoCAD LT User's Guide

No other AutoCAD LT reference should be needed when using this worktext. However, the author has referenced the major topic areas to the corresponding *AutoCAD LT User's Guide* chapters for your convenience. You will find the following abbreviation to the right of most major headings in this text:

ALTUG 8

The number to the right of each abbreviation identifies the related chapter in the *AutoCAD LT User's Guide*. For example, a reference such as ALTUG 8 refers to Chapter 8 of the *AutoCAD LT User's Guide*.

Introducing the AutoCAD LT commands

There are several ways to select AutoCAD LT drawing and editing commands. The format is slightly different when typing commands from the keyboard when compared to selecting commands from the toolbar, toolbox, or pull-down menus. For this reason, all AutoCAD LT commands and related options in this text are presented as if they were typed at the keyboard (unless otherwise specified). This allows you to see the full command name and the prompts that appear on screen. Since you are encouraged to enter commands in the most convenient manner, shortened command aliases are also presented.

Commands, options, and values you must enter are given in bold text as shown in the following example. Pressing the [Enter] key is indicated with the enter symbol (↵). (Also, refer to the earlier section *Fonts used in this text*.)

> Command: *(type* LINE *or* L *and press* [Enter]*)*
> From point: **2,2** ↵
> To point: **4,2** ↵
> To point: ↵

General input tasks such as picking a point or selecting an object are presented in italics.

> Command: *(type* LINE *or* L *and press* [Enter]*)*
> From point: *(pick a point)*
> To point: *(pick another point)*
> To point: ↵

Selecting commands from the pull-down menus is discussed and illustrated throughout the text. Where applicable, toolbar and toolbox button alternatives are also covered. These buttons are illustrated in the margin next to the text reference. The text will indicate where the button is located. As shown here, a grayscale button is used to represent an AutoCAD LT-related button.

Prerequisites

AutoCAD LT—Fundamentals and Applications has been developed for the user or student with experience using MS-DOS based personal computers. While prior exposure to Microsoft Windows is certainly helpful, it is by no means required. The text takes you through the entire AutoCAD LT command structure and applies AutoCAD LT functions to basic drafting concepts. Thus, readers should already possess a good working knowledge of drafting principles, such as orthographic projection, line and lettering standards, and industrial dimensioning practices.

Flexibility in design

Flexibility is the key word when using *AutoCAD LT—Fundamentals and Applications*. This worktext is an excellent training aid for individual, as well as classroom instruction. *AutoCAD LT—Fundamentals and Applications* teaches you AutoCAD LT and its applications to common drafting tasks. It is also a useful resource for professionals using AutoCAD LT in the work environment.

There are a variety of notices you will see throughout the text. These notices consist of technical information, hints, and cautions that will help you develop your AutoCAD LT skills. The notices that appear in the text are identified by icons and rules around the text. The notices are as follows:

PROFESSIONAL TIPS These are ideas and suggestions aimed at increasing your productivity and enhancing your use of AutoCAD LT commands and techniques.

NOTES A note alerts you to important aspects of the command or activity that is being discussed.

CAUTIONS A caution alerts you to potential problems if instructions or commands are used incorrectly, or if an action could corrupt or alter files, directories, or disks. If you are in doubt after reading a caution, always consult your instructor or supervisor.

The chapter exercises, tests, and drawing problems are set up to allow an instructor to select individual or group learning goals. Thus, the structure of *AutoCAD LT—Fundamentals and Applications* lends itself to the development of a course devoted entirely to AutoCAD LT training. To that end, several optional course syllabi are provided in the *Solution Manual* for you to use or revise to suit individual classroom needs.

AutoCAD LT—Fundamentals and Applications offers several ways for you to evaluate your performance. Included are:

- **Tutorials.** Several of the chapters include mini-tutorials that offer step-by-step instructions for producing AutoCAD LT drawings. The tutorials also serve to help reinforce key chapter concepts.
- **Exercises.** Each chapter is divided into short sections covering various aspects of AutoCAD LT. An exercise composed of several instructions is found at the end of most sections. These exercises help you become acquainted with the commands just introduced at your own pace.
- **Chapter Tests.** Each chapter also includes a written test. Questions may require you to provide the proper command, option, or response to perform a certain task.
- **Drawing Problems.** A variety of drawing problems follow each chapter. These problems are presented as "real-world" CAD drawings and, like some real-world applications, may contain mistakes, inaccuracies, or omissions. Always be sure to modify the drawings as needed and apply accurate dimensions to the completed drawings where required. The problems are designed to make you think, solve problems, research proper drafting standards, and correct possible errors in the drawings. Each drawing problem deals with one of five technical disciplines. Although doing all of the problems will enhance AutoCAD LT skills, you may have a particular discipline upon which you wish to focus. The discipline that a problem addresses is indicated by a text graphic in the margin next to the problem number. Each graphic and its description is as follows:

Mechanical Drafting	These problems address mechanical drafting and design applications, such as manufactured part design.
Architecture	These problems address architectural drafting and design applications, such as floor plans and presentation drawings.
Electronics Drafting	These problems address electronics drafting and design applications, such as electronic schematics, logic diagrams, and electrical part design.
Graphic Design	These problems address graphic design applications, such as text creation, title blocks, and page layout.
General	These problems address a variety of general drafting and design applications, and should be attempted by everyone learning AutoCAD LT for the first time.

ENHANCING THE TEXT WITH CD-ROM

To aid you in the AutoCAD LT endeavors, a CD-ROM is packaged with this text. This CD-ROM contains a variety of "tools" that can be used to enhance your productivity efforts. In addition, demos of several programs that can enhance your productivity and maximize your efforts are included on the disc.

The CD-ROM is organized into separate directories, each containing a README.TXT file that describes the installation and use of the program(s) in that particular directory. (You can access the README.TXT files from Windows 3.x Notepad.) The following list indicates the names of the directories and provides a brief description of the contents of each:

Directory	Description
ARCHNOTE	Contains typical architectural notes and symbols, which can be incorporated in drawings. Also includes an architectural font.
BONUS	Includes a variety of sample drawings that were created with AutoCAD and AutoCAD LT.
CADSYM	Contains a demonstration program, which includes electrical and fluid power symbols.
CREATCAD	Provides several different fonts.
MNU&BUTT	Includes a compilation of buttons, toolbars, and menus found in AutoCAD LT.
MNU_UTIL	Includes several subdirectories, which contain a variety of AutoCAD LT menu enhancements.
PROTOTYP	Provides several prototype drawing files, which can be used to expedite drawing set up for A-size through E-size drawings.
TITLBLOC	Contains a variety of title blocks and borders for A-size through E-size drawings.
RXHIGHLI	Includes a working version of a "redlining" program and several sample drawings from manufacturers.
VIACAD1	Contains over 70 electrical symbols, which can be used in the development of electrical/electronic schematics.
VIACAD2	Includes a self-paced demo of a program used to create printed circuit board (PCB) artwork.
VIADEV	Contains a self-running demo, which shows how the process of electrical controls design can be automated.

ABOUT THE AUTHOR

Ted Saufley is an AutoCAD certified instructor for the Premier Authorized Autodesk Training Center at Clackamas Community College, Oregon City, Oregon. In addition to community college experience, Ted was also an AutoCAD instructor at the University of Oregon Continuation Center in Portland, Oregon. In 1992, he was recognized by Autodesk as one of the top ten rated AutoCAD instructors in the Autodesk Training Center network. Ted has extensive industrial experience in both mechanical and software engineering, and has been involved with CAD/CAM for over a decade as a user, software developer, and consultant. He is the author of Goodheart-Willcox's *AutoCAD AME—Solid Modeling for Mechanical Design,* and the co-author of *AutoCAD and its Applications—Release 12 for Windows.*

NOTICE TO THE USER

This worktext is designed as a complete entry-level AutoCAD LT teaching tool. The author presents a typical point of view. Users are encouraged to explore alternative techniques for using and mastering AutoCAD LT. The author and publisher accept no responsibility for any loss or damage resulting from the contents of information presented in this text. This text contains the most complete and accurate information that could be obtained from various authoritative sources at the time of production. The publisher cannot assume responsibility for any changes, errors, or omissions.

ACKNOWLEDGMENTS

Lisa Senauke, Autodesk, Inc.

Contribution of materials

Melissa Martin, Geo Engineers, Portland, OR
Doug Millican, Pesznecker Bros., Clackamas, OR

CD-ROM software contributions

Autodesk, Inc.
CADSYM
Creative CAD
Dean Saadallah
Expert Graphics, Inc.
VIACAD, Inc.
Via Development Corporation

Dedicated to...

Elizabeth and Matthew Saufley

Table of Contents

Chapter *1*

Getting Started with AutoCAD LT

Learning objectives

After you have completed this chapter, you will be able to:

○ Start Microsoft Windows and load AutoCAD LT from Program Manager.
○ Describe the AutoCAD LT graphics window and user interface.
○ Understand the function and components of dialog boxes.
○ Select and use the various keyboard and function keys and identify their command equivalents.
○ Use the **HELP** command and other on-line services for assistance.

INTRODUCTION TO AUTOCAD LT

In December of 1982, a small company in Sausalito, California, introduced a new PC-based computer-aided drafting (CAD) software package. The small company was called Autodesk and they named their bold new product AutoCAD. Within five years, AutoCAD rapidly became the market leader and standard bearer for the CAD industry worldwide.

Slightly over a decade later, Autodesk set another industry milestone with the release of AutoCAD LT for Windows. With AutoCAD LT, you can prepare engineering drawings for mechanical objects, architectural floor plans for residential and commercial structures, or site plans for subdivided parcels of land. Sharing the same easy-to-use interface and command syntax as its "big brother" AutoCAD, AutoCAD LT has quickly emerged as the new market leader in low-cost desktop CAD solutions.

While many people mistakenly believe that the "LT" in AutoCAD LT means "Lite," it really stands for "Laptop." This is because AutoCAD LT requires less *random access memory (RAM)* and hard disk space than big brother AutoCAD. Thus, AutoCAD LT can be installed and run on relatively modest laptop and notebook computers. As you experiment with the exercises, tutorials, and drawing problems found in this text, you will probably come to agree with thousands of other users that there is nothing light about AutoCAD LT.

As with other Microsoft Windows-compatible programs, AutoCAD LT must first be installed on the hard disk drive of your computer. The AutoCAD LT program is contained on several floppy disks and contains a Windows-based installation program called SETUP.EXE. Instructions are given on-screen during the installation process to assist you in proper installation. The setup program automatically transfers files from the release disks to subdirectories it creates on your computer's hard disk, and then creates a *program group* in the Program Manager window. A program group contains program items graphically displayed as *icons*. Icons are small pictures that represent applications, accessories, files, or commands. An icon that starts an application like AutoCAD LT, is called a *program-item* icon. The AutoCAD LT program *group window* is a separate window within Program Manager and contains the AutoCAD LT program-item icon, a README.DOC icon, and an icon labeled LT Tutor. See Figure 1-1. The AutoCAD LT tutorial program is discussed in more detail later in this chapter.

Figure 1-1.
The AutoCAD LT installation
procedure creates a new
program group in the
Program Manager window.
Double-clicking the
AutoCAD LT program-item
icon starts AutoCAD LT.

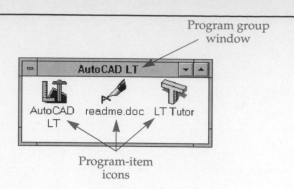

NOTE   Typically, a README.DOC file is in Windows Write format. It includes useful information about AutoCAD LT and special functions which may not be covered in the printed *AutoCAD LT User's Guide*. Be sure to read this additional documentation after installing AutoCAD LT on your hard disk.

Starting Microsoft Windows

After turning on and booting up your computer, the ***command prompt*** that appears on the display monitor indicates the current disk drive (the drive being addressed by the computer). To run Microsoft Windows, the prompt must display the letter of the hard disk drive. In the unlikely event that the screen prompt appears as A:\) or B:\), you must change to the hard drive. To change drives, type C: and then press the [Enter] key. You are now addressing the hard drive and the prompt should appear as C:\).

If your command prompt does not look like the example, you may need to change to the root directory of the hard drive. To do so, type the following:

CD \ ⏎

If the display prompt was already C:\), you are ready to start Windows and run AutoCAD LT. To load Windows, type in the following at the DOS prompt:

C:\)**WIN** ⏎

As Windows loads, the Microsoft Windows logo will appear briefly. The display screen will then present you with the Program Manager window. Program Manager is an application that is central to the Windows operating environment, and continues to run as long as you are working with a Windows application, like AutoCAD LT.

Starting AutoCAD LT from Program Manager

The Program Manager window can assume one of several different screen representations, depending on the way Windows has been configured on your computer. In Figure 1-2, Program Manager is shown with the Main group window open inside the Program Manager window. Each of the other group windows have been minimized and are represented by ***group icons*** located at the lower edge of the Program Manager window. The group icons are clearly labeled so that each may be easily distinguished from one another.

Figure 1-2.
The Main group window is shown open within the Program Manager window. Each of the other group windows have been minimized.

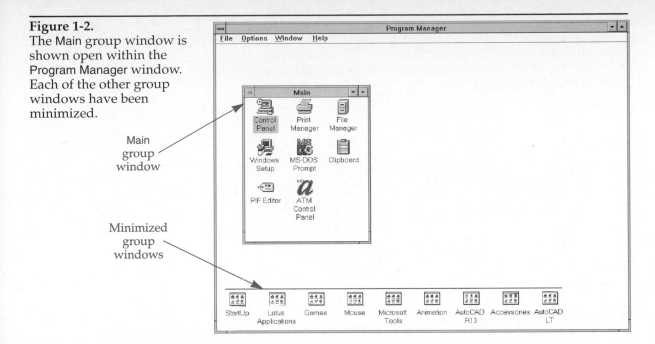

Main group window

Minimized group windows

Before AutoCAD LT can be run, you must first open the group window that contains the AutoCAD LT program-item icon. To open the AutoCAD LT group window, do one of the following:

- Double-click the AutoCAD LT group icon with the left mouse button. This is probably the fastest method.
- Select AutoCAD LT from the list at the bottom of the Window pull-down menu. This method is also fast.
- You can also press [Ctrl]+[F6] or [Ctrl]+[Tab] until the AutoCAD LT group icon is selected and then press [Enter].

Once the AutoCAD LT group window is open, you may start AutoCAD LT by double-clicking the AutoCAD LT program-item icon.

Another way the Program Manager window may appear on screen is in a *tiled* display, Figure 1-3A. In this representation, the AutoCAD LT group window (as well as several other group windows) is already open and arranged side-by-side in the Program Manager workspace. Program item icons are clearly visible in each of the open group windows, although there may not be enough room to display all of the program item icons in the allotted space for each group. To rearrange the open group windows in a tiled display, select Tile from the Window pull-down menu. To start AutoCAD LT from the tiled display, double-click the AutoCAD LT program-item icon.

As an alternative to a tiled display, the Program Manager may also be displayed with open group windows arranged in a *cascading*, or layered, fashion. This option orients and resizes each group window to overlap one another with the *title bar* of each group window clearly visible, Figure 1-3B. To rearrange all the open group windows in a cascading display, select Cascade from the Window pull-down menu. To start AutoCAD LT from a cascading display, double-click the program-item icon labeled AutoCAD LT.

Once you double-click the AutoCAD LT program-item icon, AutoCAD LT begins loading into memory and a small hourglass icon appears on-screen. The *graphics window* is then presented and it displays the AutoCAD LT logo, copyright, and login messages. It is within the **AutoCAD LT** graphics window that all drawing and editing operations are performed. Depending on how AutoCAD LT has been configured on your computer, you may also be presented with the **Create New Drawing** dialog box shown in Figure 1-4. Dialog boxes are widely used in Windows-based applications to request information about a task you are performing, provide information or options you may require, or to display important warning messages. Dialog boxes, and their various components, are described in detail in a later section of this chapter.

Figure 1-3.
A—Program groups displayed in a tiled fashion in Program Manager. B—Program groups displayed in a cascading fashion in Program Manager.

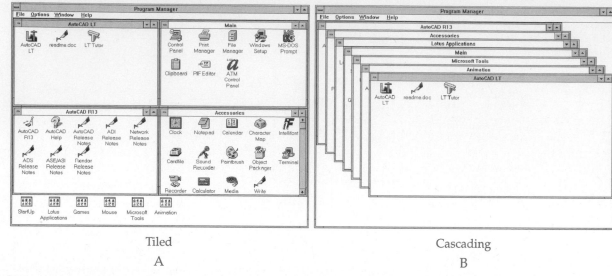

Tiled
A

Cascading
B

Figure 1-4.
The **Create New Drawing** dialog box is displayed as AutoCAD LT is loaded and provides a handy means of setting up new drawing parameters.

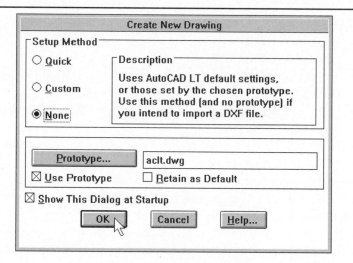

This **Create New Drawing** dialog box allows you to quickly and easily set up drawing parameters, such as drawing size and units. For now, just click the **None** option button at the left of the dialog box and then click the **OK** button. The dialog box then disappears, AutoCAD LT finishes loading, and the **Command:** prompt appears at the bottom of the graphics window. You are now ready to begin drawing with AutoCAD LT.

NOTE

The drawing setup parameters offered in the **Create New Drawing** dialog box are covered in detail in Chapter 2 of this text. Other functions available in this dialog box are more fully described in Chapter 16 of this text.

THE AUTOCAD LT USER INTERFACE

The AutoCAD LT user interface consists of all the items you will need to interact with the program. These items consist of the graphics window, graphics area, command line, menus, toolbar, toolbox, buttons, and dialog boxes. All of these elements play a part in the interaction with AutoCAD LT.

The AutoCAD LT graphics window

The **AutoCAD LT** graphics window is composed of various elements and icons. Located at the very top of the screen display is the *title bar* which tells you the name of the current drawing file. Just below the title bar, is the *menu bar*, which is where the AutoCAD LT pull-down menus are located. The *toolbar* is located directly beneath the menu bar. The toolbar contains buttons that are used as shortcuts to some of the more frequently used commands. The *toolbox* appears on the screen in a movable, or floating, window. It also contains buttons for commonly used commands. Each of these graphics window components are discussed in detail in the following sections.

Standard screen layout

The standard screen layout provides a large workspace called the *graphics area*. The graphics area is bordered by the toolbar at the top, and the command line at the bottom. In its default format, the graphics area is white and the text appearing in the command line area is black on a white background . Look at your screen now while you study the illustration in Figure 1-5.

Figure 1-5.
The standard **AutoCAD LT** graphics window. Note the location of the floating toolbox.

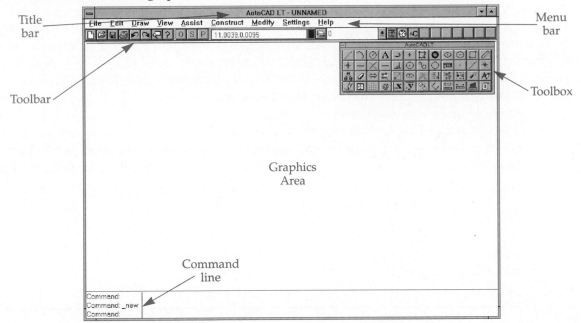

NOTE

Do not be alarmed if your display screen may appear differently than that shown in Figure 1-5. Various factors, chiefly screen resolution, affect the appearance of the **AutoCAD LT** graphics window. At high screen resolutions, for example, the toolbar contains more buttons than would be displayed at low resolutions. The screen examples illustrated in this text are at 800 × 600 resolution.

Take a few moments now to become familiar with the various areas and functions of the **AutoCAD LT** graphics window. Doing so will quickly increase your comfort level with the program and shorten the learning curve. The following list describes each area of the graphics window:

- **Command line.** The *command line*, or *prompt area*, consists of three text lines located along the bottom of the graphics window. This area displays the **Command:** prompt. The commands that you enter, and the messages and prompts issued by AutoCAD LT, are displayed here. Since this area of the graphics window is your primary communication with AutoCAD LT, make a habit of glancing at the **Command:** prompt from time-to-time as you are working.
- **Toolbar.** The toolbar is located directly above the top edge of the graphics window. As shown in Figure 1-6, the toolbar contains buttons which provide handy shortcuts for interacting with AutoCAD LT.

Figure 1-6.
The standard **AutoCAD LT** toolbar and its components.

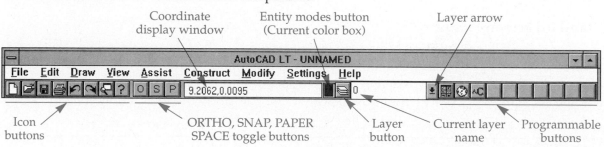

When you move your mouse over the toolbar, the screen crosshairs revert to the familiar Windows arrow pointer. If you momentarily pause over one of the buttons, the corresponding AutoCAD LT command name appears in a small text box attached to your cursor. These handy command identifiers are called *tooltips.* See Figure 1-7. Beginning from the far left of the toolbar, each of the display buttons is described as follows:

- **New button**—Displays the **Create New Drawing** dialog box. This dialog box and the **NEW** command are discussed in Chapter 2.
- **Open button**—Displays the **Open Drawing** dialog box where you can select an existing drawing file to work with. The **OPEN** command is discussed in Chapter 2.
- **Save button**—This button is used to quickly save your drawing to disk. If your drawing does not yet have a name, the **Save Drawing As** dialog box automatically appears so that you may specify a name for the drawing. As with the **NEW** and **OPEN** commands, saving your drawing files to disk is described in Chapter 2.
- **Print/Plot button**—Displays the **Plot Configuration** dialog box where you specify the parameters for printing or plotting a drawing. The **PLOT** command is discussed in detail in Chapter 13.

Figure 1-7.
The sixteen default toolbar buttons.

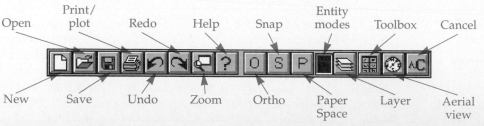

- **Undo button**—This button reverses, or undos, the most recent operation or command. The **U** and **UNDO** commands are covered in Chapter 3.
- **Redo button**—Reverses the effects of the last **U** or **UNDO** operation and is also discussed in Chapter 3.
- **Zoom button**—Invokes the **ZOOM** command. Zooming and other drawing display options are covered in Chapter 4.
- **Help button**—Opens the **AutoCAD LT Help** window. Detailed instructions for using on-line **Help** are provided at the end of this chapter.
- **Ortho button**—Toggles **ORTHO** mode on and off. When **Ortho** is on, the button appears pressed in. The button is out when **Ortho** is off. **ORTHO** mode is discussed in Chapter 3.
- **Snap button**—Toggles **SNAP** mode on and off. When **Snap** is on, the button appears pressed in. The button is out when **Snap** is off. The **SNAP** command is discussed in Chapter 2.
- **Paper Space button**—Toggles paper space on and off. When the button appears pressed in, **TILEMODE** = 0 (Off). The button is out when **TILEMODE** = 1 (On). Paper space, model space, and the **TILEMODE** system variable are covered in detail in later chapters of this text.
- **Coordinate display window**—Displays the current screen coordinates. The coordinate display window and its options are covered in Chapter 3.
- **Entity Modes button**—Clicking this button displays the **Entity Creation Modes** dialog box. This box is discussed in Chapter 5. Observe also that this button displays the current setting of the **COLOR** command or the color assigned to the current layer. For this reason, it is often referred to as the *Current Color Box*.
- **Layer button**—Enables the **Layer Control** dialog box where you can create and manage drawing layers. The **LAYER** command and its options is discussed in Chapter 5.
- **Current layer name box and arrow**—Displays the current layer name. Clicking on the down arrow to the right of the box displays a drop-down list of the layers defined in the drawing. Selecting a layer from the drop-down list quickly sets the selected layer current.
- ⊙ **Toolbox button**—The **Toolbox** button on the toolbar is used to change the physical status of the toolbox. Successive clicks of the toolbox button toggles the toolbox through the following states:
  - ⊙ Locked to the upper-left corner of the graphics window.
  - ⊙ Hidden.
  - ⊙ Locked to the upper-right corner of the graphics window.
  - ⊙ Floating (the default state).
- **Aerial View button**—Displays the **Aerial View** window which permits you to zoom and pan in a separate display window. **Aerial View** and its options is discussed in detail in Chapter 4.
- **Cancel button**—Clicking this button cancels a command in progress. You can also cancel a command using the [Ctrl]+[C] keyboard combination.

The remainder of the buttons on the toolbar are left blank so that you may easily add your own customized functions. Chapter 19 contains coverage of button customization.

- **Toolbox.** The toolbox contains many commonly used **AutoCAD LT** commands in a movable window that may be conveniently placed anywhere you choose on the face of the drawing—hence the term *floating*. As with the toolbar, if you move your mouse arrow over one of the toolbox buttons and momentarily pause, the corresponding **AutoCAD LT** tooltip appears, Figure 1-8A. You can use the toolbox button on the toolbar to anchor the window at the predefined locked locations described previously or hide the toolbox entirely. However, keep in mind that when the toolbox is locked (no longer floating) at the upper-left or upper-right corner of the graphics window, the toolbox appears as shown in Figure 1-8B and may not be moved.

Figure 1-8.
A—As with a toolbar button, the corresponding AutoCAD LT command name is displayed in a tooltip as the mouse is moved over a toolbox button.
B—The toolbox may be locked to the upper-left or upper-right corners of the graphics window but may not be moved when in a locked position.

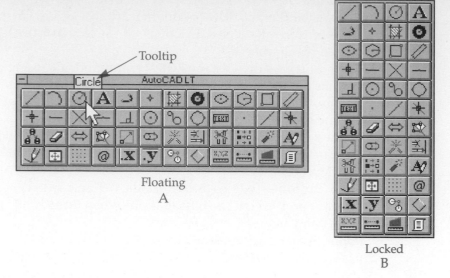

Floating
A

Locked
B

Pull-down menus

The AutoCAD LT pull-down menus are located on the menu bar directly above the toolbar. As with the toolbar and toolbox, when you move your mouse over the menu bar, the crosshairs change to the arrow pointer. From Figure 1-9, you can see that the menu bar is composed of nine pull-down menu items. They are titled **File**, **Edit**, **Draw**, **View**, **Assist**, **Construct**, **Modify**, **Settings**, and **Help**.

Figure 1-9.
The nine pull-down menu titles on the **AutoCAD LT** menu bar.

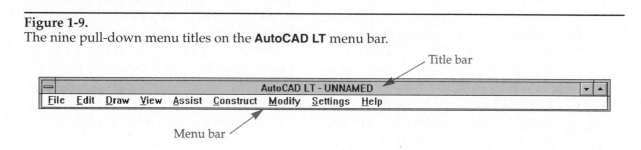

Title bar

Menu bar

The placement of the pull-down menus enables you to quickly select a variety of commands not ordinarily found in the toolbar or toolbox. Move your cursor to the **Draw** pull-down menu and click the leftmost button on your mouse. A pull-down menu appears below **Draw**, Figure 1-10A. Commands within this menu are easily selected by picking the desired menu item with your mouse. Several of the menu selections are followed by an *ellipsis* (...). If you pick one of these items, a dialog box is displayed. Dialog boxes are discussed in a later section of this chapter.

You will observe that several of the commands in the **Draw** pull-down menu have a small arrow to the right. When one of these items is selected with the mouse, a *cascading submenu* appears. This submenu offers you additional options for the selected command, Figure 1-10B. Each of these commands and options are discussed in the appropriate chapters of this text.

If you pick the wrong pull-down menu, simply move the cursor to the menu you want and click on it. The first menu is removed and the one you clicked is displayed. The pull-down menu disappears after you pick an item from the menu, pick a point in the drawing area, or type on the keyboard.

Figure 1-10.
A—The **Draw** pull-down menu. B—When a pull-down menu item is followed by an arrow, a cascading submenu appears when it is selected.

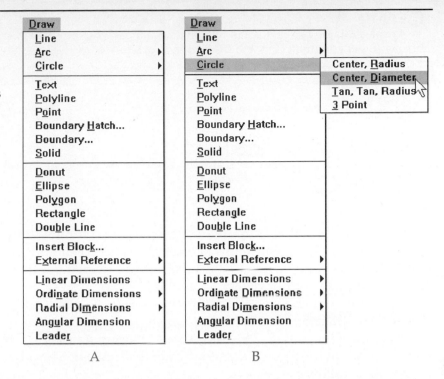

A   B

Accessing pull-down menus from the keyboard

Even the most casual perusal of the pull-down menu titles on the menu bar will reveal one underlined character in each of the menu names. This is consistent with the Microsoft Windows user interface that permits access to any pull-down menu from the keyboard using an [Alt] key combination shortcut. For instance, the **File** menu may be accessed by pressing [Alt]+[F]. Pressing [Alt]+[A] accesses the **Assist** menu, and so on. These types of key combinations are called *accelerator* keys.

Once a pull-down menu is displayed, a menu item within it may be selected using a single character key. As an example, suppose you wanted to construct a circle defined by its center point and its diameter. Referring once again to Figure 1-10B, you would first press [Alt]+[D] to access the **Draw** menu, then press C to select the **Circle** command, and then press D to select **Center, Diameter**. These single key shortcuts for pull-down menu items are call *mnemonic* keys.

Admittedly, it is far more efficient to make your menu selections with your mouse than from the keyboard. However, if your pointing device should suddenly become inoperative and stop responding, the accelerator and mnemonic keys provide a handy means of exiting the program without rebooting your computer.

NOTE   There are many individual character key and key combination shortcuts available for Windows and Windows-based applications. Refer to the *Microsoft Windows User's Guide* for a complete list of keyboard shortcuts.

Dialog boxes

As mentioned previously, anytime you pick a pull-down menu item which is followed by an *ellipsis* (...), a dialog box is displayed. In their simplest form, dialog boxes are used to display informational or warning messages to you. These types of dialog boxes, or *alert boxes*, remain on the screen until you acknowledge the displayed message by clicking the **OK** button. Two examples of this type of dialog box are shown in Figure 1-11.

Figure 1-11.
The simplest dialog boxes display informational messages shown in A, or warnings shown in B. For each type, you must click the **OK** button to acknowledge the message.

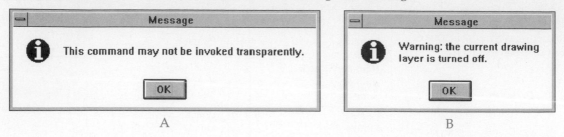

A   B

Since many of the features of dialog boxes are common throughout Microsoft Windows and Windows-based applications like AutoCAD LT, you should spend a few moments reviewing the various components found within them. Remember that a number of the items you need to complete your drawings are found in dialog boxes.

Common dialog boxes all contain the same basic areas, and work the same way regardless of the application you are using. One type of common dialog box you will encounter is illustrated in Figure 1-12. This is the **Save Drawing As** dialog box. Observe that its name is clearly shown at the top of the dialog box in the *title bar*. The other areas of the dialog box are described as follows:

- **Filename list box.** A list of existing filenames is shown at the left of the dialog box. You use your mouse to select the desired filename from this list. When the list of filenames is long, you can use a *vertical scroll bar* to view the filenames that exist beyond the borders of the box.

- **Scroll bars.** Scroll bars can appear in either vertical or horizontal orientations depending on the particular application. As shown in Figure 1-13, a scroll bar contains a scroll arrow and a scroll box. Use the scroll arrow to scroll up or down one line at a time. You can scroll continuously if you hold down the mouse button. If you click just above or below the scroll box in a vertical scroll bar, you can scroll a whole page at a time. For a horizontal scroll bar, click to the left or right of the scroll box to scroll one page horizontally.

Figure 1-12.
The basic elements of a dialog box.

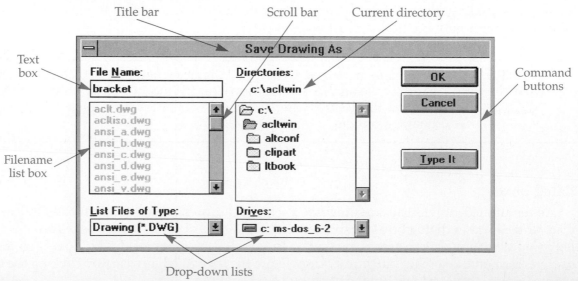

Figure 1-13.
Both vertical and horizontal
scroll bars contain scroll
arrows and a scroll box.

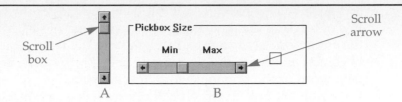

A   B

- **Directory list box.** The current directory name is shown at the top-middle of the dialog box. In the example shown, the ACLTWIN directory on the C: drive is the current directory. Just below is a list of the subdirectories under C:\ACLTWIN. Note that the ACLTWIN directory is currently open as evidenced by the "open" file folder icon to the left of the directory name.
- **Drop-down lists.** A *drop-down* list is a rectangular box that displays a list of choices. The list of available items does not appear, however, until you click the down arrow in the small box at the right. Two types of drop-down lists occur in the sample dialog box. The **List Files of Type:** drop-down list is located at the bottom left. This section specifies the type of file listed in the filename list box as well as in the **File Name:** area at the upper left. The **Drives** drop-down list is located at the bottom-right of the dialog box. This drop-down list allows you to change to a different drive on your computer. A typical **Drives** drop-down list is shown in Figure 1-14A. Another type of drop-down list is illustrated in Figure 1-14B. This list provides a handy means of changing the system of drawing units. In both drop-down list examples, the current selection is shown highlighted in the list.

Figure 1-14.
A—The **Drives** drop-down list box provides a handy means of setting another drive current. The highlighted item indicates the current selection. B—Drop-down list boxes may also be used to change system settings, like units of measurement.

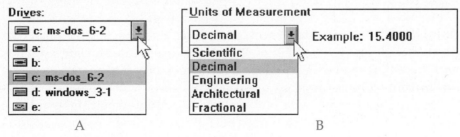

A   B

- **Text box.** A text box is used to insert a single line of textual information, such as a filename or a numeric value. When a text box is empty, a flashing vertical bar called the *insertion point* appears at the far left of the box. See Figure 1-15. The text you type starts at this point. In the example shown in Figure 1-12, a user has typed in the name bracket in the **File Name:** text box. If the text box you want to use already contains text, the existing text is highlighted. You can type over the text if you choose, or press the [Del], [Backspace], or [Spacebar] keys on your keyboard to remove the existing text from the text box. You can edit the existing text using the keyboard cursor keys,

Figure 1-15.
You can enter a filename,
numeric value, or any single
line of information in
a text box.

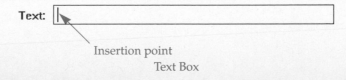

[Home], [End], [→], and [←]. The [Home] key moves the cursor to the beginning of the line of text and the [End] key moves to the end of the line. The [→] and [←] keys move the cursor one character to the right or to the left, respectively. By using the [Ctrl] key in conjunction with the right arrow or left arrow key, you can move the cursor to the next word or the previous word, respectively.

- **Filename list box.** Every type of common dialog box used for file operations, such as opening or saving a drawing, displays a filename list box. This is the bordered area at the left of the dialog box that contains a listing of existing filenames. You can use your mouse to select a file from the list or type in the desired filename in the text box as previously described. When filenames in a list box appear "grayed-out", they are not available for selection.

- **Command buttons.** These buttons usually appear at the far right or very bottom of dialog boxes and are used to initiate an immediate action. The **OK** and **Cancel** buttons are the most common type of command buttons. Click **OK** to accept the changes or information shown in a dialog box. To discard any changes made, click the **Cancel** button. Clicking a button that contains an ellipsis (...) opens another dialog box, or what is often called a *subdialog box*. Several examples of these types of buttons are shown in Figure 1-16. Note the appearance of the **OK** button in this illustration. Notice the button has a heavier border and is highlighted with a dashed rectangle. This is the default selection and may be quickly selected by pressing [Enter].

Figure 1-16.
A button label with an ellipsis (...) opens another dialog box. The heavier border around the **OK** button indicates that this is the default selection.

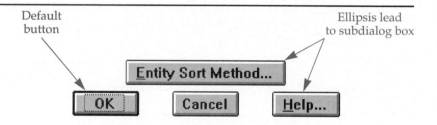

Default button

Ellipsis lead to subdialog box

- **Check boxes.** Clicking inside a check box makes a setting active. An active check box is indicated with an "X." See Figure 1-17A. To deactivate the setting, click the check box and the "X" is removed. More than one check box setting can be active at a time.
- **Option buttons.** Option buttons are used the same way as check boxes. See Figure 1-17B. Simply click the desired option button to activate a setting. Unlike check boxes, however, only one option button may be active at a time. As soon as you click a different option button in a group, the previous selection is deactivated.

Figure 1-17.
A—An "X" in a check box indicates an active setting. More than one check box may be selected. B—Only one option button in a group can be active at any one given time.

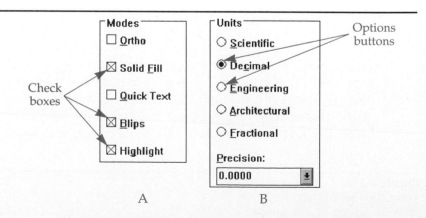

- **Image tiles.** Several of the dialog boxes in AutoCAD LT use pictorial images to display the available options, Figure 1-18. These pictorial images are called *image tiles*, or *icon menus*. Simply click the graphical representation of the option you desire, and then click the **OK** button. The dialog box is closed and the option you selected is made current.

Figure 1-18.
Some dialog boxes contain icon menus, or image tiles, that graphically display options or selections.

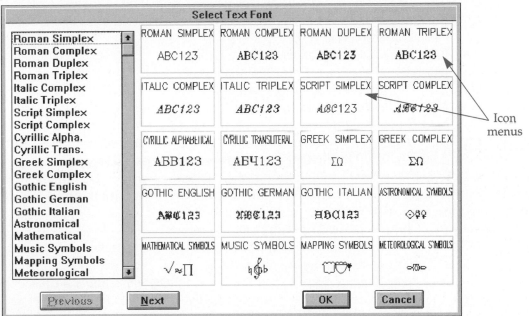

Icon menus

PROFESSIONAL TIP

As a new user, you may occasionally find yourself inside a dialog box without realizing how you got there. If you find yourself in just such a situation, be sure to click the **Cancel** button to exit the dialog box. You can also press the [Esc] key on your keyboard to quickly exit the dialog box. Doing so will discard any unnecessary (and undesirable) changes you may have made inadvertently.

SELECTING AUTOCAD LT COMMANDS

You will learn that there are usually several different ways to accomplish exactly the same task in AutoCAD LT. Apart from the toolbar, toolbox, pull-down menus, and dialog boxes, commands may also be entered from the keyboard.

The advantage in using the toolbar and toolbox buttons, as well as the pull-down menus, is that you do not have to remove your eyes from the screen. Unless you are an excellent typist, typed commands often require that you do look away from the screen. However, the commands and their options can be learned more quickly by typing them. Therefore, the examples shown in this text illustrate each of the AutoCAD LT commands as they appear when typed at the command prompt. Alternate command entry forms are also presented where appropriate.

Control keys and function keys

Earlier in this chapter, you learned how accelerator and mnemonic keys can be used to activate and make selections from the nine AutoCAD LT pull-down menus. Other functions may be performed with keyboard shortcuts as well. Many of these tasks are activated using *control key* combinations. To perform a control key function, simply press and hold the [Ctrl] key while pressing another key. The available control key combinations and their functions are as follows:

[Ctrl]+[B]   *Toggles* **SNAP** *mode on and off.*

[Ctrl]+[C]   *Cancels a command in progress.*

[Ctrl]+[D]   *Toggles the coordinate display window on and off.*

[Ctrl]+[E]   *Toggles through the right, left, and top* **ISOPLANE** *modes for isometric constructions.*

[Ctrl]+[G]   *Toggles the grid on and off.*

[Ctrl]+[H]   *Works the same as the* [Backspace] *key.*

[Ctrl]+[O]   *Toggles* **ORTHO** *mode on and off.*

[Ctrl]+[V]   *Cycles through a multiple viewport configuration, successively setting each viewport current.*

[Ctrl]+[X]   *Deletes all the entered characters on the command line.*

An even easier method for instant access to commands exists through the use of *function keys*. The function keys are located either at the left or the very top of your keyboard and are labeled F1 through F12. Eight of the function keys are pre-programmed by AutoCAD LT to perform the following tasks:

[F1]   *Invokes the on-line* **Help** *system.*

[F2]   *Toggles between the graphics window and the text window. The* **text window** *is a window that displays prompts, messages, and the command history for the current drawing session. You can use it to view the lengthy output of certain commands, as well as to review previously entered commands. A typical text window display appears in Figure 1-19.*

[F5]   *Toggles the* **ISOPLANE** *mode (same as* [Ctrl]+[E]*).*

[F6]   *Toggles the coordinate display window on and off (same as* [Ctrl]+[D]*).*

[F7]   *Toggles the grid on and off (same as* [Ctrl]+[G]*).*

[F8]   *Toggles* **ORTHO** *mode on and off (same as* [Ctrl]+[O]*).*

[F9]   *Toggles* **SNAP** *mode on and off (same as* [Ctrl]+[B]*).*

[F10]   *Highlights the* **File** *pull-down menu title. Once highlighted, simply press the* [Enter] *key to pull the menu down.*

Figure 1-19.
The **AutoCAD LT** text window displays all prompts, messages, and commands for the current drawing session.

```
                        AutoCAD LT Text - UNNAMED
Command: CHAMFER
Polyline/Distances/<Select first line>: D
Enter first chamfer distance <0.5000>:  75


CHAMFER Polyline/Distances/<Select first line>:
Select second line:

CHAMFER Polyline/Distances/<Select first line>:
Select second line:

Command: FILLET
Polyline/Radius/<Select first object>: R

FILLET Polyline/Radius/<Select first object>:
Select second object:

FILLET Polyline/Radius/<Select first object>:
Select second object:


Select objects: 1 found

                CIRCLE    Layer: 0
                          Space: Model space
                  Handle = 7
        center point, X=   7.0000  Y=   6.0000  Z=   0.0000
             radius   1.0000
      circumference   6.2832
             area   3.1416

Command:
```

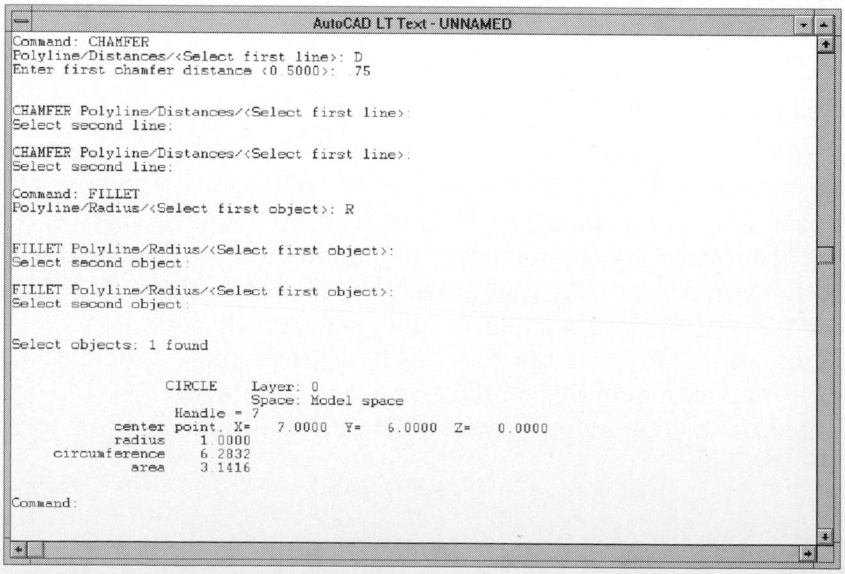

GETTING HELP

ALTUG 2

If you need some help with a specific command, option, or program feature, AutoCAD LT provides a powerful and convenient on-line **Help** system. There are several ways to access on-line **Help**. The two fastest methods are to simply click the **Help** button on the toolbar or press the [F1] key on your keyboard. Either action displays the **Contents** for the **Help** system in the **AutoCAD LT Help** window. See Figure 1-20. You may also display the **Contents** by selecting **Contents** from the **Help** pull-down menu or by typing a ? or HELP at the **Command:** prompt. The five major categories listed within the **Help Contents** are as follows:

- **How do I...**
- **Toolbar**
- **Toolbox**
- **Menus**
- **Command line**

Figure 1-20.
The **Contents** for the
AutoCAD LT Help window.

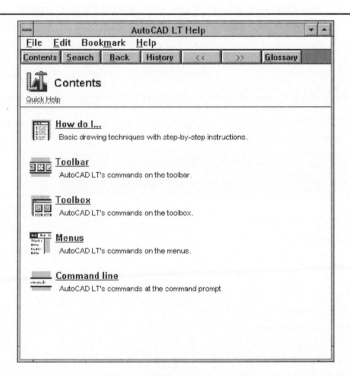

When you move the arrow pointer to one of the underlined topics, the arrow changes to a hand. If you click the underlined topic, you can get more information on that category. For example, suppose you need help with the **LINE** command. Click anywhere on the underlined topic **Command line** in the **Contents** window. A new **Help** window appears that displays a list of the AutoCAD LT command names that begin with the letters A through D. If you click the underlined letters **E-P**, all command names starting with the letters E through P are displayed. See Figure 1-21.

Figure 1-21.
AutoCAD LT commands are
displayed alphabetically in
the **Help** window.

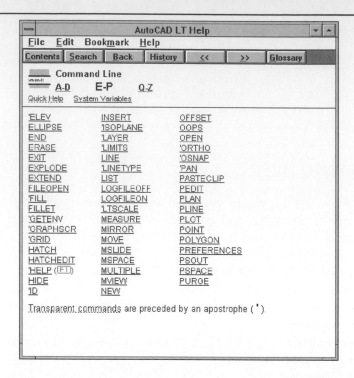

Click the underlined word **LINE** in the middle column, and another **Help** window
appears that contains information about the **LINE** command and its usage. See Figure 1-22.
Clicking the ***See Also*** item at the top of the **Help** window presents you with the small dialog
box. This dialog box directs you to the appropriate chapter in the *AutoCAD LT User's Guide*
for further information as well as the names of related commands. You may exit **Help** and
return to the graphics window by selecting **Exit** from the **File** pull-down menu.

Figure 1-22.
The **LINE** command **Help** window. Additional information and related commands are displayed in
a box when you click **See Also**.

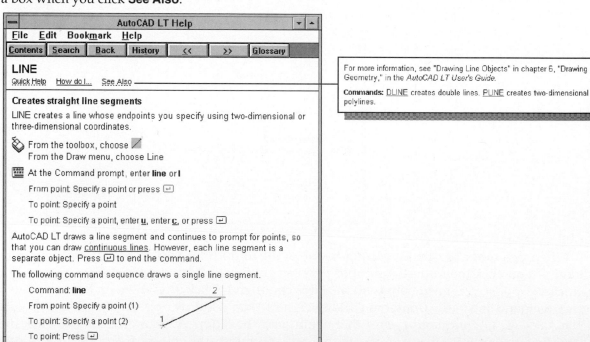

Help window buttons

Controls for moving through **Help** are provided by the seven buttons located near the top of the **Help** window. Any button which appears "grayed-out" is not currently available for selection. The seven buttons and the functions which they perform are:

- **Contents.** After researching a **Help** topic, select the **Contents** button to return to the **Contents** window.
- **Search. Search** enables you to research topics associated with particular words or phrases and is described in the next section.
- **Back.** Returns you to the previously displayed **Help** window.
- **History.** Select the **History** button to obtain a list of every **Help** topic researched during a current **Help** session. You can return to a topic by double-clicking on it.
- **》.** If this button appears in the **Help** window, it means certain **Help** topics have been grouped together in a sequence. To view the next topic in the sequence, click the 》 button or press the period [.] key. When you reach the last topic in the sequence, or if there is no browse sequence, the 》 button is dimmed.
- **《.** Click this button to view the previous topic in the sequence or press the comma [,] key. When you reach the first topic in the sequence, or if there is no sequence, the 《 button is dimmed.
- **Glossary.** The **Glossary** button displays a separate window containing an alphabetical list of AutoCAD LT terms. If you click an item from the list, its definition pops up in a box as shown in Figure 1-23. When you are through using the glossary, click the **Close** button to exit and return to the previous **Help** window.

Figure 1-23.
The **Glossary** button displays a separate window containing an alphabetical list of AutoCAD LT terms. Clicking an item from the list displays the item's definition in a box.

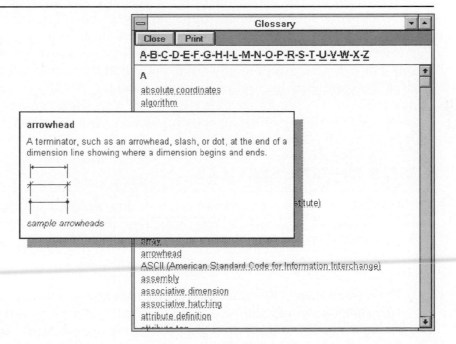

Using Search

Just as you might look up a topic in a textbook by using the book's index to locate a particular word, you can also research AutoCAD LT topics using a single word or phrase. The **Search** function in **Help** is enabled from the **AutoCAD LT** graphics window by selecting **Search for Help on...** in the **Help** pull-down menu. If you are already in **Help**, click the **Search** button near the top of the **Help** window.

The **Search** dialog box appears on screen on top of the **Contents** window. There are several components in the **Search** dialog box. See Figure 1-24. In the upper-left of the **Search**

Figure 1-24.
The **Search** dialog box.

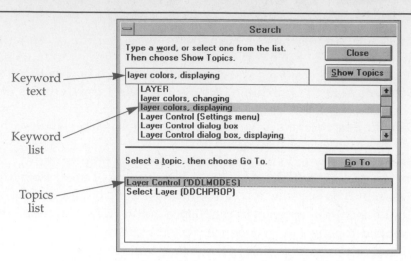

dialog box there are instructions for using **Search**. Near the top is located the *keyword text box*. Just below the keyword text box, the *keyword list box* is found. The *topics list box* is located at the very bottom of the dialog box. You can use the scroll bar to find the word or phrase you want in the keyword list box, or you can type in the word you want directly in the keyword text box.

Once the word or phrase you want to research is specified, click the **Show Topics** button. All related topics are then displayed in the topics list box. Double-clicking a word or phrase from the keyword list box will also display all related topics in the topics list box.

Click the topic you want from the topics list box, and then click the **Go To** button. You can also double-click a topic from the topics list box to obtain the same results. The **Search** dialog box is then closed, and the topic information you desire appears in the **Help** window.

Keep in mind that you can also ask for help while you are working inside another command. For example, suppose you are using the **PLINE** command and forget the meaning of each of the command line options. Simply press the [F1] key and the help you need for that command and its options are then displayed in the **Help** window. You can accomplish the same thing by entering either an apostrophe and a question mark, or an apostrophe and the word HELP at the **Command:** prompt for any command.

OTHER ON-LINE SERVICES

AutoCAD LT offers a number of other on-line services with which you should become familiar. These services include cue cards, new user orientation, what's new, and tutorials. The following sections discuss these on-line services.

Using Cue Cards

The on-line **Help** in AutoCAD LT also provides task-specific assistance. If you click **How do I...** in the **Help Contents** window, a small window called a *cue card* is displayed at the right of the screen with a list of basic drawing and editing operations.

In the example shown in Figure 1-25, a user has invoked the **How do I...** function and clicked the **Draw a line** button from the first cue card. A second cue card then appears and the user clicks the **Draw a line using the cursor** button. The third displayed cue card provides textual information and graphical examples about drawing lines using the cursor.

Figure 1-25.
AutoCAD LT cue cards
provide on-line task-specific
assistance.

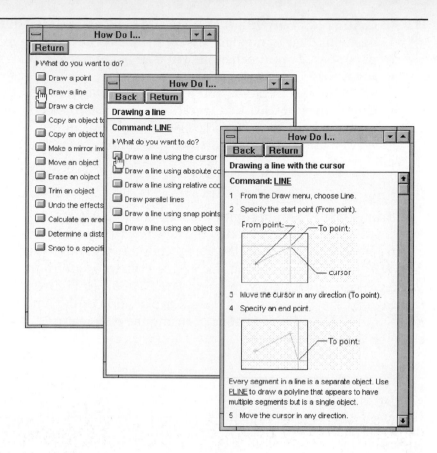

New user orientation

For users with no prior CAD experience, AutoCAD LT provides a handy on-line overview of the program's basic features and capabilities. This unique approach to new user orientation is actually a separate Windows-based application named ORIENT.EXE and is automatically placed in the ACLTWIN directory by the SETUP.EXE installation program. This application is accessed within AutoCAD LT by clicking the word **Orientation** in the **Help** pull-down menu. See Figure 1-26. The on-line orientation consists of three major categories and are described as follows:

Figure 1-26.
The **Orientation** program
helps the novice user make
a smooth transition from the
drafting board to the
computer.

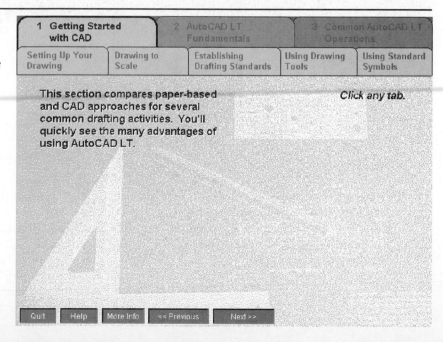

- **Getting Started with CAD.** This section compares traditional drafting board activities with their equivalent CAD functions. The advantages of using AutoCAD LT over paper-based approaches are made apparent to the novice user.
- **AutoCAD LT Fundamentals.** A general overview of AutoCAD LT viewing, drawing, and editing commands and features is provided in this section.
- **Common AutoCAD LT Operations.** Basic features common to all CAD systems are explained in a more specific fashion in this section.

Once the orientation program is loaded and running, it may be exited at any time by clicking the **Quit** button.

Finding out what's new

Users already familiar with the first version of AutoCAD LT Release 1 can quickly learn what is new and/or improved in the new release by clicking **What's New** from the **Help** pull-down menu. This action launches another separate Windows-based program called WNEW.EXE. With this on-line service, new features are divided into three categories titled **EASE OF USE, PRODUCTIVITY**, and **NEW TOOLS**. See Figure 1-27. By clicking one of the new feature topics, a graphical and textual explanation of the new feature is displayed in a separate window. Once you are done perusing the new features of AutoCAD LT Release 2, simply click the **Quit** button to exit.

Figure 1-27.
AutoCAD LT Release 1 veterans can learn all about the new features offered with Release 2.

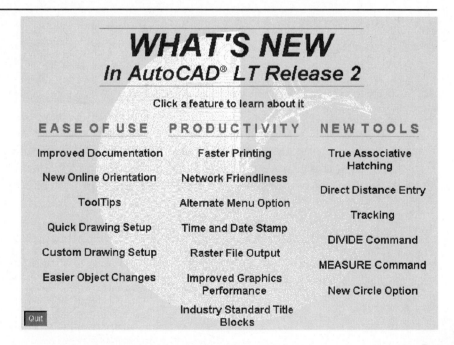

On-line tutorials

Designed for brand-new users who are anxious to get started, AutoCAD LT provides three application-specific tutorials for architecture and construction, mechanical drafting, and facilities management. The tutorials may be started by selecting **Tutorial** in the **Help** pull-down menu. The tutorial main menu is shown in Figure 1-28A. If you click the **Expand** button, a detailed listing of tutorial topics is displayed as illustrated in Figure 1-28B. Clicking the first tutorial, **Architecture and Construction**, displays a help window that describes the tutorial and how to use it. See Figure 1-28C.

Figure 1-28.
A—The on-line tutorial **Main Menu**. B—The **Expand** button displays a fuller listing of tutorial topics.
C—Each of the three available tutorials provide assistance and instructions in their use.

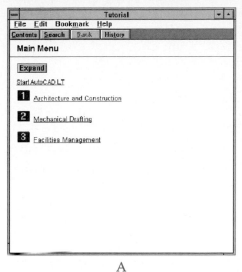

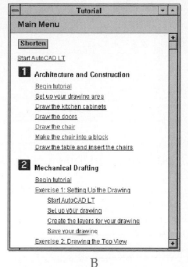

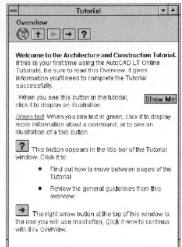

A   B   C

NOTE You can also start the tutorial independent of AutoCAD LT by clicking the LT Tutor icon in the AutoCAD LT group window as shown in Figure 1-1. However, to run the tutorial AutoCAD LT must be loaded.

CHAPTER TEST

Write your answers in the spaces provided.

1. What does the "LT" in AutoCAD LT stand for? _____

   _____

2. What do you type at the DOS prompt to load Windows? _____

   _____

3. Name five areas that comprise the **AutoCAD LT** graphics window. _____

   _____

   _____

   _____

4. Which area displays the communication between AutoCAD LT and the user? _____

   _____

   _____

5. What is the major difference between the toolbar and the toolbox? _____

   _____

   _____

   _____

---

6. What is a tooltip? _____

   _____

   _____

7. What is an accelerator key? What is a mnemonic key? How are they used? Give an example of each. _____

   _____

   _____

   _____

   _____

8. List the nine AutoCAD LT pull-down menus. _____

   _____

   _____

   _____

   _____

9. What are the functions of the following control keys?

   A. [Ctrl]+[B] _____

   B. [Ctrl]+[C] _____

   C. [Ctrl]+[D] _____

   D. [Ctrl]+[E] _____

   E. [Ctrl]+[G] _____

   F. [Ctrl]+[O] _____

10. Name the function keys that execute the same task as the following control keys.

Control key	**Function Key**

   A. [Ctrl]+[B] _____

   B. [Ctrl]+[D] _____

   C. [Ctrl]+[E] _____

   D. [Ctrl]+[G] _____

   E. [Ctrl]+[O] _____

11. What is the text window and which function key displays it? _____

   _____

   _____

12. What type of pull-down menu has an arrow to the right of the item? _____

   _____

13. What does an ellipsis (...) after a menu item represent? _____

   _____

   _____

14. What is an image tile? Where might you find one? _____

_____

_____

15. Describe the purpose of a scroll bar and how it is used. _____

_____

_____

16. What is the difference between a check box and an option button? _____

_____

_____

_____

17. If you find yourself inadvertently in a dialog box, what should you do? Why?_____

_____

_____

18. What is a cue card? How is it accessed?_____

_____

_____

_____

CHAPTER PROBLEMS

1. Start AutoCAD LT as described earlier in this chapter and spend a few moments exploring the new user orientation program. In preparation for the topics to be discussed in Chapter 2, carefully read the two sections titled *Setting Up Your Drawing* and *Drawing to Scale*.

General

2. Draw a freehand sketch of the toolbar. Using your very best upper-case block lettering, label each button with its corresponding tooltip.

General

3. Run the orientation program again and read the section titled *Using Drawing Tools*. Based on what you learn from this section, draw a freehand sketch of the toolbox and label the appropriate toolbox drawing buttons with the name of the traditional drafting instrument that would perform the same function on a drafting board.

General

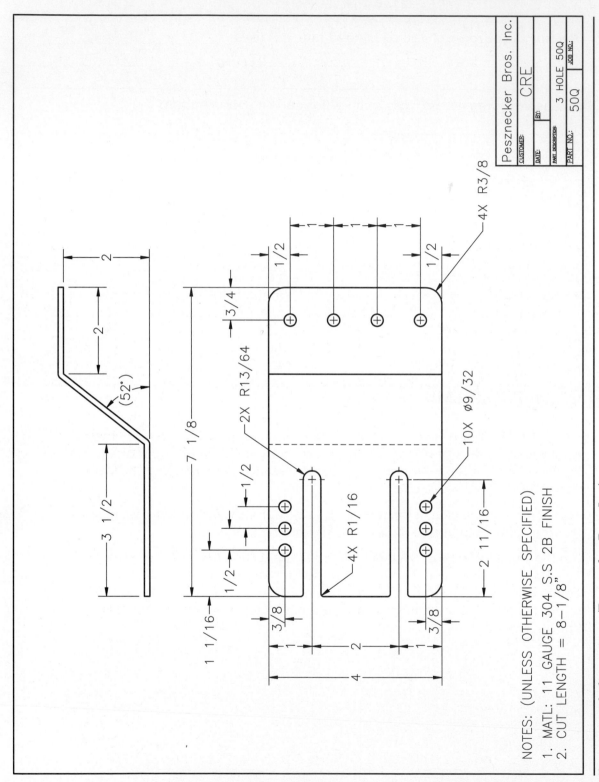

NOTES: (UNLESS OTHERWISE SPECIFIED)
1. MATL: 11 GAUGE 304 S.S 2B FINISH
2. CUT LENGTH = 8-1/8"

Pesznecker Bros. Inc.

CUSTOMER:	CRE	
DATE:	BY:	
PART DESCRIPTION:	3 HOLE 50Q	
PART NO.:	50Q	JOB NO.:

Drawing with dimensions. (Pesznecker Bros. Inc.)

Drawing Setup and File Operations

Learning objectives

After you have completed this chapter, you will be able to:
- ☉ Set up drawing parameters as you begin a new drawing.
- ○ Select appropriate drawing units.
- ○ Size the drawing area.
- ○ Understand and use grid and snap settings.
- ○ Describe the purpose and advantage of prototype drawings.
- ○ Save your work and access existing drawing files.
- ○ End a drawing session.

If you have ever created engineering or architectural drawings on a drafting board, you know that there are several factors to be considered before you start any new drawing. First, you must carefully study the object you are to draw so that you can decide how many views are required to adequately describe the object. Second, you need to determine if any additional detail, section, or auxiliary views are required. It is only then that you know what size sheet of drafting media (vellum or mylar) to tape down to your drafting board.

Planning ahead is just as important when using AutoCAD LT. In this chapter, you will learn to set up new drawings to your exact specifications using the various AutoCAD LT units of measurement and drawing aids. You will also learn to save your work, access existing drawings, and end a drawing session.

SETTING UP A DRAWING WITH THE NEW COMMAND | ALTUG 4 |

A new drawing session is launched automatically by simply starting up AutoCAD LT. Once the program is running and you are working on a drawing, you can begin an entirely new drawing by issuing the **NEW** command. If the current drawing in the graphics window has not yet been saved, AutoCAD LT first prompts you to save or discard the changes before starting a new drawing. To access the **NEW** command type NEW at the **Command:** prompt, select **New...** from the **File** pull-down menu, or click the **NEW** button at the far left of the tool-bar. Regardless of the method you use, the **Create New Drawing** dialog box is automatically displayed whenever you issue the **NEW** command or start up AutoCAD LT. As shown in Figure 2-1, the **Create New Drawing** dialog box contains several sections and buttons designed to facilitate drawing setup. If you would prefer not to see this dialog box when AutoCAD LT starts up, click the **Show This Dialog at Startup** check box. This action removes the "X" from the check box effectively disabling this option. Each of the other dialog box components are described in the following sections.

Figure 2-1.
The **Create New Drawing** dialog box provides a handy means of setting up new drawing parameters and is displayed when AutoCAD LT starts up or when the **NEW** command is issued.

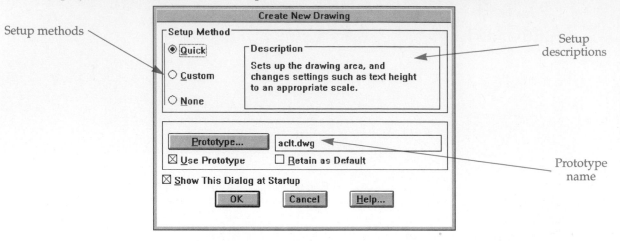

Setup methods

Setup descriptions

Prototype name

Using **Quick** setup

The **Setup Method** area at the top of the dialog box contains the **Quick**, **Custom**, and **None** option buttons. If you would rather not make any specific changes to system settings, click the **None** option button. When **None** is selected, new drawings use the default values set by AutoCAD LT. However, when you do want to set up various drawing parameters, one of the easiest and most commonly used methods is offered by the **Quick** option button. If this button is selected, the **Quick Drawing Setup** subdialog box appears as shown in Figure 2-2. This dialog box permits you to select the appropriate system of units for your drawing and specify the size, or limits, of the drawing area. You can also use this dialog box to set the spacing for the grid and snap drawing aids. Grid and snap is discussed later in this chapter.

Figure 2-2.
The **Quick Drawing Setup** subdialog box allows you to quickly select units of measurement, size the drawing area, and set grid and snap spacings.

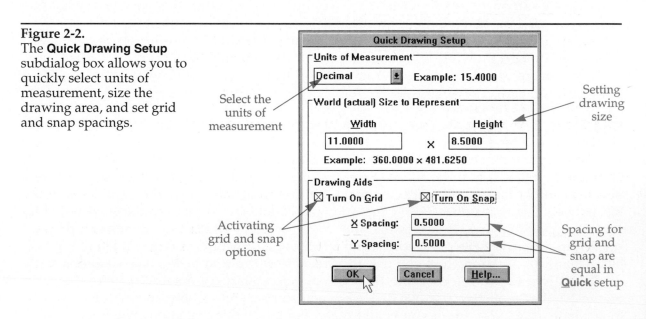

Select the units of measurement

Setting drawing size

Activating grid and snap options

Spacing for grid and snap are equal in **Quick** setup

Selecting Drawing Units. AutoCAD LT provides you with five system of units measurements from which to choose. The five systems are Scientific, Decimal (the default units of measurement), Engineering, Architectural, and Fractional. You can select the desired system of units from the drop-down list located at the top of the **Quick Drawing Setup** subdialog box. See Figure 2-2. For each system of units, AutoCAD LT displays an example to the right of the drop-down list. To better understand the formats of each system, the examples are repeated below:

Scientific	1.5400E+01
Decimal	15.4000
Engineering	1'-3.4000"
Architectural	1'-3 3/8"
Fractional	15 3/8

UNITS (handwritten)

Figure 2-3.
Drawing units are conveniently selected from the **Units of Measurement** drop-down list.

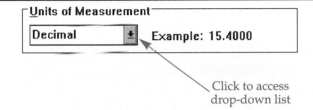

Click to access drop-down list

The system of units that you select is used for all displayed numeric values in the current drawing. That applies to the values shown on the command line, in dialog boxes, and for the dimensions placed on the drawing when using AutoCAD LT dimensioning commands.

Sizing the Drawing Area. Perhaps the greatest difference between computer-aided drafting and traditional, paper-base drafting is the ability to draw nearly anything imaginable at full scale using CAD. Whether you are drawing a jumbo jet or a threaded fastener, a commercial shopping mall or a residential deck, everything is drawn at full scale. The finished size of a drawing is determined at plotting time. Plotting parameters and plot scales are discussed in Chapter 13 of this text.

Although AutoCAD LT can draw almost anything at full scale, it is usually a good idea to size the drawing area on the screen before beginning a new drawing. This makes it easier to use title blocks with your drawings as well as helping to determine the final plot scale. Sizing the drawing area is also known as setting the *drawing limits*. By default, AutoCAD LT places the origin of the drawing at the lower-left corner (0,0) of the display screen, while the upper-right corner is set to 12 units on the X axis and 9 units on the Y axis (12,9). These drawing limits represent an architectural A-size sheet of paper.

You can set the drawing limits using the **World (actual) Size to Represent** area in the **Quick Drawing Setup** subdialog box. For example, to construct a drawing that is to be fitted onto a mechanical A-size (8.5 × 11) sheet, set the drawing **Width** to 11 inches and the drawing **Height** to 8.5 inches as shown in Figure 2-2. For a mechanical C-size sheet, set the drawing **Width** to 22 inches and the drawing **Height** to 17 inches. Remember to always use "real-world" units when you set your drawing limits, such as feet, inches, or millimeters.

SET LIMITS (handwritten)
0,0 — 12,9 (handwritten)
dEFALT (handwritten)
"A" A-SIZE 8½ (handwritten)

Setting the Grid. AutoCAD LT provides several handy drawing aids to help you draw accurately in the graphics window. One of these drawing aids is called the *grid*. It is very similar to grid paper. However, unlike grid paper that uses lines, the grid created by AutoCAD LT is a series of dots on the screen. You can specify the spacing between the dots on both the horizontal (X) and vertical (Y) axes. As shown in the **Quick Drawing Setup** subdialog box in Figure 2-2, the grid spacing is set to .5 units on both axes. Normally, the values in the **X Spacing:** and **Y Spacing:** text boxes appear grayed out, or disabled. Before setting new values, or accepting the default spacing, be sure to click the **Turn On Grid** check box to activate the text boxes. A grid with .5 × .5 spacing appears on screen as shown in Figure 2-4. The screen area covered by the grid corresponds to the current drawing limits. If you want to increase or decrease the size of the grid, increase or decrease the drawing limits accordingly.

Figure 2-4.
The drawing screen as it appears with drawing limits set to 0,0 and 11,8.5 and the grid X and Y spacing set to .5 units.

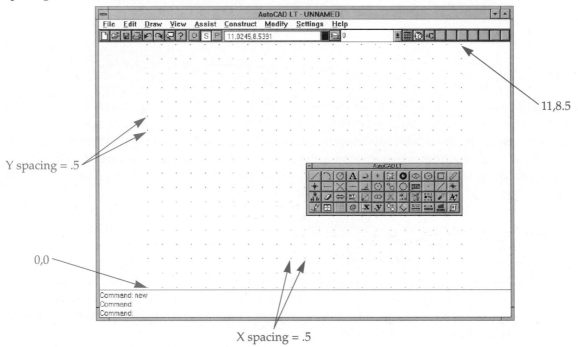

It is also possible to set the grid X and Y spacing independently. For example, if the Y spacing remains at .5 units and the X spacing is set to 1 unit, then the grid appears as shown in Figure 2-5. If you set the grid spacing too close, AutoCAD LT cannot display it and you will receive the following message:

    Grid too dense too display

Keep in mind that the grid dots are for construction purposes only. They will not plot, neither can they be erased. When you no longer want to see the grid, it can quickly be turned off by pressing the [F7] function key, or the [Ctrl]+[G] control key combination.

Figure 2-5.
The drawing screen as it appears with the grid X spacing set to 1 unit and the Y spacing set to .5 units.

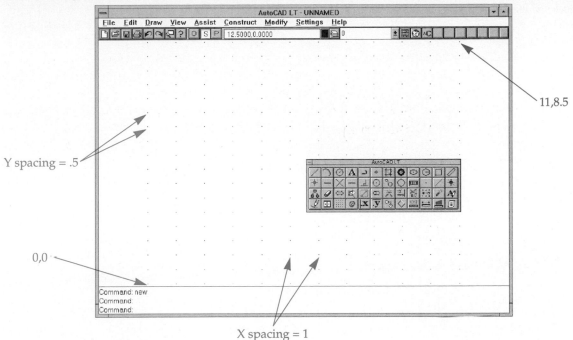

Y spacing = .5

11,8.5

0,0

X spacing = 1

Setting the Snap. While the grid is a handy visual aid, its real value becomes apparent when used in conjunction with another drawing aid called *snap*. Normally, the screen crosshair cursor can be freely moved about the drawing area. When the snap function is enabled, the cursor movement is restricted to user-specified increments. The cursor then moves from snap point to snap point. Although, the grid does not have to be on to use snap, by setting grid and snap spacing to be equal, you can draw lines and other entities by snapping onto the displayed grid dots. If you set the snap spacing smaller than the grid spacing, you can draw between the grid dots.

The grid and snap spacing is always set equal when you use the **Quick Drawing Setup** subdialog box. As with the grid, click the **Turn on Snap** check box so that the snap can be used. To quickly turn off the snap, click the **Snap** toolbar button, press [F9], or press [Ctrl]+[B].

PROFESSIONAL TIP

Here are two quick ways to set the X and Y grid and snap spacing equal. First turn both grid and snap on by clicking the **Turn on Grid** and **Turn on Snap** check boxes. Next, double-click inside the **X Spacing:** text box and enter the value you desire. Now, simply click inside the **Y Spacing:** text box and its value changes automatically to match that of the X spacing. Click the **OK** button in the **Quick Drawing Setup** subdialog box to accept the settings.

The second method is even faster. After setting the X spacing, simply press the [Enter] key. The Y spacing is set to match that of the X spacing and the **Quick Drawing Setup** subdialog box is automatically exited.

Once you have made your changes to the **Quick Drawing Setup** subdialog box, look over your settings carefully to be sure they are correct. If any changes are required, make them or click the **Cancel** button to start over. When everything is set to your satisfaction, click the **OK** button. The dialog box is exited, the AutoCAD LT graphics window appears, and you are ready to begin drawing.

EXERCISE 2-1

❑ Load Windows and start AutoCAD LT.

❑ When the **Create New Drawing** dialog box appears, click the **Quick** option button and then click **OK**.

❑ Using the **Units of Measurement** drop-down list, set Architectural units.

❑ Set the drawing **Width** to 80′ and the drawing **Height** to 60′. Do not forget to type in the foot mark (′), otherwise AutoCAD LT will use inch units.

❑ Click the **Drawing Aids** check boxes to turn grid and snap on and set the X and Y spacing to 2′. The **Quick Drawing Setup** subdialog box should appear as shown here. Click **OK** when you are finished.

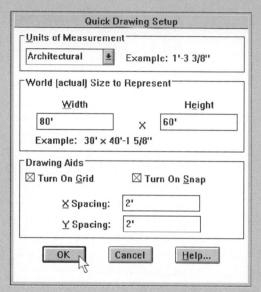

❑ Using your mouse, move the cursor around the drawing area. Observe the motion of the cursor as it snaps from one grid dot to the next.

❑ Now, turn the snap off using the **Snap** toolbar button, [F9], or [Ctrl]+[B]. Do you notice the difference in the cursor movement?

❑ Now try turning the grid on and off using function key [F7] or [Ctrl]+[G].

❑ When you are done, leave the screen as is, do not exit AutoCAD LT, and continue reading the following sections.

Using **Custom** setup

When you use the **Quick** method for a new drawing, your setup options are somewhat limited. For example, you cannot set the snap spacing different from the grid spacing or enable any other drawing aids. Also, you cannot select a system of measurement for angular values. Additionally, the **Quick** method affects only *model space*. Model space is where you construct your drawing, or model. Normally, this is precisely the space you want to be working in. However, there may be instances when you want to enter *paper space*. Paper space may be used to arrange the final layout of your drawing prior to plotting. AutoCAD LT uses paper space to insert a title block or border, as well as a date and time stamp, on your drawing.

When you want to perform a more detailed drawing setup, select the **Custom** option button from the **Setup Method** area in the **Create New Drawing** dialog box. This action displays the **Custom Drawing Setup** subdialog box shown in Figure 2-6. Using **Custom** setup, you still size the drawing area as you do with **Quick** setup, but you have additional options for units of measurement and drawing aids selection. What is more, you can use **Custom** setup to automatically insert a border or title block around the drawing limits.

Figure 2-6.
The **Custom Drawing Setup** subdialog box.

Select to
set units

Setting drawing
size

Setting drawing
aids

Select to insert
title block

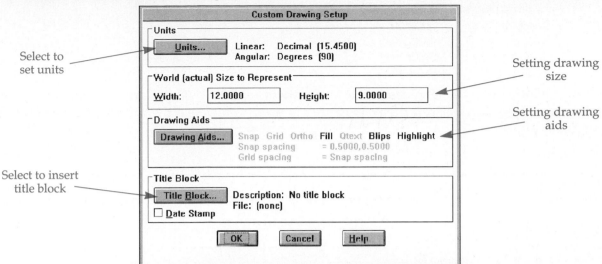

Setting custom units of measurement. AutoCAD LT defaults to four digits of precision for Scientific, Decimal, and Engineering units. If you want to change the number of displayed digits to the right of the decimal point, select the **Units...** button from the **Custom Drawing Setup** subdialog box. This displays the **Units Control** subdialog box. See Figure 2-7. Click the appropriate option button for the system of units you desire, and use the **Precision:** drop-down list to select the number of places of precision. In the example shown, the **Decimal** option button has been clicked, and three decimal places has been selected from the **Precision:** drop-down list.

Figure 2-7.
Both linear and angular units of measurement, as well as the number of decimal places of precision may be selected from the **Units Control** subdialog box.

Setting precision
for units

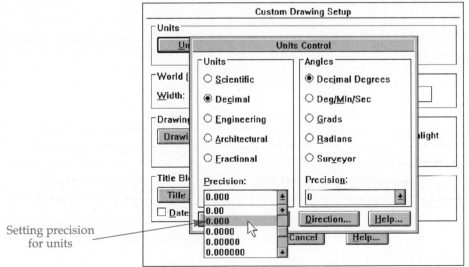

In the **Angles** area of the **Units Control** subdialog box, there are five different units of angular measurement available. The type and format for each are as follows:

De<u>c</u>imal Degrees	0.00
Deg/<u>M</u>in/Sec	0d00'00"
<u>G</u>rads	0.00g
<u>R</u>adians	0.00r
Sur<u>v</u>eyor	N 0d00' E

In Figure 2-8, the <u>**Engineering**</u> and **Sur<u>v</u>eyor** option buttons are selected, and the **Precision<u>:</u>** drop-down list in the **Angles** area is used to increase the accuracy of displayed angular values.

Figure 2-8.
The units selected in this example are appropriate for civil engineering and surveying applications.

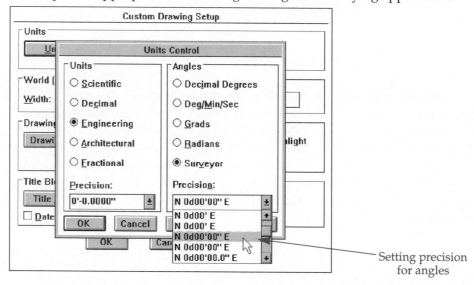

Setting precision
for angles

NOTE

Keep in mind that the number of decimal places you select for linear or angular measurement is for display purposes only. These displayed values are used by AutoCAD LT on the command line, in dialog boxes, and for dimensioning operations. They are also used when you query the system for the length of a line, the radius of a circle, or the area of a closed shape, for example. But regardless of the number of decimal places you specify, AutoCAD LT's database is accurate to 14 decimal places.

Using Drawing Aids to set Snap and Grid. In the middle of the **Custom Drawing Setup** dialog box is the **Drawing Aids** area. This area shows which drawing aids are turned on and which are off. The drawing aids and values that appear "grayed-out" are turned off. If you want to make any changes to the current settings, click the **Drawing <u>A</u>ids...** button and the **Drawing Aids** subdialog box appears.

From the example illustrated in Figure 2-9, you can see that the snap spacing is set to .25 and the grid spacing to .5. After setting the spacing, click the **<u>S</u>nap** and **<u>G</u>rid** check boxes to turn on the snap and grid. When you are done, click the **OK** button to exit the subdialog box. Remember the handy shortcut previously mentioned. Set the X spacing first, and then press [Enter] or click in the **<u>Y</u> Spacing** text box to set both X and Y values equal.

Figure 2-9.
The **Drawing Aids** dialog box.

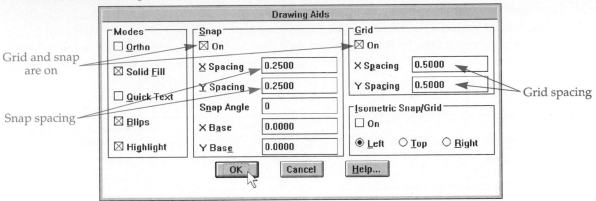

Grid and snap are on

Snap spacing

Grid spacing

It is also possible to rotate the entire snap and grid around a base point at a specified angle. You might find such an orientation handy when drawing angled features or auxiliary views. An example of a drawing with the snap and grid rotated at 45° is shown in Figure 2-10. To obtain a rotated orientation, enter the desired rotation angle in the **Snap Angle** text box. Normally, the drawing is rotated about the 0,0 origin, but if you want to rotate about some other coordinate, enter the appropriate X and Y values in the **X Base** and **Y Base** text boxes.

Other drawing aids appear at the far left of the dialog box in the **Modes** area. Each of these items will be discussed as they are encountered in later sections of this text. You will also note that at the lower-right of the dialog box is the **Isometric Snap/Grid** area. These options are covered in Chapter 15 of this text.

Figure 2-10.
Both the snap and grid are rotated 45° around the drawing origin.

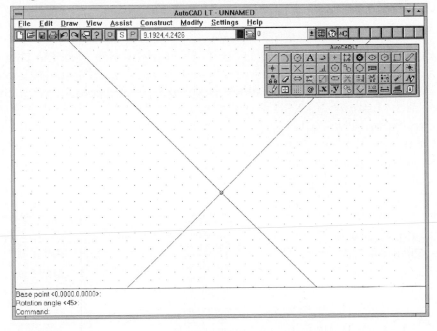

Inserting a title block

Located at the very bottom of the **Custom Drawing Setup** dialog box is the **Title Block** area. This area contains one button and one check box, which are used to insert a title block or drawing border around the limits of your drawing. Remember to first set the drawing limits in the **World (actual) Size to Represent** area of the dialog box. AutoCAD LT automatically inserts a border, not a title block, around your drawing limits when you use the **Custom** setup method. A drawing with just such a border appears in Figure 2-11.

Figure 2-11.
A drawing border is automatically placed around the drawing limits when using **Custom** setup.

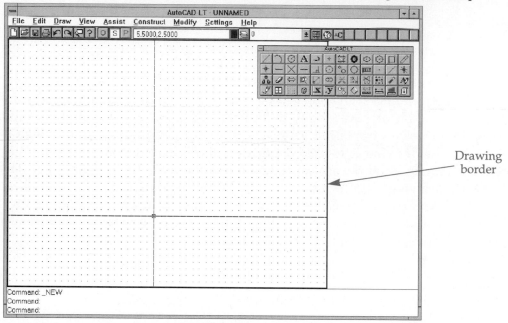

If you want to use a title block sheet instead of a plain border, click the **Title Block...** button to obtain a list of available title block formats. In Figure 2-12, an A-size title block is selected from the list. This particular title block is drawn in accordance with the American National Standards Institute (ANSI) specification, ANSI Y14.1, *Drawing Sheet Sizes and Format*. Hence the appropriate title block name ANSI A. Use the vertical scroll bar in the **Title Block** subdialog box to display a complete listing of title blocks provided by AutoCAD LT. The ISO title blocks at the bottom of the list are in metric format, and are in accordance with the specifications set forth by the International Standards Organization.

Figure 2-12.
A list of available title blocks is shown in the **Title Block** subdialog box.

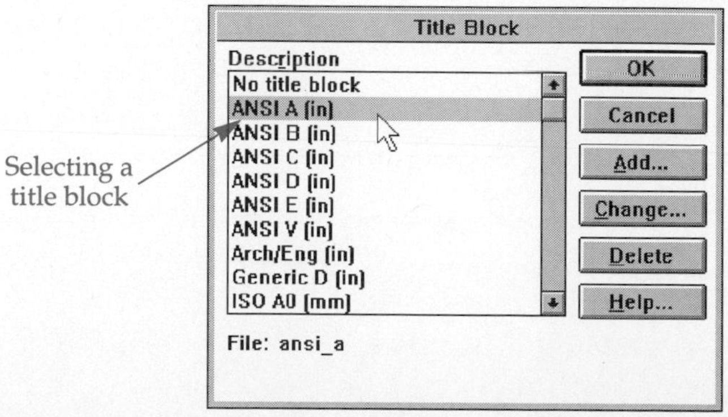

NOTE The ANSI V option in the list is also an A-size title block, but it is in vertical format. The ANSI A title block is in horizontal format.

Keep in mind, if you choose to insert a title block or border during **Custom** setup, then the title blocks and borders are inserted in paper space. The ANSI A title block is shown in Figure 2-13A and the ISO A4 title block appears in Figure 2-13B. Observe that a rectangular border appears inside both title blocks. This border is a paper space *viewport.* A viewport is a bounded area that displays some portion of a drawing in model space. It is in model space that all of our drawing and editing tasks are typically performed. This is why the grid and crosshair cursor are only displayed inside the viewport and not outside.

Figure 2-13.
A—The ANSI A title block. B—The ISO A4 title block.

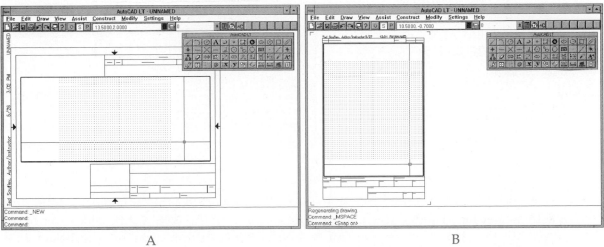

A   B

NOTE To fill out the title block information, you will need to work outside the boundary of the viewport. To do this, model space must be exited and paper space entered. This is done by clicking the **Paper Space** button on the toolbar. When you wish to return to model space and your drawing, simply click the **Paper Space** button again, or type MSPACE, or MS at the **Command:** prompt. Paper space is covered in detail in Chapter 16 of this text.

Additional title block options. Each of the available title blocks are separate drawing files that reside in the \ACLTWIN directory. This directory, and the title blocks themselves, are created by the SETUP.EXE installation program. Make sure you do not delete these files or you will lose your automatic access to title block formats. Additionally, you can customize these title block drawings to make them more closely conform to your school or company standards.

Note the **Add...**, **Change...**, and **Delete** buttons on the right side of the **Title Block** subdialog box. Descriptions of these buttons and their functions are as follows:

- **Add....** Use this button if you have additional title blocks that you would like to add to the list. In Figure 2-14A a custom E-size title block has been created for architectural applications and an appropriate description is entered into the **Description:** text box. Next, the **File...** button is clicked to bring up the **Select Title Block File** subdialog box shown in Figure 2-14B. So that AutoCAD LT can find the new title block, the user enters the name of the title block, ARCH-E, in the **File Name:** text box and then clicks the **OK** button. The new architectural E-size title block is then automatically added to the title block list for future use.

Figure 2-14.
A—Adding the description for a new title block. B—The new title block is selected from the **Select Title Block File** subdialog box.

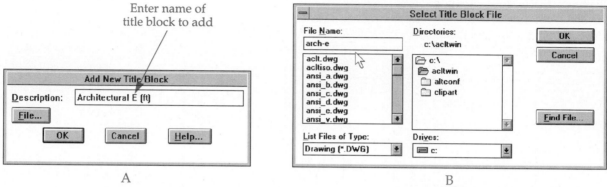

A

B

- **Change....** Use this button to change the description of existing title blocks. In Figure 2-15, a user has decided to change the description of the ANSI C title block to CSIZE. As with the **Add...** button, you must use the **File...** button to access the **Select Title Block File** subdialog box in order to select the title block that is being changed.

Figure 2-15.
Changing the description for an existing title block.

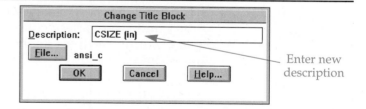

- **Delete.** To permanently remove one or more title blocks from the list, select the title block name, and then click the **Delete** button. The title block is removed from the list only, and not from the hard disk. Should you accidentally remove a title block from the list, use the **Add...** button to add it back.

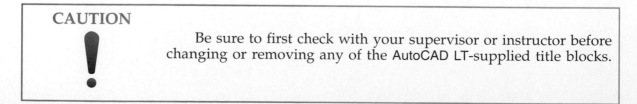

CAUTION

Be sure to first check with your supervisor or instructor before changing or removing any of the AutoCAD LT-supplied title blocks.

Adding a date and time stamp. If you like, the <u>C</u>ustom setup will conveniently add the user name, date, time of day, and drawing name to your drawing. This option is activated by clicking the <u>D</u>ate Stamp check box in the lower-left of the **Custom Drawing Setup** subdialog box. If you select one of the horizontal title block formats for your drawing, the data stamp is placed outside the left-vertical margin of the title block. If a vertical title block format is selected, such as ANSI V or ISO A4, then the date stamp is placed outside the top horizontal margin. Refer to Figure 2-13. If you choose to have just a border for your drawing, (the No title block option), then you can specify the date stamp location when AutoCAD LT prompts you on the command line with the following:

REVDATE block insertion point ⟨0,0⟩: *(enter coordinates or press* [Enter]*)*
REVDATE block rotation (0 or 90 degrees) ⟨0⟩: *(enter 0 or 90 and press* [Enter]*)*

Whenever you see alpha or numeric data enclosed within angle brackets like the examples shown above, that means that those values are the default settings. Unless you enter a different X and Y location, the date stamp is inserted at the 0,0 drawing origin. To accept the default insertion point values shown in the angle brackets, simply press the [Enter]. If you want the date stamp information to read left to right in a horizontal orientation (0°), simply press [Enter] again to accept the default. On the other hand, if you would prefer to have the date stamp read from the bottom to the top in a vertical orientation, type in 90 before you press [Enter].

It may be necessary to adjust the screen display somewhat so that the date stamp can be seen. To do so, you must enter paper space, issue the **ZOOM** command, and then return to model space to begin drawing. These operations are performed as follows:

Command: *(enter* PSPACE *or* PS *and press* [Enter]*)*
Command: *(enter* ZOOM *or* Z *and press* [Enter]*)*
All/Center/Extents/Previous/Window/⟨Scale(X/XP)⟩: **A** ↵
Command: *(enter* MSPACE *or* MS *and press* [Enter]*)*

PROFESSIONAL TIP

    Remember that by clicking the **Paper Space** toolbar button on and off, you can quickly toggle between model space and paper space and save yourself some typing. For more information about the **ZOOM** command, refer to Chapter 4 of this text.

Revising the date stamp information. Every new drawing started in AutoCAD LT is automatically given the name UNNAMED until it is first saved with a specific name. Saving your drawing files is covered later in this chapter. Because a new drawing is unnamed, the date stamp cannot yet show the proper name that the drawing will have when it is complete. This also applies to the date shown on the drawing. You may begin a new drawing on Monday, yet not finish it until Thursday. How can you update the drawing name, date, and time information on a drawing when it is finished?

Fortunately, this capability is provided by selecting **Date and Time** from the <u>M</u>odify pull-down menu. See Figure 2-16. This menu item enables the **REVDATE** command and automatically updates the date stamp information on your drawing. The **REVDATE** command may also be entered from the keyboard and can be used at any time. You can also use **REVDATE** to add date stamp information to a drawing that has no date stamp.

Figure 2-16.
Selecting **Date and Time** from the **Modify** pull-down menu updates the date stamp information on a drawing.

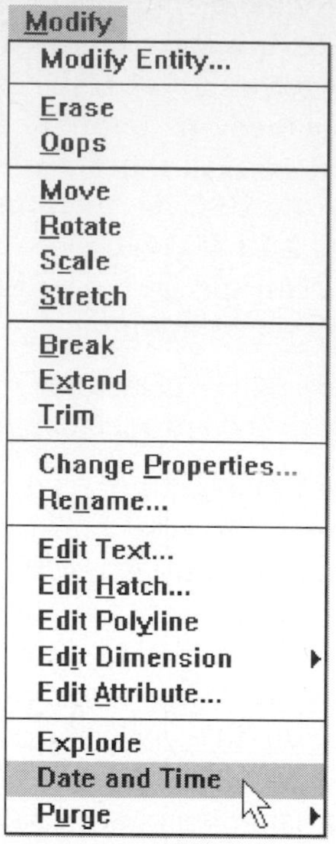

```
Modify
    Modify Entity...

    Erase
    Oops

    Move
    Rotate
    Scale
    Stretch

    Break
    Extend
    Trim

    Change Properties...
    Rename...

    Edit Text...
    Edit Hatch...
    Edit Polyline
    Edit Dimension        ▶
    Edit Attribute...

    Explode
    Date and Time
    Purge                 ▶
```

EXERCISE 2-2

❑ Exercise 2-1 should still be displayed on your screen. If it is not, perform Exercise 2-1 at this time.

❑ Issue the **NEW** command by clicking the **New** button on the toolbar, or selecting **New...** from the **File** pull-down menu. A dialog box appears asking you to save the changes made to the current drawing. Click the **No** button.

❑ When the **Create New Drawing** dialog box appears, click the **Custom** option button and then click **OK**.

❑ Use the **Units...** button to display the **Units Control** subdialog box and set Decimal units. Next, use the scroll bar in the **Precision** drop-down list to set the number of decimal places to 0.00. Click **OK** when you are through.

❑ When the **Custom Drawing Setup** dialog box reappears, set the drawing **Width** to 17 and the drawing **Height** to 11.

❑ Now, click the **Drawing Aids...** button. Set the snap X and Y spacing to .25 and the grid X and Y spacing to .5. Be sure to activate the **Snap** and **Grid** check boxes.

❑ Next, click the **Title Block...** button and select ANSI B (in) from the **Title Block** subdialog box. Click **OK** after selecting the title block from the list.

❑ Finally, click the **Date Stamp** check box. Click the **OK** button.

❑ So that you can see the date and time stamp on the drawing, perform the **PSPACE** and **ZOOM** commands previously described.

❑ Return to model space as described in the previous section.

❑ Leave this exercise displayed on your screen and do not exit AutoCAD LT.

ALTERNATIVE DRAWING SETUP OPTIONS

From the previous sections you have learned that it is quick and easy to specify drawing setup parameters whenever you begin a new drawing with AutoCAD LT. However, what if you wanted to change your snap and grid settings, or perhaps increase or decrease the drawing limits for an existing drawing? Fortunately, it is not necessary to start all over again. You can easily change the snap and grid, units of measurement, or drawing limits for any drawing at anytime. These setup options are all located in the **Settings** pull-down menu, Figure 2-17.

Figure 2-17.
The **Settings** pull-down menu contains the needed commands for changing drawing parameters without beginning a new drawing.

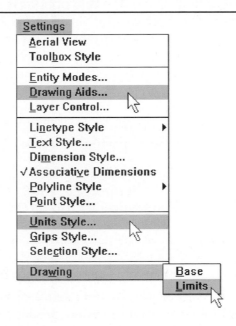

The **DDRMODES, SNAP,** and **GRID** commands

Perhaps the easiest way to specify or change snap and grid settings is with the **Drawing Aids** dialog box shown in Figure 2-9. You may recall that this dialog box is displayed automatically when you begin a new drawing and select the **Custom** setup method option button. However, you can bring up this dialog box at any time during a drawing session by issuing the **DDRMODES** (dynamic drawing modes) command. To do so, type in **DDRMODES** from the keyboard, click the **DDRMODES** button in the toolbox, or select **Drawing Aids...** from the **Settings** pull-down menu.

If you prefer to change snap and grid settings at the command line instead of using a dialog box, you can also use the **SNAP** and **GRID** commands. The **SNAP** command and its options are as follows:

Command: *(enter* SNAP *or* SN *and press* [Enter]*)*
Snap spacing or ON/OFF/Aspect/Rotate/Style ⟨*current*⟩: *(specify a value, enter an option, or accept the default)*

The description of each of the **Snap** options is as follows:
- ⟨*current*⟩. The current snap spacing for both X and Y axes is displayed here. By default, this value is set to .5000.
- **ON/OFF.** Turns snap mode on and off. This is the same as clicking the toolbar **Snap** button, pressing the [F9] key, or using [Ctrl]+[B].
- **Aspect.** The **Aspect** option lets you set the snap X spacing different from the Y spacing.
- **Rotate.** Discussed earlier in this chapter, you will recall that this option permits you to rotate the snap at an angle and about a specified point.

- **Style.** Snap has two styles, which are Standard and Isometric. The Standard style is orthogonal and is the default. Set the style to Isometric when you want to create isometric drawings. This capability is discussed in Chapter 15 of this text.

The **GRID** command offers features nearly identical to that of the **SNAP** command. These options are described below.

> Command: *(enter* GRID *or* G *and press* [Enter]*)*
> Grid spacing(X) or ON/OFF/Snap/Aspect ⟨*current*⟩: *(specify a value, enter an option, or accept the default)*

The description of each of the **Grid** options is as follows:
- ⟨*current*⟩. The current grid spacing for both X and Y axes is displayed here. By default, this value is set to .0000. If you are using the **Quick** or **Custom** setup options, however, the grid defaults to .5000 spacing.
- **ON/OFF.** Turns the grid on and off. This is the same as pressing function key [F7], or using [Ctrl]+[G].
- **Snap.** This handy option sets the grid spacing equal to the current snap spacing.
- **Aspect.** As with the **SNAP** command, the **Aspect** option lets you set the grid X spacing differently than the Y spacing.

NOTE   Entering the **SNAP** and **GRID** commands from the keyboard automatically turns on the snap and grid.

Selecting units of measurement with DDUNITS

As explained earlier, the **Custom** setup option allows you to specify both linear and angular units of measurement for a new drawing. You can change the units of measurement for an existing drawing at any time using the **DDUNITS** command. Whenever an AutoCAD LT command is prefaced with "DD", it means that a *dynamic dialog* box is used with the command. Typing DDUNITS at the **Command:** prompt, or selecting **Units Style...** from the **Settings** pull-down menu, will display the **Units Control** dialog box. See Figure 2-18. As previously described, simply click the appropriate option button for the system of linear and angular units you desire, and select the number of places of precision using the drop-down lists.

Figure 2-18.
The **DDUNITS** command displays the **Units Control** dialog box.

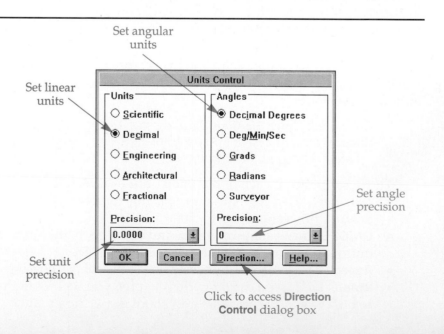

AutoCAD LT—Fundamentals and Applications

Using the **Direction...** button

AutoCAD LT uses the polar coordinate system to measure angles. With this system, all angles are measured in a *positive*, or counterclockwise, direction. Thus, 0° is to the right (east), 90° is straight up (north), 180° is to the left (west), and 270° is straight down (south). This convention is illustrated in Figure 2-19. If you want to measure angles in a clockwise fashion, simply enter the angles as negative (–) values.

Figure 2-19.
AutoCAD LT measures angles in a positive, or counter-clockwise, direction.

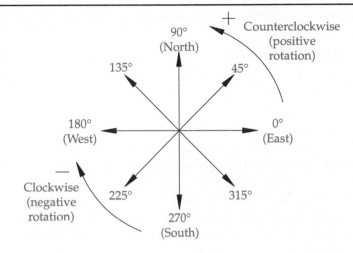

You can change this default method of angular measurement by clicking the **Direction...** button in the **Units Control** dialog box. This displays the **Direction Control** subdialog box. See Figure 2-20. If you want to set some arbitrary direction for angle 0, click the option button labeled **Other**. You can then enter the desired angle in the **Angle** text box. Alternatively, you can click the **Pick ⟨** button and then pick a point in the graphics window to represent angle 0.

Figure 2-20.
You can change the location of angle 0 and direction of angular measurement using the **Direction Control** subdialog box.

The LIMITS command

Although AutoCAD LT can draw virtually any object at virtually any scale, it is still helpful to size the drawing area before beginning construction. Normally, the drawing limits are set when the **NEW** command is used, but can be changed at any time using the **LIMITS** command. Before setting the drawing limits, be sure to set the units of measurement accordingly. In other words, if you want to size the drawing area large enough to accommodate a residential or commercial structure, first set architectural units before changing the limits. The same provision applies for mechanical or civil engineering drawings.

Referring once more to Figure 2-17, you can see that to specify new limits, you must first select **Drawing** from the **Settings** pull-down menu and then select **Limits** from the cascading submenu. If you choose to type in the command, its syntax and options are as follows:

Command: *(enter LIMITS or LM and press* [Enter]*)*
Reset Model space limits:
ON/OFF/⟨Lower left corner⟩ ⟨0.0000,0.0000⟩: *(specify a point, enter on or off,*
   or accept the default)
Upper right corner ⟨12.0000,9.0000⟩: *(specify a point or accept the default)*

From the prompt above, you can see that AutoCAD LT is asking for the lower-left corner of the drawing area. It is usually a good idea to leave the corner at the default 0,0 values, so just press [Enter] at this prompt. If you do decide to change the values though, always set the limits by first entering the horizontal distance, followed by a comma, and then entering the vertical distance. Also notice that the **LIMITS** command allows you to turn the limits ON and OFF. The limits are off by default. That means that even though you set the lower-left and upper-right of the drawing area, you may still freely draw outside those specified points. If you attempt to draw outside the defined points when the limits are turned on, however, you are prevented from doing so and receive the following error message: **Outside limits. Turning the limits on is also called *limits checking*. Should you find yourself constrained by limits checking in any of your drawings, simply return to the **LIMITS** command and turn the limits off.

After specifying the lower-left corner, you are then prompted to set the upper-right of the drawing area. The default values are 12 units on the X (horizontal) axis, and 9 units on the Y (vertical) axis. It is often useful to set the upper-right values to match the size of the media on which you intend to plot the finished drawing. As an example, if you intend to plot on a B-size piece of vellum or mylar, set the upper-right corner to 17,11. For a D-size drawing, set the upper-right corner to 34,22. Once you have manually set your new limits, do not forget to zoom your screen to display them. As discussed earlier, this is accomplished using the **ZOOM** command's **All** option. This option zooms the screen to the drawing limits or to the drawing extents—whichever is greater. The command sequence is as follows:

Command: *(enter ZOOM or Z and press* [Enter]*)*
All/Center/Extents/Previous/Window/⟨Scale(X/XP)⟩: **A** ↵

One of the benefits of setting the limits with the **Quick** or **Custom** setup methods is that the screen is zoomed for you automatically. The **ZOOM** command and each of its options is covered in Chapter 4 of this text.

> **NOTE** Remember that the grid display matches the current drawing limits. To increase or decrease the grid coverage, increase or decrease the drawing limits, and perform a **ZOOM All**. Also, do not be concerned that the drawing limits and grid do not extend all the way to the right side of the screen. This is because drawing limits are calculated in "real-world" units and the aspect ratio (ratio of horizontal width to vertical height) of a computer display monitor usually differs from the aspect ratio of standard drawing sheet sizes. Remember too that you may freely draw both inside and outside the drawing limits unless limits checking has been enabled.

Canceling a command in progress

If you make a typing error when entering characters from the keyboard, you can use the [Backspace] key to fix the error, or you can cancel *all* of the characters on the command line with the [Ctrl]+[X] key combination. If you are in the middle of a command and would like to cancel, use the [Ctrl]+[C] combination instead. You can also cancel a command in progress by clicking the **Cancel** button on the toolbar. Also, remember that you can cancel out of a dialog box by clicking the **Cancel** button or pressing the [Esc] key on the keyboard.

PROTOTYPE DRAWINGS   ALTUG 4

A prototype drawing is a framework, or template, that is used to create new drawings. A typical prototype drawing can contain the default settings for units of measurement, drawing limits, and snap and grid spacing, for example. Other settings might include layers, colors, and linetypes, as well as text and dimension styles. These types of settings are covered in later chapters of this text. Thus, you can create prototype drawings to reflect settings consistent with your specific discipline, design application, or company standards.

AutoCAD LT provides several prototype drawings that you can use "right-out-of-the-box", or you can create your own. Refer now to the **Create New Drawing** dialog box shown in Figure 2-21. To use a prototype drawing, click the **None** option button in this dialog box instead of using the **Quick** or **Custom** options. You will observe the filename ACLT.DWG appears in the text box just to the right of the **Prototype...** button, and that the **Use Prototype** check box is active. The default prototype drawing used by AutoCAD LT is called ACLT.DWG (all AutoCAD LT drawings have the file extension .DWG). The reason that AutoCAD LT defaults to decimal units of measurement with four digits to the right of the decimal point is because the ACLT.DWG prototype is set this way. Similarly, the reason that every new drawing defaults to 12,9 for the upper-right corner drawing limits is because the ACLT drawing has these limits set. For that matter, *all* of the settings in the ACLT drawing carry over into every new AutoCAD LT drawing, unless you specify a different prototype.

Figure 2-21.
Click the **Prototype...** button to select a drawing other than ACLT.DWG as your prototype.

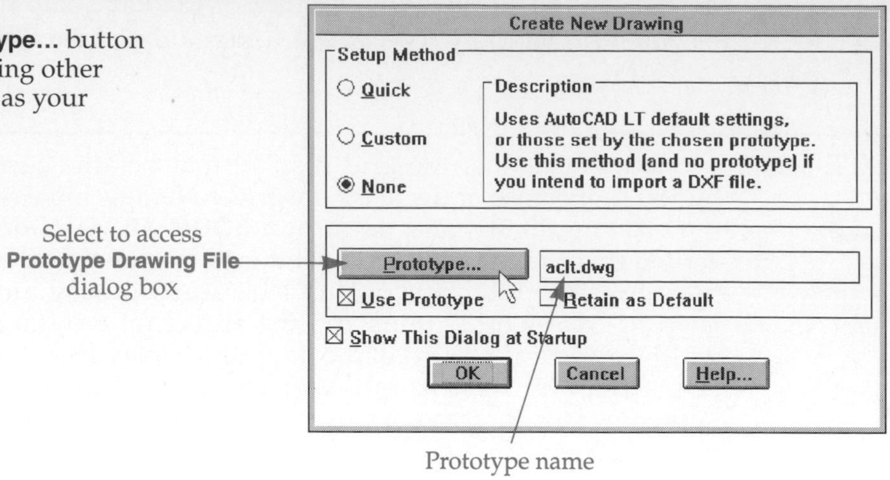

Select to access
Prototype Drawing File
dialog box

Prototype name

Selecting a prototype drawing

If you would like to use a prototype drawing other than ACLT.DWG, click the **Prototype...** button to display the **Prototype Drawing File** subdialog box. See Figure 2-22. You can type a new prototype drawing name in the **File Name:** text box, or select a drawing from the file list at the left of the subdialog box. Keep in mind that *any* drawing may be used as a prototype. From the file list, note the drawing file named ACLTISO.DWG. This drawing contains metric settings in accordance with the International Standards Organization (ISO). Observe also that each of the title blocks available with AutoCAD LT appear in the file list, as well.

Figure 2-22.
The **Prototype Drawing File** subdialog box.

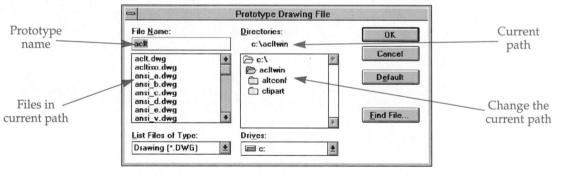

Prototype name

Files in current path

Current path

Change the current path

Advantages of prototype drawings

The key to using AutoCAD LT productively is to *never perform the same operation twice*. If you are an architect, it is far more efficient to have a prototype drawing set up for architectural drafting than it is to set architectural units and limits every time you begin a new drawing. Once you have a drawing with architectural parameters set, save it to disk to be used in future as a prototype. The same can be said for mechanical or civil engineering applications. When you create your prototypes, give them logical names like MECH.DWG, ARCH.DWG, or CIVIL.DWG so they can easily be identified. Once you have completed the remainder of this text, you will have learned all of the other types of settings and variables that control the AutoCAD LT drawing and dimensioning environment. You will then be better prepared to make your prototype drawings as complete as possible.

Because the entire concept of prototype drawings is to construct one drawing based on another, you can easily create similar types of drawings very quickly. As an example, consider the three simple objects illustrated in Figure 2-23.

Figure 2-23.
The prototype drawing method can be used to quickly produce similar drawings.

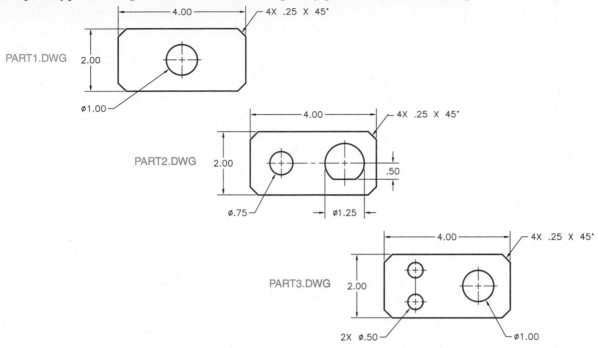

Except for the hole patterns, observe that all three drawings are identical. To quickly produce the three drawings, you would do the following:

1. Create the PART1 drawing. Be sure to make the drawing as complete as possible.
2. When finished, save the drawing to the hard disk.
3. Now begin a new drawing session. When the **Create New Drawing** dialog box appears, click the **None** option button and then click the **Prototype...** button to access the **Prototype Drawing File** subdialog box.
4. Select PART1.DWG from the file list and click **OK**.
5. The name PART1.DWG should now appear in the **Prototype** text box. Be sure that the **Use Prototype** check box is activated, and then click **OK** to exit the **Create New Drawing** dialog box.
6. A copy of the PART1 drawing is displayed in the graphics window. Make the required changes to the hole pattern and then use the **SAVEAS** command to save the new drawing as PART2.DWG.
7. Repeat the procedure for the PART3 drawing.

PROFESSIONAL TIP

Customize each of the title block drawings that are supplied with AutoCAD LT. Be sure to check with your instructor or supervisor before doing so, however. Set the units, snap, grid, etc., to your liking and add your school or company logo to the title blocks. It might also be a good idea to save the revised title blocks with different filenames. Use descriptive names like TITLEA, BSIZE, or FORMATC for example. When you need to create a new drawing in a title block format, use the prototype procedure outlined above. Simply select the appropriate size title block from the file list in the **Prototype Drawing File** dialog box. See Chapter 14 for additional ideas on title block customization.

Now that you know how to begin a new drawing session and set up a few drawing parameters, it is time you learned how to save your work. An AutoCAD LT drawing does not have a name until it is saved. It is the **SAVEAS** command that allows you to provide a name for your drawing while simultaneously saving it to disk. This command also allows you to redirect the drawing to a different drive and/or directory. Once a drawing has been given a name, the **SAVE** command is used instead of **SAVEAS**. Of course, if you want to save a drawing with a different name, or to a different directory path, then you should use the **SAVEAS** command.

To save a drawing, click the **Save** toolbar button, or select **Save** from the **File** pull-down menu. See Figure 2-24. If the drawing has not yet been saved, AutoCAD LT automatically invokes the **SAVEAS** command instead of **SAVE** so that a name can be provided for the drawing.

Figure 2-24.
The **SAVE** command can be issued by selecting **Save...** from the **File** pull-down menu.

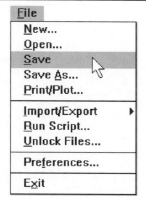

The **SAVEAS** command displays the **Save Drawing As** dialog box as shown in Figure 2-25. In this example, a user has entered the name BRACKET in the **File Name:** text box. It is not necessary to append the file extension .DWG to the drawing name—AutoCAD LT does this for you automatically. Observe that the drawing will be saved to the ACLTWIN directory on the hard drive (C:\ACLTWIN). If you want to redirect the drawing to another directory, double-click the appropriate directory icon in the directory window. These are the icons that appear as open

---

Figure 2-25.
The **Save Drawing As** prototype dialog box is used to save a drawing with a different name or to a different drive or directory.

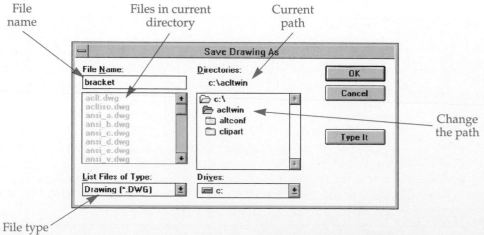

---

and closed folders. Open folders represent the current directory and/or subdirectory. If you wish to save the drawing to a different disk drive, select the desired drive from the **Drives** drop-down list at the bottom center of the dialog box. After providing a name for the drawing, click the **OK** button to save the drawing and exit the dialog box.

Saving your work automatically

It is critically important to save your drawing on a frequent basis. Doing so protects you from losing work due to hardware or electrical power failures. A good rule of thumb is to save every 10–15 minutes. If something should go wrong, then the most work you will lose is only about fifteen minutes worth. AutoCAD LT has a system variable called **SAVETIME** that can be set to save your work automatically at regular intervals. You can set this variable by typing the command PREFERENCES, or by selecting **Preferences...** from the **File** pull-down menu. Either method displays the **Preferences** dialog box shown in Figure 2-26.

Figure 2-26.
The **Preferences** dialog box can be used to automatically save your drawing at specified time intervals.

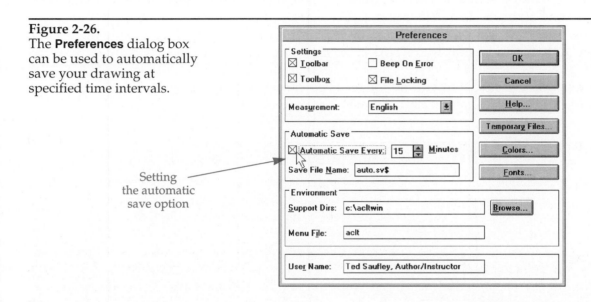

Setting the automatic save option

When the dialog box is displayed on your screen, locate the **Automatic Save** section in the middle of the dialog box. Use the up and down arrows to set the desired time interval (in minutes) and then click the **Automatic Save Every:** check box to activate your new setting. When this feature is enabled, AutoCAD LT saves your drawing with the name AUTO.SV$. You can use the **Save File Name:** text box to specify a different name if you like, but you cannot change the file extension. When you are through with your settings, click **OK** to exit the dialog box.

> **NOTE** The other options available in the **Preferences** dialog box are covered in detail in Chapter 19.

Assume that you have set the automatic save feature to save your drawing every 15 minutes. If you are in the middle of a drawing or editing command when 15 minutes has elapsed, AutoCAD LT will wait until you are finished before saving the drawing. You will not be interrupted. As the drawing is saved, the following message appears in the command line area at the bottom of the graphics window:

    Automatic save to C:\ACLTWIN\AUTO.SV$...

The **Command:** prompt reappears when the automatic save is complete. If you should ever need to work on this file inside AutoCAD LT, you will need to rename it. This is because AutoCAD LT will not read a file with the extension .SV$. It must be renamed with a .DWG file extension. To accomplish this, use the DOS RENAME command or the Windows File Manager. If you are not familiar with File Manager, be sure to refer to Chapter 21 of this text.

Backup (.BAK) files

The first time a new drawing is saved to disk, AutoCAD LT automatically appends the file extension .DWG to the drawing. After 10–15 minutes of additional work, the drawing is saved again. What happens to the original drawing on disk?

The second time that the drawing is saved, the original .DWG file is renamed with a .BAK (backup) file extension. The newly saved drawing is now the .DWG file. Thus, AutoCAD LT always maintains the previous version of a drawing as a .BAK file. This can be very handy should you make several changes to a drawing, save it, and then realize that you do not need the revisions after all. To retrieve the earlier version, you must first delete the unwanted drawing from the disk. Then, since AutoCAD LT will not read a .BAK file, rename the backup version .BAK file extension to a .DWG extension. The older version may now be used by AutoCAD LT.

When you are sure that you no longer need earlier backup versions of your drawings, delete the .BAK files from your hard drive to conserve disk space.

EXERCISE 2-3

❑ Exercise 2-2 should still be displayed on your screen. If it is not, do that exercise now.
❑ Be sure that you are in model space before completing this exercise. If you are still in paper space, click the **Paper Space** button on the toolbar, or type in MSPACE, or MS, to return to model space.
❑ Use the **DDUNITS** command to change to fractional units of measurement. Change the angular units to Deg/Min/Sec.
❑ With the **SNAP** command, set the snap spacing to 1/8. Use the **GRID** command to set the grid spacing to 1/4.
❑ Set the **SAVETIME** variable to save the drawing every 10 minutes.
❑ Now, use the **SAVEAS** command to save the drawing with the name MYFIRST.
❑ Once saved, use the **REVDATE** command to revise the date stamp on your drawing. Observe that the stamp now reflects the current drawing name.
❑ Finally, issue the **SAVE** command. Since the drawing now has a name, it is quickly saved without displaying a dialog box.
❑ Now, exit AutoCAD LT by issuing the **QUIT** command. You will be returned to the Windows Program Manager.
❑ Activate File Manager and open the ACLTWIN directory. You should have two versions of the MYFIRST drawing, .BAK and .DWG.

ACCESSING AN EXISTING DRAWING | ALTUG 2 |

Before you can work with a previously created drawing file, it must first be opened using the **OPEN** command. You can type in **OPEN**, click the **Open** button on the toolbar, or select **Open...** from the **File** pull-down menu. If the drawing you are currently working with has not yet been saved to disk, AutoCAD LT displays the alert box shown in Figure 2-27. This dialog box gives you the option to save your drawing changes, discard them, or cancel the command entirely. Always slow down and think a moment before clicking the appropriate button.

Figure 2-27.
AutoCAD LT displays an alert box if you attempt to open another drawing without saving your current changes.

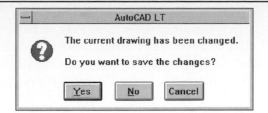

Whether you choose to save your changes or not, you are next presented with the **Open Drawing** dialog box. See Figure 2-28. As with other common file dialog boxes of this type, enter the desired file name in the **File Name:** text box or use your mouse to select the file from the file list at the left of the dialog box. If the file you want to open is in a different directory or on a different drive, use the **Directories:** list box and **Drives:** drop-down list as appropriate.

Observe the button labeled **Type It**. If you click this button, the dialog box is closed and you are prompted on the command line with the following:

Enter name of drawing: *(type in a drawing name and press* [Enter]*)*

Figure 2-28.
The **Open Drawing** dialog box. Notice the drawing PLANE.DWG has been selected from the file list and appears in the **File Name:** text box.

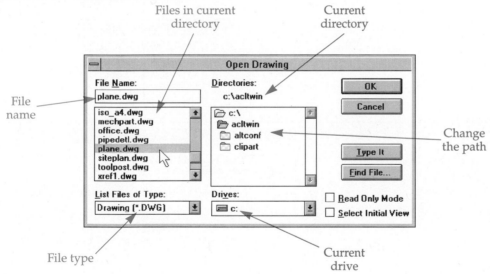

Notice also the two check boxes labeled **Read Only Mode** and **Select Initial View** at the lower-right corner of the dialog box. If you activate **Read Only Mode**, you may make changes to the opened drawing, but you cannot save the changes. To save your changes, use the **SAVEAS** command and provide a new drawing name. If you attempt to save the drawing with its original name, you will receive a message in a dialog box informing you that the drawing is write-protected.

AutoCAD LT allows you to save specified views of your drawing. The views are saved with names so that they may easily be restored for viewing, or deleted when no longer needed. The **Select Initial View** option displays a dialog box permitting you to select one of the saved views. The view that you select is then automatically displayed on screen as the drawing is opened. The **VIEW** command and its options are covered in Chapter 4 of this text.

Opening a drawing from the File pull-down menu list

AutoCAD LT remembers up to a maximum of four drawing files most recently opened in the drawing editor. These file names are listed at the bottom of the **File** pull-down menu as shown in Figure 2-29. Any one of these files may be quickly opened by clicking the file name with your mouse. You will observe that the drive and directory for each drawing is included with the file name.

If you should try to open one of these drawing files after it has been deleted or moved to a different drive or directory, AutoCAD LT will be unable to locate it. An alert box like that shown in Figure 2-30 is displayed.

Figure 2-29.
AutoCAD LT lists the four most recently opened drawings at the bottom of the **File** pull-down menu.

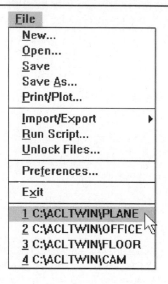

Figure 2-30.
AutoCAD LT displays an alert box if you attempt to open a file that has been deleted or moved from a directory.

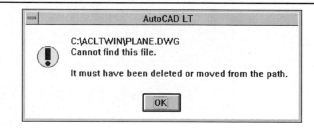

Using Find File

There may be instances when you need to edit an existing drawing file, but you cannot remember the drawing name or where the drawing resides on disk. A drawing file, (or any other AutoCAD LT file type) may be located by its name, type, date, or time created. To locate a file:

1. Click the **Find File...** button at the lower right of the **Open Drawing** dialog box. This action displays the **Find File** subdialog box shown in Figure 2-31.
2. Select the type of file you want to find from the **File Spec:** text box.
3. If desired, use the **Date** and **Time** text boxes to limit the search to files created after a date or time (or both) that you specify. When you use these features, you must follow these formats:

   Date   *mm-dd-yy*
   Time   *hh:mm:ss*

4. Use the **Drives** drop-down list to specify the drive(s) you want searched.
5. Use the **Path** text box to specify the directory you want searched.
6. Click the **Start Search** button.

Figure 2-31.
The **Find File** subdialog box. File search parameters can include drives and directories, file types, and be limited by the date and/or time when the files were created.

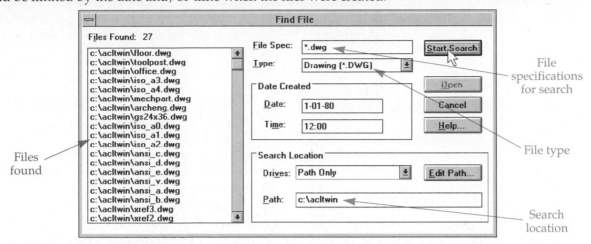

A status window appears to update you on the progress of the search. If the search takes too long, you can click the **Cancel** button.

When the search is completed, the list box on the left side of the **Find File** subdialog box displays the files that matched the search criteria. In the example shown, a total of 27 .DWG files were found in the C:\ACLTWIN directory. To open a drawing from the list, double-click the filename in the list or click once on the filename and then click the **Open** button at the right of the dialog box.

Building a search path

Normally AutoCAD LT searches only the current directory when the **Start Search** button is clicked. However, you can have AutoCAD LT search a number of directories on the same drive or on different drives by building a search path. To build a search path, do the following:

1. In the **Find File** subdialog box, select Path Only in the **Drives** list box.
2. Click the **Edit Path...** button and the **Edit Path** subdialog box appears. See Figure 2-32.
3. In the **Drives** and **Directories** list boxes, locate the directories you want searched, highlight each directory, and click the **Add** button to add them to the search path. If you later decide to delete a directory from the **Search Path:** list box, highlight it and click the **Delete** button. Any directories you select will appear in the **Search Path:** list box. In the example shown in Figure 2-32, the ACAD13 directory on the C: drive has been selected.
4. Click the **Close** button to close the **Edit Path** subdialog box and update the **Path:** text box in the **Find File** subdialog box.

Figure 2-32.
The **Edit Path** subdialog box. The \ACAD13 directory on the C: drive has been added to the search path.

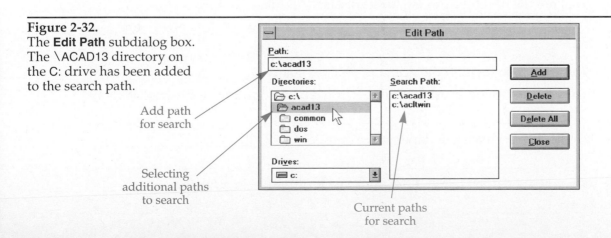

ENDING A DRAWING SESSION

When you have completed a drawing session, you can save your drawing, exit AutoCAD LT, and return to the Program Manager in one operation using the **END** command. Since this command does not appear in the toolbar, toolbox, or pull-down menus, type END at the **Command:** prompt as follows:

Command: **END** ↵

The drawing is automatically appended with a .DWG file extension as explained earlier.

QUITTING A DRAWING SESSION

If you choose, you may also exit AutoCAD LT without saving your drawing changes. This is handy when you have just been experimenting with the program and have no intent on saving the drawing. To do so, select **Exit** from the **File** pull-down menu or type in QUIT at the **Command:** prompt. If your drawing has not yet been saved, AutoCAD LT displays the dialog box shown in Figure 2-27. Click the **No** button to discard your changes and exit AutoCAD LT. Should you decide that you want to save the drawing after all, click the **Yes** button. If the drawing does not yet have a name, the **Save Drawing As** dialog box is then displayed as described previously. Click the **Cancel** button to return to the drawing editor if you decide not to exit AutoCAD LT.

CHAPTER TEST

Write your answers in the spaces provided.

1. How can the **Create New Drawing** dialog box be turned off? _____

   _____

2. The snap and grid spacings can be set independently using the **Quick** setup option. (True/False) _____

3. What is the default number of digits to the right of the decimal point in AutoCAD LT?

   _____

4. How many types of linear units of measurement are available in AutoCAD LT? How many types of angular units? _____

   _____

5. What are the default drawing limits in AutoCAD LT? _____

   _____

   _____

6. Is it possible to turn off the grid, but still use snap? _____

7. Which setup option is used to place a title block around the drawing limits? _____

   _____

8. Is a title block created in paper space or model space? _____

   _____

9. What must be done before filling out the information in a title block? _____

   _____

10. List two different ways to exit paper space. _____

_____

11. How do you update the date stamp information on a drawing? _____

_____

12. List two methods to cancel a command in progress. _____

_____

13. What must you do after changing your drawing limits with the **LIMITS** command? _____

_____

14. AutoCAD LT keeps displaying the error message: **Outside limits. What is wrong and how can it be corrected? _____

_____

15. How can you have AutoCAD LT automatically save your drawing at specified time intervals?_____

_____

_____

16. What are the advantages of using a prototype drawing? _____

_____

_____

_____

_____

17. What are some of the differences between the **SAVE** and **SAVEAS** commands?

_____

_____

_____

_____

_____

18. Every time you attempt to save your drawing, you receive a message stating that the drawing is write-protected. What is the cause of this message? _____

_____

19. What must be done before a .BAK backup file can be read by AutoCAD LT?_____

_____

20. What is the difference between the **END** and **QUIT** commands? _____

_____

_____

_____

_____

General

1. Begin a new drawing and set the following parameters:
   A. Linear decimal units with 3 digits to the right of the decimal point.
   B. Angular decimal degrees with 0 digits to the right of the decimal point.
   C. Snap spacing = .25
   D. Grid spacing = .5
   E. Limits set to 0,0 (lower-left corner) and 11, 8.5 (upper-right corner). Perform a **ZOOM All** after setting the limits.
   F. Save the drawing with the name PROTOA (for A-size prototype).

   This drawing will be used for many of the subsequent drawing problems in this text.

General

2. Edit the PROTOA drawing from Problem 1. Change the drawing limits to 17,11 for the upper-right corner. Remember to zoom the drawing after changing the limits. Save the revised drawing with the name PROTOB. This B-size prototype drawing will also be used for future drawing problems.

General

3. Edit the PROTOB drawing from Problem 2. Change the drawing limits to 22,17 for the upper-right corner. Once again, zoom the drawing after changing the limits. Save the revised drawing with the name PROTOC. As with PROTOA and PROTOB, this C-size prototype drawing will be used for subsequent drawing problems.

General

4. Open the AutoCAD LT-supplied drawing ANSI-A. Set the grid, snap, etc., as described in Problem 1. Save the revised title block drawing with the name TITLEA. Your new title block drawing will be used for future drawing problems in this text.

General

5. Open the ANSI-B and ANSI-C title block drawings, and perform identical operations done for Problem 4. Set the limits accordingly for each and do not forget to zoom afterwards. Save the revised title blocks with the names TITLEB and TITLEC, respectively.

Chapter 3

AutoCAD LT

Drawing and Erasing Lines

Learning objectives:
After you have completed this chapter, you will be able to:
- ❍ Understand and use **Direct Distance Entry** for drawing lines.
- ❍ Use **ORTHO** mode and the coordinate display box as drawing aids.
- ❍ Undo, redo, and continue line segments.
- ❍ Enter absolute, relative, and polar coordinates for line constructions.
- ❍ Erase unwanted lines and restore them again.
- ❍ Understand and use selection set options.
- ❍ Describe the difference between verb/noun and noun/verb entity selection.
- ❍ Undo and redo AutoCAD LT commands.

Perhaps the most commonly used function of any CAD system is drawing lines. In AutoCAD LT, lines are the most common drawn objects, or *entities*. In this chapter, you will learn to construct lines using a variety of techniques. Since some of the lines you draw will invariably have to be erased, you will also learn the various methods used to select entities for erasing and other editing functions.

ACCURACY AND SCALING

Precision is, or should be, the standard for every drafter, designer, and engineer. In a truly integrated CAD working environment, precise geometry creation is of great importance. This is because the electronic geometry contained in the CAD file is used to drive most, if not all, downstream operations. In mechanical engineering, such operations include prototype and production manufacturing, testing and analysis, as well as technical documentation such as product manuals and illustrations. In such cases, the original CAD geometry is used to satisfy those functions. Indeed, it is quite common for a *numerical control (N/C)* programmer or machinist to completely ignore the dimensions on a CAD drawing and generate the machining tool paths on the displayed geometry alone. Inaccurate geometry results in inaccurate tool paths—inaccurate tool paths result in inaccurate parts.

Accurate and precise geometry construction is important in the *AEC (Architecture, Engineering, Construction)* trades also. It is now quite common for subcontractors and vendors to share a set of CAD working drawings electronically. Since the same drawings are used for a variety of applications, including wiring, piping, landscaping, *HVAC (heating, ventilating, air conditioning)*, it is critically important that the drawings are as precise as possible. A single geometric error in a simple residential floor plan can cause serious downstream repercussions for everyone involved in the building project.

Sloppy, imprecise geometry is often called *dirty geometry*. This usually occurs because of incorrect coordinate entry, as well as through the improper use of the AutoCAD LT editing commands. Other instances of dirty geometry occur when entities are inadvertently duplicated one on top of another or where corners do not meet. Such mistakes can be a major source of grief for other users who must work with these drawing files.

One of the most common ways of creating inaccurate geometry is through the practice of rounding off, or truncating, decimal values when entering decimal coordinates. When using decimal units to construct your geometry, always enter decimal values in full. For example, enter .0625 for 1/16, .09375 for 3/32, .21875 for 7/32, etc. A fraction-to-decimal conversion chart appears in the appendices of this text. Remember that AutoCAD LT's database is accurate to 14 decimal places. Use this high-degree of accuracy to your advantage when entering decimal coordinates. Proper coordinate entry will eliminate rounding errors and/or tolerance buildup.

If you prefer to enter your coordinates using fractional units, the numerator and denominator must be whole numbers greater than zero. When entering values greater than one that contain fractions, there must be a hyphen between the whole number and the fraction—for example, 3-1/2. You must use a hyphen (-) as a separator because a space (pressing the space-bar) acts just like pressing the [Enter] key or clicking the right mouse button. Either action on your part ends the command line input.

Another common mistake made by users new to CAD is failing to create drawings at full scale. From the previous chapter you learned that AutoCAD LT can draw virtually anything at virtually any size. The drawings are scaled up or down as necessary using a predetermined scale factor at plot time. Think of the scale factor as the size of what is being drawn relative to the size of the plotted drawing. It is important to consider the appropriate scale factor to ensure that drawing annotation, such as notes and dimensions, have the proper lettering height when plotted. Creating text and dimensions with the correct height is covered in later chapters of this text. For complete information on plotting and plot scales, refer to Chapter 13 of this text.

DRAWING LINES   ALTUG 6

A line is drawn in AutoCAD LT by using the **LINE** command and specifying a starting point and an ending point for the line. The endpoints of the line can be selected interactively by simply picking points on the screen with your cursor, or by entering precise coordinates. You can type LINE at the **Command:** prompt, click the **Line** button in the toolbox, or select **Line** from the **Draw** pull-down menu. See Figure 3-1. The **LINE** command presents you with the following prompts:

    Command: (*type* LINE *or* L *and press* [Enter])
    From point: (*pick a start point for the line*)
    To point: (*pick an endpoint for the line*)
    To point: (*pick another point or press* [Enter] *to end the command*)

Figure 3-1.
The **LINE** command
can be issued by selecting
Line from the **Draw**
pull-down menu.

AutoCAD LT draws a single-line segment between the **From point:** and **To point:** selections. The **LINE** command continues to prompt for points, so you can continue drawing additional lines. No matter how many line segments you draw, however, each segment is a separate entity. When you are done drawing lines, click the right button on your mouse or press [Enter] to end the command.

In the example illustrated in Figure 3-2, a line is drawn between two points selected with the screen crosshair cursor. When you draw lines interactively using the cursor, a *rubberband* line connects to the end of the last point selected. As you move your mouse around the graphics window, the rubberband line follows the motion of your cursor.

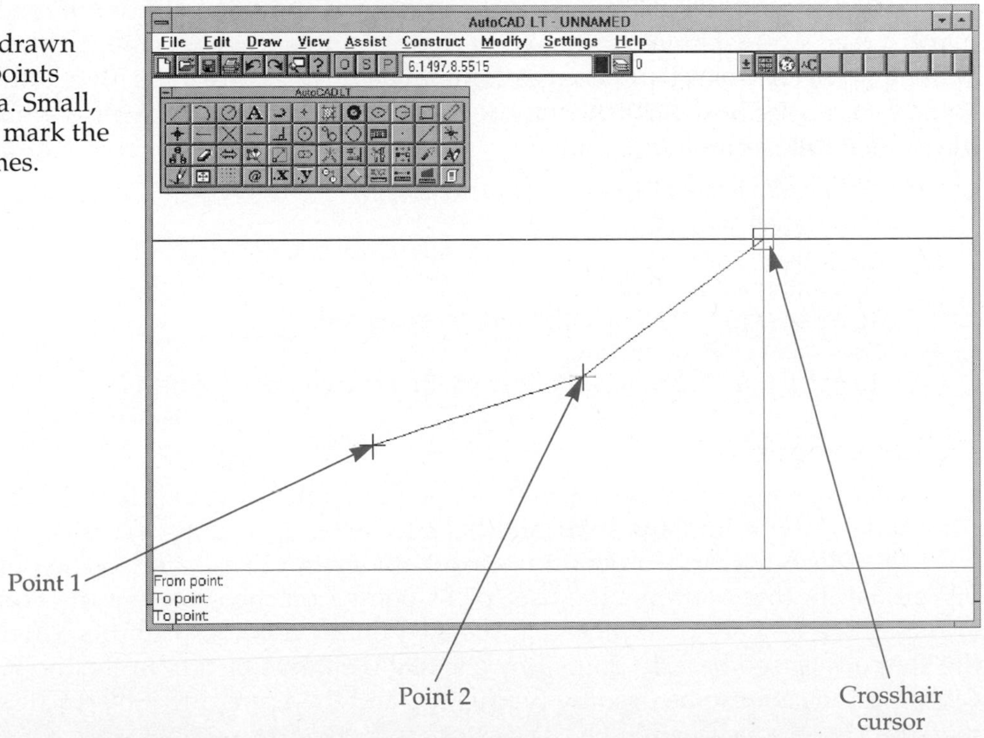

Figure 3-2.
Line segments are drawn
between selected points
in the graphics area. Small,
cross-shaped blips mark the
endpoints of the lines.

Point 1

Point 2

Crosshair
cursor

Blips and the REDRAW command

The points you select on the screen with the cursor are marked with small crosses called *blips*. These are temporary markers that appear on screen when a location is indicated with an entered coordinate or a pointing device, like your mouse. Blips are on by default, but may be turned off with an AutoCAD LT system variable called **BLIPMODE**. As you will learn in later chapters, blips can actually be considered reference points and it is recommended that you do not turn them off. Although blips do not plot, most users prefer to refresh their drawing screens regularly so that the blips disappear.

There are two ways to quickly refresh the drawing display. One way is to turn the grid on and off quickly using the [F7] function key. A better way exists using the **REDRAW** command. You can redraw your screen by typing REDRAW at the **Command:** prompt, clicking the **Redraw** button in the toolbox, or by selecting **Redraw** from the **View** pull-down menu. See Figure 3-3. The command sequence is as follows:

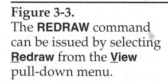

Command: *(type* REDRAW *or* R *and press* [Enter]*)*

Figure 3-3.
The **REDRAW** command can be issued by selecting **Redraw** from the **View** pull-down menu.

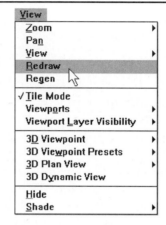

The **REDRAW** command is one of a small subset of AutoCAD LT commands that may be invoked *transparently*. That means the command may be used while inside another command. Once a transparent command is complete, the previous command is resumed. To use a transparent command, preface the command with an apostophe ('). In the sequence that follows, you can see how **REDRAW** can be invoked to remove screen blips while still in the middle of the **LINE** command.

Command: *(type* LINE *or* L *and press* [Enter]*)*
From point: *(pick point 1)*
To point: *(pick point 2)*
To point: *(pick point 3)*
To point: *(type* 'REDRAW *or* 'R *and press* [Enter]*)*
Resuming LINE command.
To point: *(pick another point or press* [Enter] *to end the command)*

The Close option

When you want to draw a closed shape using lines, it is a simple matter to have the **LINE** command draw a line automatically back to its starting point. This capability is provided with the **Close** option. To obtain a clearer understanding, refer to the object illustrated in Figure 3-4. In this example, the user picks point 1 on the screen at the **From point:** prompt. Points 2, 3, and 4 are then picked at the next three **To point:** prompts. After picking point 4, the shape is closed back to point 1 by clicking the **Close** button in the toolbox as shown. The **Close** option can also be used by typing in C and then pressing [Enter]. The sequence of steps to draw the object shown in Figure 3-4 looks like this:

Command: *(type* LINE *or* L *and press* [Enter]*)*
From point: *(pick point 1)*
To point: *(pick point 2)*
To point: *(pick point 3)*
To point: *(pick point 4)*
To point: **C** ↵
Command:

Whether you use the **Close** toolbox button, or type in C from the keyboard, the **Close** option closes the shape you are drawing and automatically ends the **LINE** command. However, keep in mind that you must draw at least two or more line segments before the **Close** option can be used.

Figure 3-4.
The **Close** option creates a closed shape by automatically drawing a line segment back to the starting point.

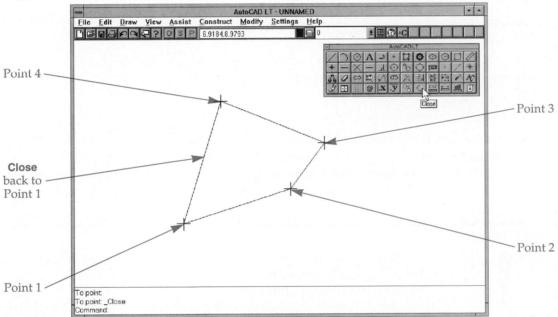

Repeating the LINE command

ALTUG 6

If after drawing several lines you would like to quickly repeat the **LINE** command, you need not reissue the command. Simply press the [Enter] key or the spacebar on your keyboard, and the **LINE** command is automatically repeated. This handy feature applies to nearly every command in AutoCAD LT. Get in the habit of using this repeat function—it can save you a lot of work.

Another way to automatically repeat commands is by using the **MULTIPLE** command modifier. To use this method, you simply preface the command name with the word MULTIPLE, or MU, as follows:

Command: **MULTIPLE LINE** ↵

or

Command: **MU L** ↵

Be sure to put a space between MULTIPLE and the command name. AutoCAD LT then repeats the command until you press [Ctrl]+[C] or click the **Cancel** button on the toolbar. You can use the **MULTIPLE** command with most of the drawing and editing commands in AutoCAD LT. However, it cannot be used with dialog box commands.

The continuation option

There will be occasions when you inadvertently end the **LINE** command without drawing all of the lines you had intended. You can easily repeat the **LINE** command and have AutoCAD LT automatically pick up where it left off. First, press [Enter] or the spacebar to repeat the **LINE** command as described above. At the **From point:** prompt, simply press [Enter] or the [Spacebar] again. The new line is automatically connected to the endpoint of the last line drawn. This method of reattachment is called the *continuation* option. Once attached, you may continue to draw more line segments.

Undoing line segments

No matter how careful or attentive, you will occasionally draw a line segment incorrectly. AutoCAD LT provides an **Undo** option that permits you to remain in the **LINE** command, remove the incorrect segment, and continue on with line construction. To use this option, simple type U while you are still in the **LINE** command as shown below:

Command: *(type* LINE *or* L *and press* [Enter]*)*
From point: *(pick point 1)*
To point: *(pick point 2)*
To point: *(pick point 3)*

If you suddenly realize that the line just drawn between points 2 and 3 is incorrect, then use the **Undo** option to remove the segment.

To point: **U** ↵
To point: *(pick a new location for point 3)*

You can also click the **Undo** button on the toolbar to undo a line segment. To undo several line segments as far back as needed, enter U followed by [Enter] a number of times, or successive clicks of the toolbar **Undo** button. The endpoints of the removed lines remain as blips for reference until you redraw the screen.

CAUTION

Try to remember to undo incorrect line segments while you are still in the **LINE** command. Once you end the command and type U (or click the toolbar **Undo** button), then the entire line operation is undone. If that should happen, click the **Redo** button just to the right of the **Undo** button to restore your lines. More about the **UNDO** and **REDO** commands later in this chapter.

Using Ortho mode

Ortho is an AutoCAD LT drawing aid that constrains cursor movement to horizontal or vertical directions only. This means that no matter how hard you try, you cannot draw a diagonal line with your cursor when **Ortho** is on. It, therefore, becomes much easier to draw perfectly horizontal or vertical lines using **Ortho**. **Ortho** is particularly handy when you have found that you have drawn two views too closely together and there is not enough room for dimensions. You simply move one of the views left or right (or up and down) to increase the spacing between the views. With **Ortho** on, motion is constrained about the horizontal and vertical axes so that the views maintain perfect alignment. There are several ways to enable **ORTHO** mode. One way is to use the **ORTHO** command as follows:

Command: *(type* ORTHO *or* OR *and press* [Enter]*)*
ON/OFF ⟨current⟩: *(type* ON *or* OFF *as desired)*

However, it is faster to use the [Ctrl]+[O] keyboard combination, press function key [F8], or simply click the **Ortho** button on the toolbar. Like **GRID** and **SNAP** modes, **Ortho** can be toggled on and off in the middle of a drawing command.

EXERCISE 3-1

❏ Load Windows and start AutoCAD LT.
❏ Begin a new drawing using the PROTOA prototype drawing you created in Problem 1 of Chapter 2. If you did not complete this drawing problem, set the snap spacing to .25 and the grid spacing to .5.
❏ Use the **LINE** command with grid and snap turned on to draw the objects shown below. Do not be concerned with dimensions. Size the objects so that they are proportional to those shown.

❏ As you draw, experiment with the **Undo** and **Continuation** options described in the preceding text.
❏ Now, turn off the grid and snap, and try drawing several of the objects.
❏ Turn on **ORTHO** mode, or click the toolbar **Ortho** button, and try drawing the two triangles. What happens?
❏ Finally, use the **MULTIPLE** command modifier to automatically repeat the **LINE** command. Remember to cancel to exit the **LINE** command.
❏ When you are done, save the drawing with the name EX3-1.

DRAWING A LINE USING DIRECT DISTANCE ENTRY   ALTUG 5

Direct Distance Entry is a construction method that allows you to specify a point by moving your cursor to indicate a direction and then typing a distance from the first point selected. The **Direct Distance Entry** method can be used for nearly every command in AutoCAD LT that requests points. With the **LINE** command, it allows you to quickly specify a line of a specific length. For example, when you are in the **LINE** command and the **To point:** prompt is displayed, you enter a real value instead of using your mouse to indicate a distance. However, before you enter the line length value you must move your cursor in the direction you want the line to be drawn. Do not pick a point, though—just move your cursor. AutoCAD LT starts drawing from the last point you selected and draws (in the direction of the cursor) a line segment with the length you specified. The line will be perfectly straight if **Ortho** is on. If **Ortho** is off, the line will be drawn at the angle formed by the last specified point and the current cursor location.

You can quickly draw the rectangle shown in Figure 3-5 by turning **ORTHO** mode on and then using the following procedure:

> Command: *(type LINE or L and press* [Enter]*)*
> From point: *(pick a location for point 1)*

Figure 3-5.
A rectangle drawn using
Direct Distance Entry. Notice
that the **Ortho** button on
the toolbar is active.

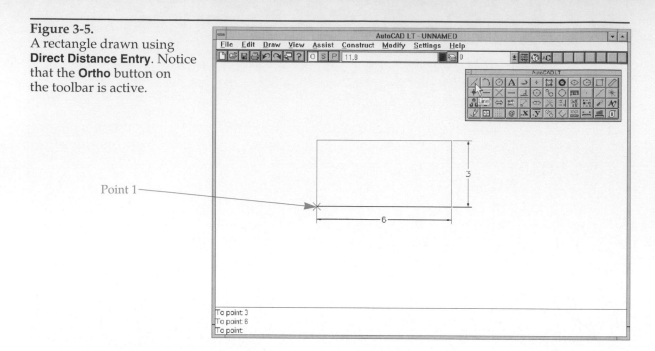

Now, move your cursor to the right but do not pick a point.

> To point: **6** ↵

Move your cursor up. Again, do not pick a point.

> To point: **3** ↵

Now move your cursor to the left.

> To point: **6** ↵

Finally, move your cursor down.

> To point: **3** ↵
> To point: ↵
> Command:

Remember that the **Close** option is a better and more efficient alternative than entering 3 for
the last line segment.

EXERCISE 3-2

❑ Begin a new drawing session. It is not necessary to use one of your prototype drawings
for this exercise.
❑ Turn **Ortho** on and use the **LINE** command with **Direct Distance Entry** to draw the rec-
tangle shown in Figure 3-5.
❑ Try drawing the rectangle with **Ortho** off. What happens?
❑ Turn **Ortho** back on and draw several other rectangular and square-shaped objects using
any length values you like.
❑ When you are done, save the drawing as EX3-2.

AutoCAD LT—Fundamentals and Applications

DRAWING LINES USING COORDINATES

While **Direct Distance Entry** is certainly quick and easy, there will be occasions when other means of point entry are required. Most of the point entry methods in AutoCAD LT use the *Cartesian*, or rectangular, coordinate system with which you are probably already familiar. With this system, all X and Y values are related to the drawing origin (usually at the very lower-left of the drawing screen) where X=0 and Y=0. Point distances are measured along the horizontal X axis and the vertical Y axis. Positive X values are to the right, or east, and positive Y values are to the top, or north as shown in Figure 3-6. It follows, that negative X values are to the left, or west, and negative Y values are to the bottom, or south.

Figure 3-6.
In the Cartesian coordinate system, the positive X direction is to the right and the positive Y direction is up. The negative X direction is to the left and the negative Y direction is down.

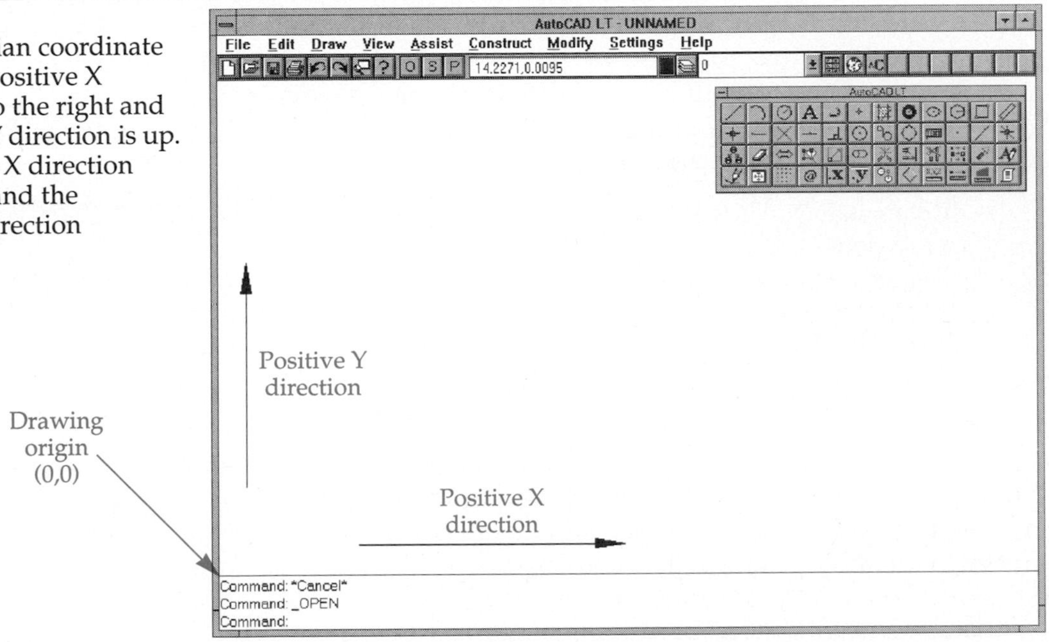

| NOTE | Since AutoCAD LT is a true 3D software program, it also has a Z axis that is perpendicular, or normal to the screen. Positive Z values are out of the screen toward you, the viewer, while negative Z values go into the screen, or away from you. The three XYZ axes, therefore, form 90° mutually perpendicular planes which allow six degrees of freedom for 3D geometry construction. Basic 3D viewing and drawing commands are introduced in Chapter 18 of this text. |

The World Coordinate System (WCS)

The Cartesian coordinate system described above is fixed in 3D space and may not be moved or altered. Because it is universal, AutoCAD LT refers to it as the *WCS*, or *World Coordinate System*. Whenever a new drawing file is created in AutoCAD LT, the graphics window defaults to a single viewport which corresponds to the WCS. In this view, the user is looking down along the positive Z axis onto the XY plane. This viewing angle is referred to as the *plan view*, or *plan to the WCS* as it is commonly called. All of the coordinates are measured along the X and Y axes relative to the 0, 0 origin at the lower left. Most of the 2D drawings that you will create using this textbook will be in the plan view with the World Coordinate System. An alternative to the WCS is the *UCS*, or *User Coordinate System*. With

---

the UCS, a user may redefine the location of 0,0 and the direction of the XYZ axes. This capability is absolutely essential for 3D geometry construction, but can also be used for certain 2D applications. Those applications and the UCS will be discussed more fully in later chapters.

Using absolute coordinates

Absolute coordinates are the most basic of the point entry methods used in AutoCAD LT. With absolute coordinates, all points are measured relative to the drawing origin (0,0). As an example, refer to the object shown in Figure 3-7. This is the same 6 × 3 rectangle that you created using **Direct Distance Entry** in the previous exercise. In this example, the object is created using absolute coordinate entry. Observe that the lower left corner of the rectangle has the absolute coordinate 3,3. This means that AutoCAD LT measures 3 units horizontally (the positive X direction), and 3 units vertically (the positive Y direction) from the drawing origin (0,0) to locate the starting point of the first line. If you are seated at your computer, use the command sequence below to construct the rectangle. Remember to separate the Y coordinate from the X coordinate with a comma (,). If you make a typing mistake, use the [Backspace] key to correct the error. If you draw a line segment incorrectly, use the **U** option to undo it while you are still in the **LINE** command.

> Command: *(type* LINE *or* L *and press* [Enter]*)*
> From point: **3,3** ↵
> To point: **9,3** ↵
> To point: **9,6** ↵
> To point: **3,6** ↵
> To point: **C** ↵
> Command:

Of course, you can enter the final coordinate of 3,3 and then press [Enter] to close the rectangle. However, typing C and then [Enter] is a much quicker method to close the shape and end the **LINE** command all in one simple operation. Better yet, you can just click the **Close** button in the toolbox to do the same operation.

Figure 3-7.
The 6 × 3 rectangle drawn using absolute coordinates.

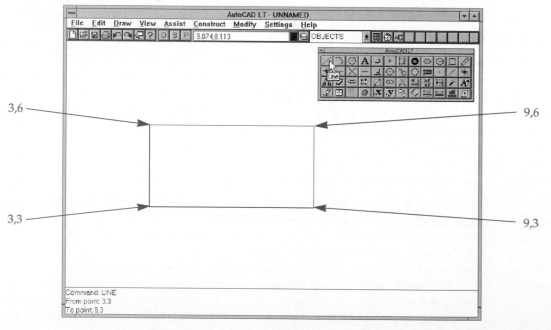

AutoCAD LT—Fundamentals and Applications

EXERCISE 3-3

❑ Begin a new drawing session. It is not necessary to use one of your prototype drawings for this exercise.

❑ Use the **LINE** command with the following absolute coordinates to draw the object shown below.

Point	Coordinate	Point	Coordinate	Point	Coordinate
1	4,2	5	7.75,3.5	9	8,5.875
2	8,2	6	7.75,4.375	10	4,5.875
3	9,3	7	9,4.375	11	4,2 *or* CLOSE
4	9,3.5	8	9,4.875		

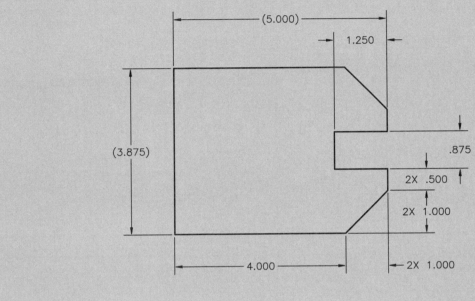

❑ Save the drawing as EX3-3.

Using relative coordinates

While absolute coordinates are useful, they are not very efficient. To explain further, think about the traditional, paper-based drafting process. If you were to work on a drafting board using the equivalent of absolute coordinates, then every line drawn would have to be measured from the very lower left corner of the sheet of vellum taped to your board. Drafting would become very laborious and time-consuming, indeed!

It is far better to draw lines and other drawing entities *relative to each other*, rather than relative to the drawing origin. This is the type of method commonly used on a drafting board. AutoCAD LT allows for this type of point entry using *relative coordinates*. With this method, the coordinates you enter are in relation to previously entered coordinates. To tell AutoCAD LT that you want to use relative coordinates, you must precede your coordinate entry with the *at symbol (@).* It is located on the number 2 key on the top row of your keyboard so you must use the [Shift] key to access it.

What does the @ symbol really represent? Every time you locate a point in the drawing area, the X, Y (and Z) coordinates of the cursor position are stored in an AutoCAD LT system variable called **LASTPOINT**. As you move your cursor around the screen and pick points, the **LASTPOINT** values constantly change. When you use the @ symbol, AutoCAD LT reads and uses the XYZ coordinates stored in **LASTPOINT**. This is why AutoCAD LT always knows where you left off in your drawing!

From Figure 3-8, you can see how relative coordinates define the 6 × 3 rectangle that was previously drawn using **Direct Distance Entry** and absolute coordinates. If you are seated at your computer, try the following command sequence to draw the rectangle using relative coordinates. Do not forget to use the @ symbol, or your line segments will be drawn relative to 0,0.

> Command: (*type* LINE *or* L *and press* [Enter])
> From point: **3,3** ↵
> To point: **@6,0** ↵
> To point: **@0,3** ↵
> To point: **@-6,0** ↵
> To point: **C** ↵
> Command:

Figure 3-8.
The 6 × 3 rectangle drawn using relative coordinates.

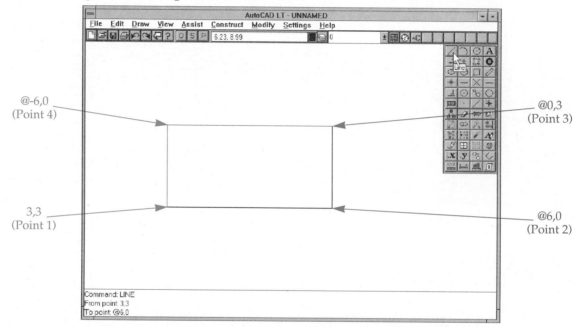

❑ Begin a new drawing session. It is not necessary to use one of your prototype drawings for this exercise.
❑ Draw the same object as in Exercise 3-3, but using the following relative coordinates:

Point	Coordinate	Point	Coordinate	Point	Coordinate
1	4,2	5	@–1,0	9	@–1,1
2	@4,0	6	@0,.875	10	@-4,0
3	@1,1	7	@1,0	11	@0,–3.875 *or*
4	@0,.5	8	@0,.5		CLOSE

❑ Save the drawing as EX3-4.

Using polar coordinates

From Chapter 2 you learned that AutoCAD LT uses a *polar coordinate system* to measure angles. Remember that in this system, angles are measured in a positive, or counterclockwise, direction where 0° is to the right (east), 90° is straight up (north), 180° is to the left (west), and 270° is straight down (south). This convention is graphically illustrated in Figure 3-9.

Figure 3-9.
In the polar coordinate system, angles are measured in a positive, or counter-clockwise, direction.

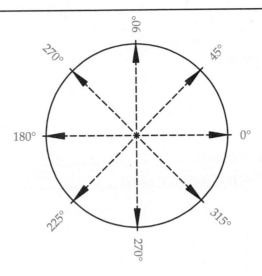

Polar coordinates can be used to locate a point by specifying its distance and angle from an existing point. To use relative polar coordinates, enter the @ symbol, the distance, a less-than sign (⟨), and then the angle (@*distance*⟨*angle*). Refer to Figure 3-10 to see how several lines are drawn using polar coordinates. If you think of the angle as direction, then you can see that polar coordinates use distance and direction values, and not X and Y values at all.

Figure 3-10.
Lines drawn using polar coordinates.

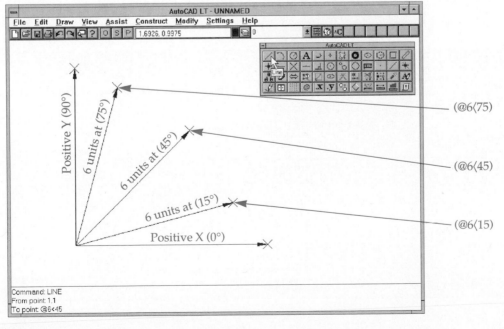

From Figure 3-11, observe how polar coordinates are used to draw the 6 × 3 rectangle that was previously drawn using the **Direct Distance Entry**, absolute, and relative coordinate methods. Once more, try the following command sequence to draw the rectangle using polar coordinates if you are seated at your computer.

> Command: *(type* LINE *or* L *and press* [Enter]*)*
> From point: **3,3** ↵
> To point: **@6⟨0** ↵
> To point: **@3⟨90** ↵
> To point: **@6⟨180** ↵
> To point: **C** ↵
> Command:

Figure 3-11.
The 6 × 3 rectangle drawn using polar coordinates.

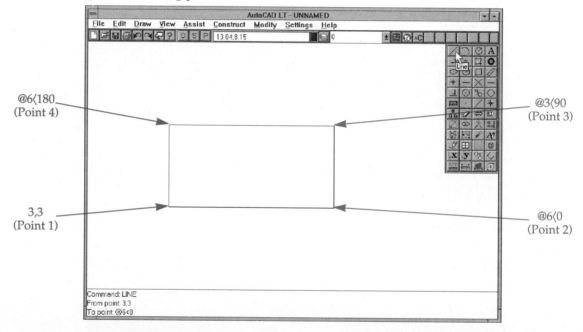

❑ Begin a new drawing session. It is not necessary to use one of your prototype drawings for this exercise.

❑ Draw the same object as in the previous three exercises, but use the following polar coordinates:

Point	Coordinate	Point	Coordinate	Point	Coordinate
1	4,2	5	@1⟨180	9	@1.414⟨135
2	@4⟨0	6	@.875⟨90	10	@4⟨180
3	@1.414⟨45	7	@1⟨0	11	@3.875⟨270 *or*
4	@.5⟨90	8	@.5⟨90		CLOSE

❑ Save the drawing as EX3-5 and QUIT.

Using the coordinate display box

AutoCAD LT displays the current cursor location with a pair of XY coordinate values in the coordinate display box on the toolbar. See Figure 3-12. These coordinates always match the current system of units. When used in conjunction with **GRID**, **SNAP**, and **ORTHO** modes, the coordinate display box can be a useful drawing aid. The coordinates can be displayed in the following three ways:

- The display is turned off (static) and only updates when you specify a point.
- The display is turned on (dynamic) and constantly updates as you move your cursor around the graphics area. This is the default setting.
- The coordinates are displayed as polar (distance⟨angle⟩ rather than Cartesian (XY). This display is available only when you draw lines or other entity types that prompt for more than one point.

Figure 3-12.
When activated, the coordinate display box indicates the cursor location using the current units of measurement.

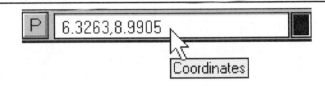

You may recall from chapter 1 that the coordinate display box can be toggled on and off using function key [F6], or the control key combination [Ctrl]+[D]. You can also turn the coordinate display on and off by simply clicking anywhere inside the box with your mouse. You can use any one of these methods to cycle through the three coordinate display states or you can use the **COORDS** system variable as follows:

Command: **COORDS** ↵
New value for COORDS ⟨*current*⟩: (*enter* 0, 1, *or* 2 *and press* [Enter])

By default, **COORDS** is set to 1 (on). To turn off the display, set **COORDS** to 0 (zero). Set **COORDS** to 2 if you want to use a polar display.

EXERCISE 3-6

❑ In this exercise, you will once again draw the 6 × 3 rectangle. However, this time you will rely solely on drawing aids to create the object.
❑ Begin a new drawing using your PROTOA prototype drawing.
❑ Be sure that snap and grid are turned on and set **COORDS** to 2.
❑ Issue the **LINE** command. At the **From point:** prompt, pick a starting point somewhere near the lower-left corner of the screen. Observe the coordinate display on the toolbar as you move your mouse to the right.
❑ Pick a second point when the display reads: 6⟨0. It may be helpful to turn on **ORTHO** mode.
❑ Move your cursor up and pick a point when the display reads: 3⟨90.
❑ Now move your cursor to the right and pick a third point when the display reads: 6⟨180.
❑ Finally, use the **Close** option to close the shape. It is not necessary to save this exercise.

When you modify a drawing to correct mistakes or to revise a design, you are editing the drawing. Whether you select only one entity to edit, or many hundreds of entities, you create a *selection set*. There are a variety of ways to create selection sets for editing. Each of the selection set options described in the following section apply to erasing entities. However, the selection options are used the same way with most of the editing commands in AutoCAD LT whenever you receive the **Select objects:** prompt. You can access the selection set options from the command line, or pick them from the **Select** cascading submenu in the **Assist** pull-down menu. See Figure 3-13.

Figure 3-13.
Selection set options may be picked from the **Select** cascading submenu in the **Assist** pull-down menu.

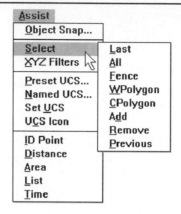

Erasing unwanted drawing entities is one of the most basic editing functions. To do so, type ERASE at the **Command:** prompt, click the **Erase** button in the toolbox, or select **Erase** from the **Modify** pull-down menu. See Figure 3-14. The **ERASE** command prompts you to select objects to be erased:

Command: *(type* ERASE *or* E *and press* [Enter]*)*
Select objects: *(select an object)*
Select objects: *(select another object or press* [Enter] *to end the command)*

Figure 3-14.
The **ERASE** command can be issued by selecting **Erase** from the **Modify** pull-down menu.

When the **Select objects:** prompt appears, the full screen crosshair cursor is replaced with a small box called the *pickbox*. Move your mouse to place the pickbox over the entity you want to select and pick. As shown in Figure 3-15A, a picked entity assumes a dotted or dashed appearance. AutoCAD LT calls this *highlighting*. The **Select objects:** prompt remains active in case you want to select another entity. When you are done picking, press [Enter] to end the **ERASE** command. The entity(s) you select is then erased from the screen and the **Command:** prompt reappears. See Figure 3-15B. Use the **REDRAW** command to remove the blips left behind from the erased entity.

Figure 3-15.
A—Locate the pickbox over the entity to be erased, pick it and press [Enter]. B—Select another entity or press [Enter] to end the command. The entity is erased and a **REDRAW** removes the blips.

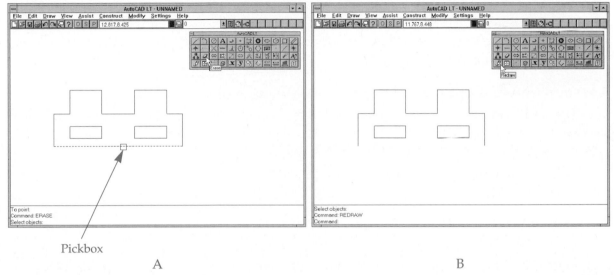

Pickbox

A   B

NOTE   You can turn off highlighting using the **HIGHLIGHT** system variable (0=OFF, 1=ON). However, since highlighting lets you know that an entity has been selected, it is suggested that it be left on. Highlighting, like blips, can also be turned on and off in the **Drawing Aids** dialog box. This dialog box is accessed by typing DDRMODES at the **Command:** prompt, clicking the **Drawing Aids** button in the toolbox, or selecting **Drawing Aids...** from the **Settings** pull-down menu.

The OOPS command

If you find that you have erased entities mistakenly, those entities may be restored using the **OOPS** command. This appropriately named command is accessed from the **Modify** pull-down menu, or by typing OO at the **Command:** prompt. However, keep in mind that the **OOPS** command can only restore entities erased with the very last **ERASE** operation.

Sizing the pickbox

The size of the pickbox can be increased to allow for a larger picking area, or decreased to provide more accurate picking when entities are spaced closely together. Use the **PICKBOX** command if you want to change the size of the pickbox.

    Command: **PICKBOX** ↵
    New value for PICKBOX⟨3⟩: *(enter an integer value)*

The pickbox can also be sized transparently while inside another command by typing in 'PICKBOX. The size of the pickbox is measured in *pixels*. Pixels, or *pels*, stands for picture elements and are the tiny dots that make up what is displayed on a computer monitor. The default value is 3 pixels, but most users prefer a slightly larger pickbox of 5 or 6 pixels. Try experimenting with various sizes to find the one that suits your preferences. Once you change the size of the pickbox, the new value is stored in an external configuration file called ACLT.CFG. This file resides in the ACLTWIN directory and is created when you first install AutoCAD LT. It contains hardware configuration settings that are used for all of your AutoCAD LT drawings. Therefore, changing the pickbox size in the current drawing changes the pickbox size for all of your drawings.

SELECTION SET OPTIONS ALTUG 9

As mentioned previously, you create a selection set when you select one or more entities at the **Select objects:** prompt. The various selection set options include **Last, Previous, All, Window, Crossing, WPolygon, CPolygon, Undo, Remove,** and **Add**. Each of these options are described in the following sections.

Last and Previous options

The **Last** option is used to select the very last visible object created. This option is accessed by entering LAST, or L. You can use this option as shown below when you have drawn an entity incorrectly and would like to quickly erase it.

```
Command: (type ERASE or E and press [Enter])
Select objects: L ⏎
1 found
Select objects: ⏎
Command:
```

AutoCAD LT remembers the most recent entity selection. For example, suppose you erase a group of entities and then decide to restore them with the **OOPS** command. You then realize that you want to erase the entities after all. You can quickly reselect the restored entities to erase using the **Previous** option by entering PREVIOUS, or P, as follows:

```
Command: (type ERASE or E and press [Enter])
Select objects: P ⏎
n found
Select objects: ⏎
Command:
```

All, Window, and Crossing options

When you want to select every entity on your drawing for an editing operation, use the **All** option. Be careful, because even objects not displayed in the current viewport, such as entities off the screen, are selected with this option. However, any entities on frozen layers are ignored. See Chapter 5 of this text for more information about frozen and thawed layers. When you use the **All** option, you must type in ALL, and not just A.

```
Command: (type ERASE or E and press [Enter])
Select objects: ALL ⏎
n found
Select objects: ⏎
Command:
```

You can also select a large number of entities by enclosing them within a selection window. As shown in Figure 3-16A, the window is defined by picking two diagonally opposite corners. Thus, the window box can be square or rectangular in shape and is displayed on screen in a solid line representation. It is important to note that only entities that lie *completely within* the window are selected. The results of the window selection are shown in Figure 3-16B. To use the Window option, type WINDOW, or W, as follows:

> Command: *(type* ERASE *or* E *and press* [Enter])
> Select objects: **W** ↵
> First corner: *(pick a point)* Other corner: *(pick a second diagonal point)*
> *n* found
> Select objects: ↵
> Command:

Figure 3-16.
A—The **Window** option requires two diagonal corners. Note that a window box is represented with a solid line. B—After pressing [Enter], all of the entities completely enclosed within the **Window** box are erased.

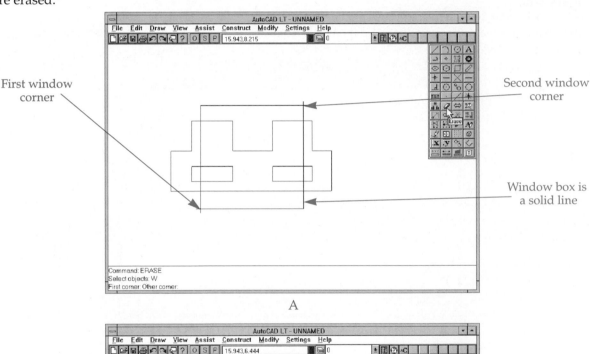

A

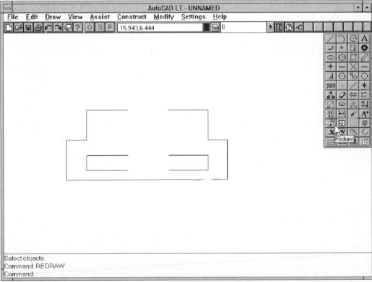

B

A second type of window selection method available in AutoCAD LT is called a *crossing*. Like a window box, a crossing box is also defined with two diagonal corners and is square or rectangular in shape. Also like a window box, any entities enclosed within the crossing box are selected. The major difference is that, in addition to all entities within the box, any entities that cross over the box are also selected. From the example illustrated in Figure 3-17A, you can see that the same two diagonal corners are selected as in the previous example. Also note that unlike a window box, the crossing box is represented with a dotted, or dashed, line instead of a solid line. Compare the results using **Crossing**, Figure 3-17B, with those using **Window**, Figure 3-16B. To use the **Crossing** option, type CROSSING, or C, as follows:

> Command: *(type* ERASE *or* E *and press* [Enter]*)*
> Select objects: **C** ↵
> First corner: *(pick a point)* Other corner: *(pick a second diagonal point)*
> *n* found
> Select objects: ↵
> Command:

Figure 3-17.
A—The **Crossing** option also requires two diagonal corners. Observe that a crossing box is represented with a dotted, or dashed, line. B—After pressing [Enter], all of the entities enclosed within or crossing over the crossing box are erased.

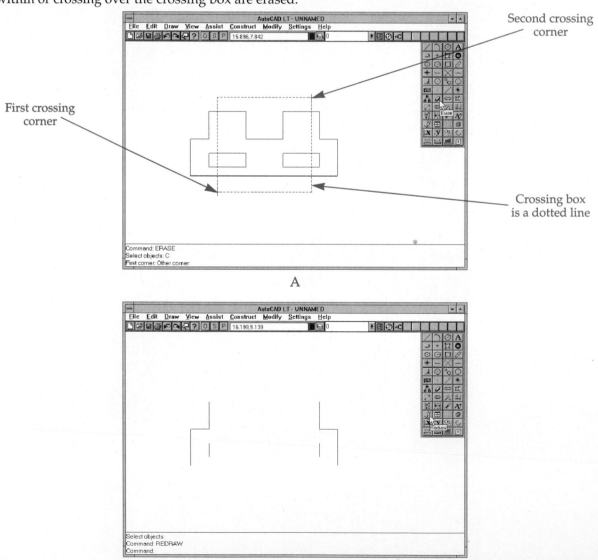

First crossing corner

Second crossing corner

Crossing box is a dotted line

A

B

AutoCAD LT—Fundamentals and Applications

To further illustrate the difference between the **Window** and a **Crossing** option, consider the circle with centerlines shown in Figure 3-18A. As you will learn in Chapter 11 of this text, AutoCAD LT creates centerlines with individual line segments. Thus, the centerline in Figure 3-18A is comprised of six separate lines. To erase all the centerlines, you might be inclined to use the **Window** option. Unfortunately, the circle gets included in the selection set as well. Although the **Remove** option can be used to remove the circle from the selection set, it requires an additional step, which will be covered later in this chapter.

A far more efficient way to select only the centerlines is shown in Figure 3-18B. Use the **Crossing** option and pick the two diagonal corners indicated. The portion of the centerlines that are completely enclosed within the box are selected, as well as the portions that cross over the box. The circle is ignored entirely.

Figure 3-18.
A—The **Window** option selects both the circle and the centerlines. B—The **Crossing** option is used to select the centerlines only.

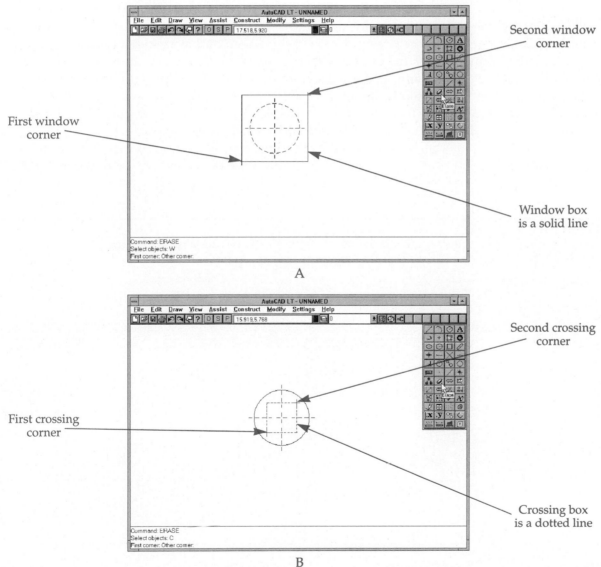

A

B

Using implied windowing

Because window and crossing boxes are so frequently used for editing operations, AutoCAD LT allows you to automatically create a window or crossing without first typing W or C. This method is called *implied windowing*. When the **Select objects:** prompt appears, pick the first corner point in an empty area of the graphics screen; AutoCAD LT then prompts you for the other corner point. If you drag your cursor from left to right, a window box is automatically created. Dragging your cursor from right to left automatically creates a crossing box. Implied windowing is on by default in AutoCAD LT, but may be turned off using the **PICKAUTO** system variable.

Verb/Noun vs. Noun/Verb selection

From the examples given so far, you can see that to perform an editing operation, such as **ERASE**, you first enter the command and then select the objects to be edited. AutoCAD LT calls this method *Verb/Noun selection*. An alternative method for entity selection is called *Noun/Verb*. This second method allows you to select the entities first, and then enter the command you want to use on the selection set. As shown in Figure 3-19A, you can use implied windowing to preselect entities with a window box without even being in a command. Simply pick a corner point on an empty area of the screen and drag to the right to completely enclose the entities. Once the entities are selected, you then enter the editing command that you wish to use with them. The small squares that appear on the preselected entities are called *grips* and are discussed in detail in Chapter 10. If you inadvertently preselect screen entities and want to remove the grips from the display, press [Ctrl]+[C], or click the **Cancel** button on the toolbar. To automatically preselect entities with a crossing selection, pick a corner point on an empty area of the screen and drag to the left. See Figure 3-19B. The noun/verb selection method is on by default in AutoCAD LT, but may be turned off using the **PICKFIRST** system variable.

Figure 3-19.
A—Picking a corner and dragging to the right automatically creates a window box.
B—Picking a corner and dragging to the left creates a crossing box.

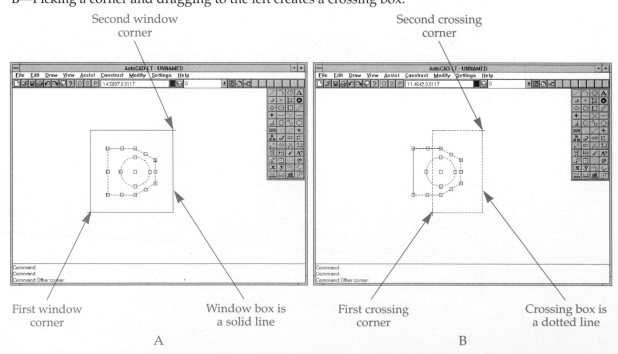

Second window corner

Second crossing corner

First window corner

Window box is a solid line

First crossing corner

Crossing box is a dotted line

A

B

WPolygon, CPolygon, and Fence options

Because the **Window** selection set option places a square or rectangle around entities, it is sometimes difficult to select the objects you want without others being selected as well. The **WPolygon** selection set option is similar to **Window**, but it lets you designate an irregular polygon (a closed figure with three or more sides) around the entities you want to select. You can draw a polygon of any shape, but it cannot touch or cross itself. Like a **Window** box, the **WPolygon** outline is drawn with a solid line. To better understand the **WPolygon** option, refer to Figure 3-20A. To use the **WPolygon** option, type WPOLYGON, or WP, as follows:

Command: *(type* ERASE *or* E *and press* [Enter]*)*
Select objects: **WP** ↵
First polygon point: *(pick point 1)*
Undo/⟨Endpoint of line⟩: *(pick point 2 or enter* U *to undo)*
Undo/⟨Endpoint of line⟩: *(pick point 3 or enter* U *to undo)*
Undo/⟨Endpoint of line⟩: *(pick point 4 or enter* U *to undo)*
Undo/⟨Endpoint of line⟩: ↵
n found
Select objects: ↵
Command:

As with the **Window** option, any entities completely enclosed by the **WPolygon** are selected, Figure 3-20B.

Figure 3-20.
A—Entities are selected by using an irregular polygon with the **WPolygon** option. B—After pressing [Enter], all of the entities completely enclosed within the polygon outline are erased.

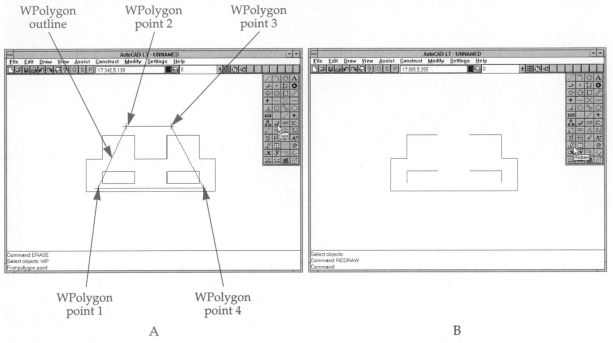

WPolygon outline

WPolygon point 2

WPolygon point 3

WPolygon point 1

WPolygon point 4

A

B

There is also a **CPolygon** option that is similar to **WPolygon** but has the same characteristics as **Crossing**. In other words, entities completely enclosed or crossed over with a **CPolygon** outline are selected. Also, the **CPolygon** outline is drawn with a dotted, or dashed, line like a **Crossing** box. See Figure 3-21A. To use the **CPolygon** option, type CPOLYGON, or CP, as follows:

Command: *(type* ERASE *or* E *and press* [Enter]*)*
Select objects: **CP** ⏎
First polygon point: *(pick point 1)*
Undo/⟨Endpoint of line⟩: *(pick point 2 or enter* U *to undo)*
Undo/⟨Endpoint of line⟩: *(pick point 3 or enter* U *to undo)*
Undo/⟨Endpoint of line⟩: *(pick point 4 or enter* U *to undo)*
Undo/⟨Endpoint of line⟩: ⏎
n found
Select objects: ⏎
Command:

The results of the **CPolygon** operation are shown in Figure 3-21B.

Figure 3-21.
A—Entities are selected by using an irregular polygon with the **CPolygon** option. Note the dotted or dashed **CPolygon** outline. B—After pressing [Enter], all of the entities completely enclosed within or crossing over the polygon outline are erased.

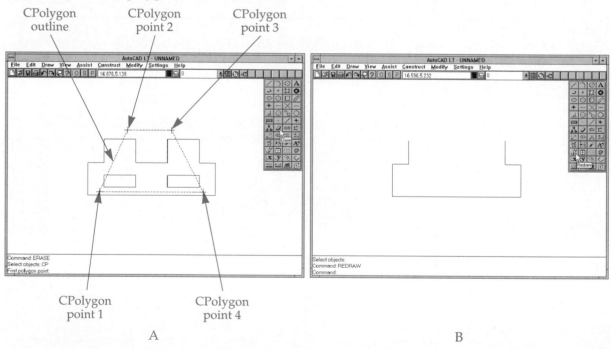

CPolygon outline   CPolygon point 2   CPolygon point 3

CPolygon point 1   CPolygon point 4

A   B

An additional method used to select more than one entity at a time exists with the **Fence** selection set option. A **Fence** is a multi-segmented line that is drawn to select entities it passes through. It is somewhat similar to **CPolygon**, but it does not close the last segment drawn. The **Fence** can be drawn straight or staggered and is represented with a dashed line. Refer to the lower object shown in Figure 3-22A. To use the **Fence** option, type FENCE, or F, as follows:

Command: *(type* ERASE *or* E *and press* [Enter]*)*
Select objects: **F** ↵
First fence point: *(pick point 1)*
Undo/⟨Endpoint of line⟩: *(pick point 2 or enter* U *to undo)*
Undo/⟨Endpoint of line⟩: *(pick point 3 or enter* U *to undo)*
Undo/⟨Endpoint of line⟩: *(pick point 4 or enter* U *to undo)*
Undo/⟨Endpoint of line⟩: ↵
n found
Select objects: ↵
Command:

The results of the **Fence** selection are shown in Figure 3-22B.

Figure 3-22.
A—A fence line may be straight or staggered. B—After pressing [Enter], all of the entities passed through with the fence line are erased.

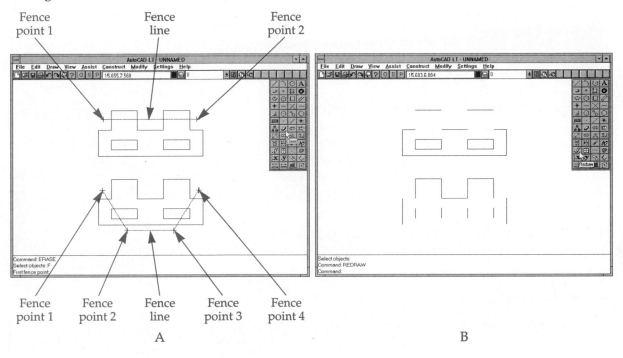

A

B

Undo, Remove, and Add options

There will be instances when you mistakenly select an entity for editing. You can undo your selection using the **Undo** selection set option. This option works identically to the **LINE** command **Undo** option described earlier in this chapter. Simply click the **Undo** button on the toolbar or type U to remove the highlighting from the selected object while the **Select objects:** prompt is still displayed.

On other occasions, it is likely that you will include one or more entities inadvertently in a selection set. This can often happen when you use the **Window** and **Crossing** options. Entities can be removed from a selection set using the **Remove** option as follows:

Command: *(type* ERASE *or* E *and press* [Enter]*)*
Select objects: *(pick one or more entities)*
Select objects: **R** ↵
Remove objects: *(pick the entities to be removed from the selection set)*
Remove objects: ↵
Command:

If you mistakenly remove some entities that you would rather retain in the selection set, use the **Add** option to add them back. The **Remove objects:** prompt then reverts back to the **Select objects:** prompt as follows:

      Remove objects: **A** ⏎
      Select objects: *(add one or more entities to the selection set)*
      Command: Select objects: ⏎

    Lastly, because all of the other selection set options are valid with the **Remove** and **Add** options, you may freely use the **Window**, **WPolygon**, **Crossing**, and **CPolygon** methods to add or remove a large number of entities to or from a selection set.

PROFESSIONAL TIP

    Here is a fast and easy way to remove an entity from a selection set without using the **Remove** option. When the **Select objects:** prompt is displayed, pick the entity you want to remove while simultaneously pressing and holding the [Shift] key.

    Remember also that as an alternative to keyboard entry, each of the selection set options discussed in this chapter may be accessed from the **Select** cascading submenu in the **Assist** pull-down menu.

CUSTOMIZING ENTITY SELECTION   ALTUG 9

    Apart from the selection set options previously described, there are several other selection modes available to you. These modes are set in the **Entity Selection Settings** dialog box. This dialog box is accessed by typing DDSELECT, or SL, at the **Command:** prompt, or by selecting **Selection Style...** from the **Settings** pull-down menu. See Figure 3-23. The command sequence is as follows:

      Command: *(type* DDSELECT *or* SL *and press* [Enter]*)*

Figure 3-23.
The **DDSELECT** command can be issued by picking **Selection Style...** from the **Settings** pull-down menu.

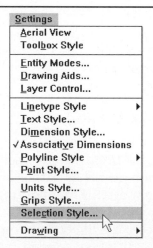

    The **Entity Selection Settings** dialog box is shown in Figure 3-24. Each of the options available in this dialog box are described below and on the next page. The **Selection Modes** area contains four check boxes that perform the following functions:

- **Noun/Verb Selection.** Activating the **Noun/Verb Selection** check box allows you to select entities first, and then enter the command you want to use on the selection set as described previously in this chapter. This option is on by default. Remember that another way to activate or deactivate this option is with the **PICKFIRST** system variable.

Figure 3-24.
The **Entity Selection Settings** dialog box.

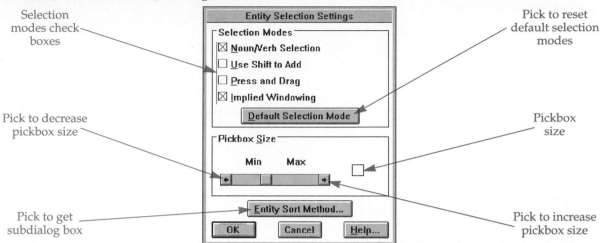

Selection modes check boxes

Pick to reset default selection modes

Pick to decrease pickbox size

Pickbox size

Pick to get subdialog box

Pick to increase pickbox size

- **Use Shift to Add.** This check box controls how you add entities to an existing selection set. When checked, it activates an additive selection mode, in which you must press and hold down the [Shift] key while adding more entitics to the selection set. While this mode is not very efficient, it is consistent with several other graphics software programs commercially available. The **Use Shift to Add** mode is off by default. You can also use the **PICKADD** system variable to turn this mode on and off.
- **Press and Drag.** This option controls how selection windows are drawn. When active, you must press and hold down the pick button on your mouse as you diagonally drag your cursor to create a window or crossing box selection. Release the button to complete the window or crossing at its second diagonal corner. As with the **Use Shift to Add** option, this method is not very efficient but it is consistent with several other commercially available software products. By default, the **Press and Drag** mode is off, but you can also use the **PICKDRAG** system variable to toggle this option on and off.
- **Implied Windowing.** As discussed previously, implied windowing allows you to automatically create a selection window when the **Select objects:** prompt appears by picking first and second diagonal corner points in empty areas of the screen. Drawing the selection window from left to right creates a window box, while drawing the selection window from right to left creates a crossing box. Enabled by default, **Implied Windowing** may be disabled using this check box or the **PICKAUTO** system variable.
- **Default Selection Mode.** Click the **Default Selection Mode** button to reset the four selection mode check boxes to their original default settings. That is, **Noun/Verb Selection** and **Implied Windowing** are activated and **Use Shift to Add** and **Press and Drag** are deactivated.

Earlier in this chapter you learned that the **PICKBOX** command may be used to adjust the size of the pickbox. You can also use the horizontal slider bar in the **Pickbox Size** area to accomplish the same task. As you move the slider button left or right, the pickbox size dynamically changes as illustrated in the pickbox image tile to the right of the slider bar.

Clicking the **Entity Sort Method...** button displays the **Entity Sort Method** subdialog box shown in Figure 3-25. The seven check boxes that appear in this subdialog box allow you to process entities in the order in which they occur in the database. That is, in the order in which the entities were created. As an example, check the **Redraws** and **Regens** check boxes to assure that redraws and regenerations always draw entities in the order in which they were created. Regenerations are covered in Chapter 4 of this text. To ensure that entities selected by the **Window** and **Crossing** options go into the selection set in a predictable order, check the **Object Selection** check box.

Figure 3-25.
The **Entity Sort Method**
subdialog box.

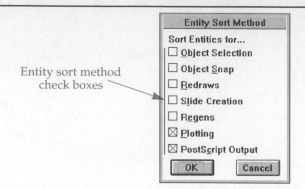

Entity sort method
check boxes

By default, only **Plotting** and **PostScript Output** are entity sorted as shown in Figure 3-25. Unless the drawing you are working on or the application you are using depends on entity order, it is recommended that you do not change the default settings in the other check boxes. This is because selecting additional sorting methods usually increases processing time and slows down system performance. This is particularly true for large drawings.

UNDOING THE EFFECTS OF A COMMAND

ALTUG 2

Earlier in this chapter you learned how an incorrectly drawn line segment can be removed using the **Undo** option in the **LINE** command. You also learned that the **OOPS** command can restore erased entities by essentially undoing the **ERASE** command. AutoCAD LT provides two other commands that reverse the most recent operation. These two commands are the **U** and **UNDO** commands. AutoCAD LT also provides the **REDO** command, which reverses an **UNDO** operation.

The U command

The **U** command reverses, or undos, the most recent AutoCAD LT operation. Operations external to the current drawing, such as plotting or saving a drawing to disk, cannot be undone, however. To use the **U** command, simple type U at the **Command:** prompt. You can also access the **U** command by clicking the **Undo** button on the toolbar, or selecting **Undo** from the **Edit** pull-down menu. You can enter U as many times as you like, backing up one step at a time. Be careful, because too many **U**'s can take you all the way back to the beginning of the current drawing session.

The UNDO command

The **UNDO** command is similar to the **U** command but with a variety of available options. Some of the options let you undo several commands at once and perform special operations, such as marking a point to return to in case things go wrong. The **UNDO** command must be entered at the **Command:** prompt, because choosing **Undo** from the **Edit** pull-down menu invokes the **U** command, and not the **UNDO** command. The **UNDO** command sequence is as follows:

    Command: **UNDO** ↵
    Auto/Back/Control/End/Group/Mark/⟨number⟩:

Each of the options offered by the **UNDO** command are described below:

- ⟨*number*⟩. The default option lets you specify the number of preceding operations to be undone. Entering 3 reverses the previous three operations. Entering 1 is the equivalent of using the **U** command.
- **Auto.** Selecting **Auto** prompts you with the following:

  ON/OFF ⟨*current*⟩: (*enter* ON *or* OFF *and press* [Enter])

  When **Auto** is on, (its default setting), AutoCAD LT commands are automatically grouped together to perform certain operations, no matter how complicated. This grouping occurs *behind the scenes* with no action necessary on your part. Each of the commands in the group are then removed as a single command when a **U** or **UNDO** operation is performed. If **Auto** is turned off, then each command in a group of commands is treated separately and several iterations of **U** or **UNDO** are required.
- **Back.** The **Back** option reverses every operation back to the beginning of the current drawing session. You are prompted with:

  This will undo everything. OK? ⟨Y⟩ (*answer* Y *or* N *and press* [Enter])

  If a mark has been inserted using the **Mark** option, then **Back** takes the drawing back to the state it was in when the mark is encountered.
- **Control.** The **Control** option limits the **UNDO** operation or disables it completely. Selecting **Control** prompts you with the following suboptions:

  All/None/One ⟨All⟩:

  - **All**—The **All** suboption enables all of the **UNDO** options. This is the default setting.
  - **None**—Selecting **None** disables the **U** and **UNDO** commands.
  - **One**—The **One** suboption limits the **UNDO** command to a single operation, so that it operates similar to the **U** command. The **Auto, Group,** and **Mark** suboptions are not available when **One** is in effect.
- **End and Group.** These options are used together. When you use the **Group** option, a group of commands is treated as a single command for the purposes of **U** and **UNDO**. Select the **End** option to terminate the command grouping. To explain further, suppose you enable the **Group** option and then perform three separate drawing commands. Because **Group** is enabled, all three commands are grouped together as if one. Then you return to the **UNDO** command, and enable the **End** option. If you now issue the **U** or **UNDO** commands, all three commands are undone at the same time. Any commands performed after using the **End** option are treated separately by the **U** and **UNDO** commands.
- **Mark.** The **Mark** option makes a special mark in the undo information. Use the **Back** option to undo back to the mark. AutoCAD LT informs you when you reach the mark if you undo one operation at a time. If the **Group** option is enabled, **Mark** and **Back** cannot be used.

The REDO command

It is inevitable that you will eventually undo an operation accidentally. Since pressing [Enter] or the spacebar automatically repeats the previous command in AutoCAD LT, you can see that performing a **U** command, and then inadvertently pressing [Enter] a second time would perform two undos! To reverse an unwanted undo, enter REDO, or RE, at the **Command:** prompt, click the **Redo** button on the toolbar, or select <u>R</u>edo from the <u>E</u>dit pull-down menu. However, keep in mind that the **REDO** command must be issued *immediately* after performing the **U** command. If you attempt to perform a **REDO** after executing several other commands since the unwanted undo, the following message is displayed:

Previous command did not undo things.

Figure 3-26.
Both the **U** and **REDO**
commands may be accessed
from the **Edit** pull-down
menu, or from the Undo
and Redo buttons on
the toolbar.

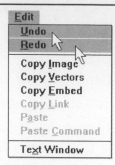

Edit
Undo
Redo
Copy Image
Copy Vectors
Copy Embed
Copy Link
Paste
Paste Command
Text Window

PROFESSIONAL TIP

The **OOPS** command can only be used to reverse the very last erase operation. The **U** and **UNDO** commands can reverse *all* drawing and editing operations. Remember also that the **REDO** command can only reverse one **U** or **UNDO** operation. Therefore, take care when undoing commands. Save your drawing often as a precaution against one-too-many undos!

EXERCISE 3-7

❑ Open drawing EX3-1.DWG that you completed earlier in this chapter.
❑ Experiment with the **Last, Previous, All, Window, Crossing, WPolygon, CPolygon, Undo, Remove,** and **Add** selection set options as you erase portions of the drawing. Use the **OOPS** command to restore the erased entities.
❑ Draw several lines and use the **U** or **UNDO** commands to remove them. Use the **REDO** command to get them back.
❑ When you are done experimenting, quit the session.

CHAPTER TEST

Write your answers in the spaces provided.

1. Why is precise coordinate entry important? _____

_____

_____

2. What are blips and how can they be removed from the screen? _____

_____

3. What is a transparent command? What must you type to use one? Give an example.

_____

_____

_____

4. List two methods to quickly repeat the previous command. _____

_____

_____

5. How can you tell AutoCAD LT to close a shape back to its starting point? _____

_____

_____

6. Why should you undo an incorrect line segment while still in the **LINE** command?

_____

_____

7. What is the **Continuation** option? How is it used? _____

_____

_____

8. What is **ORTHO** mode? List two ways to toggle **ORTHO** mode on and off. _____

_____

_____

_____

9. Define **Direct Distance Entry**. _____

_____

_____

_____

10. How do absolute coordinates differ from relative coordinates? What symbol must you type to tell AutoCAD LT that you want to use relative coordinates? _____

_____

_____

_____

_____

11. What is the **LASTPOINT** system variable? _____

_____

12. What are polar coordinates? How are they used? _____

_____

_____

_____

13. List four ways to change the status of the coordinate display box. _____

_____

_____

14. When an entity is picked, it assumes a dotted or dashed appearance. What is this appearance called? _____

_____

15. What is the difference between the **Last** and **Previous** selection set options? _____

_____

_____

16. Describe the similarities between a window box and a crossing box. How are they different?

_____

_____

_____

17. List two methods to remove an entity from a selection set. _____

_____

_____

18. What is the purpose of the **PICKFIRST** variable? _____

_____

19. Which option of the **UNDO** command reverses every operation back to the beginning of the current drawing session? _____

20. List three ways to access the **REDO** command. _____

_____

_____

_____

CHAPTER PROBLEMS

General

1. Using your **PROTOA** prototype drawing, draw the two views of the object shown below. Note that the dimensions for this object are in fractional format. You need not set fractional units to enter fractional coordinates on the AutoCAD LT command line. When entering these fractions, do not forget to separate the whole number from the fractional value with a ˉ.yphen (-). Save the completed drawing as P3-1.

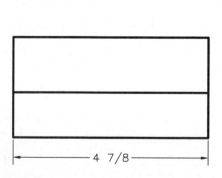
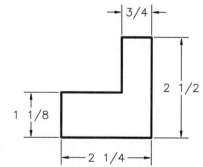

2. Once again using **PROTOA** as your prototype, draw the object shown. Note that the decimal dimensions are expressed with 3 digits to the right of the decimal point. Two of the dimensions (1.188 and 1.063) are really four-place decimals. Since accuracy is of paramount importance, be sure to refer to the decimal/fractional equivalency chart in the Appendices at the end of this text so that these two coordinates may be entered without rounding error. Save the completed drawing as P3-2.

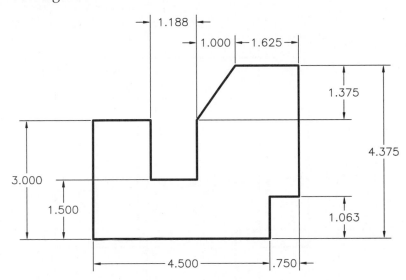

3. Using **PROTOA** as your prototype, draw the object shown. Start this object at a known coordinate such as 0,0 or 1,1 so that it is easier to locate the internal features. Save the completed drawing as P3-3.

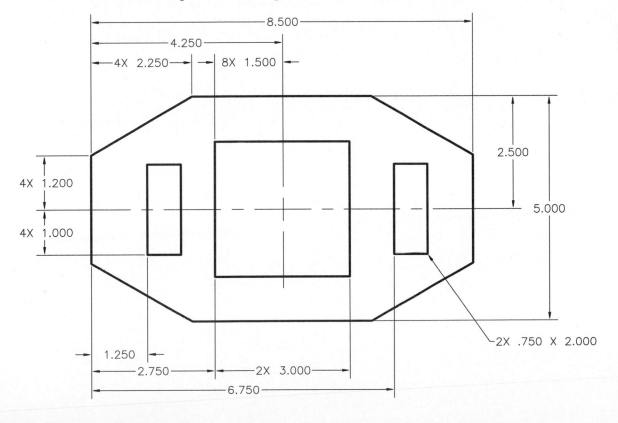

4. Draw this object using PROTOB as your prototype drawing. To facilitate the construction of this object's internal cutout, set your grid to 1/8 and your snap to 1/16. Note that each of the dimensions are expressed as two-place decimals. As with P3-2, be sure to refer to the decimal/fractional equivalency chart in the Appendices at the end of this text so that all coordinates are entered without rounding error. Save the completed drawing as P3-4.

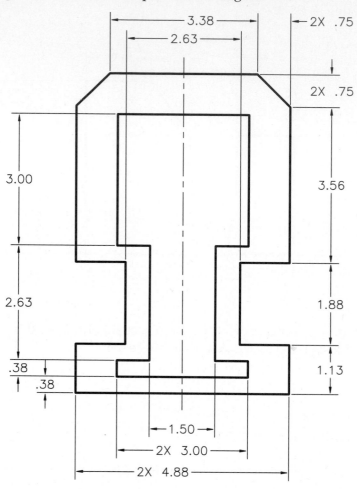

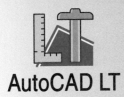

AutoCAD LT

Chapter 4

Display Commands

Learning objectives:

After you have completed this chapter, you will be able to:

- ○ Zoom selected drawing areas to magnify details.
- ○ Describe the difference between a screen redraw and a screen regeneration.
- ○ Pan the display window to change the viewing area.
- ○ Invoke and navigate the **Aerial View** window.
- ○ Save, recall, and delete named views.
- ○ Divide the graphics window into multiple viewports.

There are several ways to view the various parts of your drawing using the AutoCAD LT display commands. The **ZOOM** command lets you change the magnification of selected drawing areas, or the entire drawing itself. Using the **PAN** command, you can reposition the drawing display in the current viewport. The **DSVIEWER** command enables the **Aerial View** window. This allows you to see the entire drawing in a separate display window, locate the particular area you want to view, and move to that area using both zoom and pan functions. Once a view is displayed to your satisfaction, you can then use the **VIEW** command to save the view with a name. Named views may be listed, restored, or deleted at any time. Finally, you can also divide the screen into multiple viewing areas using the **VPORTS** command.

MAGNIFYING DRAWING DETAILS WITH THE ZOOM COMMAND

ALTUG 8

It is the **ZOOM** command that allows you to magnify (*zoom in*) or shrink (*zoom out*) the image in the graphics window. Think of the zoom function as you would a telephoto lens on a camera. Just as a telephoto lens does not actually change the absolute size of objects, neither does zooming. So when you zoom, the apparent size of the view in the graphics window changes—not the actual size of the objects. However, unlike a telephoto lens the potential zoom ratio in AutoCAD LT is 10 trillion to one! This is another reason why AutoCAD LT can draw virtually anything at full scale.

Each option of the **ZOOM** command can be accessed by selecting **Zoom** from the **View** pull-down menu. See Figure 4-1. When you click the **Zoom** button on the toolbar or enter ZOOM at the **Command:** prompt, you are presented with the following command sequence:

> Command: (*type ZOOM or Z and press* [Enter])
> All/Center/Extents/Previous/Window/⟨Scale(X/XP)⟩: (*select an option*)

Each of the **ZOOM** options are described in the following sections.

Figure 4-1.
The **ZOOM** command can be issued by selecting **Zoom** from the **View** pull-down menu.

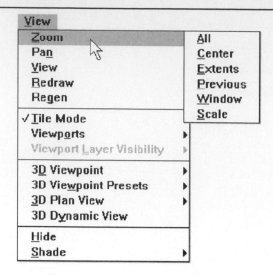

Zooming to the drawing limits—ZOOM All option

Use **ZOOM All** after changing your limits or when you want to display your entire drawing. This is because the **All** option zooms the display to the current drawing limits or to the drawing extents, whichever is greater.

> Command: *(type* ZOOM *or* Z *and press* [Enter]*)*
> All/Center/Extents/Previous/Window/⟨Scale(X/XP)⟩: **A** ↵

A zoomed-up portion of a wrench handle is shown in Figure 4-2A. After performing a **ZOOM All**, the entire wrench drawing is displayed. See Figure 4-2B.

Figure 4-2.
A—Current view of the wrench. B—The view after performing a **ZOOM All**.

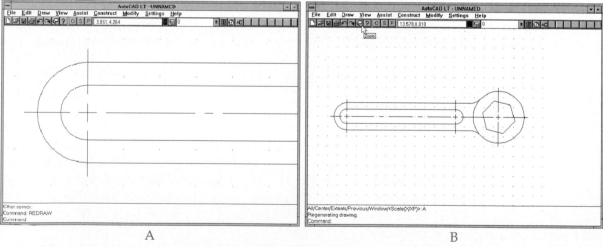

A   B

Zooming about a center point—ZOOM Center option

You can zoom about the center of a selected point using the **ZOOM Center** option. After selecting a point about which to zoom, you are prompted to enter a magnification or height scale factor.

> Command: *(type* ZOOM *or* Z *and press* [Enter]*)*
> All/Center/Extents/Previous/Window/⟨Scale(X/XP)⟩: **C** ↵
> Center point: *(select a point)*
> Magnification or Height ⟨*current height*⟩: *(enter a value and press* [Enter]*)*

The height represents the current screen height in the current units. Enter a smaller height value to zoom up the view; enter a larger height value to zoom out. You also can zoom the image with a magnification scale factor. Refer to the wrench shown in Figure 4-3A. In this example, a center point is first located and the view is zoomed up with a magnification scale factor of 4X. Remember to always enter X when you use the magnification option, otherwise AutoCAD LT will interpret the number you enter as a height value. The results of the **ZOOM Center** option are shown in Figure 4-3B.

Figure 4-3.
A—**ZOOM Center** requests a center point around which the zoom is performed.
B—The result of **ZOOM Center** at 4X scale.

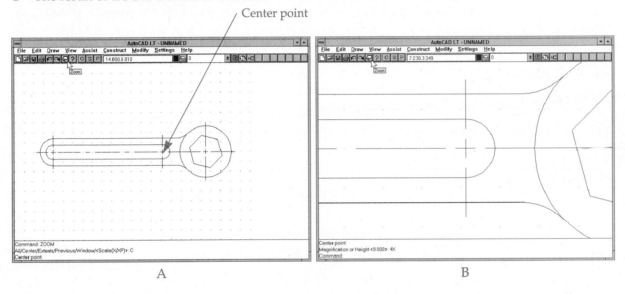

A   B

Zooming all the entities in the drawing—ZOOM Extents option

The **ZOOM Extents** option displays the largest possible view of all the entities in the drawing. If nothing has been drawn yet, then **ZOOM Extents** zooms to the screen limits.

    Command: *(type* ZOOM *or* Z *and press* [Enter]*)*
    All/Center/Extents/Previous/Window/⟨Scale(X/XP)⟩: **E** ↵

Refer to Figure 4-4 to see the effect of a **ZOOM Extents** operation on the wrench drawing.

Figure 4-4.
The wrench drawing after performing a **ZOOM Extents**.

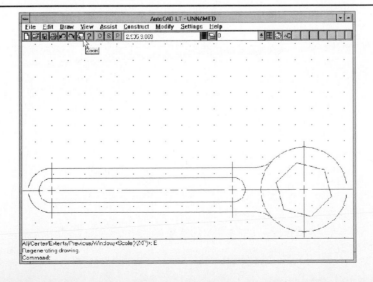

Returning to a previous view—ZOOM Previous option

The **ZOOM Previous** option lets you quickly return to a previous view. You can restore up to 10 previous views.

> Command: *(type* ZOOM *or* Z *and press* [Enter]*)*
> All/Center/Extents/Previous/Window/⟨Scale(X/XP)⟩: **E** ↵

If you attempt to back up more than 10 previous views, AutoCAD LT displays the message:

> No previous view saved.

Zooming with a window—ZOOM Window option

The **ZOOM Window** option is probably the most often used of the **ZOOM** options. It is used the same way as the **Window** selection set option described in Chapter 3 of this text. Simply pick a corner point, and then select a diagonal corner point to form a square or rectangular window around the area to be zoomed. See Figure 4-5A.

> Command: *(type* ZOOM *or* Z *and press* [Enter]*)*
> All/Center/Extents/Previous/Window/⟨Scale(X/XP)⟩: **W** ↵
> First corner: *(pick a corner)* Other corner: *(pick a second corner)*

The result of the **ZOOM Window** operation is shown in Figure 4-5B.

Figure 4-5.
A—Two diagonal corners form a window around the objects to be zoomed.
B—The result of a **ZOOM Window** operation.

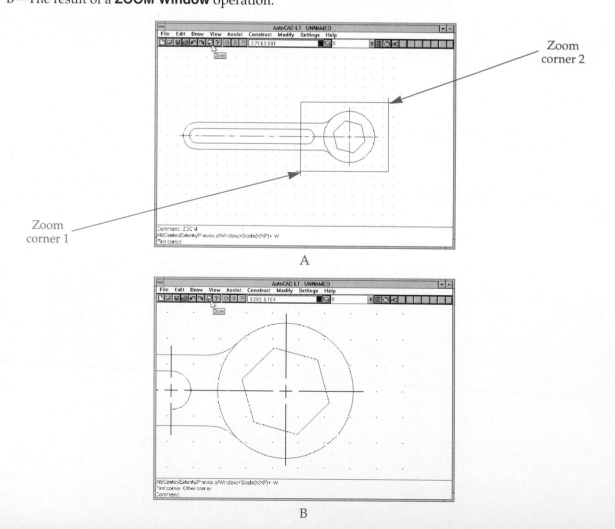

You can quickly zoom with a window by issuing the **ZOOM** command and, when presented with the command options, simply pick a point in an empty area of the screen. You are then prompted: **Other corner**. Now pick a diagonal corner point forming a window around the objects to be zoomed. You need not type a W at all.

Zooming with a scale factor—ZOOM Scale(X/XP) options

You can also zoom the screen display using a known scale factor. The scale factor can be relative to the current drawing limits (**ZOOM Scale**), the current display (**ZOOM Scale X**), or a paper space view (**ZOOM Scale XP**). To zoom with a scale *relative to the drawing limits*, enter the desired scale factor as follows:

> Command: *(type* ZOOM *or* Z *and press* [Enter]*)*
> All/Center/Extents/Previous/Window/⟨Scale(X/XP)⟩: **.5** ↵

The result of this operation is shown in Figure 4-6A.

It is often better to zoom an image *relative to the current display* rather than relative to the drawing limits. The result of the zoom operation is more predictable. To scale the image relative to the current display, you must enter a scale factor appended with an "X" as shown below. Do not put a space between the value and the letter X.

> Command: *(type* ZOOM *or* Z *and press* [Enter]*)*
> All/Center/Extents/Previous/Window/⟨Scale(X/XP)⟩: **.5X** ↵

This method is illustrated in Figure 4-6B. Observe that the wrench drawing has been zoomed by another factor of one-half relative to the display shown in Figure 4-6A.

Figure 4-6.
A—Zooming with a scale factor zooms the display relative to the drawing limits.
B—Using **Scale X** to scale the image relative to the current display.

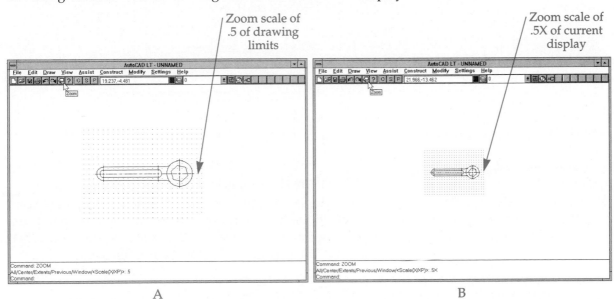

To zoom the model space display relative to paper space, type XP after the scale factor as follows:

Command: *(type* ZOOM *or* Z *and press* [Enter]*)*
All/Center/Extents/Previous/Window/⟨Scale(X/XP)⟩: **.5XP** ↵

Refer to Figure 4-7 to obtain a clearer understanding of the **XP** option. In this example, a D-size title block is drawn in paper space. Now imagine cutting three rectangular cutouts through the title block sheet with a pair of scissors. The three cutouts represent paper space viewports through which a model space drawing (such as the wrench) can be viewed. The **Scale XP** option scales the contents of each viewport (model space) relative to the D-size sheet (paper space). At the upper left, the wrench is scaled 1:1 (1XP) relative to paper space. In the middle, the wrench is scaled 1:2 (.5XP) relative to paper space. The viewport at the bottom right displays the wrench scaled 1:4 (.25XP) relative to paper space. See Chapter 16 in this text for more information on paper space and paper space viewports.

Figure 4-7.
The **Scale XP** option zooms the view in each viewport relative to paper space.

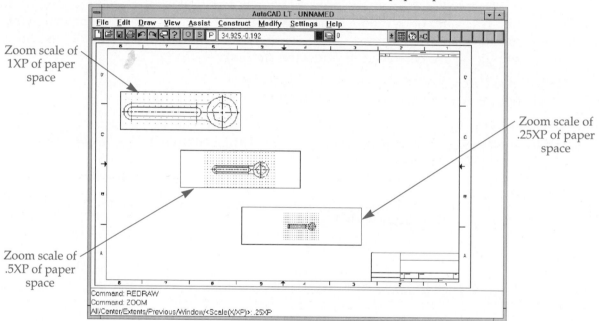

Zoom scale of 1XP of paper space

Zoom scale of .25XP of paper space

Zoom scale of .5XP of paper space

SHIFTING THE DISPLAY WITH THE PAN COMMAND · ALTUG 8

The **PAN** command moves or shifts the drawing display in the current viewport without changing the magnification. You can issue the **PAN** command by clicking the **Pan** button in the toolbox or by selecting **Pan** from the **View** pull-down menu. See Figure 4-8. It is possible to pan the display in one of two different ways. With the first method, you specify a single point that indicates the relative displacement of the drawing with respect to the graphics window. When prompted for the second point, press [Enter]. The procedure looks like the following:

Command: *(type* PAN *or* P *and press* [Enter]*)*
Displacement: *(pick a point on the screen)*   Second point: ↵

This first method, unfortunately, shifts the view so that the lower-left origin of the drawing is moved to the point you specify. The results are often unpredictable and undesirable.

Figure 4-8.
The **PAN** command
can be issued by selecting
Pan from the **View**
pull-down menu.

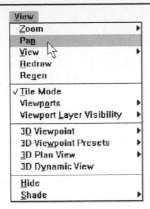

With the second panning method, you specify two points instead of just one. AutoCAD LT then computes the screen displacement from the first point to the second point and displays the drawing accordingly. This method is far more predictable than the first method described. The second method is illustrated in Figure 4-9A and looks like the following on the command line:

> Command: *(type PAN or P and press* [Enter]*)*
> Displacement: *(pick a point on the screen)*   Second point: *(pick a second point)*

The result of the pan operation on the wrench drawing is shown in Figure 4-9B.

Figure 4-9.
A—The **PAN** command shifts the display with a displacement equal to the distance and angle between two specified points. B—The result of the pan operation.

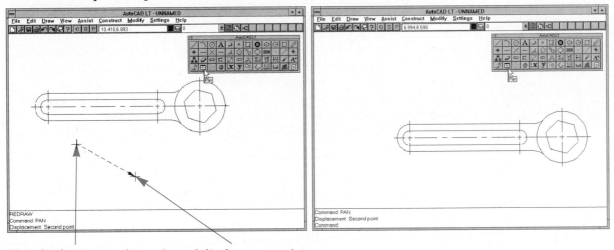

First displacement point   Second displacement point

A   B

REDRAWING THE DISPLAY vs.
REGENERATING THE DISPLAY

From Chapter 3 you learned that the **REDRAW** command is used to quickly remove marker blips and stray pixels left behind by drawing and editing commands. Remember that you can **REDRAW** the display by clicking the **Redraw** button in the toolbox, selecting **Redraw** from the **View** pull-down menu, or typing the command as follows:

Command: *(type REDRAW or R and press* [Enter]*)*

When multiple viewports are displayed, all of the viewports are redrawn with the **REDRAW** command. Remember also that **REDRAW** can be used transparently by preceding the command name with an apostrophe, such as 'REDRAW or 'R.

The other command that can be used to refresh the drawing display is the **REGEN** command. **REGEN** *regenerates*, or *rebuilds*, the entire drawing as it updates the drawing database and recomputes the screen coordinates for all objects. In AutoCAD LT the information for each drawing entity is stored as a real, or double-precision floating point, number. When a regeneration occurs, the floating point values in the database are converted to the appropriate screen coordinates. Because this process can be somewhat slow, expect some delay when regenerating a large drawing. When multiple viewports are displayed, the contents of each viewport are also regenerated. Some commands regenerate the drawing for you automatically; other commands require that you force the regeneration manually. To do so, select **Regen** from the **View** pull-down menu or enter the following at the **Command:** prompt:

Command: *(type REGEN or RG and press* [Enter]*)*

The REGEN command may not be used transparently.

NOTE

The **ZOOM** and **PAN** commands, like the **PICKBOX** and **REDRAW** commands previously discussed, are several other AutoCAD LT commands that may be used transparently. Two of the zoom options, All and Extents, may not be used transparently, however, because these options force a screen regeneration. If you type in 'ZOOM, or 'Z, or click the **Zoom** button on the toolbar while in the middle of another command, you receive a shortened list of **ZOOM** options:

⟩⟩Center/Previous/Window/⟨Scale(X/XP)⟩: *(select an option)*

You can see that the **All** and **Extents** options are not available.

EXERCISE 4-1

❏ Open one of the drawings from the Chapter 3 exercises or problems.
❏ Change the drawing limits to any values you like. Use **ZOOM All** to zoom the drawing to the new limits.
❏ Now, use **ZOOM Extents** to fill the graphics window with your drawing. Return to the previous view with **ZOOM Previous**.
❏ Use **ZOOM Center** to zoom about the center of a specified point. Try using both the **Magnification** and **Height** options.
❏ Use **ZOOM Window** to magnify a portion of the drawing. Use it again to zoom in a little closer.
❏ Experiment with the **ZOOM Scale** and **Scale X** options. In your opinion, which of the options seems more predictable?
❏ Try performing a few transparent zoom operations while drawing some lines.
❏ Finally, shift the display up and down, left and right with the **PAN** command.
❏ Do not save the drawing when you are finished experimenting.

USING THE AERIAL VIEW WINDOW

ALTUG 8

When you work on a large drawing, you can spend a lot of time zooming and panning the graphics window trying to locate a particular detail or feature. One of the most powerful features in AutoCAD LT is the **Aerial View** window. **Aerial View** is a navigation tool that lets you see the entire drawing in a separate window, locate the detail or feature you want, and move to it quickly. You can zoom in on an area, change the magnification, and match the view in the graphics window to the one in the **Aerial View** window, or vice versa. Best of all, you can use the **Aerial View** zoom and pan functions while a drawing or editing command is in progress.

To open the **Aerial View** window, enter DSVIEWER, or DS, at the **Command:** prompt, click the **Aerial View** button on the toolbar, or select **Aerial View** from the **Settings** pull-down menu. See Figure 4-10. The entire drawing is then displayed in the **Aerial View** window.

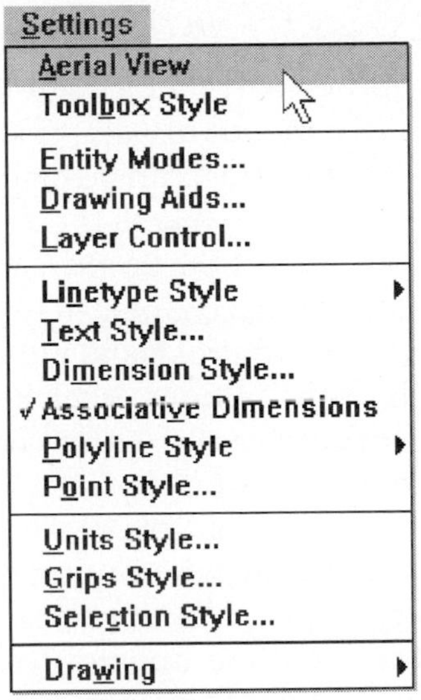

Figure 4-10.
The **DSVIEWER** command can be issued by selecting **Aerial View** from the **Settings** pull-down menu.

Settings
Aerial View
Toolbox Style
Entity Modes...
Drawing Aids...
Layer Control...
Linetype Style ▶
Text Style...
Dimension Style...
✓Associative Dimensions
Polyline Style ▶
Point Style...
Units Style...
Grips Style...
Selection Style...
Drawing ▶

Whichever view is currently displayed in the graphics window appears in the **Aerial View** window with its background reversed as shown in Figure 4-11. Like the floating toolbox, the **Aerial View** window can be moved to any convenient location on the screen. To do so, simply click in the title bar of the **Aerial View** window, hold down the left mouse button, and drag the **Aerial View** window to a new location. You can also resize the **Aerial View** window by dragging its border left or right, or up and down as desired. If you drag the border by one of its corners, the window is resized both horizontally and vertically so that the correct aspect ratio is maintained.

Figure 4-11.
The entire drawing with its background reversed is displayed in the **Aerial View** window.

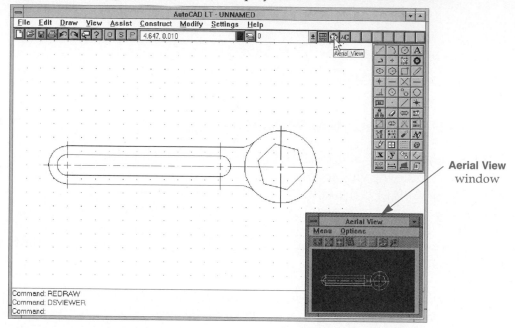

Aerial View
window

Aerial View window description

The **Aerial View** window contains eight toolbar buttons, the **Control Menu** button, and a menu bar with two pull-down menus titled **Menu** and **Options**. See Figure 4-12. The available options in the pull-down menus are described as follows:

- **Menu.** Only one viewport can be displayed in the **Aerial View** window when multiple viewports are in use. To match the display in the **Aerial View** window with that of the current viewport, select the **Set To Current VP** option in this menu. Multiple viewports are covered later in this chapter. To exit the **Aerial View** window, select the **Exit** option or double-click the **Control Menu** button at the upper-left corner of the window.

- **Options.** Each of the options available from this pull-down menu are active when a check mark appears to the left of each menu item. You can increase the size of the **Aerial View** toolbar buttons by selecting **Big Icons** and toggle the toolbar display on and off with the **Tool Bar** option. As you zoom, pan, and edit your drawing, the contents of the **Aerial View** window are dynamically updated to reflect the changes you make. For very large or complex drawings, you can improve system performance by turning off the real-time update. To do so, select the **Auto-Update** option from this menu. When real-time updating is turned off, the **Aerial View** display is not updated until you use one of the pull-down menu or toolbar options.

Figure 4-12.
The **Aerial View** window buttons.

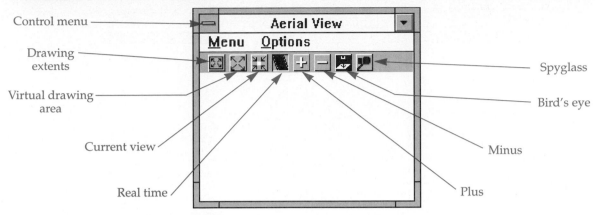

Each of the **Aerial View** toolbar buttons are described below.

- **Drawing Extents.** Use this button to display the entire drawing in the **Aerial View** window.
- **Virtual Drawing Area.** Click this button to display the largest amount of space provided to the current drawing for **Aerial View** zooming and panning functions.
- **Current View.** This button matches the display in the **Aerial View** window with that of the graphics window.
- **Real Time.** Identical to the **Auto-Update** item in the **Options** pull-down menu, this button toggles dynamic updating on and off.
- **Plus (+) and Minus (–).** These options control the magnification of the image in the **Aerial View** window. Click **+** to zoom in incrementally; click **–** to incrementally zoom out. Keep in mind that the **Minus** button has no effect after using the **Virtual Drawing Area** button because the **Aerial View** is then already zoomed out to its maximum.
- **Bird's Eye.** The **Bird's Eye** button actually performs two functions. It is used to position a view in the **Aerial View** window. It can also be used to magnify the view in the window. It does not affect the view in the graphics window, however.
- **Spyglass.** The **Spyglass** button is somewhat similar to **Bird's Eye** except that it changes the view in both the graphics window and the **Aerial View** window.

Zooming with Aerial View

To zoom using **Aerial View**, do the following:

1. Position your cursor over the reverse background area in the **Aerial View** window.
2. Click the right button on your mouse. As shown in Figure 4-13, a box with an X at its center is then displayed. This box is called the *view box*. The X at the center of the view box represents the cursor pick point.

Figure 4-13.
The X at the center of the view box represents the cursor pick point in the **Aerial View** window.

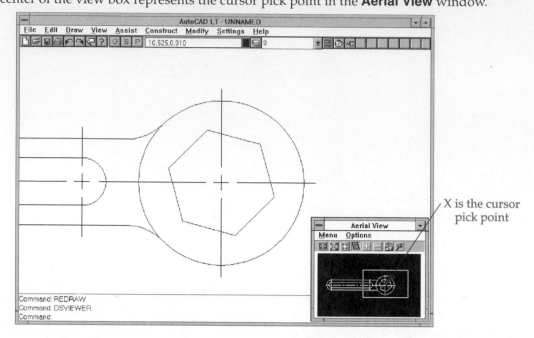

X is the cursor pick point

3. To zoom in, move your mouse to the left. The size of the view box decreases as the magnification in the graphics window increases. To zoom out, move your mouse to the right. Now the size of the view box grows as the magnification in the graphics window is reduced.
4. Once you are satisfied with the zoom display in the graphics window, click the left button on your mouse to set the view. The view that you specify replaces the previous reverse background image in the **Aerial View** window.

Using the Spyglass button to zoom

You can also use the **Spyglass** button to zoom the display in the graphics window with the following procedure:
1. Click the **Spyglass** button on the **Aerial View** toolbar.
2. Move your mouse into the graphics window. As shown in Figure 4-14A, the view box is displayed with crosshairs outside the box and a small cross (+) at its center. As you move your mouse around the graphics window, the view in the **Aerial View** window is constantly updated to match the current view in the view box.
3. To enter zoom mode, click the right button on your mouse.
4. To zoom in, move your mouse to the left. The size of the view box decreases as the magnification in the **Aerial View** window increases. To zoom out, move your mouse to the right. Now the size of the view box grows as the magnification in the **Aerial View** window shrinks.
5. Once you are satisfied with the zoom display in the **Aerial View** window, click the left button on your mouse to set the view in the graphics window. The view that you specify replaces the previous reverse background image in the **Aerial View** window. See Figure 4-14B.

Figure 4-14.
A—Using **Aerial View** to zoom the graphics window. B—The result of the zoom operation.
The reverse background represents the display in the graphics window.

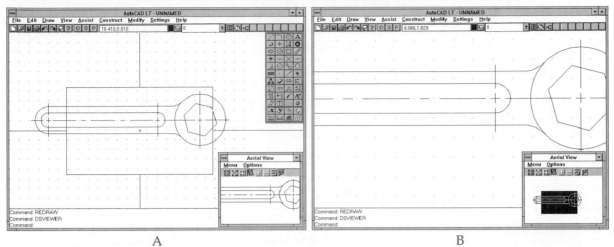

A   B

Panning with Aerial View

You can also use **Aerial View** to reposition, or pan, the image in the graphics window. To pan a view without changing its magnification, do the following:

1. Position your cursor over the reverse background area in the **Aerial View** window.
2. Click the left button on your mouse. As shown in Figure 4-15A, the view box is displayed inside the **Aerial View** window with crosshairs outside the box and a small cross (+) in the view box center.
3. Move your mouse in the **Aerial View** window to position the view box over the portion of the drawing you want to display in the graphics window. The view in the graphics window is dynamically updated as you move your mouse.
4. When you are satisfied with the display in the graphics window, click the left button on your mouse to set the view. The view that you specify replaces the previous reverse background image in the **Aerial View** window. See Figure 4-15B.

Figure 4-15.
A—Using the view box to pan the display. B—The reverse background represents the display in the graphics window.

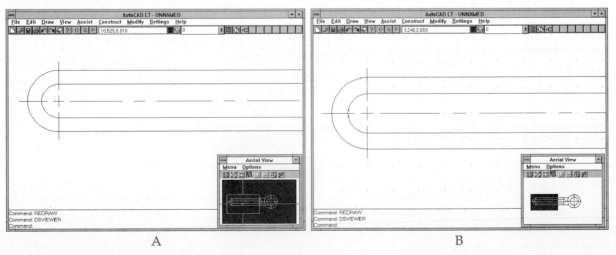

A   B

Using the Spyglass button to pan

You can also pan the graphics window display using the **Spyglass** button as follows:
1. Click the **Spyglass** button on the **Aerial View** toolbar.
2. Move your mouse into the graphics window. The view box is displayed with crosshairs outside the box and a small cross (+) at its center. As you move your mouse around the graphics window, the view in the **Aerial View** window is updated to match the current view in the view box.
3. Once you have a view positioned to your satisfaction in the **Aerial View** window, click the left button on your mouse to set the view in the graphics window. The view that you specify replaces the previous reverse background image in the **Aerial View** window.

Using Bird's Eye to change the Aerial View display

As previously mentioned, the **Bird's Eye** button may be used to position or magnify the view in the **Aerial View** window. However, the changes you make with **Bird's Eye** are not reflected in the graphics window. To position the view in the **Aerial View** window, do the following:
1. Click the **Bird's Eye** button on the **Aerial View** toolbar.
2. Position your cursor inside the **Aerial View** window.
3. A view box the size of the reverse background area is displayed inside the **Aerial View** window with crosshairs outside the box and a small cross (+) in the view box center.
4. Move your mouse to position the view box over the portion of the drawing you want to display in the **Aerial View** window.
5. Click the left button on your mouse to display the image that was in the view box.
6. To redisplay the entire drawing in the **Aerial View** window, click the **Drawing Extents** button.

To magnify the view in the **Aerial View** window, do the following:
1. Click the **Bird's Eye** button on the **Aerial View** toolbar.
2. Position your cursor inside the **Aerial View** window.
3. A view box the size of the reverse background area is displayed inside the **Aerial View** window with crosshairs outside the box and a small cross (+) in the view box center.
4. Click the right button on your mouse. The small cross at the center of the view box is replaced with an X.
5. To zoom in, move your mouse to the left. To zoom out, move your mouse to the right.
6. Once you are satisfied with the zoom display in the **Aerial View** window, click the left button on your mouse to set the view.
7. To redisplay the entire drawing in the **Aerial View** window, click the **Drawing Extents** button.

NOTE

The **Aerial View** window cannot be used in paper space, or when a perspective view is created with the **DVIEW** command. See Chapter 18 for complete information regarding **DVIEW** and other 3D viewing commands.

EXERCISE 4-2

❑ Open one of the drawings from the Chapter 3 exercises or problems.
❑ Activate the **Aerial View** window. Move and resize the window to your personal preferences. Also, try using the **Big Icons** option to increase the size of the toolbar buttons.
❑ Use **Aerial View** as described in the preceding section to zoom and pan various portions of your drawing. Spend some time familiarizing yourself with the function of each toolbar button.
❑ Do not save the drawing when you are finished experimenting.

Regardless of the method you use to display a view to your satisfaction, it is often a good idea to save the view so that you may easily return to it at any time without reissuing the **ZOOM**, **PAN**, or **DSVIEWER** commands. Views can be saved with names using the **VIEW** command, and the view name can be up to 31 characters in length. The view names must conform to standard AutoCAD LT naming convention—no spaces or punctuation marks are permitted. Therefore, named views can have *real-world* descriptions such as DETAILA, or SECTIONB-B, and can be renamed at any time.

NOTE	A named entity, like a view, can contain a dollar sign ($), hyphen (-), and underscore (_) in its name. Refer to Chapter 10 of the *AutoCAD LT User's Guide* for a complete description of valid names and wild-card characters.

You can save as many views as needed—restoring or deleting them as necessary. Since saved view names are occasionally forgotten, they can be listed for quick reference. This option is particularly handy when you find yourself working with a drawing file that was created a long time ago, or with a file created by another user. The **VIEW** command and its options are accessed by typing VIEW, or V, at the **Command:** prompt, or by selecting one of the options from the **View** cascading submenu in the **View** pull-down menu. See Figure 4-16. At the command line, you are presented with the following options:

Command: *(type* VIEW *or* V *and press* [Enter]*)*
?/Delete/Restore/Save/Window: *(select an option)*

Figure 4-16.
The **VIEW** command and its options can be accessed by selecting **View** from the **View** pull-down menu.

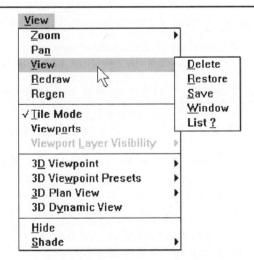

The **VIEW** options are described as follows:
- **?.** This option lists all saved views in the AutoCAD LT text window. See Figure 4-17. An M (model space) or a P (paper space) appears in a column to the right of each view name in the list to indicate in which space the view was defined. The **?** option looks like this:

        ?/Delete/Restore/Save/Window: **?** ↵
        View(s) to list ⟨*⟩: ↵

Figure 4-17.
The **VIEW** command **List** option lists all saved views in the AutoCAD LT text window.

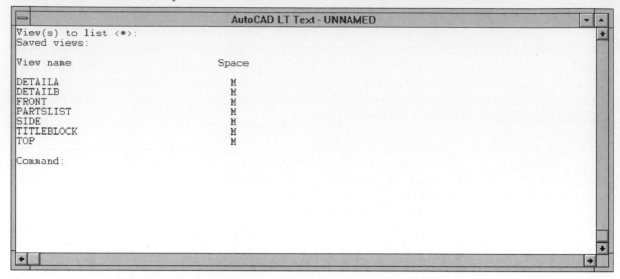

```
AutoCAD LT Text - UNNAMED
View(s) to list <*>:
Saved views:

View name                      Space

DETAILA                        M
DETAILB                        M
FRONT                          M
PARTSLIST                      M
SIDE                           M
TITLEBLOCK                     M
TOP                            M

Command:
```

Since the asterisk is a *wildcard* character, press [Enter] to list all the views saved in the drawing. If you only want to list several views, separate the view names with a comma; FRONT,TOP,SIDE. Do not put a space between the view names. The graphics window automatically flips to the text window to display the view names. If no views exist in the drawing, the following message is displayed:

> No matching views found.

When you are done, press function key [F2] to flip back to the graphics window.

- **Delete.** The **Delete** option removes one or more saved views. Multiple view names must be separated by commas as shown below.

  > ?/Delete/Restore/Save/Window: **D** ↵
  > View name(s) to delete: **DETAILA,FRONT** ↵

- **Restore.** Use the **Restore** option to display a saved view in the current viewport.

  > ?/Delete/Restore/Save/Window: **R** ↵
  > View name to restore: **SECTIONB-B** ↵

- **Save.** Once you have a view that you want to save displayed in the current viewport, use the **Save** option and provide a name for the view. Remember that the view name can be up to 31 characters in length, but no spaces are permitted. Also, be advised that no warning is issued if a view is saved with the same name of an existing view.

  > ?/Delete/Restore/Save/Window: **S** ↵
  > View name to save: **LEFTSIDE** ↵

- **Window.** The **Window** option allows you to define a view with two diagonal points. The view is named and saved, but not displayed until the **Restore** option is invoked.

  > ?/Delete/Restore/Save/Window: **W** ↵
  > View name to save: **PARTSLIST** ↵
  > First corner: *(pick a point)* Other corner: *(pick a point)*

The Select Initial View option

AutoCAD LT permits a saved view name to be specified for display *before* entering the drawing editor. This procedure is performed using the **Open Drawing** file dialog box illustrated in Figure 4-18A. With this method, you issue the **OPEN** command and select the drawing file you wish to load into AutoCAD LT as you would normally. Next, activate the **Select Initial View** check box in the lower-right corner of the dialog box and then click the **OK** button to exit the **Open Drawing** dialog box. This displays the **Select Initial View** subdialog box. Use the subdialog box to select the named view you wish to preload. See Figure 4-18B. After clicking the **OK** button, the view you selected from the list is then displayed in the graphics window.

Figure 4-18.
A—The **Select Initial View** check box is activated at the lower right of the **Open Drawing** dialog box. B—The **Select Initial View** subdialog box lists all saved views in the drawing.

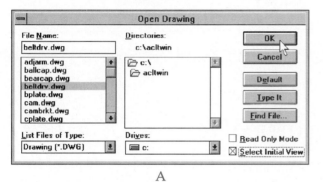

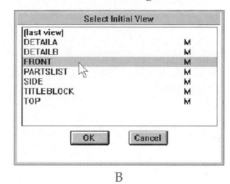

A   B

Renaming a saved view

ALTUG 10

Views may be renamed at any time with the **DDRENAME** command. This command permits you to rename your saved views, and other AutoCAD LT named objects, using a dialog box. Enter DDRENAME, or DR, at the **Command:** prompt or select **Rename...** from the **Modify** pull-down menu to display the **Rename** dialog box. See Figure 4-19.

Figure 4-19.
A—Selecting **Rename...** from the **Modify** pull-down menu displays the **Rename** dialog box.
B—Using the **Rename** dialog box to rename a saved view.

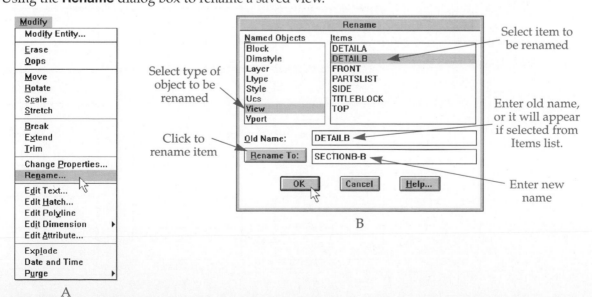

The **Named Objects** list appears in the upper-left corner of the dialog box and contains the types of objects that may be named or renamed in AutoCAD LT. Each of these objects will be explored fully as they are encountered in this text. From the example, observe that View has been selected from the list at the left. A listing of all the views saved in the current drawing appears at the right of the dialog box. To rename view DETAILB, first select the view name from the list. The name of the view you select is then displayed in the **Old Name:** text box. With your mouse, click anywhere inside the **Rename To:** text box and enter the new view name. In the example, view DETAILB is renamed to SECTIONB-B. When you are done typing, click the **Rename To:** button and the new view name appears in the list at the right of the dialog box. When you are finished renaming objects, click the **OK** button to exit the **Rename** dialog box.

It is also possible to rename objects from the command line instead of using a dialog box. In the following example, the **RENAME**, or **RN**, command is used to perform the identical renaming operation described above.

```
Command: (type RENAME or RN and press [Enter])
Block/Dimstyle/LAyer/LType/Style/Ucs/VIew/VPort: VI ↵
Old view name: DETAILB ↵
New view name: SECTIONB-B ↵
Command:
```

DIVIDING THE SCREEN INTO MULTIPLE VIEWPORTS | ALTUG 8

The AutoCAD LT **VPORTS** command allows you to divide the model space display screen into multiple viewing windows, or *viewports*. Several typical viewport configurations are shown in Figure 4-20. The viewports are *tiled*; which means they are adjacent to one another with no gaps in between. Each viewport can display a different view of your drawing, and can have independent **GRID**, **SNAP**, and **LIMITS** settings. However, if **ORTHO** mode is on, it is on in all viewports. For 2D drawings, one viewport may take an isometric, or pictorial, style, while the others remain orthographic. Whether 2D or 3D, you can pan or zoom independently in each viewport. The **REDRAW** and **REGEN** commands redraw or regenerate *all* displayed viewports. It is the **MAXACTVP** system variable that sets the maximum number of active viewports to regenerate at one time. By default, that number is 16. The value range is determined by your operating system and display driver.

Figure 4-20.
The display screen can be divided into 2, 3, or 4 multiple viewports in a variety of configurations.

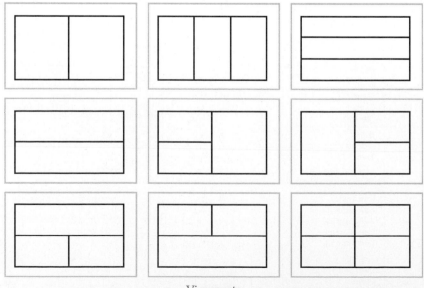

Viewports

Regardless of the number of displayed viewports, only one viewport can be active at any one time. The active viewport is surrounded by a wider border, and the screen crosshair cursor is only displayed within that viewport, Figure 4-21. For the other displayed viewports, the cursor appears as an arrow. The viewports are interactive; thus a drawing or editing command may be started in one viewport, but completed in another. An inactive viewport may be made current by a simple click of your left mouse button anywhere within its border. You may also use the [Ctrl]+[V] keyboard combination to cycle through multiple viewports, making each one current in succession.

Figure 4-21.
The active viewport is represented with a wide border and displays the full screen crosshair cursor.

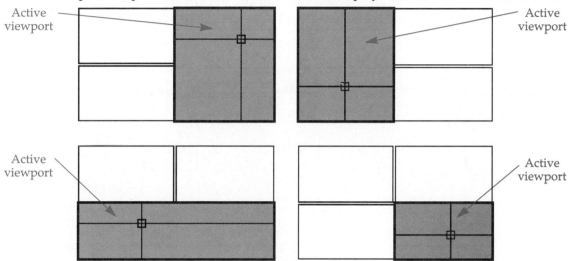

The **VPORTS** command has similar functionality to the **VIEW** command in that it allows a multiple viewport configuration to be saved with a name, restored, listed, or deleted. Single viewports can be returned to at any time, and more than one configuration can be saved. Like view names, viewport configuration names can be up to 31 characters in length and the same naming restrictions apply. Furthermore, an inactive viewport can be joined to an active viewport providing that the resulting viewport forms a rectangle. See Figure 4-22. You may find that joining viewports together can be quicker than defining an entirely new viewport configuration. However, keep in mind that the newly joined viewport inherits all aspects of the dominant viewport to which it was joined—**LIMITS**, **GRID**, **SNAP**, etc.

Figure 4-22.
The **Join** option joins one viewport to another providing the joined viewports form a rectangle.

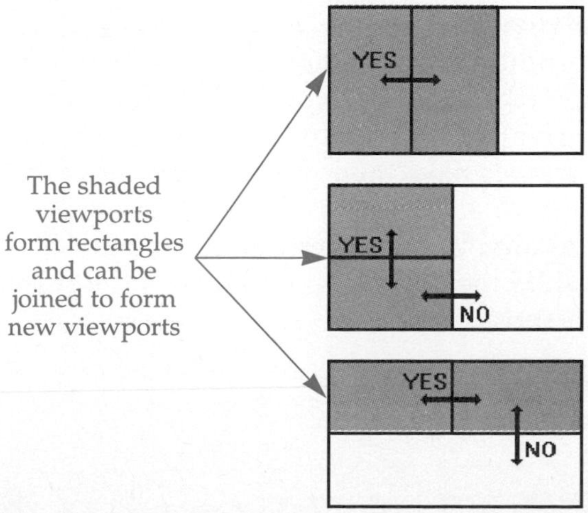

The shaded viewports form rectangles and can be joined to form new viewports

YES

YES

NO

YES

NO

By default, the **VPORTS** command divides the screen into three viewports with the active, or dominant viewport, to the right and the two inactive viewports arranged in a vertical orientation to the left. The **VPORTS** command is found as **Viewports** in the **View** pull-down menu. See Figure 4-23. The command sequence is as follows:

Command: *(type* VPORTS *or* VW *and press* [Enter]*)*
Save/Restore/Delete/Join/SIngle/?/2/⟨3⟩/4: *(select an option)*

The **VPORTS** options are as follows:
- **Save.** Saves a defined viewport configuration with a name. The configuration name may not exceed 31 characters.
- **Restore.** Redisplays a saved viewport configuration.
- **Delete.** Deletes a saved viewport configuration.
- **Join.** Combines two adjacent viewports into one viewport providing the new viewport forms a rectangle.

Figure 4-23.
The **VPORTS** command can be issued by selecting **Viewports** from the **View** pull-down menu.

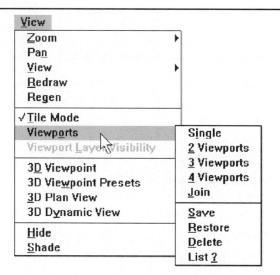

- **Single.** Disables multiple viewports and displays the current viewport as a single view.
- **?.** Lists any or all saved viewport configurations in the AutoCAD LT text window. The listing includes a unique identification number and coordinate location for each viewport. The coordinate location is based on the lower left of the display screen as 0.0000, 0.0000 and the upper right of the display as 1.0000, 1.0000.
- **2.** Divides the current viewport into two viewports. You can choose between a horizontal or vertical division.
- **3.** Divides the current viewport into three viewports. The dominant viewport may be placed to the right (the default), to the left, or above the other two viewports.
- **4.** Divides the current viewport into four equally sized viewports.

While multiple viewports have their greatest benefit for 3D modeling, they can also be useful for 2D applications. Consider the assembly drawing illustrated in Figure 4-24. In this example, the screen is divided into two vertical viewports. The drawing parts list is created in the right viewport, while the left viewport displays the relevant portion of the assembly drawing for reference purposes.

Figure 4-24.
A practical application of 2D viewports. The drawing parts list is created in the right viewport, while the assembly drawing is referenced in the left viewport.

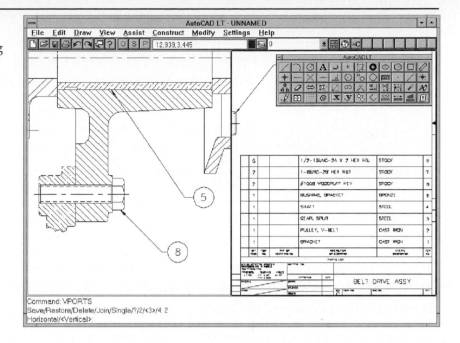

Finally, keep in mind that when plotting multiple viewports, only the current viewport is plotted.

PROFESSIONAL TIP

Named viewport configurations, like named views, take up space in a drawing file. Create and save only those views and multiple viewports necessary to detail your drawing. Should you no longer require certain views or viewport configurations, remove them using the **Delete** option of the **VIEW** or **VPORTS** commands.

CHAPTER TEST

Write your answers in the spaces provided.

1. Which two **ZOOM** command options cannot be used transparently? Why not? _____

2. Which **ZOOM** option should be used after changing the drawing limits? _____

3. Which **ZOOM** option should be used to display every entity in the drawing? _____

4. Describe the difference between **ZOOM Scale** and **ZOOM Scale X**.

5. What is the maximum number of views that may be recalled using **ZOOM Previous**?

   _____

6. When using the **ZOOM Center** option, what character should be entered with the scale factor to tell AutoCAD LT to use magnification instead of height? _____

   _____

   _____

   _____

7. The **PAN** command is used to move drawing entities to a new screen location. (True/False) _____

8. Identify two ways to activate the **Aerial View** window. _____

   _____

   _____

9. Can **Aerial View** zooming and panning functions be used transparently? (Yes/No) _____

10. What is the purpose of the **VIEW** command? _____

    _____

11. Which option of the **VIEW** command allows you to save a view without having the view displayed?_____

    _____

12. Which option of the **VIEW** command allows you to display a previously saved view?___

    _____

13. What is the maximum number of characters permitted for a view name? Are spaces allowed? _____

    _____

14. AutoCAD LT alerts you if you attempt to save a view with the name of an existing view. (True/False) _____

15. Can each viewport in a multiple viewport configuration have separate grid and snap settings? (Yes/No) _____

16. Which **VPORTS** option is used to display one viewport? _____

    _____

17. All the viewports in a multiple viewport configuration can be plotted simultaneously. (True/False) _____

18. Redraws and regenerations occur in the current viewport only. (True/False) _____

19. Which system variable determines the number of viewports that can be regenerated at one time? What is the number?_____

    _____

CHAPTER PROBLEMS

1. Begin a new drawing using your PROTOA prototype drawing created in Chapter 2. If you have not done this already, refer to Chapter 2 and do so now.

   A. Using the **LINE** command, draw a square, triangle, and rectangle as shown. Make the objects proportional to the drawing limits.

   B. Save a view of all displayed objects. Name the view ALL.

   C. Create one saved view of each shape. The view names should be SQUARE, TRIANGLE, and RECTANGLE.

   D. Set up a four viewport configuration and save it with the name 4VIEWS.

   E. Activate the upper-left viewport and restore view SQUARE.

   F. Activate the lower-left viewport and restore view TRIANGLE.

   G. Activate the upper-right viewport and restore view RECTANGLE.

   H. Activate the lower-right viewport and restore view ALL.

   I. Use **PAN** or **Aerial View** to center each view in its respective viewport.

   J. Save the drawing as P4-1.

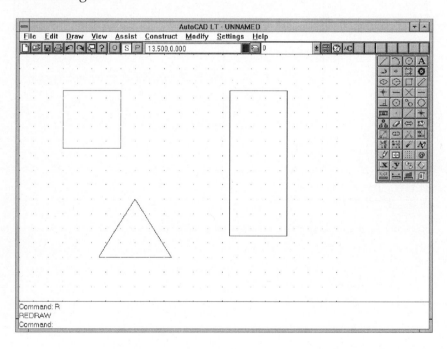

2. Open the sample drawing OFFICE.DWG from the ACLTWIN directory. Notify your instructor or supervisor if this drawing cannot be found on your workstation.

A. Zoom in on room 2202 and save the view with the name RM2202.

B. Zoom in on room 2222 and save the view with the name RM2222.

C. Zoom in on room 2225 and save the view with the name RM2225.

D. Create a three viewport configuration with the dominant viewport to the left. Save the viewport configuration with the name 3ROOMS.

E. Activate the upper-right viewport and restore view RM2202.

F. Activate the lower-right viewport and restore view RM2225.

J. Activate the left viewport and restore view RM2222.

H. Save the drawing as P4-2.

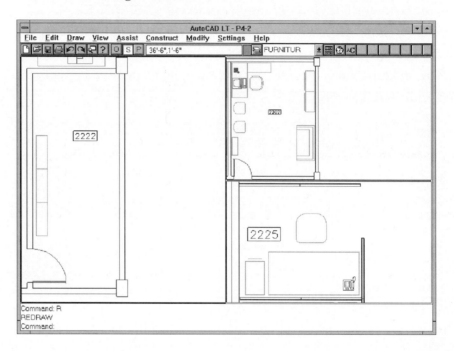

AutoCAD LT—Fundamentals and Applications

AutoCAD LT

Chapter 5

Colors, Linetypes, and Layers

Learning objectives:

After you have completed this chapter, you will be able to:

○ Select and use the colors available in AutoCAD LT.

○ Load and use various linetypes.

○ Create your own custom linetypes using both AutoCAD LT and the Microsoft Windows Notepad editor.

○ Create and manage drawing layers.

○ Change the properties of existing entities.

○ Purge unused linetypes and layers from your drawing.

Controlling the entities in your drawings plays a very important role in the efficient use of AutoCAD LT. Using various colors adds clarity and visual appeal to CAD drawings. It is also necessary to use various linetypes to describe objects without ambiguity and to comply with industry standards. In the traditional, paper-based drafting environment, transparent overlays are often used to separate various drawing elements. For an architectural application, one overlay may feature doors and windows, while another might include piping symbols. The overlays are perfectly aligned with one another. Other drawing elements, like receptacles, floor plans, and foundations may also be created on separate overlays. AutoCAD LT provides a similar capability using *layers*. With layers, you can separate your drawing objects into logically named groupings. Colors and linetypes may be assigned to individual layers, and the layers can be made visible or invisible as required. Objects can be moved from one layer to another, and linetypes and layers can be purged from a drawing if not required.

USING COLORS

ALTUG 8

There are 255 colors available for your use in AutoCAD LT. Every color has a number assigned by the *AutoCAD Color Index*, or *ACI*. The first seven colors can also be addressed by their names. AutoCAD LT refers to these first seven colors as the *standard colors*. Their names and numbers are given below:

Color Number	Color Name
1	R *or* Red
2	Y *or* Yellow
3	G *or* Green
4	C *or* Cyan
5	B *or* Blue
6	M *or* Magenta
7	W *or* White

Color 7 is the default color in AutoCAD LT. It is white on a dark background and black on a light background.

When printing or plotting your drawing, individual colors can be set to print/plot at different line widths. See Chapter 13 of this text for complete information about plotter pens and colors.

Setting a color from the command line

To set a different color for new drawing entities at the **Command:** prompt, use the **COLOR** command and enter the first letter of the color name, the full color name, or the color number. In the following example, the color green is selected.

> Command: *(type* COLOR *or* CO *and press* [Enter]*)*
> New entity color ⟨*current*⟩: *(type* 3 *or* G *or* GREEN *and press* [Enter]*)*

The **COLOR** command can also be used transparently by entering 'COLOR or 'CO while in the middle of another command. However , be aware that the new color does not take effect until the current command is terminated.

Setting a color from a dialog box

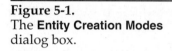

Colors can also be set using the **Entity Creation Modes** dialog box shown in Figure 5-1. To access this dialog box, type in DDEMODES, or EM. You can also click the **Current Color** button just to the right of the coordinate display box on the toolbar, or select **Entity Modes...** from the **Settings** pull-down menu. See Figure 5-2.

Figure 5-1.
The **Entity Creation Modes** dialog box.

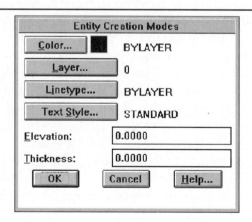

Figure 5-2.
A—Click the **Current Color** button on the toolbar to open the **Entity Creation Modes** dialog box.
B—Selecting **Entity Modes...** from the **Settings** pull-down menu.

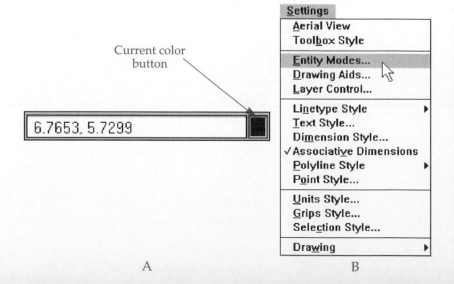

A   B

> **NOTE** Although the **Entity Modes** button shown does not appear in the toolbox or on the toolbar, it may easily be added. This function is covered in detail in Chapter 19 of this text.

To set a color using the **Entity Creation Modes** dialog box, first click the **Color...** button at the top of the dialog box. See Figure 5-1. The **Select Color** subdialog box then appears. In the example shown in Figure 5-3, the color red is selected from the **Standard Colors** section at the top of the subdialog box. Observe that the color name appears in the **Color:** text box at the bottom and the color is displayed in the image tile just to the right of the text box. Click **OK** to exit the **Select Color** subdialog box, and then click **OK** one more time to exit the **Entity Creation Modes** dialog box. Whether you set a color from the command line or from the dialog box, the new color is then displayed by the **Current Color** button on the toolbar.

Figure 5-3.
Selecting a color from the
Select Color subdialog box.

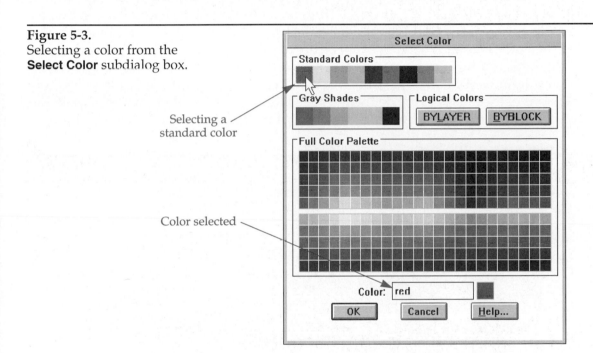

Components of **Select Color** subdialog box

The other sections of the **Select Color** subdialog box are described as follows:

- **Gray Shades.** The **Gray Shades** area displays color numbers 250-255. Use this section to specify a shade of gray for new entities.
- **Full Color Palette.** The **Full Color Palette** contains color numbers 10-249. Your display device determines the number of colors that are available from the **Full Color Palette**.
- **Logical Colors.** The two buttons in this section specify how color assignments are made. In the default **BYLAYER** mode, new entities assume the color of the layer upon which they are drawn (layers are described in a later section of this chapter). If you select **BYBLOCK** mode, AutoCAD LT draws new entities in the default color. That color is white or black, depending on your screen background color, and is maintained until the entities are made into a block. A *block* is one or more entities grouped together into a single object. When the block is inserted into a drawing, the entities in the block inherit the current setting of the **COLOR** command. See Chapter 14 for a complete description of blocks and block attributes.

EXERCISE 5-1

- ❑ Begin a new drawing. It is not necessary to use one of your prototype drawings for this exercise.
- ❑ Use the **COLOR** command and draw a line with each of the seven standard colors (1 through 7).
- ❑ Now, use **DDEMODES** to draw lines using each of the available gray shades.
- ❑ Use **DDEMODES** again to draw lines using any of the colors in the **Full Color Palette**.
- ❑ It is not necessary to save the drawing when you are finished.

LINETYPES

ALTUG 4

All of the lines you have drawn in the exercises and problems from the previous chapters have been in a solid, unbroken linetype. In drafting terminology, you might refer to this linetype as an object line. AutoCAD LT calls it the ***continuous linetype***. The continuous linetype is the default linetype in AutoCAD LT and is always loaded and ready for use in every new drawing. There are 24 other linetypes available to you as well. From Figure 5-4, you can see that each linetype is a repeating pattern of dashes or dots separated with blank spaces. The linetypes are defined in an external library file called ACLT.LIN in the \ACLTWIN directory. Metric versions of the linetypes are defined in a second library file called ACLTISO.LIN. Before you can draw with one of these linetypes, it must first be loaded into the drawing editor.

Figure 5-4.
The 24 standard linetypes defined in the ACLT.LIN linetype file.

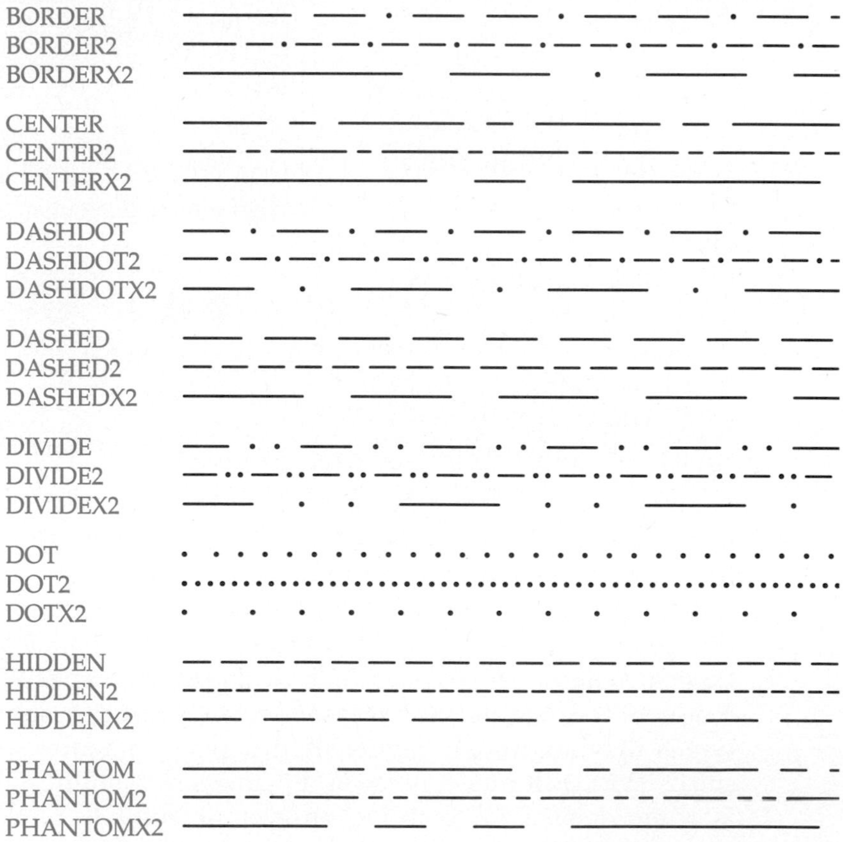

The LINETYPE Command

The **LINETYPE** command is accessed by typing LINETYPE or LT at the **Command:** prompt, or by selecting **Linetype Style** from the **Settings** pull-down menu. This menu item displays the cascading submenu shown in Figure 5-5. The command sequence is as follows:

Command: *(type* LINETYPE *or* LT *and press* [Enter]*)*
?/Create/Load/Set: *(select an option)*

Figure 5-5.
Selecting **Linetype Style** from the **Settings** pull-down menu displays a cascading submenu of linetype options.

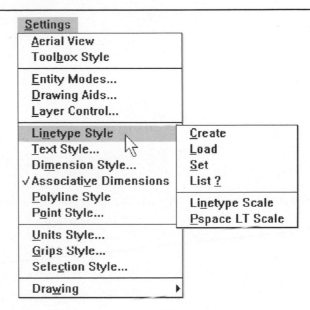

The **LINETYPE** options are described as follows:

- **?.** The **?** option is used to list the available linetypes. When you select the list option, you are presented with the **Select Linetype File** dialog box shown in Figure 5-6. Observe that linetype files have a .LIN file extension and that the two files ACLT.INI and ACLTISO.LIN appear in the file list at the left of the dialog box. Select the linetype file that you wish to list and click the **OK** button. The graphics window automatically flips to the text window to display the linetypes available in the file you selected. See Figure 5-7. After listing each of the linetypes, the **LINETYPE** command options are redisplayed. Select an option or press [Enter] to end the command. Press function key [F2] to flip back to the graphics window.

Figure 5-6.
Selecting a linetype file from the **Select Linetype File** dialog box. The ACLTISO.LIN file is used for metric drawings.

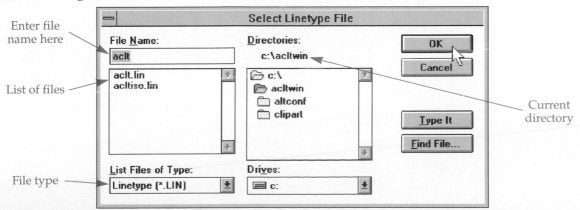

Figure 5-7.
The **LINETYPE** command **List** option displays the available linetypes in the text window.

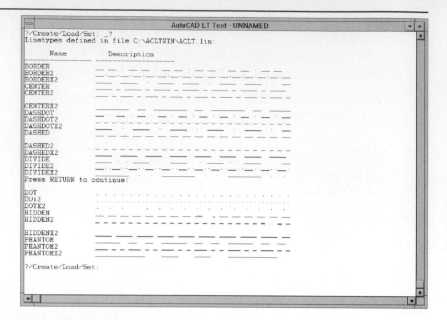

- **Create.** AutoCAD LT allows you to define your own custom linetypes. This capability is discussed in a later section of this chapter.
- **Load.** Use the **Load** option to load one or more linetypes into the drawing editor. You must enter the linetype name(s) in full—abbreviations are not accepted. When loading multiple linetypes, separate each linetype name with a comma as shown below:

> Command: *(type LINETYPE or LT and press* [Enter]*)*
> ?/Create/Load/Set: **L** ↵
> Linetype(s) to load: **CENTER,HIDDEN,PHANTOM** ↵

After you enter the linetype name(s) and press [Enter], you are presented with the **Select Linetype File** dialog box. Select the linetype file that you wish to load from and click the **OK** button. Remember to select the ACLTISO.LIN file for your metric drawings. AutoCAD LT then loads the linetypes you requested and redisplays the **LINETYPE** command options. Select another option or press [Enter] to end the command. If you would like to quickly load all 24 linetypes defined in the linetype file, enter the * wildcard character at the **Linetype(s) to load:** prompt.

- **Set.** Once a linetype is loaded, it must be set current before you can draw with it. Only one linetype can be current at a time. In the following example, the HIDDEN linetype is set current:

> Command: *(type LINETYPE or LT and press* [Enter]*)*
> ?/Create/Load/Set: **S** ↵
> New entity linetype (or ?) ⟨*current*⟩: **HIDDEN** ↵

If you forget the name of the linetype you wish to set current, use the **?** option to list the loaded linetypes as follows:

> New entity linetype (or ?) ⟨*current*⟩: **?** ↵
> Linetype(s) to list ⟨*⟩: ↵

Since the * symbol is a wildcard character, simply press [Enter] to list all loaded linetypes. After setting a linetype current, the LINETYPE command options are redisplayed. Select another option or press [Enter] to end the command.

| NOTE | The **LINETYPE** command may also be used transparently by entering 'LINETYPE or 'LT while in the middle of another command. However, like the transparent '**COLOR** commands, a different linetype does not take effect until the current command is terminated. |

Setting a linetype using a dialog box

Once a linetype is loaded, you can bypass the **LINETYPE** command **Set** option and quickly set the linetype current using the **Entity Creation Modes** dialog box. See Figure 5-8. To do so, open the dialog box as previously described and click the **Linetype...** button. The **Select Linetype** subdialog box then appears. Only the linetypes that have been loaded into the drawing editor with the **LINETYPE** command appear in this dialog box. In the example shown in Figure 5-8, the HIDDEN linetype is selected from the list and the linetype name appears in the **Linetype:** text box at the bottom. When you use this method, click the image tile of the linetype you wish to set—not the word to the right of the image tile. Click **OK** to exit the **Select Linetype** subdialog box, and then click **OK** one more time to exit the **Entity Creation Modes** dialog box.

Figure 5-8.
Selecting a linetype from the **Select Linetype** subdialog box.

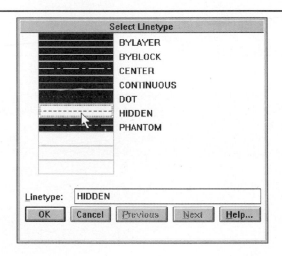

Changing the linetype scale factor

ALTUG 10

Occasionally, you will draw a line that is too short to hold even one dash sequence. This often occurs when you are drawing very short hidden or centerlines in a confined area. In these instances, AutoCAD LT uses a continuous linetype instead. To correct the problem, change the linetype scale factor using the **LTSCALE** system variable. **LTSCALE** changes the relative length of dashed and dotted linetypes per drawing unit. A value greater than one increases the length; a value less than one decreases the length. Negative values are not permitted. You can change **LTSCALE** by selecting **Linetype Style** and then **Linetype Scale** from the **Settings** pull-down menu. See Figure 5-5. The command sequence is as follows:

> Command: *(type* LTSCALE *or* LC *and press* [Enter]*)*
> New scale factor ⟨current⟩: *(enter a positive value and press* [Enter]*)*

Several examples of lines with varying linetype scales appear in Figure 5-9. However, keep in mind that changing the linetype scale factor automatically forces a drawing regeneration.

Figure 5-9.
Several examples of linetype
scale factors using **LTSCALE**.

LTSCALE = 1

LTSCALE = 2

LTSCALE = .5

PROFESSIONAL TIP

Because the **LTSCALE** variable is global, all of the lines in your drawing are affected by a change in linetype scale. To change the linetype scale for specific entities, select one of the variations from the ACLT.LIN or ACLTISO.LIN library files. As an example, if you are satisfied with the scale of the hidden lines on your drawing but would like to increase the spacing of the centerlines only, use the CENTERX2 linetype instead of CENTER or CENTER2.

EXERCISE 5-2

❑ Begin a new drawing using your PROTOA prototype drawing.
❑ Use the **LINETYPE** command **Load** option to load the CENTER and HIDDEN linetypes as previously described.
❑ Draw the objects shown to approximate size.

❑ Make the hidden lines red and the centerline blue.
❑ Try both the **LINETYPE** command **Set** option as well as the **Entity Creation Modes** dialog box when setting a different linetype current. Of the two methods, which do you prefer?
❑ After constructing the drawing objects, set **LTSCALE** to 2, then to .5, and then back to 1. Observe the effects on the linetypes.
❑ Save the drawing as EX5-2.

CUSTOM LINETYPES

As mentioned previously, AutoCAD LT stores linetype definitions in the external library files ACLT.LIN and ACLTISO.LIN. To create a custom linetype, you must edit one of the existing linetype files or create an entirely new one. There are two methods to accomplish this task. The first method uses the **LINETYPE** command **Create** option inside AutoCAD LT. The second method permits you to edit the linetype library file directly with an ASCII (American Standard Code for Information Interchange) text editor such as Windows Notepad or MS-DOS EDIT. A portion of ACLT.LIN is shown in the Notepad in Figure 5-10.

Figure 5-10.
A portion of ACLT.LIN is shown in the Notepad text editor.

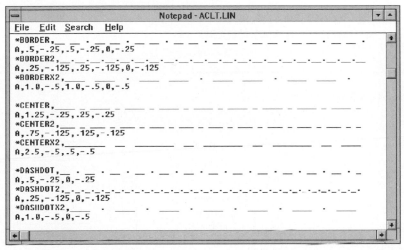

Interpreting a linetype definition is really quite simple. As you can see from the illustration, each linetype name is preceded with an asterisk and followed with a comma and a pictorial representation of the linetype. The A on the second line specifies the line pattern alignment used at the ends of individual lines, arcs, and circles. AutoCAD LT refers to this as *A-type alignment*. The pattern alignment ensures that lines and arcs start and end with a dash (or dot).

However, it is the number values that really define a linetype. A positive number specifies the length of the dash segment, while a negative number specifies the length of the space in the line. A 0 (zero) results in a dot being drawn. AutoCAD LT automatically repeats the sequence for any given line length.

CUSTOM LINETYPE TUTORIAL

➪ Use the following procedure to create a custom linetype called MYBORDER. It is similar to the BORDER linetype which draws two dashes and a dot, except that it draws two dots and then a dash.

> Command: *(type* LINETYPE *or* LT *and press* [Enter]*)*
> ?/Create/Load/Set: **C** ↵
> Name of linetype to create: **MYBORDER** ↵

➪ When the **Create or Append Linetype File** dialog box appears, enter the name MYLINES in the **File Name:** text box and then click the **OK** button. See Figure 5-11. You are then informed that the new linetype file is created, and are prompted to enter some descriptive text.

> Creating new file
> Descriptive text: **TWO DOTS AND A DASH** ↵

Figure 5-11.
The **Create or Append Linetype File** dialog box.

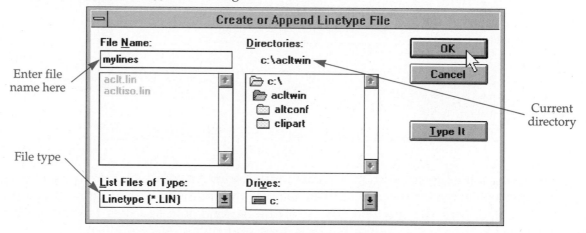

Enter file name here · File type · Current directory

➪ Now enter the linetype pattern definition. Observe that AutoCAD LT automatically places the "A" for A-type alignment at the beginning of the line for you.

> Enter pattern (on next line):
> **A, 0,−.25,0,−.25,.5,−.25** ↵
> New definition written to file.
> ?/Create/Load/Set: **L** ↵
> Linetype(s) to load: **MYBORDER** ↵

➪ When the **Select Linetype File** dialog box appears, select the file MYLINES.LIN and click **OK**.

> Linetype MYBORDER loaded.
> ?/Create/Load/Set: **S** ↵
> New entity linetype (or ?) ⟨*current*⟩: **MYBORDER** ↵
> ?/Create/Load/Set: ↵

➪ Remember that you can also use the **Entity Creation Modes** dialog box to set the MYBORDER linetype current. An example of the new linetype is shown in Figure 5-12.

Figure 5-12.
A rectangle drawn with the custom MYBORDER linetype.

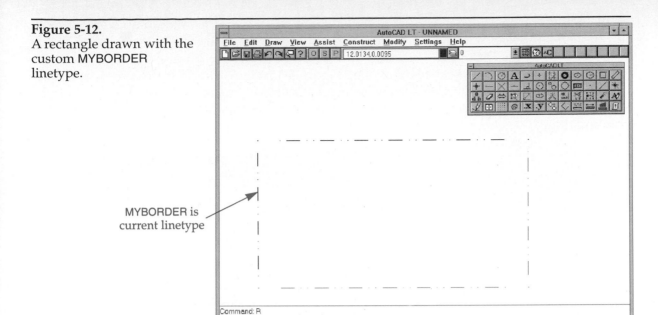

MYBORDER is current linetype

Using the Windows Notepad to create a custom linetype

The Microsoft Windows Notepad is an ASCII text editor that you can use to edit small text files (not exceeding 50K in size). This makes Notepad very handy for creating a custom line-type library file or for editing the existing ACLT.LIN or ACLTISO.LIN files. The MYLINES.LIN linetype file can be easily created using Notepad without exiting AutoCAD LT. First, use the [Ctrl]+[Esc] key combination to activate the Windows Task List, select Program Manager from the list and click the Switch To button. When the Accessories group window appears, double-click the Notepad program item icon shown in Figure 5-13. Notepad launches in its own display window, and you can begin entering the following text at the flashing text insertion point located at the top left of the window. Although this step is optional, you can use the period (.) and underscore (_) keys to duplicate the line representation shown as follows:

```
*MYBORDER, . . _ . . _ . . _ . . _
A, 0,-.25,0,-.25,.5,-.25 ⏎
```

Figure 5-13.
Notepad is launched from the Accessories group window in Program Manager.

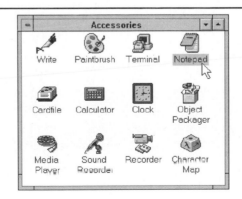

When you have finished entering the text, the Notepad window should appear as shown in Figure 5-14. Select Save As... from the File pull-down menu to access the Save As dialog box. Change to the \ACLTWIN directory and save your linetype library file with the name MYLINES.LIN in the File Name: text box. See Figure 5-15. Click the OK button to save the file and exit the dialog box. Quit Notepad by selecting Exit from the File pull-down menu and you are returned to Program Manager. To immediately return to AutoCAD LT, use the [Alt]+[Tab] key combination.

Figure 5-14.
The MYBORDER custom linetype pattern definition in the Notepad.

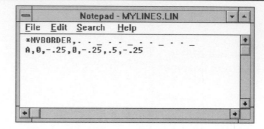

Figure 5-15.
The linetype is saved as MYLINES.LIN in the \ACLTWIN directory.

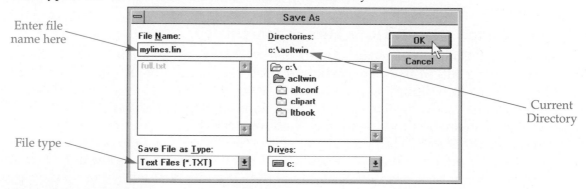

Enter file name here

File type

Current Directory

PROFESSIONAL TIP

Make a backup copy of the original ACLT.LIN or ACLTISO.LIN library files before you experiment with creating or modifying linetype definitions. It might be a good idea to create linetypes in a separate file as described in the two previous examples, and leave the ACLT.LIN or ACLTISO.LIN files undisturbed. Check with your instructor or supervisor to verify which procedures should be used.

EXERCISE 5-3

❑ Use Notepad to edit the MYLINES.LIN linetype file.
❑ Add these three dotted linetype patterns:
 *MYDOT1,.
  A,0,–.125
 *MYDOT2,.
  A,0,–.1
 *MYDOT3,.
  A,0,–.05
❑ Save the edited MYBORDER.LIN linetype file.
❑ Start AutoCAD LT, load your new linetypes and draw several lines with them.
❑ Save the drawing as EX5-3.

CREATING AND USING LAYERS

As mentioned at the beginning of this chapter, layers in AutoCAD LT are used much like the transparent overlays used in the traditional paper-based drafting environment. They provide the most powerful and efficient means of drawing organization and management. Because colors and linetypes can be assigned to individual layers, you can set up a drawing so that hidden features appear on a layer called HIDDEN, in red, and in a DASHED linetype. When you wish to view your drawing without the dashed lines, the HIDDEN layer can be turned off. Dimensions could be placed on a layer called DIMS and assigned the color green, while drawing annotation could be placed on a yellow layer called NOTES. The default layer in AutoCAD LT is layer 0. Layer 0 is assigned color 7 and the continuous linetype.

The two ways to create and manage layers in AutoCAD LT are to use the **LAYER** command, or use the **Layer Control** dialog box. The **Layer Control** dialog box is discussed later in this chapter. The command sequence for the **LAYER** command is as follows:

> Command: *(type* LAYER *or* LA *and press* [Enter]*)*
> ?/Make/Set/New/ ON/OFF/Color/Ltype/Freeze/Thaw/LOck/Unlock:

To better understand layers, each option of the **LAYER** command is described below.

- **?.** Use the **?** option to list any existing layers in the drawing. When you select the list option, you are presented with the following prompt:

> Layer name(s) to list ⟨*⟩: *(press* [Enter] *to list all layers)*

  The graphics window flips to the text window to display all the layers defined in the drawing. The colors, linetypes, and status of the layers (on/off, frozen/thawed, etc.) also appear in the list. After listing the layers, the **LAYER** command option line is redisplayed. Select an option, press [F2] to flip back to the graphics window, or press [Enter] to end the command.

- **Make.** The **Make** option makes a new layer and sets it current. The layer name can be up to 31 characters in length, but no spaces are permitted.

> New current layer ⟨0⟩: *(enter a name for the new layer)*

  The new layer is automatically assigned color 7 and the continuous linetype.

- **Set.** The **Set** option is used to set a different layer current.

> New current layer ⟨current⟩: *(enter the name of an existing layer)*

  If the layer you specify is turned off, it is automatically turned back on.

- **New.** Use the **New** option to create an entirely new layer. When creating multiple layers, separate each layer name with a comma as shown below:

> New layer name(s): **NOTES,DIMS,CENTERLINES** ↵

  Color 7 and the continuous linetype are automatically assigned to new layers. However, unlike the **Make** option a newly created layer is not automatically set current.

- **ON.** New layers are on by default. Once turned off, use the **ON** option to turn one or more layers back on. For multiple layers, separate each layer name with a comma. If you enter an asterisk (*), all layers are turned on.

> Layer name(s) to turn On: *(enter layer names separated by commas)*

- **OFF.** Use the **OFF** option to turn one or more layers off. For multiple layers, separate each layer name with a comma. If you enter an asterisk (*), all layers are turned off, including the layer you are presently working with. AutoCAD LT displays a warning message in a dialog box when you turn off the current layer. When a layer is turned off, it becomes invisible and does not plot. However, it still redraws and regenerates.

> Layer name(s) to turn Off: *(enter layer names separated by commas)*

- **Color.** The **Color** option is used to assign a color to a layer. You are first prompted to enter the color. Remember that for the seven standard colors, you can enter a number, the full color name, or just the first letter of the color name. You are then asked to name the layer(s) for the color assignment. In the example that follows, the color green is assigned to a layer called CABLES.

> Color: **G** ↵
> Layer name(s) for color 3 (green) ⟨*current layer*⟩: **CABLES** ↵

- **Ltype.** The **Ltype** option is used to assign a linetype to a layer. The linetype must first be loaded into the drawing editor with the **LINETYPE** command **Load** option. You are prompted to enter the linetype and then asked to name the layer(s) for the linetype assignment. Use the **?** option to list the linetypes loaded in the current drawing. In the following example, the CENTER2 linetype is assigned to the CENTERLINES layer.

> Linetype (or ?) ⟨*current linetype*⟩: **CENTER2** ↵
> Layer name(s) for linetype CENTER2 ⟨*current layer*⟩: **CENTERLINES** ↵

- **Freeze.** The **Freeze** option is used to remove one or more layers from the display list. However, you cannot freeze the current layer. Unlike entities on layers that are merely turned off, objects on frozen layers do not redraw or regenerate. This can significantly improve system performance. Also, keep in mind that frozen layers do not plot. For this reason, it is a good idea to create a special layer in your prototype drawing(s) for construction purposes. You might name the layer CONSTRUCT, or TEMPORARY. Place entities that you do not want plotted on this layer. Before you plot the drawing, freeze the layer.

> Layer name(s) to Freeze: *(enter layer names separated by commas)*

- **Thaw.** Use this option to thaw one or more frozen layers. The **Thaw** option regenerates the drawing as the frozen layer(s) are restored to the display list.

> Layer name(s) to Thaw: *(enter layer names separated by commas)*

- **LOck.** A locked layer is displayed on screen, but it cannot be selected. This is done to prevent accidental editing operations, such as erasing, on the locked layer objects. It is possible to draw with a locked layer.

> Layer name(s) to Lock: *(enter layer names separated by commas)*

- **Unlock.** Use this option to unlock one or more locked layers.

> Layer name(s) to Unlock: *(enter layer names separated by commas)*

LAYER CREATION TUTORIAL

To better understand the **LAYER** command and its options, spend a few moments with the following tutorial.
➪ Start AutoCAD LT.
➪ Use the **LINETYPE** command as described earlier in this chapter to load the DASHED and CENTER linetypes.

⮑ Now, use the **LAYER** command options listed below to create three layers called OBJECT, HIDDEN, and CENTERLINES. You will then assign colors and linetypes to your newly created layers.

Command: *(type* LAYER *or* LA *and press* [Enter]*)*
?/Make/Set/New/ ON/OFF/Color/Ltype/Freeze/Thaw/LOck/Unlock: **N** ⏎
New layer name(s): **OBJECT,HIDDEN,CENTERLINES** ⏎
?/Make/Set/New/ ON/OFF/Color/Ltype/Freeze/Thaw/LOck/Unlock: **C** ⏎
Color: **4** ⏎
Layer name(s) for color 4 (cyan)⟨*current layer*⟩: **OBJECT** ⏎
?/Make/Set/New/ ON/OFF/Color/Ltype/Freeze/Thaw/LOck/Unlock: **C** ⏎
Color: **3** ⏎
Layer name(s) for color 3 (green)⟨*current layer*⟩: **HIDDEN** ⏎
?/Make/Set/New/ ON/OFF/Color/Ltype/Freeze/Thaw/LOck/Unlock: **L** ⏎
Linetype (or ?) ⟨*current linetype*⟩: **DASHED** ⏎
Layer name(s) for linetype DASHED ⟨*current layer*⟩: **HIDDEN** ⏎
?/Make/Set/New/ ON/OFF/Color/Ltype/Freeze/Thaw/LOck/Unlock: **C** ⏎
Color: **2** ⏎
Layer name(s) for color 2 (yellow)⟨*current layer*⟩: **CENTERLINES** ⏎
?/Make/Set/New/ ON/OFF/Color/Ltype/Freeze/Thaw/LOck/Unlock: **L** ⏎
Linetype (or ?) ⟨*current linetype*⟩: **CENTER** ⏎
Layer name(s) for linetype CENTER ⟨*current layer*⟩: **CENTERLINES** ⏎
?/Make/Set/New/ ON/OFF/Color/Ltype/Freeze/Thaw/LOck/Unlock: **?** ⏎
Layer names(s) to list ⟨*⟩: *(press* [Enter] *to list all layers)*
?/Make/Set/New/ ON/OFF/Color/Ltype/Freeze/Thaw/LOck/Unlock: **S** ⏎
New current layer ⟨*current*⟩: **OBJECT** ⏎
?/Make/Set/New/ ON/OFF/Color/Ltype/Freeze/Thaw/LOck/Unlock: ⏎
Command:

⮑ Draw several lines with the OBJECT layer.
⮑ Set the HIDDEN layer current and draw some more lines.
⮑ Set the CENTERLINES layer current and draw a few more lines.
⮑ Turn off the OBJECT layer and then turn it back on.
⮑ Try freezing the CENTERLINES layer. What happens?
⮑ Freeze the OBJECT layer and then thaw it.
⮑ Lock the HIDDEN layer and try erasing several lines on that layer. What happens?
⮑ It is not necessary to save the drawing when you are finished experimenting.

MANAGING LAYERS WITH A DIALOG BOX

ALTUG 4

From the Layer Creation tutorial, it can be seen that a great amount of work is required to create a layer, assign it a color and linetype, and then set it current. Fortunately, layers can be created and managed quickly and easily using the **Layer Control** dialog box shown in Figure 5-16A. To access this dialog box, type in DDLMODES or LD, click the **Layer** button on the toolbar, or select **Layer Control...** from the **Settings** pull-down menu. See Figure 5-16B. Each of the buttons in the **Layer Control** dialog box are described on the next page.

Figure 5-16.
A—The **Layer Control** dialog box. B—Click the **Layer** button on the toolbar or select **Layer Control...**
from the **Settings** pull-down menu to access the **Layer Control** dialog box.

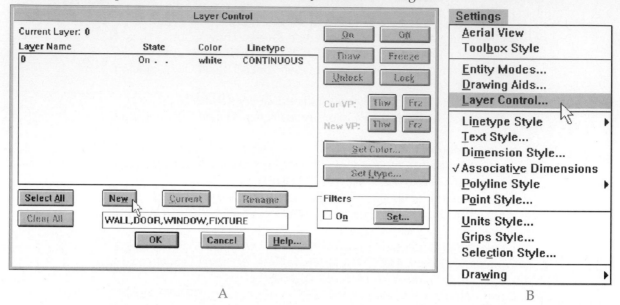

A

B

- **New.** In the example illustrated in Figure 5-16A, four layer names (WALL, DOOR, WINDOW, and FIXTURE) are entered in the text box at the bottom of the dialog box. A comma is used to separate the multiple layer names. After entering the names, select the **New** button to create the new layers.
- **Select All.** To assign a color or linetype to a layer, or to change its status, you must first select the layer from the list. In the example shown in Figure 5-17, the DOOR layer is selected and highlighted. Click the **Select All** button to select all the layers in the list.
- **Clear All.** Click this button to unselect and remove the highlighting from layers in the list.
- **Current.** After selecting a layer from the list, click the **Current** button to set it current. The current layer name is displayed at the top left of the dialog box.
- **Rename.** To rename a layer, first select the layer to be renamed from the list. The layer name then appears in the text box at the bottom of the dialog box. Double-click the

Figure 5-17.
Selecting and highlighting a layer from the layer list.

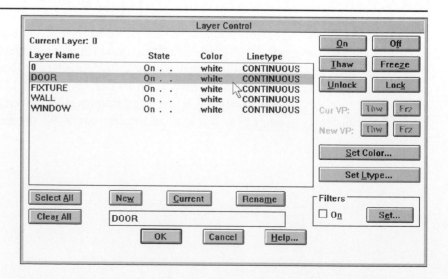

name in the text box so that it is highlighted and type over it with a new name. Click the **Rename** button and the renamed layer appears in the list.

- **Set Color....** To assign a color to a layer, click the **Set Color...** button to access the **Select Color** subdialog box. See Figure 5-3. Select one of 255 colors and click **OK**.
- **Set Ltype....** To assign a linetype to a layer, click the **Set Ltype...** button to display the **Select Linetype** subdialog box. See Figure 5-8. Remember that this subdialog box only displays linetypes that have first been loaded with the **LINETYPE** command. Select one of the loaded linetypes and click **OK**.
- **On/Off.** Select one or more layers from the list and click the appropriate button to turn the layer(s) on or off. When a layer is off, the word **On** in the **State** column is replaced with a period (.).
- **Thaw/Freeze.** Select one or more layers from the list and click the appropriate button to thaw or freeze the layer(s). When a layer is frozen, the letter **F** appears in the **State** column. Remember that you cannot freeze the current layer.
- **Unlock/Lock.** Select one or more layers from the list and click the appropriate button to unlock or lock the layer(s). When a layer is locked, the letter **L** appears in the **State** column.
- **Cur VP:/New VP:.** The buttons in this section are used for viewport-specific layer control in paper space. This capability is covered in Chapter 16 of this text.

Filtering layers in the list

For very large drawings that may contain dozens of layers, it is possible to limit the number of layers that appear in the **Layer Control** dialog box listing. The layers can be screened out, or filtered, based on name, color, or linetype. You can also choose to list only those layers that are on or off, thawed or frozen, or locked or unlocked. Consider the layer listing shown in Figure 5-18.

Figure 5-18.
A layer list may be shortened using layer filters.

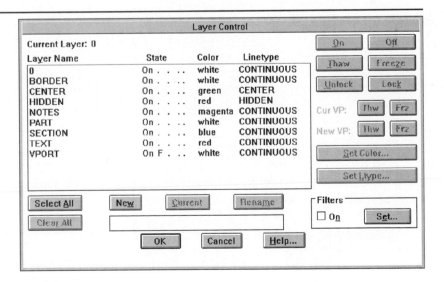

To list only the red layers, do the following:
1. Click the **Set...** button in the **Filters** section at the lower right of the dialog box to display the **Set Layer Filters** subdialog box shown in Figure 5-19.
2. Enter the color name RED (or 1) in the **Colors:** text box. Click the **OK** button.

Figure 5-19.
The **Set Layer Filters** subdialog box is used to filter only red layers.

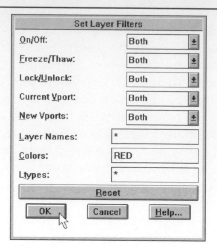

3. When the **Layer Control** dialog box reappears, observe that only the red layers are displayed in the layer listing. See Figure 5-20.

Figure 5-20.
The layer list as it appears with filters activated.

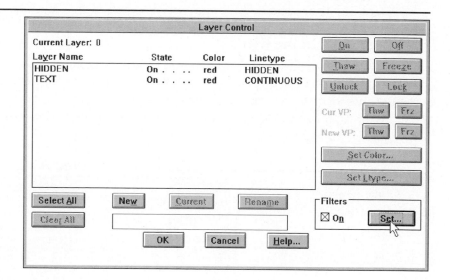

4. To restore the complete layer list again, click the **On** check box in the **Filters** section to deactivate the filters. Exiting the **Layer Control** dialog box also deactivates the filters.

Keep in mind that layer filters only limit the number of layers that appear in the **Layer Control** dialog box listing. They do not affect the display of layers on screen.

PROFESSIONAL TIP

When filtering layer names and linetypes, you can use the wildcard (*) character. As an example, to display only those layer names that start with the letter B, place your cursor in the **Layer Names:** text box and enter B*.

Setting a layer current quickly

You can quickly change to another layer using the arrow located in the **Current Layer** box on the toolbar. This box prominently displays the current layer name. Click the down arrow in the box and a drop-down list appears that contains all of the layers defined in the current drawing. Click the desired layer name, and that layer is set current. See Figure 5-21. When many layers are defined in the drawing, a vertical scroll bar can be used to move up and down through the list.

Figure 5-21.
Click the down arrow to the right of the **Current Layer** box on the toolbar to display a drop-down list of layer names. You can then click on a layer name to change to that layer. The **Layer** button at the left of the **Current Layer** box provides quick access to the **Layer Control** dialog box.

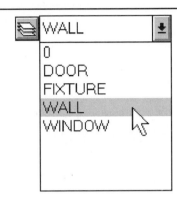

You can also use the **CLAYER** system variable to make a layer current. Type CLAYER at the **Command:** prompt as follows:

> Command: **CLAYER** ↵
> New value for CLAYER ⟨*current layer*⟩: (*enter the name of an existing layer and press* [Enter]*)*

EXERCISE 5-4

❑ Open your PROTOA prototype drawing.
❑ Use the **LINETYPE** command to load the HIDDEN, CENTER, and PHANTOM linetypes.
❑ Use **DDLMODES** to create the following layers. Assign the colors and linetypes shown.

Layer Name	Color	Linetype
OBJECTS	WHITE	CONTINUOUS
HIDDEN	CYAN	HIDDEN
CENTERLINES	YELLOW	CENTER
DIMS	GREEN	CONTINUOUS
HATCHING	MAGENTA	CONTINUOUS
NOTES	RED	CONTINUOUS
CUTPLANE	BLUE	PHANTOM

❑ Set the OBJECTS layer current before exiting the **Layer Control** dialog box.
❑ Save the revised PROTOA drawing as it will be used for many of the subsequent drawing exercises and problems in this text.
❑ Open PROTOB from Chapter 3 and repeat the procedure. Save the revised PROTOB drawing.
❑ Open PROTOC from Chapter 3 and repeat the procedure. Save the revised PROTOC drawing.
❑ Exit AutoCAD LT.

RENAMING LINETYPES AND LAYERS

ALTUG 10

Linetypes and layers can be renamed with the **DDRENAME** command. Remember in Chapter 4 that this command was used to rename objects, such as saved views, using a dialog box. To display the **Rename** dialog box, enter DDRENAME or DR at the **Command:** prompt or select **Rename...** from the **Modify** pull-down menu. See Figure 5-22.

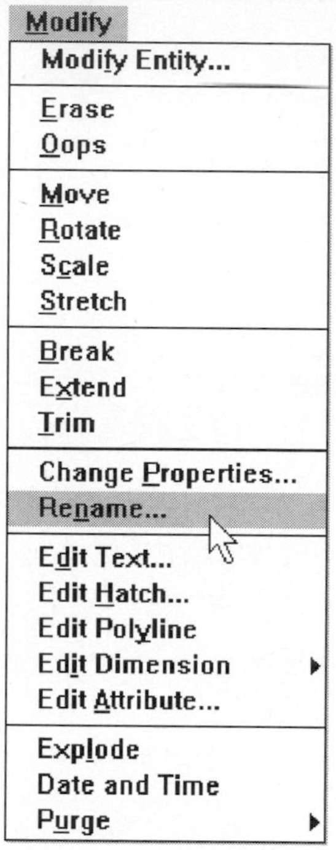

Modify
Modify Entity...
Erase
Oops
Move
Rotate
Scale
Stretch
Break
Extend
Trim
Change Properties...
Rename...
Edit Text...
Edit Hatch...
Edit Polyline
Edit Dimension
Edit Attribute...
Explode
Date and Time
Purge

Figure 5-22.
Selecting **Rename...** from the **Modify** pull-down menu issues the **DDRENAME** command and displays the **Rename** dialog box.

The **Named Objects** list appears at the left of the **Rename** dialog box. See Figure 5-23. This list contains the types of objects that can be named or renamed in AutoCAD LT. Observe in Figure 5-23A that Ltype has been selected. A listing of all the linetypes loaded in the current drawing appears in the **Items** list at the right of the dialog box. To rename the CENTER linetype, first select the linetype name from the **Items** list. The name of the linetype you select is then displayed in the **Old Name:** text box. With your mouse, click anywhere inside the **Rename To:** text box and enter the new linetype name. In the example, the CENTER linetype is renamed to CENTERLINE. When you are done typing, click the **Rename To:** button and the new linetype name appears in the list at the right of the dialog box. When you are finished renaming objects, click the **OK** button to exit the **Rename** dialog box.

A similar procedure is performed with layers in Figure 5-23B. In this example, the PART layer is renamed to OBJECT.

Figure 5-23.
A—Renaming a linetype using the **Rename** dialog box. B—Renaming a layer using the
Rename dialog box.

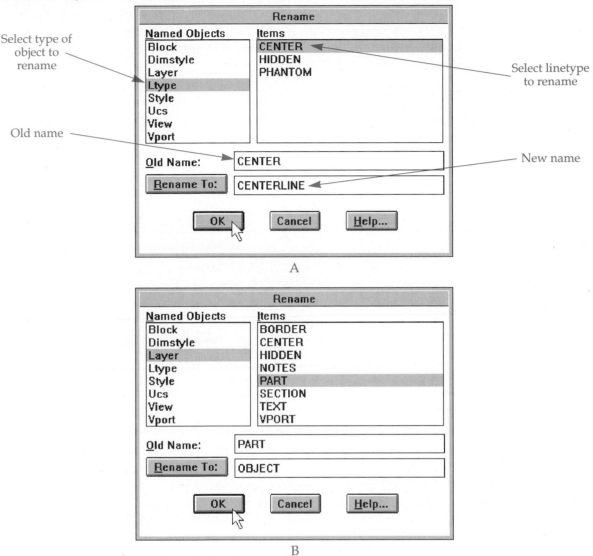

A

B

Renaming linetypes and layers at the **Command:** prompt

It is also possible to rename objects at the **Command:** prompt instead of using a dialog
box. In the following example, the **RENAME** command is used to perform the linetype renaming operation described in the previous section.

```
Command: (type RENAME or RN and press [Enter])
Block/Dimstyle/LAyer/LType/Style/Ucs/VIew/VPort: LT ↵
Old linetype name: CENTER ↵
New linetype name: CENTERLINE ↵
Command:
```

> **NOTE**   Layer 0 and the continuous linetype *cannot* be renamed and
> therefore do not appear in the **Rename** dialog box list of named
> objects.

Color, linetype, and layer are considered properties of entities. It is a simple matter to change the properties of existing entities using the **Change Properties** dialog box shown in Figure 5-24. To access this dialog box, type in DDCHPROP or DC. You can also click the **Change Properties** button in the toolbox, or select **Change Properties...** from the **Modify** pull-down menu. The command procedure looks like this:

> Command: *(type* DDCHPROP *or* DC *and press* [Enter]*)*
> Select objects: *(select one or more entities)*
> Select objects: ⌐

All of the selection set options described in Chapter 2, (window, crossing, etc.) are valid at the **Select objects:** prompt. Select the entity(s) with the properties you wish to change, press [Enter], and you are then presented with the **Change Properties** dialog box.

Figure 5-24.
The **Change Properties**
dialog box.

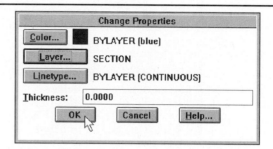

The Change Properties dialog box

This dialog box displays the current color, layer, and linetype of the object you selected. If you select several entities with different values for the property you wish to change, AutoCAD LT displays the word "varies" as the current value. Each of the components of the **Change Properties** dialog box are described as follows:

- **Color....** To change the color of an existing entity, click this button to display the **Select Color** subdialog box. Select one of 255 available colors and click **OK**.
- **Layer....** Click this button to display the **Select Layer** subdialog box shown in Figure 5-25. This is an abbreviated version of the **Layer Control** dialog box discussed previously. To move the selected entity to a different layer, select the desired layer from the list or enter the layer name in the **Set Layer Name:** text box. Click the **OK** button to exit the subdialog box. Remember that an entity placed on a different layer inherits the color and linetype properties of that layer.
- **Linetype....** To change the linetype of an existing entity, click this button to display the **Select Linetype** subdialog box. Select one of the loaded linetypes in the dialog box and click the **OK** button.
- **Thickness:.** Thickness is a property of three-dimensional objects. It determines the height of an entity above or below the zero elevation plane. See Chapter 18 of this text for more information on thickness.

Figure 5-25.
The **Select Layer** subdialog box is used to move one or more entities to a different layer.

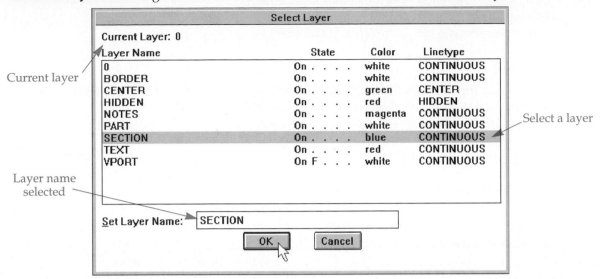

Current layer

Layer name
selected

Select a layer

When you are finished changing entity properties, click the **OK** button to exit the **Change Properties** dialog box. The object(s) you selected are immediately displayed with the new properties.

Changing entity properties at the Command: prompt

Entity properties can also be changed by using the **CHPROP** command at the **Command:** prompt. In the following example, one or more entities on the TEXT layer is selected and moved to the NOTES layer.

```
Command: (type CHPROP or CR and press [Enter])
Select objects: (select one or more entities)
Select objects: ↵
Change what property (Color/LAyer/LType/Thickness)? LA ↵
New layer ⟨TEXT⟩: NOTES ↵
Change what property (Color/LAyer/LType/Thickness)? ↵
Command:
```

If you select a single entity, AutoCAD LT displays the current value of the property in the ⟨⟩ brackets. If you select several entities with different values for the property you wish to change, AutoCAD LT displays ⟨varies⟩ as the current value.

RESTORING BYLAYER MODE

At the beginning of this chapter, you learned that color and linetype may be explicitly set before drawing any entities. However, the preferred method is to assign colors and linetypes to layers. This method ensures that drawing objects inherit the color and linetype properties of the layers they are on. AutoCAD LT refers to this convention as *bylayer* mode.

When you set a different color or linetype current using the **COLOR** or **LINETYPE** commands, you override bylayer mode. This can be a major source of frustration, because everything drawn will appear in one color, or one linetype, regardless of your layer assignments. Should you experience this problem with colors, use the **COLOR** command as follows:

```
Command: (type COLOR or CO and press [Enter])
New entity color ⟨current⟩: BYLAYER ↵
Command:
```

For linetypes, use the **LINETYPE** command as follows:

```
Command: (type LINETYPE or LT and press [Enter])
?/Create/Load/Set: S ↵
New entity linetype (or ?) ⟨current⟩: BYLAYER ↵
?/Create/Load/Set: ↵
Command:
```

It is also possible to use **DDEMODES** to restore bylayer mode in the **Select Color** and **Select Linetype** subdialog boxes. For any existing entities drawn with explicit color or line-type set, use **DDCHPROP** (or **CHPROP**) and change the properties to BYLAYER.

PURGING UNUSED ENTITIES

ALTUG 17

Unused linetypes and layers can be removed from your drawing with the **PURGE** command. This command can only be used before the drawing database has been modified in a drawing session. This means that the **PURGE** command must be issued when the drawing is opened into the drawing editor. Linetypes and layers are not the only types of named objects in AutoCAD LT that can be purged. Other named objects include blocks, dimension styles, and text styles. These types of objects are explored fully as they are encountered in this text.

You can purge unused linetypes and/or layers by entering the **PURGE** command at the **Command:** prompt, or by selecting **Purge** from the **Modify** pull-down menu. This menu item displays the cascading submenu shown in Figure 5-26. The command sequence is as follows:

```
Command: (type PURGE or PR and press [Enter])
Purge unused Blocks/Dimstyles/LAyers/LTypes/Styles/All:
```

Select an object type to purge, or enter A to purge all named object types from the drawing. Before each item is purged, you are first asked to confirm the operation. Respond with a Y or N as required.

Figure 5-26.
Selecting **Purge** from the **Modify** pull-down menu displays a cascading submenu of options.

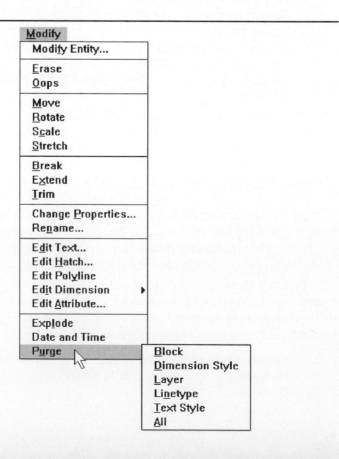

CHAPTER TEST

Write your answers in the spaces provided.

1. List the seven standard colors and their respective color numbers. What is the maximum number of colors available in AutoCAD LT? _____

   _____

   _____

   _____

   _____

2. What is the keyboard command used to access the **Entity Creation Modes** dialog box?

   _____

3. Which toolbar button accesses the **Entity Creation Modes** dialog box? _____

   _____

4. Name the two default linetype library files in AutoCAD LT. Of the two, which should be used for metric drawings? _____

   _____

   _____

5. When used transparently, the **COLOR** and **LINETYPE** commands take effect immediately. (True/False) _____

6. What is the purpose of the **LTSCALE** system variable? How is it used? _____

   _____

   _____

7. Give the command and entries needed to make the PHANTOM linetype current.

   Command: _____

   ?/Create/Load/Set: _____

   New entity linetype (or ?) ⟨*current*⟩: _____

   ?/Create/Load/Set: _____

   Command: _____

8. What is the purpose of A-type alignment? _____

   _____

   _____

   _____

9. What is the keyboard command used to access the **Layer Control** dialog box? _____

   _____

10. It is possible to turn off the current layer. (True/False) _____

11. Which **LAYER** command option should be used to remove a layer from the display list?

_____

_____

12. Layers that are turned off do not redraw or regenerate. (True/False) _____

13. What is the purpose of the **LAYER** command **Lock** option? Is a locked layer visible?

_____

_____

14. Identify two ways to rename a layer. _____

_____

_____

_____

15. Identify four ways to make a layer current. _____

_____

_____

_____

_____

16. Layer filters can be used to limit the number of layers displayed on screen. (True/False)

_____

17. Name the command used to change the properties of an existing entity. _____

_____

18. Everything on a drawing is drawn in green, regardless of the layer being drawn on. What is the problem, and how can it be fixed?_____

_____

_____

_____

19. On a drawing, lines are all displayed as phantom lines, but they are being drawn on different layers and each layer has a different assigned linetype. What is the problem, and how can it be fixed?_____

_____

_____

_____

20. The **PURGE** command can be used at any time during a drawing session. (True/False)

_____

CHAPTER PROBLEMS

1. Use your PROTOB prototype drawing to draw the object shown. Draw all three views. Place object lines on the OBJECTS layer, hidden lines on the HIDDEN layer, and centerlines on the CENTERLINES layer. Do not draw the dimensions. Save the drawing as P5-1.

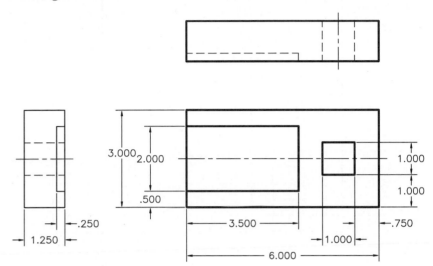

2. Use your PROTOB prototype drawing to draw the object shown. Draw all three views. As with P5-1, place object lines on the OBJECTS layer, hidden lines on the HIDDEN layer, and centerlines on the CENTERLINES layer. Do not draw the dimensions. Save the drawing as P5-2.

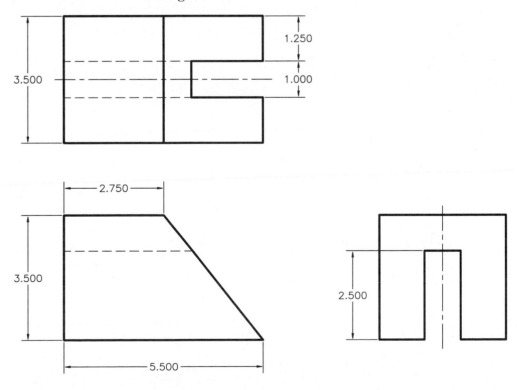

3. Use your **PROTOA** prototype drawing to draw the object shown. Draw both views. As with the previous two drawing problems, place object lines on the **OBJECTS** layer, hidden lines on the **HIDDEN** layer, and centerlines on the **CENTERLINES** layer. Do not draw the dimensions. Save the drawing as P5-3.

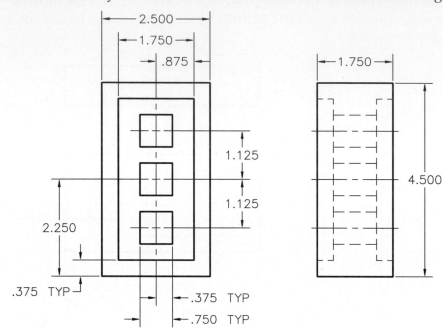

AutoCAD LT

Chapter 6

Drawing Commands

Learning objectives:
After you have completed this chapter, you will be able to:
- ❍ Draw curved objects using the **CIRCLE**, **ARC**, **ELLIPSE**, and **DONUT** commands.
- ❍ Create double lines and double arcs with **DLINE**.
- ❍ Construct multi-sided shapes using the **PLINE**, **RECTANG**, and **POLYGON** commands.
- ❍ Explode multi-sided shapes into individual line segments.
- ❍ Create chamfers and angled corners with the **CHAMFER** command.
- ❍ Draw fillets and rounded corners using the **FILLET** command.

Previous chapters described how to set up and save drawings, as well as how to draw and erase lines. You have also learned how to zoom and pan the graphics window using a variety of display control options. In addition, you now have the ability to assign colors and linetypes to layers to help manage drawing elements. It is now time to explore several other AutoCAD LT drawing commands at your disposal to create a wide variety of geometric shapes.

DRAWING CIRCLES

ALTUG 6

The **CIRCLE** command is accessed by typing CIRCLE, or C, at the **Command:** prompt, or issued by clicking the **Circle** button in the toolbox. Selecting **Circle** from the **Draw** pull-down menu displays a cascading submenu of circle construction options. See Figure 6-1. The default method for creating a circle involves locating a point for the circle center, and then providing a radius value as illustrated in Figure 6-2. The **CIRCLE** command sequence is as follows:

> Command: *(type CIRCLE or C and press* [Enter]*)*
> 3P/TTR/⟨Center point⟩: *(pick a point for the circle center)*
> Diameter/⟨Radius⟩: *(enter a positive radius value and press* [Enter]*)*
> Command:

If you prefer to specify a circle by its diameter, do the following:

> Command: *(type CIRCLE or C and press* [Enter]*)*
> 3P/TTR/⟨Center point⟩: *(pick a point for the circle center)*
> Diameter/⟨Radius⟩: *(type D, for diameter, and press* [Enter]*)*
> Diameter: *(enter a positive diameter value and press* [Enter]*)*
> Command:

Figure 6-1.
Select **Circle** from the **Draw** pull-down menu to display a cascading submenu of options.

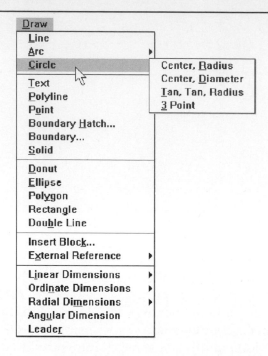

Figure 6-2.
Locate a point for the circle center, and then enter a radius value or drag to a point and pick to set the size.

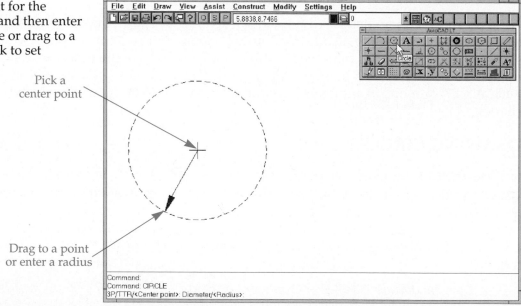

Pick a center point

Drag to a point or enter a radius

Drawing a circle through three points

A circle may also be created by locating three points in the graphics window. The three points define the circumference of the circle as shown in Figure 6-3.

Command: *(type* CIRCLE *or* C *and press* [Enter]*)*
3P/TTR/⟨Center point⟩: **3P** ↵
First point: *(locate point 1 or enter a coordinate value)*
Second point: *(locate point 2 or enter a coordinate value)*
Third point: *(locate point 3 or enter a coordinate value)*
Command:

Figure 6-3.
Defining the circumference of a circle through three points.

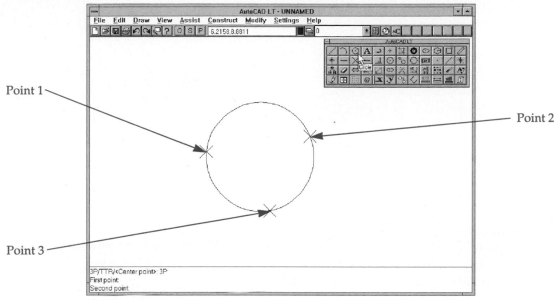

Drawing a circle tangent to two objects

A circle can also be drawn tangent to two existing entities by selecting the desired points of tangency and providing a radius value for the new circle. See Figure 6-4. The circle is drawn with its tangent points closest to the points you select on the existing entities. AutoCAD LT calls this the **TTR** (tangent, tangent, radius) method.

> Command: *(type* CIRCLE *or* C *and press* [Enter]*)*
> 3P/TTR/⟨Center point⟩: *(type* TTR *or* T *and press* [Enter]*)*
> Enter Tangent spec: *(pick first object)*
> Enter second Tangent spec: *(pick second object)*
> Radius ⟨*current*⟩: *(enter a positive radius value)*
> Command:

Figure 6-4.
The **TTR** option creates a circle tangent to two other entities.

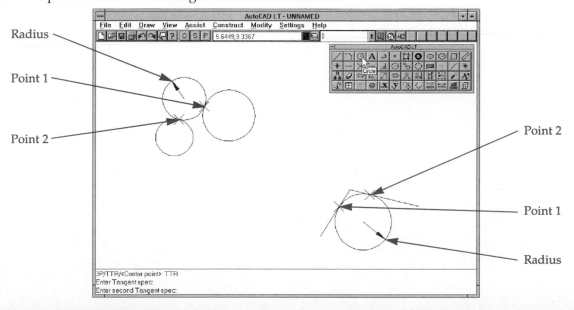

DRAWING ARCS

ALTUG 6

AutoCAD LT offers a variety of ways to draw arcs. An arc can be constructed by locating three points, or specified by its included angle, which is the angle formed between an arc's center, starting point, and ending point. By default, arcs are drawn in a counterclockwise direction. The **ARC** command is accessed by entering ARC, or A, at the **Command:** prompt, or issued by clicking the **Arc** button in the toolbox. Selecting **Arc** from the **Draw** pull-down menu displays a cascading submenu of arc construction options. See Figure 6-5. The **ARC** command sequence is as follows:

> Command: *(type* ARC *or* A *and press* [Enter]*)*
> Center ⟨Start point⟩:

Figure 6-5.
Select **Arc** from the **Draw** pull-down menu to display a cascading submenu of options.

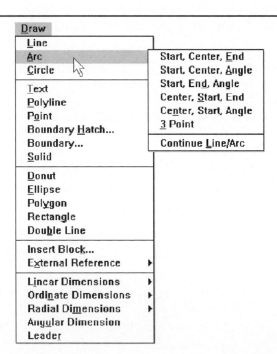

Drawing an arc through three points

The **3 Point** option is the default method when the **ARC** command is issued from the command line or selected from the toolbox. This method draws an arc using three specified points on the circumference of the arc. You are first prompted to pick a starting point for the arc. The second point you specify locates a point on the circumference of the arc, and the arc is terminated with a third point. The command sequence for a three-point arc appear as follows:

> Command: *(type* ARC *or* A *and press* [Enter])
> Center ⟨Start point⟩: *(pick a starting point for the arc)*
> Center/End/⟨Second point⟩: *(pick a second point for the arc)*
> End point: *(pick the arc's endpoint)*
> Command:

Three-point arcs can be drawn clockwise or counterclockwise, depending on the direction of the pick points. A counterclockwise arc is illustrated at the upper left of Figure 6-6.

Figure 6-6.
Arcs can be constructed in several ways. Counterclockwise from the upper left: an arc drawn with the default **3 Point** option, an arc drawn by locating center, start, and end points, an arc drawn with start and center points and an included angle, an arc drawn with start and end points and an included angle.

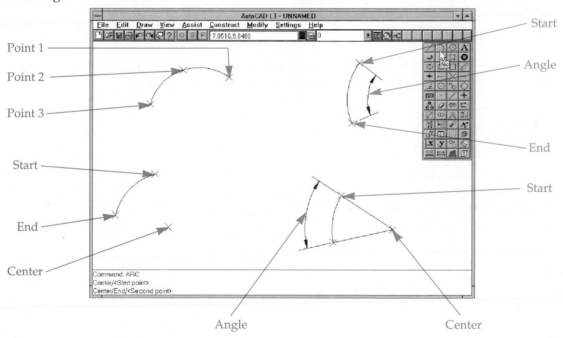

Drawing an arc with start, center, and end points

There are several other ways to construct arcs with three points. If you know the starting point, center point, and ending point for an arc, select **Start, Center, End** from the **Arc** cascading submenu. The command sequence for this option is as follows:

> Command: *(type* ARC *or* A *and press* [Enter])
> Center ⟨Start point⟩: *(pick a starting point for the arc)*
> Center/End/⟨Second point⟩: **C** ↵
> Center: *(pick a center point for the arc)*
> Angle/⟨End point⟩: *(pick the arc's endpoint)*
> Command:

Alternatively, you can start the arc at its center point using the **Center, Start, End** option.

> Command: *(type* ARC *or* A *and press* [Enter]*)*
> Center ⟨Start point⟩: **C** ↵
> Center: *(pick a center point for the arc)*
> Start point: *(pick a starting point for the arc)*
> Angle/⟨End point⟩: *(pick the arc's endpoint)*
> Command:

An arc drawn using start, center, and ending points is shown at the lower left in Figure 6-6.

Drawing an arc by its included angle

As stated previously, the angle formed between an arc's center, starting, and ending points is called the *included angle*. When you know the included angle for an arc, you can construct it using a starting point and a center point by selecting **Start, Center, Angle** from the **Arc** cascading submenu. The following command sequence creates an arc with a 45° included angle:

> Command: *(type* ARC *or* A *and press* [Enter]*)*
> Center ⟨Start point⟩: *(pick a starting point for the arc)*
> Center/End/⟨Second point⟩: **C** ↵
> Center: *(pick a center point for the arc)*
> Angle/⟨End point⟩: **A** ↵
> Included angle: **45** ↵
> Command:

The **Center, Start, Angle** option allows you to specify the center point first and then the starting point. The command sequence for a 45° arc appears as follows:

> Command: *(type* ARC *or* A *and press* [Enter]*)*
> Center ⟨Start point⟩: **C** ↵
> Center: *(pick a center point for the arc)*
> Start point: *(pick a starting point for the arc)*
> Angle/⟨End point⟩: **A** ↵
> Included angle: **45** ↵
> Command:

Either the **Start, Center, Angle** or **Center, Start, Angle** options can be used to draw the 45° arc shown at the lower right of Figure 6-6.

When you know the included angle and you have a starting and ending point for the arc, (but not a center point), select the **Start, End, Angle** option in the **Arc** cascading submenu. The 60° arc shown at the upper right of Figure 6-6 is drawn using the following command sequence:

> Command: *(type* ARC *or* A *and press* [Enter]*)*
> Center ⟨Start point⟩: *(pick a starting point for the arc)*
> Center/End/⟨Second point⟩: **E** ↵
> End point: *(pick an end point for the arc)* Included angle: **60** ↵
> Command:

Using the ARC Continuation option

In Chapter 3 you learned that AutoCAD LT provides a means of quickly attaching a new line to a previously drawn line segment using the continuation option. You may continue a new arc from a previous arc in a similar fashion. First, press [Enter] or the [Spacebar] to repeat the **ARC** command and when the ⟨**Start point**⟩: prompt appears, simply press [Enter] or the [Spacebar] again. The new arc is automatically connected to the endpoint of the last arc or line drawn. It is also drawn tangent to the previous arc or line entity. Once attached, you can continue to draw more arcs.

The **Continuation** option can also be used by selecting **Continue Line/Arc** from the **Arc** cascading submenu. For example, the **Continuation** option can be used to produce the fully-radiused slot illustrated in Figure 6-7. The command sequence for this object is as follows:

> Command: *(type* LINE *or* L *and press* [Enter]*)*
> From point: *(pick the starting point* P1*)*
> To point: **@3〈0** ↵
> To point: *(press* [Enter] *or the* [Spacebar] *to exit the* **LINE** *command)*
> Command: *(type* ARC *or* A *and press* [Enter]*)*
> Center/〈Start point〉: *(press* [Enter] *or the* [Spacebar] *to place the starting point of the arc,*
>   *point* P2, *at the end of the previous line)*
> End point: **@1〈90** ↵
> Command: *(type* LINE *or* L *and press* [Enter]*)*
> From point: *(press* [Enter] *or the* [Spacebar] *to place the starting point of the line,*
>   *point* P3, *at the end of the previous arc)*
> Length of line: **3** ↵
> To point: *(press* [Enter] *or the* [Spacebar] *to exit the* **LINE** *command)*
> Command: *(type* ARC *or* A *and press* [Enter]*)*
> Center/〈Start point〉: *(press* [Enter] *or the* [Spacebar] *to place the starting point of the arc,*
>   *point* P4, *at the end of the previous line)*
> End point: **@1〈270** ↵
> Command:

Figure 6-7.
Fully radiused features such as this slot may be drawn quickly and easily using **LINE** and **ARC** command continuation options.

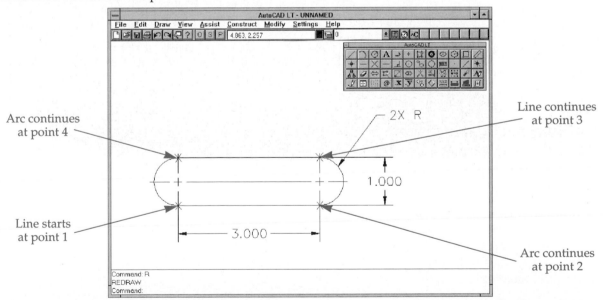

DRAWING ELLIPSES

When a circle is rotated from the line of sight, an ellipse is created. The longer axis of an ellipse is called the *major axis*, and the shorter axis is called the *minor axis*. In AutoCAD LT, you can draw an ellipse by locating axis endpoints or selecting a center point and a rotation angle. To issue the **ELLIPSE** command, type ELLIPSE or EL at the **Command:** prompt, click the **Ellipse** button in the toolbox, or select **Ellipse** from the **Draw** pull-down menu. See Figure 6-8. The command sequence is as follows:

> Command: *(type* ELLIPSE *or* EL *and press* [Enter])
> ⟨Axis endpoint 1⟩/Center:

Figure 6-8.
Select **Ellipse** from the **Draw** pull-down menu.

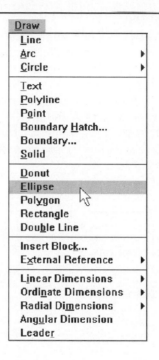

Drawing an ellipse using axis endpoints

The default method for creating an ellipse requires that you select two axis endpoints, and then a third point to specify the other axis distance. Refer to Figure 6-9 and follow the **ELLIPSE** command sequence as follows:

> Command: *(type* ELLIPSE *or* EL *and press* [Enter])
> ⟨Axis endpoint 1⟩/Center: *(pick axis endpoint 1)*
> Axis endpoint 2: *(pick axis endpoint 2)*
> ⟨Other axis distance⟩/Rotation: *(pick a third point)*
> Command:

Figure 6-9.
An ellipse can be drawn by locating points that define the major and minor axes of the ellipse.

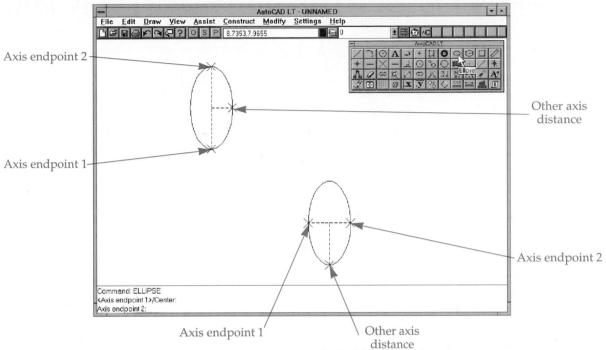

From Figure 6-9, you can see that the two axis endpoints can specify the major axis or minor axis depending on the point selected for the other axis distance. If you select the **Rotation** option after locating the two axis endpoints, AutoCAD LT then assumes that the two points define the major axis for the ellipse. You then provide the angle of the ellipse as it rotated from the line of sight. The **Rotation** option looks like this:

> Command: *(type* ELLIPSE *or* EL *and press* [Enter]*)*
> ⟨Axis endpoint 1⟩/Center: *(pick axis endpoint 1)*
> Axis endpoint 2: *(pick axis endpoint 2)*
> ⟨Other axis distance⟩/Rotation: **R** ⏎
> Rotation around major axis: **45** ⏎
> Command:

A rotation angle from 0° to 89.4° can be entered. However, an angle of 0° produces a circle. The greater the angle, the greater the degree of elongation along the major axis.

Drawing an ellipse by its center point

It is also possible to create an ellipse based on a center point, an endpoint of one axis, and half the length of the other axis. This method is illustrated by the ellipse shown at the upper left in Figure 6-10. The command sequence for this ellipse is as follows:

> Command: *(type* ELLIPSE *or* EL *and press* [Enter]*)*
> ⟨Axis endpoint 1⟩/Center: **C** ⏎
> Center of ellipse: *(pick a center point)*
> Axis endpoint: *(pick a second point)*
> ⟨Other axis distance⟩/Rotation: *(pick a third point)*
> Command:

Figure 6-10.
Ellipses may also be constructed by first locating their centers. At the upper left, three points define the ellipse center, half of its major axis, and half of its minor axis. At the bottom right, two points define the ellipse center and half the major axis. The rotation of the ellipse from the line of sight is specified using the **Rotation** option.

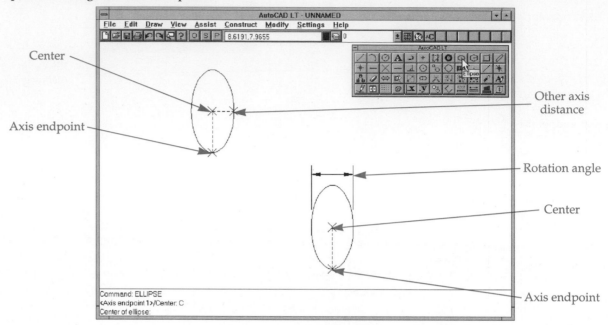

Possibly the best method to use for ellipse construction is shown at the lower right in Figure 6-10. With this method, first select a point for the ellipse center, and then select a point that defines half of the length of the major axis. Next, use the **Rotation** option to specify the angle of the ellipse as it is rotated from the line of sight. The following command sequence draws a 60° ellipse with a diameter of 3.50 units.

```
Command: (type ELLIPSE or EL and press [Enter])
⟨Axis endpoint 1⟩/Center: C ↵
Center of ellipse: (pick a center point)
Axis endpoint: @1.75⟨270 ↵
⟨Other axis distance⟩/Rotation: R ↵
Rotation around major axis: 60 ↵
Command:
```

NOTE   When the **Isometric snap** style is enabled, the **ELLIPSE** command offers the additional option of creating isometric ellipses, or isocircles. See Chapter 15 for more information about isometric drawing and dimensioning.

DRAWING DONUTS

A donut in AutoCAD LT is a filled circle or ring constructed with closed polylines comprised of wide polyarc segments. Polylines and polyarcs are covered later in this chapter. To draw a donut, you must specify a value for the donut's inside diameter, a value for its outside diameter, and then locate the donut's center point. To access the **DONUT** command type DONUT or DO at the **Command:** prompt, click the **Donut** button in the toolbox, or select **Donut** from the **Draw** pull-down menu. See Figure 6-11. The command sequence is as follows:

> Command: *(type DONUT or DO and press* [Enter]*)*
> Inside diameter ⟨*current*⟩: *(enter a value and press* [Enter]*)*
> Outside diameter ⟨*current*⟩: *(enter a value and press* [Enter]*)*
> Center of doughnut: *(pick a point for the donut center)*
> Center of doughnut: *(pick another point or press* [Enter] *to end the command)*
> Command:

Figure 6-11.
Select **Donut** from the **Draw** pull-down menu.

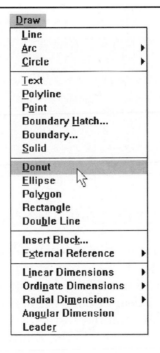

A filled circle can be drawn by specifying an inside diameter of zero. Several different donuts are illustrated in Figure 6-12A. The interior of a donut is filled or unfilled depending on the current setting of the **FILL** system variable. **Fill** mode is on by default, but can be turned off using the **FILL** command. To observe the effects of the changed **FILL** status, you must force a drawing regeneration.

> Command: *(type FILL or FL and press* [Enter]*)*
> ON/OFF/⟨On⟩: **OFF** ↵
> Command: *(type REGEN or RG and press* [Enter]*)*

The donuts are shown with **FILL** turned off in Figure 6-12B. Keep in mind that although the **FILL** command can be used transparently ('**FILL**), a regeneration must still be performed to change the drawing display.

Figure 6-12.
A–Various donuts with **FILL** on. B–The same donuts with **FILL** off.

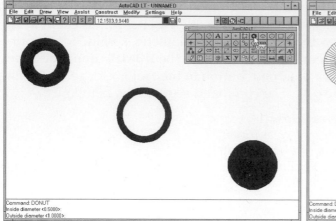

A

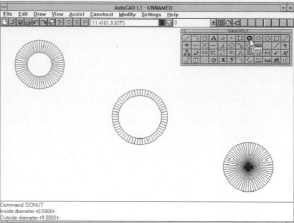

B

EXERCISE 6-3

❑ Begin a new drawing with your PROTOA prototype, or use your own variables.
❑ Draw several ellipses using the methods illustrated in Figure 6-9.
❑ Create several more ellipses using the methods shown in Figure 6-10.
❑ Draw a variety of donuts with different inside and outside diameters. Turn **FILL** mode off, regenerate the drawing and observe the effects.
❑ Save the drawing as EX6-3 and quit.

DRAWING DOUBLE LINES WITH DLINE

ALTUG 6

The **DLINE** command can be used to draw continuous double lines and arcs with a specified width. Each line and arc segment is a separate entity. For architectural and facilities management applications, **DLINE** is a handy way to draw walls in floor plans. Included among the various **DLINE** options are several that allow you to set the width of the double lines, cap the line ends, undo incorrectly drawn line and arc segments, and break the double lines at intersections. To access the **DLINE** command, type DLINE or DL at the **Command:** prompt, click the **Dline** button in the toolbox, or select **Double Line** from the **Draw** pull-down menu. See Figure 6-13. The command sequence is as follows:

    Command: (type DLINE or DL and press [Enter])
    Break/Caps/Dragline/Offset/Snap/Undo/Width/⟨start point⟩:

Figure 6-13.
Select **Double Line** from the
Draw pull-down menu.

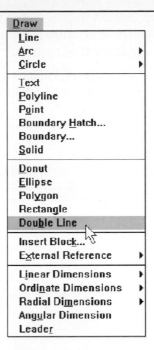

Each of the **DLINE** command options is described below:

- **⟨start point⟩.** This is equivalent to the **From point:** prompt in the **LINE** command. Pick a point on the screen or enter a coordinate for the double line starting point.
- **Break.** The **Break** option determines whether a gap is created at the intersection of two double lines. An example of double lines drawn with **Break** on and off is shown in Figure 6-14. Break is **ON** by default, but may be turned off as follows:

> Break/Caps/Dragline/Offset/Snap/Undo/Width/⟨start point⟩: **B** ↵
> Break Dline's at start and end points? OFF/⟨ON⟩: **OFF** ↵

Figure 6-14.
Using the **DLINE Break** option.

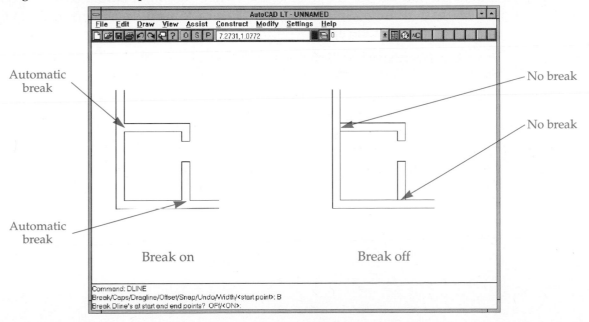

- **Caps.** Use this option to determine the type of endcaps for a double line as shown in Figure 6-15. The default **Auto** option automatically closes ends that are not snapped to (intersected with) another object.

> Break/Caps/Dragline/Offset/Snap/Undo/Width/⟨start point⟩: **C** ↵
> Draw which endcaps? Both/End/None/Start/⟨Auto⟩:

Figure 6-15.
The various **DLINE Cap** options.

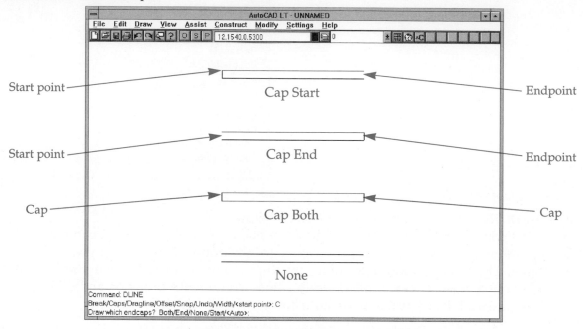

- **Dragline.** By default, the center of a double line is determined by the starting and ending points you select. You can offset to the left or to the right of the center of the double line using the **Dragline** option. As shown in Figure 6-16, the **Left** option sets the pick points to the left side of the double line, while the **Right** option sets the pick points to the right. Left and right are determined by looking from the starting point to the ending point of the double line.

> Break/Caps/Dragline/Offset/Snap/Undo/Width/⟨start point⟩: **D** ↵
> Set dragline position to Left/Center/Right/⟨Offset from center=*current*⟩:

Figure 6-16.
The **Dragline Left**, **Center**, and **Right** options.

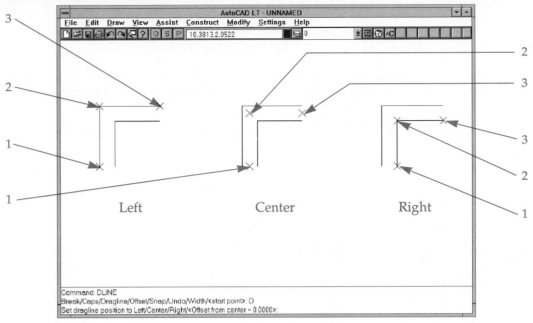

- **Offset.** This option allows you to start a new double line at a specified distance and direction from a base point. You are first prompted to locate the base point, then indicate the direction of the offset, and finally the offset distance. Refer to Figure 6-17 as you follow the command sequence below:

  Break/Caps/Dragline/Offset/Snap/Undo/Width/〈start point〉: **O** ↵
  Offset from: *(pick a base point)*
  Offset toward: *(pick a point to specify the offset direction)*
  Enter the offset distance: *(enter a value and press* [Enter]*)*

Figure 6-17.
Using the **DLINE Offset** option for a new double line.

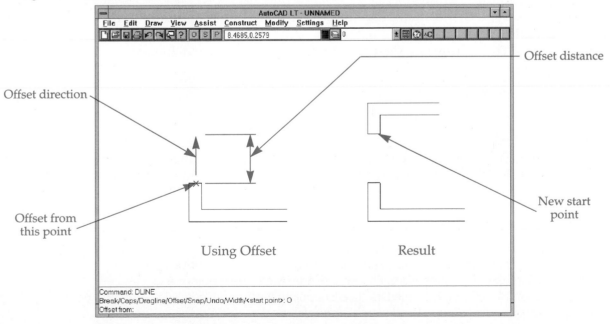

- **Snap.** The **Snap** option is used to start or end a double line by snapping to an existing entity. When both **Snap** and **Break** are on, (the defaults), an automatic *clean-up* occurs at the intersection of the two double lines. See Figure 6-18.

> Break/Caps/Dragline/Offset/Snap/Undo/Width/⟨start point⟩: **S** ↵
> Set snap size or snap On/Off. Size/OFF/⟨ON⟩: *(select an option)*

You can use the **Size** option to set the size of the area from the crosshair cursor that is searched for entity snapping. This area is called the pixel search area.

> Set snap size or snap On/Off. Size/OFF/⟨ON⟩: **S** ↵
> New snap size (1-10) ⟨3⟩: *(enter a size in pixels and press* [Enter]*)*

Figure 6-18.
Effects of **DLINE Snap** on and off.

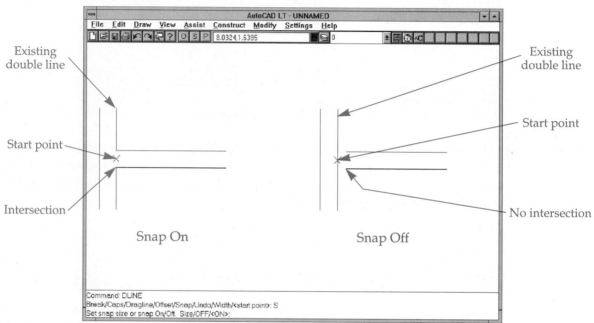

- **Undo.** Type U and then press [Enter] to use the **Undo** option to remove the previous double line or arc segment before you close the double line or end the command.
- **Width.** This option sets the width of the double line or double arc.

> Break/Caps/Dragline/Offset/Snap/Undo/Width/⟨start point⟩: **W** ↵
> New DLINE width ⟨current⟩: *(enter a value or locate two points)*

Drawing double arcs

Once you have picked a starting point for the double line, the **Arc** option is added at the beginning of the **DLINE** command options. The default double line arc is constructed like the **ARC** command's **3 Point** option described earlier in this chapter. After picking the double line starting point and entering A for arc, you are then prompted to select a second point and an endpoint for the arc. The command sequence is as follows:

> Command: *(type* DLINE *or* DL *and press* [Enter]*)*
> Break/Caps/Dragline/Offset/Snap/Undo/Width/⟨start point⟩: *(pick a point)*
> Arc/Break/CAps/CLose/Dragline/Snap/Undo/Width/⟨next point⟩: **A** ↵
> Break/CAps/CEnter/CLose/Dragline/Endpoint/Line/Snap/Undo/Width/⟨second point⟩:
>   *(pick a second point on the arc's circumference)*
> Endpoint: *(pick an endpoint for the arc)*

Alternatively, you can choose the **CEnter** option to define the center point of the arc. Once the center is located, you complete the arc by selecting an endpoint, or specifying an included angle.

Break/CAps/CEnter/CLose/Dragline/Endpoint/Line/Snap/Undo/Width/
　⟨second point⟩: **CE** ⏎
Center point: *(pick a center point for the arc)*
Angle/⟨Endpoint⟩: *(pick an endpoint for the arc or A for angle)*

Both double arc methods are illustrated in Figure 6-19.

Figure 6-19.
Drawing with **DLINE** arcs.

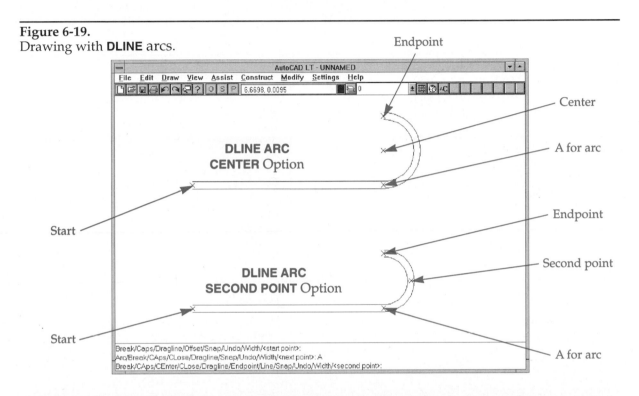

❏ Begin a new drawing with architectural units.
❏ Set the drawing limits to 40′,30′ and **ZOOM All**.
❏ Use the **DLINE** command with the **Width** set to 6″ to make a drawing similar to that shown below. Do not be concerned with dimensions.

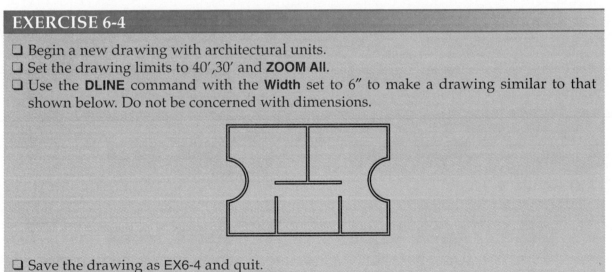

❏ Save the drawing as EX6-4 and quit.

Polylines are one of the most powerful entity types in AutoCAD LT and offer capabilities not found in normal line entities. Multiple polyline segments created in one operation are treated as one object. In addition, a polyline can be drawn with a specified width and contain arc segments (polyarcs). To draw polylines, type PLINE or PL at the **Command:** prompt, click the **Polyline** button in the toolbox, or select **Polyline** from the **Draw** pull-down menu. See Figure 6-20. The command sequence is as follows:

Command: (*type* PLINE *or* PL *and press* [Enter])
From point: (*pick a starting point*)

Figure 6-20.
Select **Polyline** from the
Draw pull-down menu.

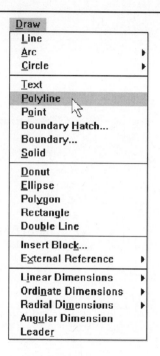

The **PLINE** command initially looks like the **LINE** command. At the **From point:** prompt, locate a point on the screen or enter a coordinate for the starting point of the polyline. After picking the starting point, the current polyline width and **PLINE** command options are displayed:

Current line-width is 0.0000
Arc/CLose/Halfwidth/Length/Undo/Width/⟨Endpoint of line⟩:

Each of the command options are described below:
* ⟨**Endpoint of line**⟩. This is the same as the **To point:** prompt in the **LINE** command. Locate a point or enter a coordinate to specify the endpoint of the polyline.
* **Undo.** Use the **Undo** option to remove the most recent polyline segment added to the polyline while still in the **PLINE** command. This option is identical to the **Undo** option found in the **LINE** and **DLINE** commands.
* **Close.** Once two or more polyline segments are drawn, use the **Close** option to draw a segment back to the starting point to create a closed shape.

- **Length.** This option draws a polyline segment of a specified length at the same angle (orientation) as the previous segment. If the previous segment is a polyarc, the new segment is drawn tangent to the arc. You are prompted as follows:

  Arc/Close/Halfwidth/Length/Undo/Width/〈Endpoint of line〉: **L** ↵
  Length of line: *(enter a positive or negative value)*

- **Width.** Use this option to specify the width of the next polyline segment. The starting width you specify becomes the ending width, by default. The width is maintained for all subsequent polylines until you change the width again. Several examples of wide polylines are illustrated in Figure 6-21. The starting and ending points of a wide polyline define the center of the line. In the example below, a uniform width of .25 is assigned for the next polyline segment to be drawn:

  Arc/Close/Halfwidth/Length/Undo/Width/〈Endpoint of line〉: **W** ↵
  Starting width 〈*current*〉: **.25** ↵
  Ending width 〈0.2500〉: ↵

Figure 6-21.
A polyline can be drawn with a constant or variable width.

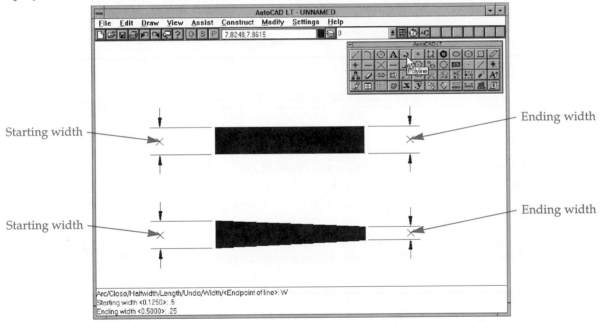

- **Halfwidth.** This option specifies the width of the next polyline segment from its center to one of its edges. The starting halfwidth you specify becomes the ending halfwidth, by default. The halfwidth is maintained for all subsequent polylines until you change the halfwidth again. Keep in mind that the halfwidth is applied equally to each side of the wide polyline. Thus, it is not possible to assign a halfwidth to just one side of the polyline segment. In the example that follows, a uniform halfwidth of .375 is assigned to the next segment to be drawn:

  Arc/Close/Halfwidth/Length/Undo/Width/〈Endpoint of line〉: **H** ↵
  Starting halfwidth 〈0.1250〉: **.375** ↵
  Ending halfwidth 〈0.3750〉: ↵

POLYLINE TUTORIAL

Because a polyline can be created with variable width, the **PLINE** command can be used to create arrowheads, or any other tapered shape. Try the following tutorial to construct the large cutting-plane line illustrated in Figure 6-22.

Figure 6-22.
A polyline in a phantom linetype is used to draw a cutting-plane line.

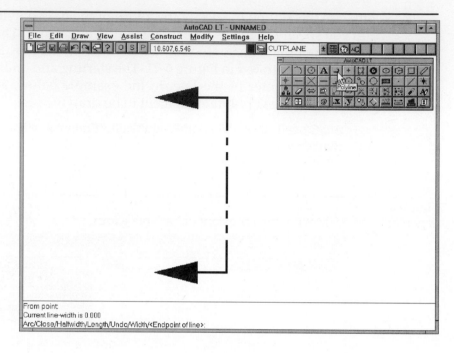

The tutorial begins as follows:

> Load AutoCAD LT and open PROTOA. Set the CUTPLANE layer current. If your proto-type drawing does not yet have a CUTPLANE layer, create one. Assign the PHANTOM linetype and color blue (5) to the new layer. Set the layer current.
> Issue the **PLINE** command and draw the cutting-plane line using the following-commands:

> Command: *(enter* PLINE *or* PL *and press* [Enter]*)*
> From point: *(pick a start point near top of screen)*
> Current line-width is 0.000
> Arc/Close/Halfwidth/Length/Undo/Width/⟨Endpoint of line⟩: **W** ⏎
> Starting width ⟨0.000⟩: ⏎
> Ending width ⟨0.000⟩: **.75** ⏎
> Arc/Close/Halfwidth/Length/Undo/Width/⟨Endpoint of line⟩: **@1.5⟨0** ⏎
> Arc/Close/Halfwidth/Length/Undo/Width/⟨Endpoint of line⟩: **W** ⏎
> Starting width ⟨0.750⟩: **.05** ⏎
> Ending width ⟨0.050⟩: ⏎
> Arc/Close/Halfwidth/Length/Undo/Width/⟨Endpoint of line⟩: **L** ⏎
> Length of line: **1** ⏎
> Arc/Close/Halfwidth/Length/Undo/Width/⟨Endpoint of line⟩: **@6⟨270** ⏎
> Arc/Close/Halfwidth/Length/Undo/Width/⟨Endpoint of line⟩: **@1⟨180** ⏎
> Arc/Close/Halfwidth/Length/Undo/Width/⟨Endpoint of line⟩: **W** ⏎
> Starting width ⟨0.050⟩: **.75** ⏎
> Ending width ⟨0.750⟩: **0** ⏎
> Arc/Close/Halfwidth/Length/Undo/Width/⟨Endpoint of line⟩: **L** ⏎
> Length of line: **1** ⏎
> Arc/Close/Halfwidth/Length/Undo/Width/⟨Endpoint of line⟩: ⏎
> Command:

> Save the completed drawing with the name CUTPLANE.DWG.

DRAWING POLYLINES WITH POLYARCS

As with double lines, the **PLINE** command also allows the drawing of arc segments. Each polyline arc (or polyarc) can have an assigned width. The polyarc is drawn tangent to the last polyline or polyarc created. Several polyarcs constructed in this fashion are shown in Figure 6-23. You can construct a polyarc by specifying its radius, center point, included angle, or direction. A polyarc may also be constructed through three points that define the radius of the entity. Before you can draw a polyarc, you must first specify a starting point as follows:

> Command: *(type* PLINE *or* PL *and press* [Enter]*)*
> From point: *(pick a point)*
> Current line-width is ⟨*current*⟩
> Arc/Close/Halfwidth/Length/Undo/Width/⟨Endpoint of line⟩: **A** ↵
> Angle/CEnter/CLose/Direction/Halfwidth/Line/Radius/Second pt/Undo/Width/
>   ⟨Endpoint of arc⟩:

Figure 6-23.
Polyline arcs (polyarcs) can also be drawn with constant or variable widths.

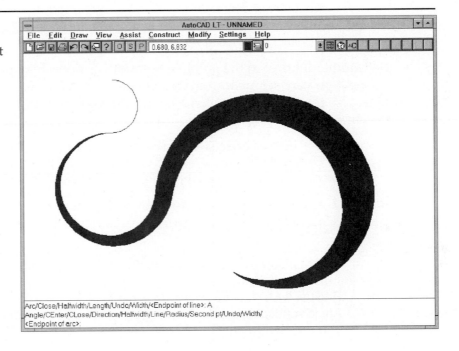

Each of the polyarc options are described below:
- **⟨Endpoint of arc⟩.** Locate a point or enter a coordinate to specify the endpoint of the polyarc.
- **Angle.** Use this option to specify the included angle of the arc segment from the starting point of the polyarc. A positive value draws a counterclockwise polyarc; a negative number draws a clockwise polyarc. After providing the included angle, you may then finish the polyarc segment by locating a center point, specifying a radius, or picking an ending point.

> Angle/CEnter/CLose/Direction/Halfwidth/Line/Radius/Second pt/Undo/Width/
>   ⟨Endpoint of arc⟩: **A** ↵
> Included angle: *(specify an angle and press* [Enter]*)*
> Center/Radius/⟨Endpoint⟩: *(pick an ending point or select an option)*

- **CEnter.** This option specifies the center of the polyarc. After locating the center point, you may then finish the polyarc segment by specifying an included angle, an ending point, or providing the arc chord length. The chord is a line segment joining two points on a circle or an arc.

  Angle/CEnter/CLose/Direction/Halfwidth/Line/Radius/Second pt/Undo/Width/
    ⟨Endpoint of arc⟩: **CE** ↵
  Center point: *(pick a center point)*
  Angle/Length/⟨Endpoint⟩: *(pick an ending point or select an option)*

- **CLose.** Use the **CLose** option to draw a polyarc segment back to the starting point to create a closed shape.

- **Direction.** The direction of polyarc segments is based on the ending direction of the previously drawn segment. This option allows an explicit starting direction to be specified, rather than using the default.

  Angle/CEnter/CLose/Direction/Halfwidth/Line/Radius/Second pt/Undo/Width/
    ⟨Endpoint of arc⟩: **D** ↵
  Direction from start point: *(pick a point to indicate direction)*
  End point: *(pick an ending point)*

- **Halfwidth.** Identical to the polyline **Halfwidth** option, this option specifies the width of the next polyarc segment from its center to one of its edges.

- **Line.** Use the **Line** option when you are through drawing polyarcs and wish to draw polylines.

  Angle/CEnter/CLose/Direction/Halfwidth/Line/Radius/Second pt/Undo/Width/
    ⟨Endpoint of arc⟩: **L** ↵
  Arc/Close/Halfwidth/Length/Undo/Width/⟨Endpoint of line⟩:

- **Radius.** Use this option to specify an explicit radius for the polyarc. You can then finish drawing the polyarc by locating an ending point, or by specifying an included angle.

  Angle/CEnter/CLose/Direction/Halfwidth/Line/Radius/Second pt/Undo/Width/
    ⟨Endpoint of arc⟩: **R** ↵
  Radius: *(enter a value or pick two points)*
  Angle/⟨Endpoint⟩: *(pick an ending point or type* A, *for Angle,*
    and press [Enter]*)*

- **Second pt.** This option is similar to the **3 Point** option of the **ARC** command. The second point you specify locates a point on the circumference of the polyarc, and the polyarc is terminated with a third point. The polyarc can be drawn clockwise or counterclockwise, depending on the direction of the pick points.

  Angle/CEnter/CLose/Direction/Halfwidth/Line/Radius/Second pt/Undo/Width/
    ⟨Endpoint of arc⟩: **S** ↵
  Second point: *(pick a second point for the polyarc)*
  End point: *(pick an ending point for the polyarc)*

- **Undo.** Use the **Undo** option to remove the most recent polyarc segment added while still in the **PLINE** command.

- **Width.** Identical to the polyline width option, this option specifies the width of the next polyarc segment. By default, the starting width specified also becomes the ending width.

DRAWING FULLY-RADIUSED FEATURES WITH POLYLINES

Earlier in this chapter, it was stated that the **LINE** and **ARC** command continuation options can be used together to quickly and easily construct fully-radiused features—like slots and cutouts. Similar features can be constructed using polylines and polyarcs in one operation without exiting the **PLINE** command. Consider the fully-radiused slot illustrated in Figure 6-24. By constructing this feature with a polyline, editing operations and inquiry commands can be performed much more efficiently than if the feature was constructed from individual lines and arcs. The command sequence is as follows:

> Command: *(type* PLINE *or* PL *and press* [Enter]*)*
> From point: *(pick point 1)*
> Current line-width is ⟨*current*⟩
> Arc/Close/Halfwidth/Length/Undo/Width/⟨Endpoint of line⟩: **@3⟨0** ⏎
> Arc/Close/Halfwidth/Length/Undo/Width/⟨Endpoint of line⟩: **A** ⏎
> Angle/CEnter/CLose/Direction/Halfwidth/Line/Radius/Second pt/Undo/Width/
>   ⟨Endpoint of arc⟩: **@1⟨90** ⏎
> Angle/CEnter/CLose/Direction/Halfwidth/Line/Radius/Second pt/Undo/Width/
>   ⟨Endpoint of arc⟩: **L** ⏎
> Arc/Close/Halfwidth/Length/Undo/Width/⟨Endpoint of line⟩: **@3⟨180** ⏎
> Arc/Close/Halfwidth/Length/Undo/Width/⟨Endpoint of line⟩: **A** ⏎
> Angle/CEnter/CLose/Direction/Halfwidth/Line/Radius/Second pt/Undo/Width/
>   ⟨Endpoint of arc⟩: **CL** ⏎
> Command:

Figure 6-24.
Fully-radiused features such as this slot may be drawn quickly and easily in one operation using polylines with polyarcs.

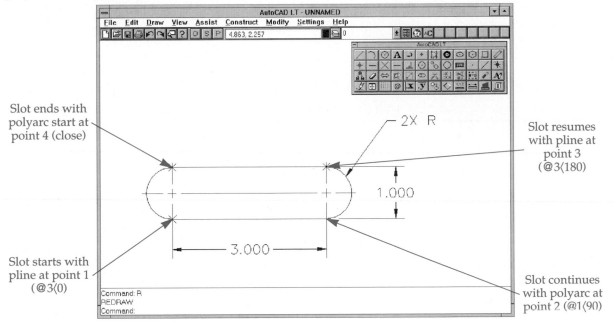

Slot ends with polyarc start at point 4 (close)

Slot starts with pline at point 1 (@3⟨0)

Slot resumes with pline at point 3 (@3⟨180)

Slot continues with polyarc at point 2 (@1⟨90)

2X R

1.000

3.000

As an alternative to entering polyline coordinates in the example above, you can use the **PLINE Length** option as you did in the previous tutorial. The **Length** option looks like this:

Arc/Close/Halfwidth/Length/Undo/Width/⟨Endpoint of line⟩: **L** ↵
Length of line: **3** ↵

EXERCISE 6-5

❏ Begin a new drawing with your PROTOA prototype, or use your own variables.
❏ Draw several polyarc segments using each of the options described in the preceding text.
❏ Using the command options and values shown above, draw the fully-radiused slot illustrated in Figure 6-24.
❏ Save the drawing as EX6-5.

DRAWING RECTANGLES

Many of the objects in engineering and architectural drawings are rectangular in shape. AutoCAD LT allows you to quickly draw a rectangular polyline using the **RECTANG** command. To access the **RECTANG** command type RECTANG or RC, click the **Rectangle** button in the toolbox, or select **Rectangle** from the **Draw** pull-down menu, Figure 6-25. The rectangle is defined by two diagonal corners as illustrated in Figure 6-26. The following command sequence creates a 6 × 4 rectangle:

Command: *(type* RECTANG *or* RC *and press* [Enter]*)*
First corner: *(pick a corner point)*
Second corner: **@6,4** ↵
Command:

Remember that rectangles are constructed with polylines.

Figure 6-25.
Select **Rectangle** from the
Draw pull-down menu.

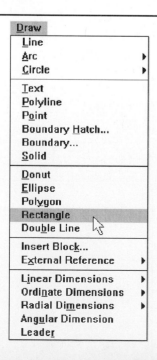

Figure 6-26.
Two diagonal points define a rectangle.

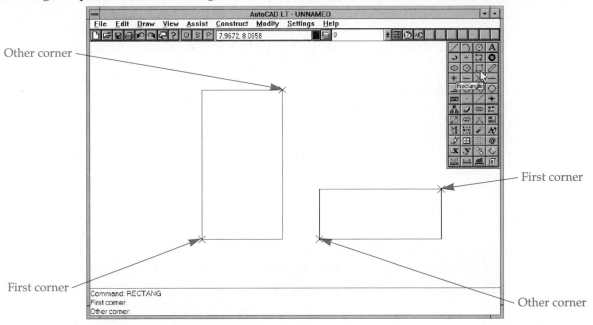

Other corner

First corner

First corner

Other corner

DRAWING POLYGONS

ALTUG 6

A regular polygon is a multi-sided figure with each side of equal length. Several examples of polygons include an equilateral triangle, a square, and a hexagon. These shapes, and many others, can be quickly and easily drawn using the **POLYGON** command. Polygons, like rectangles, are constructed with polylines. To access the **POLYGON** command type POLYGON or PG at the **Command:** prompt, click the **Polygon** button in the toolbox, or select **Polygon** from the **Draw** pull-down menu. See Figure 6-27. As shown in Figure 6-28, polygons can be constructed using two different methods. Regardless of the method selected, the **POLYGON** command first prompts you for the desired number of sides. A polygon can have between 3 and 1,024 sides—the default number is 4. The two construction methods are described in the following sections.

Figure 6-27.
Select **Polygon** from the
Draw pull-down menu.

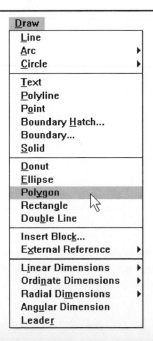

Drawing a polygon by its center and radius

The default method for creating a polygon requires you to locate a center point around which the polygon is constructed. You are then prompted to enter a radius value which defines an imaginary circle that is used to size the polygon. The polygon is circumscribed around the imaginary circle. Consider the 3-sided polygon shown at the upper left in Figure 6-28. This object can be drawn with the following sequence of steps:

```
Command: (type POLYGON or PG and press [Enter])
Number of sides ⟨4⟩: 3 ↵
Edge/⟨Center of polygon⟩: (pick a center point)
Radius of circle: 1.25 ↵
Command:
```

Figure 6-28.
Polygon construction options.

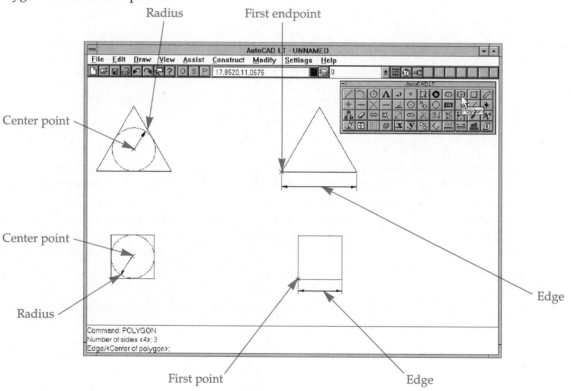

The center and radius method is useful when you know the distance from the center of the polygon to the midpoint of one of its sides.

Drawing a polygon by specifying the length of an edge

The **POLYGON Edge** option provides a handy alternative when the length of a polygon segment is known, and where it is to be placed is known. As an example, look at the 4-sided polygon at the lower right in Figure 6-28. The command sequence for this polygon is as follows:

```
Command: (type POLYGON or PG and press [Enter])
Number of sides ⟨current⟩: 4 ↵
Edge/⟨Center of polygon⟩: E ↵
First endpoint of edge: (pick the first endpoint)
Second endpoint of edge: @2.5⟨0 ↵
Command:
```

THE EXPLODE COMMAND

AutoCAD LT defines a compound object as an entity that comprises more than one object. Multiple segmented entities like polylines, rectangles, and polygons are all considered compound objects. You can convert compound objects into their component entities using the **EXPLODE** command. Exploding polylines, rectangles, and polygons converts them into individual line segments. To access the **EXPLODE** command type EXPLODE, EP, or X at the **Command:** prompt, click the **Explode** button in the toolbox, or select **Explode** from the **Modify** pull-down menu. See Figure 6-29. The command sequence is as follows:

    Command: (type EXPLODE, EP, or X and press [Enter])
    Select objects: (select one or more compound objects)
    Select objects: ↵
    Command:

Figure 6-29.
Select **Explode** from the
Modify pull-down menu.

All of the selection set options are valid with EXPLODE so you can select more than one compound object at a time. However, keep in mind that width is lost when you explode a wide polyline. In those instances, AutoCAD LT displays the following message:

    Exploding this polyline has lost width information.
    The UNDO command will restore it.

 NOTE   Other types of compound objects will be covered as they are encountered in this text.

EXERCISE 6-6

❑ Begin a new drawing with your PROTOB prototype, or use your own variables.
❑ Draw a rectangle that measures 8 units on the X axis and 4 units on the Y axis. Draw a second rectangle that measures 2.4375 on the X axis and 4.5625 on the Y axis.
❑ Using the **Edge** option of the **POLYGON** command, draw a square that measures 1.875 along each edge.
❑ Draw a hexagon with a radius of 2.3125 units and an octagon with a radius of 3.625 units.
❑ Finally, draw a .5 wide polyline that is 6 units long. Explode the polyline and observe the results. Perform an **UNDO** to retrieve the wide polyline.
❑ Save the drawing as EX6-6 and quit.

PRESETTING POLYLINE WIDTHS

You can preset the constant width of polylines, polyarcs, and rectangles with the AutoCAD LT system variable **PLINEWID**. Setting the width beforehand can save you valuable drafting time. The **PLINEWID** system variable is entered at the **Command:** prompt as follows:

Command: **PLINEWID** ⏎
New value for PLINEWID ⟨*current value*⟩: *(enter a width and press* [Enter]*)*

Although polygon entities are constructed with polylines, they are not affected by the **PLINEWID** variable. When you are done drawing wide polylines, polyarcs, or rectangles, be sure to set the value of **PLINEWID** to 0 (zero).

CREATING CHAMFERS   ALTUG 10

A *chamfer* is a slight surface angle, or bevel, used to relieve both internal and external sharp edges on mechanical parts. Chamfers are also used to facilitate the assembly of mating parts. An example of this is a bolt or other type of threaded fastener being screwed into a tapped hole. By adding a slight chamfer around the edge of the mating hole, it is easier for an assembler to insert the fastener and engage the threads.

In AutoCAD LT, a chamfer may be constructed between one line and another line, or between one polyline and another polyline. You cannot create a chamfer between a line and a polyline. Chamfers are drawn by first setting the first and second chamfer distances. As shown in Figure 6-30, the chamfer distance is the amount each entity is trimmed (or extended) to intersect the chamfer line.

Figure 6-30.
Creating a chamfer.

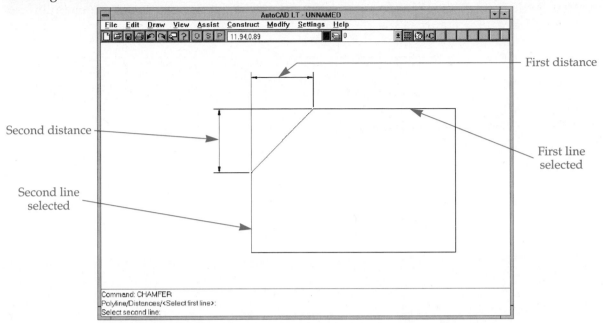

To construct a chamfer, type in CHAMFER, or CF at the **Command:** prompt, or select **Chamfer** from the **Construct** pull-down menu. See Figure 6-31. In the example below, the **Distance** option is used to first specify the chamfer distances. Since 45° chamfers are the most common, the second chamfer distance automatically defaults to the first chamfer distance entered.

> Command: *(type* CHAMFER *or* CF *and press* [Enter]*)*
> Polyline/Distances ⟨Select first line⟩: **D** ⏎
> Enter first chamfer distance ⟨*current*⟩: **.75** ⏎
> Enter second chamfer distance ⟨0.7500⟩: ⏎

Figure 6-31.
Selecting **Chamfer** from the **Construct** pull-down menu.

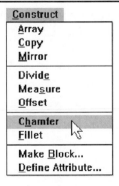

Now that the distances are set, press [Enter] to repeat the **CHAMFER** command, and select the lines (or polylines) to be chamfered.

> Command: ⏎
> CHAMFER Polyline/Distances ⟨Select first line⟩: *(pick a line)*
> Select second line: *(pick a second line)*
> Command:

As soon as the second line is selected, the chamfer is created and the lines are automatically trimmed. AutoCAD LT allows you to chamfer nonintersecting lines as well as lines that overlap. In addition, you can extend two lines to make a corner if you set the chamfer distances to 0 (zero). See Figure 6-32.

Figure 6-32.
Chamfers can be constructed between nonintersecting lines as well as lines that overlap. Setting the chamfer distances to 0 makes a corner.

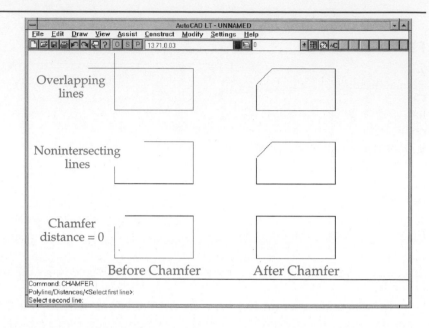

Chamfering a 2D polyline

The **Polyline** option allows all the edges of a polyline to be chamfered in one operation. However, only those edges of the polyline long enough to accommodate the new segments are chamfered. Each of the chamfers is joined to the existing polyline as a new polyline segment. The **Polyline** option is used as follows:

Command: (*type* CHAMFER *or* CF *and press* [Enter])
Polyline/Distances ⟨Select first line⟩: **P** ↵
Select 2D polyline: (*select a polyline, rectangle, or polygon*)
Command:

A polyline with all edges chamfered in one operation is illustrated in Figure 6-33.

Figure 6-33.
All contiguous vertices of a polyline are chamfered in one operation.

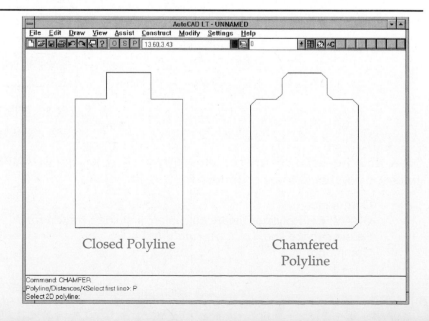

NOTE   Although the **Chamfer** button shown does not appear in the toolbox or on the toolbar, it may easily be added. This function is covered in detail in Chapter 19 of this text.

FILLETS AND ROUNDS ALTUG 10

A *fillet* is a radius at the interior intersection of two or more surfaces. A radius added at the intersection of two or more exterior surfaces is called a *round*. In mechanical design, fillets and rounds are often used to strengthen an inside corner or to relieve stress on an outside corner. Sometimes fillets and rounds are added to a design simply to provide a more aesthetically pleasing appearance.

In AutoCAD LT, fillets and rounds are created using the **FILLET** command. Before you can draw a fillet, you must first specify the fillet radius. You are then prompted to select the entities to fillet. AutoCAD LT allows you to create fillets between lines, arcs, and circles. See Figure 6-34. As with the **CHAMFER** command, you can fillet between lines or polylines. You cannot fillet between a line and a polyline—nor can you fillet polyarcs.

Figure 6-34.
Creating a fillet.

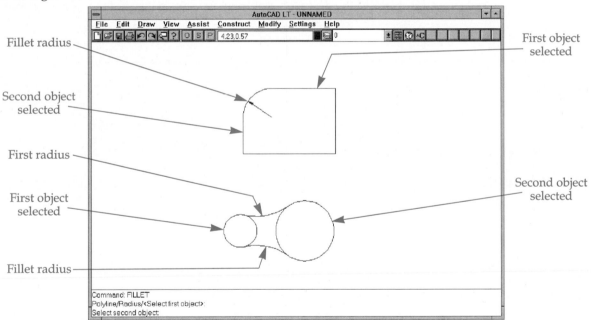

To create a fillet, type FILLET or F at the **Command:** prompt, or select **Fillet** from the **Construct** pull-down menu. See Figure 6-35. In the example below, the **Radius** option is first used to specify the size of the fillet.

    Command: *(type* FILLET *or* F *and press* [Enter])
    Polyline/Radius ⟨Select first object⟩: **R** ↵
    Enter fillet radius ⟨*current*⟩: **.25** ↵
    Command:

Now that the radius is set, press [Enter] to repeat the **FILLET** command and select the lines (or polylines), arcs, or circles to be filleted.

Command: ↵
FILLET Polyline/Radius ⟨Select first object⟩: *(pick an entity)*
Select second object: *(pick a second entity)*
Command:

Figure 6-35.
Selecting **Fillet** from the **Construct** pull-down menu.

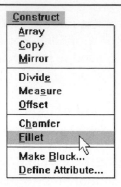

As soon as the second object is selected, the fillet is created and the entities are automatically trimmed. Like the **CHAMFER** command, AutoCAD LT allows you to fillet nonintersecting lines as well as lines that overlap. You can also extend two lines to make a corner if you set the fillet radius to 0 (zero). See Figure 6-36.

Figure 6-36.
Fillets can be constructed between nonintersecting entities as well as entities that overlap. Setting the fillet radius to 0 makes a corner.

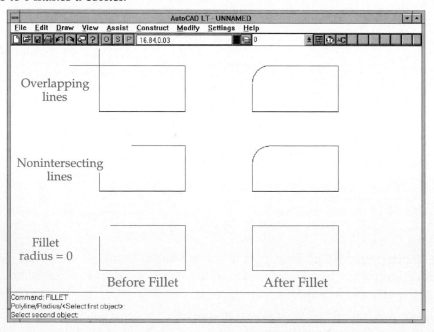

Filleting a 2D polyline

The **FILLET** command also has a **Polyline** option that lets you fillet all the edges of a polyline in one operation. As with the **Polyline** option of the **CHAMFER** command, only those edges of the polyline long enough to accommodate the new segments are filleted. Each of the fillets is joined to the existing polyline as a polyarc segment. The **Polyline** option is used as follows:

> Command: *(type* FILLET *or* F *and press* [Enter]*)*
> Polyline/Radius ⟨Select first object⟩: **P** ↵
> Select 2D polyline: *(select a polyline, rectangle, or polygon)*
> Command:

A polyline with all edges filleted in one operation is illustrated in Figure 6-37.

Figure 6-37.
All contiguous vertices of a polyline are filleted in one operation.

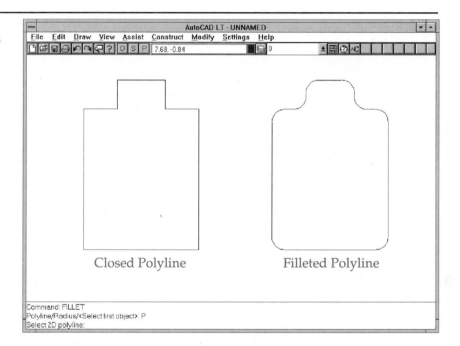

Closed Polyline   Filleted Polyline

 NOTE   Like the **Chamfer** button, the **Fillet** button shown does not appear in the toolbox or on the toolbar, but may easily be added. To learn how to customize the toolbar and toolbox, see Chapter 19 of this text.

EXERCISE 6-7

❑ Begin a new drawing with your PROTOA prototype, or use your own variables.
❑ Create several shapes similar to those illustrated in Figure 6-32. Experiment with different distance values as you chamfer the objects.
❑ Draw two lines that do not intersect. Set the chamfer distance to 0 and make a corner of the two lines.
❑ Create several shapes similar to those illustrated in Figure 6-34. Experiment with different radius values as you fillet the objects.
❑ Draw two lines that do not intersect. Set the radius to 0 and make a corner of the two lines.
❑ Save the drawing as EX6-7 and quit.

CHAPTER TEST

Write your answers in the spaces provided.

1. Describe the **TTR** option of the **CIRCLE** command. _____
   _____

2. What is an included angle? _____
   _____

3. Provide the command and entries required to draw a 30° ellipse with a major axis of 4.625 units. The ellipse is to be located by a center point and horizontally oriented.

   Command: _____

   ⟨Axis endpoint 1⟩/Center: _____

   Center of ellipse: _____

   Axis endpoint: _____

   ⟨Other axis distance⟩/Rotation: _____

   Rotation around major axis: _____

4. How do you draw a completely filled circle? _____
   _____

5. What should you do after turning **FILL** mode on or off? _____
   _____

6. What is the purpose of the **Break** option of the **DLINE** command? _____
   _____
   _____

7. What is the purpose of the **Dragline** option of the **DLINE** command? _____
   _____
   _____

8. Each line and arc segment in a double line is a separate entity. (True/False) _____

9. How do polylines differ from lines? _____
   _____
   _____
   _____

10. What is the purpose of the **PLINE Length** option? _____
    _____
    _____

11. Rectangles and polygons are comprised of what type of entity? _____

12. What are the minimum and maximum number of sides for a polygon? _____
    _____
    _____

13. When should the **POLYGON Edge** option be used? _____
    _____
    _____

14. What is a compound object? Name the command that converts a compound object.

_____

_____

15. What is the purpose of the **PLINEWID** variable? _____

_____

16. Which one of the following three entity types cannot be drawn with assigned width—polylines, polygons, or rectangles? _____

17. What must you do before you can create a chamfer? _____

_____

18. Can a fillet be created between a line and a polyline? (Yes/No) _____

19. A polyline must be exploded before it can be chamfered or filleted. (True/False) _____

20. How can you bring two lines together to make a corner? _____

_____

_____

CHAPTER PROBLEMS

1. Using your PROTOA prototype drawing, draw the GASKET with the **CIRCLE** and **FILLET** commands. Place object lines on the OBJECTS layer and centerlines on the CENTERLINES layer. Do not draw the dimensions. Save the drawing as P6-1.

Mechanical Drafting

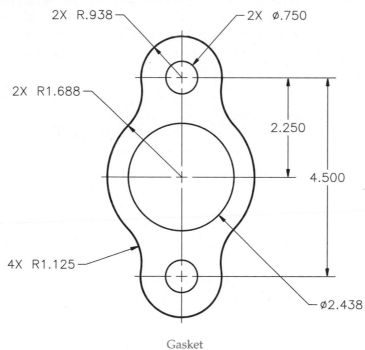

Gasket

2. Draw the **ADJUSTING ARM** using fillets, chamfers, and the arc continuation option described in this chapter. Use your **PROTOB** prototype drawing. As with P6-1, place object lines on the **OBJECTS** layer and centerlines on the **CENTERLINES** layer. Do not draw the dimensions. Save the drawing as **P6-2**.

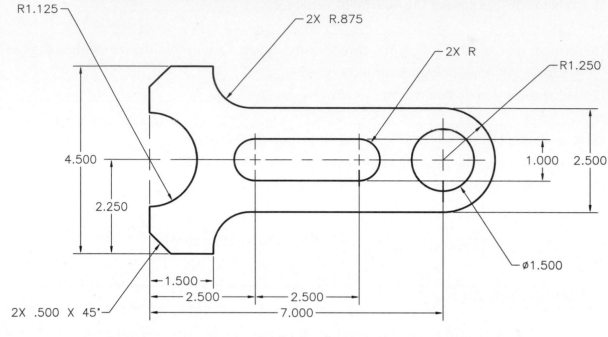

Adjusting Arm

3. Use your **PROTOB** prototype drawing to draw the **CLOSED-END WRENCH**. Rotate the snap and grid as required to draw the hexagon at the proper orientation. As with the previous two drawing problems, place object lines on the **OBJECTS** layer and centerlines on the **CENTERLINES** layer. Do not draw the dimensions. Save the drawing as **P6-3**.

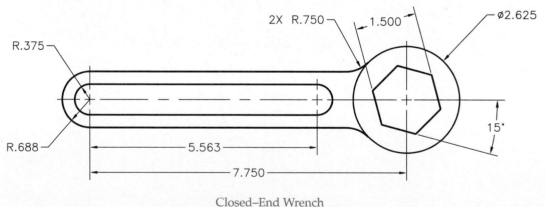

Closed–End Wrench

4. Use your **PROTOB** prototype drawing to draw the object shown. Draw the outer profile with a polyline and chamfer as specified. Draw the inside features with a 4-sided polygon and two rectangles. Save the drawing as P6-4.

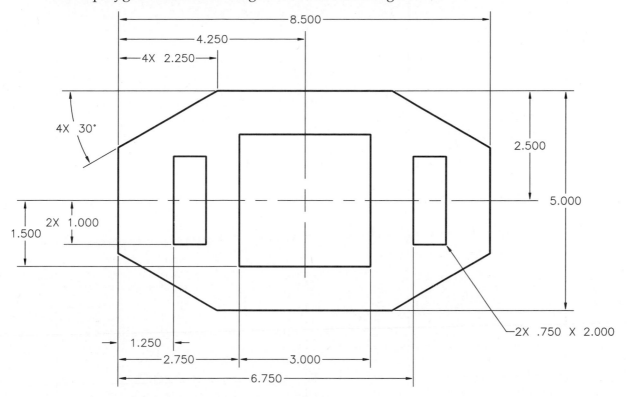

5. On a green layer named FLRPLAN, draw the floorplan shown below using the **DLINE** command. Use architectural units and set the drawing limits to 36',30'. The exterior walls are 6' thick, and the interior walls are 4" thick. Set the **DLINE Width** and **Dragline** options appropriately. Save the drawing as P6-5.

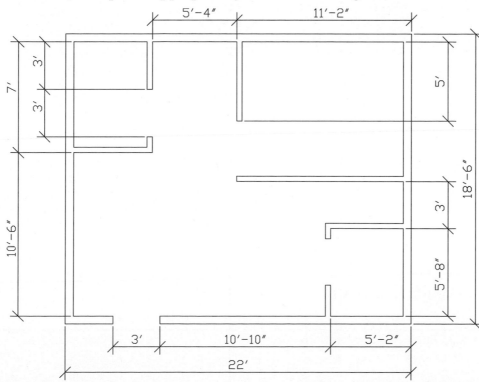

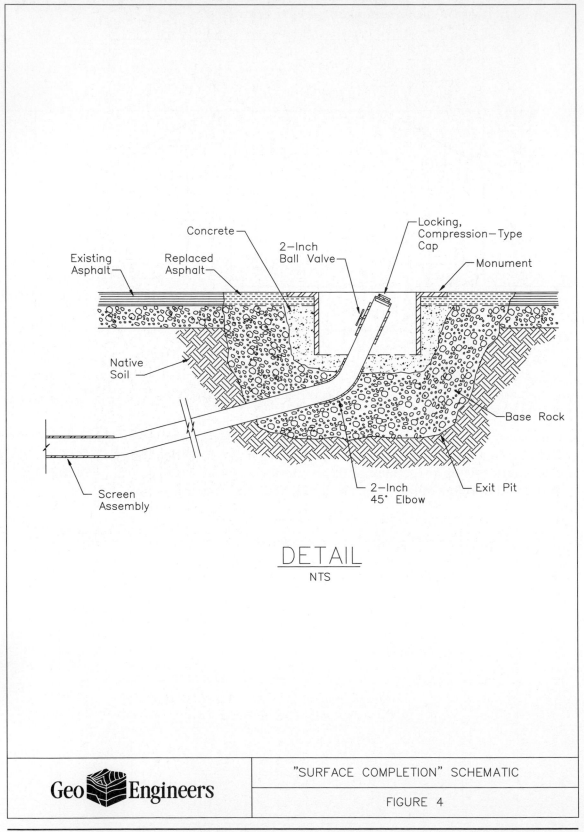

Existing Asphalt — Replaced Asphalt — Concrete — 2-Inch Ball Valve — Locking, Compression-Type Cap — Monument — Native Soil — Base Rock — Screen Assembly — 2-Inch 45° Elbow — Exit Pit

DETAIL
NTS

Geo Engineers

"SURFACE COMPLETION" SCHEMATIC

FIGURE 4

AutoCAD LT

Learning objectives:

After you have completed this chapter, you will be able to:

- ○ Select entities at precise pick points using object snap modes.
- ○ Use **X** and **Y** point filters to locate and project features and views.
- ○ Describe and use **TRACKING**.
- ○ Select and use **POINT** entities.
- ○ Divide a selected entity into a specified number of segments.
- ○ Measure a selected entity with specified length segments.
- ○ Offset an object at a specified distance or through a point to create a new object.
- ○ Create auxiliary views.

Perhaps more than anything else, AutoCAD LT is a geometry construction tool. In this chapter, you will learn how to select entities at precise locations to aid in geometry construction and editing. You will also learn how to project features and views using several different methods. This chapter also explains how to divide and measure selected objects with **POINT** entities, create parallel entities, and construct auxiliary views.

USING OBJECT SNAP MODES

ALTUG 7

The AutoCAD LT object snap modes allow you to precisely select entities at designated pick points. This is called *object snap* and means you snap to an object at a precise location. The object snap modes are commonly referred to as *osnaps* and each has a specific application. Some examples of osnaps include selecting a line at its endpoint or midpoint, or picking a circle or arc by its center point. Endpoint, midpoint, and center are three of the eleven object snap modes available.

The greatest advantage of osnaps is the extreme accuracy their use provides. For example, when you use the midpoint object snap on a line, AutoCAD LT always finds the *exact* midpoint of the line. Osnaps are quick and easy to use, too. If you use the endpoint osnap to select the end of a line, you need only pick somewhere near the line's endpoint. The endpoint osnap mode snaps to the exact end of the line you select.

Osnaps are not commands themselves, but modes that are used in conjunction with drawing and editing commands when a point is requested. When entered at the **Command:** prompt, each osnap mode may be abbreviated by its first three letters. Refer to the circle illustrated at the upper left of Figure 7-1 as you study the command sequence that follows. In this example, a line is started from the exact center point of the circle.

> Command: (*type* LINE *or* L *and press* [Enter])
> From point: **CEN** ↵
> of (*locate the cursor over some portion of the circle and pick*)
> To point: (*pick a point for the end of the line*)

Figure 7-1.
Using the **CENter** object snap.

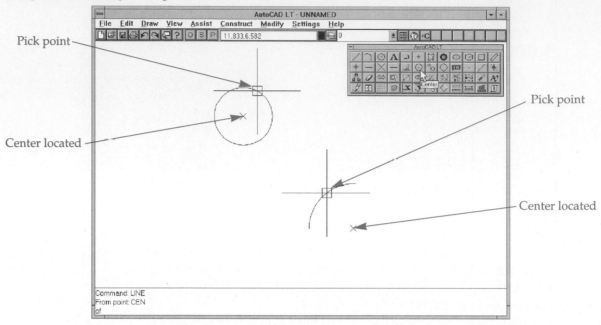

The eleven object snap modes are defined as follows:

- **CENter.** Locates the center of a circle, donut, or arc. See Figure 7-1. When you use the **CENter** osnap, do not place the cursor target, or *aperture*, over the center of the entity. You must place the aperture directly on the circle, donut, or arc. AutoCAD LT will find the object's true center.
- **ENDpoint.** As shown in Figure 7-2, osnap **ENDpoint** finds the endpoint of a line, polyline, or arc.

Figure 7-2.
Using the **ENDpoint** object snap.

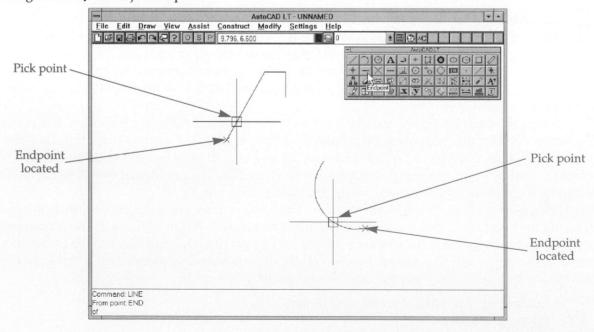

- **INSert.** This mode snaps to the insertion point of text or a block. See Figure 7-3. See Chapters 9 and 14 for complete information regarding text and block entities.

Figure 7-3.
Using the **INSert** object snap.

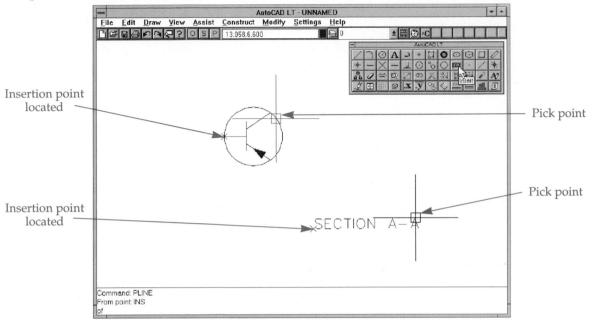

- **INTersection.** Picks the closest intersection of two or more entities. When using osnap **INTersection**, place the aperture directly over the intersecting entities you wish to snap to, Figure 7-4. With this mode, therefore, the aperture location and the pick point must be the same.

Figure 7-4.
Using the **INTersection** object snap.

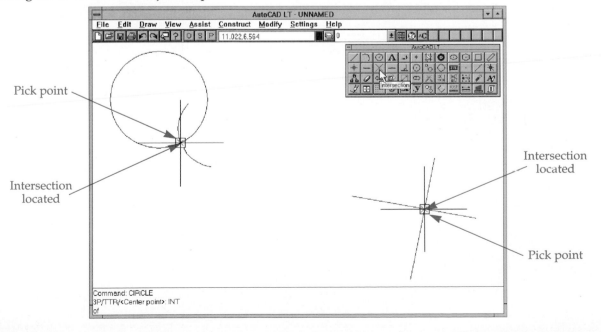

- **MIDpoint.** As shown in Figure 7-5, osnap **MIDpoint** locates the midpoint of a line, poly-line, or arc.
- **NEArest.** Locates a point on an object nearest to the crosshair cursor. Only use this mode when a precise pick location is of secondary importance.

Figure 7-5.
Using the **MIDpoint** object snap.

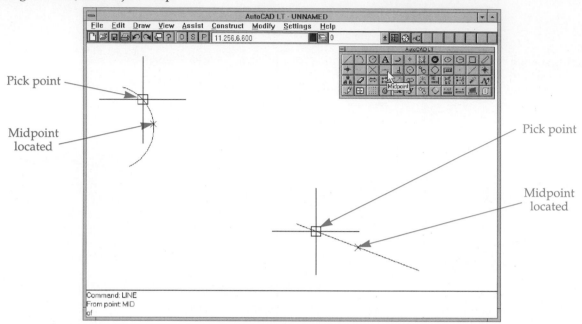

- **NODe.** Snaps to a point drawn with the **POINT** command. In the example illustrated in Figure 7-6, point entities on the two horizontal lines are connected with lines using osnap **NODe.** Points are discussed in a later section of this chapter.
- **NONe.** Use osnap **NONe** to override or turn off one or more running object snap modes.

Figure 7-6.
Using the **NODe** object snap.

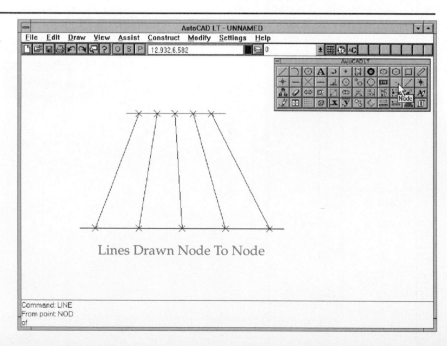

- **PERpendicular.** Creates a perpendicular line or polyline to one feature. In the example illustrated at the upper left of Figure 7-7, a line is drawn from the **QUAdrant** of a circle perpendicular to a line. At the lower right, a line is drawn from the **MIDpoint** of a polygon perpendicular to a rectangle.

Figure 7-7.
Using the **PERpendicular** object snap.

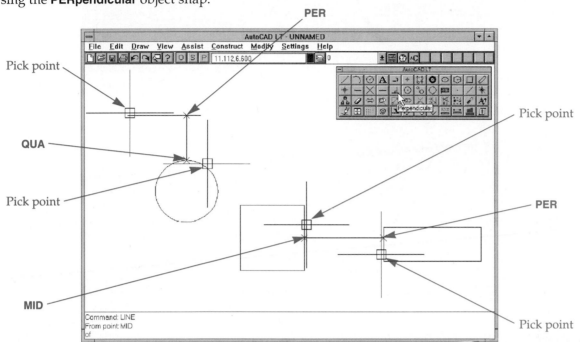

- **QUAdrant.** Picks one of four quadrants on a circle or donut closest to the target aperture. The quadrants correspond to the 0°, 90°, 180°, and 270° polar coordinate points, Figure 7-8A. As shown in Figure 7-8B, osnap **QUAdrant** can also be used to snap to the closest quadrant of an arc.

Figure 7-8.
A—**QUAdrant** points on circles and arcs. B—Using the **QUAdrant** object snap.

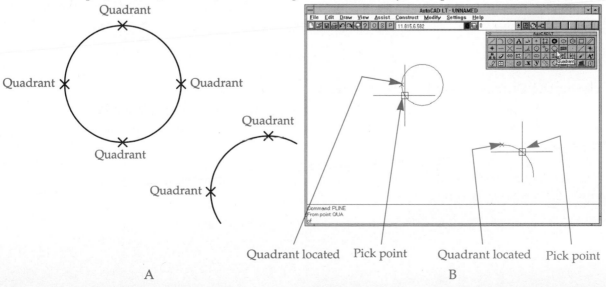

- **TANgent.** Use this object snap mode to draw a line or polyline tangent to a circle or arc. Several examples of osnap **TANgent** are illustrated in Figure 7-9.

Figure 7-9.
Using the **TANgent** object snap.

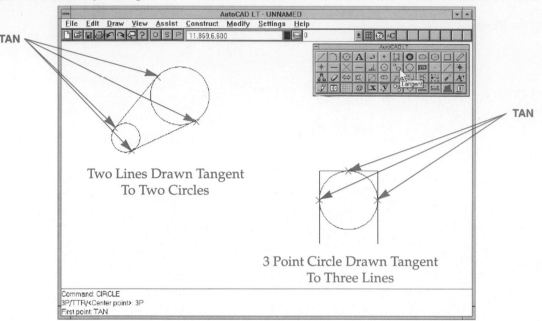

Accessing osnaps from the toolbox

If you prefer not to type in the osnap names, you can access all of the object snap modes from the toolbox. Each of the osnaps has a separate tool button as shown in Figure 7-10. Whenever you need a particular osnap, simply move your mouse pointer over the appropriate button and click.

Figure 7-10.
Each of the object snaps can be accessed from the toolbox.

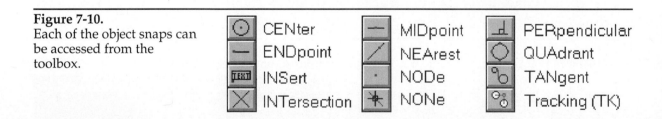

Using the Cursor Menu for object snaps

It is also possible to access the object snap modes from a floating **Cursor Menu**. See Figure 7-11. This menu is called the **Cursor Menu** because it displays at the location of the screen crosshair cursor. To activate the **Cursor Menu**, hold down the [Shift] key and click the right mouse button. When the **Cursor Menu** appears, simply move your mouse pointer to the desired osnap and click. The **Cursor Menu** disappears and the object snap you select is enabled for one pick only.

Figure 7-11.
The **Cursor Menu**
provides quick access
to object snap modes.

Tracking
Center
Endpoint
Insert
Intersection
Midpoint
Nearest
Node
Perpendicular
Quadrant
Tangent
None
XYZ Filters ▸

PROFESSIONAL TIP

Remember that object snaps are not commands, but modes that are used in conjunction with drawing and editing functions. For example, if you were to type in MID or PER at the **Command:** prompt, then AutoCAD LT would display an error message. If you do choose to type in the desired object snap mode from the keyboard, take particular care when using the **ENDpoint** osnap. Should you type in END at the **Command:** prompt, you will end the drawing session. For this reason, it is recommended that you enter ENDP instead until you become more familiar with AutoCAD LT.

SETTING RUNNING OBJECT SNAPS

ALTUG 7

A *running object snap* is an osnap that is permanently enabled. This is particularly handy if you plan to use the same object snap mode repeatedly. As an example, you might set the **ENDpoint** osnap running if you need to connect a series of line endpoints. A running osnap stays on until you turn it off, and you can have more than one osnap mode running at a time.

When you have multiple running osnaps, AutoCAD LT selects the most appropriate osnap to use depending on the entity you select or where the entity is picked. For example, suppose you set both **MIDpoint** and **ENDpoint** as running osnaps and then pick a line. Which is selected—the midpoint or endpoint of the line? If you pick closer to the middle of the line, then the midpoint is selected. If you pick closer to the end of the line, then the endpoint of the line is selected. However, be advised that some osnap modes conflict with one another. As an example, if you were to set osnap **QUAdrant** and **CENter** running simultaneously, **CENter** would be ignored and **QUAdrant** would take precedence. Can you think of other object snap modes that might conflict?

Setting a running object snap with a dialog box

To set one or more running osnaps, click the **Object Snap** button in the toolbox or select **Object Snap...** from the **Assist** pull-down menu. See Figure 7-12. The command sequence is as follows:

Command: (*type* DDOSNAP *or* OS *and press* [Enter])

Figure 7-12.
Selecting **Object Snap...**
from the Assist pull-down
menu issues the **DDOSNAP**
command.

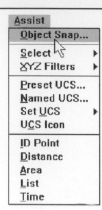

The **DDOSNAP** command displays the **Running Object Snap** dialog box illustrated in Figure 7-13. In the example shown, both the **Endpoint** and **Center** osnap modes are selected. To turn off a running osnap, click the appropriate check box to deactivate the osnap. Keep in mind that you can override one or more running osnaps at any time by simply selecting a different osnap for one pick only. Once that pick is completed, any running osnaps are again in effect until overridden once more.

Figure 7-13.
Setting **ENDpoint** and
CENter running osnaps from
the **Running Object Snap**
dialog box.

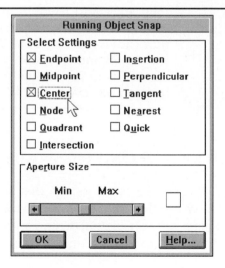

Sizing the aperture

As previously mentioned, the crosshair cursor displays a square target, or *aperture*, when an object snap mode is used. You can make the aperture larger or smaller using the **Aperture Size** horizontal slider bar in the **Running Object Snap** dialog box. The aperture size is measured in pixels and defaults to a value of 10 pixels. If you set the slider to the **Max** position, the aperture is set to 20 pixels. Sliding to the **Min** position sets the aperture size to 1 pixel. As you move the slider, the image tile to the right grows and shrinks accordingly. When you are done making your changes, click the **OK** button to exit the **Running Object Snap** dialog box.

Setting the aperture size on the command line

It is also possible to set the aperture size from the command line using the **APERTURE** system variable. This method allows you to set the aperture to its maximum size of 50 pixels.

Command: *(type* APERTURE *or* AP *and press* [Enter])
Object snap target height (1-50 pixels) ⟨*current*⟩: *(enter a value 1 to 50)*

You can also change the aperture size transparently by typing 'APERTURE or 'AP in the middle of another command.

A very large aperture size increases the risk of selecting the wrong entity since it is likely that two or more objects may fall into the increased target area. On the other hand, a very small aperture slows you down because it takes more time to position the aperture over the desired object. Most users find that a size of 5–6 pixels works well. Experiment with various sizes to find out which size suits your personal taste and work habits. Changing the aperture size automatically updates the AutoCAD LT configuration file (ACLT.CFG) in the \ACLTWIN directory. Therefore, the new size is used for all subsequent drawing sessions until changed again.

Setting a running object snap on the command line

To set one or more running object snaps, type OSNAP, or O, at the **Command:** prompt. For example, if you want to set **MIDpoint** as a running object snap, do the following:

> Command: *(type* OSNAP *or* O *and press* [Enter])
> Object snap modes: **MID** ⏎

To set multiple running osnaps, enter the first three letters of each mode separated by commas. For example:

> Command: *(type* OSNAP *or* O *and press* [Enter])
> Object snap modes: **END,CEN,MID** ⏎

When you want to turn off any running osnaps, do the following:

> Command: *(type* OSNAP *or* O *and press* [Enter])
> Object snap modes: *(type* NONE *or* OFF *or press* [Enter])

Using osnaps greatly increases your productivity and accuracy. As an additional time-saver, enable those object snap modes you use most often as running object snaps in your prototype drawing(s).

EXERCISE 7-1

❑ Begin a new drawing with your PROTOA prototype drawing, or use your own setup variables.
❑ Draw the objects shown below. As a construction hint, start with the two arcs and then draw a rectangle and a circle.

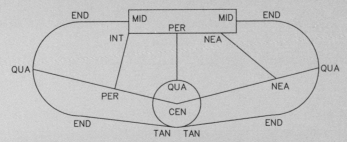

❑ Use the osnap modes indicated to draw the required lines.
❑ Save the drawing as EX7-1 and quit.

Point filters allow you to locate a point by extracting, or "filtering out", the X, Y, and Z coordinate values of existing entities. You can use one or more filters whenever AutoCAD LT requests a point. The point filters can be accessed from a cascading submenu by selecting **XYZ Filters** from the **Assist** pull-down menu. See Figure 7-14. Conveniently, you can also find the **.X** filter and **.Y** filter buttons in the toolbox. Another fast way to select point filters is from the **Cursor Menu** by pressing and holding the [Shift] key while you click the right button on your mouse. Picking **XYZ Filters** from the **Cursor Menu** displays the various point filter options in a cascading submenu.

Figure 7-14.
Selecting **XYZ Filters** from the **Assist** pull-down menu displays a cascading submenu of filter selections.

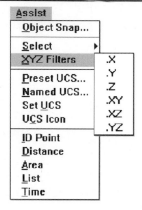

NOTE

Although the **.Z** filter button shown in the margin does not normally appear in the toolbox, it may easily be added. If you are planning on doing much three-dimensional work in the future, this would be a handy toolbox or toolbar addition. See Chapter 19 of this text to learn how to customize the toolbox and toolbar.

Using point filters

Suppose you wanted to place the center of a circle (or a polygon) at the center of a rectangle or square. See Figure 7-15. Point filters accomplish this task by extracting the midpoint X value of one of the horizontal lines, and the midpoint Y value of one of the vertical lines. In the example that follows, the filters are entered on the command line and the X value is filtered before the YZ value. However, the same operation could be performed by filtering the Y value first, and then the XZ value. The command sequence is as follows.

> Command: *(type* CIRCLE *or* C *and press* [Enter]*)*
> 3P/TTR/⟨Center point⟩: **.X** ⏎
> of *(pick the* **MIDpoint** P1 *of the top horizontal line)*
> of (need YZ): *(pick the* **MIDpoint** P2 *of the right vertical line)*
> Diameter/⟨Radius⟩ ⟨*current*⟩: *(enter the desired radius at* P3*)*
> Command:

Figure 7-15.
Locating a circle center using X and Y point filters.

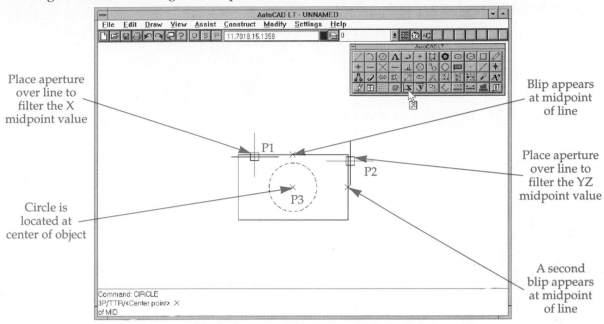

Place aperture over line to filter the X midpoint value

Circle is located at center of object

Blip appears at midpoint of line

Place aperture over line to filter the YZ midpoint value

A second blip appears at midpoint of line

Using X and Y point filters to project views and view features

Consider the drawing illustrated in Figure 7-16A. If you were drawing this object on a drafting board, you would probably draw the front view first. Then, using conventional drafting instruments, orthogonally project lines and points in the front view to complete the right side view. Point filters can be used to perform similar projection operations. The front view can be drawn very efficiently using the **RECTANG** command, and the circle constructed using X filters and Y filters as previously described. See Figure 7-16B. The command sequence to draw the side view is as follows:

> Command: *(type* RECTANG *or* RC *and press* [Enter]*)*
> First corner: **.Y** ↵
> of *(pick line* **ENDpoint** P1*)*
> of (need XZ): *(pick point* P2 *to set distance between the views)*
> Other corner: **@2,3** ↵
> Command:

Figure 7-16.
A—Orthographic views with projected features can be created using X and Y point filters.
B—Drawing a side view with X and Y point filters.

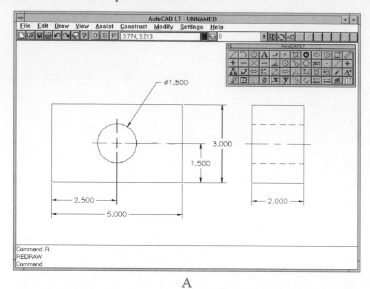

A

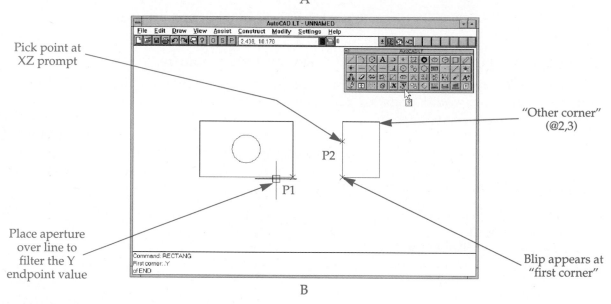

Pick point at
XZ prompt

"Other corner"
(@2,3)

Place aperture
over line to
filter the Y
endpoint value

Blip appears at
"first corner"

B

The rectangle that represents the side view is now complete. Because its lower left corner is located by filtering the Y value of the front view's lower right corner, it is aligned orthogonally with that view.

It is also a simple matter to draw the hidden lines which represent the circle seen in the side view. This operation is performed using both **QUAdrant** and **PERpendicular** object snap modes. See Figure 7-17. The command sequence is as follows:

Command: *(type* LINE *or* L *and press* [Enter]*)*
From point: **.Y** ↵
of *(pick* **QUAdrant** *point* P1 *on circle)*
of (need XZ): *(pick* **PERpendicular** *point* P2 *anywhere on line)*
To point: *(draw to* **PERpendicular** *point* P3 *on opposite line)*
To point: *(press* [Enter] *or space bar to exit the command)*
Command:

Now that one of the hidden lines is drawn, repeat the procedure to draw the second hidden line.

AutoCAD LT—Fundamentals and Applications

Figure 7-17.
Projecting a line using X and Y point filters.

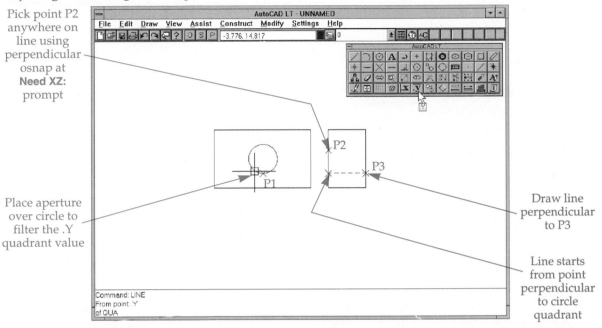

Pick point P2 anywhere on line using perpendicular osnap at **Need XZ:** prompt

Place aperture over circle to filter the .Y quadrant value

Draw line perpendicular to P3

Line starts from point perpendicular to circle quadrant

EXERCISE 7-2

❑ Begin a new drawing with your PROTOA prototype drawing, or use your own setup variables.
❑ Turn off the grid and snap if they are on.
❑ Draw the front view of the object shown in Figure 7-15 and locate the circle center using the X and Y point filter technique discussed in this chapter.
❑ Construct the top view (not the side view) of the object using the appropriate running object snap modes and X and Y filters. For the top view, which coordinate values are filtered—X or Y?
❑ Save the drawing as EX7-2 and quit.

USING THE @ SYMBOL AS A CONSTRUCTION REFERENCE POINT

From Chapter 3 you learned that the AutoCAD LT **LASTPOINT** system variable stores the X, Y, and Z coordinates of the last point entered from the keyboard, or selected on screen. You will recall that it is the @ symbol that retrieves the **LASTPOINT** coordinates when entering relative coordinates.

Consider the simple object illustrated in Figure 7-18A. Suppose, for example, that you were the drafter who had originally drawn this object. Six months later, a drawing change is required to add the two holes shown in Figure 7-18B. There is a very simple method to locate the required holes at the dimensions shown. This method requires object snap modes and the use of the **ID** command. The **ID** command is one of the standard AutoCAD LT inquiry commands which are covered in detail in Chapter 8. Essentially, the **ID** command displays the X,Y,Z coordinates of a designated point in the graphics window. The coordinate values returned by the **ID** command are then stored in the **LASTPOINT** system variable, and are therefore accessible using the @ symbol. To locate the 1.250 diameter circle at the dimensions shown in Figure 7-18A, use the following command sequence:

Command: **ID** ↵
Point: *(pick the* **MIDpoint** *of the top line)*

Figure 7-18.
A—Object as originally drawn. B—A Drawing Change Notice requires the addition of two holes.

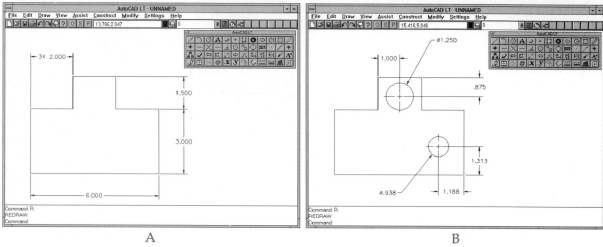

A   B

A blip appears at the midpoint of the top line. See Figure 7-19A. The screen coordinates of the line midpoint are displayed on the prompt line and stored in the **LASTPOINT** variable. The required circle is now located relative to that point.

Command: *(type* CIRCLE *or* C *and press* [Enter])
3P/TTR/⟨Center point⟩: **@.875⟨270** ↵
Diameter/⟨Radius⟩ ⟨*current*⟩: **.625** ↵
Command:

The .938 diameter circle at the lower-right of the object is located in a similar fashion. For this operation, the **ENDpoint** object snap mode is used. See Figure 7-19B. The command sequence is as follows:

Command: **ID** ↵
Point: *(pick the right* **ENDpoint** *of the bottom line)*

A blip appears at the endpoint of the bottom line. The screen coordinates of the line endpoint are displayed on the prompt line and stored in the **LASTPOINT** variable. The required circle is then located relative to that point.

Command: *(type* CIRCLE *or* C *and press* [Enter])
3P/TTR/⟨Center point⟩: **@−1.1875,1.3125** ↵
Diameter/⟨Radius⟩ ⟨*current*⟩: **.46875** ↵
Command:

Figure 7-19.
A—Using **ID** and **MIDpoint** osnap to locate the top hole. B—Using **ID** and **ENDpoint** osnap to locate the hole at bottom right.

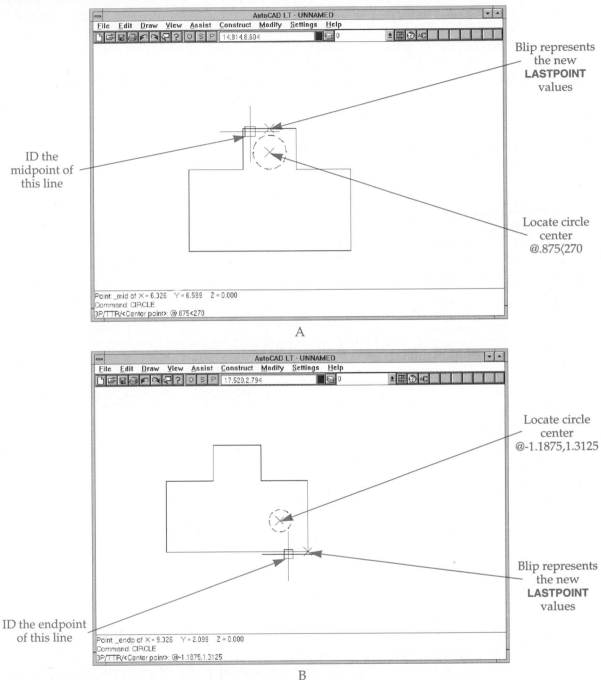

EXERCISE 7-3

❑ Begin a new drawing with your PROTOA prototype drawing, or use your own setup variables.
❑ Using any dimensions you'd like, draw the object shown in Figure 7-18A.
❑ Add the two circles shown in Figure 7-18B using the **ID** command and the method just described.
❑ Save the drawing as EX7-3 and quit.

Chapter 7 Geometry Construction Techniques

Tracking is a feature unique to AutoCAD LT. Like point filters, you can use tracking to specify a point relative to existing points. However, unlike point filters, tracking is limited to X and Y values and cannot be used for 3D constructions. This is because tracking is always performed orthogonally, or parallel to the snap axes. If you rotate the snap axes using the **SNAP** command's **Rotate** option, you also rotate the tracking axes.

As with osnaps and point filters, tracking works only when AutoCAD LT prompts for a point. If you try to use tracking at the **Command:** prompt, you will receive an error message. To use tracking, click the **Tracking** button in the toolbox, or select **Tracking** from the **Cursor Menu**. At the **Command:** prompt, enter TRACKING, or TK, or TRA. Consider the object shown in Figure 7-20. Tracking can be used to locate a circle at the center of the object using the following procedure:

Command: *(type* CIRCLE *or* C *and press* [Enter]*)*
3P/TTR/⟨Center point⟩: *(type* TRACKING, TK, *or* TRA *and press* [Enter]*)*
First tracking point: **MID** ↵
of *(pick the* **MIDpoint** P1 *of the top horizontal line)*

Figure 7-20.
Locating a circle center using tracking.

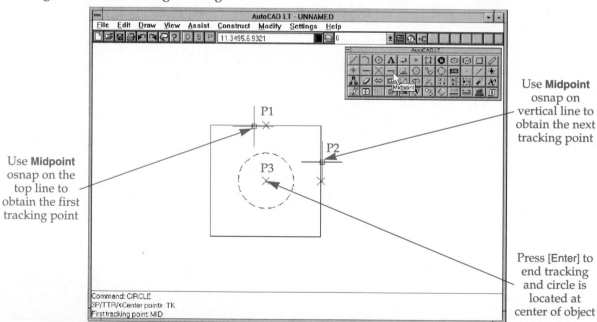

Use **Midpoint** osnap on the top line to obtain the first tracking point

Use **Midpoint** osnap on vertical line to obtain the next tracking point

Press [Enter] to end tracking and circle is located at center of object

Now, move your cursor up and down until you see the rubber-band line. When the rubber-band line appears, you are ready to continue.

Next point (Press RETURN to end tracking): **MID** ↵
of *(pick the* **MIDpoint** P2 *of the right vertical line)*
Next point (Press RETURN to end tracking): ↵
Diameter/⟨Radius⟩ ⟨*current*⟩: *(enter the desired radius at* P3*)*
Command:

When you use tracking, it is very important to move your cursor directly up, down, left, or right until you see the rubber-band line. This is because the direction of your cursor movement affects the tracking direction. If you fail to move your cursor as required, it is likely that tracking will not work properly.

Using tracking to project view features

Tracking can also be used to project views and view features. In Figure 7-21, tracking is used to project hidden lines that represent the circle in the top view. Study Figure 7-21 as you follow the sequence of steps below:

Command: *(type* LINE *or* L *and press* [Enter]*)*
From point: *(type* TRACKING, TK, *or* TRA *and press* [Enter]*)*
First tracking point: **QUA** ↵
of *(pick* **QUAdrant** *point* P1 *on the circle)*

Figure 7-21.
Projecting a line using tracking.

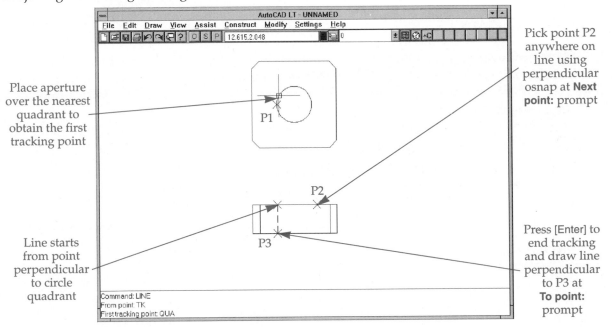

Place aperture over the nearest quadrant to obtain the first tracking point

Line starts from point perpendicular to circle quadrant

Pick point P2 anywhere on line using perpendicular osnap at **Next point:** prompt

Press [Enter] to end tracking and draw line perpendicular to P3 at **To point:** prompt

Now, move your cursor up and down until you see the rubber-band line. When the rubber-band line appears, you may continue.

Next point (Press RETURN to end tracking): **PER** ↵
to *(pick* **PERpendicular** *point* P2 *anywhere on the top line)*
Next point (Press RETURN to end tracking): ↵
To point: **PER** ↵
to *(draw to* **PERpendicular** *point* P3 *on the bottom line)*
To point: *(press* [Enter] *or space bar to exit the command)*
Command:

Do you see how tracking can also be used to project the edges of the top view chamfers to the bottom view?

PROFESSIONAL TIP

You can greatly increase your productivity when you use object snap modes in conjunction with tracking by setting the required object snap modes to be running osnaps.

CREATING POINTS

ALTUG 6

Have you ever seen a connect-the-numbered-dots game that draws a picture? You can think of the point objects created with the **POINT** command much the same way as the numbered dots. Because points can be snapped to using the **NODE** object snap mode, points can be useful construction aids.

You can draw a point by clicking the **Point** button in the toolbox, or selecting **Point** from the **Draw** pull-down menu. See Figure 7-22. The command sequence is as follows:

Command: *(type* POINT *or* PT *and press* [Enter]*)*
Point: *(pick a screen location or enter a coordinate)*

Figure 7-22.
Selecting **Point** from the **Draw** pull-down menu.

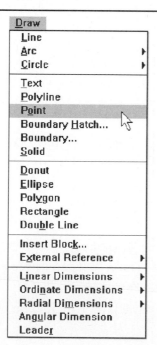

Setting the point style and size in a dialog box

Point entities are available in a variety of styles. The default point style is a small dot. This makes the points difficult to see, especially if the points are located on top of another entity. To change the point style using a dialog box, select **Point Style...** from the **Settings** pull-down menu. See Figure 7-23. The command sequence is follows:

Command: *(type* DDPTYPE *or* 'DDPTYPE *and press* [Enter]*)*

Figure 7-23.
Selecting **Point Style...** from the **Settings** pull-down menu issues the **DDPTYPE** command.

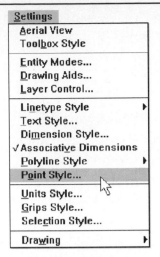

This action displays the **Point Style** dialog box shown in Figure 7-24. Each of the available point styles are displayed as image tiles. The default point style, a small dot, is shown at the upper left of the dialog box. To change your point style, simply click the image tile that represents the point style you wish to use and then click the **OK** button. As shown in the illustration, the point style that looks like an "X" has been selected. The other items in this dialog box are described as follows:

- **Point Size: text box.** Use this text box to increase or decrease the size of your points. By default, the size of points is set as a percentage of the screen size.
- **Set Size Relative to Screen.** This is the default point sizing method in AutoCAD LT. The points are sized relative to the screen based on the percentage set in the **Point Size:** text box. Using this method, point sizes do not change as you zoom the display in and out.
- **Set Size in Absolute Units.** Click this option button when you want your points to have an absolute size. Enter the absolute size value in the **Point Size:** text box. With this method, points get larger and smaller as you zoom the display in and out.

Figure 7-24.
The **Point Style** dialog box.

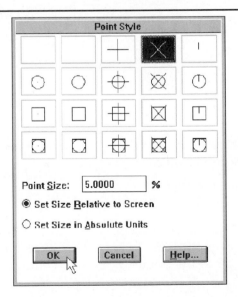

NOTE	Changes made to a point style or size do not take effect until the next screen regeneration.

The PDMODE and PDSIZE variables

If you prefer, you can set the point style from the command line using the **PDMODE**, or point display mode, system variable:

Command: **PDMODE** ↵
New value for PDMODE ⟨*current*⟩: *(enter one of the values from Figure 7-25)*

As shown in Figure 7-25, each of the AutoCAD LT points has an identifying value. **PDMODE** values 0, 2, 3, and 4 select a figure to draw for the point. Setting **PDMODE** to 1 selects nothing to be displayed. Adding 32, 64, or 96 to the values on the top line selects a circle, a square, or both to draw around the point figure.

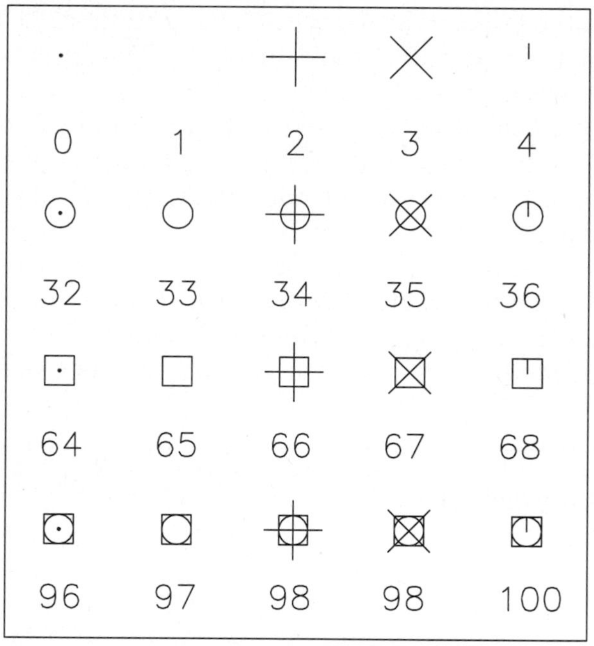

Figure 7-25.
The available point styles and their corresponding **PDMODE** values.

.		+	×	ı
0	1	2	3	4
⊙	○	⊕	⊗	◔
32	33	34	35	36
⊡	□	⊞	⊠	⊡
64	65	66	67	68
⊡	◻	⊕	⊠	◻
96	97	98	98	100

The point size can also be set at the **Command:** prompt using the **PDSIZE**, or point display size, system variable.

Command: **PDSIZE** ↵
New value for PDSIZE ⟨*current*⟩:

When **PDSIZE** is set to zero, a point is created at 5% of the viewport size. This is the default setting for **PDSIZE**. To specify an absolute point size, enter a positive value. A negative value specifies the point size as a percentage of the viewport size.

THE DIVIDE COMMAND

ALTUG 7

The **DIVIDE** command places point entities along an object to divide it into a number of user-specified segments. It is important to note that **DIVIDE** does not actually break an entity into individual objects. Instead, it uses points to identify the locations of the divisions. Because points are used, be sure to change the point style as previously described so that the points are visible. To divide an entity, select **Divide** from the **Construct** pull-down menu. See Figure 7-26. The command sequence is as follows:

Command: **DIVIDE** ↵
Select object to divide: *(select the entity to divide)*
⟨Number of segments⟩/Block: *(enter a number between 2 and 32767)*

Figure 7-26.
Selecting **Divide** from the **Construct** pull-down menu.

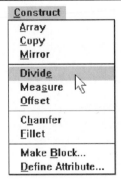

In the examples shown in Figure 7-27, a line has been divided into 5 equal segments and a circle into 12 equal segments. For a circle, the first dividing point is normally on its circumference just to the right of the circle center (0°). If the snap rotation angle is set to 180°, for example, the first dividing point starts to the left of center. You can see that **PDMODE** has been set appropriately so that the points are visible.

The **DIVIDE** command also provides you with the **Block** option to divide a selected entity with a block. You may recall that a block is one or more AutoCAD LT entities grouped together to form a single object. Blocks are an extremely handy way to create special symbols intended for multiple use. See Chapter 14 of this text for complete information about these powerful objects.

NOTE

Although the Divide tool button shown in the margin does not normally appear in the toolbox or toolbar, it can easily be added. See Chapter 19 of this text.

Figure 7-27.
A line and a circle divided into equal segments with the **DIVIDE** command.

Point entities ——

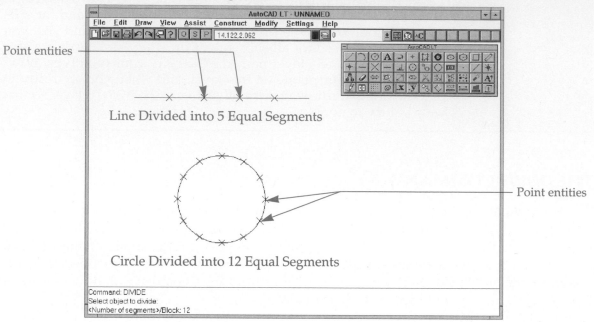

Line Divided into 5 Equal Segments

Circle Divided into 12 Equal Segments

—— Point entities

THE MEASURE COMMAND

The **MEASURE** command can be used to place point entities at specified length intervals along a selected object. As with the **DIVIDE** command, be sure to change the point style as previously described so that the points are visible. Also like **DIVIDE**, the **MEASURE** command does not actually break an entity into individual objects but uses points to identify the ending point of each segment. To measure an entity, select **Measure** from the **Construct** pulldown menu. See Figure 7-28. The command sequence is as follows:

Command: **MEASURE** ↵
Select object to measure: *(select the entity to measure)*
⟨Segment length⟩/Block: *(enter a positive value)*

Figure 7-28.
Selecting **Measure** from the **Construct** pull-down menu.

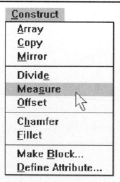

In the examples shown in Figure 7-29, points are placed every .625 units along the length of the line entity. Note the location of the pick point on the line. Measurement is started at the endpoint closest to the pick point. You can see from the illustration that there may occasionally be an unequal, or short, segment remaining at the end of the line.

Figure 7-29.
The **MEASURE** command places point markers at specified length segments on a line and a circle.

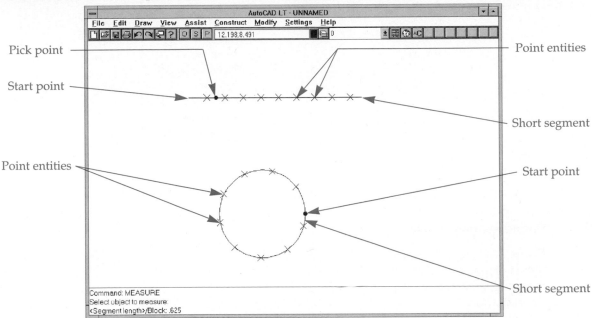

Pick point

Start point

Point entities

Point entities

Short segment

Start point

Short segment

For a circle, measurement normally starts on its circumference just to the right of the circle center (0°). If the snap rotation angle is set to 90°, for example, the measurement starts at the top of the circle.

As with the **DIVIDE** command, you may also select the **Block** option to measure an entity with a block. See Chapter 14 for more information about dividing and measuring entities with blocks.

NOTE

Although the **Measure** tool button shown in the margin does not normally appear in the toolbox or toolbar, it can easily be added. See Chapter 19 of this text.

THE **OFFSET** COMMAND

ALTUG 9

The **OFFSET** command creates a new object parallel to a selected entity. The new object can be offset at a specified distance or through a point. You can offset 2D polylines, ellipses, circles, arcs, and lines. Refer to figure used for Exercise 7-5. An offset entity retains the entity properties (color, layer, linetype) of the original object. To offset an entity, select **Offset** from the **Construct** pull-down menu. See Figure 7-30.

NOTE

Although the **Offset** tool button shown in the margin does not normally appear in the toolbox or toolbar, it can easily be added. See Chapter 19 of this text.

Figure 7-30.
Selecting **Offset** from the
Construct pull-down menu.

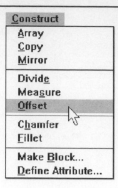

Offsetting through a point

You may offset an entity to pass through a selected point using the **OFFSET** command's **Through** option. Refer to the 4-sided polygon shown at the top of Figure 7-31 as you follow the command sequence below:

> Command: *(type* OFFSET *or* OF *and press* [Enter]*)*
> Offset distance or Through ⟨*current*⟩: **T** ⏎
> Select object to offset: *(pick the polygon)*
> Through point: *(locate a point outside the polygon)*
> Select object to offset: *(pick another entity or press* [Enter] *to end)*

In this example, a point is selected outside the perimeter of the object producing in a larger polygon. Selecting a point inside the polygon would result in a smaller polygon. This same convention applies to arcs, circles, and ellipses.

Finally, keep in mind that when prompted **Through point:**, you can enter a coordinate or osnap to an existing entity to locate the offset through point.

Figure 7-31.
An entity can be offset at a specified distance or through a point.

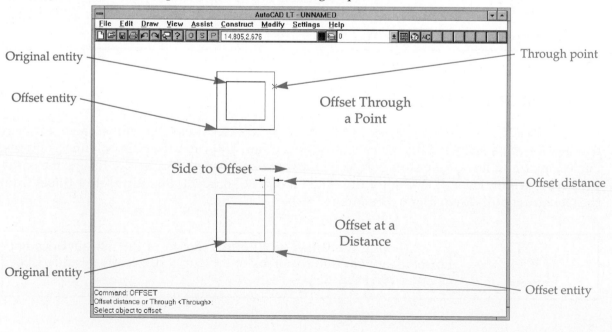

AutoCAD LT—Fundamentals and Applications

Offsetting at a distance

It is also possible to create an entity at a specified distance from an existing object. Of the two offset methods, this second approach is probably the most commonly used. Refer now to the 4-sided polygon shown at the bottom of Figure 7-31 as you follow the command sequence below:

> Command: *(type* OFFSET *or* OF *and press* [Enter]*)*
> Offset distance or Through ⟨Through⟩: *(enter a positive distance)*
> Select object to offset: *(pick the polygon)*
> Side to offset? *(pick a point to indicate the desired side)*
> Select object to offset: *(pick another entity or press* [Enter] *to end)*

As with the **Through** option, picking a point outside the perimeter of an object offsets to the outside. Picking a point on the inside of an object's perimeter offsets to the inside.

EXERCISE 7-5

❑ Begin a new drawing with your PROTOA prototype drawing, or use your own setup variables.
❑ Make a drawing similar to that shown here. Be sure to include one polyline, ellipse, circle, arc, and line.

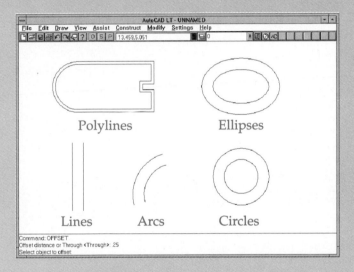

❑ Offset each entity using the **OFFSET** command. Try offsetting with specified distances as well as through selected points.
❑ Now create a new layer named POINTS. Assign to it the color of your choice and set it current.
❑ Set **PDMODE** equal to 3 and use the **DIVIDE** and **MEASURE** commands on several of your objects.
❑ Now set **PDMODE** equal to 2 and regenerate the drawing. Observe the difference in the point display.
❑ Experiment with other **PDMODE** and **PDSIZE** values. Use Figure 7-25 as a reference. Be sure to force a regeneration after each change.
❑ When you are through experimenting, save the drawing as EX7-5 and quit.

AUXILIARY VIEWS

There may be occasions when the object you are drawing has one or more slanted surfaces. In these instances, an auxiliary view is required to show the true shape and size of the surfaces that are not parallel to the six principal views of orthographic projection. AutoCAD LT provides two different methods to help you construct an auxiliary view. The first method requires you to rotate the snap and grid; the second method involves the creation of a new coordinate system. Both methods are described in the following sections. Before you begin the auxiliary view, however, first draw the principal front, top, and side views as required using point filters and/or tracking to project drawing features between the views.

Using the SNAP Rotate option to create an auxiliary view

ALTUG 7

In Chapter 2 you learned that the **SNAP** command provides the option to rotate the snap axes around a specified point and at an angle. When you set the snap angle, the grid angle also changes. This method can be useful when constructing an auxiliary view. You can set the snap angle by clicking the **Drawing Aids** button in the toolbox or selecting **Drawing Aids...** from the **Settings** pull-down menu. See Figure 7-32.

Figure 7-32.
Selecting **Drawing Aids...**
from the **Settings** pull-down menu.

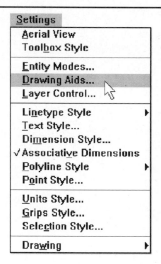

This action displays the **Drawing Aids** dialog box illustrated in Figure 7-33. In the example shown, the snap rotation angle is set to 60° in the **Snap Angle** text box. Normally, the snap is rotated around the 0,0 drawing origin. If you would like to rotate the snap around a different point, enter the desired X and Y coordinates in the **X Base** and **Y Base** text boxes, respectively. Remember that you can also use this dialog box to set your grid spacing and turn on the grid. Once you have made the necessary changes, click the **OK** button to exit the **Drawing Aids** dialog box.

Figure 7-33.
Setting the snap angle in the **Drawing Aids** dialog box.

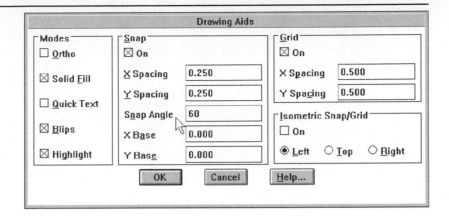

An example of an auxiliary view with the snap and grid rotated at 60° is shown in Figure 7-34. Observe that the screen crosshair cursor is realigned to match the new snap angle. As a further aid in the construction of your auxiliary view, be sure to turn **Ortho** is on. When **Snap** and **Ortho** are both on, the cursor movement is constrained to the new rotation alignment.

Figure 7-34.
Using a rotated snap and grid to construct an auxiliary view. Note the orientation of the crosshair cursor

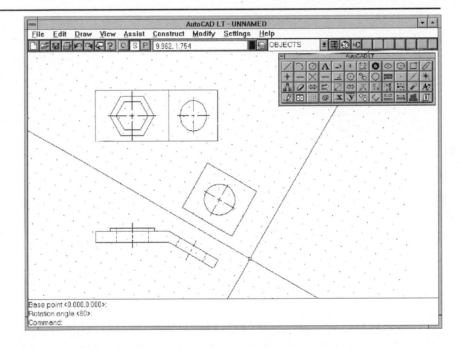

If you prefer to set the snap angle at the **Command:** prompt, do the following:

Command: *(type* SNAP *or* SN *and press* [Enter]*)*
Snap spacing or ON/OFF/Aspect/Rotate/Style ⟨*current*⟩: **R** ↵
Base point ⟨0.0000,0.0000⟩: *(pick a point or accept the default)*
Rotation angle ⟨0⟩: **60** ↵
Command:

Remember to set the snap rotation angle back to 0° when you are finished drawing the auxiliary view.

Chapter 7 Geometry Construction Techniques

Using a UCS to define an auxiliary view

In Chapter 3 you learned that the Cartesian coordinate system used by AutoCAD LT is fixed in 3D space and may not be moved or altered. AutoCAD LT refers to it as the *World Coordinate System*, or *WCS*. A better way to construct an auxiliary view is by creating your own *User Coordinate System*, or *UCS*. With the UCS, you can redefine the location of 0,0 and the direction of the XYZ axes. Using this method, the whole system is rotated and not just the snap axes. This greatly simplifies detailing and dimensioning operations in the auxiliary view.

Before you create a UCS, it is a good idea to turn on the UCS icon. The UCS icon is a small graphical marker at the lower left of the screen that displays the origin and the viewing plane of the current UCS in model space. The icon is shown at the lower left in Figure 7-35.

Figure 7-35.
The UCS icon appears at the lower left of the drawing.

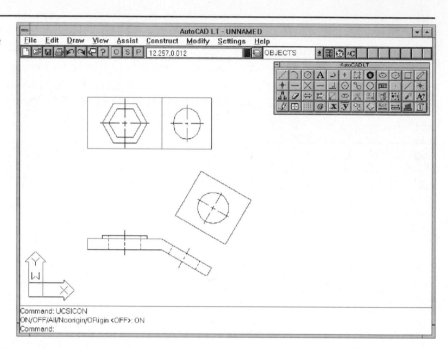

Turning on the UCS icon

ALTUG 5

In its default representation, the X, Y, and Z axes of the UCS icon are positioned 90° relative to one another, with the Z axis perpendicular to the XY plane and along the line of sight. You will notice a box drawn at the vertices of the X and Y axes. The box indicates that the viewpoint is from the positive Z direction. Therefore, the viewing angle is from a position above the XY plane looking down. Note also the small W just above the box. The W indicates that the World Coordinate System is active.

You can turn the UCS icon on and off using the **UCSICON** command. The **UCSICON** command can be issued by selecting **UCS Icon** from the **Assist** pull-down menu. The command sequence is as follows:

> Command: (*type* UCSICON *or* UI *and press* [Enter])
> ON/OFF/All/Noorigin/ORigin ⟨OFF⟩: **ON** ↵

Since it is very helpful to display the UCS icon at the origin of the current UCS, repeat the **UCSICON** command and use the **ORigin** option.

> Command: (*type* UCSICON *or* UI *and press* [Enter])
> ON/OFF/All/Noorigin/ORigin ⟨OFF⟩: **OR** ↵

The other options of the **UCSICON** command will be covered in Chapter 18 of this text.

Creating a UCS

Now that the UCS icon is turned on, it is time to create a UCS that represents the orientation of the auxiliary view under construction. You can issue the **UCS** command at the **Command:** prompt, or select **Set UCS** from the **Assist** pull-down menu. Each of the **UCS** command options are then displayed in a cascading submenu. Use the following procedure to locate the UCS origin at a point that coincides with a corner of the auxiliary view.

> Command: **UCS** ↵
> Origin/ZAxis/3point/Entity/View/X/Y/Z/Prev/Restore/Save/Del/?/⟨World⟩: **O** ↵
> Origin point ⟨0,0,0⟩: *(pick a point at the desired corner of the auxiliary view)*

From the example shown in Figure 7-36, the UCS icon displays at the point that was selected for the origin of the new UCS. Observe the plus symbol (+) that appears in the middle of the box at the X and Y vertices. This indicates that the icon origin and the UCS origin are identical.

Figure 7-36.
A plus symbol (+) appears at the vertices of the X and Y axes in the UCS icon. This indicates that the icon is at the origin of the current UCS.

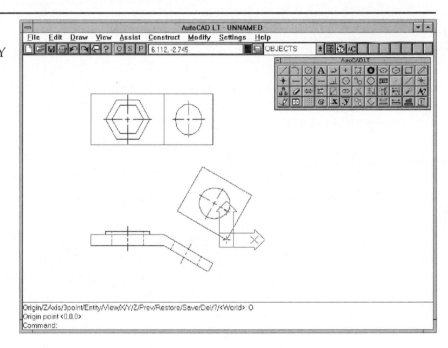

In this example, the auxiliary view is projected 60° from the slanted surface in the front view. It is now necessary to rotate the UCS about the Z axis to match the orientation of the auxiliary view:

> Command: **UCS** ↵
> Origin/ZAxis/3point/Entity/View/X/Y/Z/Prev/Restore/Save/Del/?/⟨World⟩: **Z** ↵
> Rotation angle about Z axis ⟨0⟩: **60** ↵

The UCS is now at the correct orientation as shown in Figure 7-37. Before continuing, it is a good idea to use the **Save** option to save the new UCS with a descriptive name. Should you need to return to the auxiliary view for further construction or modification, it is faster to restore the named UCS than to create a new one. A UCS name may contain up to 31 characters, but spaces are not permitted.

> Command: **UCS** ↵
> Origin/ZAxis/3point/Entity/View/X/Y/Z/Prev/Restore/Save/Del/?//⟨World⟩: **S** ↵
> ?/Desired UCS name: **AUXIL** ↵

If you decide at some point that you wish to change the name of the saved UCS, use the **DDRENAME** command to do so.

Chapter 7   Geometry Construction Techniques   *221*

Figure 7-37.
The UCS is rotated 60°
about the Z axis.

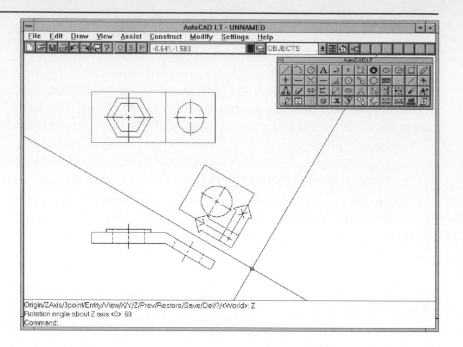

Now that the entire system matches the orientation of the auxiliary view, use point filters and/or tracking techniques as described in this chapter to project features between the auxiliary view and the slanted surface of the front view.

When you need to return to the World Coordinate System, issue the **UCS** command again and use the default **World** option as follows:

Command: **UCS** ↵
Origin/ZAxis/3point/Entity/View/X/Y/Z/Prev/Restore/Save/Del/?/⟨World⟩: ↵

You can also return to the WCS by selecting **Named UCS...** from the **Assist** pull-down menu. This action issues the **DDUCS** command and displays the **UCS Control** dialog box shown in Figure 7-38. You can use this dialog box to set a saved UCS current, return to a previous UCS or the WCS, rename an existing UCS, or delete a UCS when no longer needed. As with the **UCSICON** command, each of the other **UCS** command options will be covered in detail in Chapter 18 of this text.

Figure 7-38.
Selecting a saved **UCS** from
the **UCS Control** dialog box.

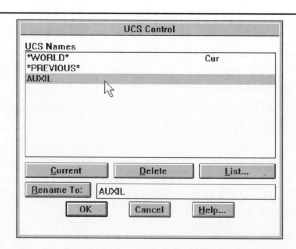

CHAPTER TEST

Write your answers in the spaces provided.

1. What is the name of the cursor target area when an osnap is used? _____

   _____

2. List three ways to access an object snap. _____

   _____

   _____

3. What is a running osnap?_____

   _____

4. Give the command and entries required to set **QUAdrant** and **PERpendicular** as the running osnaps.

   Command: _____

   Object snap modes: _____

5. List three ways to access the **Running Object Snap** dialog box. _____

   _____

   _____

6. Name the system variable that changes the size of the cursor target area. Can this system
   variable be used transparently? _____

   _____

   _____

7. How do you access the **Cursor Menu**? _____

   _____

   _____

8. Give the command and entries required to disable any running osnaps.

   Command: _____

   Object snap modes: _____

9. What is the purpose of point filters? _____

   _____

   _____

10. Identify four ways to access X and Y point filters._____

    _____

    _____

    _____

    _____

11. What must you do with your cursor when using tracking? Why? _____

_____

_____

_____

12. What is the purpose of the **PDMODE** variable? _____

_____

_____

_____

13. What is the purpose of the **PDSIZE** variable? Describe its use. _____

_____

_____

_____

14. A drawing can contain several types of points. (True/False) _____

15. Describe the difference between the **DIVIDE** and **MEASURE** commands. How are they similar? _____

_____

_____

_____

16. What should you do before you divide or measure an entity? _____

_____

_____

_____

17. What is the purpose of the **OFFSET** command? _____

_____

_____

_____

18. An offset object inherits the current system color, linetype, and layer. (True/False)

_____

19. What should be done before creating a UCS? _____

_____

_____

20. Why is is a good idea to save a UCS? _____

_____

_____

_____

1. Draw the object shown below using the correct layers in your PROTOA prototype drawing. Make your drawing proportional to that shown. Study the object carefully before beginning construction. Determine which AutoCAD LT entity types best describe the object and draw accordingly. Plan to use the **CENter**, **QUAdrant**, **ENDpoint**, **MIDpoint**, **INTersection**, and **TANgent** object snap modes as required. Save the drawing as P7-1.

General

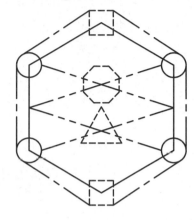

2. Construct the two views of the BEARING CAP using the point filtering and/or tracking techniques described in this chapter. Use your PROTOB prototype drawing and create the entities on the proper layers. Study the drawing carefully to determine if the **OFFSET** command can be used. Do not draw the dimensions. Save the drawing as P7-2.

Mechanical Drafting

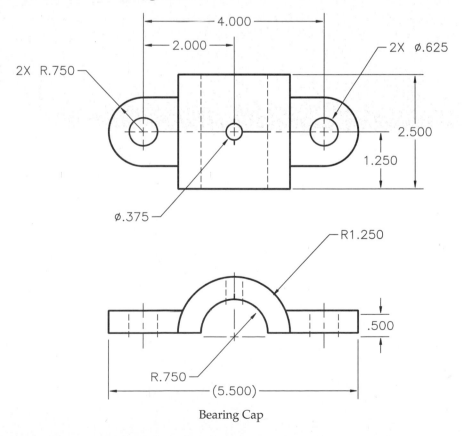

Bearing Cap

3. Use your PROTOB prototype drawing to draw the CAM BRACKET. As with P7-2, project views and features using point filters and/or tracking, and use the **OFFSET** command where appropriate. Do not draw the dimensions. Save the drawing as P7-3.

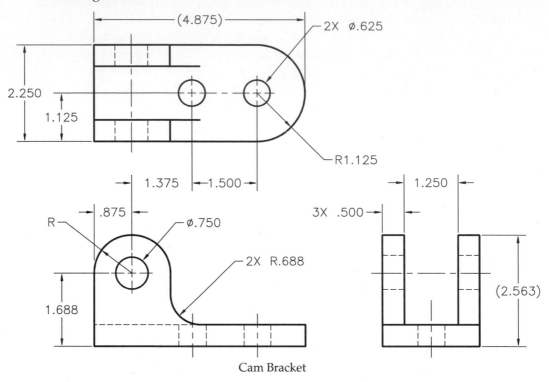

Cam Bracket

4. Use your PROTOA prototype drawing to draw the object shown. Create the auxiliary view as described in this chapter. Use point filters and/or tracking to project the counterbored feature between the auxiliary view and the slanted surface of the front view. Do not draw the dimension. Save the drawing as P7-4.

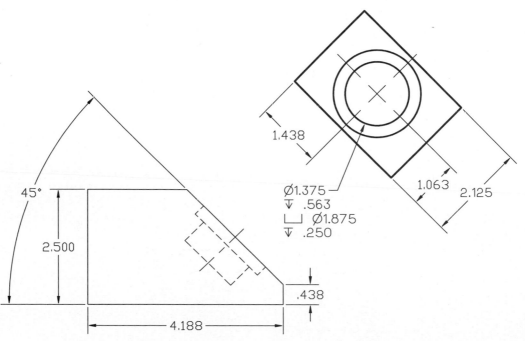

AutoCAD LT—Fundamentals and Applications

Chapter 8

Inquiry
Commands

AutoCAD LT

Learning objectives:

After you have completed this chapter, you will be able to:
- ❍ Display the XYZ coordinates of a selected point.
- ❍ Find the true 3D distance between two points.
- ❍ Obtain the angle between two points.
- ❍ Explain the purpose of the **LUPREC** and **AUPREC** system variables.
- ❍ Calculate the area and perimeter of an object or shape.
- ❍ List the database information for selected entities.
- ❍ Display the date and time statistics of a drawing.
- ❍ Use the Microsoft Windows Control Panel to set your computer's clock and date.

The AutoCAD LT inquiry commands display useful information about the entities in your drawings. Their proper use will enable you to verify the accuracy and correctness of your designs. The commands are the **ID**, **DIST**, **AREA**, **LIST**, and **TIME** commands. Each of them is located in the **Assist** pull-down menu and described in this chapter.

THE ID COMMAND

ALTUG 7

The **ID** command displays the XYZ coordinates of a screen location or selected point in the **Command:** prompt area. In Chapter 7 you learned that the coordinate values returned by the **ID** command are stored in the **LASTPOINT** system variable and accessed using the @ symbol. To access the **ID** command, type ID at the **Command:** prompt, click the **ID** button in the toolbox, or select **ID Point** from the **Assist** pull-down menu. See Figure 8-1. The command sequence is as follows:

> Command: **ID** ↵
> Point: *(pick a point)*

Figure 8-1.
Select **ID Point** from the
Assist pull-down menu to
issue the **ID** command.

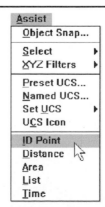

If the point selected is in an empty portion of the graphics window, **ID** displays the XY location and the Z coordinates of the current elevation. Elevation is the Z value above or below the XY plane. The current screen elevation is used whenever a 3D point is requested. By default, elevation is set to 0 (zero). However, if you use an osnap to snap to an object, then **ID** displays the Z coordinate of the selected point on the entity and not the current elevation. For 2D constructions, a point on an entity and the current elevation will have identical Z values.

EXERCISE 8-1

❏ Begin a new drawing with your PROTOA prototype drawing, or use your own setup variables.
❏ Draw the object shown below with the center of the object located at 5, 4.5. As a construction hint, start with a 4-sided polygon and then draw the circles. Be sure to enter all decimal values in full. If necessary, refer to the decimal/fractional equivalency chart in the appendices at the rear of this text.

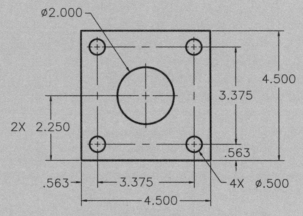

❏ Save the drawing as EX8-1, but do not exit AutoCAD LT. This drawing is to be used for several more exercises in this chapter.

THE **DIST** (Distance) COMMAND   ALTUG 7

The **DIST** command is used to calculate the distance and angle between two points. To access the **DIST** command type DIST or DI at the **Command:** prompt, click the **Distance** button in the toolbox, or select **Distance** from the **Assist** pull-down menu. See Figure 8-2. The command sequence is as follows:

Command: *(type DIST or DI and press [Enter])*
First point: *(pick a point)* Second point: *(pick a second point)*

Figure 8-2.
Select **Distance** from the
Assist pull-down menu to
issue the **DIST** command.

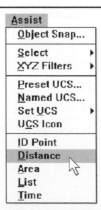

To obtain the highest degree of accuracy, be sure to use an osnap when selecting points. **DIST** reports the true 3D distance between the two points. See Figure 8-3. The angle in the XY plane is measured relative to the current X axis. The angle from the XY plane is returned for 3D points and is measured relative to the current XY plane. The distance and angle values reported by **DIST** are displayed using the current units format. Delta values are displayed to report the change in XYZ coordinates between the two selected points.

Figure 8-3.
The **DIST** command reports the distance and angle between two points on the command line.

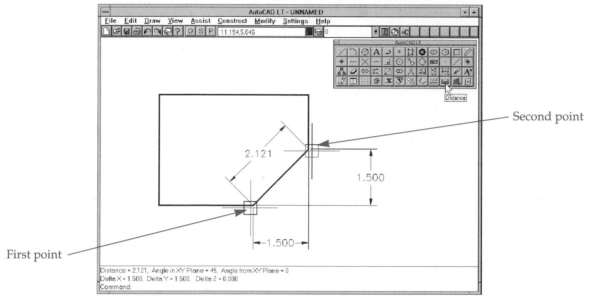

The LUPREC and AUPREC system variables

If you use decimal values in your work, it is helpful to increase the number of displayed decimal places when using the inquiry commands. This provides the greatest degree of accuracy for calculations. **LUPREC** (linear units precision) is an AutoCAD LT system variable that stores the linear units decimal places. The valid range for **LUPREC** is 0 through 8, with 4 as the default. This value is stored in the drawing and is used for all displayed decimal values including dimensions and tolerances. Use **LUPREC** at the **Command:** prompt as follows:

> Command: **LUPREC** ↵
> New value for LUPREC ⟨4⟩: *(enter a new value and press* [Enter]*)*

AUPREC (angular units precision) is another AutoCAD LT system variable that stores the angular units decimal places. The valid range for **AUPREC** is 0 through 8, with 0 as the default. As with **LUPREC**, this value is also stored in the drawing and is used for all displayed decimal values including dimensions and tolerances. Use **AUPREC** at the **Command:** prompt as follows:

> Command: **AUPREC** ↵
> New value for AUPREC ⟨0⟩: *(enter a new value and press* [Enter]*)*

The **LUPREC** and **AUPREC** system variables are a convenient way to set the system decimal places without issuing the **DDUNITS** command.

EXERCISE 8-2

❑ Open EX8-1 if it is not on your screen.
❑ Set the **LUPREC** system variable to 6 and **AUPREC** to 4.
❑ Use the **DIST** and **ID** commands to calculate the following:
Distance between circle centers A & B: _____
Angle between circle centers A & B: _____
Distance between points C & D: _____
Angle between points C & F: _____
ID of point E: _____
ID of point F: _____

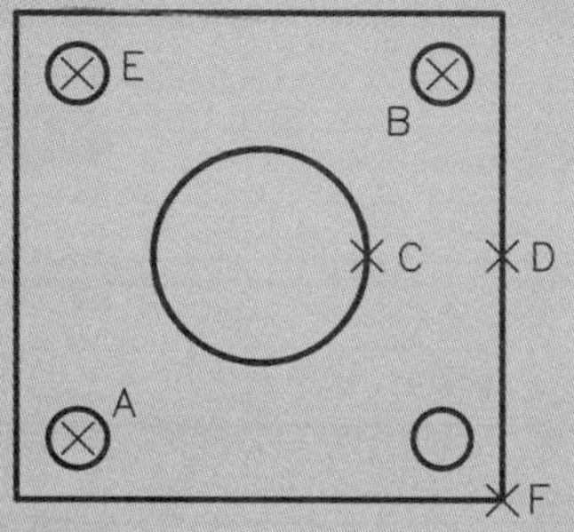

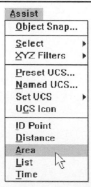

❑ When you are done, do not exit AutoCAD LT. This drawing is to be used for several more exercises in this chapter.

THE AREA COMMAND

ALTUG 7

The **AREA** command calculates the area and perimeter of objects or of defined areas. **AREA** is also used to combine the areas of two or more objects, as well as to subtract the area of an object from the area of another. To access the **AREA** command, type AREA or AA at the **Command:** prompt, click the **Area** button in the toolbox, or select **Area** from the **Assist** pull-down menu. See Figure 8-4. The command sequence is as follows:

Command: *(type AREA or AA and press [Enter])*
⟨First point⟩/Entity/Add/Subtract: *(select a point or enter an option)*

Each of the **AREA** command options are described below:
- ⟨**First point**⟩. This is the default method for area calculations. With **First point**, first set an endpoint (using **END**) or an intersection (using **INT**) running osnap and pick points at each vertex of an object. The area and perimeter of the shape enclosed by the points is reported. This method is illustrated in Figure 8-5. If a shape is not closed, the area is calculated as if a line were drawn from the last point selected to the first. That line length is automatically added to the perimeter calculation.

Figure 8-4.
Select **Area** from the **Assist** pull-down menu to issue the **AREA** command.

Figure 8-5.
With the **First point** option, each vertex of an object is selected using an appropriate osnap, such as **END**(endpoint) or **INT** (intersection).

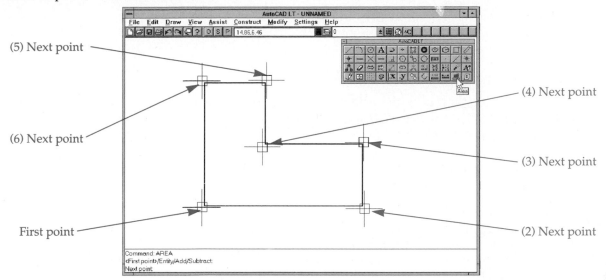

Therefore, the **First point** method reports the area between three or more points picked on the screen, even if the three points are not connected by lines. The **First point** option appears as follows:

> Command: *(type* AREA *or* AA *and press* [Enter]*)*
> ⟨First point⟩/Entity/Add/Subtract: *(pick a point)*
> Next point: *(pick a second point)*
> Next point: *(pick a third point)*
> Next point: *(pick a fourth point or press* [Enter] *to end)*
> Area = *nnnn*, Perimeter = *nnnn*

- **Entity.** The **Entity** option is used to find the area and perimeter of a selected object. This option is particularly handy because selecting every vertex of an object can be very time consuming. Additionally, this option allows you to easily calculate the area of shapes that contain fillets and rounds as long as the shape is drawn with a polyline and filleted with the **Polyline** option. If necessary, refer to Chapter 6 to review the **POLYLINE** and **FILLET** commands. You can use the **Entity** option on circles, ellipses, polygons, rectangles, polylines, and solids. A solid is a 2D fill pattern and is covered in Chapter 12 of this text. For a wide polyline, the area and perimeter (or length) calculations use the centerline of the object. If an open polyline is selected, the area is calculated as if a line were drawn from the last point selected to the first. However, unlike the **First point** option, the line length is not included in the perimeter (or length) calculation of the open polyline. The **Entity** option looks like this:

> Command: *(type* AREA *or* AA *and press* [Enter]*)*
> ⟨First point⟩/Entity/Add/Subtract: **E** ↵
> Select circle or polyline: *(select a circle or polyline)*
> Area = *nnnn*, Perimeter = *nnnn*

- **Add.** This mode allows you to pick additional points or select another object for area calculation. The additional area and perimeter is automatically added to calculate the total area of all selected objects. The **Add** mode stays in effect until you press [Enter] to end it.

> Command: *(type* AREA *or* AA *and press* [Enter]*)*
> ⟨First point⟩/Entity/Add/Subtract: **A** ↵
> ⟨First point⟩/Entity/Subtract:

- **Subtract.** This mode allows you to remove the area and perimeter of selected points or an object from the total area calculated. As with **Add**, the **Subtract** mode stays in effect until you press [Enter] to end it.

> Command: *(type* AREA *or* AA *and press* [Enter]*)*
> ⟨First point⟩/Entity/Add/Subtract: **S** ↵
> ⟨First point⟩/Entity/Add:

Adding and subtracting areas

To better understand how the **Add** and **Subtract** modes are used, refer to the object illustrated in Figure 8-6. This object is constructed with a rectangle and all four corners filleted with the **Polyline** option of the **FILLET** command. Remember that rectangles and polygons are polylines. Study the following command sequence to learn how to subtract the areas of the two circles from the filleted rectangle. Observe how the total area decreases as each circle is subtracted. Notice also that the **AREA** command reports the circumferences of the selected circles.

> Command: *(type* AREA *or* AA *and press* [Enter]*)*
> ⟨First point⟩/Entity/Add/Subtract: **A** ↵
> ⟨First point⟩/Entity/Subtract: **E** ↵
> (ADD mode) Select circle or polyline: *(pick the rectangle)*
> Area = 6.785, Perimeter = 10.142
> Total area = 6.785
> (ADD mode) Select circle or polyline: *(press* [Enter] *to exit* **ADD** *mode)*
> ⟨First point⟩/Entity/Subtract: **S** ↵
> ⟨First point⟩/Entity/Add: **E** ↵
> (SUBTRACT mode) Select circle or polyline: *(pick one of the circles)*
> Area = 0.196, Circumference = 1.571
> Total area = 6.589
> (SUBTRACT mode) Select circle or polyline: *(pick the other circle)*
> Area = 0.196, Circumference = 1.571
> Total area = 6.393
> (SUBTRACT mode) Select circle or polyline: *(press* [Enter] *to exit* **SUBTRACT** *mode)*
> ⟨First point⟩/Entity/Add: ↵
> Command:

Figure 8-6.
The **Add** and **Subtract** modes are both used to subtract the area of the two circles from the area of the filleted rectangle.

Add this entity ——

Subtract these entities ——

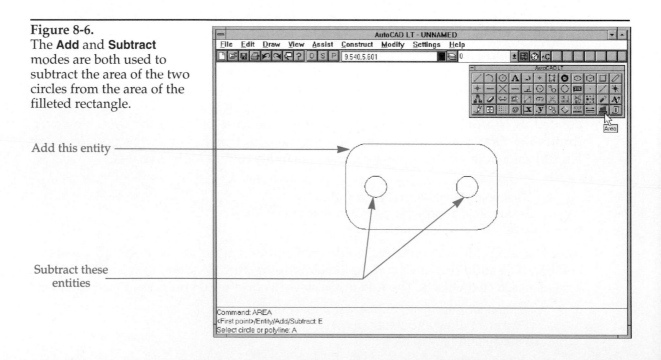

EXERCISE 8-3

❏ Open EX8-1 if it is not on your screen.
❏ Use the **AREA** command to calculate the following:

Area of Object 1 _____

Perimeter of Object 1 _____

Area of Object 2 _____

Circumference of Object 2_____

Area of Object 3 _____

Circumference of Object 3_____

Area of Object 1 minus the area of all circles _____

Total area of Objects 3, 4, 5, and 6 _____

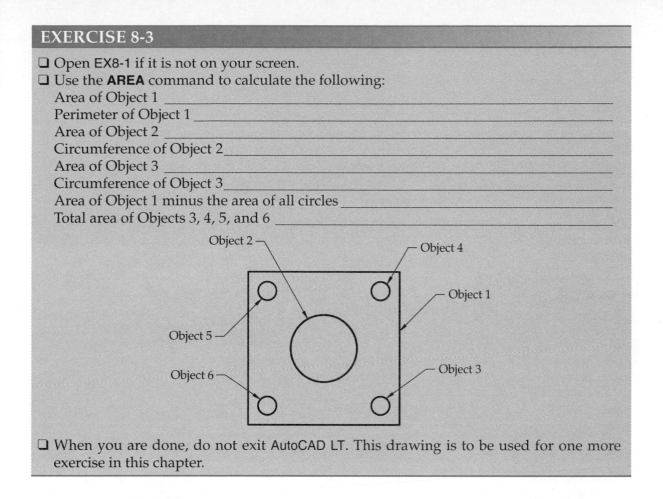

❏ When you are done, do not exit AutoCAD LT. This drawing is to be used for one more exercise in this chapter.

THE **LIST** COMMAND

ALTUG 7

The **LIST** command is particularly useful because it displays the complete database information for a selected entity. To access the **LIST** command, type LIST or LS, click the **List** button in the toolbox, or select **List** from the **Assist** pull-down menu. See Figure 8-7. The command sequence is as follows:

Command: *(type* LIST *or* LS *and press* [Enter]*)*
Select objects: *(select one or more entities)*

Figure 8-7.
Select **List** from the **Assist** pull-down menu to issue the **LIST** command.

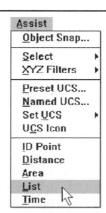

For each entity selected, AutoCAD LT lists its type, its layer, its XYZ position relative to the current UCS, and whether it was created in model space or paper space. If color and linetype are not set to **BYLAYER** mode, then color and linetype information is listed as well. Because so much information is reported by the **LIST** command, AutoCAD LT automatically flips the graphics window to the text window to display it all.

Consider the line and circle entities shown in Figure 8-8A. Both entities are selected for listing and the database information for each is displayed in the text window. See Figure 8-8B. You can see from the listing that both objects have a handle designation. A *handle* is a unique alphanumeric tag used to identity each entity in the drawing database.

Figure 8-8.
A—A line and a circle are selected for listing. B—The database information for the selected entities is displayed in the AutoCAD LT text window.

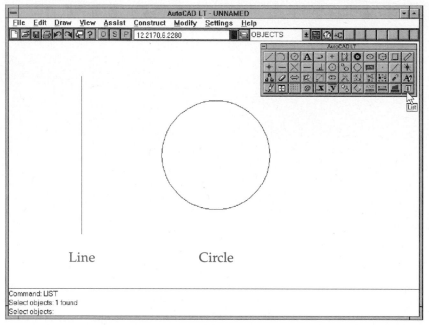

A

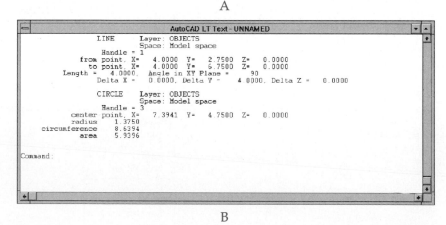

B

For 3D objects, the thickness of an entity is displayed if it is not zero. Like color, linetype, and layer, thickness is also a property of AutoCAD LT entities. It represents the distance that a 2D entity is extruded above or below its current screen elevation. Remember that the Z coordinate information reported by **LIST** represents the elevation. See Chapter 18 of this text for more information on thickness and elevation. Once you have obtained the list information that you need, press function key [F2] to flip back to the graphics window.

AutoCAD LT—Fundamentals and Applications

THE TIME COMMAND

The **TIME** command displays the date and time statistics of your drawing in the AutoCAD LT text window. It displays the current time to the nearest millisecond using a 24-hour clock. **TIME** also displays the date and time that the drawing was originally created, when it was last saved, and how much time has elapsed in the current drawing session. To access the **TIME** command, type TIME or TI at the **Command:** prompt, or select **Time** from the **Assist** pull-down menu. See Figure 8-9. The command sequence is as follows:

Command: *(type* TIME *or* TI *and press* [Enter]*)*

Figure 8-9.
Selecting **Time** from the **Assist** pull-down menu.

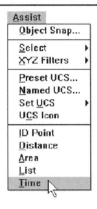

The graphics window automatically flips to the text window as **TIME** displays information similar to the following example:

Current time: 15 Aug 1996 at 01:27:19.520
Times for this drawing:
Created: 25 Jan 1996 at 17:10:00.648
Last updated: 22 March 1996 at 19:30:00.771
Total editing time: 0 days 01:44:10.520
Elapsed timer (on): 0 days 00:07:05.312
Next automatic save in: ⟨disabled⟩
Display/On/OFF/Reset: *(select an option or press* [Enter] *to end the command)*

Each of the **TIME** command options are described as follows:
- **Display.** Use this option to repeat the text window display with update times.
- **On/OFF.** Turns the elapsed timer on and off as desired. The timer is on by default.
- **Reset.** This option resets the elapsed timer to 0 days, 0 hours, 0 minutes, and 0 seconds.

If the **SAVETIME** system variable has been set to automatically save your drawing at specified time intervals, the time remaining until the next automatic save is also displayed. See Chapter 2 to review how to set the **SAVETIME** variable.

PROFESSIONAL TIP

If you are a consultant or contractor, use the **TIME** command to keep accurate time spent in a drawing. This will enable you to bill your clients accurately and fairly.

Setting your computer's date and time

If the current date and/or time reported by the **TIME** command is incorrect, they can be reset from the Windows Control Panel. The **Control Panel** provides you with a visual way of modifying your system while working with Microsoft Windows and is located in the Program Manager Main group window. See Figure 8-10.

Figure 8-10.
The Control Panel icon is located in the Program Manager Main group window.

As shown in Figure 8-11, each option that you can change is represented by an icon in the Control Panel window. Using the Date/Time option, you can change your computer's date and time. It is important that your system date and time are always accurate. Date and time changes are recognized by other Windows applications that use the system clock like the File Manager, Clock, and Calendar. File Manager functions are covered in Chapter 21 of this text.

Figure 8-11.
Options that can be changed are represented by icons in the Control Panel window.

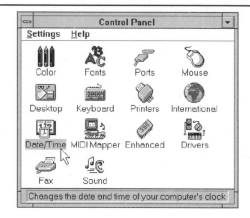

To change the system date and time, do the following:
1. Start Microsoft Windows.
2. Activate the Program Manager Main group window.
3. Double-click the Control Panel icon to activate the Control Panel window.
4. In the Control Panel window, double-click the Date/Time icon.
5. Select the part of the date or time you want to change, and then type a new value or click the up or down arrow to increase or decrease the number by one. See Figure 8-12.
6. Click the OK button and select Exit from the Settings pull-down menu in the Control Panel window.

Figure 8-12.
The system date and time may be easily changed in the Date & Time window.

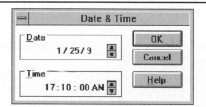

PROFESSIONAL TIP

You need not exit AutoCAD LT to return to Program Manager. Simply press [Ctrl]+[Esc] to activate the Windows Task List. Select Program Manager from the list and click the **Switch To** button. Now set the system date and time as described previously. When you are done, press [Alt]+[Tab] to immediately return to AutoCAD LT.

EXERCISE 8-4

❑ Open EX8-1 if it is not on your screen.
❑ Use the **TIME** command and study the information that is displayed.
❑ If the current date and time are incorrect, inform your instructor or supervisor. Then use the Windows Control Panel to set the correct date and time.
❑ Use the **Display** option to update the **TIME** display.
❑ If the **SAVETIME** system variable is on, note the remaining time until the next automatic save.
❑ Exit AutoCAD LT without saving.

CHAPTER TEST

Write your answers in the spaces provided.

1. What is the purpose of the **ID** command? Why would you use it? _____

   _____

   _____

   _____

2. Identify the command used to calculate the distance and angle between two points.

   _____

3. Why should you use osnaps when using the inquiry commands? _____

   _____

   _____

   _____

4. Name the system variable that allows you to quickly change the number of displayed decimal places for linear units without using the **DDUNITS** command. _____

   _____

5. What information is reported by the **AREA** command? _____

   _____

6. You need to calculate the area of an object that is fully radiused at one end. The object has been constructed with a polyline and polyarc. Which **AREA** command option should be used to perform the calculation?_____

   _____

   _____

7. What is meant by entity thickness? _____

_____

_____

_____

8. Besides the **AREA** command, which other inquiry command reports the area and circumference of a circle? _____

_____

9. What information is reported by the **TIME** command? _____

_____

_____

_____

10. You must exit AutoCAD LT to reset the date and time. (True/False)_____

CHAPTER PROBLEMS

Mechanical Drafting

1. Draw the extrusion shown below with a polyline using your **PROTOA** prototype drawing. When the object is complete, answer the following:

   A. What is the distance between Endpoints A and B? _____

   B. What is the distance between the midpoint of Line C and the midpoint of Line D? _____

   C. What is the distance and angle between Point E and the midpoint of Line F? _____

   D. What is the area of the extrusion? _____

   E. What is the perimeter? _____

   Save the drawing as **P8-1**.

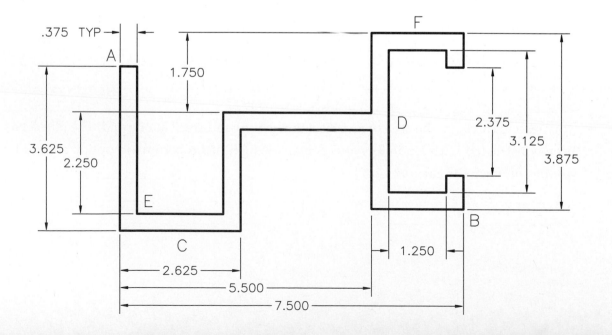

2. Draw the residential floor plan shown below using the **DLINE** command. Each of the walls is 4" thick. Before beginning construction, do the following:

Architecural Drafting

- Set architectural units.
- Set the limits to 36', 30' and **ZOOM All**.
- Set the grid spacing to 4" and the snap spacing to 2".

When the floor plan is complete, answer the following questions:

A. What is the area of the living room? _____

B. What is the combined area of the kitchen and living room? _____

C. What is the total area of the bedroom, bathroom, hall, and closet? _____

D. What is the area of the entire floor plan minus the area of the hall and closet?

_____

E. What is the perimeter of the kitchen? _____

Save the drawing as P8-2.

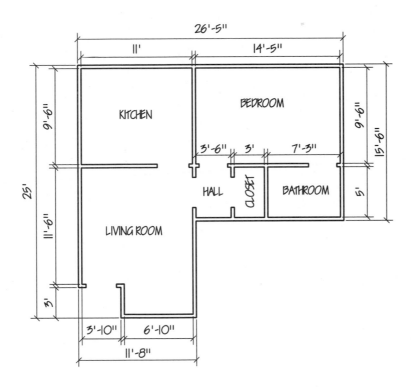

3. Draw the ADJUSTING ARM shown below using your PROTOA prototype drawing. This is the identical object from Problem 2 of Chapter 6. However, this time draw both the outer profile and the fully radiused inner slot with polylines and polyarcs. When the drawing is complete, answer the following:

A. What is the area of the fully radiused slot? _____

B. What is the slot's perimeter? _____

C. What is the area of the 1.500 diameter hole? _____

D. What is the hole's circumference? _____

E. What is the area of the adjusting arm minus the area of the inner slot and the hole?_____

Save the drawing as P8-3.

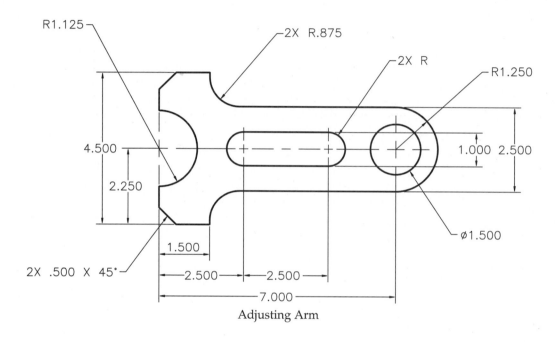

Adjusting Arm

Creating Drawing Notes

Learning objectives:

After you have completed this chapter, you will be able to:

- ❍ Add annotation to your drawings.
- ❍ Draw unique characters using special character codes.
- ❍ Describe the purpose of the **QTEXT** command.
- ❍ Create text with a specified height, orientation, slant, and width factor.
- ❍ Understand the difference between font and style.
- ❍ Modify and move existing text.

No engineering or architectural drawing is complete until it has been annotated. Typical drawing annotation includes local and general notes, parts lists, and title block information. This chapter describes the use of the **DTEXT** and **TEXT** commands so that you can begin adding notes to your drawings. You will also learn how to create your own text styles using different fonts and orientations. In addition, several text editing methods are presented in the chapter.

USING DYNAMIC TEXT

ALTUG 12

The **DTEXT**, or dynamic text, command is used to create text. When you use **DTEXT**, the characters you enter from the keyboard are displayed on the screen as well as on the command line. The text can be rotated, justified, and created at any height. The **DTEXT** command also allows you to enter multiple lines of text. When you reach the end of a sentence, press [Enter] and the text insertion cursor drops down one line and aligns itself below the previous line of text. Pressing [Enter] two times in a row terminates the **DTEXT** command.

To use **DTEXT**, click the **Text** button in the toolbox, or select <u>Text</u> from the <u>Draw</u> pull-down menu, Figure 9-1. On the command line, **DTEXT** displays the following prompts and options:

Command: *(type DTEXT, DT, or T and press* [Enter]*)*
Justify/Style/⟨Start point⟩: *(pick a starting point for the text)*
Height ⟨current⟩: *(specify a text height or accept the default)*
Rotation angle ⟨current⟩: *(enter the text rotation or accept the default)*
Text: *(enter the desired text and press* [Enter] *to drop down one line)*
Text: *(enter additional text or press* [Enter] *to end the command)*
Command:

Figure 9-1.
Select **Text** from the **Draw** pull-down menu to issue the **DTEXT** command.

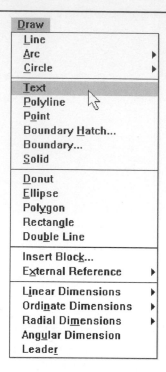

If **DTEXT** was the last command entered, pressing [Enter] at the ⟨**Start point**⟩: prompt skips the additional prompts for height and rotation angle and immediately displays the **Text:** prompt. The previous text string appears highlighted in the graphics window. Any new text you enter uses the text height and rotation angle previously specified and is placed directly beneath the line of highlighted text.

Each of the **DTEXT** options are described in the following sections.

Text start point and justification

By default, AutoCAD LT text is left justified. That is, the start point is at the lower-left corner of the text string as shown in Figure 9-2. You can specify the start point for text by picking a screen location, entering a coordinate, or using one of the object snap modes to snap to an existing entity. When selecting a start point, remember that the point specified at the ⟨**Start point**⟩: prompt can later be accessed using the **INSert** osnap.

Figure 9-2.
Text in AutoCAD LT is left justified by default.

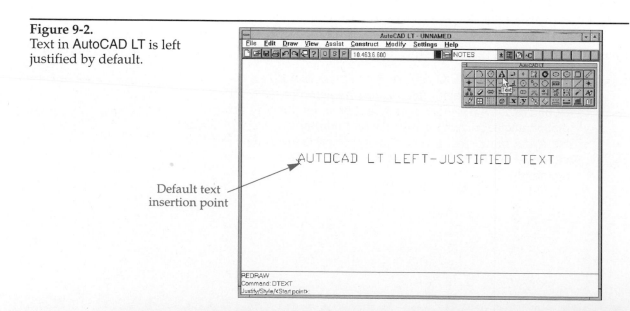

Default text insertion point

Left justification is suitable for most text operations. However, there are occasions when one of the other text justification modes is more appropriate. To change text justification, use the **Justify** option as follows:

Command: *(type DTEX, DT, or T and press [Enter])*
Justify/Style/⟨Start point⟩: **J** ⏎
Align/Fit/Center/Middle/Right: *(select a justification mode and press [Enter])*

Each of the **Justify** sub-options are described below:

- **Align.** The **Align** option justifies text between two selected points. If the two points are not aligned horizontally, the text string is created at a corresponding angle. Regardless of the number of characters entered, AutoCAD LT fits the text between the two points and adjusts the text height as necessary to do so. From Figure 9-3, you can see that the longer the character string, the shorter the text height. Fewer characters results in an increased text height. The **Align** option also adjusts the width factor automatically. The *width factor* is the width of a character in proportion to its height. Use the **Align** option as follows:

    Align/Fit/Center/Middle/Right: **A** ⏎
    First text line point: *(select a start point)*
    Second text line point: *(select an end point)*
    Text: *(enter the text)*

Figure 9-3.
An example of three text strings created with the **Align** option.

Longer text strings result in shorter character heights

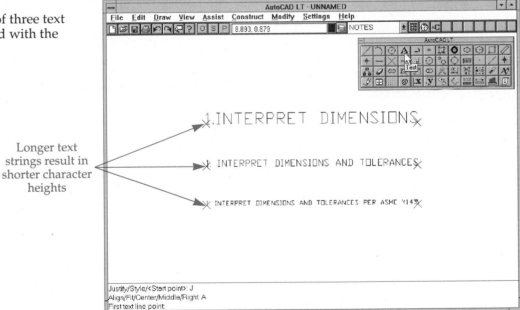

- **Fit.** The **Fit** option is very similar to the **Align** option with one important difference. With **Fit**, you are prompted to specify a character height after locating the text start and end points. As shown in Figure 9-4, the specified height is maintained regardless of the length of the text string. However, the longer the text string, the narrower the characters. A shorter text string results in wider characters. The **Fit** option looks like this:

    Align/Fit/Center/Middle/Right: **F** ⏎
    First text line point: *(select a start point)*
    Second text line point: *(select an end point)*
    Height ⟨current⟩: *(specify a text height or accept the default)*
    Text: *(enter the text)*

Figure 9-4.
An example of three text strings created using the **Fit** option.

Note the difference in character widths

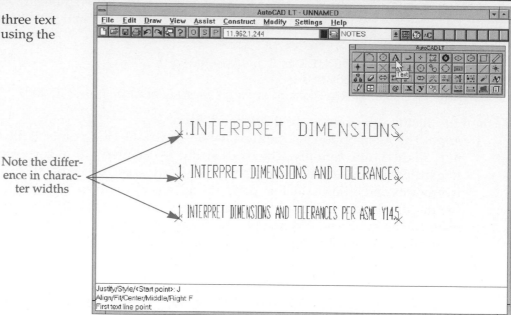

- **Center.** The **Center** option centers text horizontally about a selected point, Figure 9-5. This is a handy option when you want to label a detail or section view. Use the **Center** option as follows:

> Align/Fit/Center/Middle/Right: **C** ⏎
> Center point: *(pick a point)*
> Height ⟨*current*⟩: *(specify a text height or accept the default)*
> Rotation angle ⟨*current*⟩: *(enter the rotation or accept the default)*
> Text: *(enter the text)*

Figure 9-5.
A comparison between **Center**, **Middle**, and **Right** justified text.

Note selected points

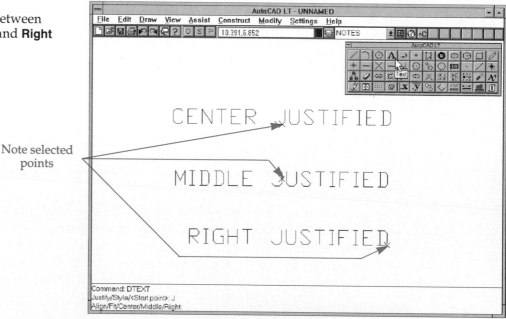

- **Middle.** As shown in Figure 9-5, the **Middle** option is used to center text both horizontally and vertically about a selected point. The **Middle** option is commonly used to locate text precisely in the middle of an object, like a rectangle or circle. It is also used to accurately place a drawing title or drawing number in the appropriate sections of a title block sheet. Since text is more accurately located using **Middle** justification, this option may be an even better way to label a detail or section view. The **Middle** option looks like this:

> Align/Fit/Center/Middle/Right: **M** ↵
> Middle point: *(pick a point)*
> Height ⟨*current*⟩: *(specify a text height or accept the default)*
> Rotation angle ⟨*current*⟩: *(enter the rotation or accept the default)*
> Text: *(enter the text)*

- **Right.** Use the **Right** option when you wish to align the right side of your text at the insertion point, Figure 9-5. The procedure is as follows:

> Align/Fit/Center/Middle/Right: **R** ↵
> End point: *(pick a point)*
> Height ⟨*current*⟩: *(specify a text height or accept the default)*
> Rotation angle ⟨*current*⟩: *(enter the rotation or accept the default)*
> Text: *(enter the text)*

As you type in text using one of the five **Justify** sub-options, the text appears on screen as if it were left justified. Do not be alarmed by this. As soon as you are through entering text and terminate the **DTEXT** command, the text will assume the justification mode you specified.

PROFESSIONAL TIP

You need not enter J for JUSTIFY when you wish to use one of the justification modes. At the ⟨**Start point**⟩: prompt, simply enter the first letter of the **Justify** sub-option you want. The procedure for middle justification looks like this:

> Command: *(type DTEXT, DT, or T and press* [Enter]*)*
> Justify/Style/⟨Start point⟩: **M** ↵
> Middle point: *(pick a point)*
> Height ⟨*current*⟩: *(specify a text height or accept the default)*
> Rotation angle ⟨*current*⟩: *(enter the rotation or accept the default)*
> Text: *(enter the text)*

Determining the correct text height

ALTUG 4

If you are using Engineering, Scientific, or Decimal units for your drawings, AutoCAD LT sets the default text height to .200 units. If you are using Architectural or Fractional units, the default text height is set to 3/16 units.

You may recall from Chapter 2 that AutoCAD LT can draw virtually anything at full scale. Very small objects are scaled up at plot time, while very large objects are scaled down. However, what happens to plotted text height?

If your drawing is to be plotted at 1:1, then you need not overly concern yourself with text height. On the other hand, if you intend to plot with a specified scale factor, it is very important to set your text height appropriately.

As an example, suppose the object you are drawing is rather small. Therefore, you intend to plot the drawing at a scale of 4:1. Since your text height will be increased by a factor of 4 at plot time, you can compensate by creating your text at 1/4 its normal size. In other words, when **DTEXT** prompts you for the text height, enter .05. The text height will be increased four times at the plotter and thus resume its default height of .200 units.

Consider another example. Suppose that the object you are drawing is very large and you intend to plot with a scale factor of 1:10 (one-tenth). Further, suppose that you want your plotted text height to be .156 (5/32). Since the drawing will be plotted ten times smaller, set your text height to be ten times larger. Therefore, set the text height to 1.56 units for this example.

As you can see, the solution to setting proper text height is to set your drawing scale factor to be the inverse, or reciprocal, of your plot scale. Use the following formula to help you determine the correct scale factor. Once you have obtained the correct scale factor, use it to multiply the height of your text.

In the following example, a drawing is to be plotted at 1:4 (quarter-scale).

$1/4'' = 1''$
$.25'' = 1''$
$1/.25 = 4$. Therefore, the scale factor is 4.

Thus, the text height should be increased four times.

The next example uses a typical architectural scale of $1/2'' = 1'$.

$1/2'' = 1'$
$1/2'' = 12''$
$(1/2)(1/2) = 12/1 \times 2/1$
$1 = 24$. Therefore, the scale factor is 24.

If the architect for this drawing wanted the plotted text height to be $3/16''$, then the drawing text height is derived by multiplying the text height by the scale factor as follows:

$3/16 \times 24$
$3/16 \times 24/1$
$72/16 = 4\ 8/16 = 4\ 1/2$

When the drawing is plotted at $1/2'' = 1'$ ($1/24$), the 4-1/2 units high text characters are reduced 24 times and resume their proper height of $3/16$.

This final example calculates the scale factor for a civil engineering drawing that is to be plotted at $1'' = 50'$.

$1'' = 50'$
$1'' = (50 \times 12)$
$1'' = 600''$
$600/1 = 600$. Therefore, the scale factor is 600.

As in the previous examples, multiply what the plotted text height should be by 600 to set the required text height in AutoCAD LT.

PROFESSIONAL TIP

The **Quick** and **Custom** drawing setup options can be used to set the proper text height for you. As an example, suppose you begin a new drawing with Decimal units that is to be plotted at 2:1. Therefore, you would set the limits to half their normal values using the **World (actual) Size to Represent Width and Height** text boxes. AutoCAD LT automatically sets the text height to .100 units. You may wish to refer to Chapter 2 to review the **Quick** and **Custom** setup options.

Text rotation angles

ALTUG 12

By default, text is generated at 0 degrees. In other words, the text reads from left to right in a horizontal orientation. You can specify a different orientation at the **Rotation angle:** prompt as follows:

Rotation angle ⟨*current*⟩: *(enter a positive or negative angle)*

A positive angle rotates text counterclockwise, while a negative angle rotates text clockwise. The ability to rotate the text at any angle is especially useful if you use AutoCAD LT to create charts and graphs. Also, some organizations use title block formats that require drawing titles and numbers to be placed in the right margin of the sheet. If your company or school uses this type of format, set the text rotation angle to 270°. Several examples of rotated text appear in Figure 9-6.

Figure 9-6.
Several examples of text at different rotation angles.

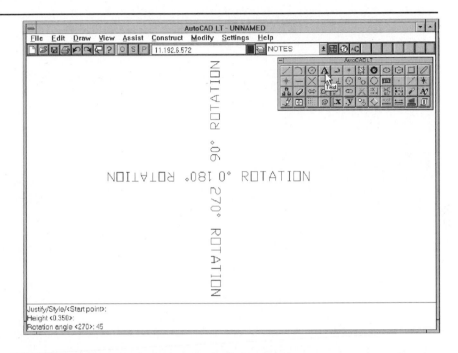

THE TEXT COMMAND   ALTUG 12

The **TEXT** command is similar to the **DTEXT** command with two exceptions. Unlike **DTEXT**, which allows you to create multiple lines of text, the **TEXT** command creates a single line of text. Pressing [Enter] after typing in text ends the **TEXT** command instead of dropping down to a new line. The other difference between **TEXT** and **DTEXT** is that text entered with the **TEXT** command appears on the command line only, and not in the graphics window. Only when the command is terminated does the text appear in the graphics window. To use the **TEXT** command, type in the following at the **Command:** prompt:

Command: *(type* TEXT *or* TX *and press* [Enter]*)*
Justify/Style/⟨Start point⟩: *(pick a point or justification option)*
Height ⟨*current*⟩: *(specify the text height or accept the default)*
Rotation angle ⟨*current*⟩: *(set the rotation angle or accept the default)*
Text: *(enter a single line of text and press* [Enter]*)*
Command:

As you can see from the above, the **TEXT** command prompts and options are the same as those for the **DTEXT** command, except the **TEXT** command displays the **Text:** prompt only once. As previously mentioned, as soon as you press [Enter] after entering your text, the **TEXT** command is terminated.

As with **DTEXT**, pressing [Enter] at the ⟨**Start point**⟩: prompt skips the additional prompts for height and rotation angle and immediately displays the **Text:** prompt if **TEXT** was the last command entered. The previous text string appears highlighted in the graphics window. Any new text you enter uses the text height and rotation angle previously specified and is placed directly beneath the line of highlighted text.

EXERCISE 9-2

❏ Begin a new drawing using your PROTOB prototype and set the NOTES layer current.
❏ Use the **TEXT** command with the proper justification modes to create text similar to that shown in Figures 9-2 through 9-5.
❏ Using the **TEXT** command, set the text rotation angles as required to duplicate the text strings illustrated in Figure 9-6.
❏ Save the drawing as EX9-2. Of the two commands, **DTEXT** and **TEXT**, which do you prefer?

SPECIAL CHARACTER CODES   ALTUG 12

Several of the text characters used in engineering and architectural drawings do not appear on a computer keyboard. For example, the Greek letter *phi* (Ø) is commonly used to represent a diameter symbol. Fortunately, AutoCAD LT provides special character codes that allow you to add these symbols to your drawing notes. Each of the codes is accessed by entering two percent signs (%%) and a designated character. The designated character can be entered in either uppercase or lowercase lettering. Each of the special character codes is listed below:

%%C	Draws a diameter symbol (Ø)
%%D	Draws a degree symbol (°)
%%P	Draws a plus or minus symbol (±)
%%O	Draws overscored characters
%%U	Draws underscored characters
%%%	Forces a single percent sign (%). This code is only used when a single percent sign precedes another control code sequence. As an example, consider the note 42%±1. To create this note you would type in the following: 42%%%%P1. When you need to use a single percent sign, simply press the percent (%) key.

The overscore and underscore character codes act as toggles that can be turned on and off in the middle of a sentence. As an example, suppose you wanted to create the following drawing note:

1. ABSOLUTELY <u>NO PAINT</u> ON THE SURFACES INDICATED.

Use the underscore toggle as follows:

1. ABSOLUTELY %%UNO PAINT%%U ON THE SURFACES INDICATED.

Both overscore and underscore modes can be on simultaneously. When using **DTEXT**, the modes are automatically turned off when you press [Enter] to add another line of text. Also, do not be alarmed to see the character codes displayed in the graphics window as you enter them from the keyboard. As soon as you terminate the **DTEXT** command, the character codes assume the proper symbols. Several examples of text using special character codes appear in Figure 9-7.

Figure 9-7.
Text created using special character codes.

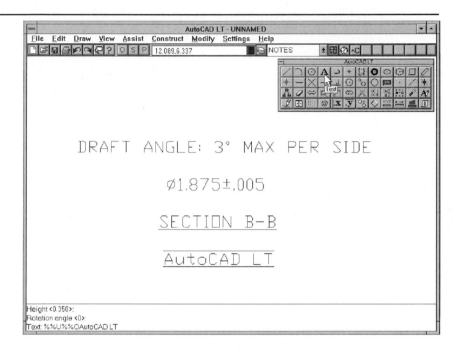

PROFESSIONAL TIP

Many drafters prefer to underline view labels such as <u>DETAIL A</u> or <u>SECTION B-B</u>. Rather than draw a line or polyline under the text, use **Middle** or **Center** justification modes and toggle underscoring on. The view labels are automatically underlined and centered under the views or details they identify.

EXERCISE 9-3

❑ Begin a new drawing using your PROTOA prototype and set the NOTES layer current.
❑ Use **DTEXT** with the appropriate special character codes to duplicate the text shown in Figure 9-7.
❑ Save the drawing as EX9-3.

THE **QTEXT** COMMAND

The **QTEXT** command controls the display and plotting of text and attribute entities. An *attribute* is informational text associated with a block entity. Blocks and attributes are covered thoroughly in Chapter 14. When **QTEXT** is on, AutoCAD LT displays each text string and attribute with a bounding box around the object. The bounding box represents the approximate height and length of the text string. In Figure 9-8, the identical text from Figure 9-7 is

---

shown with **QTEXT** turned on. If your drawing contains a lot of text, you can reduce the redraw and regeneration times by turning on **QTEXT** as follows:

Command: *(type* QTEXT *or* QT *and press* [Enter]*)*
ON/OFF ⟨*current*⟩: *(enter* ON *or* OFF *and press* [Enter]*)*

A change in **QTEXT** status does not take effect until a regeneration is performed.

Command: *(type* REGEN *or* RG *and press* [Enter]*)*

Finally, do not forget to turn **QTEXT** off before plotting.

Figure 9-8.
The text from Figure 9-7 shown with **QTEXT** turned on.

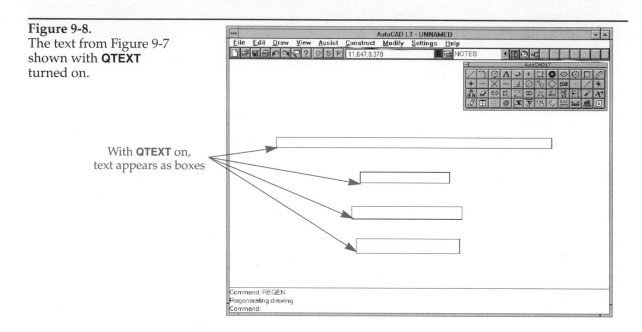

With **QTEXT** on, text appears as boxes

AUTOCAD LT TEXT FONTS

A *font* is a character set of distinctive design. It contains letters, numerals, punctuation marks, and symbols. The standard AutoCAD LT fonts are shown in Figure 9-9. The default text font used by AutoCAD LT is called TXT. This font redraws and regenerates quickly because it contains few vectors. However, it is not particularly attractive. Many users prefer to use the ROMANS (Roman Simplex) font instead. It redraws and regenerates quickly and looks more like the single-stroke Gothic lettering typically used in the traditional paper-based drafting environment.

Figure 9-9.
The standard AutoCAD LT text fonts. (Autodesk, Inc.)

FAST FONTS

Txt   The quick brown fox jumps over the lazy dog.   ABC123

Monotxt   The quick brown fox jumps over the lazy dog.   ABC123

SIMPLEX FONTS

Romans   The quick brown fox jumps over the lazy dog.   ABC123

Scripts   *The quick brown fox jumps over the lazy dog.   ABC123*

Greeks   Τηε θυιχκ βροων φοξ θυμπσ οϵερ τηε λαζψ δογ.   ABX123

DUPLEX FONTS

Romand   The quick brown fox jumps over the lazy dog.   ABC123

Figure 9-9.
Continued

COMPLEX FONTS

Romanc	The quick brown fox jumps over the lazy dog. ABC123
Italicc	*The quick brown fox jumps over the lazy dog. ABC123*
Scriptc	*The quick brown fox jumps over the lazy dog. ABC123*
Greekc	Τηε ϑυιχκ βροων φοξ ϑυμπσ οϵερ τηε λαζψ δογ. ΑΒΧ123
Cyrillic	Узд рфивк бсоцн еоч йфмпт охдс узд лащш гож. АБВ123
Cyriltlc	Тхе цуичк брошн фож щумпс овер тхе лазй дог. АБЧ123

TRIPLEX FONTS

Romant	**The quick brown fox jumps over the lazy dog. ABC123**
Italict	***The quick brown fox jumps over the lazy dog. ABC123***

GOTHIC FONTS

Gothice	The quick brown fox jumps over the lazy dog. ABC123
Gothicg	The quick brown fox jumpſ over the lazy dog. ABC123
Gothici	The quick brown fox jumps over the lazy dog. ABC123

From Figure 9-10, you can see that a variety of special symbol fonts are also included with AutoCAD LT. They include astronomical, mapping, mathematical, meteorological, and musical symbols. Each of these symbols is mapped to a specific key on your keyboard. The character mapping for each symbol font set is shown in Figure 9-11.

Figure 9-10.
The AutoCAD LT symbol fonts. (Autodesk, Inc.)

SYMBOL FONTS

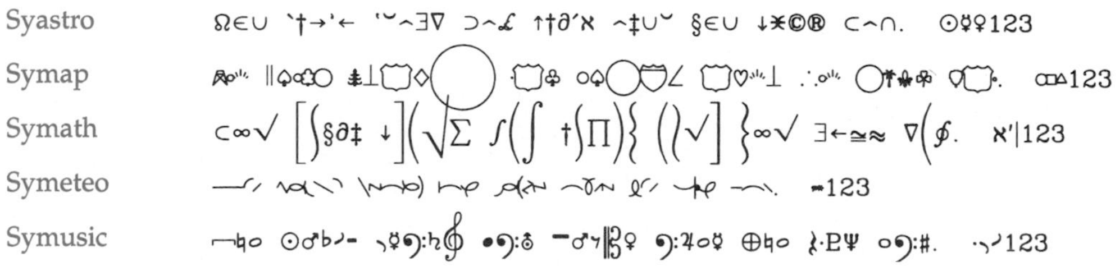

Figure 9-11.
Character mapping for nonroman and symbol fonts. (Autodesk, Inc.)

	A	B	C	D	E	F	G	H	I	J	K	L	M	N	O	P	Q	R	S	T	U	V	W	X	Y	Z	[	\	]	^	_	‘
Cyrillic	А	Б	В	Г	Д	Е	Ж	З	И	Й	К	Л	М	Н	О	П	Р	С	Т	У	Ф	Х	Ц	Ч	Ш	Щ	Ъ	Ы	Ь	Э	Ю	Я
Cyriltlc	А	Б	Ч	Д	Е	Ф	Г	Х	И	Щ	К	Л	М	Н	О	П	Ц	Р	С	Т	У	В	Ш	Ж	Й	З	Ь	Ы	Ъ	Ю	Э	Я
Greekc	Α	Β	Χ	Δ	Ε	Φ	Γ	Η	Ι	ϑ	Κ	Λ	Μ	Ν	Ο	Π	Θ	Ρ	Σ	Τ	Υ	∇	Ω	Ξ	Ψ	Ζ	[	\	]	^	_	‘
Greeks	Α	Β	Χ	Δ	Ε	Φ	Γ	Η	Ι	ϑ	Κ	Λ	Μ	Ν	Ο	Π	Θ	Ρ	Σ	Τ	Υ	∇	Ω	Ξ	Ψ	Ζ	[	\	]	^	_	‘
Syastro	☉	☿	♀	⊕	♂	♃	♄	♅	♆	♇	☾	☄	✱	☊	☋	♈	♉	♊	♋	♌	♍	♎	♏	♐	♑	♒	[	\	]	^	_	‘
Symap	○	□	△	◊	☆	+	×	✱	●	■	▲	◀	▼	▶	★	⚑	‡	†	⚒	⩓	⛪	⛰	✜	©	✡	🔔	[	\	]	^	_	‘
Symath	ℵ	′	|	‖	±	∓	×	·	÷	=	≠	≡	<	>	≦	≧	∝	∼	√	⊂	∪	⊃	∩	∈	→	↑	[	\	]	^	_	‘
Symeteo	,	.	*	▲	▬	◣	^	∩	⌒	◡	‿	›	’	‘	S	∾	∞	℞	6	—	⁄	|	\	—	⁄	/	[	\	]	^	_	‘
Symusic	·	͝	♪	o	o	●	#	♮	♭	—	-	×	ᒣ	𝄞	𝄢	𝄃	•	›	---	⌐	^	≡	▽				[	\	]	^	_	‘

In addition, AutoCAD LT provides a variety of industry-standard PostScript™ fonts for your use. *PostScript* is a page description language and is commonly used in illustration and desktop publishing. Look closely at the CIBT (City Blueprint) font in Figure 9-12. This font is particularly popular for architectural and facilities layout applications. More information about PostScript fonts is included in Chapter 13 of this text.

The AutoCAD LT fonts are stored in the \ACLTWIN directory. Each of the standard fonts has a file extension of .SHX. The PostScript fonts have a .PFB file extension.

Figure 9-12.
The AutoCAD LT PostScript fonts. (Autodesk, Inc.)

POSTSCRIPT FONTS

Cibt	The quick brown fox jumped over the lazy dog.	ABC12
Cobt	The quick brown fox jumped over the lazy dog.	ABC12
Rom	The quick brown fox jumped over the lazy dog.	ABC12
Romb	The quick brown fox jumped over the lazy dog.	ABC12
Sas	The quick brown fox jumped over the lazy dog.	ABC12
Sasb	The quick brown fox jumped over the lazy dog.	ABC12
Saso	The quick brown fox jumped over the lazy dog.	ABC12
Sasbo	The quick brown fox jumped over the lazy dog.	ABC12
Te	THE QUICK BROWN FOX JUMPED OVER THE LAZY DOG.	ABC12
Tel	THE QUICK BROWN FOX JUMPED OVER THE LAZY DOG.	ABC12
Teb	THE QUICK BROWN FOX JUMPED OVER THE LAZY DOG.	ABC12
Eur	The quick brown fox jumped over the lazy dog. àáâãäåæçèéêëìíîïðñòóÛÝßØµ¶©™®¢£¤¥¦§±‡†‡¿¡	ABC12
Euro	The quick brown fox jumped over the lazy dog. àáâãäåæçèéêëìíîïðñòóÛÝÞßØµ¶©™®¢£¤¥¦§±‡†‡¿¡	ABC12
Pan	The quick brown fox jumped over the lazy dog. ə√ÆæŊŋ¿ʰᵃðθßÐÐS¶áàâãǎāã'aa'ÂÁÄÄ	ABC12
Suf	The quick brown fox jumped over the lazy dog. £₫ø±ß«»¶{}∈Ł÷ħſˊ¿ªáàâã'aa'aÂÄ	ABC12

CREATING A TEXT STYLE ALTUG 12

Before you can use any of the available AutoCAD LT fonts, you must first create a text style. A *text style* is a named collection of settings that affect the appearance of text characters for each of the available fonts. For example, text characters can be wide or narrow, slanted or vertical, upside-down, or backwards. Several examples of text styles are illustrated in Figure 9-13. Text styles are created with the **STYLE** command and are saved with a name in the current drawing. The name you provide can contain up to 31 characters, but no spaces are allowed. When you begin a new drawing in AutoCAD LT, the default style is used. This style is called STANDARD and has the TXT font assigned to it.

Figure 9-13.
A variety of different text styles and fonts.

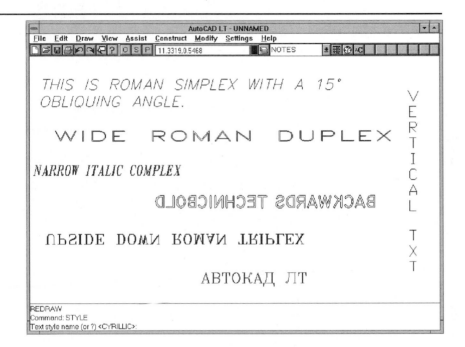

There are two ways to define a new text style. The first method allows you to provide a descriptive name of your own choosing for the style. To create a text style, enter STYLE or ST at the **Command:** prompt. The **STYLE** command displays the following prompts and options:

```
Command: (type STYLE or ST and press [Enter])
Text style name (or ?) 〈STANDARD〉: ↵
Height 〈0.0000〉: ↵
Width factor 〈1.0000〉: ↵
Obliquing angle 〈0〉: ↵
Backwards? 〈N〉 ↵
Upside-down? 〈N〉 ↵
Vertical? 〈N〉 ↵
```

Each of the **STYLE** command options are described as follows:
* **Text style name (or ?).** You can use the **?** option at this prompt to list any existing text styles defined in the current drawing. If you enter a text style name and press [Enter], the **Select Text Font** dialog box is displayed. From the example shown in Figure 9-14, the ROMANS font is selected from the file list at the left of the dialog box. You can also type in the desired font name directly over the existing highlighted font name in the **File Name:** text box. Be sure to add the extension .SHX to the font name you enter. (Do

not use this method for PostScript font names, however.) If you click the **Type It** button at the right of the dialog box, the dialog box disappears and you are prompted to enter the desired font name, without a file extension, on the command line:

Font file ⟨*current*⟩: **ROMANS** ↵

Figure 9-14.
Selecting the Roman Simplex font (ROMANS.SHX) from the **Select Font File** dialog box.

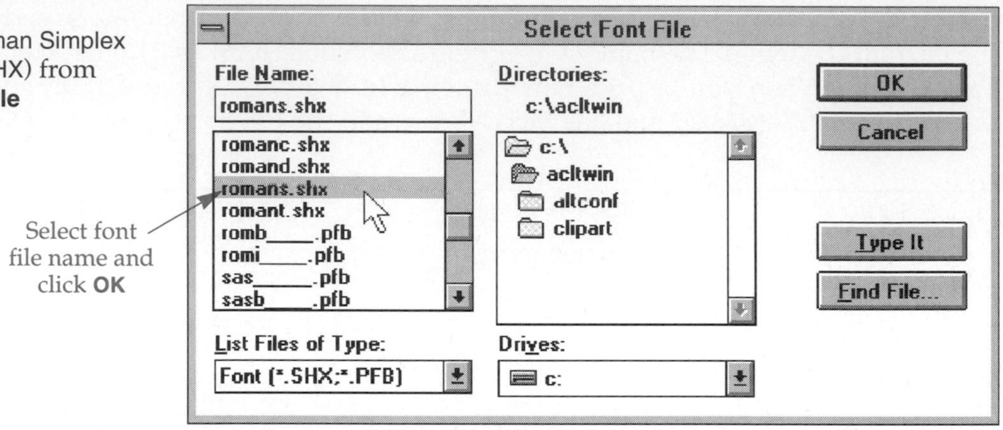

- **Height.** It is strongly recommended that you leave the height set to 0. Doing so allows you to specify the text height each time you enter text using this style. If you specify an explicit height here, then the text height you enter is always used for this style and you are not prompted for height.
- **Width factor.** As mentioned previously, the width factor is the width of a character in proportion to its height. A value less than 1 condenses characters, making them narrow. A value greater than 1 expands the characters, making them wider.
- **Obliquing angle.** The obliquing angle is used to create a slanted text style. You can enter a value greater than 0 and less than 85. Slanted text created with an obliquing angle of 15° is shown in Figure 9-13.
- **Backwards.** Answer Y if you want text generated backwards. The default is N.
- **Upside-down.** Answer Y if you want text generated upside-down. The default is N.
- **Vertical.** Answer Y if you want text generated in a vertical format. The default is N. An example of vertical text is shown in Figure 9-13. This aspect of style might be useful for charts and graphs. Keep in mind, however, that not all the fonts supplied with AutoCAD LT support the Vertical orientation.

Once each of the prompts has been answered, the **STYLE** command displays a message stating the style name you specified is now the current text style. In the following exercise, you will create a new text style named SLANTED. The style will use the Roman Simplex font with an obliquing angle of 15°.

EXERCISE 9-4

❑ Begin a new drawing using your PROTOA prototype.
❑ Enter the **STYLE** command and answer the prompts as shown below:

        Command: *(type* STYLE *or* ST *and press* [Enter])
        Text style name (or ?) ⟨STANDARD⟩: **SLANTED** ↲

❑ When the **Select Font File** dialog box appears, locate and select ROMANS.SHX from the file list at the left of the dialog box. Click **OK** to exit the dialog box.

        New style. Height ⟨0.000⟩: ↲
        Width factor ⟨1.000⟩: ↲
        Obliquing angle ⟨0⟩: **15** ↲
        Backwards? ⟨N⟩ ↲
        Upside-down? ⟨N⟩ ↲
        Vertical? ⟨N⟩ ↲
        SLANTED is now the current text style.
        Command:

❑ Set the NOTES layer current and create some text with your new text style.
❑ When you are done experimenting, save the drawing as EX9-4.

Creating a style using a dialog box

The second method you can use to create a text style can be found in the **Settings** pull-down menu, Figure 9-15. Selecting **Text Style...** from this menu displays the **Select Text Font** dialog box shown in Figure 9-16A. You can use the vertical slider bar at the left of the dialog box to select the font that you wish to use or, more simply, select the font by clicking its representative icon. Click the **Next** button to display the other available fonts in a second dialog box. See Figure 9-16B. Click the **Previous** button to return to the first dialog box.

When you use this method, you are not allowed to provide a unique name for the text style. Instead, AutoCAD LT automatically gives the style the same name as the font you select. However, you are still prompted to change the other aspects of the text style (width factor, obliquing angle, etc.) as previously described.

Figure 9-15.
Selecting **Text Style...** from the **Settings** pull-down menu displays the **Select Text Font** dialog box.

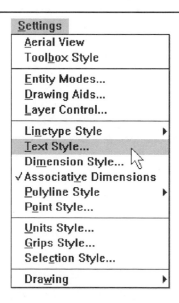

Figure 9-16.
A—Selecting the **Roman Simplex** font using the **Select Text Font** dialog box. Clicking the **Next** button displays additional text fonts. B—The second **Select Text Font** dialog box.

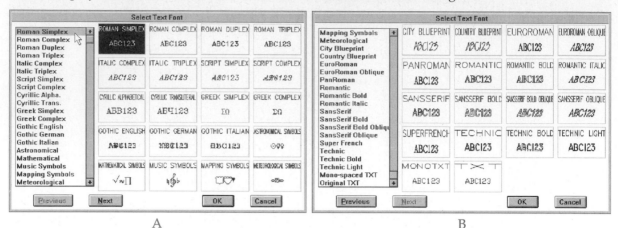

A   B

SETTING A TEXT STYLE CURRENT

Once you have two or more text styles defined in your drawing, it is a simple matter to make one of them current. There are several ways to accomplish this. One method is to use the **Style** option offered by both the **DTEXT** and **TEXT** commands. This option looks like this:

> Command: *(type DTEXT, DT, or T and press* [Enter]*)*
> Justify/Style/⟨Start point⟩: **S** ⏎
> Style name (or ?) ⟨*current*⟩: *(enter an existing text style name)*

After providing a valid name, the **DTEXT** (or **TEXT**) command resumes as usual. If you enter a text style name that does not exist, AutoCAD LT displays an error message. If this happens, use the **?** option to list the styles defined in the current drawing or to double-check the correct spelling of the style names.

You can also preset the text style name before you create any text. This is done using the **TEXTSTYLE** system variable. In the following example, the SLANTED style is set current.

> Command: **TEXTSTYLE** ⏎
> New value for TEXTSTYLE ⟨"STANDARD"⟩: **SLANTED** ⏎
> Command:

Setting a text style current using a dialog box

ALTUG 12

It is also possible to set a text style current using the **Entity Creation Modes** dialog box. You may recall from Chapter 5 that this dialog box was introduced as a means to set current a specific color or linetype. It is accessed by clicking the **Current Color** button on the toolbar, by selecting **Entity Modes...** from the **Settings** pull-down menu (Figure 9-17), or by clicking the **Entity Modes** button. Although the **Entity Modes** button shown here does not appear in the toolbar or toolbox by default, it may easily be added. You can also enter the following at the **Command:** prompt:

> Command: *(type DDEMODES or EM and press* [Enter]*)*

Figure 9-17.
Select **Entity Modes...** from the **Settings** pull-down menu to issue the **DDEMODES** command.

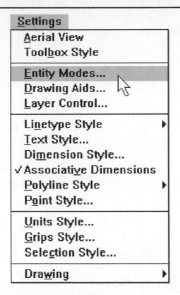

As shown in Figure 9-18, the current text style is displayed just to the right of the **Text Style...** button. Click this button to display the **Select Text Style** subdialog box, Figure 9-19. The text styles defined in the current drawing are displayed at the upper left of the dialog box. To set one of them current, either select the style name with your mouse or enter the name in the **Style Name:** text box. You can see a graphical representation of the current style in the image tile at the upper right of the dialog box. The dialog box also reports the assigned font, height, width factor, and obliquing angle of the current text style. If the current style is upside-down, backwards, or in a vertical orientation, it is noted on the line labeled **Generation:**. Once you have selected the desired text style to set current, click **OK** to exit the **Select Text Style** sub-dialog box. Click **OK** once more to exit the **Entity Creation Modes** dialog box.

Figure 9-18.
The **Text Style...** button in the **Entity Creation Modes** dialog box is used to set a text style current.

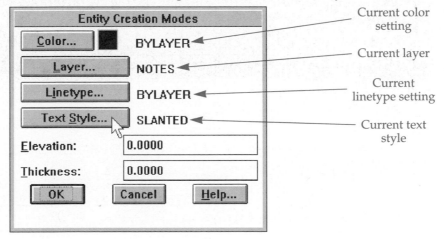

Figure 9-19.
The **Select Text Style** dialog box.

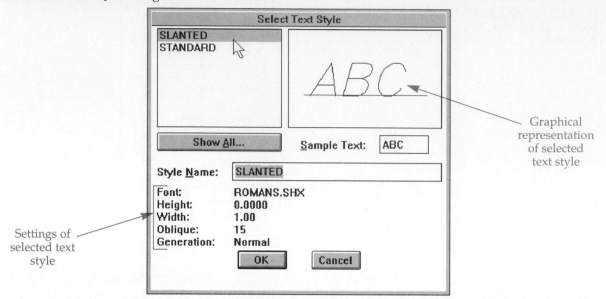

Graphical representation of selected text style

Settings of selected text style

Using other special character codes

Earlier in this chapter you learned that character codes are used by AutoCAD LT to display certain symbols. There are many other special control codes that work with the standard AutoCAD LT fonts, as well as the PostScript fonts. Each character is represented by a special numeric ASCII (American Standard Code for Information Interchange) code. There is a specific code for 128 characters. Once you know the code number, it is entered using two percent signs as follows: %%nnn.

You can determine the ASCII code for each character of the current text style by clicking the **Show All...** button in the **Select Text Style** subdialog box. This action displays the **Text Style Symbol Set** subdialog box shown in Figure 9-20. Each character shown has a corresponding symbol set number. You can estimate the character number you need by starting on the top row and counting the characters from left to right.

Figure 9-20.
The **Show All...** button displays the symbol set for a specified text style.

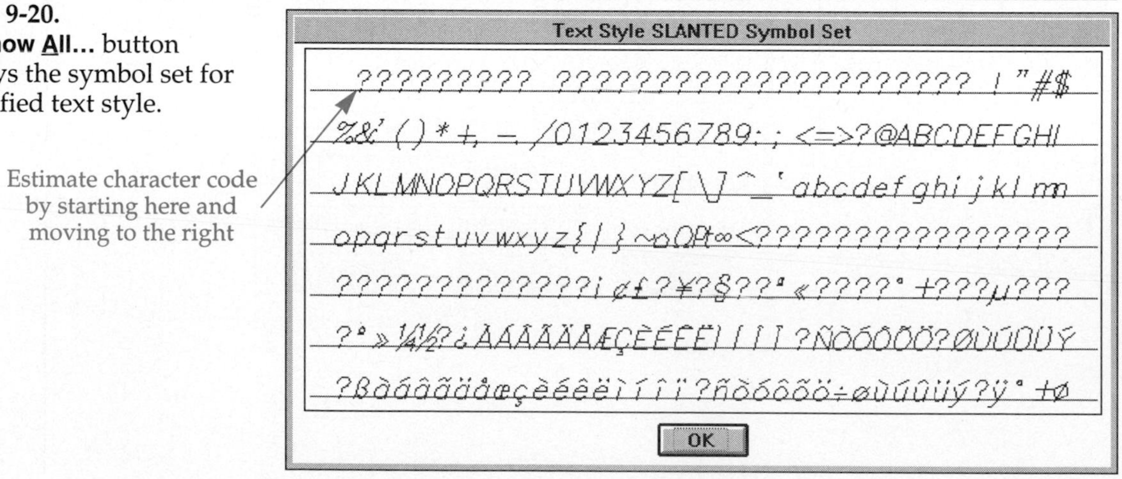

Estimate character code by starting here and moving to the right

Text Style SLANTED Symbol Set

```
?????????  ??????????????????? ! " #$
%&' ( ) * +, −. /0123456789: ; <=>?@ABCDEFGHI
JKLMNOPQRSTUVWXYZ[ \] ^_`abcdefghi jkl mn
opqrstuvwxyz{ | } ~◦○Ωℓ∞<???????????????
?????????????¡ ¢£?¥?§??° «????° +???µ???
?° »¼½?¿ÀÁÂÃÄÅÆÇÈÉÊEÌ Í Î ?ÑÒÓÔÕÖ?ØÙÚÛÜÝ
?ßàáâãäåæçèéêëì í î ï ?ñòóôõö÷øùúûüý?ÿ° +ø
```

OK

AutoCAD LT—Fundamentals and Applications

Enter the number you estimated in the **Sample Text:** box shown in Figure 9-19. As an example, to enter the 188th character in the set, enter %%188 and press [Enter]. The 1/4 character appears in the image tile at the upper right. Once you have identified one of the symbols with a known ASCII code, it is fairly easy to count forward or backward from that point to locate a desired character. For example, suppose that you are drawing an electronic schematic diagram and you need to use the Greek alphabet letter μ (*mu*) to specify the rating on a capacitor. Since you know that the 1/4 character is 188, count back seven characters to locate the μ symbol. Then, enter %%181 in the **Sample Text:** box and press [Enter]. The μ symbol appears in the image tile.

PROFESSIONAL TIP   As with layers, create various text styles in your prototype drawing(s) so that they are always available when needed. Also, write down the special character codes for the symbols you use most often in your work.

RENAMING A TEXT STYLE

ALTUG 12

Text styles, like views, linetypes, and layers, can be renamed at any time with the **DDRENAME** command. You may recall from previous chapters that this command permits you to rename objects using a dialog box. Select **Rename...** from the **Modify** pull-down menu to display the **Rename** dialog box shown in Figure 9-21, or enter the following at the **Command:** prompt:

Command: *(type* DDRENAME *or* DR *and press* [Enter]*)*

The **Named Objects** list appears at the left of the dialog box and contains the types of objects that can be named or renamed in AutoCAD LT. In the example shown in Figure 9-21, observe that **Style** has been selected from the list at the left. A listing of all the text styles defined in the current drawing appears at the right of the dialog box. To rename the SLANTED text style, first select the style name from the list. The name of the text style you select is then displayed in the **Old Name:** text box. With your mouse, click anywhere inside the **Rename To:** text box and enter the new style name. In the example, the SLANTED text style is renamed to OBLIQUE. When you are done typing, click the **Rename To:** button and the new style name appears in the list at the right of the dialog box. When you are finished renaming objects, click the **OK** button to exit the **Rename** dialog box.

Figure 9-21.
Using the **Rename** dialog box to rename a text style.

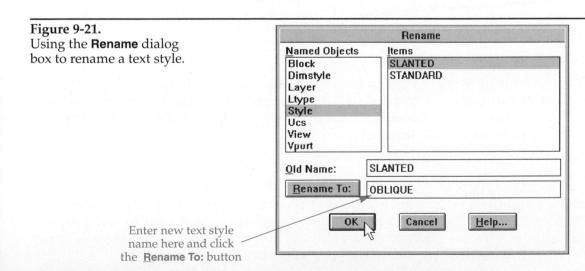

Enter new text style name here and click the **Rename To:** button

---

It is also possible to rename text styles from the command line instead of using the dialog box. In the following example, the **RENAME** command is used to perform the identical renaming operation described on the previous page.

Command: **RENAME** ↵
Block/Dimstyle/LAyer/LType/Style/Ucs/VIew/VPort: **S** ↵
Old text style name: **SLANTED** ↵
New text style name: **OBLIQUE** ↵
Command:

EDITING EXISTING TEXT

ALTUG 12

Occasionally, it will be necessary to modify the notes on your drawings. You can edit text in a dialog box by clicking the **Edit Text** button in the toolbox or selecting **Edit Text...** from the **Modify** pull-down menu, Figure 9-22. At the **Command:** prompt, enter the **DDEDIT** command as follows:

Command: *(type* DDEDIT, ED, *or* TE *and press* [Enter]*)*
⟨Select a TEXT or ATTDEF object⟩/Undo: *(select one line of text)*

Figure 9-22.
Select **Edit Text...** from the **Modify** pull-down menu to issue the **DDEDIT** command.

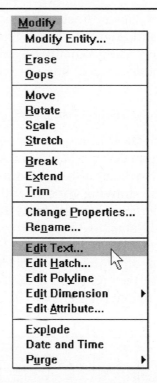

You are prompted to select a text or attribute entity. (As stated earlier in this chapter, an attribute is informational text associated with a block entity.) Only one entity can be selected at a time with **DDEDIT**. In the example shown in Figure 9-23A, the following note has been selected and appears in the **Edit Text** dialog box:

NOTS: (UNLESS OTHERWISE SPECIFIED)

To correct the typing error, move the text insertion cursor (the flashing vertical bar) between the T and the S in the word NOTS. Now, type in the letter E and click the **OK** button (or press [Enter]) to exit the dialog box, Figure 9-23B. You are prompted to select another object for editing, or to use the **Undo** option to undo the editing operation that you just performed. When you are finished, press [Enter] to end the **DDEDIT** command.

Figure 9-23.
A—The cursor is located at the desired text insertion point. B—After editing the text, click the **OK** button or press [Enter] to exit the **Edit Text** dialog box.

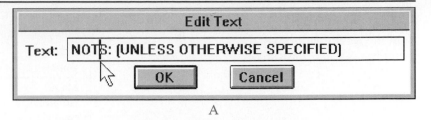

A

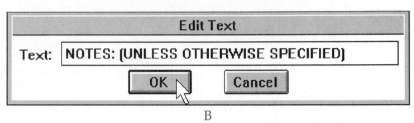

B

DDEDIT editing methods

The text string that you select for editing with **DDEDIT** appears highlighted in the **Edit Text** dialog box. If you begin entering any new text, the highlighted text is automatically removed. You can also remove the highlighted text by pressing the space bar, by using the [Ctrl]+[X] key combination, or by pressing the [Delete] or [Backspace] keys on your keyboard. If you make a typing error, use the [Backspace] key or click the **Cancel** button and reselect the text you wish to edit.

You can freely pick with your mouse to locate the text insertion cursor at the desired point in the character string. You can also use several of the editing keys on your keyboard. The left and right arrow keys move the cursor one character to the left or to the right, respectively. The [End] key places the text cursor at the very end of the character string. The [Home] key places the text cursor at the very start of the character string. The [Delete] key deletes the character just to the right of the text cursor.

CHANGING OTHER ASPECTS OF TEXT   ALTUG 12

The **DDEDIT** command described above is very handy when you need to correct a spelling error or amend some existing text. However, when you need to change style aspects such as height and rotation, or the color or layer of text, use the **DDMODIFY** command instead. To issue the **DDMODIFY** command, select **Modify Entity...** from the **Modify** pull-down menu, or click the **Modify Entity** button. See Figure 9-24. Although the **Modify Entity** button shown in the margin does not appear in the toolbar or toolbox by default, it may easily be added. Enter the following at the **Command:** prompt:

> Command: **DDMODIFY** ↵
> Select object to modify: *(select one text entity)*

Select one text entity and the **Modify Text** dialog box is then displayed. As shown in Figure 9-25, the selected text is highlighted in the **Text:** text box and can be edited using the same keyboard techniques as would be used for **DDEDIT**. If you wish to change the text properties of color, linetype, or layer, click the appropriate buttons at the top of the dialog box. Text height, rotation, width factor, and obliquing angle can all be changed using the corresponding text boxes. If you wish to change the existing justification or style, make your choices using the **Justify:** and **Style:** drop-down lists at the right of the dialog box. Click the **Upside Down** or **Backward** check boxes if you want the selected text to assume one of these orientations. (Observe that the Vertical style format is not available in this dialog box.) If you need to change the location of the text, you can enter new X and Y coordinates in the **X:** and **Y:**

Figure 9-24.
Selecting **Modify Entity...**
from the **Modify** pull-down
menu issues the **DDMODIFY**
command.

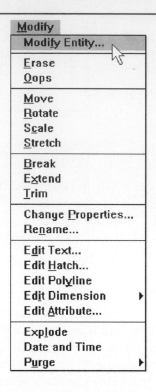

Figure 9-25.
The **Modify Text** dialog box
can be used to change
nearly every aspect of an
existing string of text.

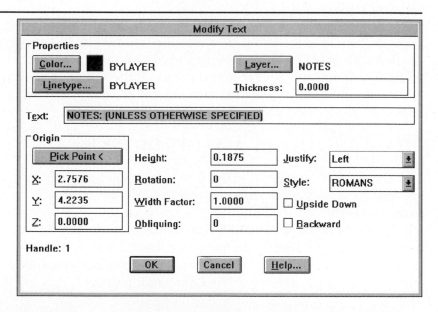

text boxes. It is faster and easier, however, to click the **Pick Point** ⟨ button. Doing so removes the dialog box and you are prompted on the command line with:

Insertion point:

Move your cursor to select a new insertion point for the text and pick. The **Modify Text** dialog box is redisplayed and the coordinates of the new insertion point are shown in the **X:** and **Y:** text boxes. Click **OK** to exit the dialog box, and the selected text appears at the new location.

THE CHANGE COMMAND

As an alternative to changing text using a dialog box, you can issue the **CHANGE** command to modify or move selected text on the command line. The procedure looks like the following:

Command: *(type* CHANGE *or* CH *and press* [Enter]*)*
Select objects: *(select one or more text strings to be changed)*
Select objects: ↵
Properties/⟨Change point⟩: ↵
Enter text insertion point: *(pick a new text location or press* [Enter]*)*
Text style: STANDARD
New style or RETURN for no change: *(enter an existing style name or press* [Enter]*)*
New height ⟨*current*⟩: *(specify a new text height or press* [Enter]*)*
New rotation angle ⟨*current*⟩: *(specify a new text rotation or press* [Enter]*)*
New text ⟨*selected text string*⟩: *(enter a new text string or press* [Enter]*)*
Command:

The **CHANGE** command allows you to select more than one text entity. If several text strings are selected, you receive the prompts shown above for each text entity as it is encountered in the selection set. After all the selected text has been changed, the **Command:** prompt returns.

Both the **DDMODIFY** and **CHANGE** commands can be used to edit other entity types, as well. This capability is described in Chapter 10 of this text.

CHAPTER TEST

Write your answers in the spaces provided.

1. Identify two ways to access the **DTEXT** command. _____

_____

2. List the differences between the **DTEXT** and **TEXT** commands. _____

_____

3. Why would the **Middle** justification mode be used? _____

_____

_____

4. You are drawing an architectural floor plan that is to be plotted at 1/4″ = 1′. The plotted text height is to be 3/16″. What is the drawing scale factor, and what size should you make the text in AutoCAD LT?_____

5. Provide the special character codes for the following text strings:
   A. Ø7.625 _____
   B. 2° MAX DRAFT _____ _____
   C. .375±.010 _____
   D. DETAIL A _____

6. Special character codes must always be entered in uppercase lettering. (True/False)_____

7. What is a font? _____

_____

8. What is a style? _____

_____

_____

9. What is **QTEXT**? Why would it be used? _____

_____

_____

10. Name the **STYLE** command option that creates slanted text. _____

_____

11. What is meant by width factor? _____

_____

12. How many characters can be used in a text style name? _____

_____

13. Why should you leave the style height set to 0 (zero)? _____

_____

14. Identify three ways to set a text style current. _____

_____

_____

15. Name three commands that can be used to modify existing text. Of the three, which command only changes the text content? _____

_____

CHAPTER PROBLEMS

Electronics Drafting

1. Use the layers in your PROTOB drawing to draw the block diagram of the modulator receiver shown below. Use the **POLYLINE**, **POLYGON**, and **RECTANG** commands to your advantage. Make the symbols proportional in size to those illustrated. Create a style with the Roman Simplex font and use **DTEXT** to letter the diagram. Save the drawing as P9-1.

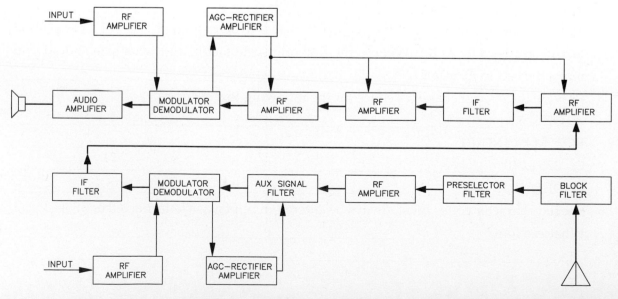

2. Draw the map title shown below using your PROTOA prototype drawing. Create a text style using the Roman Triplex font and place all lettering on the NOTES layer. Using **DTEXT**, set the text height appropriately to approximate the lettering height shown. Use **DDMODIFY** to increase the width factor as required to duplicate the "IN THE" and "SCALE~MILES" text strings. Draw the solid lines in the legend with wide polylines. Save the drawing as P9-2.

General

MAP SHOWING
IRON ORE DEPOSITS
IN THE
WESTERN STATES

SCALE~MILES

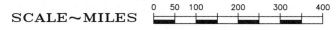

3. Draw the architectural title shown below using your PROTOA prototype drawing. Create a text style using the City Blueprint font and place all lettering on the NOTES layer. Save the drawing as P9-3.

Architectural Drafting

FIRST
FLOOR
PLAN

A RESIDENCE FOR
MR. & MRS. JOHN DOE
BROOKINGS, OREGON

COMMISSION
524
11-18-

SCALE
1/ 4" = 1'0"

DESIGNED BY
MATTHEW TRAVERS
REGISTERED ARCHITECT
EUGENE, OREGON

SHEET NO.
2
OF 7

4. Use the layers in your PROTOB drawing to draw the flow diagram of the digital numerical control (DNC) system shown below. Make the diagram proportional in size to that illustrated and use the **POLYLINE** and **RECTANG** commands to your advantage. Create a style with the Roman Simplex font and use **DTEXT** to letter the diagram. Save the drawing as P9-4.

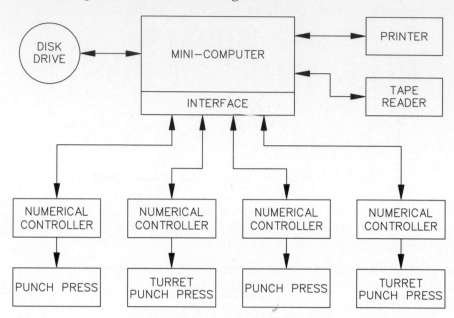

AutoCAD LT—Fundamentals and Applications

Modifying the Drawing

Learning objectives:
After you have completed this chapter, you will be able to:
- ○ Trim one or more objects against an edge.
- ○ Extend one or more objects to a boundary.
- ○ Break an object at selected points.
- ○ Move and rotate drawing objects.
- ○ Resize objects using the **SCALE** and **STRETCH** commands.
- ○ Use the **CHANGE** command to modify line endpoints and the size of circles.
- ○ Create a mirror image of an object.
- ○ Make one or more copies of selected entities.
- ○ Perform various polyline editing operations.
- ○ Edit a selected entity using a dialog box.
- ○ Use grips to modify entities.

Regardless of the technical discipline, most detail drawings are eventually revised to implement design improvements, reduce costs, and to correct drafting errors. Fortunately, AutoCAD LT provides a vast array of editing commands that allow you to quickly and easily modify your drawings. These editing commands are also used to aid in the construction of new drawings and are described in this chapter.

TRIMMING OBJECTS

ALTUG 10

The **TRIM** command is used to trim one or more entities against existing objects. You can trim arcs, circles, donuts, lines, rectangles, polygons, and open 2D and 3D polylines. The entities that you trim against are called *cutting edges*. To use **TRIM**, type TRIM or TR at the **Command:** prompt, click the **Trim** button in the toolbox, or select **Trim** from the **Modify** pull-down menu. See Figure 10-1. The command sequence is as follows:

> Command: *(type* TRIM *or* TR *and press* [Enter]*)*
> Select cutting edge(s)...
> Select objects: *(select one or more entities to trim against)*
> Select objects: ↵

After selecting the cutting edge(s), it is very important to terminate the selection by pressing [Enter]. The prompt now changes to:

> ⟨Select object to trim⟩/Undo: *(select an entity to trim)*
> ⟨Select object to trim⟩/Undo: *(select another entity or press* [Enter] *to end)*
> Command:

Figure 10-1.
Select **Trim** from the **Modify**
pull-down menu to issue
the **TRIM** command.

As shown in Figure 10-2A, select the entities on the side that you wish to trim. If you select the wrong entity, or the wrong side, use the **Undo** option to undo the selection and try again. Occasionally, there may be instances when more than one cutting edge exists. Such an example is illustrated by the "D" hole shown in Figure 10-2B.

Figure 10-2.
A—An example of several lines trimmed against one cutting edge. B—Trimming with two cutting edges.

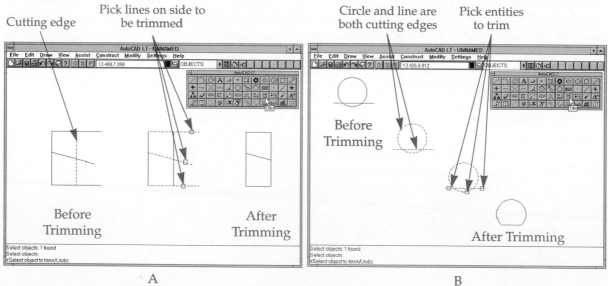

EXERCISE 10-1

- ❑ Draw an object similar to that illustrated in Figure 10-2A and use **TRIM** as shown.
- ❑ Undo the trim operation and try picking the lines on the other side of the cutting edge.
- ❑ Now, draw a line and circle like that shown in Figure 10-2B. Use **TRIM** to produce the "D" hole illustrated.
- ❑ Save the drawing as EX10-1.

EXTENDING OBJECTS

ALTUG 10

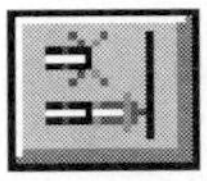

The **EXTEND** command extends an entity to meet, or intersect, another entity. The intersecting entity is called the ***boundary edge***. Entities that you may extend include arcs, lines, and open 2D and 3D polylines. Since polygons and rectangles are considered closed polylines, these entity types may not be extended. To use **EXTEND**, type EXTEND or EX at the **Command:** prompt, click the **Extend** button in the toolbox, or select **Extend** from the **Modify** pull-down menu. See Figure 10-3. The command sequence is as follows:

Command: *(type* EXTEND *or* EX *and press* [Enter]*)*
Select boundary edge(s)...
Select objects: *(select one or more entities to extend to)*
Select objects: ↵

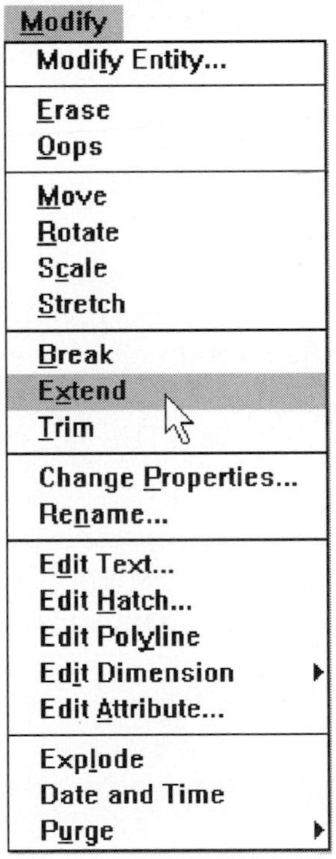
Modify
Modify Entity...
Erase
Oops
Move
Rotate
Scale
Stretch
Break
Extend
Trim
Change Properties...
Rename...
Edit Text...
Edit Hatch...
Edit Polyline
Edit Dimension
Edit Attribute...
Explode
Date and Time
Purge

Figure 10-3.
Select **Extend** from the **Modify** pull-down menu to issue the **EXTEND** command.

After selecting the boundary edge(s), it is necessary to terminate the selection by pressing [Enter]. The prompt now changes to:

⟨Select object to extend⟩/Undo: *(select an entity to extend)*
⟨Select object to extend⟩/Undo: *(select another entity or press* [Enter] *to end)*
Command:

As shown in Figure 10-4A, an arc and a line are selected at the endpoints closest to the boundary edge they are to meet. When two boundary edges are selected, it is then possible to extend an object in two directions. This method is illustrated in Figure 10-4B. As with the **TRIM** command, if you select the wrong entity, or the wrong endpoint, use the **Undo** option to undo the selection and try again. If you attempt to extend an entity where no intersection exists, AutoCAD LT displays the following error message:

Entity does not intersect an edge.

Figure 10-4.
A—An example of an arc and a line extended to one boundary. B—Extending several lines to two boundary edges.

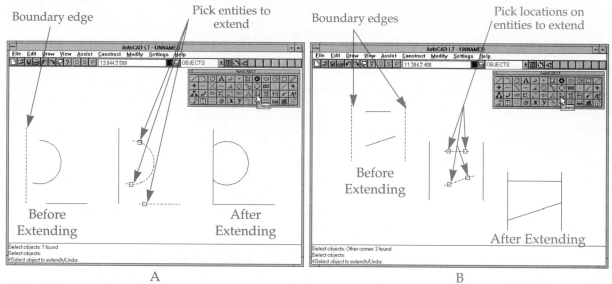

NOTE You cannot trim against, or extend to, a block. See Chapter 14 for complete information about block entities.

EXERCISE 10-2

❏ Draw two lines and an arc similar to those illustrated in Figure 10-4A and use **EXTEND** as shown.
❏ Next, draw the line pattern shown in Figure 10-4B. Extend both lines to the two boundary edges as shown.
❏ Draw a rectangle with the **RECTANG** command, and a square with the **POLYGON** command. Try to extend these entities to a line. What happens? Why?
❏ Save the drawing as EX10-2.

THE BREAK COMMAND

The **BREAK** command allows you to put a space in an entity by breaking out a section. You can also break an object at a selected point, resulting in two separate entities. To use the **BREAK** command, type BREAK or BR at the **Command:** prompt, click the **Break** button in the toolbox or select **Break** from the **Modify** pull-down menu. See Figure 10-5. Using the **BREAK** command is described in the following two sections.

Figure 10-5.
Select **Break** from the **Modify** pull-down menu to issue the **BREAK** command.

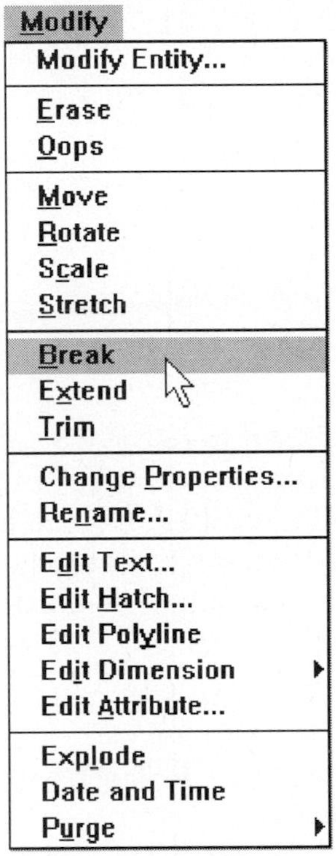

Modify
Modify Entity...
Erase
Oops
Move
Rotate
Scale
Stretch
Break
Extend
Trim
Change Properties...
Rename...
Edit Text...
Edit Hatch...
Edit Polyline
Edit Dimension ▶
Edit Attribute...
Explode
Date and Time
Purge ▶

Breaking between two points

The **BREAK** command is most commonly used to remove a section from an object by breaking between two selected points. While the **TRIM** command is a faster and more reliable way to remove a section from an entity, there are certain instances where **BREAK** must be used. One example occurs when there are no cutting edges to trim against. Another example exists when the edge you need to trim against belongs to a block entity. As mentioned previously, blocks cannot be used as cutting edges.

There are several ways to use **BREAK** to remove a section. The first method requires that you select the entity to break and then pick the two points to break between. This method is illustrated using a circle in Figure 10-6. The procedure looks like the following:

> Command: *(type* BREAK *or* BR *and press* [Enter]*)*
> Select object: *(select the circle)*
> Enter second point (or F for first point): **F** ⏎
> Enter first point: *(pick the first point on the circle)*
> Enter second point: *(pick the second point on the circle)*
> Command:

For both circles and arcs, the order in which points are selected determines whether the break is performed in a clockwise or counterclockwise direction. See Figure 10-6.

Figure 10-6.
Sections removed from
circles using the **BREAK**
command.

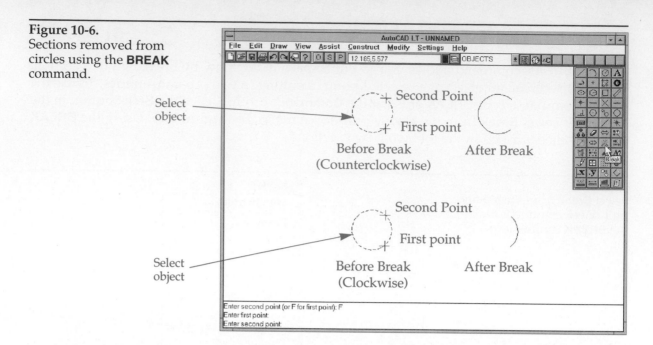

When you use **BREAK** to remove a section from an entity, be sure to use the appropriate object snap mode if necessary. As an example, consider the portion of an electronic schematic diagram shown in Figure 10-7. Here, a line passes completely through a transistor symbol and must be removed where it intersects with the transistor. Since the transistor is a block entity, the **TRIM** command cannot be used. To break the line accurately, osnap **INTersection** is used twice at the intersections of the transistor and the line. The procedure looks like this:

    Command: *(type BREAK or BR and press [Enter])*
    Select object: *(select the line)*
    Enter second point (or F for first point): **F** ↵
    Enter first point: **INT** ↵
    of *(pick the first intersection of the line and the block)*
    Enter second point: **INT** ↵
    of *(pick the second intersection of the line and the block)*
    Command:

Figure 10-7.
Using **BREAK** on a
line entity.

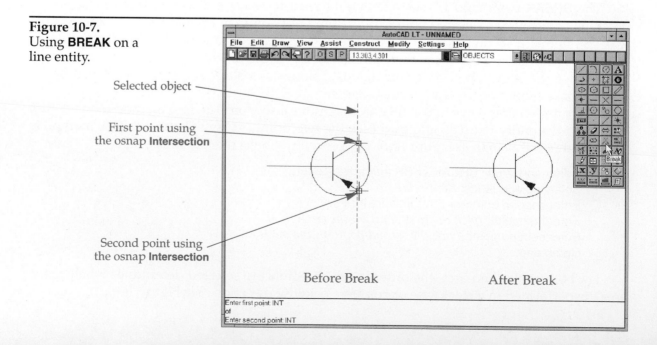

AutoCAD LT—Fundamentals and Applications

You can also break a section out of an object without explicitly selecting the first point with the **F** option. With this method, the point you select on the entity when prompted **Select object:** automatically becomes the first break point. To ensure precision, use an osnap if necessary when picking the first point.

Command: *(type* BREAK *or* BR *and press* [Enter]*)*
Select object: *(pick the first point on the object)*
Enter second point (or F for first point): *(pick a second point on the object)*
Command:

Breaking at a single point

As mentioned previously, the **BREAK** command may also be used to break an entity at a selected point, resulting in two separate entities. This procedure uses the **@** symbol and is shown below:

Command: *(type* BREAK *or* BR *and press* [Enter]*)*
Select object: *(select an entity)*
Enter second point (or F for first point): **@** ↵
Command:

Using this method, an entity is broken at precisely the point at which it is selected. Therefore, be sure to use the appropriate osnap when selecting the entity to break. For example, if you want to break a line at its midpoint into two separate lines, do the following:

Command: *(type* BREAK *or* BR *and press* [Enter]*)*
Select object: *(select the line using the* **MIDpoint** *osnap)*
Enter second point (or F for first point): **@** ↵
Command:

EXERCISE 10-3

❏ Draw several lines, polylines, arcs, and circles. Experiment with the **BREAK** command as described in the preceding sections. For the arcs and circles, try selecting points in both counterclockwise and clockwise directions.
❏ When you are done experimenting with the **BREAK** command, begin a new drawing without saving the current drawing. It is not necessary to use one of your prototypes for the new drawing.
❏ Construct the object shown below. *Construction hint:* Draw all radiused features with circles and use the **TRIM** command to produce the arcs. Connect the arcs with the **TANgent** object snap mode.
❏ Do not draw the centerlines or dimensions.

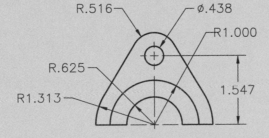

❏ Save the drawing as EX10-3 when you are finished, but do not exit AutoCAD LT.

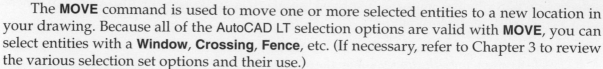

The **MOVE** command is used to move one or more selected entities to a new location in your drawing. Because all of the AutoCAD LT selection options are valid with **MOVE**, you can select entities with a **Window**, **Crossing**, **Fence**, etc. (If necessary, refer to Chapter 3 to review the various selection set options and their use.)

After selecting the entities, you are prompted to select a base point or enter a displacement. The base point is a reference point from which to move. After selecting the base point, you are prompted for the second displacement point. The two points you specify define the distance and direction the objects are to be moved. To issue the **MOVE** command, type MOVE or M at the **Command:** prompt, click the **Move** button in the toolbox, or select **Move** from the **Modify** pull-down menu. See Figure 10-8.

Figure 10-8.
Select **Move** from the **Modify** pull-down menu to issue the **MOVE** command.

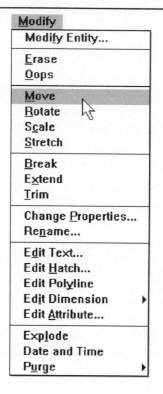

Moving from a reference point

Moving an object relative to a known base point, or reference point is quite commonly used and is described as follows:

```
Command: (type MOVE or M and press [Enter])
Select objects: (select the object(s) to move)
Select objects: ↵
Base point or displacement: (pick a point close to the selected entities)
Second point of displacement: (pick the point to move to)
Command:
```

Be sure to use the appropriate object snap modes when the base point and/or displacement point must be precisely selected. As an example, consider the object shown in Figure 10-9. This is the same object that you constructed in Exercise 10-3. In this example, the lower left corner of the object is selected as the base point using osnap **ENDpoint**. The object is then dynamically "dragged" with the mouse to a new screen location. Once the object is located to your satisfaction, click the left mouse button to set the object and end the command.

Figure 10-9.
Using the **MOVE** command.

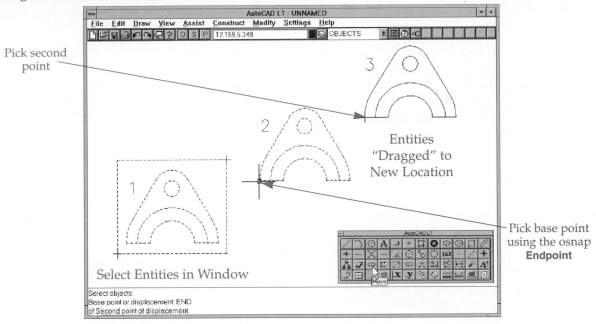

Pick second point

Select Entities in Window

Entities "Dragged" to New Location

Pick base point using the osnap **Endpoint**

Moving a circle to its correct location on an object using the **CENter** osnap is shown in Figure 10-10. In this example, the base point of the circle is its center and the second point of displacement is the center of the arc.

Figure 10-10.
Using object snap modes with the **Move** command.

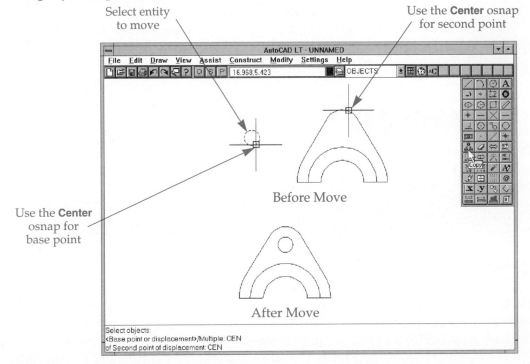

Select entity to move

Use the **Center** osnap for second point

Use the **Center** osnap for base point

Before Move

After Move

Moving with a known displacement

If you know the exact distance that an object must be moved, you can enter that distance on the command line. For example, suppose that an object needs to be relocated 4 units to the right. There are two ways to accomplish this. The first method looks like this:

    Command: (type MOVE or M and press [Enter])
    Select objects: (select the object)
    Select objects: ↵
    Base point or displacement: (pick a point or use an osnap)
    Second point of displacement: @4,0 ↵
    Command:

Since polar coordinates may be used, you can use the method just described to move selected entities at any distance and at any angle from a known base point.

An even faster method exists to move an object at a known displacement. With this second method, only the displacement is entered—no base point is selected at all.

    Command: (type MOVE or M and press [Enter])
    Select objects: (select the object)
    Select objects: ↵
    Base point or displacement: 4,0 ↵
    Second point of displacement: ↵
    Command:

As shown above, AutoCAD LT still prompts for a second point of displacement even though the displacement has been entered. If you press [Enter] at this prompt, the values you originally entered are then interpreted as the relative X, Y, and Z displacement from the 0,0,0 drawing origin and the object is moved accordingly.

PROFESSIONAL TIP

When using **MOVE** to increase or decrease the space between views, be sure to toggle **ORTHO** mode on. Doing so ensures that the views stay in alignment during the move operation. **Ortho** can be used for both orthogonal and auxiliary views. Refer to Chapter 7 to review the construction of auxiliary views.

EXERCISE 10-4

❑ Open EX10-3 if it is not on your screen.
❑ Move the entire object 3 units straight down.
❑ Next, move the circle off the object at an unspecified distance and angle.
❑ Using the example shown in Figure 10-10, move the circle back to its original position.
❑ When you are through, save the drawing as EX10-4 but do not exit AutoCAD LT.

ROTATING OBJECTS

ALTUG 9

The **ROTATE** command rotates entities around a selected base point at a specified angle. As with the **MOVE** command, all of the AutoCAD LT selection set options are valid. To use the **ROTATE** command, type ROTATE or RO at the **Command:** prompt, click the **Rotate** button in the toolbox, or select **Rotate** from the **Modify** pull-down menu. See Figure 10-11. The command options are described in the following sections.

AutoCAD LT—Fundamentals and Applications

Figure 10-11.
Select **Rotate** from the **Modify** pull-down menu to issue the **ROTATE** command.

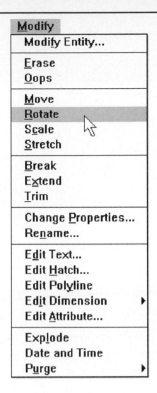

Modify
Modify Entity...
Erase
Oops
Move
Rotate
Scale
Stretch
Break
Extend
Trim
Change Properties...
Rename...
Edit Text...
Edit Hatch...
Edit Polyline
Edit Dimension ▶
Edit Attribute...
Explode
Date and Time
Purge ▶

Rotating around a reference point

The default method for rotating objects involves selecting a base point and then specifying a rotation angle. A positive rotation angle rotates in a counterclockwise direction and a negative angle rotates in a clockwise direction. As with other editing commands, the proper use of object snap modes helps to facilitate the operation. In the example shown in Figure 10-12, the object is first selected in a window and then rotated 45° about the center of the arc. The command sequence is as follows:

> Command: *(type* ROTATE *or* RO *and press* [Enter]*)*
> Select objects: **W** ↵
> First corner: *(pick a point)* Other corner: *(pick a diagonal point)*
> Select objects: ↵
> Base point: *(use osnap* **CENter** *and pick the arc)*
> 〈Rotation angle〉/Reference: **45** ↵
> Command:

Remember that implied windowing can be used as an efficient alternative to entering W at the **Select objects:** prompt.

Rotating using the Reference option

The **ROTATE** command's **Reference** option allows you to rotate entities relative to an existing angle or entity. With this method, you are prompted to specify the reference (existing) angle and then the new angle. When you know the reference angle, it may be entered at the keyboard. If you do not know the reference angle, you can use osnaps to select two specific points on an entity. The angle between the two points you select defines the reference

Figure 10-12.
Using an osnap with the **ROTATE** command.

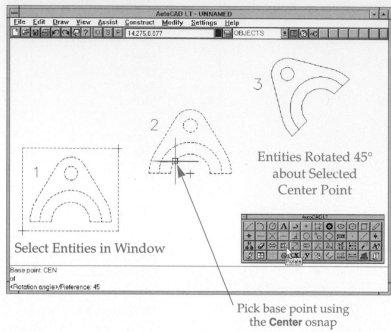

Pick base point using
the **Center** osnap

angle. This method is illustrated in Figure 10-13. In this example, the object previously rotated 45° is rotated another 15° relative to the angle specified by the two selected endpoints. The procedure looks like the following:

> Command: *(type ROTATE or RO and press [Enter])*
> Select objects: **W** ⏎
> First corner: *(pick a point)* Other corner: *(pick a diagonal point)*
> Select objects: ⏎
> Base point: *(select a base point)*
> ⟨Rotation angle⟩/Reference: **R** ⏎
> Reference angle ⟨0⟩: *(pick two points using osnap ENDpoint)*
> New angle: **15** ⏎
> Command:

Figure 10-13.
The **ROTATE Reference** option rotates objects relative to an existing entity or angle.

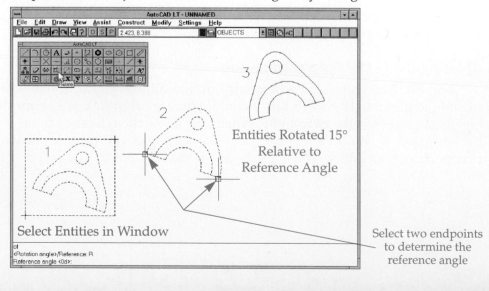

Select two endpoints
to determine the
reference angle

SCALING OBJECTS

ALTUG 10

The **SCALE** command is used to reduce or enlarge selected entities. When you use the scale command, objects are scaled equally in the X, Y, and Z directions. To issue the **SCALE** command, type SCALE or SC at the **Command:** prompt, click the **Scale** button in the toolbox, or select **Scale** from the **Modify** pull-down menu. See Figure 10-14. As with the **MOVE** and **ROTATE** commands, all of the AutoCAD LT selection set options are valid with **SCALE**. The **SCALE** command options are described in the following two sections.

Figure 10-14.
Select **Scale** from the **Modify** pull-down menu to issue the **SCALE** command.

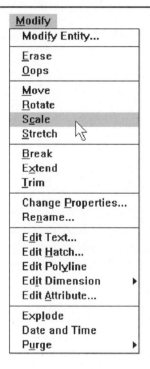

Scaling with a known scale factor

The default scaling method scales objects with a known scale factor relative to a selected base point. A scale factor greater than 1 enlarges the objects, while a scale factor between 0 and 1 shrinks the objects. A negative value is disallowed. Once again, consider the familiar object shown in Figure 10-15. In the two examples illustrated, the object is scaled from a base point at the lower left and with a specified scale factor. The procedure looks like this:

    Command: (type SCALE or SC and press [Enter])
    Select objects: (select the object using any selection set option)
    Select objects: ↵
    Base point: (pick a base point)
    〈Scale factor〉/Reference: 2 ↵
    Command:

Figure 10-15.
Scaling object with the **SCALE** command.

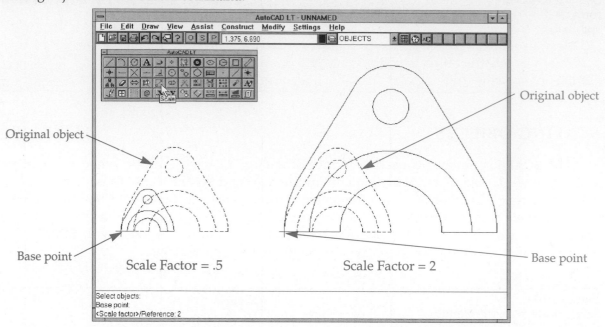

In the example above, the object is doubled in size. It is also possible to scale an object dynamically by "dragging" the object to the desired size at the ⟨**Scale factor**⟩/**Reference:** prompt. Using this method, a rubber-band line connected to the selected base point follows the motion of your mouse. Move your mouse up or down, or left and right to scale the object. Once the object is scaled to your satisfaction, click the left mouse button to set the new size and end the command.

Scaling using the Reference option

The **Reference** option allows you to scale an object using an existing dimension as the basis for a new size. You are first prompted to specify the current length and then to enter a new length. In the example shown in Figure 10-16, a line is changed from 5 units to 7 units in length using the **Reference** option. The procedure is as follows:

```
Command: (type SCALE or SC and press [Enter])
Select objects: (select the line)
Select objects: ⏎
Base point: (pick the base point using osnap ENDpoint)
⟨Scale factor⟩/Reference: R ⏎
Reference length ⟨1⟩: 5 ⏎
New length: 7 ⏎
Command:
```

Scaling the entire drawing

It may occasionally be necessary to scale an entire drawing. This can occur if a change in drawing units is required. As an example, use the following procedure to convert an entire drawing to millimeters:

```
Command: (type SCALE or SC and press [Enter])
Select objects: ALL ⏎
Select objects: ⏎
Base point: 0,0 ⏎
⟨Scale factor⟩/Reference: 25.4 ⏎
Command:
```

Figure 10-16.
Using the **SCALE**
command's **Reference**
option.

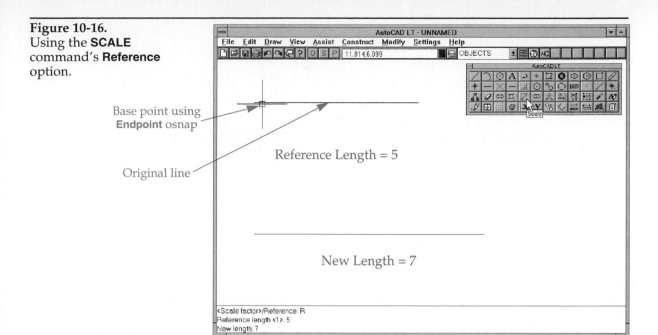

Base point using
Endpoint osnap

Original line

Reference Length = 5

New Length = 7

```
<Scale factor>/Reference: R
Reference length <1>: 5
New length: 7
```

Since there are 25.4 millimeters to an inch, the entire drawing is scaled 25.4 times larger. Now, perform a **ZOOM Extents** operation to view the entire drawing.

> Command: *(type* ZOOM *or* Z *and press* [Enter]*)*
> All/Center/Extents/Previous/Window/⟨Scale(X/XP)⟩: **E** ↵
> Command:

Also, do not forget to set the appropriate drawing limits for a metric drawing.

PROFESSIONAL TIP   You can also use the procedure described above to convert a metric drawing to Imperial units. Enter .03937 when prompted for the scale factor.

STRETCHING OBJECTS   ALTUG 10

The **STRETCH** command stretches (or shrinks) selected entities. To use **STRETCH**, you must use a crossing box or crossing polygon to select the objects. This is because AutoCAD LT can only stretch entities that cross the selection window. The endpoints that lie inside the crossing box are moved, while those that are outside the crossing box are unchanged. The crossing selection set option is automatically enabled when you click the **Stretch** button in the toolbox or select **S**tretch from the **M**odify pull-down menu. See Figure 10-17. When you enter STRETCH or S at the **Command:** prompt, you receive the following message:

> Select objects to stretch by window or polygon...

This message is misleading because a window box or window polygon cannot be used with **STRETCH**. The entities *must* be selected with a crossing box (C) or crossing polygon (CP).

The **STRETCH** command prompts and options are identical to the **MOVE** command discussed earlier in this chapter. In other words, you may stretch from a selected base point, with a known displacement, or both. These **STRETCH** command options are described in the following sections.

Figure 10-17.
Select **Stretch** from the
Modify pull-down menu to
issue the **STRETCH**
command.

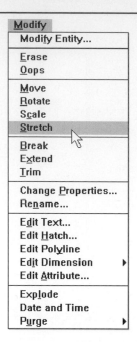

Stretching from a reference point

Consider the simple object shown at the top of Figure 10-18. This object is to be stretched to the right. Observe that the crossing box only encloses those entities that are to be moved. The remainder of the object is outside the crossing box and stays *anchored* at its current location. This is very important because if you select the entire object in the selection set, the entities are moved and not stretched. Additionally, it is a good idea to toggle **ORTHO** mode on before stretching an object. This ensures that entities do not get skewed, or misaligned, during the operation. The procedure for stretching the object shown at the top of Figure 10-18 is given below:

        Command: *(type* STRETCH *or* S *and press* [Enter]*)*
        Select objects to stretch by window or polygon…
        Select objects: **C** ↵
        First corner: *(pick the point indicated)* Other corner: *(pick the diagonal point)*
        Select objects: ↵
        Base point or displacement: *(select the circle using osnap* **CENter***)*
        Second point of displacement: *(pick a location to the right of the object)*
        Command:

Remember that implied windowing can be used as an efficient alternative to entering a C at the **Select objects:** prompt.

Stretching with a known displacement

If you know the exact distance that an object must be stretched, you can enter that distance on the command line. For example, suppose that the object shown at the bottom of Figure 10-18 needs to be stretched 2 units straight down. There are two ways to accomplish this stretching. The first method looks like this:

        Command: *(type* STRETCH *or* S *and press* [Enter]*)*
        Select objects to stretch by window or polygon…
        Select objects: **C** ↵
        First corner: *(pick the point indicated)* Other corner: *(pick the diagonal point)*
        Select objects: ↵
        Base point or displacement: *(pick the lower right corner using osnap* **ENDpoint***)*
        Second point of displacement: **@2⟨270** ↵
        Command:

Figure 10-18.
Using the **STRETCH** command.

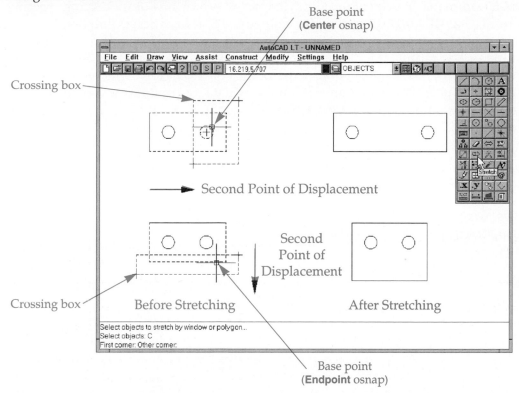

Since polar coordinates may be used, you can use the method just described to stretch selected entities at any distance and at any angle from a known base point.

An even faster method exists to stretch an object at a known displacement. With this second method, only the displacement is entered—no base point is selected at all.

> Command: *(type* STRETCH *or* S *and press* [Enter]*)*
> Select objects to stretch by window or polygon...
> Select objects: **C** ↵
> First corner: *(pick the point indicated)* Other corner: *(pick the diagonal point)*
> Select objects: ↵
> Base point or displacement: **0, –2** ↵
> Second point of displacement: ↵
> Command:

As just shown, AutoCAD LT still prompts for a second point of displacement even though the displacement has been entered. If you press [Enter] at this prompt, the values you originally entered are then interpreted as the relative X, Y, and Z displacement from the 0,0,0 drawing origin and the object is stretched accordingly.

EXERCISE 10-6

❑ Draw a rectangle with two circles similar to that shown in Figure 10-18.
❑ Use the **STRETCH** command to resize the object along both axes. Also try shrinking the object.
❑ Next, use the **SCALE** command and scale the object by a factor of 4.
❑ Finally, draw a line similar to that shown in Figure 10-16. Use the **SCALE** command's **Reference** option to change the length of the line.
❑ Do not save the drawing when you are finished.

EDITING LINES AND CIRCLES WITH THE CHANGE COMMAND

The **CHANGE** command was introduced in Chapter 9 as a means of modifying existing text. You may recall that **CHANGE** allows you to change the text insertion point, height, rotation angle, style, and character string. However, **CHANGE** may also be used to modify the endpoint of a line or the radius of a circle. When changing the endpoint of a line, you are prompted ⟨**Change point**⟩. The *change point* is the point you select for the new endpoint of the line. You can pick a point on the screen, enter a coordinate, or osnap to an existing entity. To gain a clearer understanding of how **CHANGE** modifies the endpoints of lines, see Figure 10-19. At the top of the illustration, a line endpoint is modified to intersect with the endpoint of a horizontal line. The procedure is as follows:

> Command: *(type* CHANGE *or* CH *and press* [Enter]*)*
> Select objects: *(pick the diagonal line nearest the endpoint to change)*
> Select objects: ⏎
> Properties/⟨Change point⟩: **END** ⏎
> of *(select the endpoint of the horizontal line)*
> Command:

Figure 10-19.
Using the **CHANGE** command to change line endpoints.

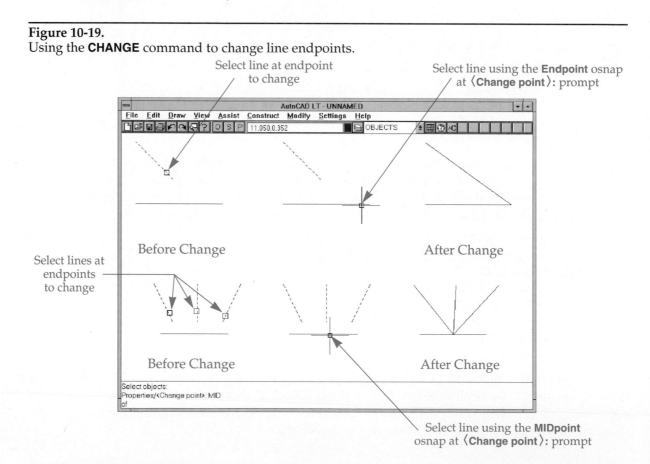

Because all of the AutoCAD LT selection set options are valid with **CHANGE**, you can select more than one line at a time. When you specify a new endpoint for several lines, the endpoints of the selected lines closest to the change point move to the new point. This is illustrated by the three lines shown near the bottom of Figure 10-19. In this example, the change point for the three lines selected is the **MIDpoint** of the horizontal line. However, if **ORTHO** mode is on, the lines are forced parallel to either the X or the Y axis, rather than moving their endpoints to the specified change point. In the example shown in Figure 10-19, the three lines would be forced vertical with **Ortho** on since their original orientation was more vertical than horizontal.

You can use **CHANGE** to specify a new circle radius for an existing circle in two different ways. The first method is to simply pick a screen location that the circle is to pass through. See Figure 10-20. The procedure looks like this:

Command: *(type* CHANGE *or* CH *and press* [Enter]*)*
Select objects: *(pick the circle to change)*
Select objects: ↵
Properties/⟨Change point⟩: *(pick a point through which the circle is to be drawn)*
Command:

When you need to be more precise for the new circle radius, do the following:

Command: *(type* CHANGE *or* CH *and press* [Enter]*)*
Select objects: *(pick the circle to change)*
Select objects: ↵
Properties/⟨Change point⟩: ↵
Enter circle radius: *(enter a positive value)*
Command:

If more than one circle is selected, AutoCAD LT repeats the prompt for each entity encountered in the selection set.

Figure 10-20.
Changing the radius of a circle with the **CHANGE** command.

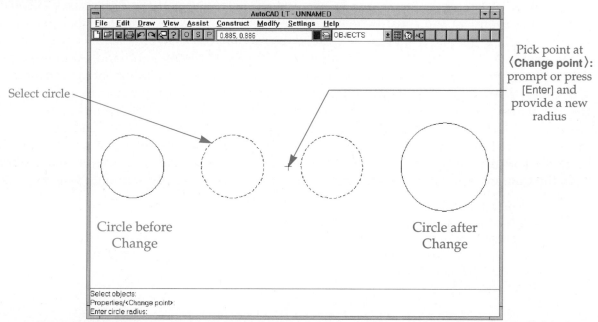

Use **CHANGE** whenever the size of a circle must be changed. It is far more efficient to revise the radius of an existing circle than it is to erase the circle and re-create it. This is particularly true when many circles must be modified.

COMMANDS THAT DUPLICATE EXISTING ENTITIES

Perhaps the greatest value in using CAD is never having to draw the same object twice. AutoCAD LT provides several commands that allow you to duplicate existing entities. One of these commands, **OFFSET**, was introduced in Chapter 7. You may recall that **OFFSET** allows you to duplicate an entity at a distance or through a selected point. The following sections describe the **MIRROR**, **COPY**, and **ARRAY** commands. These commands allow you to duplicate many entities at once using a variety of methods.

CREATING MIRROR IMAGES

ALTUG 9

The **MIRROR** command creates a mirror image of selected entities. This makes **MIRROR** particularly useful in the construction of complex symmetrical objects. For these types of shapes, simply draw one half of the object and mirror it across its symmetrical center line. All of the AutoCAD LT selection set options are valid with the **MIRROR** command. After selecting the entities to mirror, you are prompted to select the first and second points of the mirror line. The *mirror line* is the axis about which the selected objects are mirrored. Be sure to turn **ORTHO** mode on if the two points you select are on the screen and not on the object itself. This ensures that the mirrored entities do not get skewed, or misaligned. At the end of the command, you are prompted to delete or retain the original entities. Answer Y or N accordingly. To issue the **MIRROR** command, type MIRROR or MI at the **Command:** prompt, or select **Mirror** from the **Construct** pull-down menu. See Figure 10-21. The command sequence is as follows:

```
Command: (type MIRROR or MI and press [Enter])
Select objects: (select the object(s) to be mirrored)
Select objects: ↵
First point of mirror line: (pick a point)  Second point: (pick a second point)
Delete old objects? ⟨N⟩ (answer Y or N)
Command:
```

Figure 10-21.
Selecting **Mirror** from the **Construct** pull-down menu issues the **MIRROR** command.

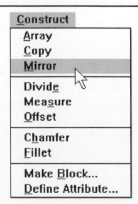

Refer to Figure 10-22 to obtain a better understanding of the **MIRROR** procedure. At the left, the entities to be mirrored are first selected using a crossing box. Observe that the two horizontal lines of the object are purposely excluded from the selection set. This is to ensure that these lines are not duplicated upon themselves during the **MIRROR** operation. Next, osnap **ENDpoint** is used to select two points that define the axis about which the entities are to be mirrored. At the far right, the object is mirrored, the original entities are retained, and the two original horizontal lines are erased. The two lines could also have been erased prior to the **MIRROR** procedure.

Figure 10-22.
Using the **MIRROR** command.

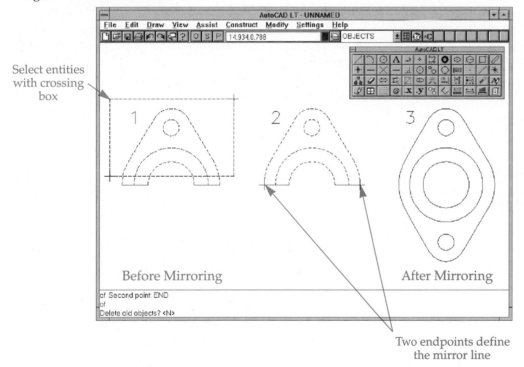

Two endpoints define
the mirror line

The MIRRTEXT System Variable

ALTUG 9

It is important to realize that the **MIRROR** command also mirrors text and dimensions. This is controlled by the **MIRRTEXT** system variable. By default, **MIRRTEXT** is turned on, which causes text and dimensions to mirror. To eliminate mirrored text and dimensions, turn **MIRRTEXT** off as follows:

Command: **MIRRTEXT** ↵
New value for MIRRTEXT ⟨1⟩: **0** ↵

Block attributes, (textual information attached to blocks), get mirrored regardless of the **MIRRTEXT** setting. See Chapter 14 for complete information about blocks and block attributes.

EXERCISE 10-8

❑ Open drawing EX10-4.
❑ Using the **MIRROR** command, create a mirror image of the object as shown in Figure 10-22.
❑ Save the drawing as EX10-8.

COPYING OBJECTS

ALTUG 9

The **COPY** command makes one or more copies of selected objects. All of the AutoCAD LT selection set options are valid with the **COPY** command. The prompts and options of the **COPY** command are nearly identical to those of the **MOVE** command. The major difference is that after selecting the desired objects, the selected entities are copied upon themselves, and it is the copies that are moved. As with the **MOVE** command, you can copy using a base point, a known displacement, or both. To use the **COPY** command, type COPY or CP at the **Command:** prompt, click the **Copy** button in the toolbox, or select **Copy** from the **Construct** pull-down menu. See Figure 10-23. The **COPY** command and its options are described in the following sections.

Figure 10-23.
Select **Copy** from the **Construct** pull-down menu to issue the **COPY** command.

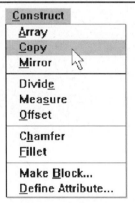

Copying from a reference point

Consider the partial schematic diagram shown in Figure 10-24. In this example, a resistor symbol is copied to another location in the diagram using the appropriate object snap modes. Study the illustration as you follow the command sequence given below:

Command: *(type COPY or CP and press [Enter])*
Select objects: **W** ↵
First corner: *(pick the first corner)* Other corner: *(pick a diagonal corner)*
Select objects: ↵
⟨Base point or displacement⟩/Multiple: **CEN** ↵
of *(select the center of the donut at the top of the resistor)*
Second point of displacement: **NEA** ↵
to *(select a point on the top line to the right of the resistor)*
Command:

Figure 10-24.
Using the **COPY** command.

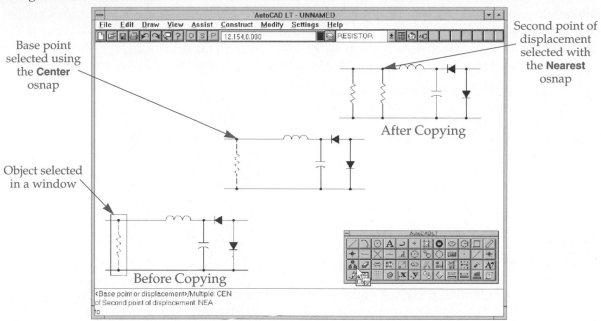

Base point selected using the **Center** osnap

Object selected in a window

Before Copying

After Copying

Second point of displacement selected with the **Nearest** osnap

Copying with a known displacement

If you know the exact distance that a copied object is to be moved, you can enter that distance on the command line. For example, suppose that an object needs to be copied 3 units to the left. There are two ways to accomplish this. The first method looks like this:

> Command: *(type* COPY *or* CP *and press* [Enter]*)*
> Select objects: *(select the object(s) to copy)*
> Select objects: ↵
> ⟨Base point or displacement⟩/Multiple: *(pick a point or use an osnap)*
> Second point of displacement: **@−3,0** ↵
> Command:

Since polar coordinates may be used, you can use the method just described to copy selected entities at any distance and at any angle from a known base point.

An even faster method exists to copy an object at a known displacement. With this second method, only the displacement is entered—no base point is selected at all.

> Command: *(type* COPY *or* CP *and press* [Enter]*)*
> Select objects: *(select the object(s) to copy)*
> Select objects: ↵
> ⟨Base point or displacement⟩/Multiple: **−3,0** ↵
> Second point of displacement: ↵
> Command:

As shown above, AutoCAD LT still prompts for a second point of displacement even though the displacement has been entered. If you press [Enter] at this prompt, the values you originally entered arc then interpreted as the relative X, Y, and Z displacement from the 0,0,0 drawing origin and the object is copied to the new location accordingly.

Making multiple copies

It is often necessary to make more than one copy of an object. The **COPY** command's **Multiple** option allows you to do so. After selecting the entities to copy, enter M for **Multiple**. Then, select a base point as usual and a second point of displacement to place the copy. The **Second point of displacement:** prompt is repeated to allow multiple copies. When you are through copying, press [Enter] to end the command. The command sequence is as follows:

Command: *(type* COPY *or* CP *and press* [Enter]*)*
Select objects: *(select the object(s) to copy)*
Select objects: ⏎
⟨Base point or displacement⟩/Multiple: **M** ⏎
Base point: ⏎
Second point of displacement: *(pick a point or use an osnap)*
Second point of displacement: *(pick another point or use an osnap)*
Second point of displacement: *(locate another copy or press* [Enter] *to end)*
Command:

THE **ARRAY** COMMAND

ALTUG 9

The **ARRAY** command creates multiple copies of objects in a rectangular or polar (circular) pattern. To issue the **ARRAY** command, type ARRAY or AR at the **Command:** prompt, or select **Array** from the **Construct** pull-down menu. See Figure 10-24. The **ARRAY** command and its options are described in the following sections.

NOTE Although the **Array** button shown in the margin does not appear in the toolbar or toolbox by default, it may easily be added.

Figure 10-25.
Selecting **Array** from the **Construct** pull-down menu issues the **ARRAY** command.

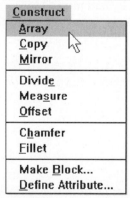

Creating a rectangular array

A rectangular array copies objects in a pattern defined by a number of rows and columns. The rows correspond to the Y axis, and the columns correspond to the X axis. Consider the rectangular array of electronic resistors shown in Figure 10-26. The first resistor in this array is located at the lower left. This is the original object that is copied and is called the *cornerstone element*. Each of the other objects in a rectangular array are called *cells*. Each cell remains a separate, discrete drawing entity that may be erased, or otherwise modified, independently from the rest of the array. In this example, there are 4 rows and 3 columns in the array. The distance between the rows and columns must also be specified. To create the array shown in Figure 10-26, do the following:

Command: *(type* ARRAY *or* AR *and press* [Enter]*)*
Select objects: *(select the resistor)*
Select objects: ↵
Rectangular or Polar array (R/P) ⟨*current*⟩: **R** ↵
Number of rows (---) ⟨1⟩: **4** ↵
Number of columns (⦙⦙⦙) ⟨1⟩: **3** ↵
Unit cell or distance between rows (---): **1.5** ↵
Distance between columns (⦙⦙⦙): **3** ↵
Command:

Figure 10-26.
In a rectangular array, the columns correspond to the X direction and the rows correspond to the Y direction.

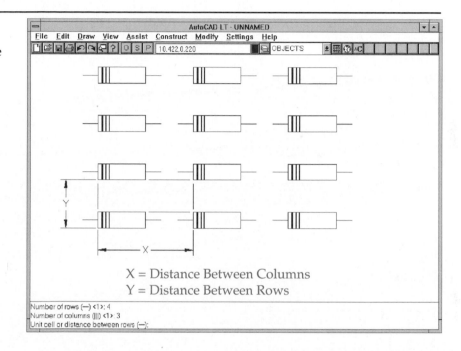

X = Distance Between Columns
Y = Distance Between Rows

The cornerstone element is usually assumed to be at the lower left so that an array is created up and to the right. However, an array can be created down and/or to the left by entering negative values for the distances between the rows and columns. It is also possible to specify the distance between cells by picking two diagonal corners with your mouse. This method is illustrated in Figure 10-27 and is performed as follows:

Command: *(type* ARRAY *or* AR *and press* [Enter]*)*
Select objects: *(select the resistor)*
Select objects: ↵
Rectangular or Polar array (R/P)⟨*current*⟩: **R** ↵
Number of rows (---) ⟨1⟩: **4** ↵
Number of columns (⦙⦙⦙) ⟨1⟩: **3** ↵
Unit cell or distance between rows (---): *(pick the first corner)*
Other corner: *(pick a diagonal corner)*
Command:

PROFESSIONAL TIP   To generate a rectangular array at an angle other than 0°, set the **SNAP Rotation** angle before issuing the **ARRAY** command.

Figure 10-27.
Two diagonal corners define the unit cell distance.

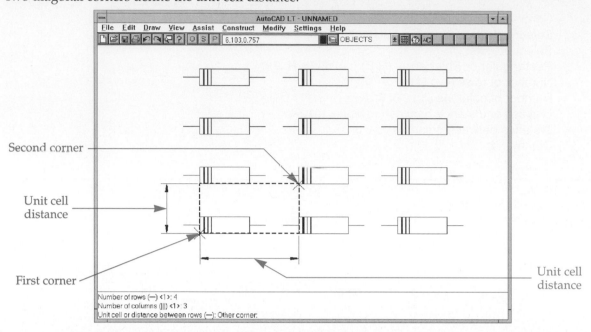

❑ Use a circle and a six-sided polygon to draw one of the hexagonal features shown in this exercise. Do not draw the centerlines or dimensions.

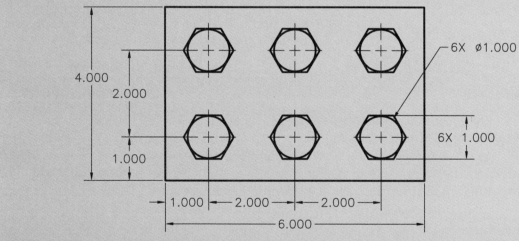

❑ Finish the construction using a rectangular array.
❑ Save the drawing as EX10-9.

Creating a polar array

A polar array copies selected objects in a circular pattern around a specified center point. As shown in Figure 10-28, a small circle with a centerline is copied 8 times around the center point of the large circle. The objects can be rotated as they are being copied, as shown in the illustration. Observe the difference in the centerlines when the array is not rotated. To create the polar array shown in Figure 10-28, do the following:

> Command: *(type* ARRAY *or* AR *and press* [Enter]*)*
> Select objects: *(select the object(s) to array)*
> Select objects: ⏎
> Rectangular or Polar array (R/P)⟨*current*⟩: **P** ⏎
> Center point of array: *(pick the large circle using osnap* **CENter***)*
> Number of items: **8** ⏎

When specifying the number of items to array, be sure to include the original selection set.

> Angle to fill (+=ccw,-=cw) ⟨360⟩: ⏎

You can array an object through a full 360° or only through a portion of the 360°. A positive value copies in a counterclockwise direction, while a negative value copies in a clockwise direction.

> Rotate objects as they are copied? ⟨Y⟩: ⏎
> Command:

The default is to rotate entities as they are arrayed. If you prefer not to rotate the objects, answer N accordingly.

There may be instances when you know the angle that must exist between the arrayed objects, but you are unsure as to the number of items. In the following example, an angle of 60° is specified between the arrayed objects:

> Command: *(type* ARRAY *or* AR *and press* [Enter]*)*
> Select objects: *(select the object(s) to array)*
> Select objects: ⏎
> Rectangular or Polar array (R/P)⟨*current*⟩: **P** ⏎
> Center point of array: *(pick the center point)*
> Number of items: ⏎
> Angle to fill (+=ccw,-=cw) ⟨360⟩: ⏎
> Angle between items: **60** ⏎
> Rotate objects as they are copied? ⟨Y⟩: ⏎
> Command:

Figure 10-28.
An example of a rotated and non-rotated polar array.

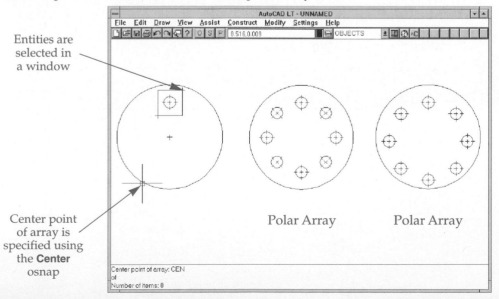

Entities are selected in a window

Center point of array is specified using the **Center** osnap

Polar Array   Polar Array

A final word about polar arrays

When objects are not rotated in a polar array, they often appear to not rotate correctly around the specified center point of the array. This is apparent with the non-rotated circles and centerlines shown at the far right in Figure 10-28. This occurs because AutoCAD LT determines the distance from the center point of the array to a reference point on the *last entity* encountered in the selection set. The reference point varies depending on the type of entity selected. AutoCAD LT uses one endpoint of a line, the start point of text, and the center point of an arc or circle as the reference point. If you pick entities singly with your mouse, the last entity selected determines the reference point. On the other hand, if you use a crossing or window box, the last object encountered in the selection set is arbitrary. This is the reason why a non-rotated polar array appears non-symmetric around the center.

To avoid this problem, remove the entity you wish to use as reference from the selection set, and then immediately add it back. This forces the entity to be the last object selected. Refer to Chapter 3 of this text to review the **Remove** and **Add** selection set options.

EXERCISE 10-10

❑ Use a polar array to draw the object shown in this exercise. Do not draw the centerlines or dimensions.
❑ *Construction hint:* Study the geometry carefully to identify how the **OFFSET** and **TRIM** commands can speed the construction of this object.

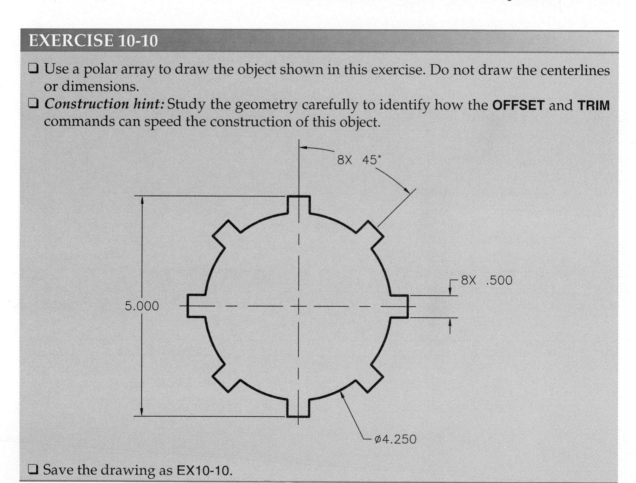

❑ Save the drawing as EX10-10.

POLYLINE EDITING

The **POLYLINE** command was introduced in Chapter 6. Polylines offer capabilities not found in normal line entities. As an example, multiple polyline and polyarc segments created in one operation can be drawn with variable widths and are treated as one object. Polylines can be edited in a variety of ways using the **PEDIT** command. To issue the **PEDIT** command, type PEDIT or PE at the **Command:** prompt, or select **Edit Polyline** from the **Modify** pull-down menu. See Figure 10-29. The command sequence is as follows:

> Command: *(type* PEDIT *or* PE *and press* [Enter]*)*
> Select polyline: *(select the object)*

Figure 10-29.
Selecting **Edit Polyline** from the **Modify** pull-down menu issues the **PEDIT** command.

 NOTE   Although the **Edit Polyline** button shown in the margin does not appear in the toolbar or toolbox by default, it may easily be added.

If you select a line or an arc, AutoCAD LT informs you that you did not select a polyline. You are then given the option to automatically convert the entity to a polyline by simply pressing [Enter].

> Entity selected is not a polyline
> Do you want to turn it into one? ⟨Y⟩ ↵
> Close/Join/Width/Edit Vertex/Fit/Spline/Decurve/Ltype gen/Undo/eXit ⟨X⟩:

Each of the **PEDIT** command options are described in the following sections.

Closing and opening a polyline

If the polyline you select is open, then the first **PEDIT** command option is **Close**. This option draws the closing segment of the polyline by connecting the last segment with the first. On the other hand, if the polyline you select is already closed, then the first command option is **Open**. An example of a closed and open polyline is shown in Figure 10-30.

Figure 10-30.
The **PEDIT** command can
close an open polyline and
open a closed one.

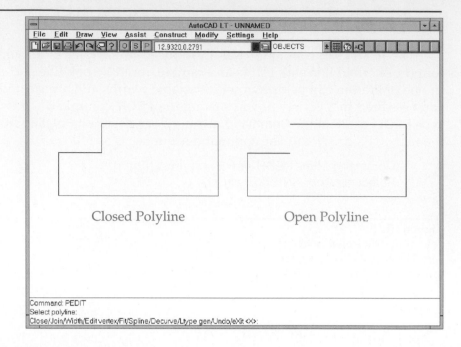

Joining entities together into one polyline

The **PEDIT Join** option allows you to join line, arc, and polyline entities together into one polyline as long as their endpoints touch. See Figure 10-31. If a line or polyline crosses the end of a polyline in a T-shape, the entities cannot be joined. Additionally, you cannot join entities to a closed polyline. The **Join** option appears as follows:

Command: *(type* PEDIT *or* PE *and press* [Enter]*)*
Select polyline: *(select the object)*

Figure 10-31.
Separate entities can be
joined into one polyline
using the **PEDIT Join** option.

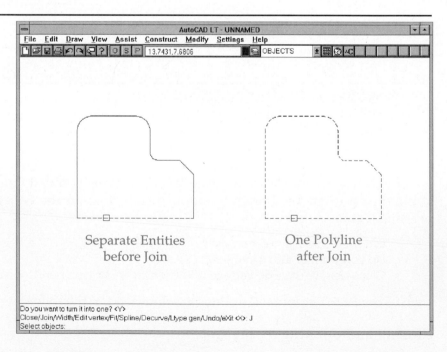

Remember that if the entity you select is a line or an arc, you are then prompted to automatically convert it into a polyline.

```
Close/Join/Width/Edit Vertex/Fit/Spline/Decurve/Ltype gen/Undo/eXit ⟨X⟩: J ↵
Select objects: (select one or more objects to join together)
Select objects: ↵
n segments added to polyline
Close/Join/Width/Edit Vertex/Fit/Spline/Decurve/Ltype gen/Undo/eXit ⟨X⟩: ↵
Command:
```

PROFESSIONAL TIP

The **PEDIT Join** option is particularly handy when you have a shape drawn with lines and would like to fillet or chamfer each vertex of the object in one operation. Once the entities are joined into a polyline, use the Polyline option of the FILLET or CHAMFER commands to modify all contiguous vertices in one step.

Changing the width of a polyline

Use the **PEDIT Width** option to add a width or specify a new width for an existing polyline. As shown in Figure 10-32, the width you specify is uniform over the entire length of the polyline. The **Width** option looks like this:

```
Command: (type PEDIT or PE and press [Enter])
Select polyline: (select the polyline)
Close/Join/Width/Edit Vertex/Fit/Spline/Decurve/Ltype gen/Undo/eXit ⟨X⟩: W ↵
Enter new width for all segments: (enter a positive value)
Close/Join/Width/Edit Vertex/Fit/Spline/Decurve/Ltype gen/Undo/eXit ⟨X⟩: ↵
Command:
```

Figure 10-32.
The **PEDIT Width** option is used to add or modify polyline width.

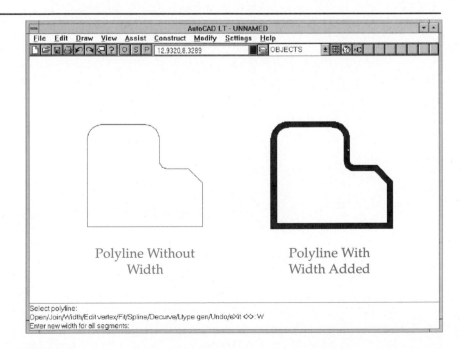

Polyline Without Width

Polyline With Width Added

Editing the vertices of a polyline

Each vertex of a polyline may be individually modified using the **PEDIT Edit Vertex** option. When this option is selected, AutoCAD LT places a marker shaped like an X at the first vertex of the selected polyline. You then move the marker to the vertex you wish to edit using the **Next** (for next vertex) and **Previous** (for previous vertex) suboptions. The **PEDIT Edit Vertex** option appears as follows:

> Command: *(type* PEDIT *or* PE *and press* [Enter])
> Select polyline: *(select the polyline)*
> Close/Join/Width/Edit Vertex/Fit/Spline/Decurve/Ltype gen/Undo/eXit 〈X〉: **E** ↵
> Next/Previous/Break/Insert/Move/Regen/Straighten/Tangent/Width/eXit 〈N〉:

Each of the **Edit Vertex** suboptions are described below:

- **Next/Previous.** As mentioned above, use these suboptions to move the X shaped marker forward or backward to the vertex you wish to edit. The **Next** suboption is the default.

- **Break.** Use this suboption to remove one or more segments from a polyline. See Figure 10-33. The break is performed between the first selected vertex and the last selected vertex as marked by the **Next** and **Previous** suboptions. Once you have identified the last vertex, use the **Go** suboption to effect the break. The **Break** suboption looks like this:

> Next/Previous/Break/Insert/Move/Regen/Straighten/Tangent/Width/eXit 〈N〉: **B** ↵
> Next/Previous/Go/eXit 〈N〉:

Figure 10-33.
The **Edit Vertex Break** suboption removes one or more segments from a polyline.

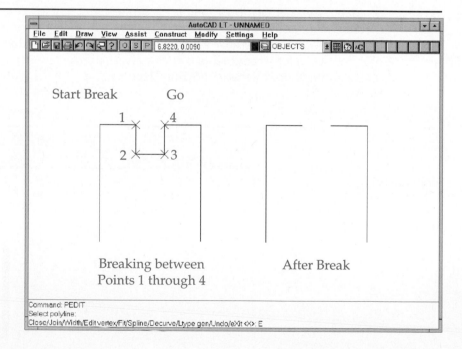

- **Insert.** This suboption allows you to insert a new vertex at a selected location after the vertex that is currently marked with the X. See Figure 10-34. The **Insert** suboption appears as follows:

  Next/Previous/Break/Insert/Move/Regen/Straighten/Tangent/Width/eXit ⟨N⟩: **I** ↵
  Enter location of new vertex: *(locate a point)*

Figure 10-34.
Using the **Edit Vertex Insert** suboption to add a new vertex.

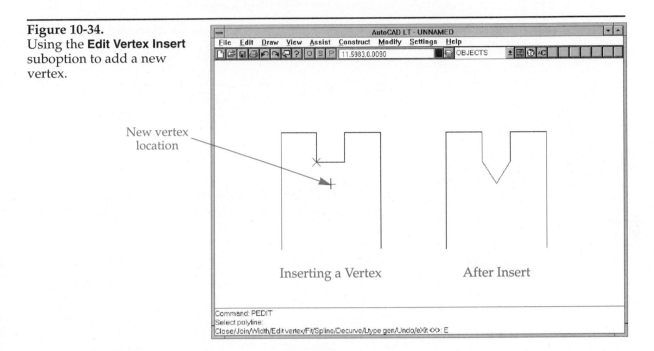

- **Move.** Use this suboption to move an X marked vertex to a new screen location. See Figure 10-35.

  Next/Previous/Break/Insert/Move/Regen/Straighten/Tangent/Width/eXit ⟨N⟩: **M** ↵
  Enter new location: *(locate a point)*

Figure 10-35.
The **Edit Vertex Move** suboption is used to move an existing vertex.

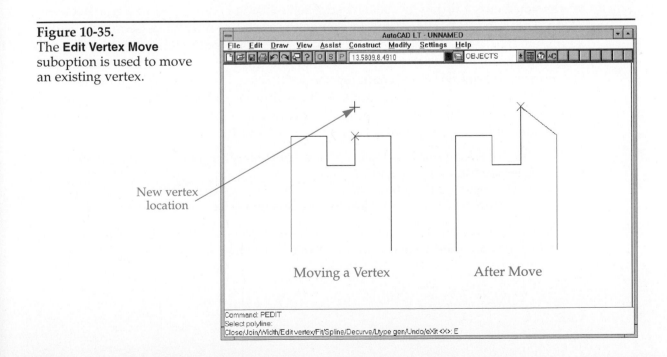

- **Regen.** After using the **Edit Vertex Width** suboption, **Regen** is used to display the changes. The **Width** suboption is described in a later section.
- **Straighten.** This suboption is used to straighten both polyline and polyarc segments between selected vertices. See Figure 10-36. The straightening is performed between the first selected vertex and the last selected vertex as marked by the **Next** and **Previous** suboptions. Once you have identified the last vertex, use the **Go** suboption to straighten the polyline. The **Straighten** suboption looks like this:

Next/Previous/Break/Insert/Move/Regen/Straighten/Tangent/Width/eXit ⟨N⟩: **S** ↵
Next/Previous/Go/eXit ⟨N⟩:

Figure 10-36.
The **Edit Vertex Straighten** suboption may be used to straighten both polyline and polyarc segments.

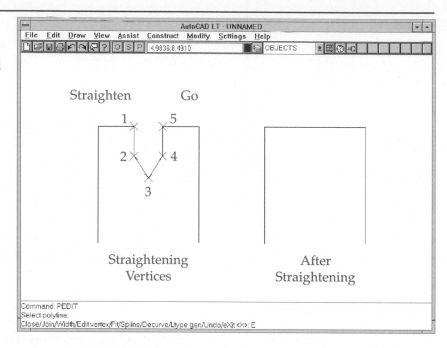

- **Tangent.** The **Tangent** suboption is used to change the tangent direction of a polyline vertex when curve fitting has been used. Curve fitting is described in a later section.
- **Width.** This suboption allows you to change the width of individual segments within a polyline. The polyline segment that immediately follows the X marked vertex is the segment whose width is changed. As shown in Figure 10-37, the segment width may be uniform or tapered. After changing the width, use the **Regen** suboption as previously described to display the change. In the following example, a starting width of 0 and an ending width of .25 is specified to produce a tapered polyline segment. The **Regen** suboption is then used to display the new width.

Next/Previous/Break/Insert/Move/Regen/Straighten/Tangent/Width/eXit ⟨N⟩: **W** ↵
Enter starting width ⟨*current*⟩: **0** ↵
Enter ending width ⟨0.0000⟩: **.25** ↵
Next/Previous/Break/Insert/Move/Regen/Straighten/Tangent/Width/eXit ⟨N⟩: **R** ↵

- **eXit.** Once you are finished editing the polyline vertices, enter X for **eXit** to end the operation. You are then returned to the **PEDIT** command options.

Figure 10-37.
The **Edit Vertex Width** suboption is used to change the width of individual segments within a polyline. After changing the width, use the **Regen** suboption to display the change.

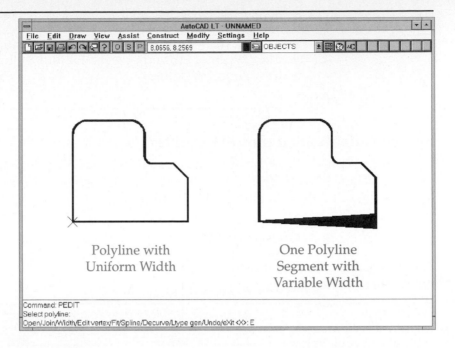

The **Fit, Spline, and Decurve options**

The **PEDIT Fit** option creates a smooth curve by converting a polyline from straight line segments into arcs. As shown in Figure 10-38, there are two arcs for every pair of vertices. Observe that the curve passes through all the vertices of the polyline. Use the **Edit Vertex Tangent** suboption if you wish to modify the tangent direction of the arcs.

It is also possible to create a spline from an existing polyline using the **PEDIT Spline** option. Unlike the **Fit** option, the **Spline** option creates a curve that passes through the first and last control points only. The curve is pulled toward the other control points but does not always pass through them. The more control points on the polyline, the more pull they exert on the curve. This type of curve is called a B-spline and it produces a much smoother curve than that produced by the **Fit** option. Use the **PEDIT Decurve** option when you want to remove the curve or spline applied to a polyline.

Figure 10-38.
The **PEDIT Fit** option is applied to a polyline.

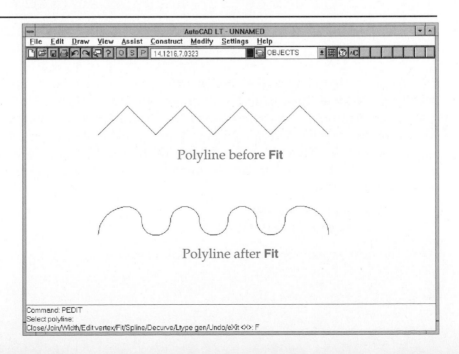

Use the **Fit** and **Spline** options to create wiring, cabling, and other types of curved objects. **Fit** and **Spline** can also be used to draw short break lines.

System variables that control B-splines

You can control the type of spline created by AutoCAD LT using the **SPLINETYPE** system variable. When **SPLINETYPE** is set to 5, a quadratic B-spline is generated. Setting **SPLINETYPE** to 6 (the default value) creates a cubic B-spline.

>   Command: **SPLINETYPE** ↵
>   New value for SPLINETYPE ⟨6⟩: *(enter a 5 or 6 and press* [Enter]*)*

The two spline types are illustrated in Figure 10-39.

Figure 10-39.
AutoCAD LT creates a quadratic or cubic spline based on the setting of the **SPLINETYPE** system variable.

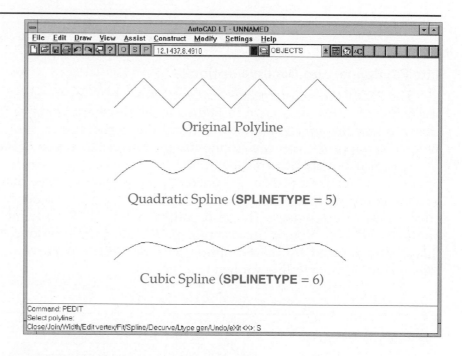

You can also change the **SPLINETYPE** system variable from a cascading submenu by selecting **Polyline Style** from the **Settings** pull-down menu. Notice that this submenu contains two additional items titled **Spline Frame** and **Spline Segments**. When a spline is applied to a polyline, AutoCAD LT remembers the original polyline *frame* so that it can be restored when you use the **Decurve** option. Normally, the spline frames are not displayed on screen. If you want to see them, select **Spline Frame** from the cascading submenu or enter the following at the **Command:** prompt:

>   Command: **SPLFRAME** ↵
>   New value for SPLFRAME ⟨0⟩: **1** ↵

After the next screen regeneration, the spline frames are displayed. See Figure 10-40.

Figure 10-40.
Spline frames are shown
when **SPLFRAME** is enabled.

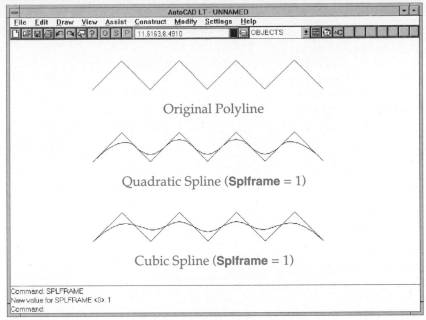

Finally, you can change the fineness or coarseness of displayed splines by selecting **Spline Segments** from the cascading submenu, or entering the following at the **Command:** prompt:

> Command: **SPLINESEGS** ↵
> New value for SPLINESEGS ⟨8⟩: *(enter a higher or lower value as desired)*

After changing the **SPLINESEGS** value, use the **PEDIT Spline** option to respline an existing curve to the new setting. Although a higher value draws more line segments and produces a more precise spline approximation, keep in mind that the new spline takes up more space in the drawing file and takes longer to redraw and regenerate.

The PEDIT Ltype gen option

When **Ltype gen** is turned off (the default), linetype generation is performed so that dashes start and stop at each vertex of an object. This is in accordance with good drafting practice. When **Ltype gen** is turned on, linetypes are drawn in a continous pattern through polylines disregarding the vertices. An example of **Ltype gen** turned on and off is shown in Figure 10-41. In the unlikely event that you need to enable **Ltype gen**, there are several ways to do so. They are listed below:

1. Use the **PEDIT Ltype gen** option as follows:

> Command: *(type* PEDIT *or* PE *and press* [Enter]*)*
> Select polyline: *(select the polyline)*
> Close/Join/Width/Edit Vertex/Fit/Spline/Decurve/Ltype gen/Undo/eXit ⟨X⟩: **L** ↵
> Full PLINE linetype ON/OFF ⟨Off⟩: **ON** ↵

2. Select **Linetype Generation** from the **Polyline Style** cascading submenu.
3. Use the **PLINEGEN** system variable at the **Command:** prompt as follows:

> Command: **PLINEGEN** ↵
> New value for PLINEGEN ⟨0⟩: **1** ↵

Remember that linetype generation affects polyline entities only. These include ellipses, polygons, and rectangles. Tapered polylines are not affected, however.

Figure 10-41.
An example of several polylines with **Ltype gen** on and off. Observe the dashes at the vertices of each polyline. The default in AutoCAD LT is to have **Ltype gen** turned off.

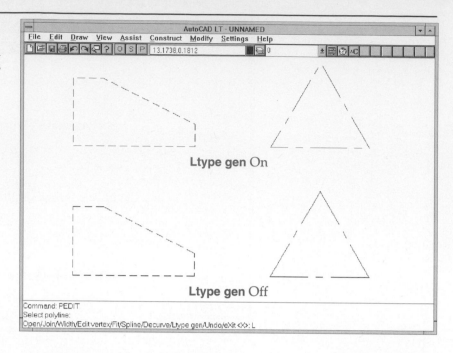

MODIFYING ENTITIES USING A DIALOG BOX ALTUG 10

The **DDMODIFY** command was introduced in Chapter 9 as a means of editing a string of text characters. However, **DDMODIFY** can be used on any entity type in AutoCAD LT. Remember, **DDMODIFY** also permits you to change the properties (color, layer, linetype, thickness) of a selected entity. To issue the **DDMODIFY** command, enter DDMODIFY at the **Command:** prompt, or select **Modify Entity...** from the **Modify** pull-down menu. See Figure 10-42. The command sequence is as follows:

Command: **DDMODIFY** ↵
Select object to modify: *(select one entity)*

Figure 10-42.
Selecting **Modify Entity...** from the **Modify** pull-down menu issues the **DDMODIFY** command.

NOTE
Although the **Modify Entity** button shown in the margin does not appear in the toolbar or toolbox by default, it may easily be added.

DDMODIFY allows only one entity to be selected for modification. After picking the entity, a dialog box appropriate for the entity type you selected is displayed. As shown in Figure 10-43A, the **Modify Circle** dialog box displays when a circle is selected. The circle's radius, diameter, circumference, and area are displayed at the right of the dialog box. Use the **Radius:** text box to change the size of the circle. At the left of the dialog box, the XYZ coordinates of the circle's center are displayed in the corresponding text boxes. You can edit the values in these text boxes to move the circle to a new location, or click the **Pick Point** ⟨ button instead. When you use this button, the dialog box temporarily disappears and you receive the **Center point:** prompt:

Pick a point on the screen, enter a coordinate, or osnap to an existing entity to locate the circle at a new origin. The dialog box then reappears showing the new XYZ coordinates of the circle's center. Click **OK** to exit the dialog box.

When a line is selected, **DDMODIFY** displays the **Modify Line** dialog box shown in Figure 10-43B. You can change the starting and ending points of a line by changing the values in the appropriate text boxes, or click th **Pick Point** ⟨ buttons to interactively change the line points. The **Delta XYZ:** values, length, and angle for the selected line are displayed at the right of the dialog box. When you are through modifying the line, click **OK** to exit the dialog box.

Figure 10-43.
A—The **Modify Circle** dialog box. B—The **Modify Line** dialog box.

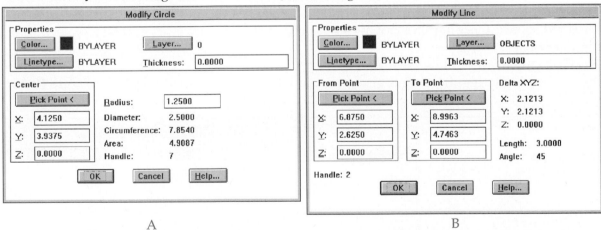

A   B

EXERCISE 10-11

❑ Open EX10-10 from the previous polar array exercise.
❑ Use **DDMODIFY** to change the length of one of the lines and the radius of one of the arcs. Select any values you like.
❑ Next, draw a polyline similar to that shown in Figure 10-39. Use **DDMODIFY** to change it to a curve, and then a cubic B-spline, and finally a quadratic B-spline.
❑ Do not save the drawing when you are through experimenting.

INTRODUCTION TO GRIPS AND GRIP EDITING

Grips are the small squares that appear on an object when an entity is selected at the **Command:** prompt. They provide a quick way to edit AutoCAD LT objects without using the standard editing commands. As shown in Figure 10-44, grips are strategically placed on entities in locations that correspond to object snap points, such as the midpoint or endpoints of a line.

Figure 10-44.
Grips appear at specific points on each entity type. The points correspond with object snap mode locations.

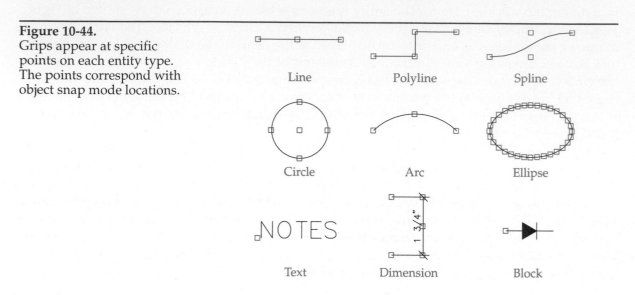

Grips can be either warm, hot, or cold. The grips that appear when an entity is selected at the **Command:** prompt are called warm grips. By default, they display as unfilled blue squares. Selecting a warm grip with your mouse makes the grip hot. It then displays as a filled red square. Once a grip is hot, it can be used to stretch, move, copy, rotate, scale, or mirror an entity.

Grips are made cold by performing a [Ctrl]+[C] or clicking the **Cancel** or **Undo** buttons on the toolbar. Entity highlighting is also removed when grips are made cold. See Figure 10-45.

Figure 10-45.
A visual comparison between warm, hot, and cold grips.

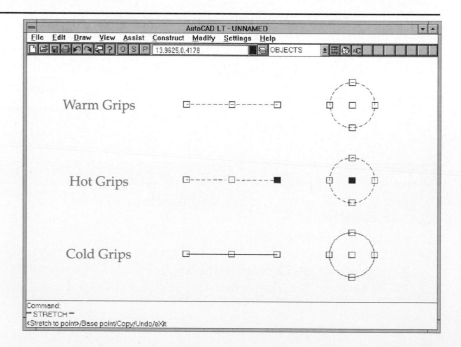

The Grips dialog box

There are several system variables that control the use of grips. These variables can be changed using a dialog box by selecting **Grips Style...** from the **Settings** pull-down menu, or by entering DDGRIPS or GR at the **Command:** prompt:

The **DDGRIPS** command activates the **Grips** dialog box shown in Figure 10-46. Each of the components of this dialog box are described below.

Figure 10-46.
The **Grips** dialog box.

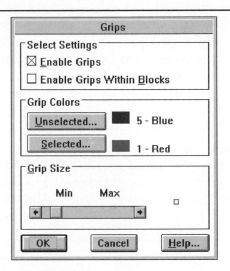

- **Select Settings.** If you wish to disable grips, click to remove the X from the **Enable Grips** check box. This action sets the **GRIPS** system variable to 0 (off). If you wish to turn on the display of grips within block entities, activate the **Enable Grips Within Blocks** check box. The new setting is stored in the **GRIPBLOCK** system variable.
- **Grip Colors.** As previously mentioned, unselected (warm) grips are blue and selected (hot) grips are red. Use the appropriate buttons in this section to assign different colors to your grips. The color selected for warm grips is stored in the **GRIPCOLOR** system variable, and the color selected for hot grips is stored in the **GRIPHOT** system variable.
- **Grip Size.** Use the horizontal slider bar in this section to dynamically increase or decrease the size of grips. By default, grips are 3 pixels in size (the same as the entity pickbox). The new grip size is stored in the **GRIPSIZE** system variable.

Once you have made your changes, click **OK** to exit the **Grips** dialog box.

Editing with grips

To modify an object using grips, first select the entity. The object is highlighted and unselected grips appear on the entity. To select a grip, move your mouse over the desired grip and pick. There is no need to use one of the object snap modes—the cursor will snap directly to the grip. Once the grip is selected, it becomes hot and appears solid. At the same time, the following is displayed in the **Command:** prompt area at the bottom of the screen:

```
**STRETCH**
⟨Stretch to point⟩/Base point/Copy/Undo/eXit:
```

If you pick a new screen location at the **⟨Stretch to point⟩/Base point/Copy/Undo/eXit:** prompt, the entity will stretch from the hot grip origin to the new selected point. See Figure 10-47. Each of the other **STRETCH** options are described as follows:

- **Base point.** Enter B and press [Enter] to select a different base point as the point of reference from which to stretch.
- **Copy.** If you wish to make one or more copies of the selected entity, enter C and press [Enter]. This activates **Multiple** mode, allowing you to make multiple copies until you exit the operation.
- **Undo.** Use the **Undo** option to undo the **Base point** or **Copy** selection.
- **eXit.** Enter X and press [Enter] to exit the grip editing procedure. The hot grip is removed from the entity, but the unselected (warm) grips remain. As previously mentioned, the warm grips are made cold by performing a [Ctrl]+[C] or clicking the **Cancel** or **Undo** buttons on the toolbar. Cancel twice to remove the cold grips, turn off entity highlighting, and return to the **Command:** prompt.

Stretching is the default grip editing mode. This mode is very powerful because it allows you to move and copy as well. To move a line using stretch, simply select the middle grip of the line and move it to a new location. If you wish to move a circle, pick the grip at the very center of the circle. Only one grip appears on text entities. This grip corresponds to the text insertion point. Pick this grip to move a string of text.

Figure 10-47.
Stretching with grips.

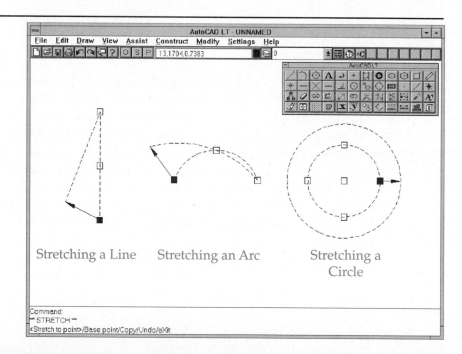

Stretching a Line   Stretching an Arc   Stretching a Circle

PROFESSIONAL TIP

More than one grip can be hot at a time. This is particularly useful when you stretch using grips. To make more than one grip hot, press and hold the [Shift] key while picking other warm grips. Once all of the required grips are selected, release the [Shift] key and pick the grip that represents the desired base point.

Other grip editing modes

You can also use the **MOVE, ROTATE, SCALE,** and **MIRROR** functions on grips. If you successively press [Enter] when you see **STRETCH** appear on the command line, you can cycle through each of the other available grip editing modes. These modes appear as follows:

```
**MOVE**
〈Move to point〉/Base point/Copy/Undo/eXit:
**ROTATE**
〈Rotation angle〉/Base point/Copy/Undo/Reference/eXit:
**SCALE**
〈Scale factor〉/Base point/Copy/Undo/Reference/eXit:
**MIRROR**
〈Second point〉/Base point/Copy/Undo/eXit:
```

As an alternative to pressing [Enter] to cycle through each of the grip editing modes, you may enter the first two characters of the desired command from the keyboard as follows: MO for **MOVE**, RO for **ROTATE**, SC for **SCALE**, MI for **MIRROR**, and ST for **STRETCH**.

The **Base point, Copy,** and **Undo** options work identically for all the grip editing modes. The **Reference** options appear only for the **ROTATE** and **SCALE** modes, and are identical to the **ROTATE** and **SCALE** command **Reference** options described earlier in this chapter.

When mirroring with grips, the hot grip automatically becomes the first point of the mirror line. Use the **Copy** option if you want to retain the original object.

EXERCISE 10-12

❏ Make a drawing similar to that shown in Figure 10-47.
❏ Use grips to stretch the line and arc endpoints to new locations.
❏ Use a grip to move the circle to a different origin.
❏ Draw one or more simple objects of your choice. Experiment with the other grip editing modes, as well.
❏ Do not save the drawing when you are finished.

CHAPTER TEST

Write your answers in the spaces provided.

1. What are cutting edges? What are boundary edges? _____

   _____

   _____

   _____

2. What is the purpose of the **BREAK** command? _____

   _____

3. When using the **MOVE** or **COPY** commands, what is meant by *base point*? _____

   _____

   _____

4. Give the command and entries required to move an object 5 units to the right and 2 units straight up *without using a base point*.

    Command:_____

    Select objects:_____

    Select objects:_____

    Base point or displacement: _____

    Second point of displacement: _____

5. What is the purpose of the **ROTATE** command's **Reference** option? How is it used?

    _____

    _____

    _____

6. Give the command and entries required to reduce the size of an object by 1/4th.

    Command:_____

    Select objects:_____

    Select objects:_____

    Base point: _____

    ⟨Scale factor⟩/Reference: _____

7. Which two selection set options are valid with the **STRETCH** command?_____

    _____

8. Why is it a good idea to turn **Ortho** on before stretching? _____

    _____

9. A stretch operation has just been performed on an object. However, instead of stretching, the object has moved to a new location. Why did this occur? _____

    _____

    _____

    _____

10. What happens when more than one line is selected using the **CHANGE** command?

    _____

    _____

11. It is more efficient to erase and redraw a circle rather than change its size. (True/False)

    _____

12. What is the mirror line? _____

    _____

13. Name the system variable that controls the mirroring of text and dimensions.

    _____

14. Give the command and entries required to make two copies of a selected object.

Command:_____

Select objects:_____

Select objects:_____

⟨Base point or displacement⟩/Multiple: _____

Base point: _____

Second point of displacement: _____

Second point of displacement: _____

Second point of displacement: _____

15. In a rectangular array, what do the rows and columns represent? _____

_____

16. What must you do to create an array that goes down and to the right?_____

_____

17. How does a polar array differ from a rectangular array? _____

_____

18. How do you specify the angle between items when creating a polar array?_____

_____

_____

19. What is the purpose of the **PEDIT Join** option?_____

_____

20. Which **Edit Vertex** suboption allows you to remove segments from a polyline?_____

_____

21. Which **Edit Vertex** suboption allows you to add a segment to a polyline? _____

_____

22. What must you do after changing the starting and ending width of a polyline segment?

_____

_____

23. Describe the difference between the **PEDIT Fit** and **Spline** options._____

_____

_____

_____

24. What must you do to create a quadratic B-spline?_____

_____

25. Describe the differences between a warm grip and a hot grip. _____

_____

_____

_____

26. Identify the six editing operations that may be performed using grips. _____

_____

27. List two ways to access the **Grips** dialog box. _____

_____

28. It is not necessary to select grips with an osnap. (True/False) _____

CHAPTER PROBLEMS

*Mechanical
Drafting*

1. Use your PROTOA prototype drawing to draw the COVER PLATE shown below. Use the **ARC** and **TRIM** commands to construct the object. Do not draw the centerlines or dimensions. Save the drawing as P10-1.

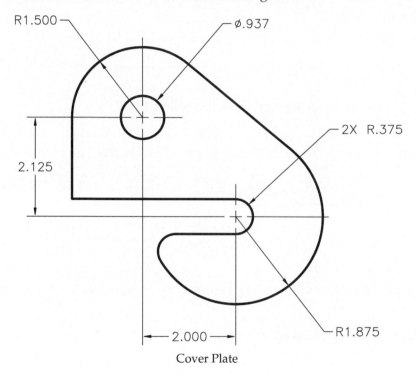

Cover Plate

2. Draw the **CUP WASHER** shown below using your PROTOA prototype drawing. Be sure to use the proper layers. Use a polar array to speed the construction of the top view. Project points and lines to the bottom view using point filters and/or tracking as described in Chapter 7. Do not draw the centerlines or dimensions. Save the drawing as P10-2.

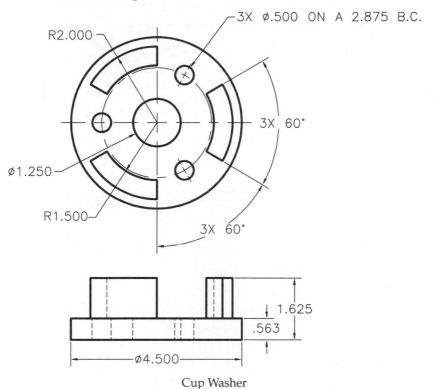

Cup Washer

3. Draw the **SLOTTED CAM** shown below using your PROTOA prototype drawing. Use the **TRIM** and **ARRAY** commands to your advantage. Do not draw the centerlines or dimensions. Save the drawing as P10-3.

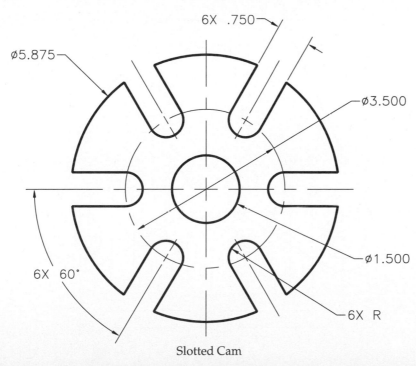

Slotted Cam

4. Use your PROTOA prototype drawing to draw the GASKET shown below. Use the **RECTANG** and **ARRAY** commands to help you construct the object. Do not draw the centerlines or dimensions. Save the drawing as P10-4.

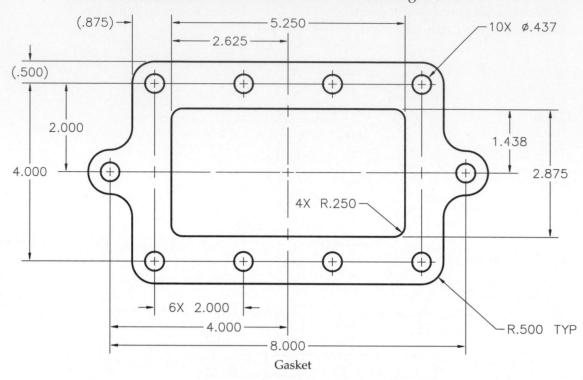

Gasket

5. Construct the MOUNTING PLATE shown below using your PROTOB prototype drawing. Draw one half of the object and mirror it across the symmetrical centerline. Use a rectangular array where appropriate to create the hole patterns. Do not draw the centerlines or dimensions. Save the drawing as P10-5.

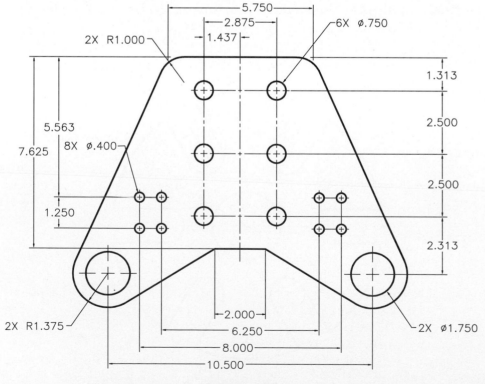

Mounting Plate

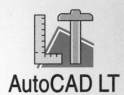

Learning objectives:

After you have completed this chapter, you will be able to:
- ○ Add linear, angular, radial, and ordinate dimensions to your drawings.
- ○ Use dimension variables to control the appearance and format of dimensions.
- ○ Create centerlines through arcs and circles.
- ○ Use leaders to place feature callouts.
- ○ Modify existing dimensions.
- ○ Create and use dimension styles.

Drawing dimensions convey feature size and location and may well be the most important aspect of any engineering or architectural drawing. AutoCAD LT provides a variety of dimensioning commands and options that enable you to quickly and accurately place dimensions on your drawings. This chapter describes each of these functions as well as the dimension variables that control the appearance and format of dimensions. In addition, you will learn how to edit existing dimensions and create your own dimension styles.

AUTOCAD LT DIMENSIONING MODE | ALTUG 13 |

All dimensioning and dimension editing in AutoCAD LT is performed in the *dimensioning mode*. To enter dimensioning mode, type the following at the **Command:** prompt

> Command: *(type* DIM *or* D *and press* [Enter]*)*
> Dim:

The **Dim:** prompt indicates that dimensioning mode is active and each of the available dimensioning commands can now be issued. Once you enter dimensioning mode, the mode remains active until you return to the normal command mode. To exit the dimensioning mode and return to the **Command:** prompt, enter E for Exit and press [Enter], press [Ctrl]+[C], or click the **Cancel** button on the toolbar.

Dimensioning commands

Once you enter the dimensioning mode, each of the dimensioning commands can be abbreviated to the capital letters indicated in the following list. The examples illustrated in this chapter show each of the dimensioning commands as they would appear on the command line in both their unabbreviated and abbreviated forms.
- **ALigned.** A linear dimension that is aligned with the extension line origins.
- **ANgular.** Angular dimension.
- **Baseline.** Continues from the first extension line of the previous dimension.
- **CEnter.** Draws a center mark or centerlines through circles and arcs.

- **COntinue.** Continues from the second extension line of the previous dimension.
- **Diameter.** Diameter dimension.
- **Exit.** Returns to the normal command mode (**Command:** prompt).
- **HORizontal.** A linear dimension with a horizontal dimension line.
- **Leader.** Draws a leader to the dimension text.
- **ORdinate.** Ordinate point (arrowless) dimensioning.
- **RAdius.** Radius dimension.
- **Redraw.** Redraws the display.
- **REStore.** Changes to a previously stored dimension style.
- **ROtated.** A linear dimension at a specified angle.
- **SAve.** Stores the current variable settings as a dimension style.
- **STAtus.** Lists dimensioning variables and their current values.
- **STYle.** Switches to a new text style.
- **Undo.** Reverses the last dimensioning command.
- **VErtical.** A linear dimension with a vertical dimension line.

The following dimension editing commands operate on a selection set of existing dimensions:
- **HOMetext.** Moves dimension text back to its home (default) position.
- **Newtext.** Modifies the text of selected dimensions.
- **OBlique.** Sets the oblique angle of dimension extension lines.
- **OVerride.** Overrides a subset of the dimension variable settings.
- **TEdit.** Changes the position of the dimension text.
- **TRotate.** Rotates the dimension text.
- **UPdate.** Redraws the dimensions in the current settings of all dimensioning variables.
- **VAriables.** Lists variable settings.

If you plan to use only one dimensioning command, type the following at the **Command:** prompt.

Command: *(type* DIM1 *or* D1 *and press* [Enter]*)*
Dim:

After performing the one dimensioning task, AutoCAD LT automatically exits the dimensioning mode and returns to the **Command:** prompt.

Accessing dimensioning commands from the pull-down menus

As an alternative to keyboard entry, the dimensioning commands can also be accessed through the **Draw** pull-down menu as shown in Figure 11-1. Three of the selections—**Linear Dimensions**, **Ordinate Dimensions**, and **Radial Dimensions**—feature cascading submenus that provide additional options. The **Dimension** button shown in the margin does not perform any dimensioning commands, but is used to enter **Dim:** mode. Although this button does not appear on the toolbar or in the toolbox by default, it can easily be added.

Figure 11-1.
The dimensioning commands can be accessed from the **Draw** pull-down menu. Three of the menu selections feature cascading submenus, that offer additional options.

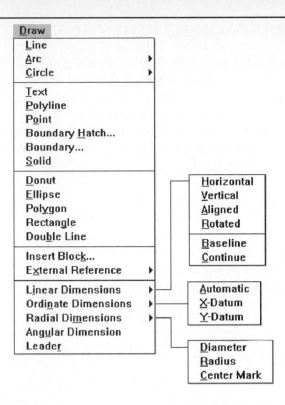

The commands which perform dimension editing can be accessed from the **Modify** pull-down menu, Figure 11-2. Click the **Edit Dimension** selection, and a cascading submenu appears containing these options: **Change Text**, **Home Text**, **Move Text**, **Rotate Text**, **Oblique Dimension**, and **Update Dimension**. Each of these editing functions are covered thoroughly later in this chapter.

Keep in mind, however, that the **Dim1:** mode is used when making selections from the pull-down menus. In other words, you do not remain in dimensioning mode after performing a dimensioning operation, but instead, are immediately returned to the **Command:** prompt.

Figure 11-2.
The dimension editing commands can be accessed from the **Modify** pull-down menu.

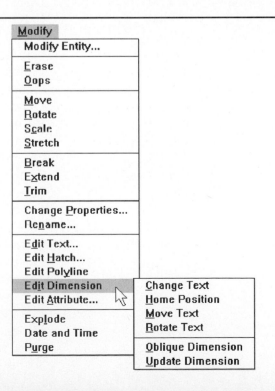

The appearance and format of AutoCAD LT dimensions is controlled through the use of dimension variables, or *dimvars*, for short. Each of the dimvars begins with the letters "DIM". The remaining letters are a code that describes the purpose of the variable. You can change the variables at the **Dim:** prompt or in a dialog box using the **DDIM** command.

To check the current status of the dimensioning variables at any time while in the dimensioning mode, enter the following at the **Dim:** prompt.

Dim: *(type* STATUS *or* STA *and press* [Enter]*)*

The graphics window automatically flips to the text window and all the dimvars and their respective values are displayed in a format similar to that shown below. From the list, you can see that some dimvars contain numeric values while others are listed as on or off. You can turn on a dimvar by entering ON or typing the numeral 1. Turn off a dimvar by entering OFF or typing a 0 (zero). Observe also that several of the dimvars show no values at all. These dimvars are set with user-specified characters.

DIMALT	Off	Alternate units selected
DIMALTD	2	Alternate unit decimal places
DIMALTF	25.4000	Alternate unit scale factor
DIMAPOST		Suffix for alternate text
DIMASO	On	Create associative dimensions
DIMASZ	0.1800	Arrow size
DIMBLK		Arrow block name
DIMBLK1		First arrow block name
DIMBLK2		Second arrow block name
DIMCEN	0.0900	Center mark size
DIMCLRD	BYBLOCK	Dimension line color
DIMCLRE	BYBLOCK	Extension line and leader color
DIMCLRT	BYBLOCK	Dimension text color
DIMDLE	0.0000	Dimension line extension
DIMDLI	0.3800	Dimension line increment for continuation
DIMEXE	0.1800	Extension above dimension line
DIMEXO	0.0625	Extension line origin offset
DIMGAP	0.0900	Gap from dimension line to text
DIMLFAC	1.0000	Linear unit scale factor
DIMLIM	Off	Generate dimension limits
DIMPOST		Default suffix for dimension text
DIMRND	0.0000	Rounding value
DIMSAH	Off	Separate arrow blocks
DIMSCALE	1.0000	Overall scale factor
DIMSE1	Off	Suppress the first extension line
DIMSE2	Off	Suppress the second extension line
DIMSHO	On	Update dimensions while dragging
DIMSOXD	Off	Suppress outside extension dimension
DIMSTYLE	*UNNAMED	Current dimension style (read-only)
DIMTAD	0	Place text above the dimension line
DIMTFAC	1.0000	Tolerance text height scaling factor
DIMTIH	On	Text inside extensions is horizontal
DIMTIX	Off	Place text inside extensions
DIMTM	0.0000	Minus tolerance
DIMTOFL	Off	Force line inside extension lines
DIMTOH	On	Text outside extensions is horizontal

DIMTOL	Off	Generate dimension tolerances
DIMTP	0.0000	Plus tolerance
DIMTSZ	0.0000	Tick size
DIMTVP	0.0000	Text vertical position
DIMTXT	0.1800	Text height
DIMZIN	0	Zero suppression

When you are done checking the current dimvar status, press function key [F2] to return to the graphics window. This chapter describes each of the dimensioning variables in the context for which they are most appropriate. Changing the value of a dimvar from the **Dim:** prompt or using the **Dimension Styles and Settings** dialog box is also presented.

PROFESSIONAL TIP   The dimension variables can be set to comply with mechanical, architectural, or civil engineering drafting standards. Set the variables appropriately for your application in your prototype drawing(s) so that they are always ready for use.

DIMENSION TEXT FORMATS

ALTUG 13

Dimensioning in AutoCAD LT is performed in the current system of units. In other words, dimensions appear in feet and inches when architectural units are current, and as fractions when fractional units are set. When using decimal units, be sure to set the number of digits to the right of the decimal point as required for your application. If necessary, refer to Chapter 2 to review the **DDUNITS** command.

Dimensions are also created using the current text style. However, keep in mind, that the default dimension height differs from the default text height. AutoCAD LT sets the dimension text height at 3/16 units, which is in accordance with industry standards. AutoCAD LT text height, on the other hand, is .200 units by default. Be sure to set text height and dimension height equally in your prototype drawing(s) to ensure uniformity.

Setting dimension text height

If you wish to change the dimension height, use the **DIMTXT** (TeXT) dimension variable. In the following example, dimension height is changed to 5/32 (.156) units:

    Dim: **DIMTXT** ↵
    Current value 〈0.1800〉 New value: **.156** ↵
    Dim:

The dimension height can also be changed using a dialog box by selecting **Dimension Style...** from the **Settings** pull-down menu, Figure 11-3. (Although the **Dimension Style** button shown in the margin does not appear on the toolbar or in the toolbox by default, it can easily be added.) From the command line, enter the following to display the **Dimension Styles and Settings** dialog box shown in Figure 11-4:

    Dim: *(type* DDIM *or* DM *and press* [Enter]*)*

Figure 11-3.
Selecting **Dimension Style...**
from the **Settings** pull-down
menu issues the **DDIM**
command.

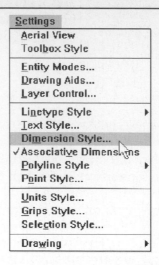

Figure 11-4.
The **Dimension Styles and
Settings** dialog box. Note
the different buttons in the
Dimension Settings section.

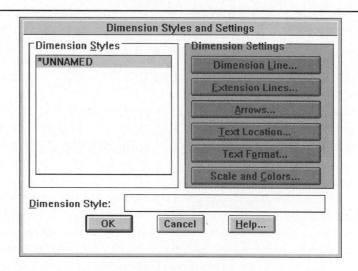

To set the dimension text height, first click the **Text Location...** button. The **Text Location** subdialog box then appears. In the example illustrated in Figure 11-5, the dimension height is changed to .156 in **the Text Height:** text box. After changing the dimension height, click OK to exit the **Text Location** subdialog box. Click OK once again to exit the **Dimension Styles and Settings** dialog box.

Figure 11-5.
Setting the dimension text
height using the **Text
Location** subdialog box.

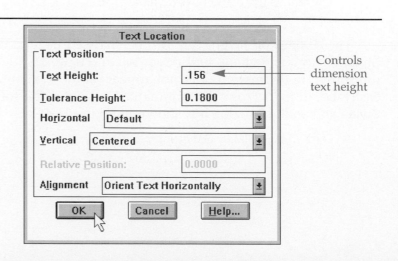

The DIMZIN variable

The **DIMZIN**, or Zero Inch, variable controls the display of leading and trailing zeros that occur in certain types of dimensions. For architectural dimensions, **DIMZIN** may contain the value 0 (the default), 1, 2, or 3. The following list provides an example of each setting:

DIMZIN = 0	Suppresses zero feet and zero inches	5/8"	4"	3'	3'-0 1/2"
DIMZIN = 1	Includes zero feet and zero inches	0'-0 5/8"	0'-4"	3'-0"	3'-0 1/2"
DIMZIN = 2	Includes zero feet suppresses zero inches	0'-0 5/8"	0'-4"	3'	3'-0 1/2"
DIMZIN = 3	Suppresses zero feet includes zero inches	5/8"	4"	3'-0"	3'-0 1/2"

For mechanical dimensions with inch units, set **DIMZIN** = 4 to omit leading zeros. As an example:

DIMZIN = 0   **DIMZIN** = 4

0.75   .75

To change **DIMZIN** using the **Dimension Styles and Settings** dialog box, issue the **DDIM** command and click the **Text Format...** button. The **Text Format** subdialog box appears with the **Zero Suppression** section at the lower left. As shown in Figure 11-6, the **0 Feet** and **0 Inches** check boxes are active by default. The **0 Feet** check box omits the 0' value for a feet and inches dimension that is less than one foot. Therefore, a six inch dimension reads as 6" when this box is checked, and as 0'-6" when it is *not* checked. The **0 Inches** check box omits the 0" portion of a dimension, such as 24'. When this box is not checked, the same dimension would read as 24'-0".

Figure 11-6.
The **Zero Suppression** section of the **Text Format** subdialog box controls the leading and trailing zeros for various types of dimensions.

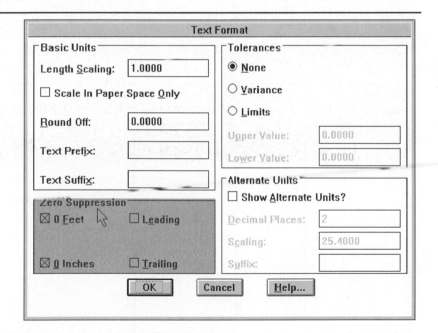

The **Leading** check box is used to drop the leading zero from a decimal inch dimension. This is equivalent to setting **DIMZIN** = 4 as previously described. Leave this box unchecked if you are performing metric dimensioning, however, since metric standards state that dimensions less than one millimeter in size require a 0 before the decimal point.

When activated, the **Trailing** check box removes all trailing zeros from a decimal dimension. Thus, a dimension that would normally read as 7.500 becomes 7.5. It is strongly recommended that you do not activate the **Trailing** check box because trailing zeros usually have tolerance significance in mechanical engineering and manufacturing. Instead, use the **DDUNITS** command to set the required number of decimal places to the right of the decimal point. This can also be quickly accomplished using the **LUPREC** system variable as follows:

Command: **LUPREC** ⏎
New value for LUPREC ⟨current⟩: (enter a value between 0 and 8 and press [Enter])
Command:

The **LUPREC** variable can be set at either the **Command:** or **Dim:** prompts.

Dimension scaling

You may recall from scaling discussions in previous chapters that AutoCAD LT can draw virtually anything at full scale. Very small objects are scaled up at plot time, while very large objects are scaled down. What happens, then, to dimension text height?

If your drawing is to be plotted at 1:1, then you need not overly concern yourself with dimension text height. If, on the other hand, you intend to plot with a specified scale factor, it is critically important to set your dimension height appropriately. This also applies to other components of a dimension as well, such as the arrowhead lengths and the distance that an extension line is offset from an object line.

Fortunately, the size of all dimensioning entities can be controlled with the **DIMSCALE** dimension variable. As an example, suppose the object you are dimensioning is somewhat small. You intend, therefore, to plot the drawing at a scale of 2:1. Since the size of your dimensions will be increased by a factor of two at plot time, you can compensate by setting **DIMSCALE** equal to .5 (1/2). As shown at the left in Figure 11-7, all the components of the dimension are then reduced by a factor of 1/2. When plotted at 2:1, the drawing geometry increases by a factor of 2 and the dimensions are restored to their normal sizes.

Figure 11-7.
An example of dimensioning entities created with different **DIMSCALE** values.

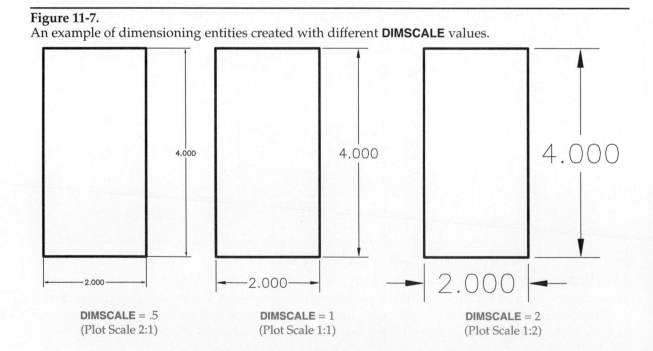

AutoCAD LT—Fundamentals and Applications

Consider another example. Suppose that the object you are drawing is rather large and you intend to plot with a scale factor of 1:2. Since the drawing geometry will be plotted two times smaller, you must ensure that the dimensions do not also reduce in scale. As shown at the right of Figure 11-7, setting **DIMSCALE** equal to 2 creates dimension entities two times larger, thus compensating for the reduced drawing size at the plotter.

At the **Dim:** prompt, **DIMSCALE** can be changed as follows:

Dim: **DIMSCALE** ↵
Current value ⟨1.0000⟩ New value: *(enter a new scale factor)*

To change **DIMSCALE** using the **Dimension Styles and Settings** dialog box, issue the **DDIM** command and click the **Scale and Colors...** button to display the **Scale and Colors** subdialog box. In the example shown in Figure 11-8, **DIMSCALE** is set to .5 in the **Feature Scaling:** text box in the **Scale** area at the top of the subdialog box.

Figure 11-8.
Changing **DIMSCALE** using the **Scale and Colors** subdialog box.

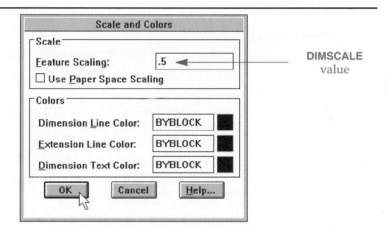

DIMSCALE value

NOTE

The **Use Paper Space Scaling** check box is used to calculate the scale factor based on the scaling between the current model space viewport and paper space. Activating this check box disables **DIM-SCALE**. Viewports in paper space are covered in Chapter 16 of this text.

The **DIMLFAC** variable

The **DIMLFAC** variable sets a global scale factor for linear and radial dimensioning measurements. The size and distance values measured by the dimensioning commands are multiplied by the **DIMLFAC** setting before being converted to dimension text. Angular dimensions are not affected, however.

DIMLFAC is convenient when dimensioning detail or section views that are scaled differently from the main views of the drawing. As an example, suppose you wanted to dimension a detail view that is at a scale of 4:1. Simply set **DIMLFAC** to a value of .25 as follows:

Dim: **DIMLFAC** ↵
Current value ⟨1.0000⟩ New value: **.25** ↵

When you dimension the view, AutoCAD LT automatically divides the values that appear in the brackets by a factor of 1/4 and displays the dimensions as if the view were drawn at 1:1. Be sure to set **DIMLFAC** back to 1 when you wish to resume full-scale dimensioning.

Setting dimension colors

Like other entities in AutoCAD LT, dimensions are created on the current layer. It is a good idea to create a separate dimensioning layer for your dimensions. The dimensions can then be turned on and off, or frozen and thawed as desired. You may recall from the discussion of colors and layers in Chapter 5 that entities (including dimensions) normally inherit the color of the layer on which they are created. AutoCAD LT calls this *bylayer mode*. It is possible to override bylayer mode by explicitly setting colors using the **COLOR** command.

It is also possible to set explicit colors for dimension lines, extension lines, and dimension text using dimension variables. The dimvars that are used for these settings are **DIMCLRD**, **DIMCLRE**, and **DIMCLRT**. **DIMCLRD** sets the color of dimension lines, arrowheads, and leaders. **DIMCLRE** sets the color of extension lines. **DIMCLRT** is used to assign color to the dimension text.

Remember that when specifying a color, you can enter the name of the color or its *ACI (AutoCAD Color Index)* number. In the following example, the dimension text color is changed to red:

> Dim: **DIMCLRT** ↵
> Current value ⟨BYBLOCK⟩ New value: *(type RED, R, or 1 and press [Enter])*
> Dim:

NOTE The **BYBLOCK** mode differs from **BYLAYER** mode such that entities assume the current color until grouped into a block. When the block is inserted into a drawing, it inherits the current color setting of that drawing. See Chapter 14 for more information about block entities.

You can also change dimension colors quickly and easily using the **Dimension Styles and Settings** dialog box. First, issue the **DDIM** command and then click the **Scale and Colors...** button. To change one or more of the dimension colors, click the corresponding color swatch in the Colors section of the **Scale and Colors** subdialog box, Figure 11-8. The **Select Color** subdialog box is then displayed. In the example shown in Figure 11-9, cyan (ACI number 4) is selected from the standard colors at the top of the subdialog box. After making your color selection, click OK to exit the **Select Color** subdialog box.

Figure 11-9.
Selecting one of 255 colors from the **Select Color** subdialog box.

Color can be selected from any of these areas

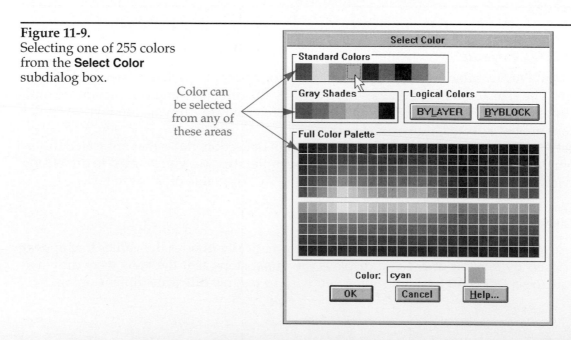

LINEAR DIMENSIONS

ALTUG 13

Linear dimensioning measures lines that are horizontal, vertical, or neither. A linear dimension includes dimension text, dimension lines, extension lines, and arrowheads, Figure 11-10. Each of the dimension components are grouped into a single dimension entity. AutoCAD LT allows you to create four types of linear dimensions—horizontal, vertical, aligned, and rotated. An example of each type is shown in Figure 11-11. The **HORIZONTAL** command is used to dimension a horizontal feature. The **VERTICAL** command places dimensions for vertical features. The **ALIGNED** option aligns a dimension so that the dimension line is parallel with a feature. The feature can be horizontal, vertical, or inclined. The **ROTATED** command is used to create a linear dimension with dimension lines drawn at a user-specified angle.

When creating a linear dimension, you are prompted to select the first and second extension line origins. These are the ends of the feature to be dimensioned. You are then asked to pick a location for the dimension line. As you move your cursor, the dimension is dynamically "dragged" to the location you specify. The only difference among the four linear dimensioning commands is the angle at which the dimension line is drawn. Each of the linear dimensioning commands are described in the following sections.

Figure 11-10.
Components of a linear dimension.

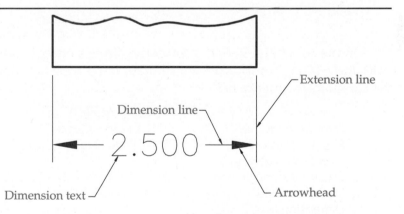

Figure 11-11.
Examples of the four types of linear dimensions available in AutoCAD LT.

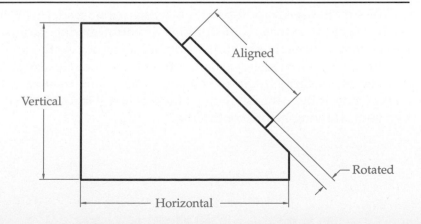

Horizontal dimensions

The **HORIZONTAL** command can be accessed by first selecting **Linear Dimensions** from the **Draw** pull-down menu, and then selecting **Horizontal** from the cascading submenu, Figure 11-12. Remember, however, that the dimensioning commands found in the **Draw** pull-down menu use **Dim1:** mode. If you use the pull-down menu, you are automatically returned to the **Command:** prompt after the dimension is drawn.

Figure 11-12.
Selecting **Linear Dimensions** from the **Draw** pull-down menu displays a cascading submenu of linear dimensioning options.

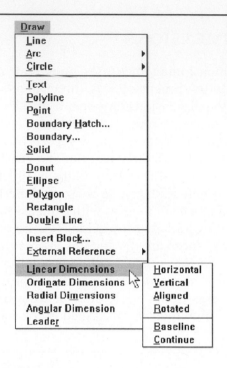

On the command line, first enter the dimensioning mode and then type HORIZONTAL or HOR at the **Dim:** prompt to create a horizontal dimension. Refer to Figure 11-13 as you follow the command sequence below:

> Command: *(type* DIM *or* D *and press* [Enter]*)*
> Dim: *(type* HORIZONTAL *or* HOR *and press* [Enter]*)*
> First extension line origin or RETURN to select: *(pick one end of the*
>   *feature to dimension)*
> Second extension line origin: *(pick the other point of the feature to dimension)*
> Dimension line location (Text/Angle): *(pick a location)*
> Dimension text ⟨2.500⟩: ↵
> Dim:

Be sure to use an appropriate object snap mode, such as **ENDpoint** or **INTersection**, to precisely select the extension line origins. If your drawing geometry is accurate, and you have used osnaps correctly, the dimension value shown in the angle brackets (⟨⟩) is the proper measurement. Press [Enter] to accept the dimension. However, if the dimension shown in the brackets is not correct, start over again making sure that the extension line origins are selected correctly. If the value shown in brackets is still incorrect, exit dimensioning mode and correct your drawing before continuing.

Figure 11-13.
Creating a linear dimension.

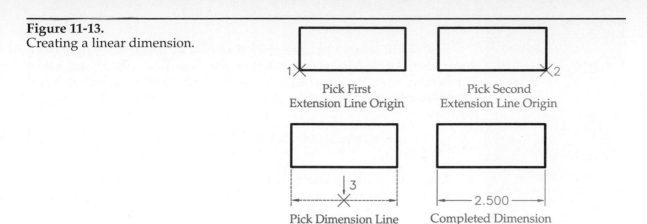

Pick First
Extension Line Origin

Pick Second
Extension Line Origin

Pick Dimension Line
Location With Cursor

Completed Dimension

Using the Text/Angle option

When creating linear or angular dimensions, AutoCAD LT allows you to append a dimension with additional text using the Text option. For example, suppose that you wish to append a dimension with the letters TYP, for TYPICAL. After selecting the extension line origins, follow the procedure given below:

> Dimension line location (Text/Angle): **T** ⏎
> Dimension text ⟨2.500⟩: ⟨⟩ **TYP** ⏎
> Dimension line location (Text/Angle): *(pick a location)*
> Dim:

In this example, you instruct AutoCAD LT to "take the value in the brackets and place a space and the letters TYP after it." There is no need to reenter the 2.500 value (even though you can if you wish). The resulting dimension is displayed as 2.500 TYP.

You can also use the **Text** option to add a prefix to a dimension. In the following example, the characters 2X are added to indicate that a dimension occurs at two places:

> Dimension line location (Text/Angle): **T** ⏎
> Dimension text ⟨2.500⟩: **2X** ⟨⟩ ⏎
> Dimension line location (Text/Angle): *(pick a location)*
> Dim:

The resulting dimension is displayed as 2X 2.500. Whether you add a prefix or a suffix, the dimension is still one entity.

The **Angle** option allows you to change the angle of the dimension text. By default, all dimensions are created in a unidirectional fashion. In other words, dimensions read horizontally from left to right. If you wish to place dimension text at a different angle, do the following:

> Dimension line location (Text/Angle): **A** ⏎
> Enter text angle: **90** ⏎
> Dimension line location (Text/Angle): *(pick a location)*
> Dim:

In architectural drafting, it is common practice to rotate dimensions so that they are aligned with the features being dimensioned. While the **Angle** option can be used for this purpose, it is far more efficient to use the **DIMTIH** and **DIMTOH** dimension variables. These two dimvars are covered later in this chapter.

It is not necessary to use the **Text** option to preface or append a dimension with additional text. Select the extension line origins and dimension line location as you would normally. Then, at the **Dimension text:** prompt, use the following procedure as a handy shortcut.

> Dimension text ⟨2.500⟩: **%%C ⟨⟩ TYP** ↵
> Dim:

AutoCAD LT does not place a diameter symbol in front of a dimension when using one of the linear dimensioning commands. In the example shown above, a diameter symbol is added by entering the %%C special character control code. This instructs AutoCAD LT to "take the value in the brackets and place a diameter symbol in front of it and then a space, and the word TYP after it." The resulting dimension is displayed as Ø2.500 TYP and is still a single entity. This option is frequently used when placing linear dimensions on cylindrical features. If necessary, refer to Chapter 9 to review the other special character control codes.

Vertical dimensions

As mentioned previously, the **VERTICAL** command places dimensions for vertical features. An example of a vertical dimension appears in Figure 11-11. As a linear dimension type, the procedure and options are identical to that of the **HORIZONTAL** command. To issue the **VERTICAL** command, first **Select Linear Dimensions** from the **Draw** pull-down menu and then select **Vertical** from the cascading submenu. On the command line, first enter the dimensioning mode and then type the following at the **Dim:** prompt to create a vertical dimension.

> Dim: *(type* VERTICAL *or* VE *and press* [Enter]*)*
> First extension line origin or RETURN to select: *(pick a point)*
> Second extension line origin: *(pick a second point)*
> Dimension line location (Text/Angle): *(pick a location)*
> Dimension text ⟨*current*⟩: ↵
> Dim:

Aligned dimensions

The **ALIGNED** command aligns a dimension so that the dimension line is parallel with a horizontal, vertical, or angled feature. An example of an aligned dimension is shown in Figure 11-11. The procedure and options of the **ALIGNED** command are identical to those of the **HORIZONTAL** and **VERTICAL** commands. To issue the **ALIGNED** command, first select **Linear Dimensions** from the **Draw** pull-down menu and then select **Aligned** from the cascading submenu. On the command line, first enter the dimensioning mode and then type the following at the **Dim:** prompt to create an aligned dimension.

> Dim: *(type* ALIGNED *or* AL *and press* [Enter]*)*
> First extension line origin or RETURN to select: *(pick a point)*
> Second extension line origin: *(pick a second point)*
> Dimension line location (Text/Angle): *(pick a location)*
> Dimension text ⟨*current*⟩: ↵
> Dim:

Since the **ALIGNED** command can dimension horizontal and vertical features, as well as angled surfaces, it can be used in place of the **HORIZONTAL** and **VERTICAL** commands. The **ALIGNED** command is also a convenient way to dimension auxiliary views. Refer to Chapter 8 to review auxiliary view construction.

Rotated dimensions

Rotated dimensions are very similar to aligned dimensions with one important distinction. An example of a rotated dimension is shown in Figure 11-11. With rotated dimensions, you must first specify the dimension line angle before selecting the extension line origins. Apart from specifying the dimension line angle, the procedure and options of the **ROTATED** command are identical to those of the other linear dimensioning commands. To issue the **ROTATED** command, first select **Linear Dimensions** from the **Draw** pull-down menu and then select **Rotated** from the cascading submenu. On the command line, first enter the dimensioning mode and then type the following at the **Dim:** prompt to create a rotated dimension.

> Dim: *(type* ROTATED *or* RO *and press* [Enter]*)*
> Dimension line angle ⟨0⟩: *(specify an angle)*
> First extension line origin or RETURN to select: *(pick a point)*
> Second extension line origin: *(pick a second point)*
> Dimension line location (Text/Angle): *(pick a location)*
> Dimension text ⟨*current*⟩: ↵
> Dim:

There may be instances when you do not know the required dimension line angle. You can use the **LIST** command to query the system for the angle, or pick two points on the line to be dimensioned when prompted for the dimension line angle. Be sure to use an osnap to pick the points precisely. If necessary, refer to Chapter 8, **The Inquiry Commands** to review the **LIST** command.

The RETURN to select option

In each of the previous linear dimensioning examples, you may have noticed the **or RETURN to select:** prompt. This powerful option allows you to place a horizontal, vertical, aligned, or rotated dimension on a line, arc, or circle without specifying the extension line origins. When prompted **or RETURN to select:**, simply press [Enter] and pick the entity you wish to dimension. Refer to the dimensioned circle at the far left of Figure 11-14 as you follow the command procedure below:

> Dim: *(type* HORIZONTAL *or* HOR *and press* [Enter]*)*
> First extension line origin or RETURN to select: ↵
> Select line, arc, or circle: *(pick anywhere on circle)*
> Dimension line location (Text/Angle): *(pick a location)*
> Dimension text ⟨1.500⟩: **%%C ⟨⟩** ↵
> Dim:

The **RETURN to select** option can also be used on polylines, donuts, rectangles, and polygons.

Figure 11-14.
Using the **Return to select:** option.

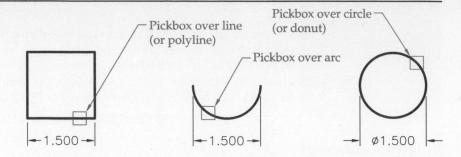

Pickbox over line (or polyline)

Pickbox over circle (or donut)

Pickbox over arc

|← 1.500 →| |← 1.500 →| |← ⌀1.500 →|

Dimensioning in AutoCAD LT, like dimensioning on a conventional drafting board, should be performed as accurately and as neatly as possible. You can achieve professional results consistently by adhering to the following guidelines:

- Always construct drawing geometry as precisely as possible. Never truncate, or round-off, decimal values when entering coordinates. In other words, enter .4375 for 7/16—not .43 or .44.
- For decimal dimensioning, set the system variable **LUPREC** (Linear Units PRECision) to the desired number of decimal places before creating any dimensions.
- Do *not* use the **DIMRND** (RouND) variable. This dimension variable rounds linear and radial dimension distances to a specified value. For example, if **DIMRND** is set to .5, all distances round to the nearest .5 unit. All dimensions round to the nearest integer when **DIMRND** is set to 1. A value of 0 (the default) turns off **DIMRND**.
- Use running object snap modes like **ENDpoint** and **INTersection** to your advantage to snap to exact extension line origins.
- *Never* type in a different dimension value than appears in the brackets. If a dimension needs to change, revise the drawing geometry accordingly. The ability to change the dimension in the brackets is provided by AutoCAD LT so that a different text format can be specified for the dimension. In addition, prefixes and/or suffixes can be added to the dimension in the brackets as previously described. A typical example of a prefix might be to specify the number of times a dimension occurs, such as: 4X 1.750. The same callout can be expressed with a suffix as follows: 1.750 4 PLCS.

Adding text to dimensions using the DIMPOST variable

Another way to add a prefix or suffix to a dimension is with the dimension variable **DIMPOST**. Suppose, for example, that you wish to create a series of dimensions each appended with the letters TYP. Set **DIMPOST** as follows:

    Dim: **DIMPOST** ↵
    Current value ⟨⟩ New value: **TYP** ↵

Every dimension you now create will automatically include the letters TYP. Be sure, however, to type a space before entering the suffix. Doing so ensures that a space exists between the dimension and the suffix. To clear the **DIMPOST** variable, type a period (.) as follows:

    Dim: **DIMPOST** ↵
    Current value ⟨⟩ New value: **.** ↵

You can also use **DIMPOST** to add a prefix to a dimension. In the following example, the prefix APPROX. is added to a series of dimensions. Note the use of the angle brackets in the following example. Entering the brackets after the **DIMPOST** value instructs AutoCAD LT to use the value as a prefix rather than a suffix.

> Dim: **DIMPOST** ⏎
> Current value 〈〉 New value: **APPROX.** 〈〉 ⏎

To change **DIMPOST** using the **Dimension Styles and Settings** dialog box, issue the **DDIM** command and click the **Text Format...** button to display the **Text Format** subdialog box, Figure 11-15. In the example shown, APPROX. appears in the **Text Prefix:** text box and FT. is entered in the **Text Suffix:** text box. Every newly created dimension will now appear as APPROX. *nnn* FT. Be sure to include spaces where appropriate as previously described.

Figure 11-15.
Adding a prefix and a suffix to dimensions using the **Text Format** subdialog box.

Setting the text prefix and suffix

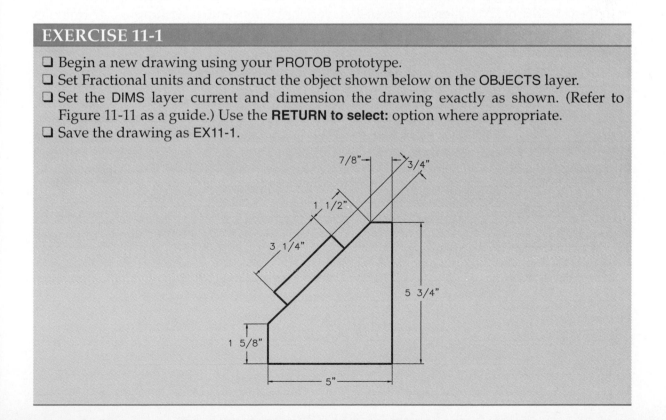

EXERCISE 11-1

❏ Begin a new drawing using your PROTOB prototype.
❏ Set Fractional units and construct the object shown below on the OBJECTS layer.
❏ Set the DIMS layer current and dimension the drawing exactly as shown. (Refer to Figure 11-11 as a guide.) Use the **RETURN to select:** option where appropriate.
❏ Save the drawing as EX11-1.

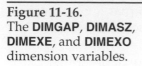
As previously stated, dimension variables control the appearance and format of all AutoCAD LT dimensions. The dimvars described in the following sections control the placement of dimension text and the appearance of dimension lines and extension lines. Four of these variables are shown in Figure 11-16 and are described below:

Figure 11-16.
The **DIMGAP**, **DIMASZ**, **DIMEXE**, and **DIMEXO** dimension variables.

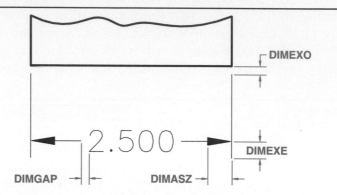

The DIMEXO and DIMEXE variables

The **DIMEXO,** or EXtension line Offset, variable controls the amount of space between the end of an object line and the start of an extension line. By default, that value is set to .0625 (1/16) units in accordance with current drafting standards. To change the extension line offset, type the following:

Dim: **DIMEXO** ↵
Current value ⟨0.0625⟩ New value: *(enter a positive value and press* [Enter]*)*

The distance that an extension line extends past the end of a dimension line is controlled with the **DIMEXE,** or EXtension line Extension, variable. This value is .18 (approx. 3/16) units by default and is also in accordance with drafting standards. To change this value, type the following:

Dim: **DIMEXE** ↵
Current value ⟨0.1800⟩ New value: *(enter a positive value and press* [Enter]*)*

You can also use the **Dimension Styles and Settings** dialog box to change the values of both **DIMEXO** and **DIMEXE**. First, issue the **DDIM** command and then click the **Extension Lines...** button to display the **Extension Lines** subdialog box shown in Figure 11-17. Change the **DIMEXE** variable by entering the desired new value in the **Extension Above Line:** text box. Use the **Feature Offset:** text box to change the value of **DIMEXO**.

Figure 11-17.
The **Extension Above Line:** and **Feature Offset:** text boxes at the top of the **Extension Lines** subdialog box are used to change **DIMEXE** and **DIMEXO**, respectively.

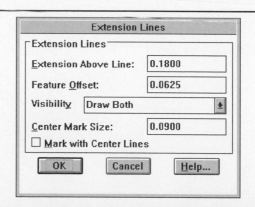

Controlling the gap between the dimension line and dimension text

The **DIMGAP** variable is used to control the spacing between the end of a dimension line and the start of the dimension text. By default, that spacing is .09 (approximately 3/32) units. It is rarely necessary to change this value. However, setting **DIMGAP** to a negative value creates a dimension like that shown in Figure 11-18. This type of dimension is called a *basic dimension,* and represents a theoretically exact dimension used in geometric dimensioning and tolerancing (GD&T). To create a basic dimension using **DIMGAP**, type the following:

Dim: **DIMGAP** ⏎
Current value ⟨0.0900⟩ New value: **–.09** ⏎

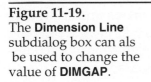

Figure 11-18.
Setting **DIMGAP** to a negative value create a basic dimension.

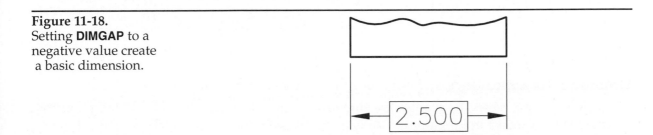

A larger negative value creates a larger box around the dimension, while a smaller negative value draws a smaller box. To change **DIMGAP** using the **Dimension Styles and Settings** dialog box, issue the **DDIM** command and click the **Dimension Line...** button to display the **Dimension Line** subdialog box, Figure 11-19. Use the **Text Gap:** text box to increase or decrease the positive value of **DIMGAP**. To create a basic dimension, click the **Basic Dimension** check box as shown.

Figure 11-19.
The **Dimension Line** subdialog box can als be used to change the value of **DIMGAP**.

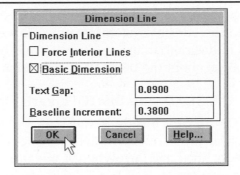

Setting the size of arrowheads

The length of the arrowheads at the end of dimension lines and leader lines is controlled with the **DIMASZ**, or Arrowhead SiZe, variable. This value is set to .18 units (approximately 3/16) by default. If you wish to change the length of your arrowheads, use **DIMASZ** as shown below:

Dim: **DIMASZ** ⏎
Current value ⟨0.1800⟩ New value: *(enter a larger or smaller value and press* [Enter]*)*

You can also use the **Dimension Styles and Settings** dialog box to change the value of **DIMASZ**. First, issue the **DDIM** command and then click the **Arrows...** button to display the **Arrows** subdialog box shown in Figure 11-20. Enter an appropriate value in the **Arrow Size:** text box to lengthen or shorten arrowheads.

Figure 11-20.
Using the **Arrows** subdialog
box to change the value
of **DIMASZ**.

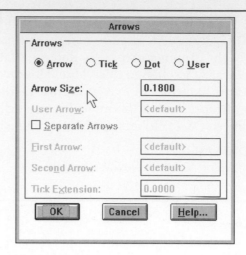

Updating the appearance and format of existing dimensions

It is often necessary to change the dimension variable status for one or more existing dimensions. As an example, suppose you need to change the arrowhead lengths for a drawing that is already completely dimensioned. It is not necessary to erase the existing dimensions and recreate them. Instead, set **DIMASZ** as required and use the **UPDATE** command as follows:

> Dim: *(type* UPDATE *or* UP *and press* [Enter]*)*
> Select objects: *(select the dimension(s) to change)*
> Select objects: ↵
> Dim:

Since all of the AutoCAD LT selection set options are valid with **UPDATE**, you can select many dimensions at one time using a Window or Crossing box. Be advised, however, that selected dimensions are updated to the current status of *all* dimension variables. The **UPDATE** command can also be used to change the text style of existing dimensions and to update dimensions to the current system of units. This is especially useful if you have a drawing dimensioned in decimal units, for example, and wish to convert the dimensions to fractions. More information about the **UPDATE** command is provided later in this chapter.

The DIMTIX, DIMSOXD, and DIMTOFL variables

The **DIMTIX,** or Text Inside eXtensions, dimension variable controls the placement of dimension text inside or outside extension lines. As shown in Figure 11-21, when **DIMTIX** = 1 (on), dimension lines and arrowheads are placed outside, and dimension text is placed between the extension lines. When **DIMTIX** is off (equal to 0), the dimension is placed on the side of the last extension line origin selected. **DIMTIX** is off by default. As shown below, it can be turned on by entering the number 1 or the word ON as follows:

> Dim: **DIMTIX** ↵
> Current value ⟨Off⟩ New value: *(type* 1 *or* ON *and press* [Enter]*)*

Turn off **DIMTIX** by entering a 0 or OFF.

When **DIMTIX** is on, arrowheads and dimension lines are always placed outside when they cannot be fit between the extension lines. To force text and arrowheads inside the extension lines, the **DIMSOXD** (Suppress Outside Dimension lines) variable is used. As shown at the lower right of Figure 11-21, **DIMSOXD** automatically suppresses arrowheads and dimension lines if they do not fit inside. **DIMSOXD** has no effect when **DIMTIX** is off.

Figure 11-21.
The effects of the **DIMTIX**, **DIMTOFL**, and **DIMSOXD** variables.

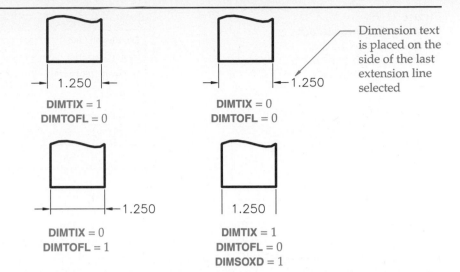

Dimension text is placed on the side of the last extension line selected

DIMTIX = 1
DIMTOFL = 0

DIMTIX = 0
DIMTOFL = 0

DIMTIX = 0
DIMTOFL = 1

DIMTIX = 1
DIMTOFL = 0
DIMSOXD = 1

To change **DIMTIX** and **DIMSOXD** using the **Dimension Styles and Settings** dialog box, issue the **DDIM** command and click the **Text Location...** button to display the **Text Location** subdialog box. As shown in Figure 11-22, the **Horizontal** drop-down list features the following three choices:

* **Default.** Turns **DIMTIX** off.
* **Force Text Inside.** Turns **DIMTIX** on.
* **Text, Arrows Inside.** This option turns on the **DIMSOXD** variable. (**DIMSOXD** is off by default.)

Figure 11-22.
DIMTIX and **DIMSOXD** can be turned on and off using the **Text Location** subdialog box.

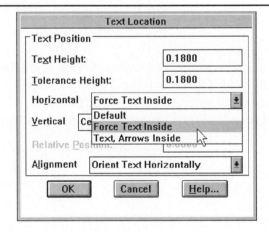

The **DIMTOFL**, or Text Outside, Force Line inside, variable draws a dimension line between the extension lines when the text is placed outside the extensions. This can be seen at the lower left of Figure 11-21. **DIMTOFL** is off by default, but can be turned on as follows:

Dim: **DIMTOFL** ↵
Current value ⟨Off⟩ New value: *(enter* 1 *or* ON *and press* [Enter]*)*

You can also use the **Dimension Styles and Settings** dialog box. First, issue the **DDIM** command and click the **Dimension Line...** button to display the **Dimension Line** subdialog box. Click the **Force Interior Lines** check box as shown in Figure 11-23 to activate **DIMTOFL**.

Figure 11-23.
Clicking the **Force Interior Lines** check box in the **Dimension Line** subdialog box activates **DIMTOFL**.

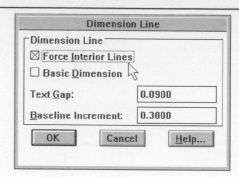

Suppressing extension lines

Linear and angular dimensions in AutoCAD LT are automatically drawn with extension lines. You may choose to suppress one or both extension lines using the **DIMSE1** (Suppress Extension line 1) and **DIMSE2** (Suppress Extension line 2) dimension variables. Several examples of extension line suppression are shown in Figure 11-24.

Dim: *(type* DIMSE1 *or* DIMSE2 *and press* [Enter]*)*
Current value ⟨Off⟩ New value: *(enter* 1 *or* ON *and press* [Enter]*)*

Figure 11-24.
The **DIMSE1** and **DIMSE2** variables control extension line suppression.

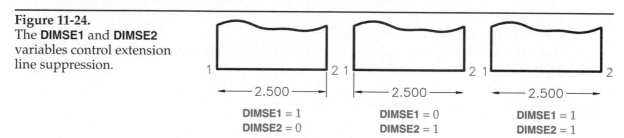

You can also use the **Dimension Styles and Settings** dialog box to change the values of both **DIMSE1** and **DIMSE2**. First, issue the **DDIM** command and then click the **Extension Lines...** button to display the **Extension Lines** subdialog box. Use the **Visibility** drop-down list shown in Figure 11-25 to control extension line suppression.

Figure 11-25.
Using the **Visibility** drop-down list in the **Extension Lines** subdialog box to control extension line suppression.

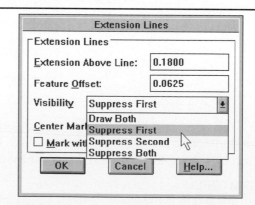

EXERCISE 11-2

❏ Open drawing EX11-1 if it is not on your screen.
❏ Try changing the values of each of the dimension variables described previously.
❏ After changing one or more dimvars, use the **UPDATE** command on your dimensions to see the effect.
❏ Do not save the drawing when you are finished experimenting.

AutoCAD LT—Fundamentals and Applications

ARCHITECTURAL DIMENSIONING VARIABLES

AutoCAD LT offers several dimension variables that are more appropriate for architectural drafting practices. These dimvars are illustrated in Figure 11-26 and are described in this section.

Figure 11-26.
The dimension variables for architectural applications.

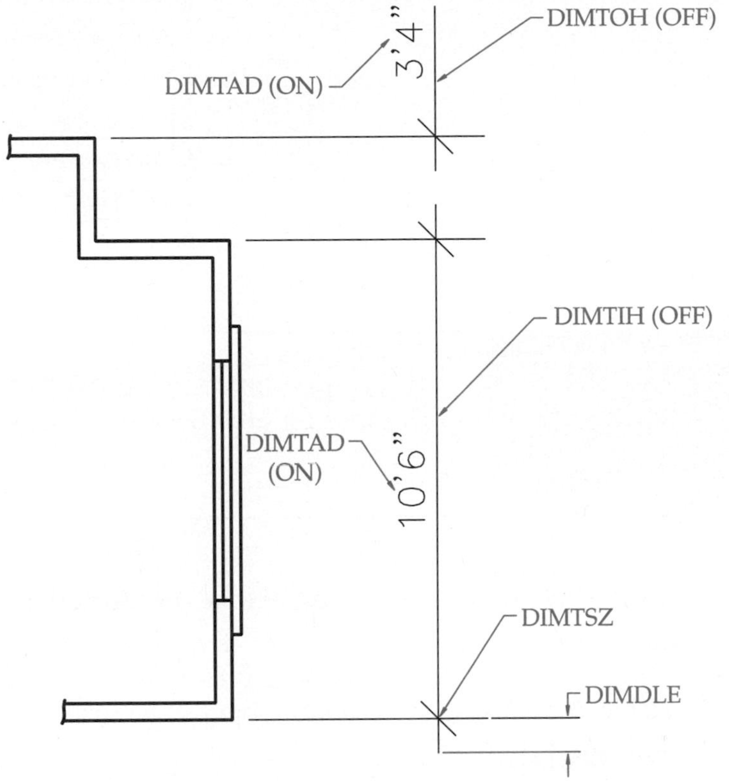

Using oblique strokes in place of arrowheads

Architects often use tick marks at the end of dimension lines instead of arrowheads. This capability is provided with the **DIMTSZ**, or Tick SiZe, variable and is illustrated in Figure 11-26. When **DIMTSZ** is set to 0 (the default), arrowheads are drawn. Enter a positive value to draw tick marks in place of arrowheads.

> Dim: **DIMTSZ** ↵
> Current value ⟨0.0000⟩ New value: *(enter a positive value and press* [Enter]*)*

Larger positive values produce larger tick marks. Once **DIMTSZ** is set, **DIMASZ** is ignored.

Extending a dimension line past extension lines

It is also common in architectural drafting to extend the dimension line so that it crosses the extension lines. This practice is shown in Figure 11-26 and can be accomplished with the **DIMDLE**, or Dimension Line Extension, variable as follows:

> Dim: **DIMDLE** ↵
> Current value ⟨0.0000⟩ New value: *(enter a positive value and press* [Enter]*)*

The **DIMTSZ** variable must be set before **DIMDLE** can be used. You can activate both **DIMTSZ** and **DIMDLE** using the **Dimension Styles and Settings** dialog box. First, issue the **DDIM** command and then click the **Arrows...** button to display the **Arrows** subdialog box. As shown in Figure 11-27, click the **Tick** button and set the tick size in the **Arrow Size:** text box to activate tick marks in place of arrowheads. Enter an appropriate value in the **Tick Extension:** text box to set the dimension line extension.

Figure 11-27.
DIMTSZ and **DIMDLE** can both be activated using the **Arrows** subdialog box.

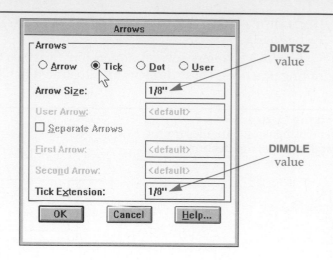

Placing dimension text above or below the dimension line

Placing dimension text above or below the dimension line

Dimensions are often placed above the dimension line in architectural and structural drafting, Figure 11-26. This capability is provided with the **DIMTAD**, or Text Above Dimension line, variable. **DIMTAD** is Off by default, but can be turned on as follows:

Dim: **DIMTAD** ↵
Current value ⟨Off⟩ New value: *(type 1 or ON and press* [Enter]*)*

Another dimension variable somewhat similar to **DIMTAD** is **DIMTVP** (Text Vertical Position). The similarities between **DIMTAD** and **DIMTVP** are illustrated in Figure 11-28. As shown in the illustration, **DIMTVP** can be used to place dimension text below the dimension line as well as above it. Entering 1 places the dimension text above the dimension line. Text is placed below the dimension line when a −1 is entered.

Dim: **DIMTVP** ↵
Current value ⟨0.0000⟩ New value: *(type 1 or −1 as appropriate and press* [Enter]*)*

To obtain a dimension text location that is not centered within the dimension line, but not completely above or below it, set **DIMTVP** to any value between 1 and −1.

Figure 11-28.
Comparisons of **DIMTAD** and **DIMTVP**.

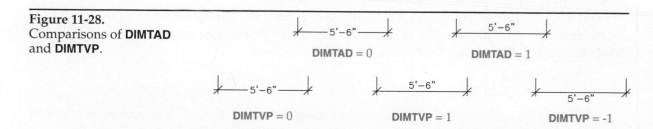

To change **DIMTAD** or **DIMTVP** using the **Dimension Styles and Settings** dialog box, issue the **DDIM** command and click the **Text Location...** button to display the **Text Location** subdialog box. As shown in Figure 11-29, the **Vertical** drop-down list features the following three choices:

- **Centered.** Turns off **DIMTAD** and sets **DIMTVP** = 0.
- **Above.** Turns on **DIMTAD**.
- **Relative.** The **Relative Position:** text box located in the **Text Location** subdialog box is normally *grayed-out*. Selecting **Relative** from the drop-down list activates this text box allowing you to enter a **DIMTVP** value. As previously mentioned, enter 1, –1, or any value in between to set the text vertical position.

Figure 11-29.
Both **DIMTAD** and **DIMTVP** can be set using the **Vertical** drop-down list in the **Text Location** subdialog box.

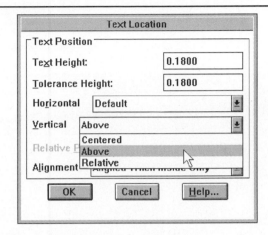

Alignment of dimension text inside and outside extension lines

By default, dimensions in AutoCAD LT are created *unidirectionally* (dimensions read from left to right in a horizontal fashion). However, it is common practice in architectural drafting to align dimension text with dimension lines. This capability is provided with two dimension variables called **DIMTIH** (Text Inside Horizontal) and **DIMTOH** (Text Outside Horizontal). As shown in Figure 11-26, **DIMTIH** controls the alignment of dimension text when the text is placed inside the extension lines. **DIMTOH** performs the same function when dimension text is located outside the extension lines. By default, **DIMTIH** and **DIMTOH** are both on. To create aligned dimensions, turn one or both of them off as follows:

Dim: *(type* DIMTIH *or* DIMTOH *and press* [Enter]*)*
Current value ⟨On⟩ New value: *(enter* 0 *or* OFF *and press* [Enter]*)*

To change the status of **DIMTIH** or **DIMTOH** using the **Dimension Styles and Settings** dialog box, issue the **DDIM** command and click the **Text Location...** button to display the **Text Location** subdialog box. As shown in Figure 11-30, the **Alignment** drop-down list features the following choices:

- **Orient Text Horizontally.** Turns on both **DIMTIH** and **DIMTOH**.
- **Align With Dimension Line.** Turns off both **DIMTIH** and **DIMTOH**.
- **Aligned When Inside Only.** Turns off only **DIMTIH**.
- **Aligned When Outside Only.** Turns off only **DIMTOH**.

PROFESSIONAL TIP

For architectural applications, create a text style using the City Blueprint or Country Blueprint fonts. These fonts closely resemble the lettering style commonly used in architectural drafting. As a matter of efficiency, create the text style in your prototype drawing so that it is always available for your use. See Chapter 9 for more information about text styles and fonts.

Figure 11-30.
DIMTIH and **DIMTOH** can be turned on and off using the **Alignment** drop-down list in the **Text Location** subdialog box.

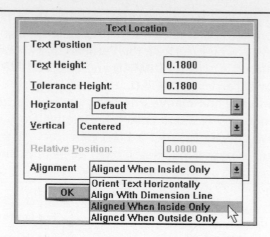

EXERCISE 11-3

❏ Begin a new drawing using your PROTOC prototype drawing.
❏ Set architectural units current and set the drawing limits to 60', 40'. Perform a **ZOOM All** after changing the limits.
❏ Next, create a text style named ARCH using the City Blueprint font.
❏ Use the **DLINE** command to draw the partial floor plan shown below. All wall thicknesses are 6".
❏ The plot scale of the drawing is 1/8" = 1'. Set **DIMSCALE** appropriately. Set other dimension variables as required to dimension the drawing exactly as shown. Be sure to create all dimensions on the DIMS layer.
❏ Save the drawing as EX11-3.

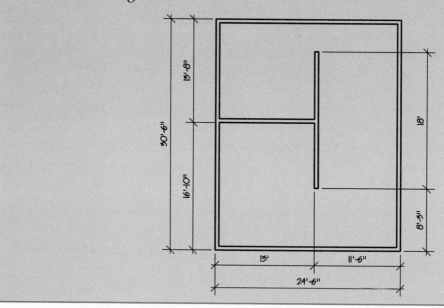

BASELINE DIMENSIONING

ALTUG 13

The **BASELINE** command continues a linear dimension from the baseline, or datum, of the previous linear dimension. This is why baseline dimensioning is also called *datum dimensioning*. An example of baseline dimensioning appears at the top of Figure 11-31. As shown in the illustration, the **BASELINE** command draws a series of related dimensions measured from the same baseline. In Figure 11-31, the baseline is at the left of the object. Before you can use the **BASELINE** command, you must first create a linear dimension to serve as the

AutoCAD LT—Fundamentals and Applications

base dimension. In the example shown, a horizontal or aligned dimension can be used to create the 2.500 base dimension.

To issue the **BASELINE** command, first select **Linear Dimensions** from the **Draw** pull-down menu. Next, select **Baseline** from the cascading submenu, Figure 11-32. The two baseline dimensions shown in Figure 11-31 are created as follows:

    Dim: *(type* BASELINE *or* B *and press* [Enter]*)*
    Second extension line origin or RETURN to select: *(pick point 1)*
    Dimension text ⟨5.750⟩: ⏎
    Dim: *(press* [Enter] *to repeat the* BASELINE *command)*
    Second extension line origin or RETURN to select: *(pick point 2)*
    Dimension text ⟨8.375⟩: ⏎
    Dim:

AutoCAD LT uses the first extension line origin of the previous dimension for the first extension line origin of the baseline dimension. After you select a second extension line origin, the baseline dimension is drawn and AutoCAD LT redisplays the **Second extension line origin** prompt.

Figure 11-31.
An example of baseline (datum) dimensioning.

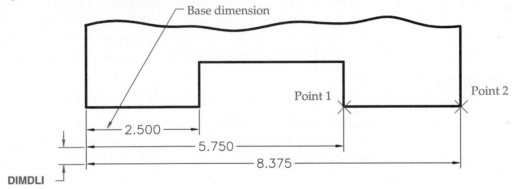

Figure 11-32.
Selecting **Baseline** from the **Linear Dimensions** cascading submenu.

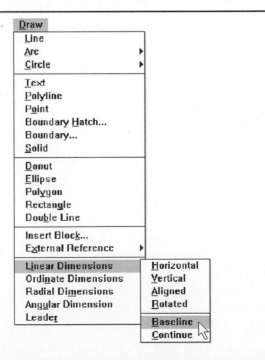

Selecting a different baseline origin

AutoCAD LT automatically uses the last dimension created as the baseline reference for the next dimension. However, there may be occasions when you wish to use a different dimension as the base for subsequent dimensions. To select a different baseline origin, do the following:

> Dim: *(type* BASELINE *or* B *and press* [Enter]*)*
> Second extension line origin or RETURN to select: ⤶
> Select base dimension: *(pick the dimension you wish to use as the new baseline reference)*
> Second extension line origin or RETURN to select: *(pick a point)*
> Dimension text ⟨*current*⟩: ⤶
> Dim:

After you select the new base dimension, the **Second extension line origin or RETURN to select:** prompt is redisplayed. Specify the point for the second extension line, press [Enter] at the **Dimension text** prompt, and the baseline dimension is drawn.

Setting the dimension line increment

As shown in Figure 11-31, AutoCAD LT uses a baseline increment value to offset each new dimension line to avoid overwriting the previous dimension line. This value is stored in the **DIMDLI**, or Dimension Line Increment, variable. By default, **DIMDLI** is set to .38 units (3/8) in accordance with drafting standards. While acceptable for most horizontal dimensions, the default value may be too close for vertical dimensions. This is particularly true if the vertical dimensions include tolerances. To change the value of **DIMDLI**, type the following:

> Dim: **DIMDLI** ⤶
> Current value ⟨0.3800⟩ New value: *(enter a positive value and press* [Enter]*)*

You can also use the **Dimension Styles and Settings** dialog box to change **DIMDLI**. First, issue the **DDIM** command and click the **Dimension Line...** button to display the **Dimension Line** subdialog box. Use the **Baseline Increment:** text box to change the dimension line spacing. See Figure 11-33.

Figure 11-33.
The value of **DIMDLI** can be changed using the **Baseline Increment:** text box in the **Dimension Line** subdialog box.

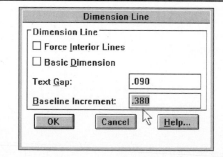

CONTINUED DIMENSIONING

ALTUG 13

The **CONTINUE** command continues a linear dimension from the second extension line of the previously created linear dimension. Continued dimensioning is also known as *chain dimensioning*. As shown in Figure 11-34, AutoCAD LT uses the origin of the previous dimension's second extension line for the origin of the next dimension's first extension line. As with baseline dimensioning, you must first create a base dimension before using the **CONTINUE** command.

Figure 11-34.
An example of continue
(chain) dimensioning.

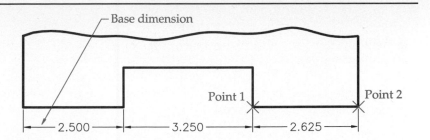

To issue the **CONTINUE** command, first select **Linear Dimensions** from the **Draw** pull-down menu. Then, select **Continue** from the cascading submenu, Figure 11-35. The two continued dimensions shown in Figure 11-34 are created using the following procedure:

> Dim: *(type* CONTINUE *or* CO *and press* [Enter]*)*
> Second extension line origin or RETURN to select: *(pick point 1)*
> Dimension text ⟨3.250⟩: ↵
> Dim: *(press* [Enter] *to repeat the* CONTINUE *command)*
> Second extension line origin or RETURN to select: *(pick point 2)*
> Dimension text ⟨2.625⟩: ↵

Figure 11-35.
Selecting **Continue** from
the **Linear Dimensions**
cascading submenu.

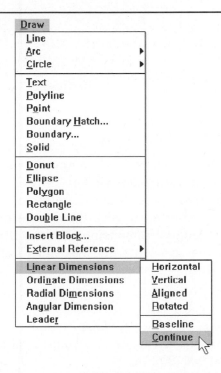

As with the **BASELINE** command, AutoCAD LT automatically uses the last dimension created as the reference for the next continued dimension. If you wish to use a different dimension as the base for subsequent dimensions, use the following procedure:

> Dim: *(type* CONTINUE *or* CO *and press* [Enter]*)*
> Second extension line origin or RETURN to select: ↵
> Select continued dimension: *(pick the dimension you wish to use as the*
> *new continue reference)*
> Second extension line origin or RETURN to select: *(pick a point)*
> Dimension text ⟨*current*⟩: ↵
> Dim:

Finally, if it is necessary to increment a continued dimension to avoid writing over an existing dimension, the current value of **DIMDLI** is used to set the dimension line spacing.

EXERCISE 11-4

❑ Begin a new drawing using your PROTOA prototype drawing.
❑ Draw the object shown below on the OBJECTS layer.
❑ Set the DIMS layer current and use baseline dimensioning to create the horizontal dimensions. Use continued dimensioning to create the vertical dimensions.
❑ Save the drawing as EX11-4.

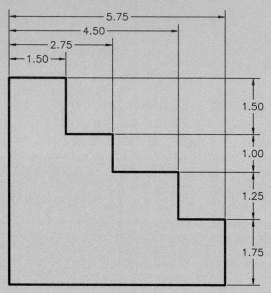

ANGULAR DIMENSIONS

Angular dimensions are most commonly used to indicate the angle between two selected lines. An angular dimension can also be used to measure the angle between two points on a circle, or the angle between the two endpoints of an arc. After selecting the extension line origins, you are prompted to pick the dimension line arc location. To issue the **ANGULAR** command, select **Angular Dimension** from the **Draw** pull-down menu, Figure 11-36. Refer to the angular dimension used with lines shown at the top of Figure 11-37 as you follow this command procedure:

        Dim: *(type* ANGULAR *or* AN *and press* [Enter]*)*
        Select arc, circle, line, or RETURN: *(pick a line)*
        Second line: *(pick a second line)*
        Dimension arc line location (Text/Angle): *(pick the dimension arc location)*
        Dimension text ⟨90⟩: ↵
        Enter text location (or RETURN): ↵
        Dim:

If you press [Enter] at the **Enter text location:** prompt, the dimension text is centered within the dimension arc. If you prefer to shift the text within the arc, or position the text outside the extension lines, pick the desired point with your cursor. AutoCAD LT automatically adds a degree symbol (°) to the dimension text.

Figure 11-36.
Selecting **Angular Dimension** from the **Draw** pull-down menu.

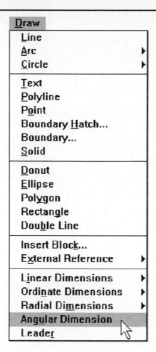

As previously mentioned, angular dimensions can also be used with circles and arcs. At the lower left of Figure 11-37, an angular dimension is used to measure the angle between two selected points on a circle. The first pick point on the circle becomes the first extension line origin. The second pick point is the second extension line origin. (The second point does not need to be on the circle.)

As shown at the lower right of Figure 11-37, the center of an arc becomes the angle vertex when placing an angular dimension. The two endpoints of the arc become the extension line origins.

Figure 11-37.
Creating angular dimensions with lines, a circle, and an arc.

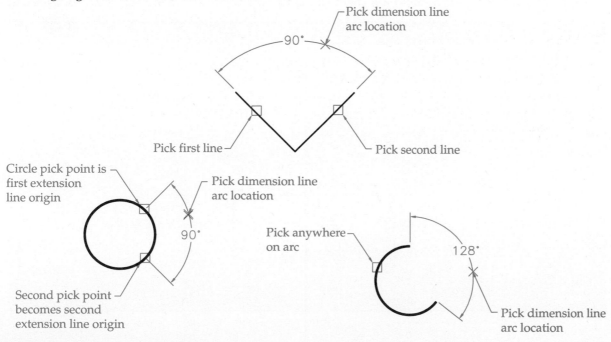

Creating an angular dimension through three points

It is also possible to create an angular dimension through three points. With this method, you first specify the angle vertex and then select the extension line origins. A practical application for this type of angular dimension is shown in Figure 11-38. Refer to the illustration as you follow the procedure below:

Dim: *(type ANGULAR or AN and press [Enter])*
Select arc, circle, line, or RETURN: ↵
Angle vertex: *(pick the CENter of the large circle)*
First angle endpoint: *(pick the QUAdrant of the top circle)*
Second angle endpoint: *(pick the QUAdrant of the circle at the right)*
Dimension arc line location (Text/Angle): *(pick the dimension arc location)*
Dimension text ⟨90⟩: ↵
Enter text location (or RETURN): ↵
Dim:

Figure 11-38.
Creating an angular
dimension through three
points.

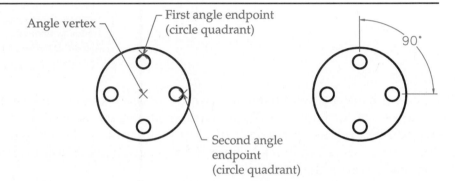

NOTE   With the exception of **DIMLFAC** and **DIMRND**, each of the dimension variables described so far in this chapter are also applicable to angular dimensions.

EXERCISE 11-5

❑ Begin a new drawing using your PROTOA prototype drawing.
❑ Draw the object shown below on the OBJECTS layer.
❑ Set the DIMS layer current and dimension the object exactly as shown.
❑ Create the centerline through the object on the CENTERLINES layer.
❑ Save the drawing as EX11-5.

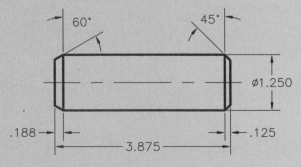

RADIAL DIMENSIONS

AutoCAD LT refers to both diameter and radius dimensions as radial dimensions. This section describes radial dimensioning operations, as well as how to place center marks and centerlines through arcs and circles. The radial dimensioning commands can be accessed from a cascading submenu by selecting **Radial Dimensions** from the **Draw** pull-down menu, Figure 11-39.

Figure 11-39.
Selecting **Radial Dimensions** from the **Draw** pull-down menu displays a cascading submenu of radial dimensioning options.

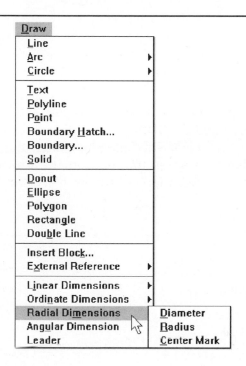

Drawing center marks and centerlines

Good drafting practice dictates that center marks be drawn through small arcs and circles when detailing a drawing. For larger arcs and circles, drawing centerlines is the preferred method. You can draw center marks or centerlines by selecting **Radial Dimensions** from the **Draw** pull-down menu, and then selecting **Center Mark** from the cascading submenu. You can also enter the following at the **Dim:** prompt:

> Dim: *(type* CENTER *or* CE *and press* [Enter]*)*
> Select arc or circle: *(pick an arc or circle)*

AutoCAD LT places a center mark in the selected arc or circle. (Center marks can also be placed in donut entities.) You can control the size of the center mark, and whether centerlines are drawn instead of center marks, using the **DIMCEN**, or CENter, variable.

> Dim: **DIMCEN** ↵
> Current value ⟨0.0900⟩ New value: *(enter a positive or negative value and press* [Enter]*)*

As shown in Figure 11-40, a positive value (the default) draws a center mark. The larger the value, the larger the center mark. A negative value draws a centerline that extends past an arc or circle at the distance specified. The larger the negative value, the greater the extension of the centerline.

Figure 11-40.
The **DIMCEN** variable controls whether center marks or centerlines are drawn.

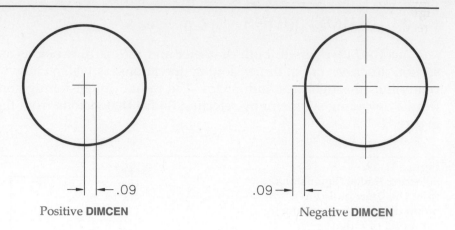

Positive **DIMCEN**　　　　　Negative **DIMCEN**

You can also use the **Dimension Styles and Settings** dialog box to change the value of **DIMCEN**. First, issue the **DDIM** command and then click the **Extension Lines...** button to display the **Extension Lines** subdialog box. Enter the desired value in the **Center Mark Size:** text box to lengthen or shorten the center mark through small arcs and circles. To draw centerlines instead of center marks, activate the **Mark with Center Lines** check box as shown in Figure 11-41.

Figure 11-41.
Using the **Extension Lines** subdialog box to set the **DIMCEN** variable.

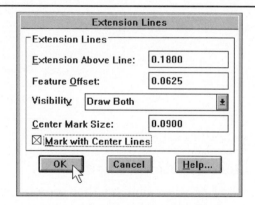

Diameter dimensions

The **DIAMETER** command is used to place a radial dimension on a circle. Although possible, it should not be used with arc entities because the command automatically places a diameter symbol (Ø) in front of the dimension text. For arcs, use the **RADIUS** command instead. The point at which a circle or arc is selected determines the angle of the leader line. This applies to both diameter and radius dimensions as shown in Figure 11-42. To create a diameter dimension, select **Radial Dimensions** from the **Draw** pull-down menu, and then select **Diameter** from the cascading submenu. At the **Dim:** prompt, enter the following:

Dim: *(type* DIAMETER *or* D *and press* [Enter]*)*
Select arc or circle: *(pick an arc or circle)*
Dimension text ⟨*current*⟩: ↵

Figure 11-42.
Creating a radial dimension.

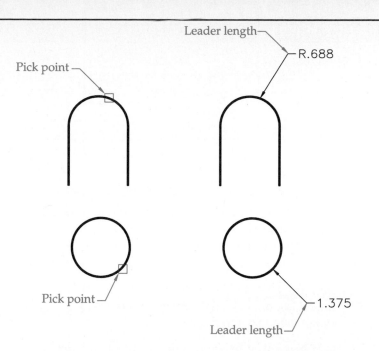

If **DIMTIX** is off, you are then prompted to enter the leader length. If you press [Enter] at the prompt, AutoCAD LT draws a small leader equal to the length of two arrowheads. For a longer leader, use your cursor to dynamically "drag" the leader to the desired position.

Enter leader length for text: *(drag to a point or press* [Enter]*)*
Dim:

Keep in mind that the **DIAMETER** command automatically places a center mark through the circle being dimensioned. If **DIMCEN** is set to a negative value, a centerline is placed instead. The center mark (or centerline) is part of the dimension and is created on the same layer. You can suppress the center mark by setting **DIMCEN** = 0. The effects of the **DIMTIX**, **DIMTOFL**, and **DIMCEN** variables on several diameter dimensions are shown in Figure 11-43.

Figure 11-43.
The effects of **DIMTIX**, **DIMTOFL**, and **DIMCEN** on diameter dimensions.

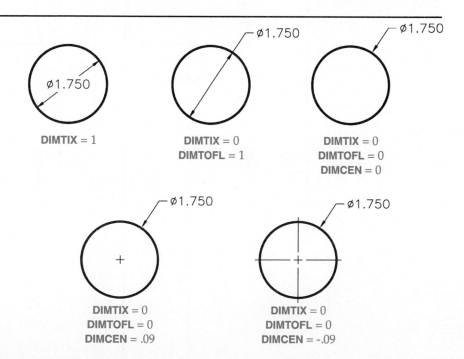

Radius dimensions

The **RADIUS** command is used to place a radial dimension on an arc and automatically places an "R" (for radius) in front of the dimension text. As with diameter dimensions, the point at which the arc is selected determines the angle of the leader line. To create a radius dimension, select **Radial Dimensions** from the **Draw** pull-down menu, and then select **Radius** from the cascading submenu. You can also type the following at the **Dim:** prompt:

Dim: *(type* RADIUS *or* RA *and press* [Enter]*)*
Select arc or circle: *(pick an arc or circle)*
Dimension text ⟨*current*⟩: ↵

If **DIMTIX** is off, you are then prompted to enter the leader length. As with the **DIAMETER** command, pressing [Enter] draws a small leader equal to the length of two arrowheads. For a longer leader, use your cursor to dynamically "drag" the leader to the desired position.

Enter leader length for text: *(drag to a point or press* [Enter]*)*
Dim:

As shown in Figure 11-44, the **DIMTIX**, **DIMTOFL**, and **DIMCEN** variables also affect the appearance of radius dimensions.

Figure 11-44.
The effects of **DIMTIX**, **DIMTOFL**, and **DIMCEN** on radius dimensions.

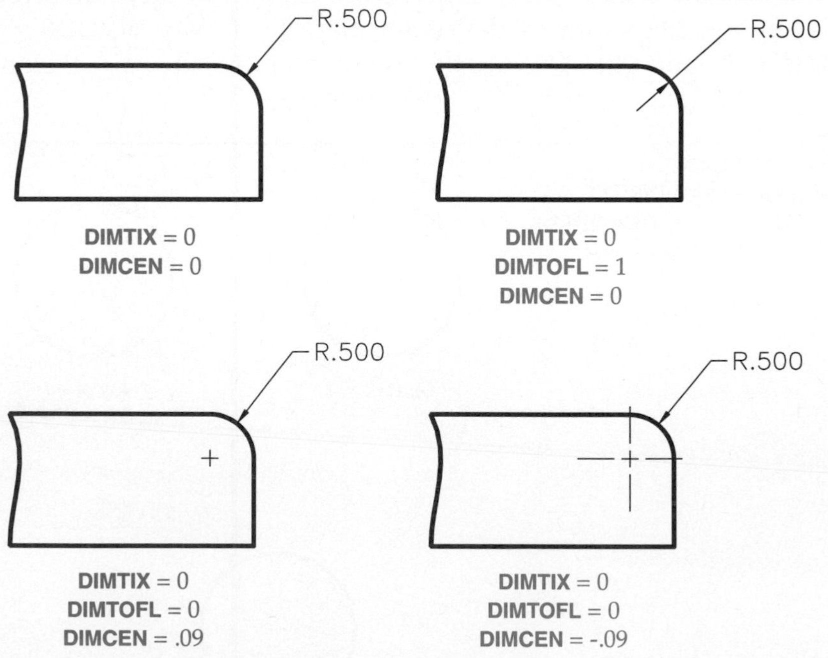

R.500

DIMTIX = 0
DIMCEN = 0

R.500

DIMTIX = 0
DIMTOFL = 1
DIMCEN = 0

R.500

DIMTIX = 0
DIMTOFL = 0
DIMCEN = .09

R.500

DIMTIX = 0
DIMTOFL = 0
DIMCEN = -.09

EXERCISE 11-7

❏ Open PROTOA.
❏ With the OBJECTS layer set current, draw an object similar to that shown in Figure 11-44. It is not necessary to draw the break line.
❏ Use the **COPY Multiple** command to create three additional copies of the object.
❏ Set the DIMS layer current. Using the appropriate dimension variables, dimension each fillet exactly as shown.
❏ Save the drawing as EX11-7.

THE LEADER COMMAND ALTUG 13

The **LEADER** command creates a leader similar to that drawn by the **DIAMETER** and **RADIUS** commands. Its purpose is to draw a leader with appended text for specification callouts. Unlike a diameter or radius dimension which is one complete entity, a leader is drawn with separate text and line entities. The arrowhead at the end of the leader is a filled solid. (The **SOLID** command is described in Chapter 12.) Unlike linear, angular, and radial dimensions, leaders are not true dimensioning types. As such, most of the dimension variables are not applicable to them.

To draw a leader, enter **LEADER** at the **Dim:** prompt or select **Leader** from the **Draw** pull-down menu, Figure 11-45.

Figure 11-45.
Selecting the **Leader** command from the **Draw** pull-down menu.

Refer to Figure 11-46 as you follow the procedure shown below.

Command: *(type* DIM *or* D *and press* [Enter]*)*
Dim: *(type* LEADER *or* L *and press* [Enter]*)*
Leader start: *(pick a point on the feature to be dimensioned—object snap mode* NEArest *is often a good choice)*

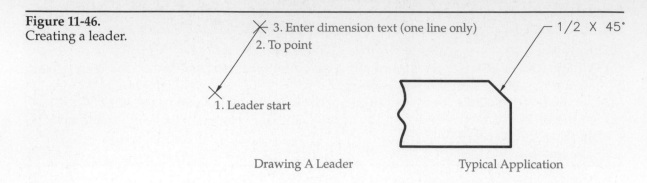

Figure 11-46.
Creating a leader.

3. Enter dimension text (one line only)
2. To point
1. Leader start

1/2 X 45°

Drawing A Leader

Typical Application

As shown above, you are first prompted for the leader start. This is the point at which the leader arrowhead will touch. Be sure to use an appropriate object snap mode when picking the start point. The command begins to resemble the **LINE** command as you are presented with the **To point:** prompt.

> To point: *(pick the second leader point—the start of the shoulder)*

Use your cursor to dynamically "drag" the leader to the desired length and angle and pick to set the second point. AutoCAD LT repeats the **To point:** prompt, allowing you to draw multiple leader segments until you press [Enter]. As with the **LINE** command, enter U and press [Enter] to undo an incorrectly drawn segment.

> To point: *(press* [Enter] *to automatically draw the shoulder)*

It is not necessary to pick a third point to define the end of the leader shoulder. After picking the second point as shown in Figure 11-46, simply press [Enter]. AutoCAD LT draws the horizontal shoulder segment for you automatically.

> Dimension text ⟨*value from the previous dimension*⟩: *(enter the desired character or numeric data, or press* [Enter] *to accept the value in the brackets)*
> Dim:

DIMENSIONING WITH CUSTOM ARROWHEADS   ALTUG 13

AutoCAD LT provides you with the option of creating your own custom arrowheads. A custom arrowhead must first be drawn 1 unit in size and saved as a block. (Block entities are covered in Chapter 14.) One custom arrowhead, in the form of a dot, is included with AutoCAD LT. This type of arrowhead is often used in architectural drafting. Several examples of the DOT arrowhead are shown in Figure 11-47.

Figure 11-47.
Examples of the DOT arrowhead.

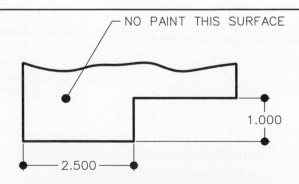

NO PAINT THIS SURFACE

1.000

2.500

The size of the dot is controlled with the **DIMASZ** (Arrowhead SiZe) variable described earlier in this chapter. To use the DOT arrowhead, set the **DIMBLK**, or BLocK, variable as follows:

> Dim: **DIMBLK** ↵
> Current value ⟨⟩ New value: **DOT** ↵

When you wish to restore normal arrowheads for your dimension lines and leaders, clear the **DIMBLK** variable by typing a period (.) as follows:

> Dim: **DIMBLK** ↵
> Current value ⟨⟩ New value: **.** ↵

You can also use the **Dimension Styles and Settings** dialog box to set the DOT arrowhead. First, issue the **DDIM** command and then click the **Arrows...** button to display the **Arrows** subdialog box. As shown in Figure 11-48, click the **Dot** option button to make dot arrowheads current. Enter an appropriate value in the **Arrow Size:** text box to increase or decrease the diameter of the dots.

Figure 11-48.
Click the **Dot** option button in the **Arrows** subdialog box to use dot terminators.

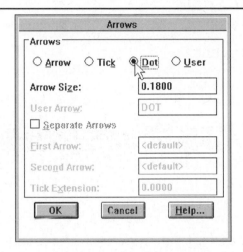

Another example of a custom arrowhead called MYARROW appears at the left of Figure 11-49. These arrowheads are open rather than filled. The arrowhead is first drawn 1 unit in size and saved as a block with the name MYARROW. (Blocks, like linetypes, layers, and text styles, are named entities.) The name MYARROW is then entered for the **DIMBLK** value.

> Dim: **DIMBLK** ↵
> Current value ⟨⟩ New value: **MYARROW** ↵

Figure 11-49.
At the left, the custom arrowhead MYARROW is used with a linear dimension. Separate custom arrowheads and the dimvars that control their use are shown at the right.

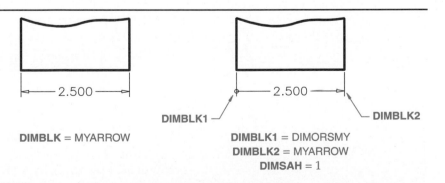

Whenever a linear, angular, or radial dimension is now created, AutoCAD LT inserts your block where the arrowheads are normally placed. The custom arrowhead is then sized using the formula **DIMASZ** × **DIMSCALE**. Also, be sure to draw an extra "tail" with your arrowheads so that they connect properly with the dimension lines. The tail is trimmed at each end of the dimension line using the formula **DIMGAP** × **DIMSCALE**.

You can also use the **Dimension Styles and Settings** dialog box to set your custom arrowhead current. Issue the **DDIM** command and then click the **Arrows...** button to display the **Arrows** subdialog box. As shown in Figure 11-50A, click the **User** option button and enter the arrowhead name in the **User Arrow:** text box.

Using separate custom arrowheads

It is also possible to have different arrowheads at each end of a dimension line as shown at the right in Figure 11-49. In this example, a custom arrowhead representing the dimension origin symbol sometimes used by mechanical engineers, appears on the left side of the dimension line. This block has been given the name DIMORSYM. The MYARROW block appears at the right of the dimension line. Three dimension variables control the use of separate arrowheads. The variables are **DIMBLK1** (first extension line), **DIMBLK2** (second extension line), and **DIMSAH** (Separate ArrowHeads). At the **Dim:** prompt, these variables are set as follows:

> Dim: **DIMBLK1** ↵
> Current value ⟨⟩ New value: **DIMORSYM** ↵
> Dim: **DIMBLK2** ↵
> Current value ⟨⟩ New value: **MYARROW** ↵
> Dim: **DIMSAH** ↵
> Current value ⟨Off⟩ New value: *(enter 1 or ON and press* [Enter]*)*

Using the **Arrows** subdialog box to set separate arrowheads is shown in Figure 11-50B. First, click the **User** option button and pick the **Separate Arrows** check box to turn on **DIMSAH**. Next, enter the DIMBLK1 name in the **First Arrow:** text box and the DIMBLK2 name in the **Second Arrow:** text box.

Figure 11-50.
A—Setting **DIMBLK** using the **Arrows** subdialog box. B—Setting **DIMSAH**, **DIMBLK1**, and **DIMBLK2** using the **Arrows** subdialog box.

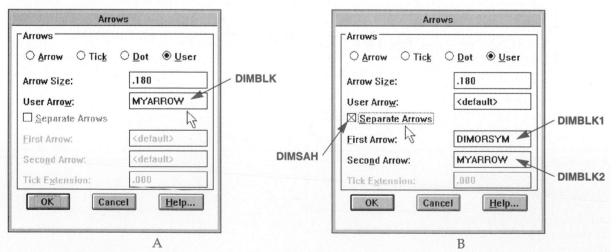

A   B

NOTE   When using separate arrowheads, diameter and radius dimensions use the arrowhead specified by **DIMBLK1**. The **LEADER** command uses the arrowhead specified by **DIMBLK2**.

ORDINATE DIMENSIONING

Ordinate dimensions, also known as *arrowless dimensions*, display the X or Y coordinate of a feature on a single leader line. As shown in Figure 11-51, no arrowheads are used with ordinate dimensions. Before dimensioning with ordinate dimensions, you must first create a UCS (User Coordinate System). AutoCAD LT uses the origin of the current UCS to determine the measured X or Y coordinates. The leader lines are then drawn parallel to the coordinate axes of the current UCS. For most applications, the UCS is created at the lower-left corner of the object. That point then becomes the 0,0 datum for all subsequent ordinate dimensions. Certain applications may require the datum to be located on a specific feature, like the center of a hole. Such a datum is shown in Figure 11-52. Although the two objects are identical, compare the dimensions in this illustration with those in Figure 11-51.

Figure 11-51.
Ordinate dimensions
display the X or Y
coordinate of a feature
on a single leader.

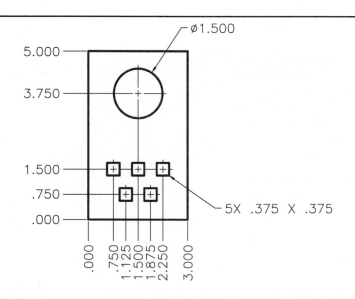

Figure 11-52.
A UCS is defined at the
datum origin of the object.

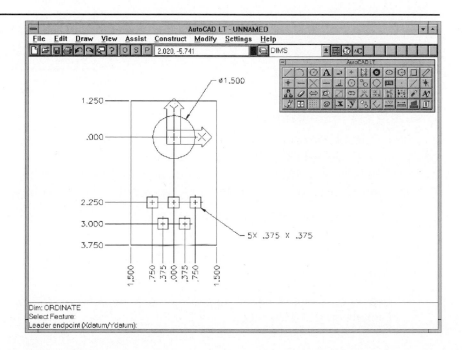

The UCS and UCSICON commands revisited

You may recall that the **UCS** command was introduced in Chapter 7 as a means of facilitating the creation of auxiliary views. The **UCS** command can be issued at the **Command:** prompt, or by selecting **Set UCS** from the **Assist** pull-down menu. Each of the **UCS** command options are then displayed in a cascading submenu. Refer to Figure 11-52 as you follow the procedure given below to create a UCS that represents the 0,0 datum:

> Command: **UCS** ⏎
> Origin/ZAxis/3point/Entity/View/X/Y/Z/Prev/Restore/Save/Del/?/⟨World⟩: **O** ⏎
> Origin point ⟨0,0,0⟩: *(select the circle using* CENter *osnap)*
> Command:

Now that the required UCS is created, it is helpful to turn on and display the UCS icon at the origin of the current UCS. You can turn the UCS icon on and off using the **UCSICON** command, or by selecting **UCS Icon** from the **Assist** pull-down menu, Figure 11-53. The procedure looks like this:

> Command: *(type* UCSICON *or* UI *and press* [Enter]*)*
> ON/OFF/All/Noorigin/ORigin ⟨OFF⟩: **ON** ⏎
> Command: ⏎
> ON/OFF/All/Noorigin/ORigin ⟨ON⟩: **OR** ⏎
> Command:

Figure 11-53.
Selecting **UCS Icon** from the **Assist** pull-down menu issues the **UCSICON** command.

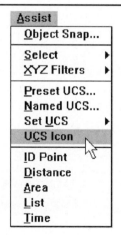

Creating ordinate dimensions

Once the UCS is defined, you are ready to begin creating ordinate dimensions. To ensure completely straight leader lines, it is recommended that you turn on **Ortho** mode. The snap and grid may be helpful, as well. Begin dimensioning by selecting **Ordinate Dimensions** from the **Draw** pull-down menu, Figure 11-54, or by entering the following at the **Dim:** prompt:

> Dim: *(type* ORDINATE *or* OR *and press* [Enter]*)*
> Select feature: *(pick a feature to be dimensioned)*

AutoCAD LT uses the point you selected as the start point of the leader line and then prompts for the endpoint.

> Leader endpoint (Xdatum/Ydatum): *(pick an endpoint for the leader)*
> Dimension text ⟨current⟩: ⏎
> Dim:

Figure 11-54.
Selecting **Ordinate**
Dimensions from the **Draw**
pull-down menu displays a
cascading submenu of
dimensioning options.

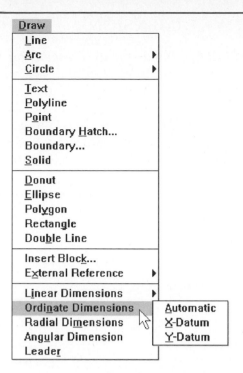

As shown above, you have the option to specify whether an **Xdatum** or **Ydatum** dimension is to be created. This is not really necessary because the default (**Automatic**) option of the **ORDINATE** command makes the determination based on the direction you pick for the leader endpoint. If the difference in the X coordinate between the feature location and the leader endpoint is greater than the Y coordinate, the dimension measures the Y coordinate. Otherwise, an X coordinate dimension is placed.

EXERCISE 11-8

❑ Open PROTOA.
❑ Set the OBJECTS layer current and draw the following object. Use the **ARRAY** and **CHAMFER** commands to your advantage.
❑ Create a UCS at the lower-left corner of the object. Turn on the UCS icon and orient it at the origin of the UCS.
❑ Set the DIMS layer current and dimension the object using ordinate dimensions exactly as shown. Turn on **Ortho** to ensure straight leader lines.
❑ Save the drawing as EX11-8.

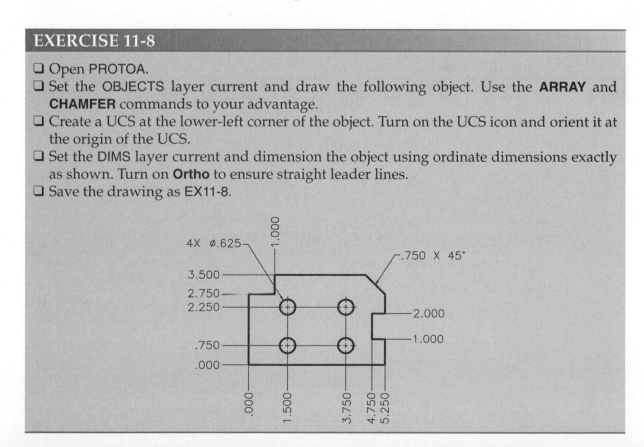

ASSOCIATIVE DIMENSIONS

AutoCAD LT defines an *associative dimension* as a dimension that adapts as the associated geometry is modified. In other words, if you stretch a dimensioned object, the dimension updates automatically. This powerful capability permits you to quickly revise drawings without having to redimension them. Consider the simple object illustrated in Figure 11-55. In this example, an object is stretched 1.375 units to the right. Since the dimension is included in the Crossing selection set, its value is automatically updated both during and after the stretch operation.

Figure 11-55.
Dimension associativity
ensures that dimensions are
updated during a **STRETCH**
operation.

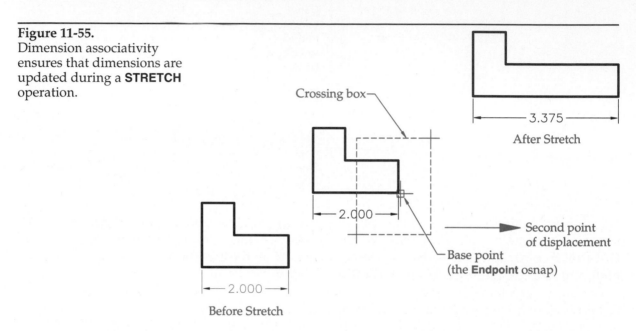

Dimension associativity is controlled with the **DIMASO**, or ASsOciativity, variable. When **DIMASO** is off (0), there is no association between the various elements of a dimension. The lines, arcs, arrowheads, and text of a dimension are drawn as separate entities and must be edited individually. When **DIMASO** is on (the default), there is association between each element of a dimension forming it into a single object. If the *definition point* of the dimension moves, the dimension value is updated. Definition points are used by AutoCAD LT to maintain associativity between geometry and dimensions. These points define extension and dimension line origins, as well as the selected points and centers of circles and arcs for diameter and radius dimensions. Although it is recommended that **DIMASO** be left on, it can be turned off as follows:

Dim: **DIMASO** ↵
Current value ⟨On⟩ New value: *(type 0 or OFF and press* [Enter]*)*

DIMASO can also be turned on and off by selecting **Associati̲ve Dimensions** from the **S̲ettings** pull-down menu, Figure 11-56. The displayed check mark indicates that **DIMASO** is turned on.

Figure 11-56.
The check mark alongside
Associative Dimensions in
the **Settings** pull-down
menu indicates that **DIMASO**
is turned on.

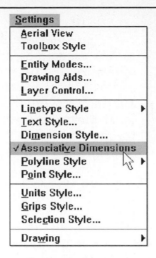

> **NOTE**
>
> Associative dimensions recompute dynamically as they are dragged. This can be a slow process on older computers, or machines that have insufficient physical memory (RAM). If you find that dimension dragging is adversely affecting system performance, it can be turned off with the **DIMSHO** variable. When turned on (the default), **DIMSHO** controls the redefinition of linear and angular dimensions while dragging. The dynamic dragging of radius or diameter leader lengths are not affected by **DIMSHO**.

The DEFPOINTS layer

As mentioned previously, definition points are used to maintain associativity between geometry and dimensions. When **DIMASO** is on and the first associative dimension is created in a drawing, AutoCAD LT automatically creates a new layer called DEFPOINTS, Figure 11-57. This layer contains the definition points needed for dimension associativity. The definition points are displayed, but not plotted, whether the DEFPOINTS layer is turned on or off. When stretching dimensioned geometry, be sure to include the definition points in the selection set or the dimensions will not update.

Figure 11-57.
The DEFPOINTS layer is
shown in the **Layer Control**
dialog box.

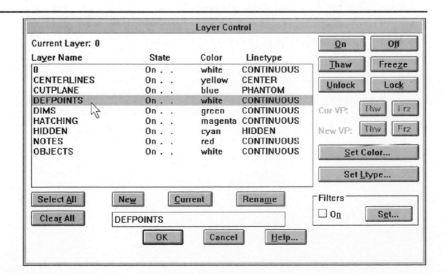

Exploding a dimension

An associative dimension is all one entity. The **EXPLODE** command returns an associative dimension to its separate elements and associativity is lost. This is the equivalent of creating a dimension with **DIMASO** turned off. Also, the entities that once comprised the dimension (lines and text) are automatically placed on Layer 0. If you inadvertently explode one or more dimensions, an **UNDO** operation will restore them.

EDITING DIMENSIONS

ALTUG 13

Eventually, one or more of the associative dimensions on your drawings may require modification. Dimension editing commands can be accessed from the **Modify** pull-down menu. As shown in Figure 11-58, clicking the **Edit Dimension** selection displays a cascading submenu containing these options: **Change Text**, **Home Text**, **Move Text**, **Rotate Text**, **Oblique Dimension**, and **Update Dimension**. These options correspond to the **NEWTEXT**, **HOMETEXT**, **TEDIT**, **TROTATE**, **OBLIQUE**, and **UPDATE** commands, respectively. Each of these commands are described in the following section. Keep in mind, however, that the dimension editing commands cannot be used with exploded, or nonassociative, dimensions.

Figure 11-58.
Selecting **Edit Dimension** from the **Modify** pull-down menu displays a cascading submenu of dimension editing options.

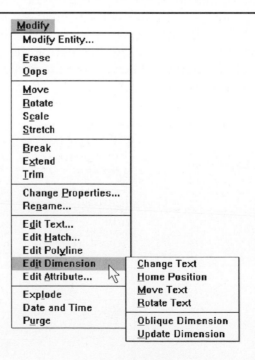

The NEWTEXT command

The **NEWTEXT** command can be used to edit the text format of, or add a prefix or suffix to, one or more existing dimensions. In the example shown in Figure 11-59, a diameter symbol (Ø) has been left off the 1.125 vertical dimension. To correct the error, issue the **NEWTEXT** command by selecting **Change Text** from the **Edit Dimension** cascading submenu or enter the following at the **Dim:** prompt:

> Dim: *(type* NEWTEXT *or* N *and press* [Enter]*)*
> Enter new dimension text: **%%C ⟨⟩** ↵
> Select objects: *(select the 1.125 dimension)*
> Select objects: ↵
> Dim:

Figure 11-59.
The **NEWTEXT** command is used to add prefixes and/or suffixes to associative dimensions.

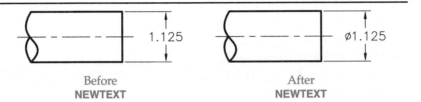

Before
NEWTEXT

After
NEWTEXT

PROFESSIONAL TIP

Never use the **NEWTEXT** command to type in a different dimensional value than appears in the brackets. Doing so destroys the associativity between the dimension and the associated feature. Should the dimensioned object then be stretched, the dimension will *not* update. If a dimension needs to be changed, revise the object geometry accordingly. Only use **NEWTEXT** to change the existing dimension text format or add a prefix/suffix to a dimension.

The TEDIT command

The **TEDIT**, or Text EDIT, command is used to shift a linear dimension left, right, up, or down within the dimension line, Figure 11-60. It is often used to stagger dimensions. For vertical dimensions, shifting to the left moves the dimension text down; shifting to the right moves the dimension text up. Rather than specifying the **Left** or **Right** options, you can also use your cursor to dynamically drag the dimension after issuing the **TEDIT** command. Doing so gives you greater control over the dimension placement.

Figure 11-60.
Using the **TEDIT** command with associative dimensions.

← 3.500 ——————→

Text Shifted Left

|←———————— 3.500 —→|

Text Shifted Right

|←——— 3.500 ——→|

Text Shifted Home

|←——— 3.500 ——→|

Text Angled at 45°

Use the **Home** option to return the dimension text to its original (centered) position. As shown in Figure 11-60, the **Angle** option rotates dimension text at any angle (positive or negative) within the dimension line. This option is useful for orienting dimensions correctly in auxiliary views. To return angled dimension text to its default text angle, enter 0 (zero).

Issue the **TEDIT** command by selecting **Move Text** from the **Edit Dimension** cascading submenu, or enter the following at the **Dim:** prompt:

> Dim: *(type* TEDIT *or* TE *and press* [Enter]*)*
> Select dimension: *(select a dimension)*
> Enter text location (Left/Right/Home/Angle): *(select an option or use your mouse to dynamically move the dimension text)*
> Dim:

The **HOMETEXT** command

The **HOMETEXT** command returns linear dimension text to its original (centered) position. It performs the same function as the **Home** option of the **TEDIT** command. The difference is that **HOMETEXT** allows you to select more than one dimension at a time. Issue the **HOMETEXT** command by selecting **Home Position** from the **Edit Dimension** cascading submenu, or enter the following at the **Dim:** prompt:

> Dim: *(type* HOMETEXT *or* HOM *and press* [Enter]*)*
> Select objects: *(select one or more dimensions)*
> Select objects: ⏎
> Dim:

The **TROTATE** command

Similar to the **Angle** option of the **TEDIT** command, the **TROTATE**, or **Text ROTATE**, command rotates dimension text at any angle (positive or negative) within the dimension line. The difference is that **TROTATE** allows you to rotate more than one dimension at a time. Issue the **TROTATE** command by selecting **Rotate Text** from the **Edit Dimension** cascading submenu, or enter the following at the **Dim:** prompt:

> Dim: *(type* TROTATE *or* TR *and press* [Enter]*)*
> Enter text angle: *(enter a positive or negative value and press* [Enter]*)*
> Select objects: *(select one or more dimensions)*
> Select objects: ⏎
> Dim:

Changing the angle of extension lines

The **OBLIQUE** command is used to change the extension line angles for existing associative dimensions. This option is occasionally used on curved surfaces when dimensions are crowded or diffficult to read. As shown at the right in Figure 11-61, an obliquing angle of 30° has been applied to two vertical dimensions. Issue the **OBLIQUE** command by selecting **Oblique Dimension** from the **Edit Dimension** cascading submenu, or enter the following at the **Dim:** prompt:

> Dim: *(type* OBLIQUE *or* OB *and press* [Enter]*)*
> Select objects: *(select one or more linear dimensions)*
> Select objects: ⏎
> Enter obliquing angle (RETURN for none): *(enter a positive or negative value and press* [Enter]*)*
> Dim:

Oblique dimensions are also used to dimension isometric drawings. This capability is explored in Chapter 15 of this text.

Figure 11-61.
A—Linear dimensions on a curved object. B—Two dimensions with oblique extension lines.

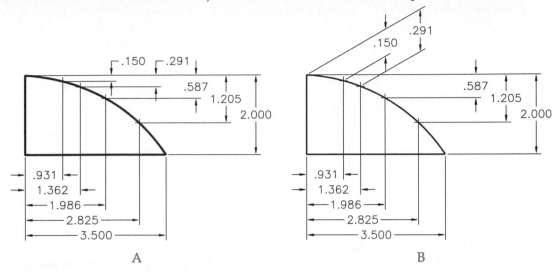

The UPDATE command revisited

As mentioned earlier in this chapter, the **UPDATE** command is used to update one or more dimensions to the current dimension variable settings. It can also be used to change the text style of existing dimensions and to update dimensions to the current system of units. Since all of the AutoCAD LT selection set options are valid with **UPDATE**, you can select many dimensions at one time using a Window or Crossing box. Exploded, or nonassociative, dimensions cannot be updated, however. Issue the **UPDATE** command by selecting **Update Dimension** from the **Edit Dimension** cascading submenu, or enter the following at the **Dim:** prompt:

Dim: *(type* UPDATE *or* UP *and press* [Enter]*)*
Select objects: *(select one or more dimensions)*
Select objects: ⏎
Dim:

NOTE   The **UPDATE** command cannot be used to increase the dimension line increment (**DIMDLI**) between **BASELINE** and **CONTINUE** dimensions. If you need to increase the spacing between existing linear dimensions, use the **STRECH** command instead. Also, **UPDATE** will not update the size of the centerlines drawn through an arc or a circle with the **CENTER** dimensioning command. You must erase the existing centerlines, change the value of **DIMCEN**, and reissue the **CENTER** command. However, the centerlines created through arcs and circles by the **RADIUS** and **DIAMETER** commands can be updated to a new **DIMCEN** value using **UPDATE**.

ADDING TOLERANCES TO DIMENSIONS

ALTUG 13

A *tolerance* is the total amount of permissible variation in size from a specified dimension. Tolerances may be expressed as plus and minus (+/−) values or as dimensional limits. A horizontal dimension expressed with tolerance limits is shown at the upper right in Figure 11-62. The three dimension variables that control this type of dimension are **DIMLIM** (LIMits), **DIMTP** (Tolerance Plus), and **DIMTM** (Tolerance Minus). In the example shown, **DIMTP** and **DIMTM** are both set to .005.

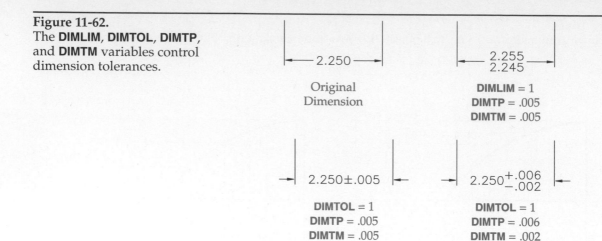

Figure 11-62.
The **DIMLIM**, **DIMTOL**, **DIMTP**, and **DIMTM** variables control dimension tolerances.

To express the same dimension with plus and minus values, the **DIMTOL** (TOLerance) variable is used in place of **DIMLIM**. (Turning **DIMTOL** on automatically disables **DIMLIM**, and vice-versa.) When **DIMTP** and **DIMTM** are set equal, the dimension is created with an equal bilateral tolerance. This type of dimension is shown at the lower left in Figure 11-62. An unequal bilateral tolerance is shown at the lower right. To create this tolerance, type the following:

> Dim: **DIMTOL** ⏎
> Current value ⟨Off⟩ New value: *(enter* 1 *or* ON *and press* [Enter]*)*
> Dim: **DIMTP** ⏎
> Current value ⟨.000⟩ New value: **.006** ⏎
> Dim: **DIMTM** ⏎
> Current value ⟨.000⟩ New value: **.002** ⏎

Any new dimension you now create automatically includes the +.006/−.002 tolerance. Use the **UPDATE** command to add the tolerance to one or more existing dimensions.

As shown in Figure 11-62, AutoCAD LT sets the tolerance height equal to the height of the dimension text. This is in accordance with current drafting standards. If you wish to set the tolerance height slightly smaller (or larger) than the dimension height, use the **DIMTFAC** (Tolerance FACtor) variable. In the following example, tolerance height is set to three-quarters of the dimension height:

> Dim: **DIMTFAC** ⏎
> Current value ⟨1.000⟩ New value: **.75** ⏎

Tolerances can also be set using the **Dimension Styles and Settings** dialog box. First, issue the **DDIM** command and click the **Text Format...** button to display the **Text Format** subdialog box. In the example shown in Figure 11-63, **DIMTOL** is turned on, **DIMTP** is set to .006, and **DIMTM** is set to .002. The option buttons and text boxes in the **Tolerances** section at the upper right of the subdialog box are described as follows:

- **None.** This option button turns off **DIMTOL** or **DIMLIM**.
- **Variance.** This option button turns on **DIMTOL**, and turns off **DIMLIM**.
- **Limits.** This option button turns on **DIMLIM**, and turns off **DIMTOL**.
- **Upper Value:.** This text box sets the **DIMTP** value.
- **Lower Value:.** This text box sets the **DIMTM** value.

Figure 11-63.
Setting an unequal bilateral tolerance using the **Text Format** subdialog box.

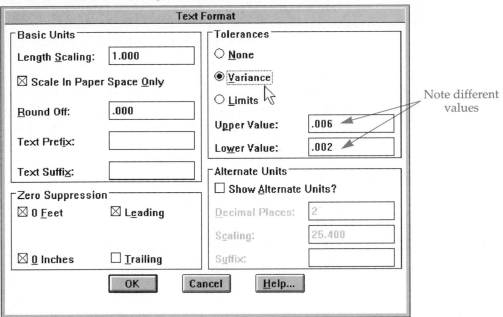

Note different values

PROFESSIONAL TIP

Keep in mind that AutoCAD LT omits the + (or –) in a unilateral or unequal bilateral tolerance when one of the tolerance values is zero. This is acceptable for metric tolerances, but inch tolerances should display the + (or –) in accordance with ANSI and ASME standards. You can "trick" AutoCAD LT into placing a + (or –) in front of a zero tolerance by setting the **DIMTP** or **DIMTM** variables to a greater number of decimal places than are actually required. For example, suppose you are dimensioning and tolerancing a drawing using three-place decimals (**LUPREC** = 3). Several dimensions on your drawing require a tolerance of +.000, –.005. Set **DIMTM** to .005, but set **DIMTP** to .0001. Because dimension and tolerance decimal places are displayed as stored in the **LUPREC** system variable, AutoCAD LT does not show the numeral 1 in the fourth decimal place. Thus, the tolerance displays on screen as +.000.

EXERCISE 11-9

❏ Open EX11-5.
❏ Set the appropriate dimension variables to create the toleranced dimensions shown below. Use the **UPDATE** command to revise the existing dimensions.
❏ Save the drawing as EX11-9.

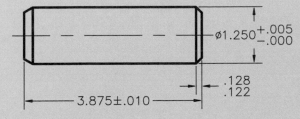

DUAL DIMENSIONING

The practice of including metric equivalents with inch dimensions on a drawing is called *dual dimensioning*. AutoCAD LT refers to it as *alternate units dimensioning*. Two examples of dual dimensions are shown in Figure 11-64. The dimension variables that create dual dimensions are described below:

- **DIMALT.** When **DIMALT** is on (**DIMALT** = 1), alternate units are displayed in brackets to the right of the primary units. The default alternate units are millimeters.
- **DIMALTD.** This variable sets the number of alternate unit decimal places. The default value is 2. **DIMALTD** is not affected by the **LUPREC** system variable, which controls system decimal places.
- **DIMALTF.** This is the alternate unit scale factor. The default value is 25.4, but can be set to any scale factor you choose. As an example, if you wish to use millimeters as the primary units and inches as the alternate units, set **DIMALTF** to .039370078. Enter this value in full to prevent round-off error.
- **DIMAPOST.** Similar to **DIMPOST**, **DIMAPOST** adds a suffix to an alternate unit dimension. Both **DIMPOST** and **DIMAPOST** are used to produce the 5.000 IN. [127.00 MM] dimension shown at the right in Figure 11-64. As with **DIMPOST**, enter a period (.) to clear the **DIMAPOST** value.

Figure 11-64.
Using dual dimensions.

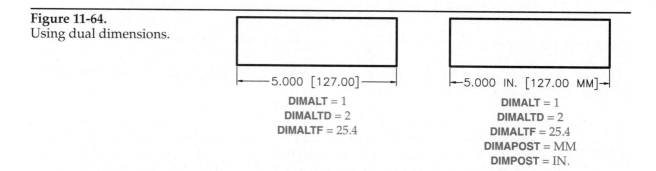

Alternate units can also be set using the **Dimension Styles and Settings** dialog box. First, issue the **DDIM** command and click the **Text Format...** button to display the **Text Format** subdialog box. The **Alternate Units** section is at the lower right. As shown in Figure 11-65, **DIMALT** is turned on by activating the **Show Alternate Units?** check box. If necessary, change the values of **DIMALTF** and **DIMALTD** in the **Scaling:** and **Suffix:** text boxes, respectively. Note that **DIMPOST** and **DIMAPOST** can also be set using the **Text Format** subdialog box.

Figure 11-65.
Dual dimensioning is controlled in the **Alternate Units** section of the **Text Format** subdialog box.

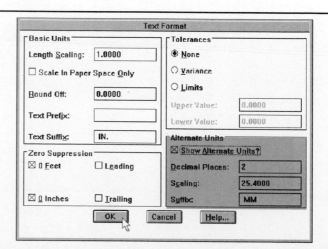

Using AutoCAD LT for metric dimensioning only

It may occasionally be necessary to create and dimension a drawing in millimeters only. This can easily be accomplished by adhering to the following guidelines:

- Set the drawing limits in millimeters and **ZOOM All**. Remember that one inch equals 25.4 millimeters.
- Set the value of the **LUPREC** system variable to 1 or 2 (decimal places) as required.
- Set the **DIMSCALE** variable to 25.4. Remember that **DIMSCALE** controls the size of *all* dimensioning entities, so you need not set each variable individually.
- When using the **DTEXT** or **TEXT** commands to create the drawing annotation, be sure to set the text height in millimeters to match that of the dimension text height.
- Adjust the **LTSCALE** variable as necessary to ensure that hidden lines, phantom lines, centerlines, etc., are scaled correctly.
- For sectioned views, set the hatch pattern scale to 25.4. Hatching parameters are discussed in Chapter 12, **Hatching Patterns and Techniques**.
- Plot the finished drawing at 1 (plotted inch) = 25.4 (drawing units). Plotting and plot scale factors are covered thoroughly in Chapter 13.

EXERCISE 11-10

❏ Open EX11-4.
❏ Turn on **DIMALT** and update the dimensions as shown below.
❏ If necessary, use the **STRETCH** command to adjust the placement of the vertical dimensions.
❏ Save the drawing as EX11-10.

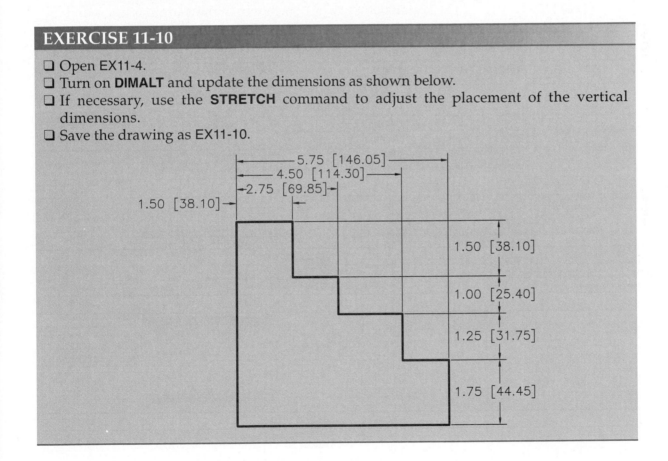

DIMENSION STYLES

ALTUG 13

A *dimension style* is a stored group of dimensioning variables with unique values. The style is saved with a name and can be recalled for use at any time. This capability allows you to create several styles to be used for different drafting applications or industry standards. The current dimension style name is stored in the **DIMSTYLE** variable. When you list the current settings of dimensioning variables with the **STATUS** dimensioning command, you can see the word *UNNAMED next to the entry for the **DIMSTYLE** variable. This is because no dimension style exists in AutoCAD LT until you create one. You can also verify the current style at the **Dim:** prompt as follows:

> Dim: **DIMSTYLE** ↵
> Current value ⟨*UNNAMED⟩
> Dim:

DIMSTYLE cannot be used to change the current style because it is a *read only* type of dimensioning variable. This means that it only stores a value.

Using a dialog box to manage dimension styles

Thus far in this chapter you have seen how the **Dimension Styles and Settings** dialog box provides quick access to dimensioning variables. It can also be used to create, list, and restore a dimension style.

To create a dimension style, issue the **DDIM** command, or select **Dimension Style...** from the **Settings** pull-down menu to display the **Dimension Styles and Settings** dialog box.

NOTE The **Dimension Style** button shown in the margin is not found on the toolbar or toolbox by default, but it can be easily added. See Chapter 19 of this text.

The name of the current dimension style is always shown highlighted in the list. Enter the desired style name in the **Dimension Style:** text box and press [Enter]. A dimension style name may contain up to 31 characters, but no spaces are allowed. As shown in Figure 11-66, the name ASME (for American Society of Mechanical Engineers) is entered. Also, note the message at the lower left of the dialog box. This message appears because AutoCAD LT makes a complete copy of the current dimension style. The style name you enter then appears in the list at the upper left of the dialog box.

Figure 11-66.
Creating a dimension style using the **Dimension Styles and Settings** dialog box.

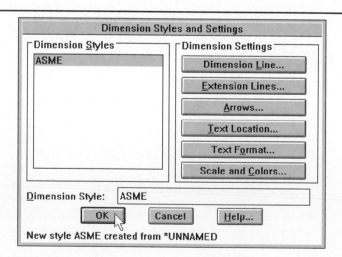

Next, make any required dimension variable changes using the applicable buttons in the **Dimension Settings** area. When you are finished changing the variables, click the **OK** button to exit the **Dimension Styles and Settings** dialog box.

Whenever you wish to use one of your saved dimension styles, issue the **DDIM** command and select its name from the list box. The style name then appears in the **Dimension Style:** text box and becomes the current dimension style, Figure 11-67.

Figure 11-67.
Existing dimension styles
are listed in the **Dimension
Styles and Settings** dialog
box. Selecting a name from
the list sets the dimension
style current.

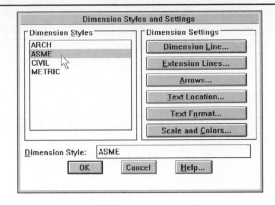

Other dimension style options

Dimension styles can also be created and managed at the **Dim:** prompt with the following commands:

- **SAVE.** After setting the dimension variables as required, use the **SAVE** command to save them with a name. This command also features the **?** option allowing you to list all existing dimension styles in the current drawing.

  > Dim: *(type* SAVE *or* SA *and press* [Enter]*)*
  > ?/Name for new dimension style: *(enter the style name and press* [Enter]*)*

- **RESTORE.** The **RESTORE** command is used to restore a previously saved dimension style. It can also be used to list existing dimension styles.

  > Dim: *(type* RESTORE *or* RES *and press* [Enter]*)*
  > Current dimension style: ASME
  > ?/Enter dimension style name or RETURN to select dimension:

  Enter the name of the style you wish to set current. If you press [Enter], you are then prompted to select a dimension. The style used to create the dimension you select then becomes the current dimension style.

- **VARIABLES.** This command lists all of the current dimension variable settings for a specified dimension style. The graphics window flips to the text window to display the complete dimension variable listing.

  > Dim: *(type* VARIABLES *or* VA *and press* [Enter]*)*
  > Current dimension style: ASME
  > ?/Enter dimension style name or RETURN to select dimension:

  As with the **RESTORE** command, you can enter the name of the style whose variable settings you wish to list, or select a dimension on the screen.

- **OVERRIDE.** This command allows you to change one or more dimension variables, update selected dimensions, and then update the dimension style of the selected dimensions to the new variable settings. As an example, suppose you have an architectural dimension style named ARCH in the current drawing. You would like to change the arrowheads on a single dimension to the DOT arrowhead style, but wish to retain the tick marks defined in the ARCH dimension style for any new dimensions you may create. The procedure looks like this:

  > Dim: *(type* OVERRIDE *or* OV *and press* [Enter]*)*
  > Dimension variable to override: **DIMBLK** ↵
  > Current value ⟨⟩ New value: **DOT** ↵
  > Dimension variable to override: ↵
  > Select objects: *(pick the dimension to change)*
  > Select objects: ↵
  > Modify dimension style "ARCH"? ⟨N⟩: ↵
  > Dim:

If you wish to permanently change the ARCH dimension style to the new **DIMBLK** setting, answer Y to the prompt shown above. An affirmative answer also changes every existing dimension in the drawing created with the ARCH dimension style to the DOT arrowheads.

PROFESSIONAL TIP

To increase your drawing productivity, create the dimension styles in your prototype drawing(s) so that they are available when needed.

CHAPTER TEST

Write your answers in the spaces provided.

1. Describe the **Dim1:** mode. _____
   _____
   _____
   _____

2. What is an associative dimension? _____
   _____

3. What happens to an exploded dimension? _____
   _____
   _____

4. What is an aligned dimension? _____
   _____

5. How does a rotated dimension differ from an aligned dimension? _____
   _____

6. What is the purpose of the **RETURN to select:** option? _____
   _____

7. Why should you never type in a different dimension value than appears in the brackets?
   _____
   _____
   _____
   _____

8. What is the purpose of the **UPDATE** command? _____
   _____

9. Identify the commands that perform datum and chain dimensioning. _____
   _____

10. Angular dimensions can only be used with lines. (True/False) _____

11. How can you prevent the **DIAMETER** or **RADIUS** commands from automatically creating a centerline? _____
    _____

12. When creating a radial dimension, what determines the angle of the leader line?_____
_____

13. What must you do to create a centerline that extends past an arc or a circle?_____
_____

14. The **LEADER** command creates an associative dimension. (True/False) _____

15. What must you do before using ordinate dimensions? Why? _____
_____

16. What is the purpose of the DEFPOINTS layer? _____
_____

17. Identify the command used to create a staggered dimension._____

18. Which command changes the angle of extension lines? _____

19. What is a dimension style? _____
_____

For Questions 20 through 40, identify the dimension variable that:

20. Controls the placement of dimension text inside extension lines._____

21. Sets dimension text height. _____

22. Controls the overall scaling of all dimensions._____

23. Forces a dimension line between extension lines. _____

24. Controls the size of arrowheads._____

25. Controls trailing and leading zeros on dimensions. _____

26. Sets the distance that an extension line is offset from an object line._____

27. Places dimension text above, but not below, a dimension line. _____

28. Turns on and sets the size of tick marks. _____

29. Sets the plus tolerance value._____

30. Sets the minus tolerance value. _____

31. Turns on limits dimensioning._____

32. Enables dual dimensioning._____

33. Assigns a color to dimension text. _____

34. Controls the dimension text alignment outside extension lines. _____

35. Sets dimension line spacing for baseline and continue dimensions._____

36. Creates dimension lines that extend past extension lines. _____

37. Suppresses the second extension line. _____

38. Disables associative dimensioning. _____

39. Controls the dimension text alignment inside extension lines. _____

40. Adds a prefix and/or suffix to a dimension._____

Mechanical Drafting

1. Use the layers in your PROTOA drawing to draw and dimension the CONTROL PLATE shown below. Use the **RECTANG** and **CHAMFER** commands to your advantage. Save the drawing as P11-1.

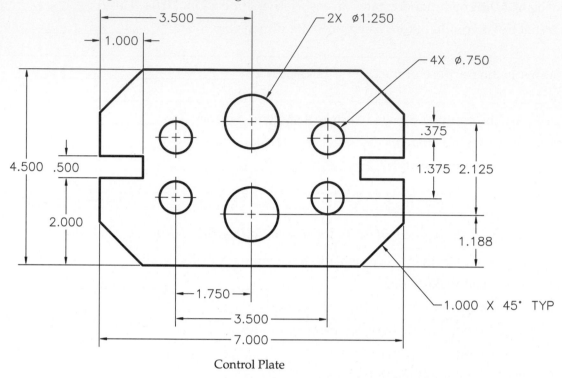

Control Plate

Mechanical Drafting

2. Draw and dimension the SHAFT shown below using your PROTOB prototype drawing. Do not draw the WOODRUFF KEY detail. It is provided for your reference. Add the drawing notes shown at the lower left in the proper layer. Save the drawing as P11-2.

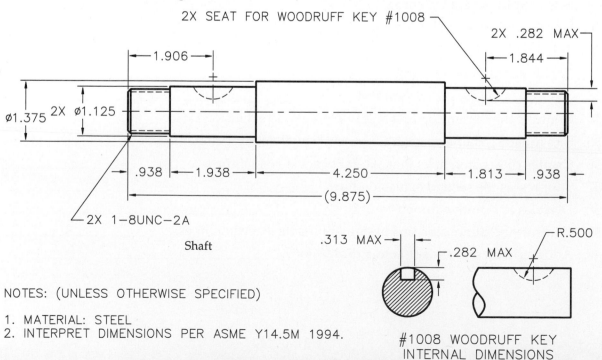

Shaft

NOTES: (UNLESS OTHERWISE SPECIFIED)

1. MATERIAL: STEEL
2. INTERPRET DIMENSIONS PER ASME Y14.5M 1994.

#1008 WOODRUFF KEY
INTERNAL DIMENSIONS

3. Draw and dimension the HUB shown below using your PROTOA prototype
    drawing. Use a polar array to aid in the construction of the front view. Save the
    drawing as P11-3.

Mechanical
Drafting

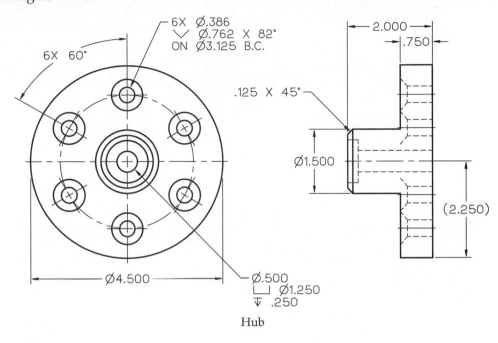

Hub

4. Draw the TRANSISTOR shown below using your PROTOA prototype drawing.
    An object this small would probably be plotted at 4:1. Set the **DIMSCALE**
    variable accordingly before dimensioning. Save the drawing as P11-4.

Electronics
Drafting

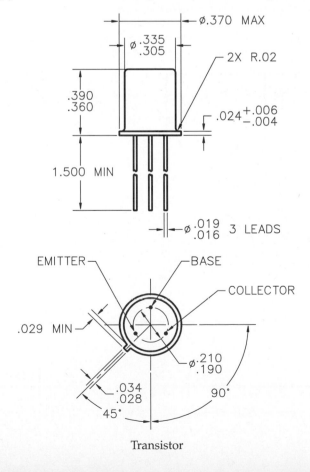

Transistor

5. Draw the TRANSISTOR shown below using your PROTOA prototype drawing. This object would probably be plotted at 2:1. As with P11-4, set the **DIMSCALE** variable accordingly before dimensioning. Save the drawing as P11-5.

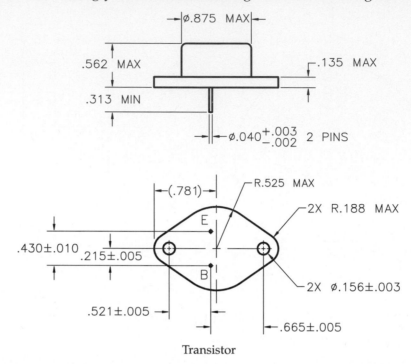

Transistor

6. Draw and dimension the SLANTED BLOCK shown below using your PROTOC prototype drawing. Draw the viewing plane line on the CUTPLANE layer. If necessary, refer to Chapter 7 to review auxiliary view construction.

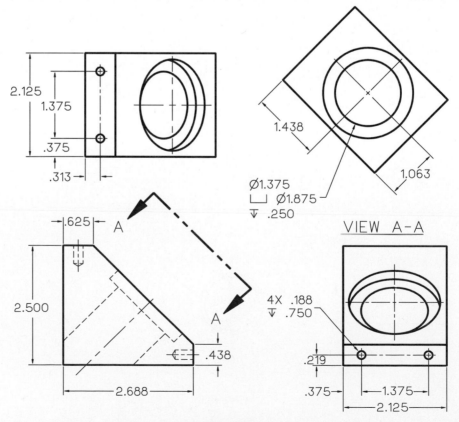

Slanted Block

AutoCAD LT

Chapter 12

Hatching Patterns and Techniques

Learning objectives:

After you have completed this chapter, you will be able to:
- ○ Draw a cutting-plane line.
- ○ Hatch a closed area with a specified hatch pattern, angle, and spacing.
- ○ Edit existing hatched areas.
- ○ Interpret a hatch pattern definition and create custom hatch patterns using the Windows Notepad.
- ○ Create solid-filled polygons with the **SOLID** command.
- ○ Construct polylines from the boundaries of objects.

Many objects designed by engineers contain complex internal structures. Attempting to convey these features using hidden lines is often confusing, and sometimes impossible. When this is the case, a sectional view, which shows a portion of the object cut away, is used. A sectional view must show which portions of the object are empty spaces and which contain solid material. This is accomplished using section lines, called *hatching*, in the areas that contain material.

In this chapter, you will learn how hatching is performed in AutoCAD LT and how to create your own custom hatch patterns. The **BOUNDARY** and **SOLID** commands are also introduced.

CUTTING-PLANE LINES

Cutting-plane lines are used to identify the plane through an object from which a sectional view is taken. As shown in Figure 12-1, sometimes the section is obvious and the cutting-plane line is unnecessary. In other objects, the cutting-plane line helps to describe the precise area viewed in the section. See Figure 12-2.

Figure 12-1.
The cutting-plane line identifies the direction of sight for the sectional view.

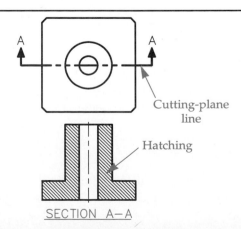

Figure 12-2.
This cutting-plane line describes the precise area being sectioned.

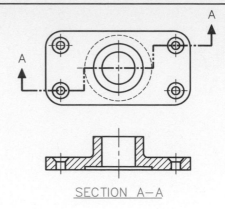

SECTION A—A

Cutting-plane lines are constructed with phantom or hidden linetypes. Each end of the line terminates with a large arrowhead. The arrowheads are drawn perpendicular to the line and are used to indicate the direction of sight for viewing the section.

When more than one sectional view exists in a drawing, letters are placed near the arrowheads to help identify the associated view. Additionally, cutting-plane lines are drawn thick to stand out clearly.

In Chapter 6, you learned that a polyline can be created with variable width and can be used to create arrowheads. This makes polylines ideal entities for cutting-plane lines. A tutorial appeared in Chapter 6 to construct a large cutting-plane line. Another tutorial is presented below to draw the cutting-plane line illustrated in Figure 12-3.

CUTTING-PLANE LINE TUTORIAL

➪ Load AutoCAD LT and open PROTOA. Set the CUTPLANE layer current.

➪ If your prototype drawing does not have a CUTPLANE layer, create one. Assign the PHANTOM linetype and color blue (5) to the new layer. Set the layer current.

➪ Use the **PLINE** command to draw the cutting-plane line:

> Command: *(type* PLINE *or* PL *and press* [Enter]*)*
> From point: *(pick point 1)*
> Current line-width is 0.000
> Arc/Close/Halfwidth/Length/Undo/Width/⟨Endpoint of line⟩: **W** ↵
> Starting width ⟨0.000⟩: ↵
> Ending width ⟨0.000⟩: **.375** ↵
> Arc/Close/Halfwidth/Length/Undo/Width/⟨Endpoint of line⟩: **@.5⟨270** ↵
> Arc/Close/Halfwidth/Length/Undo/Width/⟨Endpoint of line⟩: **W** ↵
> Starting width ⟨0.375⟩: **.04** ↵
> Ending width ⟨0.040⟩: ↵
> Arc/Close/Halfwidth/Length/Undo/Width/⟨Endpoint of line⟩: **L** ↵
> Length of line: **.75** ↵
> Arc/Close/Halfwidth/Length/Undo/Width/⟨Endpoint of line⟩: **@5⟨0** ↵
> Arc/Close/Halfwidth/Length/Undo/Width/⟨Endpoint of line⟩: **@.75⟨90** ↵
> Arc/Close/Halfwidth/Length/Undo/Width/⟨Endpoint of line⟩: **W** ↵
> Starting width ⟨0.040⟩: **.375** ↵
> Ending width ⟨0.375⟩: **0** ↵
> Arc/Close/Halfwidth/Length/Undo/Width/⟨Endpoint of line⟩: **L** ↵
> Length of line: **.5** ↵
> Arc/Close/Halfwidth/Length/Undo/Width/⟨Endpoint of line⟩: ↵
> Command:

➪ After drawing the cutting-plane line, use the **DTEXT** command to create the identification letters. Use a height of .25. It is not necessary to save the drawing when you are finished.

Figure 12-3.
The **PLINE** command with a phantom linetype is used to draw a cutting-plane line.

AUTOCAD LT HATCH PATTERNS

ALTUG 6

There are 53 predefined hatch patterns supplied with AutoCAD LT. Each pattern has a descriptive name and is stored in an external file called ACLT.PAT. This file is located in the \ACLTWIN directory.

The default hatch pattern is ANSI31. This pattern represents cast iron, but is used for general purpose hatching. Each of the patterns are shown in Figure 12-4.

Many other hatch patterns are available from software vendors. Creating a custom hatch pattern is described later in this chapter.

Figure 12-4.
Standard AutoCAD LT hatch patterns. (Autodesk, Inc.)

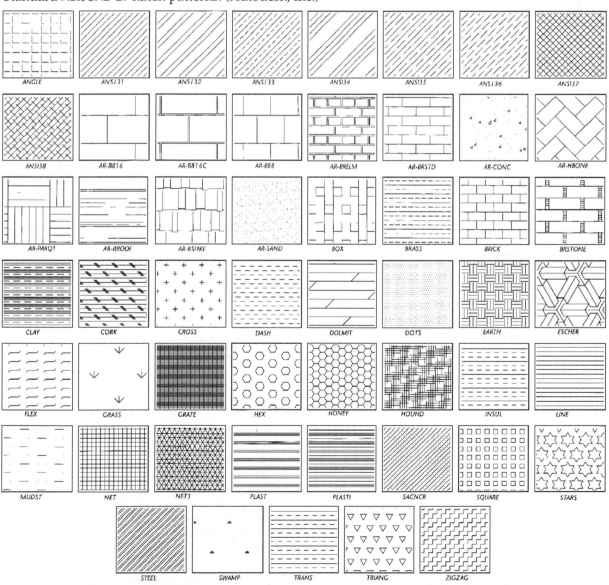

Figure 12-14.
Hatching is updated
automatically after islands
and boundaries are edited.

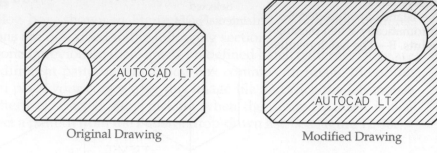

Original Drawing   Modified Drawing

NOTE   Drawings created with AutoCAD LT for Windows 3.1 (formerly
Release 2) are compatible with AutoCAD LT 1.0 and AutoCAD Release
12. However, if the boundaries or islands of associative hatching are
modified using one of the other programs, the hatch will not be
updated.

Boundary hatching with a user-defined pattern

The **BHATCH** command also permits you to create a user-defined hatch pattern using the
current linetype. With this option, you specify an explicit hatch scale and angle. You can also
choose to double hatch an area.

To create a user-defined hatch pattern, select **User-defined** from the **Pattern Type** drop-
down list. See Figure 12-15. Enter the desired hatch angle in the **Angle:** text box. Use the
Spacing: text box to specify the distance between the hatch lines. Activate the check box
labeled **Double** if you wish to use double hatching. Several examples of user-defined hatching are shown in Figure 12-16.

Figure 12-15.
Selecting **User-defined**
from the **Pattern Type**
drop-down list.

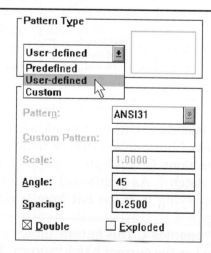

Figure 12-16.
Examples of user-defined
hatch patterns.

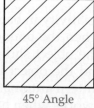
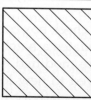
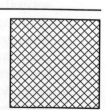

45° Angle   135° Angle   45° Angle
.25 Spacing   .25 Spacing   .125 Spacing
Single Hatch   Single Hatch   Double Hatch

ADVANCED BOUNDARY HATCH OPTIONS

ALTUG 6

The **BHATCH** command offers additional options that are accessed by clicking the **Advanced...** button in the **Boundary Hatch** dialog box.. This displays the **Advanced Options** subdialog box shown in Figure 12-17. The properties of the **Advanced Options** subdialog box are described in the following sections.

Figure 12-17.
The **Advanced Options** subdialog box.

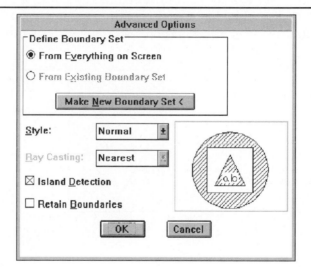

Defining a boundary set

The **BHATCH** command analyzes every object displayed on screen when determining islands and boundaries. This is a time-consuming process for very large or complex drawings. You can limit the area to be evaluated by defining a boundary set. There are three options:

- **From Everything on Screen.** When this is set, the entire screen is examined to determine islands and boundaries. This option button is active by default.
- **From Existing Boundary Set.** This option is not available until a new boundary set is created.
- **Make New Boundary Set** ⟨. Use this button to limit what is evaluated during the hatching operation. When **Select Objects:** prompt appears, use a window box to define the area of the screen to be evaluated for hatching. This area remains the only area examined during future hatching operations. Creating another boundary set replaces the existing set.

Selecting a Hatch Style

There are three hatch styles: **Normal, Outer,** and **Ignore**, as shown in Figure 12-18. The **Style:** drop-down list is used to choose one of the three styles. A graphical representation of the current hatch style appears in the image tile to the right of the drop-down list. The hatch styles are described as follows:

- **Normal.** This is the default style. Normal hatches inward from the outermost boundary. When an internal boundary is encountered, hatching is turned off and remains off until another boundary is encountered. The Normal style hatches every other boundary.
- **Outer.** This style also hatches inward and turns off hatching when an internal boundary is encountered. However, the hatching is not turned back on. Only the outermost areas are hatched.
- **Ignore.** This option ignores all internal areas and hatches through the entire object.

Figure 12-18.
The three hatching styles. Normal is the default.

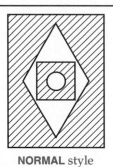 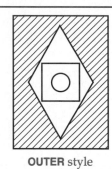 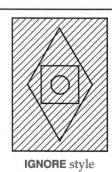

NORMAL style   **OUTER** style   **IGNORE** style

Island Detection and Ray Casting

The **Island Detection** check box is on by default. If you disable island detection, AutoCAD LT uses a technique called *ray casting* to identify hatch boundaries. When you pick an internal point, a ray detects the nearest entity and turns in a counterclockwise direction to trace the boundary. By default, AutoCAD LT looks in all directions for the nearest entity. You can use the **Ray Casting:** drop-down list to specify which direction (+X, –X, +Y, or –Y) the ray originates. This method can be useful for very complex drawings, where entities are closely-spaced. For most applications, however, it is recommended that the default island detection method be used instead.

Retaining hatch boundaries

The **BHATCH** command creates a temporary polyline boundary using the entities that define an enclosed area. Once the hatching is applied, the temporary polyline is erased. You can choose to keep the boundary as a permanent polyline entity by activating the **Retain Boundaries** check box. By default, this check box is not active.

Turning off the Boundary Hatch dialog box

Most dialog boxes are controlled by the **FILEDIA** (file dialog) system variable. However, the variable that controls the **Boundary Hatch** dialog box is **CMDDIA** (command dialog). The dialog box is disabled by setting the variable to zero:

> Command: **CMDDIA** ↵
> New value for CMDDIA ⟨1⟩: **0** ↵

Once the dialog box is disabled, the **BHATCH** command options are displayed on the **Command:** prompt as follows:

> Command: **BHATCH** ↵
> Properties/Select/Remove islands/Advanced/⟨Internal point⟩:

Set **CMDDIA** back to 1 to restore the **Boundary Hatch** dialog box.

NOTE   The current status of both the **FILEDIA** and **CMDDIA** variables are stored in the ACLT.CFG file in the \ACLTWIN directory. Therefore, turning either variable off (or on) in one drawing affects *all* drawings.

THE HATCH COMMAND

The **HATCH** command can be used if you do not wish to use boundary hatching. Because there is no island or boundary detection, the **HATCH** command functions like the **Select Objects** option of the **BHATCH** command.

The **HATCH** command displays the following prompts and options:

> Command: *(type HATCH or H and press [Enter])*
> Pattern (? or name/U,style) ⟨ANSI31⟩: *(enter a pattern name)*
> Scale for pattern ⟨1.0000⟩: *(enter the hatch scale)*
> Angle for pattern ⟨0⟩: *(enter the hatch angle)*
> Select objects: *(select one or more objects)*
> Select objects: ↵
> Command:

Listing available hatch patterns

If you forget the name of a hatch pattern, a list of the available patterns can be displayed:

> Command: *(type HATCH or H and press [Enter])*
> Pattern (? or name/U,style) ⟨ANSI31⟩: **?** ↵
> Pattern(s) to list ⟨*⟩: ↵

An alphabetical list of hatch pattern names and descriptions is then displayed in the text window. See Figure 12-19. When the listing is finished, press [F2] to flip back to the graphics window.

The U option

The **U** option of the **HATCH** command allows you to specify a user-defined pattern. You set the hatch angle, spacing, and double hatching. The prompts are easily followed:

> Command: *(type HATCH or H and press [Enter])*
> Pattern (? or name/U,style) ⟨ANSI31⟩: **U** ↵
> Angle for crosshatch lines ⟨0⟩: **45** ↵
> Spacing between lines ⟨1.0000⟩: **.125** ↵
> Double hatch area? ⟨N⟩ *(enter Y or N)*
> Select objects: *(select objects)*
> Select objects: ↵
> Command:

Figure 12-19.
The list of available hatch patterns is displayed in the text window.

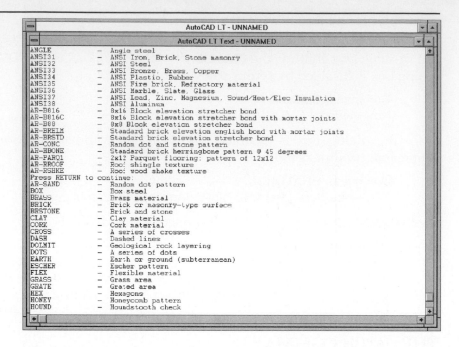

Using the HATCH Style option

The **HATCH** command permits you to specify one of the three hatch style options (Normal, Outer, or Ignore). When you use the **Style** option, it is more efficient to select the entities to be hatched with a window or crossing box. In the following example, the Outer style is being used with the ANSI32 pattern. Separate the hatch style from the pattern name with a comma, as shown:

Command: *(type HATCH or H and press [Enter])*
Pattern (? or name/U,style) ⟨ANSI31⟩: **ANSI32,O** ↵
Scale for pattern ⟨1.0000⟩: ↵
Angle for pattern ⟨0⟩: ↵
Select objects: *(pick a corner)* Other corner: *(pick a diagonal point)*
Select objects: ↵
Command:

MODIFYING HATCHED AREAS

ALTUG 10

The **HATCHEDIT** command allows you to modify associative hatching. To edit an existing hatched area, type HATCHEDIT at the **Command:** prompt or select **Edit Hatch...** from the **Modify** pull-down menu. See Figure 12-20. The **Edit Hatch** button shown in the margin is not located in the toolbar or toolbox by default, but it can be easily added. See Chapter 19 of this text.

Command: **HATCHEDIT** ↵
Select hatch object: *(select the hatching to change)*

Only one hatched area can be edited at a time. After selecting the hatch to change, the **Hatchedit** dialog box appears. See Figure 12-21. This dialog box is identical to the **Boundary Hatch** dialog box. However, many of the buttons are "grayed-out" and are unavailable for use.

The **Hatchedit** dialog box displays all of the characteristics of the selected hatch. Change the hatch properties and click the **Apply** button. The dialog box disappears and the hatching is modified to the new specifications.

AutoCAD LT—Fundamentals and Applications

Figure 12-20.
Select **Edit Hatch...** from the
Modify pull-down menu to
issue the **HATCHEDIT**
command.

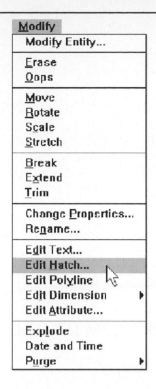

Figure 12-21.
The **Hatchedit** dialog box
displays the characteristics
of the selected hatch.

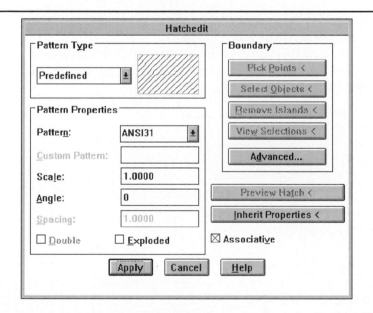

NOTE Hatching created with the **HATCH** command is not associative
and cannot be modified with **HATCHEDIT**.

EXERCISE 12-2

❑ Open EX12-1.
❑ Using **HATCHEDIT**, change the three ANSI31 patterns to BRICK, ESCHER, and EARTH as shown below.
❑ Use any pattern, angle, or spacing you choose to modify the remaining three hatched squares.
❑ Save the drawing as EX12-2.

 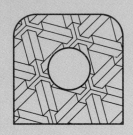 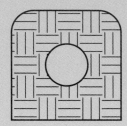

CREATING A CUSTOM HATCH PATTERN

ALTUG 21

Like linetypes, hatch patterns are stored in an external library file (ACLT.PAT). This file can be modified to create your own custom hatch patterns. Unlike linetypes, custom hatch patterns cannot be modified or created using AutoCAD LT. The ACLT.PAT file must be edited with an ASCII (American Standard Code for Information Exchange) text editor, such as Windows Notepad or MS-DOS EDIT.

The ACLT.PAT library file contains the definitions for the standard hatch patterns. Three of the patterns, LINE, NET, and NET3, are shown in Figure 12-22. These patterns are defined in the ACLT.PAT file as follows:

```
*LINE,Parallel horizontal lines
0, 0,0, 0,.125
*NET,Horizontal / vertical grid
0, 0,0, 0,.125
90, 0,0, 0,.125
*NET3,Network pattern 0-60-120
0, 0,0, 0,.125
60, 0,0, 0,.125
120, 0,0, 0,.125
```

Figure 12-22.
The LINE, NET, and NET3 hatch patterns.

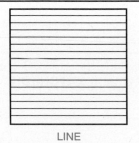 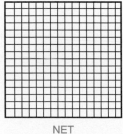 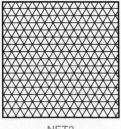

LINE   NET   NET3

Deciphering a hatch pattern definition is not difficult. The word after the asterisk (*) is the hatch pattern name. The text string after the comma is a description of the pattern. This description is displayed in the text window when you list hatch patterns.

Each line of numbers under the pattern description represents a group of repeated parallel lines. The numbers represent the angle, X-origin, Y-origin, delta-X, and delta-Y, respectively. Dashes, dots, and gaps can also be included.

In the first hatch pattern example, LINE, the first 0 represents the angle at which the lines are drawn. The 0,0 is the X and Y origin, and the last pair of numbers specifies where to start subsequent parallel lines. After drawing the first horizontal line of the pattern, the second line starts 0 units to the left and .125 units up from the starting point of the first line.

The NET pattern has two parallel line groups, with the first pattern being identical to the LINE pattern group. It then draws a second group of 90° lines spaced .125 apart. The NET3 pattern is very similar, but it has three groups of lines, at 0°, 60°, and 120°.

There are many types of hatch patterns designed for specific drawing applications. Many of these patterns are included with AutoCAD LT, others can be purchased.

Using the Windows Notepad to create a custom hatch pattern

The Microsoft Windows Notepad is an ASCII text editor that can edit small text files (less than 50K in size). It can be used to create a custom hatch pattern file, or for editing the ACLT.PAT file.

Consider the roof shingle hatch pattern shown in Figure 12-23. This pattern can be easily created using Notepad without exiting AutoCAD LT. First, use [Ctrl]+[Esc] to activate the Windows Task List. Select Program Manager from the list and click the **Switch To** button. Open the Accessories group window and double-click the Notepad icon, shown in Figure 12-24.

Notepad launches in its own display window, and you can begin entering the following lines of text:

```
*ROOF,Custom shingles
0, 0,0, 0,6
90, 0,0, 6,18, 6,-6
90, 12,0, 6,18, 3,-9
90, 24,0, 6,18, 3,-9
```

Figure 12-23.
The ROOF custom hatch pattern.

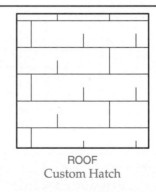

ROOF
Custom Hatch

Figure 12-24.
Notepad is launched from the Accessories group window in the Windows Program Manager.

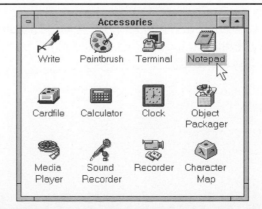

When you have finished entering the text, the Notepad window should appear as shown in Figure 12-25. Select **Save As...** from the **File** pull-down menu. Change to the \ACLTWIN directory and save your hatch pattern file with the name ROOF.PAT. See Figure 12-26.

Figure 12-25.
The ROOF custom hatch pattern definition as entered in Notepad.

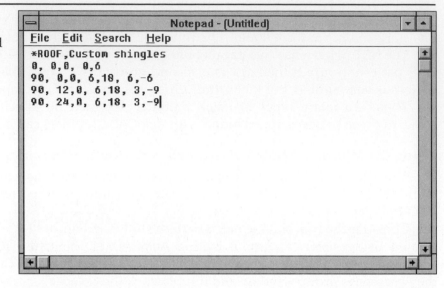

Figure 12-26.
The hatch pattern is saved with the name ROOF.PAT in the \ACLTWIN directory.

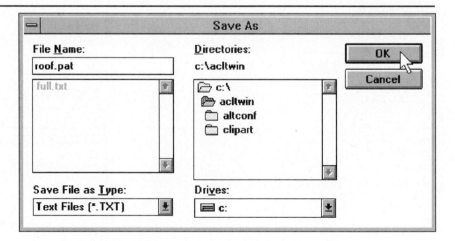

Quit Notepad by selecting **Exit** from the **File** pull-down menu and you are returned to Program Manager. To return to AutoCAD LT, use [Alt]+[Tab].

A custom hatch pattern does not need to be included in the ACLT.PAT library file. The pattern can be stored in a separate file, as long as the file name matches the hatch pattern name. In this example, the ROOF pattern resides in a file called ROOF.PAT.

To use your custom hatch pattern, select **Custom** from the **Pattern Type** drop-down list in the **Boundary Hatch** dialog box. Enter the hatch pattern name in the **Custom Pattern:** text box, as shown in Figure 12-27.

Figure 12-27.
Selecting **Custom** from the
Pattern Type drop-down list.
The ROOF custom hatch
pattern is entered in the
Custom Pattern: text box.

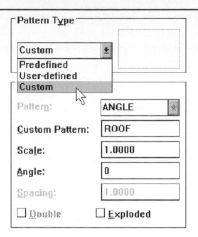

Pattern Type	
Custom	±
Predefined	
User-defined	
Custom	

Pattern:	ANGLE ±
Custom Pattern:	ROOF
Scale:	1.0000
Angle:	0
Spacing:	1.0000
☐ Double	☐ Exploded

PROFESSIONAL TIP

Be sure to make a backup copy of the original ACLT.PAT file before you experiment with creating or modifying hatch patterns. It is a good idea to create hatch patterns in separate files as described in the previous section and leave the ACLT.PAT file undisturbed. Check with your instructor or supervisor to verify which procedures should be used.

EXERCISE 12-3

❑ Use Notepad to create the ROOF hatch pattern described in the preceding text.
❑ Be sure to save the Notepad file with the name ROOF.PAT in the \ACLTWIN directory.
❑ Start AutoCAD LT and open PROTOC. Set **UNITS** to architectural, **LIMITS** to 80′, 60′, and **ZOOM All**.
❑ Use the **RECTANG** command on the OBJECTS layer to draw a 60′ × 30′ rectangle.
❑ Set the HATCHING layer current and use **BHATCH** to hatch the rectangle with the ROOF pattern.
❑ Use **HATCHEDIT** to experiment with different hatch pattern scales.
❑ Save the drawing as EX12-3.

THE SOLID COMMAND

ALTUG 6

Polylines, polyarcs, and donuts can be filled solid when **FILL** mode is on. When **FILL** is off, these entities are drawn as outlines.

The **SOLID** command creates solid-filled polygons. It can be used to fill shapes that are already drawn, or to fill an area defined by selected points.

To draw a solid-filled object, begin the **SOLID** command by selecting **Solid** from the **Draw** pull-down menu. See Figure 12-28. The command sequence is as follows:

Command: *(type* SOLID *or* SO *and press* [Enter]*)*
First point: *(pick a point)*
Second point: *(pick a second point)*

The first two points that you select define one edge of the polygon.

Third point: *(pick a point diagonally opposite the second point)*
Fourth point: *(pick point 4 or press* [Enter] *to end the command)*

Figure 12-28.
Selecting **Solid** from the
Draw pull-down menu to
use the **SOLID** command.

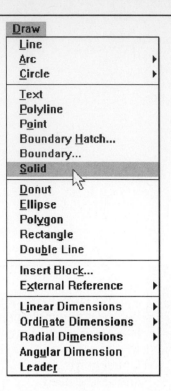

If you press [Enter] at the **Fourth point:** prompt, AutoCAD LT creates a filled triangle. However, picking a fourth point can also create a quadrilateral area, depending on the four point locations. Several examples of solids are shown in Figure 12-29. Observe how the picking sequence determines the final shape of the solid.

When drawing a solid, the last two points selected form the first edge of the next filled area. This helps to create multiple connected triangles and four-sided polygons in a single solid-filled object. AutoCAD LT repeats the **Third point:** and **Fourth point:** prompts so that you can create additional figures in a single operation. When you are through, press [Enter] to end the **SOLID** command.

Figure 12-29.
Several examples of solids
defined with different
picking sequences.

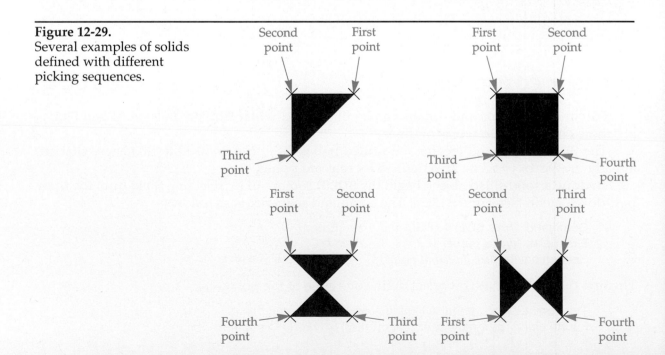

The **SOLID** command is often used when sectioning very thin features, such as seals and gaskets. See Figure 12-30. It is a better alternative to using a densely spaced hatch pattern. A wide polyline can also be used for this type of application.

Figure 12-30.
This gasket between mating parts is drawn with the **SOLID** command.

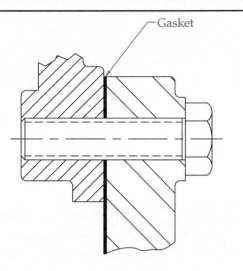

Gasket

CREATING POLYLINES USING THE **BOUNDARY** COMMAND

ALTUG 6

The **BOUNDARY** command creates a polyline entity from overlapping objects. This function is the same as the component of the **BHATCH** command that creates a boundary object.

To create a polyline boundary, enter BOUNDARY at the **Command:** prompt or select **Boundary...** from the **Draw** pull-down menu. See Figure 12-31. The **Boundary** button shown in the margin is not located in the toolbar or toolbox by default, but it can be easily added. See Chapter 19 in this text.

Figure 12-31.
Selecting **Boundary...** from the **Draw** pull-down menu to use the **BOUNDARY** command.

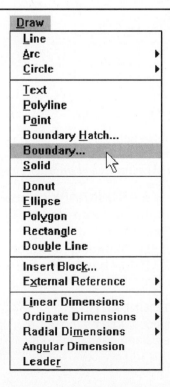

Refer to Figure 12-32 as you follow the command procedure described below.

Command: **BOUNDARY** ↵

Figure 12-32.
The **BOUNDARY** command creates a polyline boundary around the enclosed area.

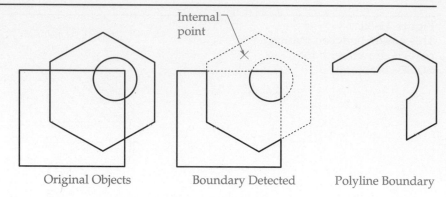

Original Objects   Boundary Detected   Polyline Boundary

The **Boundary Creation** dialog box appears. See Figure 12-33. Note that the options are identical to those offered by the **Advanced Options** subdialog box in the **BHATCH** command. Pick the **Pick Points** button. The dialog box disappears and you receive the following prompt:

Select internal point: *(pick anywhere inside the closed area)*

Figure 12-33.
The **Boundary Creation** dialog box offers the same options as the **Advanced Options** subdialog box of the **BHATCH** command.

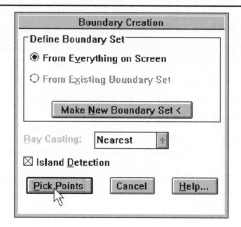

If you pick the wrong area, enter U for undo and pick again.

Analyzing the selected data...
Analyzing internal islands...
Select internal point: *(select another closed area or press* [Enter]*)*

Pressing [Enter] ends the **BOUNDARY** command and you are informed of the number of polylines created. The boundary is created on the current layer, color, and linetype. It can be edited using the **PEDIT** command.

The display of the **Boundary Creation** dialog box is controlled by the **CMDDIA** system variable. When the dialog box is off, the **BOUNDARY** command appears at the **Command:** prompt as follows:

Command: **BOUNDARY** ↵
Advanced options/⟨Internal point⟩: **A** ↵
Boundary set/Island detection/⟨eXit⟩:

CHAPTER TEST

Write your answers in the spaces provided.

1. What is the ACLT.PAT file? _____

   _____

   _____

2. Identify two ways to access the **BHATCH** command. _____

   _____

3. How does **BHATCH** differ from the **HATCH** command? _____

   _____

4. Which button in the **Boundary Hatch** dialog box lets you use an existing hatch pattern in your drawing as the pattern for the next hatch operation? _____

5. What is associative hatching? What must be done before it can be used? _____

   _____

   _____

6. List the three hatch style options. Of the three, which style hatches completely through an object? _____

   _____

   _____

7. What type of entity is used for a hatch boundary? _____

   _____

8. Identify the system variable that controls the display of the **Boundary Hatch** and **Boundary Creation** dialog boxes. _____

9. Name the command that allows you to change existing hatched areas. In which pull-down menu is it located? _____

   _____

10. Hatching created with the **HATCH** command can be edited. (True/False) _____

11. What is the purpose of the **SOLID** command? _____

    _____

    _____

12. As with **BHATCH**, the polyline created with the **BOUNDARY** command is automatically erased when the command is terminated. (True/False) _____

Electronics Drafting

1. Use the layers in your **PROTOA** drawing to draw and hatch the cross-section of the multilayer circuit board shown. Use the **SOLID** command to draw the conductor patterns. Save the drawing as P12-1.

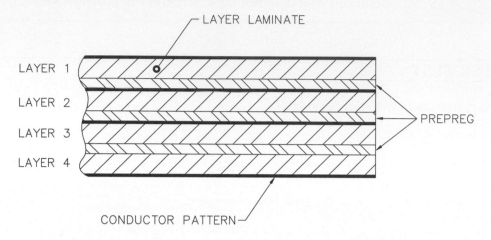

General

2. Draw, label, and hatch the pie chart shown using your **PROTOA** prototype drawing. Create the text and hatch patterns as shown, using separate layers. Save the drawing as P12-2.

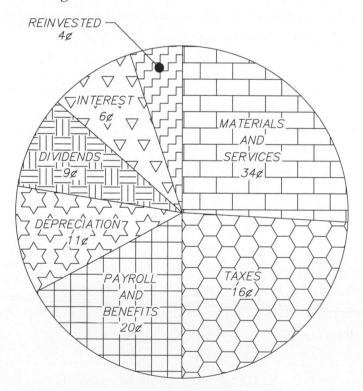

3. Draw, dimension, and hatch the HUB LEVER shown using your PROTOB prototype drawing. Save the drawing as P12-3.

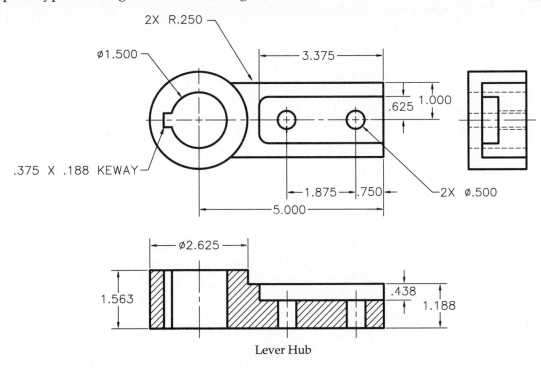

Lever Hub

4. Draw, dimension, and hatch the BELL CRANK shown using your PROTOC prototype drawing. Construct the cutting-plane line as described in this chapter. Create the drawing notes at the lower left in the proper layer. Save the drawing as P12-4.

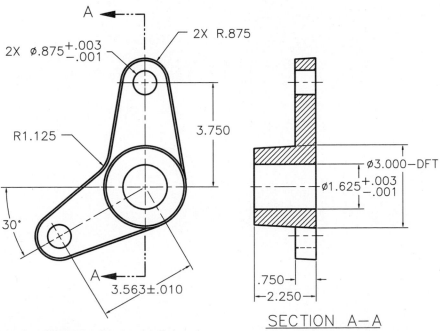

SECTION A—A

NOTES: (UNLESS OTHERWISE SPECIFIED)

1. DRAFT ANGLE: 3° MAX PER SIDE.
2. MATERIAL: CAST IRON
3. INTERPRET DIMENSIONS PER ASME Y14.5M 1994.

Bell Crank

5. Draw, dimension, and hatch the V-BELT PULLEY shown below using your PROTOC prototype drawing. Construct the cutting-plane line as described in this chapter. Create the drawing notes at the lower right in the proper layer. Save the drawing as P12-5.

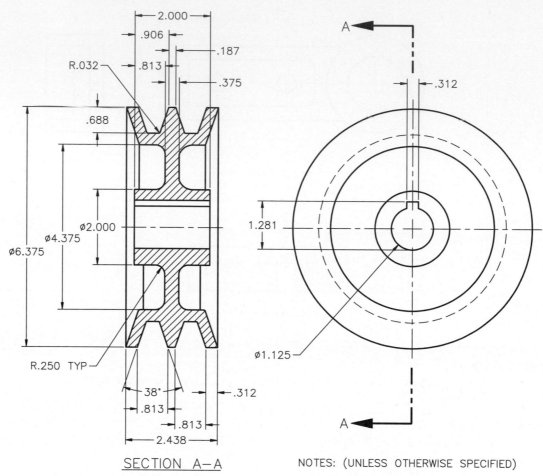

SECTION A—A

NOTES: (UNLESS OTHERWISE SPECIFIED)

1. MATERIAL: CAST IRON
2. INTERPRET DIMENSIONS PER ASME Y14.5M 1994.

AutoCAD LT

Chapter *13*

Plotting a Drawing

Learning objectives:

After you have completed this chapter, you will be able to:
- ○ Print or plot a drawing.
- ○ Output a drawing in a variety of raster graphics formats.
- ○ Export a drawing in PostScript format.

THE PLOT COMMAND

ALTUG 16

You can reproduce your drawing on a printer or plotter using the **PLOT** command. You can also use this command to save your drawing on disk in one of several industry-standard graphics formats. This allows your drawing to be used with other computer applications.

Before printing or plotting, make sure that your output device is configured properly, as described in Appendix F of the *AutoCAD LT Release 2 for Windows User's Guide*. Once the output device is configured, the **PLOT** command can be entered in several ways. You can select **Print/Plot...** from the **File** pull-down menu, click the **Print/Plot** button on the toolbar, or enter the command as follows:

Command: *(type* PLOT *or* PP *and press* [Enter]*)*

The **Plot Configuration** dialog box appears, Figure 13-1. This dialog box allows you to define and then preview each one of the parameters you specify for the final printing or plotting of your drawing.

Unlike most other dialog boxes in AutoCAD LT that are controlled with the **FILEDIA** system variable, this dialog box is controlled with the system variable **CMDDIA**. By default, **CMDDIA** is set to 1 (on) and will display the **Plot Configuration** dialog box. When **CMDDIA** is set to 0 (off), all printing and plotting parameters must be specified on the command line. Each of the areas and options of the **Plot Configuration** dialog box are described in the following sections.

Figure 13-1.
The **Plot Configuration** dialog box.

Output device
information
and setup

Click to change
the pen settings

Select what
to plot

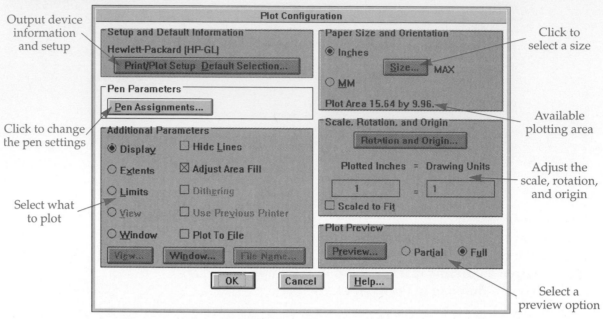

Click to
select a size

Available
plotting area

Adjust the
scale, rotation,
and origin

Select a
preview option

Selecting the output device

The **Setup and Default Information** section at the top left of the **Plot Configuration** dialog box is used to select the type of output device you will be using. Click the **Print/Plot Setup Default Selection...** button to display the **Print/Plot Setup & Default Selection** subdialog box, Figure 13-2. A list of available output devices and raster file formats appears at the top of the dialog box. The raster file format options are described later in this chapter.

In Figure 13-2, System Printer is selected from the list. The System Printer is the device used to print all Microsoft Windows applications. Use the buttons in the **Device Specific Configuration** area to review or change your printer or plotter settings. The **Show Device Requirements...** button at the lower left opens the **Show Device Requirements** subdialog box. This subdialog box displays the manufacturer of the currently configured device and the port

Figure 13-2.
Selecting the desired output device from the **Print/Plot Setup & Default Selection** subdialog box.

Select an
output device

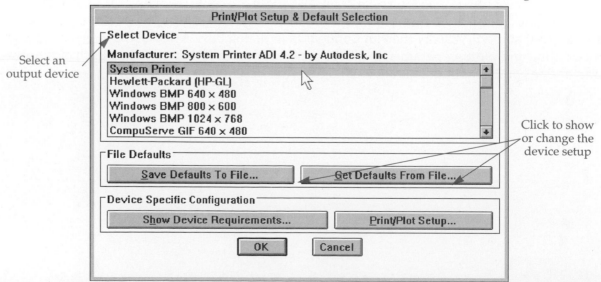

Click to show
or change the
device setup

to which it is connected. Check the current device settings and click **OK** when you are satisfied. In Figure 13-3A, the device requirements for the currently configured system printer are shown. In the Windows environment, the system printer is the output device specified in the Print Manager. Click the **Print/Plot Setup...** button to make any changes.

If your currently configured device is the system printer, several dialog boxes similar to those shown in Figure 13-3B and Figure 13-3C are displayed. When you print or plot using the system printer, AutoCAD LT uses the default printer specified in the Windows Print Manager in the Control Panel. This device is listed as the **Default Printer** in the **Print Setup** subdialog box. If you wish to use a different printer, activate the **Specific Printer** option button and select the desired printer from the drop-down list. Make any other changes as required and click **OK** to continue.

Remember that the type and number of dialog boxes presented are a function of your currently configured printer or plotter. If you have selected the Hewlett-Packard (HP-GL) driver, the **Show Device Requirements** and **HPGL Driver Setup** dialog boxes shown in Figure 13-4A and Figure 13-4B are displayed. Use the **HPGL Driver Setup** drop-down list to select the type of plotter you are using and specify the appropriate serial port in the **Output to:** text box. Regardless of the type of output device you are using, be sure to refer to the manufacturer's instructions supplied with your printer or plotter to help you configure the device properly.

Figure 13-3.
A—The **Show Device Requirements** subdialog box for the currently configured system printer. B and C—Clicking the **Print/Plot Setup...** button in the **Print/Plot Setup & Default Selection** subdialog box presents additional options for this particular printer.

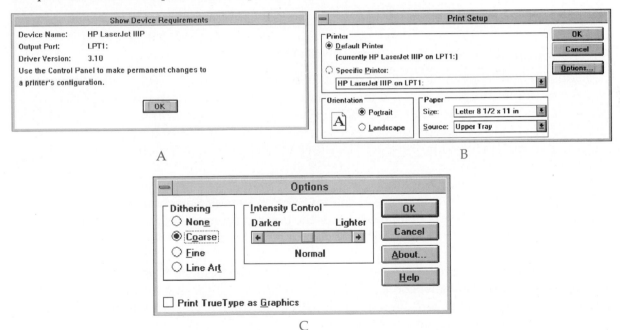

Figure 13-4.
A—The **Show Device Requirements** subdialog box for the currently configured Hewlett-Packard pen plotter. B—Clicking the **Print/Plot Setup...** button in the **Print/Plot Setup & Default Selection** subdialog box presents configuration options for the plotter.

A   B

> **NOTE**
>
> HP-GL means *Hewlett-Packard Graphics Language*. A plot file written in the HP-GL language is a series of instructions for pen motions (pen up, pen down, draw). Even if your plotter is from a different manufacturer, it is likely to conform to the HP-GL standard. Also, the changes that you make to the system printer only affect printed AutoCAD LT drawings. If you want the changes to be in effect for *all* printed Windows applications, make the changes permanent using the Windows **Print Manager** located in the Control Panel. Refer to the *Microsoft Windows User's Guide* for a complete description of Print Manager.

Saving and reusing plot parameters

You can save your plot specifications in an external .PCP (*Plot Configuration Parameters*) file. For example, a typical .PCP file may contain information about the output device, pens, plot scale, and rotation. You can have .PCP files for various size drawings, printers, and plotters. Even if you do not have a plotter, you can still use this capability to specify the required plotting parameters for your drawing. The file can then be given to a plotting service that can plot the drawing for you.

Before creating a .PCP file, first specify all the required plot parameters. Then, click the **Save Defaults To File...** button in the **Print/Plot Setup & Default Selection** subdialog box. The **Save to File** subdialog box is displayed. Enter the desired filename in the **File Name:** text box at the upper left and click the **OK** button, Figure 13-5A. By default, the .PCP file is stored in the \ACLTWIN directory.

When you wish to retrieve a saved .PCP file, click the **Get Defaults From File...** button in the **Print/Plot Setup & Default Selection** subdialog box. Any saved .PCP files appear at the left of the **Obtain from File** subdialog box, Figure 13-5B. Select the file that you wish to use from the file list, or enter the desired filename in the **File Name:** text box. Click **OK** when you are finished.

> **PROFESSIONAL TIP**
>
>
>
> Keep backup copies of your saved .PCP files on a floppy disk. Should you need to reinstall AutoCAD LT, or upgrade to a new version, simply restore your saved .PCP files onto your hard disk to avoid recreating the plotting parameters again.

Figure 13-5.
A—Saving a .PCP file. B—Retrieving a stored .PCP file.

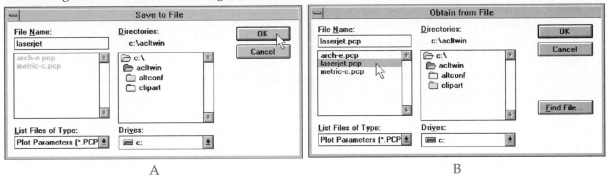

A   B

Pen assignments

The **Pen Parameters** area in the **Plot Configuration** dialog box allows you to set pen parameters based on your drawing standards or the type of printer/plotter you are using. Refer to Figure 13-1. To change the pen parameters, click the **Pen Assignments...** button to open the **Pen Assignments** subdialog box, Figure 13-6. Selecting a pen from the list displays the current pen values in the **Modify Values** text boxes at the right of the subdialog box. You can change the pen number, linetype, and width of the selected pen.

When you plot a drawing with a pen plotter, you must assign the color numbers used on-screen to the corresponding pen number in the plotter. This is called *mapping.* For example, suppose you have created a drawing using the first seven colors available in AutoCAD LT. Those colors—red, yellow, green, cyan, blue, magenta, and white (or black)—are mapped to color numbers 1 through 7, respectively. These color numbers are by default assigned pen numbers 1 through 7 by AutoCAD LT. In other words, all red entities on screen are plotted with pen number 1, all yellow entities with pen number 2, all green entities with pen number 3, and so on. If you do not change this convention, you will need a separate pen for every color used in your drawing!

It is far more efficient and cost-effective to map the various colors used in your drawing to only a few pens. To further illustrate, refer to the **Pen Assignments** subdialog box shown in Figure 13-6. In this example, colors 1 through 6 have been assigned to pen number 1. The entities drawn with these colors will be plotted with a thin pen. These entities include dimensions, text, hatching, and centerlines. The object lines in the drawing were drawn with color

Figure 13-6.
The **Pen Assignments** subdialog box.

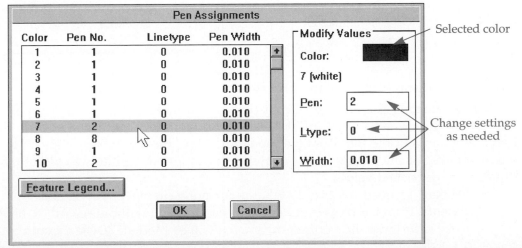

number 7. Since object lines should be drawn thick, color number 7 has been assigned to pen number 2. This pen has a tip size that produces a line weight of .032" to conform to the ANSI standard for object lines. Therefore, only two pens are required to accurately plot all the drawing entities.

Most pen plotters are capable of using various pen sizes. These type of pens are similar to the ink pens used for manual inking on mylar and are available in a range of tip sizes. If your pen plotter is compatible with these types of pens, you do not need to set the pen width in the **Pen Assignments** subdialog box. Simply insert the correct pen size in the assigned pen position on your plotter.

Other types of output devices, such as laser printers or electrostatic plotters, do not use pens. However, you can still produce finished plots with the proper line weights by assigning the desired pen widths to the color numbers used in your drawing. This is a particularly convenient feature for users who do not have pen plotters.

You will also note that a specific linetype can be assigned to a pen using the **Ltype:** text box in the **Pen Assignments** subdialog box. For most pen plotters, the drawing linetypes are controlled by the installed plotter driver. Therefore, entities drawn in linetypes other than continuous will plot correctly as a function of the software itself. It is very unlikely that you will need to change the linetype assignments unless everything in your drawing has been drawn with the continuous linetype. To make a linetype assignment, click the **Feature Legend...** button at the lower-left of the **Pen Assignments** subdialog box to display the **Feature Legend** subdialog box shown in Figure 13-7. The linetypes and their respective **Ltype:** values shown in this subdialog box reflect the linetypes that are generated by your plotter, and are different than the linetypes created in your drawing by AutoCAD LT. Thus, assigning linetype value 6 to a pen in the **Pen Assignments** subdialog box plots a phantom line rather than a continuous line. Keep in mind that the linetype values displayed in the **Feature Legend** subdialog box vary from one device to another.

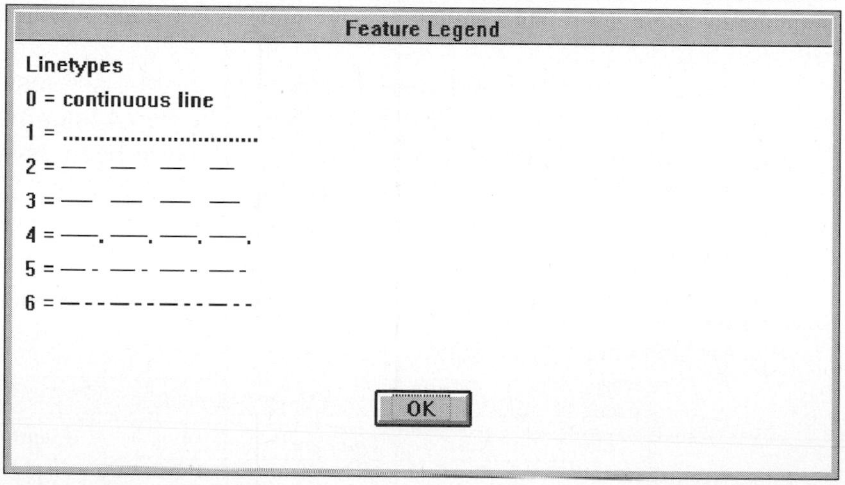

Figure 13-7.
The **Feature Legend** subdialog box displays the linetypes generated by the currently configured output device—not AutoCAD LT.

Additional parameters—choosing what to plot

After selecting the desired output device and making the necessary pen assignments, you must decide what part of the drawing you want to plot. Look at the **Additional Parameters** area of the **Plot Configuration** dialog box shown in Figure 13-1. This section provides options for the portion of the drawing to be plotted, and how to plot it. The five option buttons are described below:

- **Display.** Prints or plots only what is currently displayed on-screen.
- **Extents.** Prints or plots every entity in the drawing without regard to the current screen display or limits. To verify exactly what will be plotted, **ZOOM Extents** before plotting.

- **Limits.** Prints or plots everything inside the defined drawing limits.
- **View.** Views saved with the **VIEW** command (see Chapter 4) are plotted using this option. Until a view name is provided, this button is grayed-out. To specify a view name, click the **View...** button to display the **View Name** subdialog box. Select the name of the view you want printed or plotted and then click **OK**. The view name you select does not have to be currently displayed on the screen. However, the **TILEMODE** system variable must be off (0) to output any saved view from either model space or paper space. Refer to Chapter 16 of this text to learn more about the **TILEMODE** variable.
- **Window.** This option button is automatically activated by clicking the **Window...** button which displays the **Window Selection** subdialog box shown in Figure 13-8. Define two diagonally opposite corners of a window around the portion of the drawing to be plotted either with your mouse or by entering absolute coordinates. Enter the **First Corner** and **Other Corner** coordinates of the desired window in the appropriate **X:** and **Y:** text boxes. If you want to define the window with your mouse, select the **Pick** ⟨ button at the upper left of the subdialog box. This clears the dialog boxes and redisplays the graphics window. You are then prompted on the command line to pick the window corners that surround the part of the drawing you want printed or plotted. After you have picked the corners, the **Window Selection** subdialog box reappears and displays the X and Y coordinates of the window. Click **OK** to return to the **Plot Configuration** dialog box.

Figure 13-8.
The **Window Selection** dialog box is used to specify a plot window.

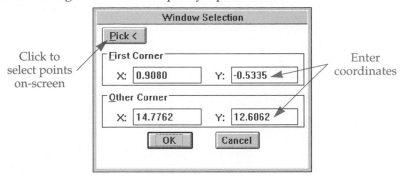

Other additional parameters

Click the **Hide Lines** check box when you wish to plot a 3D model with hidden lines removed. This function works the same as the **HIDE** command described in Chapter 18. Plotting takes somewhat longer when removing hidden lines since AutoCAD LT must calculate each of the entities to be removed. Do not check this box when plotting 2D drawings.

The **Adjust Area Fill** check box should be activated when you want entities such as wide polylines, donuts, and solids filled with a higher degree of precision. AutoCAD LT does this by adjusting the pen inside the boundary of the solid-filled object by one-half the pen width. This option is only necessary for very precise applications, such as printed circuit artwork. The pen moves at the center of the boundary when this check box is not active.

The **Dithering** check box is active if you have a system printer capable of color output. If your color printer has few available colors, dithering is used automatically. *Dithering* blends several colors together with white space. This tricks the eye into seeing more color hues than are available. Dithering is also used on black and white printers to differentiate between colors.

Earlier in this chapter, you learned that you can specify a specific printer in place of the default printer using the **Print Setup** dialog box. If you have done so and wish to use the specific printer the next time you print, activate the **Use Previous Printer** check box. Otherwise, the default printer will be used instead.

Creating a plot file

Some computer operating systems allow you to continue working on a drawing, while other instructions are being handled by the computer. This capability is called *multitasking* and is a standard feature of the Windows NT, Windows 95, and UNIX operating systems. For those operating systems capable of true multitasking, it can be extremely handy to redirect plot output to an external file. This plot file can then be sent directly to a configured plotter while a user continues working on a drawing.

Unfortunately, MS-DOS is not a multitasking operating system and can only run one program at a time. Many people confuse the Windows 3.1 and Windows for Workgroups 3.11 environments with multitasking operating systems. Since Windows has the ability to display multiple open windows on the display screen at one time, it gives the impression that several applications are running simultaneously. This is not the case, however. Only the application in the active window is running—another application is "dormant" until its window is reactivated.

Since MS-DOS and Windows are not multitasking operating environments, redirecting plot output to a .PLT file is especially useful if there is only one department or classroom lab computer connected to a printer or plotter. The plot file can be written to a floppy disk and loaded onto the hard disk of the computer connected to the output device and plotted accordingly.

If you want to redirect plot output to a file, click the **Plot To File** check box. The plot file name automatically defaults to the current drawing name. If you have not yet provided a name for the current drawing, the plot file is saved with the name UNNAMED.PLT. If you wish to enter a different filename, click the **File Name...** button to display the **Create Plot File** subdialog box shown in Figure 13-9. Saved plot files are automatically given the extension .PLT. To provide a different name for the plot file, enter the desired name in the **File Name:** text box and click **OK**. You are then returned to the **Plot Configuration** dialog box. Click **OK** once more to close the dialog box and create the plot file. When the plot file is complete, a message appears on the command line.

Figure 13-9.
Entering a plot filename in the **Create Plot File** subdialog box.

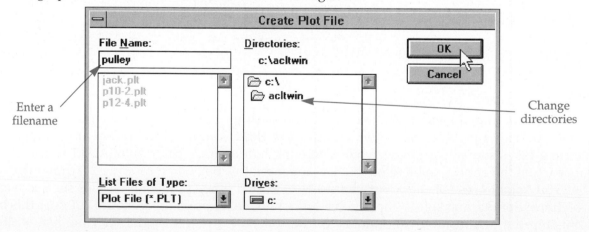

Paper size and orientation

As shown in Figure 13-1, the area at the upper right of the **Plot Configuration** dialog box controls the paper size and orientation. Click either the **Inches** or **MM** option buttons to specify the appropriate units for the plotted drawing. Clicking the **Size...** button displays the **Paper Size** subdialog box shown in Figure 13-10. Select the desired size from the list on the left of the dialog box, or enter your own size specifications in one of the **USER:** text boxes. If you enter your own size specifications, make sure the values you enter do not exceed the maximum (MAX) size indicated in the list. The MAX size is the largest size plot media your plotter can accommodate. Therefore, the sizes listed in the **Paper Size** subdialog box will vary according to the manufacturer and size of printer or plotter you have.

Keep in mind that all pen plotters require margins around the edges of the plot media. This space is used to secure the media to the plotter drum using clamps, grit wheels, or other holding devices. As a result, the available plotting area is smaller than the standard sheet sizes specified by industry standards. Whether you select a standard size from the list in the **Paper Size** subdialog box, or enter your own size specifications, the available plotting area is reported in the **Paper Size and Orientation** area of the **Plot Configuration** dialog box, Figure 13-1.

Figure 13-10.
Available sheet sizes for the current output device are listed in the **Paper Size** subdialog box.

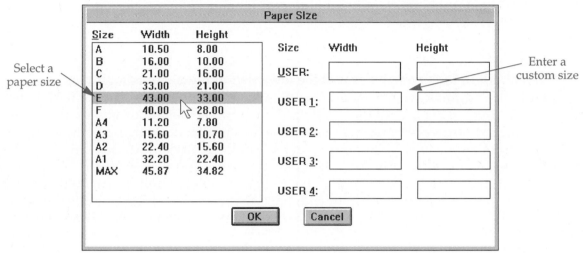

Select a paper size

Enter a custom size

Plot rotation

Options to control the plot scale, rotation, and origin are located in the **Scale, Rotation, and Origin** area of the **Plot Configuration** dialog box, Figure 13-1. Clicking the **Rotation and Origin...** button displays the **Plot Rotation and Origin** subdialog box shown in Figure 13-11. AutoCAD LT rotates plots in 90° clockwise increments. Buttons for 0, 90, 180, and 270 degree rotation settings appear in the **Plot Rotation** area of this subdialog box. The results of different plot rotation values are shown in Figure 13-12.

For system printers, the **Portrait** and **Landscape** settings in the Windows Control Panel also affect plot rotation. As shown in Figure 13-12A, a portrait orientation corresponds to a 0° rotation. The landscape orientation shown in Figure 13-12B corresponds to a 90° rotation.

Figure 13-11.
The **Plot Rotation and Origin** subdialog box.

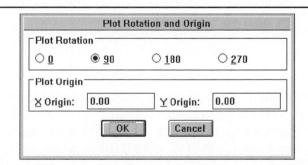

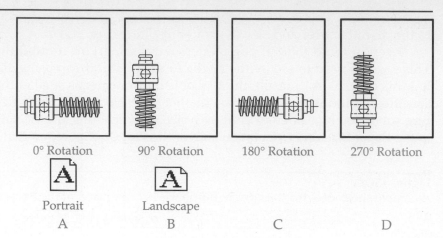

Figure 13-12.
Plot rotation is performed in 90° clockwise increments. For the system printer, the Windows Control Panel also affects plot rotation by specifying either portrait mode or landscape mode.

0° Rotation   90° Rotation   180° Rotation   270° Rotation

Portrait   Landscape
A   B   C   D

Plot origin

The plot origin for a pen plotter is at the lower left of the plot media. If you wish to use the default plot origin, leave the values shown in the **Plot Origin** text boxes at 0.00. Refer to Figure 13-11. If you want to shift the drawing away from the default origin, set the required values in the text boxes accordingly. For example, to shift the drawing one unit to the right and one-half unit above the plotter origin, enter 1 in the **X Origin:** text box, and .5 in the **Y Origin:** text box. For printers, the origin is at the upper left corner of the paper. These coordinates will shift the print origin one unit to the right and one-half unit down. Remember that the units you enter should be consistent with the units specified (inches or millimeters) with the option buttons in the **Paper Size and Orientation** area of the **Plot Configuration** dialog box, Figure 13-1.

Setting the plot scale

Scaling of text height and dimensions was covered in previous chapters. You may recall from those discussions that, unless a drawing is to be plotted at 1:1, the plot scale factor is always the reciprocal of the drawing scale. For example, if you wish to plot an architectural drawing at a scale of 1/8″ = 1′-0″, calculate the scale factor as follows:

1/8″ = 1′-0″
.125″ = 12″
12 ÷ .125 = 96 *(The scale factor is 96)*

A mechanical drawing plotted at a scale of 1:4 is calculated as follows:

1″ = 4″
1″ / 4″
1/4 = .25 *(The scale factor is .25)*

Finally, the scale factor of a civil engineering drawing that has a scale of 1″ = 50′ is calculated as:

1″ = 50′
1″ = (50 × 12) = 600 *(The scale factor is 600)*

As explained in previous chapters, AutoCAD LT drawing geometry should *always* be created at full scale. The drawing is then scaled up or down accordingly when plotting to fit onto the plot media sheet size. The **Plotted Inches = Drawing Units** section in the **Scale, Rotation, and Origin** area of the **Plot Configuration** dialog box is used to specify the plot scale. Refer to Figure 13-1. The **Plotted Inches = Drawing Units** text boxes allow you to specify the plot scale as a ratio of plotted units to drawing units. A mechanical drawing to be plotted at a scale of 1/2″ = 1″ is entered in the text boxes in one of the following formats:

1/2″ = 1″ *or* .5 = 1 *or* 1 = 2

An architectural drawing to be plotted at 1/2″ = 1′-0″ can be entered in the text boxes as:

1/2″ = 1′ *or* .5 = 12 *or* 1 = 24

If you would like to have AutoCAD LT automatically adjust your drawing to fit on the sheet, click the **Scaled to Fit** check box. This option is convenient if you only have a C-size pen plotter, for example, but need to plot a D-size or E-size drawing. The **Scaled to Fit** feature is also useful if you are printing a large drawing on a dot matrix or laser printer that can accommodate A-size sheets only. The drawing is automatically scaled down to fit the size of printer paper.

Previewing the plot

The size and complexity of some drawings can result in long plot times. By previewing a plot before it is sent to the output device, you can save ink, sheet media, and time. Preview options appear in the **Plot Preview** area at the lower right of the **Plot Configuration** dialog box, Figure 13-1. You can choose between a partial or full preview before clicking the **Preview...** button. The two preview options are described below:

- **Partial.** This button displays the **Preview Effective Plotting Area** subdialog box shown in Figure 13-13. It is used to verify the position of the plotted drawing on the sheet. Two outlines are displayed. The red outline represents the paper size. The blue outline represents the area occupied by the plotted image and is called the *effective area*. The dimensions of both the paper size and the effective area are reported just below the outlines. The **Warnings:** area at the bottom of the dialog box alerts you if the plotted image extends outside the effective area. When the effective area and the paper size are the same, AutoCAD LT displays a red and blue dashed line. In Figure 13-13, the reported values indicate that a B-size drawing is being plotted on a C-size sheet of plot media. Also, notice the small triangular symbol in the lower left corner of the effective area. This symbol is called the *rotation icon*. The 0° default rotation angle is indicated when the icon is in the lower-left corner. The icon displays in the upper-left corner when the plot rotation is 90°, the upper-right corner for a 180° rotation, and in the lower-right corner for a 270° rotation.
- **Full.** This button displays the drawing in the graphics window as it will appear on the plotted hard copy. The **Plot Preview** dialog box appears at the center of the screen, Figure 13-14. This small dialog box features a button labeled **Pan and Zoom** that

Figure 13-13.
The **Partial** preview option button displays the **Preview Effective Plotting Area** subdialog box.

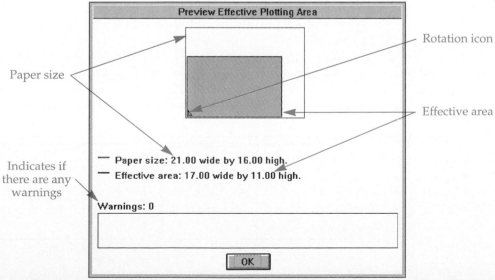

Paper size

Rotation icon

Effective area

Indicates if there are any warnings

Paper size: 21.00 wide by 16.00 high.
Effective area: 17.00 wide by 11.00 high.

Warnings: 0

OK

allows you to inspect details on the drawing before plotting. If you click the **Pan and Zoom** button, a small pan box with an X inside appears on the screen, Figure 13-15A. Use your mouse to move the pan box anywhere you like over the face of the drawing. Using the pick button on your mouse changes the pan box to a zoom box. The zoom box contains an arrow, Figure 13-15B. Make the zoom box bigger by moving your mouse to the right, or smaller by moving it to the left. When you have the size and position of the box where you want it, press [Enter] or the rightmost button on your mouse. The preview is then displayed at the pan location and zoom scale that you specified. The results of a pan and zoom are shown in Figure 13-16. After performing the zoom, the **Plot Preview** subdialog box features a **Zoom Previous** button that allows you to return to the original full preview display. Click the **End Preview** button when you wish to return to the **Plot Configuration** dialog box.

Once you are satisfied with all printer or plotter parameters and are ready to plot, click the **OK** button to exit the **Plot Configuration** dialog box. The following messages are then displayed on the command line:

Effective plotting area: (*xx*) wide by (*yy*) high
Position paper in plotter.
Press RETURN to continue or S to stop for hardware setup

AutoCAD LT reports the actual dimensions of the effective plotting area on the first line. Before pressing [Enter], be sure that your printer or plotter is plugged in and turned on, and that all cabling is secure. For pen plotters, make sure that the correct size and number of pens are in place, and that the plot media is properly loaded in the plotter.

Figure 13-14.
The **Full** preview option button displays the portion of the drawing that will plot. A **Pan and Zoom** option is offered in the **Plot Preview** subdialog box (shown here highlighted).

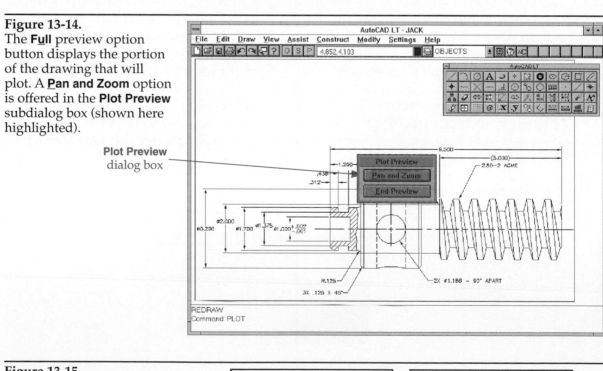

Plot Preview
dialog box

Figure 13-15.
The plot preview pan and zoom boxes.

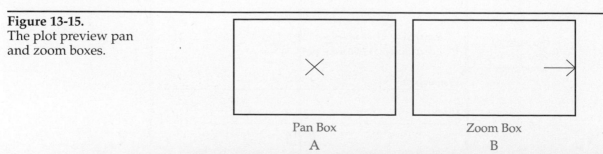

Pan Box
A

Zoom Box
B

Figure 13-16.
A detail is examined before plotting.

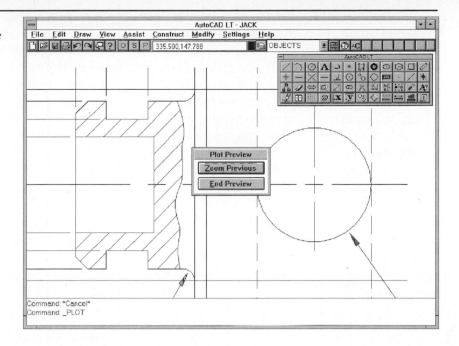

PLOTTING TO A RASTER FILE

ALTUG 16

The **PLOT** command also allows you to export a drawing in one of four industry-standard raster file formats. A *raster file* is a file where graphical objects are defined by the location and color of screen pixels. Raster file formats are used in a variety of both MS-DOS and Windows-based presentation graphics and desktop publishing applications. The four available raster formats are:

- Windows bitmap (.BMP)
- CompuServe (.GIF)
- Z-Soft (.PCX)
- Tag Image File Format (.TIF)

Each of the four formats offers the choice of 640×480, 800×600, or 1024×768 screen resolutions. Select the desired file format as you would the output device. In the example shown in Figure 13-17, the Z-Soft .PCX format with 800×600 screen resolution is selected from the list in the **Print/Plot Setup & Default Selection** subdialog box.

Figure 13-17.
Selecting a raster file format from the **Print/Plot Setup & Default Selection** subdialog box.

Pick to select a color output option →

Print/Plot Setup & Default Selection

Select Device

Manufacturer: Raster file export ADI 4.2 - by Autodesk, Inc

Windows BMP 1024 × 768
CompuServe GIF 640 × 480
CompuServe GIF 800 × 600
CompuServe GIF 1024 × 768
Z-Soft PCX format 640 × 480
Z-Soft PCX format 800 × 600

File Defaults

Save Defaults To File...   Get Defaults From File...

Device Specific Configuration

Show Device Requirements...   Print/Plot Setup...

OK   Cancel

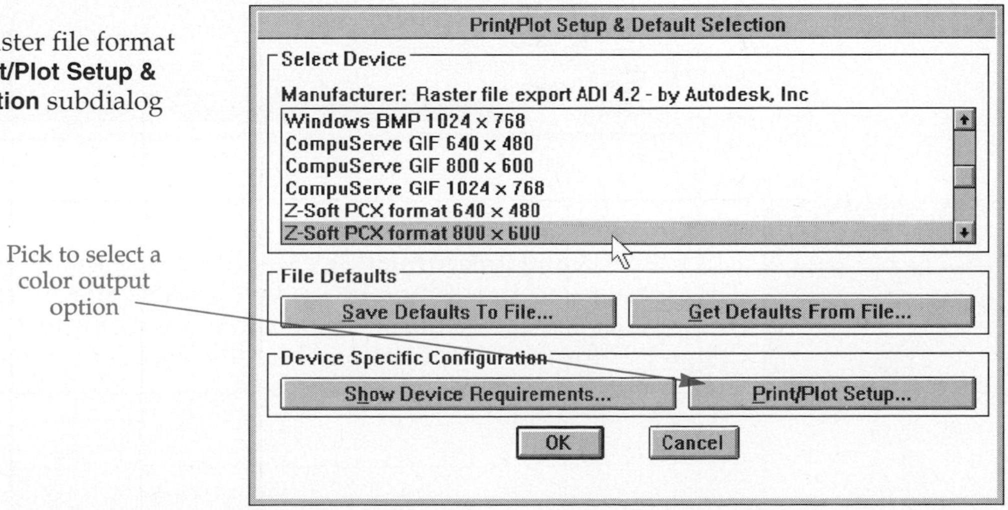

Once you have selected the format, click the **Print/Plot Setup...** button to display the **Print/Plot Setup** subdialog box shown in Figure 13-18. Use this subdialog box to select one of three color output options—monochrome, 16 color, or 256 color. You can also specify the background color (1 - 255) using this subdialog box. The default background color is black. When you are finished making your changes, click **OK** to exit the **Print/Plot Setup** subdialog box. Click **OK** once more to return to the **Plot Configuration** dialog box.

Next, specify any required plot parameters (such as scale and rotation) as described in this chapter. When all parameters are set to your satisfaction, click **OK** to exit the **Plot Configuration** dialog box. The output file is then saved to disk in the raster format you specified. An example of an AutoCAD LT drawing in .PCX monochrome format appears in the Windows Paintbrush, Figure 13-19.

Figure 13-18.
Use the **Print/Plot Setup** subdialog box to specify color output options and the background color.

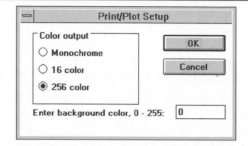

Figure 13-19.
An AutoCAD LT drawing in .PCX format displayed in Windows Paintbrush.

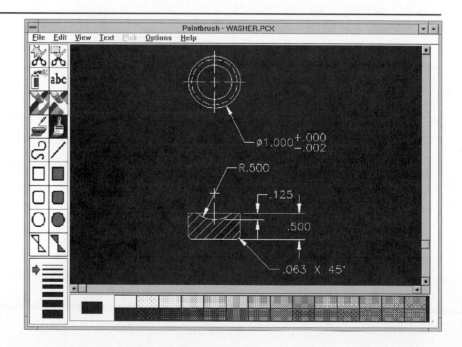

PROFESSIONAL TIP

The .PCX and .GIF formats are smaller in size than the .BMP and .TIF formats, and therefore take up far less disk space. Also, monochrome files are the smallest of the three color output options. See Chapter 22 for more information about file export options.

PostScript is a page description language commonly used in desktop publishing applications. You can export an AutoCAD LT drawing in PostScript format using the **PSOUT** command. The output file is saved with a .EPS (Encapsulated PostScript) file extension. The **PSOUT** command can be issued by first selecting **Import/Export** from the **File** pull-down menu, and then selecting **PostScript Out...** from the cascading submenu. You can also enter the following at the **Command:** prompt:

> Command: *(type* PSOUT *or* PU *and press* [Enter]*)*

The **Create PostScript File** dialog box is displayed, Figure 13-20. AutoCAD LT automatically appends an .EPS file extension to the filename that you provide. Enter the desired filename in the **File Name:** text box and click **OK**.

> What to plot - Display, Extents, Limits, View, or Window ⟨D⟩: *(select an option)*
> Include a screen preview image in the file? (None/EPSI/TIFF) ⟨None⟩:

If you choose, you can include a screen preview image to display in desktop publishing applications. If you select **E** for EPSI or **T** for TIFF, you are then prompted to select a screen resolution of 128, 256, or 512 pixels. Accept the default 128 pixels to speed the display of the preview image.

> Size units (Inches or Millimeters) ⟨Inches⟩: *(select inches or millimeters)*
> Output Inches=Drawing Units or Fit or ? ⟨Fit⟩:

Enter the output scale for plotting, as described earlier in this chapter. For example, if you wish to have the output at quarter-scale, enter 1 = 4. Use the **Fit** option to scale the output to fill the paper. The graphics window then flips to the text window and you are prompted with the following:

> Enter the Size or Width,Height (in Inches) ⟨USER⟩:

A list of available paper sizes is displayed. Enter a standard paper size (such as A or B) or enter a custom size as required. When entering a custom size, specify the width first, enter a comma, and then specify the height, like this: 7.5,10.

> Effective plotting area: (*xx*) wide by (*yy*) high
> Command:

As with the **PLOT** command, AutoCAD LT reports the actual dimensions of the effective plotting area. The file now resides on disk and can be used with a PostScript application or output to a printer with PostScript capability.

Figure 13-20.
The **Create PostScript File** dialog box.

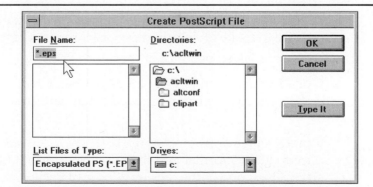

CHAPTER TEST

Write your answers in the spaces provided.

1. What is the system printer? _____

2. Define HP-GL. _____

    _____

3. What is a .PCP file? Why is it used? _____

    _____

4. What is the purpose of the **Pen Assignments** subdialog box? _____

    _____

5. Why would you create a plot file? _____

6. Plots are rotated in 90° counterclockwise increments. (True/False) _____

7. Describe the purpose and appearance of the **Preview Effective Plotting Area** subdialog box. _____

8. Identify the system variable that controls the display of the **Plot Configuration** dialog box. _____

    _____

9. What is a raster file? List the file extensions of the four types of raster files that can be output by AutoCAD LT. _____

10. What is PostScript and where is it used? Identify the command that allows you to export a drawing in PostScript format. _____

CHAPTER PROBLEMS

General

1. Open Problem 3 from Chapter 9 (P9-3). Obtain a print on your printer.

General

2. Open Problem 5 from Chapter 11 (P11-5). Set the line weights accordingly using the **Pen Assignments** dialog box. Use the **Fit** option to obtain a print on your printer.

General

3. Open the BELL CRANK from Chapter 12 (P12-4).

    A. Zoom-in on SECTION A-A and produce a pen plot using the **Display** option. Be sure to make all required pen assignments before plotting.

    B. Next, make a pen plot of the entire drawing.

General

4. Open Problem 2 from Chapter 12 (P12-2). Create a pen plot of the pie chart using a different color ink pen for each hatch pattern in the drawing.

General

5. Open Problem 1 from Chapter 12 (P12-1). Output the drawing in Windows bitmap (.BMP) format and then in Z-Soft format (.PCX). Compare the two file sizes. Open one of the files in Windows Paintbrush and use the Print... command to obtain a printed copy.

General

6. If you have access to a desktop publishing or other PostScript-compatible program, try exporting a drawing of your choice using the **PSOUT** command.

Chapter 14

Blocks, Attributes, and External References

Learning objectives:

After you have completed this chapter, you will be able to:
- ❍ Create, insert, and redefine a block.
- ❍ Save a block to disk.
- ❍ Divide and measure selected entities with blocks.
- ❍ Assign and edit attributes.
- ❍ Use attributes to automate drafting documentation tasks.
- ❍ Extract attribute information in a bill of materials.
- ❍ Link existing drawings to new drawings.

Many types of drawing symbols exist in the engineering and architectural fields. Symbols can be used for items such as for fasteners, gears, doors, windows, piping, resistors, and diodes. In traditional drafting, plastic templates are used to quickly draw common symbols. In CAD, a symbol is drawn once and then can be inserted many times. Symbols in AutoCAD LT are created as *blocks*. Textual information, called *attributes*, can be included with the block symbols if desired. This chapter describes how blocks and block attributes can be used to automate repetitive drafting tasks. You will also learn how one drawing can be linked, or attached, to another drawing using the **XREF** command.

CREATING A BLOCK

ALTUG 14

There are two types of blocks in AutoCAD LT. The first type remains in the drawing where it was created. This type of block is created with either the **BMAKE** or **BLOCK** command. The second type of block is a *wblock*. These blocks are saved to disk so that they can be used with any number of different drawings. Wblocks are created using the **WBLOCK** command, described later in this chapter. Both types of blocks take up much less space in a drawing file than other types of entities. Therefore, use blocks whenever there are multiple occurrences of a symbol or feature.

Regardless of the type of block you define, the procedure for creating a block is very simple. To create a block, use the following steps:

1. Construct the object to be made into a block. Draw it as completely and as accurately as possible. Any layers, colors, and linetypes used to create the object are retained when the object is made into a block and inserted. However, if the object is constructed on layer 0, the block will assume the properties of the drawing layer it is inserted on.
2. Name the block. A block name cannot exceed 31 characters. No spaces are permitted.
3. Select an *insertion base point*. This is a point of reference on the block for when it is inserted into a drawing. Use an appropriate object snap mode or enter a known coordinate to ensure accuracy. The location should be logical for the symbol. For example, the center of a hex nut or the corner of a door are good insertion points, Figure 14-1.
4. Select the objects that will comprise the block using any of the selection set methods.

Figure 14-1.
Creating a block. Choose a
logical place for the insertion
point, such as the center of
the nut shown here.

  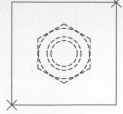

A. Draw the object   B. Pick the insertion point   C. Select the object

Creating a block using a dialog box

You can use the **Block Definition** dialog box to define a block, Figure 14-2. To access this dialog box, select **Make Block...** from the **Construct** pull-down menu. You can also type BMAKE at the **Command:** prompt as follows:

    Command: **BMAKE** ↵

Figure 14-2.
The **Block Definition** dialog box.

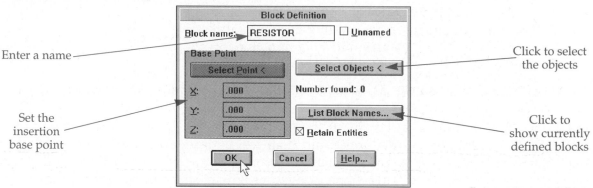

Enter a name

Set the
insertion
base point

Click to select
the objects

Click to
show currently
defined blocks

Each of the components of this dialog box are described below.
- **Block name:.** Enter a name for the block in this text box. Remember that a block name cannot exceed 31 characters.
- **Base Point.** Use this area to specify the insertion base point for the block. You can enter the X, Y, and Z values of a known point. However, it may be faster to click the **Select Point 〈** button. When you do, the dialog box disappears and you are prompted for the insertion base point on the command line. Pick the point using an osnap to ensure accuracy. The endpoint of the resistor shown in Figure 14-3 was selected using the **Endpoint** object snap mode. After picking the insertion base point, the **Block Definition** dialog box reappears.

Figure 14-3.
The insertion base point of
the resistor symbol is
selected using the osnap
Endpoint.

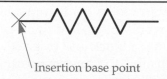

Insertion base point

- **Select Objects** ⟨. Click this button to select the objects that will make up the block. When the button is picked, the dialog box disappears and the **Select objects:** prompt is displayed on the command line. Use any selection set option to select the objects. The dialog box then reappears and reports the number of objects selected just below the **Select Objects** ⟨ button.
- **List Block Names....** Clicking this button displays a subdialog box listing all of the blocks defined in the current drawing, Figure 14-4.
- **Retain Entities.** When this check box is active (the default), the original objects are retained in the drawing. Deactivate this check box if you wish to have the original objects erased after the block is created.

Figure 14-4.
Clicking the **List Block Names...** button in the **Block Definition** dialog box lists the blocks defined in the current drawing in a separate subdialog box.

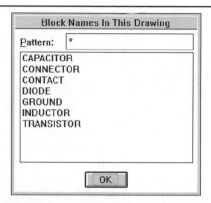

Once you have provided a name, identified the insertion base point, and selected the objects, click the **OK** button. The **Boundary Definition** dialog box disappears and the command is terminated. The block is now created and can be inserted into the current drawing as many times as necessary using the **INSERT** command. However, the block is defined in the current drawing *only.* It cannot be used in a different drawing until it has been written to disk using the **WBLOCK** command.

PROFESSIONAL TIP

If you wish to change the name of an existing block, use the **DDRENAME** or **RENAME** commands as described in previous chapters.

CAUTION

A user-defined block without a name cannot be accessed. Therefore, *do not* activate the **Unnamed** check box in the **Boundary Definition** dialog box.

Creating a block on the command line

If you prefer, you can define a block on the command line using the **BLOCK** command or by clicking the **Block** button. The command sequence is as follows:

Command: *(type* BLOCK *or* B *and press* [Enter]*)*
Block name (or ?): **RESISTOR** ↵
Insertion base point: *(pick the insertion point)*
Select objects: *(select the objects that make up the symbol)*
Select objects: ↵
Command:

NOTE The **Block** button does not appear on the toolbar or toolbox by default, but it can be easily added. See Chapter 19 of this text.

Unlike the **BMAKE** ccommand, the **BLOCK** command automatically erases the original objects after the block is defined. If you wish to restore the original objects, enter OOPS at the **Command:** prompt, or select **Oops** from the **Modify** pull-down menu. The original objects reappear on-screen in their original locations.

To verify that the block was saved properly, repeat the **BLOCK** command. Use the **?** option at the **Block name (or ?):** prompt, as shown below:

Command: *(type* BLOCK *or* B *and press* [Enter]*)*
Block name (or ?): **?** ↵
Block(s) to list ⟨*⟩: ↵

After pressing [Enter], the name and number of all blocks defined in the current drawing is reported in the AutoCAD LT text window, Figure 14-5. The column labeled User Blocks contains the block names created using the **BMAKE** or **BLOCK** commands. Drawings that are *referenced*, or attached, with the **XREF** command are listed in the column labeled External References. The **XREF** command is discussed later in this chapter. Any blocks that are part of a referenced drawing are listed under Dependent Blocks. The Unnamed Blocks column reports the number of anonymous blocks, such as hatch patterns and associative dimensions.

Figure 14-5.
The **?** option of the **BLOCK** command lists all blocks defined in the current drawing in the text window.

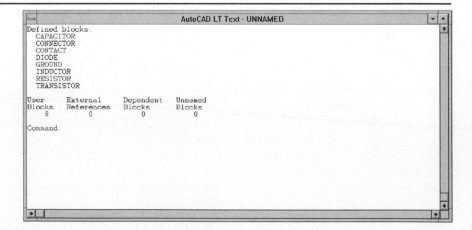

Depending on the application, some block symbols will vary in size from one drawing to another. In these instances, it is helpful to create the symbol so that it fits inside a one unit square. When the block is inserted, it can then be scaled to the required size. As an example, create a circle one unit in diameter. Next, place a centerline (or center mark) through the circle as described in Chapter 11. Create a block of the circle and the centerline. Now, whenever a hole of a given diameter is required, insert the circle block at the required scale. You then have a circle of the correct diameter with a centerline drawn through it and scaled accordingly in one operation.

EXERCISE 14-1

❏ Begin a new drawing.
❏ Draw the resistor symbol shown in Figure 14-3 on layer 0. Leave the color set to white and the linetype as continuous.
❏ Use the **BMAKE** command to create a block named RESISTOR. Select the insertion base point indicated in Figure 14-3.
❏ Save the drawing as EX14-1.

SAVING A BLOCK TO DISK—THE WBLOCK COMMAND | ALTUG 14

A block exists in the current drawing only and cannot be used in another drawing. A *wblock* is a block saved to disk so that it can be used in other drawings. To create a wblock, use the **WBLOCK** (write block) command. This command writes an existing block to disk. When using **WBLOCK**, you are first prompted to provide a filename for the block. The filename can be entirely different from the block name, but cannot have more than eight characters.

To access this command, select **Import/Export** from the **File** pull-down menu, and then select **Block Out...** from the cascading submenu, Figure 14-6. You can also enter WBLOCK at the **Command:** prompt.

Figure 14-6.
Selecting **Block Out...** from the **Import/Export** cascading submenu issues the **WBLOCK** command.

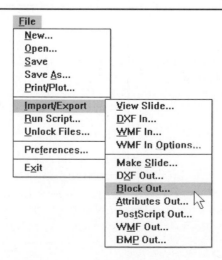

The **Create Drawing File** dialog box then appears on-screen, Figure 14-7. Enter a filename in the **File Name:** text box. Note that blocks written to disk assume the file extension .DWG just like an AutoCAD LT drawing. After entering a filename, click the **OK** button to exit the **Create Drawing File** dialog box. The following prompt is then displayed on the command line:

    Block name: = ↵
    Command:

If the block name and filename are identical, enter an "=" symbol, as shown above. If they are not the same, enter a block name at the prompt. For example, the block name CAPACITOR has more than eight characters. Therefore, CAPACITOR cannot be used as the filename. This block can be written to disk with a filename such as CAP, and given the block name CAPACITOR.

Figure 14-7.
The **Create Drawing File** dialog box.

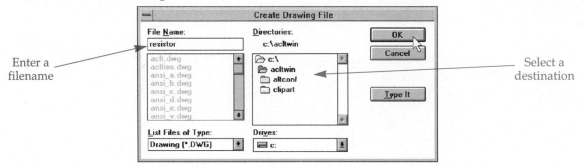

Enter a filename → Select a destination

Once the block has been saved to disk, it can be used in any other drawing at any time. It is a good idea to make a backup copy of the block on a floppy disk so that it can be shared with co-workers and clients.

Creating and saving a block simultaneously

It is also possible to define a block and write it to disk at the same time with the **WBLOCK** command. This option is convenient because you do not need to use the **BLOCK** command at all. First, draw the object. Then, issue the **WBLOCK** command. Enter a filename for the object when the **Create Drawing File** dialog box appears. Since a block has not yet been defined, press [Enter] when prompted for a block name and continue as follows:

    Block name: ↵
    Insertion base point: (pick the insertion point)
    Select objects: (select the entities that make up the block)
    Select objects: ↵
    Command:

Compressing a drawing with WBLOCK

Suppose you have a drawing where several linetypes have been loaded, but not used, and there are some layers that contain no drawing entities. The **WBLOCK** command can be used to remove unneeded linetypes, layers, blocks, and other named objects from a drawing. AutoCAD LT refers to unused named objects as *unreferenced objects*. Removing unreferenced objects compresses a drawing and saves disk space. To compress a drawing do the following:

    Command: **WBLOCK** ↵

Enter the current drawing filename when the **Create Drawing File** dialog box appears and click **OK**. An alert box appears indicating that the current drawing file exists and asks if you want to replace it. Click the **Yes** button. When prompted for a block name on the command line, enter an asterisk (*) as follows:

    Block name: * ⏎
    Command:

Because an asterisk is used, this procedure is often called *star-blocking*. As the drawing is saved to disk, unreferenced objects are discarded and every entity is stored in a new sequential order. The re-ordering process closes "gaps" in the data structure and helps greatly to reduce the overall file size.

CAUTION Do not save the drawing after star-blocking or you will write over the new compressed version on disk with the earlier uncompressed version.

PROFESSIONAL TIP It is best to perform star-blocking when a drawing is complete and you are certain that the unreferenced objects are no longer needed.

Compressing a drawing with the PURGE command ALTUG 17

The **PURGE** command can also be used to remove unreferenced objects from the drawing database. Keep in mind, however, that **PURGE** can be used only before the drawing database has been modified in the current drawing session. Therefore, when you wish to purge a drawing, do so when you first open the drawing. To issue the **PURGE** command, select **Purge** from the **Modify** pull-down menu. See Figure 14-8. The command sequence is as follows:

    Command: (type PURGE or PR and press [Enter])
    Purge unused Blocks/Dimstyles/LAyers/LTypes/Styles/All:

Select an object type to purge from the cascading submenu or enter the type on the command line. **All** purges all named object types.

PURGE removes only one level of reference. Therefore, it may be necessary to repeat the operation several times. To purge every unused object from a drawing, use the **PURGE** command with the **All** option and end the current drawing session. Then, restart AutoCAD LT and try purging again. Repeat the procedure until **PURGE** reports that there are no unreferenced objects. Finally, drawing files are not as greatly reduced in size as with the **WBLOCK** command because **PURGE** does not reorder the drawing database.

Figure 14-8.
Selecting **Purge** from the **Modify** pull-down menu displays a cascading submenu of named objects that can be purged.

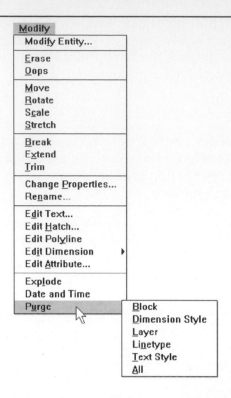

INSERTING A BLOCK

ALTUG 14

The **INSERT** command inserts a defined block or an entire drawing into the current drawing at a specified point, applying scale factors and rotation. If the block is not defined in the current drawing, but another drawing with that name exists on disk, a block definition is first created from the other drawing. The **INSERT** command displays the following prompts and options:

Command: *(type* INSERT *or* IN *and press* [Enter]*)*
Block name (or ?): **RESISTOR** ↵

Enter ? to list each of the blocks currently defined in the drawing. If you wish to insert a drawing rather than a block, enter a tilde (~) to display the **Select Drawing File** dialog box. The drawing name can then be selected from the dialog box file list, rather than entering the name on the command line. The command sequence then continues:

Insertion point: *(locate the insertion point)*
X scale factor ⟨1⟩/Corner/XYZ: *(enter the X scale factor or select an option)*
Y scale factor (default=X): *(enter a different Y scale factor or accept the default)*
Rotation angle ⟨0⟩: *(enter a rotation angle or press* [Enter]*)*
Command:

If you wish to separate the block or drawing into individual entities while inserting it, preface the block name with an asterisk (*) as shown below. Keep in mind, however, that you can only specify an X scale factor when exploding a block during insertion.

Command: *(type* INSERT *or* IN *and press* [Enter]*)*
Block name (or ?): ***RESISTOR** ↵

Once a block has been inserted, or referenced, into a drawing, it can be selected with a single pick. Use the **Insert** object snap mode to select a block at its insertion point.

Insertion scaling options

The Y scale factor defaults to the X scale factor. When you wish both the X and Y dimensions of a block to be identical, press [Enter] when prompted for the Y scale factor. By default, blocks are inserted at full scale (1:1). However, the X and Y scale factor prompts allow you to provide different scale factors for both axes of a block. For example, suppose you created a block one unit square. However, when inserted, you want the block to be 4.5 units long and 2.25 units high. When prompted for the scale factors, enter the following:

> X scale factor ⟨1⟩/Corner/XYZ: **4.5** ↵
> Y scale factor (default=X): **2.25** ↵

You can obtain mirror images of inserted blocks by entering negative values for the X and Y scale factors. The effects of this technique on a block are illustrated in Figure 14-9.

Figure 14-9.
Negative scale factors produce mirrored images of an inserted block.

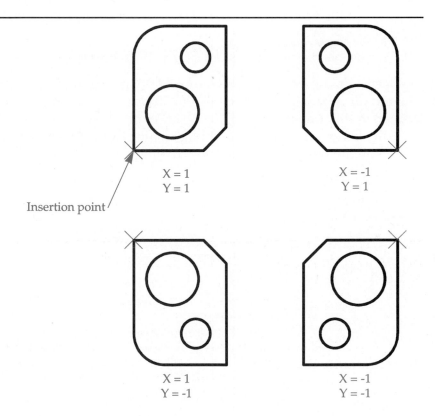

The **Corner** option allows you to specify the X and Y scale factors simultaneously by using the insertion point as the lower-left corner of a box, and a new diagonal point as the upper-right corner. The procedure looks like this:

> X scale factor ⟨1⟩/Corner/XYZ: **C** ↵
> Other corner: *(pick a diagonal point)*

The block is then scaled to fit between the two diagonal corners.

For three-dimensional blocks, enter XYZ at the X scale factor prompt to specify different scale factors as follows:

> X scale factor ⟨1⟩ / Corner / XYZ: **XYZ** ↵
> X scale factor ⟨1⟩ / Corner: *(enter a scale or C for Corner)*
> Y scale factor (default = X): *(enter a Y scale factor)*
> Z scale factor (default = X): *(enter a Z scale factor)*

See Chapter 18 of this text for more information on three-dimensional objects.

> **NOTE**
> Before a block can be edited, it must be exploded. However, a block inserted with a different X, Y, or Z scale factor cannot be exploded. This restriction also applies to a block inserted as a mirror image, if one scale factor is positive and the other negative (for example: X = 1, Y = –1). Block editing and redefinition is covered later in this chapter.

Inserting a block using a dialog box

You can also use the **Insert** dialog box to insert a block or drawing. To access this dialog box, use the **DDINSERT** command. Issue the command by clicking the **Insert Block** button or selecting **Insert Block...** from the **Draw** pull-down menu. The **Insert Block** button is not included in the toolbox or toolbar by default. You can also type **DDINSERT** at the **Command:** prompt as follows:

Command: *(type* DDINSERT *or* I *and press* [Enter]*)*

The **Insert** dialog box appears, Figure 14-10. If you know the name of the block or file, you can enter it in the appropriate text box. If not, click the **Block...** button to display the **Blocks Defined in this Drawing** subdialog box, Figure 14-11. Select the block that you wish to insert from the list or enter the desired block name in the **Selection:** text box. Click the **OK** button when you are finished and the **Insert** dialog box reappears.

Figure 14-10.
The **Insert** dialog box.

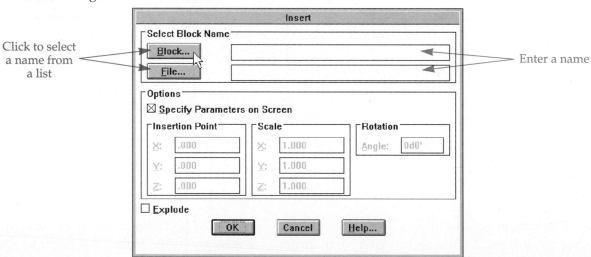

If you wish to insert a drawing file rather than a block, click the **File...** button. When the **Select Drawing File** dialog box appears, select the drawing you wish to insert and click **OK**. The **Insert** dialog box is then redisplayed.

Notice in Figure 14-10 that the **Insertion Point, Scale**, and **Rotation** text boxes are grayed-out. This is because the **Specify Parameters on Screen** check box is active by default. When this check box is active, the insertion point, scale, and rotation are entered on the command line. If you wish to enter these parameters in the corresponding text boxes, deactivate the check box. If you wish to separate the block into individual entities during insertion, activate the **Explode** check box at the lower left of the **Insert** dialog box.

Figure 14-11.
Selecting a block for insertion from the list in the **Blocks Defined in this Drawing** subdialog box.

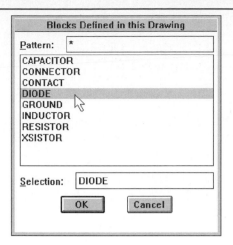

Blocks Defined in this Drawing

Pattern: | *

CAPACITOR
CONNECTOR
CONTACT
DIODE
GROUND
INDUCTOR
RESISTOR
XSISTOR

Selection: | DIODE

OK   Cancel

PROFESSIONAL TIP

It is common practice in industry to refer to other drawing prints to check features or dimensions while working on a drawing. Unfortunately, the hard copy prints are occasionally out of date, resulting in erroneous information. In other instances, the prints are not available and must be plotted. This is usually handled by a Document Control department after a formal Print Request is issued. You can avoid such problems and delays by using the **INSERT** or **DDINSERT** commands. When you need to reference another drawing, insert it into your current drawing. When you are done checking the features or dimensions you need, simply undo the insert operation or erase the inserted drawing. Drawings can also be inserted into other drawings using the "drag and drop" capability of the Windows File Manager. See Chapter 21 for a complete description of this powerful feature.

EXERCISE 14-2

❏ Open EX14-1 if it is not on your screen.
❏ Create three layers named RED, GREEN, and BLUE. Assign the corresponding color to each of the layers.
❏ Set the RED layer current and use **INSERT** or **DDINSERT** to insert the RESISTOR block at 1:1 (full scale).
❏ Set the GREEN layer current and insert the RESISTOR block at 2:1.
❏ Set the BLUE layer current and insert the RESISTOR block at 4:1 with a 270° rotation angle.
❏ What color are the three inserted blocks? Why?
❏ Save the drawing as EX14-2.

THE BASE COMMAND

When a drawing is inserted, it automatically becomes a block entity. If you want to modify it, you must explode the block into individual entities. Also, AutoCAD LT uses the 0,0 drawing origin of the inserted drawing as the base point. You can change the insertion base point for a drawing using the **BASE** command.

To access the **BASE** command, select **Drawing** from the **Settings** pull-down menu, and then select **Base** from the cascading submenu, Figure 14-12. You can also enter the following on the command line:

Command: *(type* BASE *or* BA *and press* [Enter])
Base point ⟨0.0000,0.0000,0.0000⟩: *(pick a point or enter new coordinates)*
Command:

Figure 14-12.
Issue the **BASE** command by first selecting **Drawing** from the **Settings** pull-down menu, and then selecting **Base** from the cascading submenu.

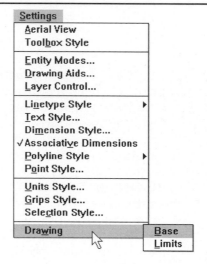

Use the **BASE** command only if the current drawing is to be inserted into another drawing and requires a base point other than (0,0).

DIVIDING AN OBJECT WITH A BLOCK

In Chapter 7, you learned that the **DIVIDE** command can be used to divide an object into a number of user-specified segments using point entities. The **DIVIDE** command also allows you to divide a selected entity with a block. When using a block, you can choose whether or not to align the block with the divided entity. In Figure 14-13, a polyline has been converted into a spline with **PEDIT** and divided into five equal segments with a block representing a D-hole. The block is shown both aligned and not aligned with the spline.

To divide an entity with a block, select **Divide** from the **Construct** pull-down menu. You can also enter the command as follows:

Command: **DIVIDE** ⏎
Select object to divide: *(select the entity to divide)*
⟨Number of segments⟩/Block: **B** ⏎
Block name to insert: **D-HOLE** ⏎
Align block with object? ⟨Y⟩ *(answer Y or N as required)*
Number of segments: **5** ⏎
Command:

Figure 14-13.
Dividing an object with a
block. The block can be
aligned or not aligned with
the divided entity.

Blocks aligned
with divided entity

Blocks not aligned
with divided entity

MEASURING AN OBJECT WITH A BLOCK

ALTUG 7

You may also recall from Chapter 7 that the **MEASURE** command is used to place points
at user-specified segment lengths along an object. The **MEASURE** command can also be used
to place a block at specified lengths along an entity. As with the **DIVIDE** command, you have
the option to align or not align the block with the object you are measuring, Figure 14-14.

To measure an entity with a block, select **Mea̲sure** from the **C̲onstruct** pull-down menu.
You can also enter the command as follows:

> Command: **MEASURE** ↵
> Select object to measure: *(select the entity to measure)*
> ⟨Segment length⟩/Block: **B** ↵
> Block name to insert: **D-HOLE** ↵
> Align block with object? ⟨Y⟩ *(answer Y or N as required)*
> Segment length: **.75** ↵
> Command:

Figure 14-14.
Measuring an object with a
block. The block can be
aligned or not aligned with
the measured entity.

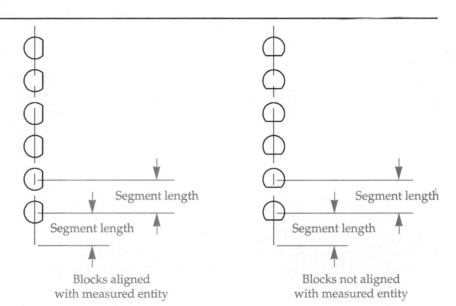

Segment length

Segment length

Blocks aligned
with measured entity

Segment length

Segment length

Blocks not aligned
with measured entity

It may be necessary to modify or edit an existing block. AutoCAD LT refers to modification of a block as *block redefinition*. Before you can modify a block, the block must first be exploded. If you change an unexploded block and attempt to make a new block from it using the same name, the following error message is displayed:

> Block *name* references itself
> *Invalid*

To redefine a block, do the following:

1. Insert the block to be redefined anywhere in the drawing.
2. Explode the inserted block. Remember that you can simultaneously explode the block as it is inserted by prefacing the block name with an asterisk (*), or activating the **Explode** check box in the **Insert** dialog box.
3. Make any required changes.
4. Issue the **BLOCK** command and provide the same name as previously used for the block. Answer Y when AutoCAD LT prompts you with **Block *name* already exists. Redefine it?**
5. Be sure to specify the same insertion base point as previously used.
6. Finally, select all of the entities that will comprise the block.

Once the block has been redefined, any existing occurrences of the block in the drawing are automatically updated to reflect the modifications. Therefore, changing one block changes them all.

Using BMAKE to redefine a block

If you use the **BMAKE** command to redefine a block, AutoCAD LT displays the alert box shown in Figure 14-15. Click the **Redefine** button to proceed with the block redefinition. Keep in mind, however, that it may be necessary to force a screen regeneration to update any existing blocks to the new definition.

Figure 14-15.
Redefining a block using the **BMAKE** command displays this alert box.

> **Warning**
> A Block with this name already exists in the drawing. Do you want to redefine it?
>
> [Redefine]   [Cancel]

EXERCISE 14-3

❏ Open EX14-2 if it is not on your screen.
❏ Use **INSERT** or **DDINSERT** to insert the RESISTOR block in the drawing. Explode the block as it is inserted. The insertion point is not important.
❏ Modify the resistor to match the object shown below.
❏ Make a new block using the same name (RESISTOR) and the same insertion base point indicated.
❏ What happens to the three previously inserted blocks?
❏ Save the drawing as EX14-3.

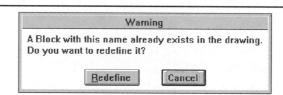

MANAGING BLOCKS

You will probably create a large number of blocks as your experience with AutoCAD LT grows. A large collection of block symbols is called a *symbol library*. Remember to use the **WBLOCK** command to store your blocks in a symbol library on disk so that they can be used in other drawings and shared with co-workers and clients. Many users prefer to keep their symbol libraries in one or more separate subdirectories or floppy disks. As an example, you might create a subdirectory called SYMBOLS under the \ACLTWIN directory. The path to the subdirectory would look like this:

      C:\ACLTWIN\SYMBOLS

If you work with many block symbols representing various professional applications, you might create several subdirectories with specific names, like the following:

      C:\ACLTWIN\ARCH
      C:\ACLTWIN\CIVIL
      C:\ACLTWIN\ELEC
      C:\ACLTWIN\MECH

Refer to Chapter 21 of this text to learn how to create subdirectories. To create a path to your new subdirectories so that AutoCAD LT can find your blocks, see Chapter 19 of this text.

In a networked environment, all of the block symbols should be stored on the network server so that they are easily accessible to everyone in the office or classroom. The CAD Manager or Network Administrator should have the responsibility to manage the symbol library. It is also this person's duty to inform everyone concerned when a block has been added to, or deleted from, the library.

Storing blocks in a prototype drawing

As an alternative to storing your blocks on disk or the network, you can also store blocks in your prototype drawing. With this method, all of your blocks are created and stored in the ACLT.DWG prototype drawing. This makes the blocks readily accessible at all times. The file size of the prototype drawing will grow, but a new drawing file can easily be reduced in size when it is completed using the **WBLOCK** and **PURGE** commands described earlier in this chapter.

Since any drawing can be used as a prototype, you can create one drawing named MECH that contains only mechanical symbols. Another named ARCH might contain only architectural symbols, and so on. Figure 14-16 shows a drawing of a symbol library. When you create such a drawing, be sure to include the name of the block and a marker, such as a point or an

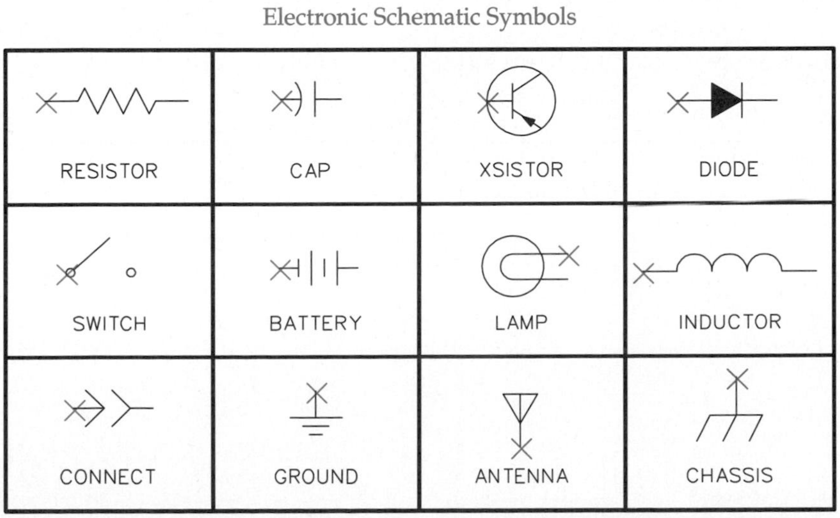

Figure 14-16.
An example of a block symbol library for electronic schematic symbols. The name and insertion point (shown in color) for each symbol is included in the drawing.

Electronic Schematic Symbols

RESISTOR	CAP	XSISTOR	DIODE
SWITCH	BATTERY	LAMP	INDUCTOR
CONNECT	GROUND	ANTENNA	CHASSIS

X, to identify the insertion point of the block. Make 8-1/2″ × 11″ printed copies of the drawing to be shared with everyone in your office or school who will use the blocks. A larger plotted copy might also be displayed on the wall where it can easily be seen.

Inserting a symbol library

Once you have a prototype drawing that contains a symbol library, it can be inserted into another drawing whenever the blocks are needed. In the following example, the drawing ELEC.DWG shown in Figure 14-16 is inserted:

> Command: *(type* INSERT *or* IN *and press* [Enter]*)*
> Block name (or ?): **ELEC** ⏎
> Insertion point: *(press* [Ctrl]+[C] *or click the toolbar* **Cancel** *button)*

After entering the prototype drawing name, AutoCAD LT first searches the current drawing for a block with that name. When the block is not found, then the current working directory is searched for a drawing with that name. Once the drawing is located, the entities defined in the drawing appear briefly on-screen. At this point, cancel the command and the entities disappear. However, all of the blocks defined in the symbol library now reside in the current drawing and are accessible to you.

PROFESSIONAL TIP

Inserting one drawing into another also inserts layers, linetypes, text styles, and dimension styles along with blocks. This is a very convenient way to transfer named objects from one drawing to another. As an example, suppose you start a new drawing but forget to use the prototype drawing that contains your layers. Simply insert the prototype drawing into the new drawing and cancel at the **Insertion point:** prompt. The layers, as well as any other named objects defined in the prototype drawing, are now in the new drawing.

BLOCK ATTRIBUTES

> **ALTUG 14**

Attributes are entities that contain textual information and can be assigned to any object that is part of a block. Several examples of blocks with attributes appear in Figure 14-17. Other attribute examples include part numbers, vendor names, prices, and sizes. Attributes can be made visible or invisible. This capability is useful when you wish to suppress the display of proprietary information, such as the price or supplier.

Attributes can be edited both before and after becoming part of a block. Attribute data can also be extracted from a drawing to help produce a drawing parts list, or bill of materials.

Figure 14-17.
Several examples of blocks with attributes.

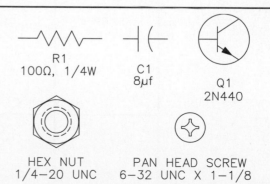

R1
100Ω, 1/4W

C1
8μf

Q1
2N440

HEX NUT
1/4−20 UNC

PAN HEAD SCREW
6−32 UNC X 1−1/8

Creating attributes with the ATTDEF command

Attributes can be created on the command line using the **ATTDEF** (attribute definition) command. An attribute has four optional modes. The four modes are described as follows:

- **Invisible.** When on, attributes are not displayed or plotted. By default, attributes are visible.
- **Constant.** This mode assigns a fixed value to an attribute that cannot be changed without redefining the block. It is best to assign **Constant** mode to only those attributes that will not change.
- **Verify.** This mode prompts for verification that the attribute value is correct when you insert the block.
- **Preset.** Similar to **Constant** except that the attribute value can be changed without redefining the block.

Enter I, C, V, or P to specify one or more of the modes. You are then prompted to provide a tag for the attribute. The *tag* is simply an identifier for the attribute and can contain any characters except spaces and exclamation marks. You *must* provide an attribute tag.

Next, you are asked to provide an attribute prompt. This step is omitted if you specified **Constant** mode. The prompt is used to help define the attribute when the block is inserted. Typical prompts include Enter the manufacturer's name: or What is the price? If you do not specify a prompt, the attribute tag is automatically used in its place.

AutoCAD LT then asks for a default attribute value. This is the value that appears with the block on-screen. You do not need to assign a default value. Even if a value is assigned, you can change it as you insert the block. If you specified **Constant** mode, however, you *must* assign a default value.

After specifying one of the four optional modes, assigning a tag, and providing a prompt and a default value, the **ATTDEF** command begins to look like the **TEXT** and **DTEXT** commands. You are prompted for the starting point of the attribute, the text height, and the text rotation. Look at the resistor symbol in Figure 14-18. Four attributes are first defined using middle text justification directly underneath the resistor. Notice that the attribute tags are displayed on-screen until included in a block definition. The resistor and attribute definitions are then made into a single block and inserted into the drawing. When inserted, the tags are replaced with the attribute values entered while inserting. Refer to the illustration as you follow the **ATTDEF** command sequence given below:

```
Command: ATTDEF ↵
Attribute modes - Invisible:N Constant:N Verify:N Preset:N
Enter (ICVP) to change, RETURN when done: ↵
Attribute tag: RESISTOR ↵
Attribute prompt: REFERENCE DESIGNATOR? ↵
Default attribute value: R1 ↵
Justify/Style/⟨Start point⟩: J ↵
Align/Fit/Center/Middle/Right: M ↵
Middle point: (locate a middle point under the resistor)
Height ⟨0.2000⟩: (enter a value or accept the default)
Rotation angle ⟨0⟩: ↵
Command:
```

Figure 14-18.
At the left, attributes tags are displayed underneath a resistor symbol before being included in a block. The attributes and the resistor are made into a block and inserted at the right.

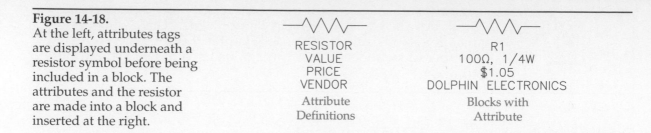

RESISTOR
VALUE
PRICE
VENDOR
Attribute
Definitions

R1
100Ω, 1/4W
$1.05
DOLPHIN ELECTRONICS
Blocks with
Attribute

To create additional attributes, press [Enter] to repeat the command. When you reach the ⟨**Start point**⟩: prompt, note that the previously created attribute appears highlighted on-screen. Simply press [Enter] to place the new attribute tag directly below the previous tag. Using this method, the new tag also inherits the text justification of the previous tag.

Once you have created the necessary attribute definitions, use the **BLOCK** or **WBLOCK** command, as described earlier in this chapter. Be sure to include the attributes in the selection set when you create the block.

Creating attributes with a dialog box

Attributes can also be created using the **Attribute Definition** dialog box, Figure 14-19. To access this dialog box, select **Define Attribute...** from the **Construct** pull-down menu. See Figure 14-20. You can also enter the following on the command line:

Command: *(type* DDATTDEF *or* DAD *and press* [Enter]*)*

Figure 14-19.
The **Attribute Definition** dialog box.

Attribute Definition

Mode
☐ Invisible
☐ Constant
☐ Verify
☐ Preset

Select a mode

Attribute
Tag: RESISTOR
Prompt: REFERENCE DESIGNATOR?
Value: R1

Enter the attributes

Insertion Point
Pick Point <
X: 0.0000
Y: 0.0000
Z: 0.0000

Define an insertion point

Text Options
Justification: Left
Text Style: STANDARD
Height < 0.2000
Rotation < 0

Select the text options

☐ Align below previous attribute

OK   Cancel   Help...

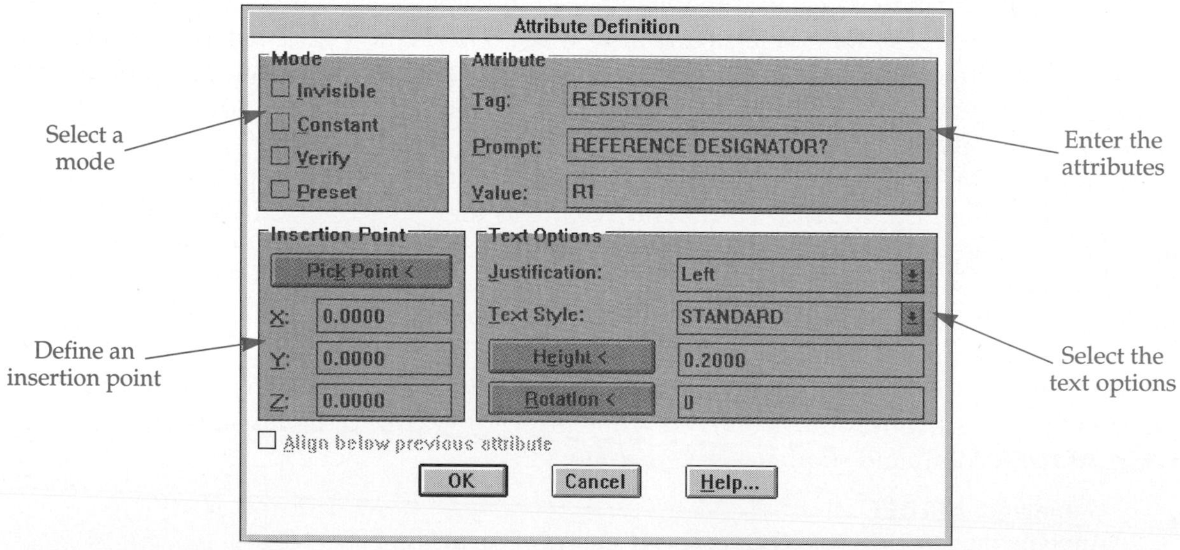

Figure 14-20.
Selecting **Define Attribute...** from the **Construct** pull-down menu issues the **DDATTDEF** command.

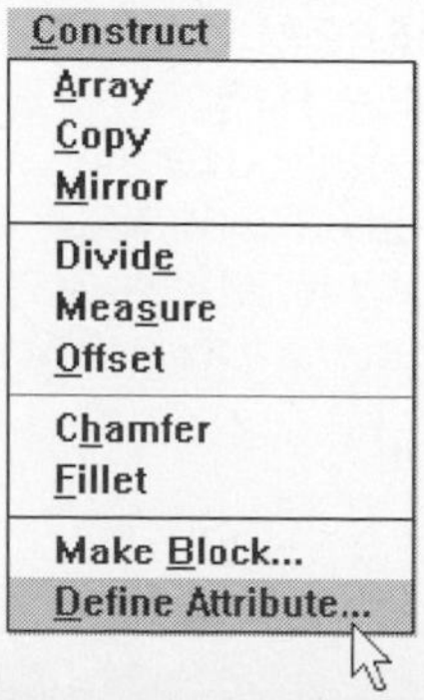

Construct
Array
Copy
Mirror

Divide
Measure
Offset

Chamfer
Fillet

Make Block...
Define Attribute...

If you wish to enable one or more of the four optional modes, activate the appropriate check box in the **Mode** area at the upper left of the dialog box. Use the text boxes in the **Attribute** area at the upper right to enter the attribute tag, prompt, and default value. Each of the text boxes can contain up to 256 characters. Remember that entering a default value is strictly optional unless you have activated the **Constant** check box. Also, the **Prompt:** text box is not available if you select **Constant** mode.

The **Text Options** section allows you to set the attribute justification, height, rotation, and text style. Use the **Justification:** drop-down list to specify the desired text justification for your attribute. Enter the attribute text height and rotation in the appropriate text boxes at the lower right. However, if you click either the **Height** ⟨ or **Rotation** ⟨ buttons, the **Attribute Definition** dialog box disappears and you are prompted for height and rotation values on the command line. If more than one text style is defined in the drawing, it can be selected from the **Text Style:** drop-down list.

The **X:**, **Y:**, and **Z:** text boxes in the **Insertion Point** area at the lower left can be used to specify the origin of the attribute. However, it is much easier to use the **Pick Point** ⟨ button for this. When you click this button, the **Attribute Definition** dialog box disappears and you are prompted for the text start point on the command line. Pick an origin point on the screen as desired. The **Attribute Definition** dialog box then reappears, and the XYZ coordinates of the screen origin you selected are displayed in the appropriate text boxes.

When you are finished entering all necessary information in the **Attribute Definition** dialog box, click the **OK** button. The dialog box disappears and the attribute tag appears at the origin you specified.

If you wish to define another attribute, press [Enter] to repeat the command. Then, enter all necessary information as required in the appropriate sections. If you want to place the new attribute directly underneath the previous attribute using the same text justification, activate the **Align below previous attribute** check box at the lower left of the **Attribute Definition** dialog box. As with the **ATTDEF** command, once you have created the necessary attribute definitions, create a block making sure that the attributes are included in the selection set.

PROFESSIONAL TIP

When attribute definitions are selected using a window or crossing selection set, the prompts are answered in a random order as the block is inserted. If you prefer to be prompted in a specific order, select the attribute definitions in the same order as you wish to be prompted when you create the block.

EDITING ATTRIBUTE DEFINITIONS

ALTUG 14

You may need to change certain aspects of attribute text before it is included in a block or wblock. The **CHANGE** command can be used to change the attribute text insertion point, text style, height, and rotation angle of selected attribute definitions. This is similar to editing normal text. The **CHANGE** command also allows you to revise the attribute tag, prompt, and default value (if initially provided). The syntax and options appear as shown on the following page.

Command: *(type* CHANGE *or* CH *and press* [Enter])
Select objects: *(select the attribute definition to change)*
Select objects: *(press* [Enter] *to close the selection set)*
Properties/⟨Change point⟩: *(press* [Enter])
Enter text insertion point: *(pick a new insertion point or press* [Enter])
Text style: STANDARD
New style or RETURN for no change: *(enter an existing style name or press* [Enter])
New height ⟨0.2000⟩: *(enter a new height or press* [Enter])
New rotation angle ⟨0⟩: *(enter a new angle or press* [Enter])
New tag ⟨RESISTOR⟩: *(provide a new tag or press* [Enter])
New prompt ⟨REFERENCE DESIGNATOR?⟩: *(enter a new prompt or press* [Enter])
New default value ⟨R1⟩: *(provide a new default value or press* [Enter])

If you only want to change the tag, prompt, or default value assigned to a text attribute, you can do so quickly using the **Edit Attribute Definition** dialog box. See Figure 14-21. Unlike the **CHANGE** command however, this dialog only allows you to change one attribute definition at a time. To access this dialog box, click the **Edit Text** button in the toolbox or select **Edit Text...** from the **Modify** pull-down menu. See Figure 14-22. You can also enter the following on the command line:

Command: *(type* DDEDIT *or* ED *or* TE *and press* [Enter])
⟨Select a TEXT or ATTDEF object⟩/Undo: *(select one attribute definition to change)*

Revise the tag, prompt, or default value in the corresponding text box. If necessary, refer to Chapter 9 to review the editing techniques available in this type of dialog box. When you are done making changes, click the **OK** button and the dialog box is closed. The **DDEDIT** prompt remains on the command line if you want to select another entity or undo the changes you made. If you are finished, press [Enter] to end the command.

Figure 14-21.
An attribute's tag, prompt, and default value can be edited in the **Edit Attribute Definition** dialog box

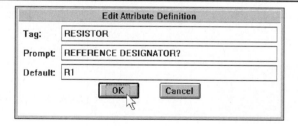

Figure 14-22.
Select **Edit Text...** from the **Modify** pull-down menu to issue the **DDEDIT** command.

Editing attribute definitions in a dialog box

The **Modify Attribute Definition** dialog box provides expanded editing capabilities for text attributes. See Figure 14-23. To activate this dialog box, click the **Modify Entity** button or select **Modify Entity...** from the **Modify** pull-down menu. See Figure 14-24. The **Modify Entity** button does not appear in the toolbox or toolbar by default. You can also enter the following at the **Command:** prompt:

Command: **DDMODIFY** ⏎

You can change the color, linetype, layer, or thickness properties of the selected attribute in the **Properties** section at the top of the dialog box. Just below the **Properties** section are the **Tag:**, **Prompt:**, and **Default:** text boxes. These text boxes provide the same functions as the **DDEDIT** command. You can change the origin of the text attribute by selecting the **Pick Point** ⟨ button and picking a new point on the screen, or entering new X, Y, or Z coordinates in the appropriate text boxes. You will also note the options to change the text height, rotation angle, width factor, and obliquing angle. Clicking the arrow to the right of the **Justify:** box activates a drop-down list where you can select a new text justification. To change the

Figure 14-23.
Every aspect of an attribute definition can be changed in the **Modify Attribute Definition** dialog box.

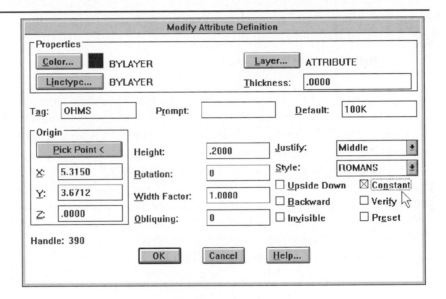

Figure 14-24.
Selecting **Modify Entity...** from the **Modify** pull-down menu issues the **DDMODIFY** command.

attribute's text style, click the arrow to the right of the **Style:** box. If another text style is defined in the current drawing, it appears in this drop-down list. Click the **Upside Down** or **Backward** check box if you want one of these conditions applied to your text attribute.

Perhaps the most powerful feature of the **Modify Attribute Definition** dialog box is the ability to change the attribute modes originally defined for a text attribute. You may recall from the discussion of the **ATTDEF** and **DDATTDEF** commands earlier in this chapter that an attribute can be defined with **Invisible**, **Constant**, **Verify**, or **Preset** modes. Remember that the **Constant** mode assumes that the values of an attribute will remain unchanged. Therefore, no prompt is defined for the attribute and no prompt is presented when the attribute is inserted. The example shown in Figure 14-23 illustrates this restriction. Since the **Constant** box is checked, no prompt appears in the **Prompt:** text box. To revise the attribute definition for normal prompting, deactivate the **Constant** check box and enter a prompt in the **Prompt:** text box. If you want to toggle the **Verify** or **Preset** modes, or change an attribute from visible to invisible, click the appropriate check box.

INSERTING BLOCKS WITH ATTRIBUTES ALTUG 14

Normally, attribute prompts are answered on the command line as a block is inserted. To accept the default attribute value, simply press [Enter] or provide a new value as required. However, you can answer attribute prompts using a dialog box if the **ATTDIA** (attribute dialog) system variable is turned on as follows:

Command: **ATTDIA** ↵
New value for ATTDIA ⟨0⟩: **1** ↵

After entering the block name, scale, and rotation angle using the **INSERT** or **DDINSERT** commands, the **Enter Attributes** dialog box appears on-screen. As shown in Figure 14-25, this dialog box can list up to ten attributes at one time. If a block has more than ten attributes, click the **Next** button to display additional attributes.

Responding to attribute prompts in a dialog box has distinct advantages over answering the prompts on the command line. With the dialog box, you can see at a glance whether all the attribute values are correct. It is therefore not necessary to use the **Verify** mode. If you decide to change a value, simply move to the incorrect value and enter a new one. You can quickly navigate forward through the attribute values and buttons in this dialog box by using the [Tab] key. Using the [Shift]+[Tab] key combination cycles through the attribute values and buttons in reverse order. When you are finished, click **OK** to close the dialog box. The inserted block with attributes then appears on-screen.

Figure 14-25.
Attribute values can be changed during a block insertion using the **Enter Attributes** dialog box.

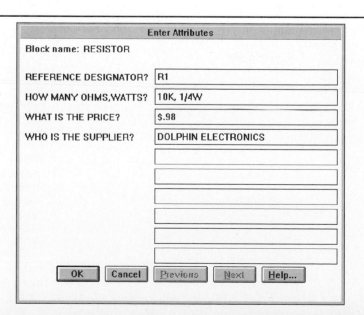

Set the value of **ATTDIA** to 1 in your prototype drawing to automatically activate the **Enter Attributes** dialog box whenever you insert a block with attributes.

CONTROLLING THE DISPLAY OF ATTRIBUTES

ALTUG 14

All attributes are displayed on screen unless they are defined as invisible. You can control attribute visibility using the **ATTDISP** system variable as follows:

Command: *(type* ATTDISP *or* AT *and press* [Enter]*)*
Normal/ON/OFF ⟨Normal⟩: *(select an option)*

Turning **ATTDISP** on displays all attributes, even those that are defined as invisible. Turning **ATTDISP** off removes the display of all attributes. The **NORMAL** option returns the display of attributes as originally defined. Keep in mind that **ATTDISP** is a global variable and controls the display of all attributes defined in the drawing.

EXERCISE 14-4

❏ Open EX14-1.
❏ Insert the RESISTOR block in the drawing using the **INSERT** or **DDINSERT** commands. Explode the block as it is inserted. The insertion point is not important.
❏ Use **ATTDEF** or **DDATTDEF** to create four attributes with the values given below. You can use **Center** or **Middle** text justification for the attributes.

Mode	Tag	Prompt	Value
(none)	RESISTER	Reference designator?	R1
(none)	VALUES	How many Ohms, Watts?	10K, 1/4W
Invisible & Verify	PRICE	What is the price?	$.98
Invisible	SUPPLIER	Who is the supplier?	Dolphin Electronics

❏ Make a new block using the same name (RESISTOR) and the same insertion base point. Be sure to include the attribute definitions in the selection set.
❏ Next, insert the block several times into the drawing. Enter different values for the attributes if you like. You will be prompted twice for the price because **Verify** mode is being used. Both the price and supplier attributes should not appear on screen if **Invisible** mode was set properly.
❏ Turn **ATTDIA** on and insert the resistor one more time. Use the dialog box to change the attribute values.
❏ Use **ATTDISP** to display all attributes. Next, turn off the display of the attributes. Finally, restore the display of attributes to their original definitions.
❏ Save the drawing as EX14-4.

RESISTOR
VALUES
PRICE
SUPPLIER

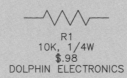

R1
10K, 1/4W
$.98
DOLPHIN ELECTRONICS

As mentioned earlier, you can freely edit attribute definitions with the **CHANGE**, **DDEDIT**, or **DDMODIFY** commands before they are included in a block. Once the block is created, however, the attributes are part of it and must be changed using the **DDATTE** or **ATTEDIT** commands. The **DDATTE** (dynamic dialog attribute editing) command is used to edit attribute text values only. The **ATTEDIT** (attribute editing) command can be used to change both attribute text and attribute properties. These properties include attribute position, height, angle, style, layer, and color.

The DDATTE command

The **DDATTE** command allows you to edit attribute text values using the **Edit Attributes** dialog box. See Figure 14-26. Select **Edit Attribute...** from the **Modify** pull-down menu. See Figure 14-27. You can also enter the following on the command line:

Command: *(type* DDATTE *or* DE *and press* [Enter]*)*
Select block: *(pick a block with attributes)*

Each of the attribute values of the selected block then appears in the dialog box. To make a change, simply move to the value you wish to edit and enter a new one. Remember that you can quickly move through the attribute text values by using the [Tab] key. When you are finished editing the attributes, click **OK** to close the dialog box. The edited block attributes are then displayed on-screen.

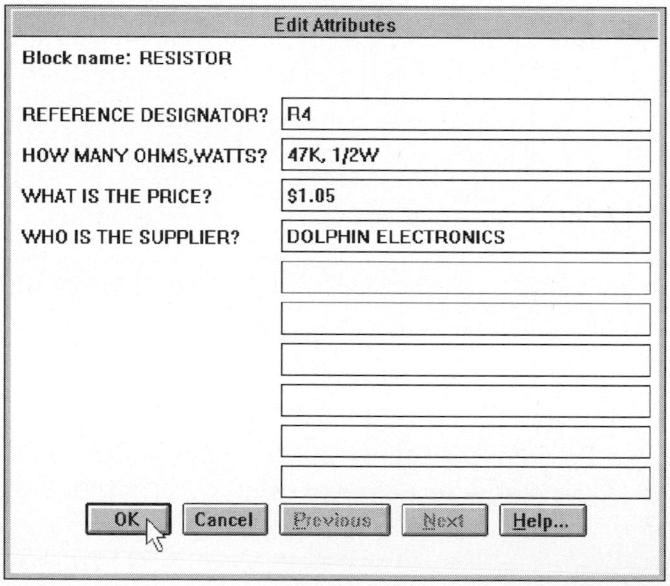

Figure 14-26.
Attribute values can be edited using the **Edit Attributes** dialog box.

Edit Attributes
Block name: RESISTOR
REFERENCE DESIGNATOR?   R4
HOW MANY OHMS,WATTS?   47K, 1/2W
WHAT IS THE PRICE? $1.05
WHO IS THE SUPPLIER?   DOLPHIN ELECTRONICS
OK   Cancel   Previous   Next   Help...

Figure 14-27.
Selecting **Edit Attribute...**
from the **Modify** pull-down
menu issues the **DDATTE**
command.

The ATTEDIT command

The **ATTEDIT** command allows you to edit attribute text values as well as properties. Attributes can be edited one at a time or globally. Attributes must be visible to be edited one at a time, so use the **ATTDISP** command if necessary. However, this restriction does not apply to global editing. The **ATTEDIT** command displays the following prompts:

> Command: *(type* ATTEDIT *or* AE *and press* [Enter]*)*
> Edit attributes one at a time? ⟨Y⟩ *(answer* Y *or* N*)*
> Block name specification ⟨*⟩: ↵
> Attribute tag specification ⟨*⟩: ↵
> Attribute value specification ⟨*⟩: ↵

If you answer N, a global edit of text values is performed. Global editing, however, limits you to replacing one text string with another. Answering Y allows you to edit the attribute properties one at a time. You can choose to restrict the attribute selection to block name, tag, or value specifications. It is usually faster to simply press [Enter] at the prompts as shown above.

Global attribute editing

To obtain a clearer understanding of global editing, refer to the resistors illustrated in Figure 14-28. In this example, the supplier is changed from Dolphin Electronics to Parker Supply on all three resistors. The procedure to change all three attributes in one operation is as follows:

> Command: *(type* ATTEDIT *or* AE *and press* [Enter]*)*
> Edit attributes one at a time? ⟨Y⟩ **N** ↵
> Global edit of attribute values.
> Edit only attributes visible on screen? ⟨Y⟩ ↵
> Block name specification ⟨*⟩: ↵
> Attribute tag specification ⟨*⟩: ↵
> Attribute value specification ⟨*⟩: ↵
> Select Attributes: *(pick* DOLPHIN ELECTRONICS *on all three resistors and press* [Enter]*)*
> 3 attributes selected.
> String to change: **DOLPHIN ELECTRONICS** ↵
> New string: **PARKER SUPPLY** ↵
> Command:

Figure 14-28.
Global editing is used to change the same attribute value on multiple block insertions.

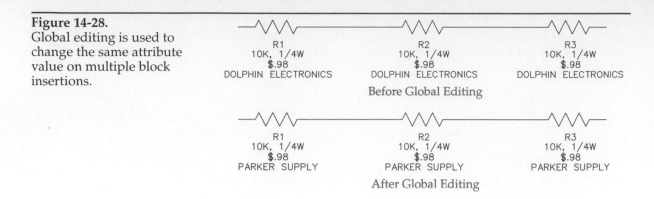

Before Global Editing

After Global Editing

Attributes do not need to be displayed when performing global editing. As an example, if you answer N to the **Edit only attributes visible on screen?** prompt shown on the previous page, the graphics window automatically flips to the text window, and you are not prompted to select attributes. You are, however, asked for the text string to change and the new text string. Be careful using this method since every occurrence of the old text string, visible or invisible, changes to the new text string you enter.

PROFESSIONAL TIP

Attribute text strings are case-sensitive. This means that they recognize both uppercase and lowercase letters. Therefore, it is a good idea to turn on **ATTDISP** so that you can verify and enter attribute values exactly as they appear on-screen.

Editing attributes one at a time

Individual attribute editing allows you to change a variety of properties for a selected attribute. The properties you can change include value, position, height, angle, style, layer, and color. When you perform individual editing, the first attribute encountered in the selection set is marked with a small "X". After changing the first attribute, press [Enter] for **Next** and the "X" moves to the next attribute it encounters in the selection set.

For example, look at the resistor shown on the left in Figure 14-29. The resistor was inserted with a 270° rotation angle. The attributes must be rotated to 0° so that they can be read horizontally. The attributes also require a new text position. The **Angle** and **Position** options are used to make the necessary changes as follows:

    Command: (type ATTEDIT or AE and press [Enter])
    Edit attributes one at a time? ⟨Y⟩ ↵
    Block name specification ⟨*⟩: ↵
    Attribute tag specification ⟨*⟩: ↵
    Attribute value specification ⟨*⟩: ↵
    Select Attributes: (pick both resistor attributes and press [Enter])
    2 attributes selected.

Figure 14-29.
Individual attribute editing is used to change attribute properties such as text angle and position.

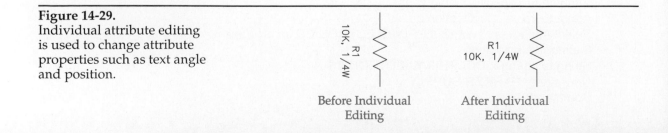

Before Individual Editing

After Individual Editing

AutoCAD LT—Fundamentals and Applications

An "X" appears on the first attribute selected.

> Value/Position/Height/Angle/Style/Layer/Color/Next ⟨N⟩: **A** ↵
> New rotation angle ⟨270⟩: **0** ↵
> Value/Position/Height/Angle/Style/Layer/Color/Next ⟨N⟩: **P** ↵
> Enter text insertion point: *(move the text string as required)*
> Value/Position/Height/Angle/Style/Layer/Color/Next ⟨N⟩: ↵

The "X" moves to the next attribute in the selection set. The identical operations are now performed for the remaining attribute.

> Value/Position/Height/Angle/Style/Layer/Color/Next ⟨N⟩: **A** ↵
> New rotation angle ⟨270⟩: **0** ↵
> Value/Position/Height/Angle/Style/Layer/Color/Next ⟨N⟩: **P** ↵
> Enter text insertion point: *(move the text string as required)*
> Value/Position/Height/Angle/Style/Layer/Color/Next ⟨N⟩: ↵
> Command:

Because there are no other attributes in the selection set, pressing [Enter] for **Next** automatically terminates the command. The edited attributes are shown on the right in Figure 14-29.

NOTE   The **ATTEDIT** command displays the following error message if you attempt to edit an inserted block attribute with a **Constant** mode setting:

> 0 attributes selected. *Invalid*

The inserted block must then be exploded and redefined as described earlier in this chapter. An error message is also displayed if you attempt to change attribute values using a different letter case (upper or lower) than originally assigned.

EXERCISE 14-5

❏ Open EX14-4 and erase all block entities on-screen.
❏ Draw the partial schematic diagram shown by inserting the RESISTOR block three times into the drawing. Resistors R1 and R2 are to be rotated 270° as they are inserted. Accept the default attribute values.
❏ Edit the attribute text values to match those shown using the **DDATTE** command.
❏ Change the angle and position attribute properties for resistors R1 and R2 using the **ATTEDIT** command.
❏ Save the drawing as EX14-5.

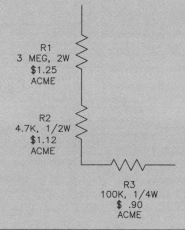

---

you have answered the prompts and clicked the **OK** button, the title block appears on-screen with each field of information completely filled out, Figure 14-33. You are now ready to begin drawing construction. Should you need to change any of the information later on, such as the completion date of the drawing, you can do so quickly and easily with the **DDATTE** command. If the position or text height of an attribute requires revision, use the **ATTEDIT** command.

Figure 14-33.
The title block after insertion. When the drawing is complete, dates and checker information can be conveniently added with the **DDATTE** command.

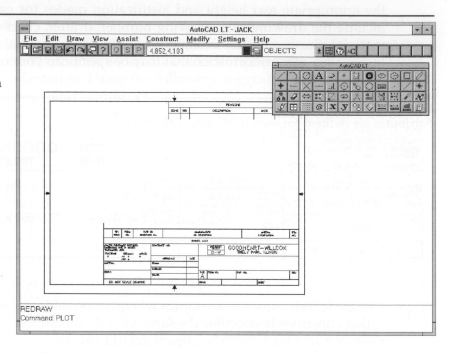

NOTE The FCSM (Federal Supply Code for Manufacturers) is a five-digit numerical code identifier applicable to any organization that produces items used by the federal government. It also applies to government activities that control design, or are responsible for the development of certain specifications, drawings, or standards that control the design of items.

Attributes and revision blocks

It is almost certain that a detail drawing will require revision at some time in the life cycle of a product. Typical changes that occur include design improvements or the correction of drafting errors. The first time that a drawing is revised, it is usually assigned the revision letter A. If necessary, revision letters continue with B through Z. However, the letters I, O, and Q are not used because they might be confused with numbers.

Title block sheet formats include an area called the *revision block* especially designated to record all drawing changes. This area is normally located at the upper-right corner of the title block sheet. The revision block provides space for the revision letter, description of the change, date, and approvals. Zones appear in the margins of a title block sheet and are indicated by alphabetical and numerical entries. They are used for reference purposes much the same way as reference letters and numbers are used to identify a street or feature on a road map. Although A and B size title blocks may include zones, they are rarely needed for these smaller formats.

Block attributes provide an easy way of completing the necessary information in a revision block. Refer to Figure 14-34 as you follow the guidelines below.

- First, create a revision block on the appropriate drawing layer(s).

Figure 14-34.
A revision block with attributes and insertion point.

- Define attributes on a separate layer that describe the zone (optional), revision letter, description of change, and change approval.
- Use left-justified text for the change description attribute, and middle-justified text for the remainder.
- Use the **WBLOCK** command to save the revision block on disk with a descriptive name like REVBLK. Use the upper-left endpoint of the revision block as the insertion point.

After a drawing has been revised, simply insert the revision block at the correct location into the edited drawing. If **ATTDIA** is set to 1, you can answer the attribute prompts in the **Enter Attributes** dialog box. After providing the change information, Click the **OK** button and the completed revision block is automatically added to the title block sheet, Figure 14-35.

Figure 14-35.
The revision block after insertion.

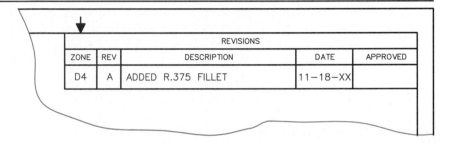

Attributes and parts lists

Assembly drawings require a parts list, or list of materials, that includes the quantity, FCSM code (optional), part number, description, and item number for each component of the assembly or sub-assembly. In some organizations, the parts list is generated as a separate document, usually in an 8-1/2″ × 11″ format. In other companies, the parts list is included on the assembly drawing. Whether as a separate document, or as part of the assembly drawing itself, parts lists provide another example of how attributes can be used to automate the documentation process.

Refer once again to the title block in Figure 14-30. You will observe a section specifically designated for a parts list located just above the title block area. Now, refer to the example in Figure 14-36 as you follow the guidelines below.

- First, create a parts list block in the appropriate drawing layer(s).
- Define attributes on a separate layer that describe the quantity, FSCM number (optional), part number, item description, material specification, and item number for the components of an assembly drawing.

Figure 14-36.
Attributes and an insertion point are defined for a parts list block.

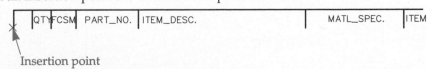

- Use left-justified text for the item description attribute, and middle-justified text for the remainder.
- Use the **WBLOCK** command to save the parts list block on disk with a descriptive name like PL for parts list or BOM for Bill of Materials. Use the lower-left endpoint of the parts list block as the insertion point.

After an assembly drawing has been completed, simply insert the parts list block at the correct location on the drawing. If the system variable **ATTDIA** is set to 1, you can answer the attribute prompts in the **Enter Attributes** dialog box. After providing the parts list information, click the **OK** button and the completed parts list block is automatically added to the title block sheet, Figure 14-37. Repeat the procedure as many times as required for each component of the assembly drawing.

Figure 14-37.
The parts list block after insertion.

1		52451	PLATE, MOUNTING	6061–T6 ALUM	1
QTY REQD	FSCM NO.	PART OR IDENTIFYING NO.	NOMENCLATURE OR DESCRIPTION	MATERIAL SPECIFICATION	ITEM NO.

PARTS LIST

ATTRIBUTE EXTRACTION

ALTUG 14

Attribute information can be taken from a drawing to create a separate text, or *extract*, file that can serve as a parts list or bill of materials. Extract files can be created in several different formats to be used with spreadsheet, database, or other CAD programs.

Before you can extract attribute data from a drawing, you must first create a template file using an ASCII text editor, like the Windows **Notepad**. Once the template file is created with a text editor, the extract file is created using AutoCAD LT.

Creating a template file

The template file is used to tell AutoCAD LT what type of attribute data to extract from the drawing. It contains information about the attribute tag name, block name, insertion point coordinates, data type (character or numeric), field length, and the number of decimal places associated with the information you wish to extract.

To obtain a clearer understanding of the structure required for a template file, refer to Figure 14-38. The template file starts at the left with a field name of any length. The data in the second column begins with a C or an N to indicate whether it is character or numeric data. The next three characters represent the total field width including a decimal point and decimal values. The last three characters represent the number of decimal places for numeric data. Notice in Figure 14-38 that the price data does not begin with an N for numeric as you might think. This is because the price information for this particular attribute begins with a "$" symbol and the symbol is character data.

Figure 14-38.
Interpreting a sample template file.

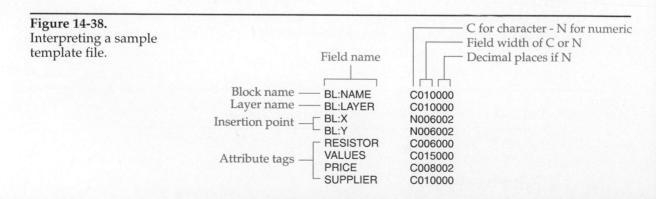

NOTE	See Chapter 14 of the *AutoCAD LT User's Guide* for a complete listing of acceptable field names and their respective formats. Also, you can use a tab between fields if you are using Notepad to create a template file. Other types of text editors, such as MS-DOS EDIT, require that you use a space between fields.

EXERCISE 14-6

❏ In this exercise, you will construct a template file for the drawing EX14-5. Use Windows Notepad to create the file.
❏ Open EX14-5.DWG if it is not already on your screen.
❏ Use the [Alt]+[Esc] key combination to activate Program Manager.
❏ Open the Accessories group window and double-click the Notepad icon to launch Notepad.
❏ Begin entering the following text at the text insertion point (flashing vertical cursor) located at the top left of the Notepad window. With Notepad, you can place either a tab or spaces between the columns:

```
BL:NAME      C010000
BL:LAYER     C010000
RESISTOR     C006000
VALUES       C015000
PRICE        C008002
SUPPLIER     C010000
```

❏ Select Save As... from the File pull-down menu, and save the file with the name EX14-6. Notepad automatically adds a .TXT extension to the filename.
❏ Select Exit from the File pull-down menu to exit Notepad and return to AutoCAD LT.

Attribute extraction using a dialog box

Once the template file is created, you can extract the attribute data. Attribute extraction can be performed using a dialog box with the **DDATTEXT** (dynamic dialog attribute extraction) command. The **DDATTEXT** command can be entered on the command line or issued by first selecting **Import/Export** from the **File** pull-down menu, and then selecting **Attributes Out...** from the cascading submenu.

Command: *(type* DDATTEXT *or* DAX *and press* [Enter]*)*

The **Attribute Extraction** dialog box then appears on-screen, Figure 14-39. Each of the buttons available in this dialog box are described below:

- **Comma Delimited File (CDF).** As shown in Figure 14-40, the CDF format uses a comma to separate the fields for each block record in the extract file. Each character field is enclosed with single quotation marks. Select this option button when you wish to transfer attribute data to an external database program.
- **Space Delimited File (SDF).** The SDF format uses spaces to separate blocks, and does not use commas or quotation marks. See Figure 14-41. This format is easier to read and many spreadsheet programs use this type of file format.
- **Drawing Interchange File (DXF).** The DXF format is used to transfer drawing data between AutoCAD LT and other CAD software programs. This option does not require a template file. The extract file is given the .DXX, not .DXF, file extension. See Chapter 22 for more information about the DXF file format.

Figure 14-39.
The **Attribute Extraction**
dialog box.

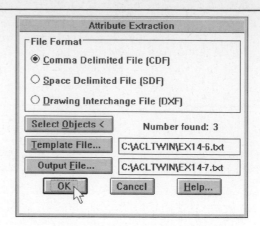

Figure 14-40.
An extract file displayed
in CDF format in the
Windows Notepad.

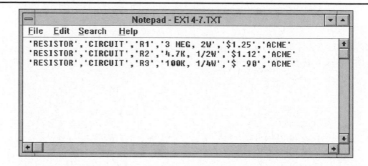

Figure 14-41.
An extract file displayed
in SDF format in the
Windows Notepad.

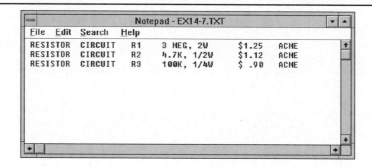

- **Template File....** Once you have specified the desired format for the extract file, click this button to display the **Template File** dialog box, Figure 14-42. Select the template file from the list at the left of the dialog box, or enter filename in **File Name:** text box. Click **OK** when you are finished and the **Attribute Extraction** dialog box is redisplayed.
- **Output File....** Click this button to display the **Output File** dialog box. You must provide a filename. Be sure to enter a different filename than that used for the template file, or the extract file will overwrite the template file. As shown in Figure 14-43, the name EX14-7 is entered in the text box. The file extension .TXT is automatically appended to the filename you provide. Click **OK** when you are finished and the **Attribute Extraction** dialog box is once again displayed.
- **Select Objects ⟨.** You are now ready to select the blocks with attribute data for extraction. When you click this button, the **Attribute Extraction** dialog box disappears and the prompt **Select objects:** appears on the command line. If you want the attribute data to be listed in a specific order in the extract file, be sure to select the blocks in a corresponding sequence. When you are done selecting the blocks with attributes, press [Enter]. The **Attribute Extraction** dialog box reappears and reports the number of blocks found. Click **OK** to exit the dialog box and create the extract file.

Figure 14-42.
The **Template File**
dialog box.

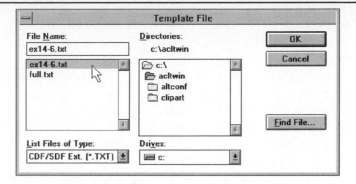

Figure 14-43.
The **Output File**
dialog box.

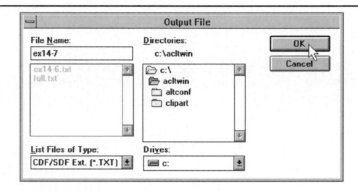

Attribute extraction on the command line

If you do not wish to use the **Attribute Extraction** dialog box, you can perform attribute extraction on the command line as follows:

Command: *(type* ATTEXT *or* AX *and press* [Enter]*)*
CDF, SDF, or DXF Attribute extract (or Entities)? ⟨C⟩: *(select a format option)*

After specifying the desired file format, the **Select Template File** and **Create Extract File** dialog boxes appear, in that order. These are used just as the **Template File** and **Output File** dialog boxes previously described. When complete, **ATTEXT** reports the number of records in the extract file on the command line.

EXERCISE 14-7

❑ Open EX14-5.DWG if it is not still on your screen.
❑ Use **DDATTEXT** and specify the template file that you created in the previous exercise.
❑ Create an extract file called EX14-7 in CDF format. When the extraction is complete, open the file in Notepad. Print the file if you have a printer.
❑ Now create another extract file with the same name, but in SDF format. Open the file in Notepad and print it if you have a printer.

EXTERNAL REFERENCES   ALTUG 14

A drawing that is linked, or attached, to another drawing is called an *external reference*. The drawing that it is attached to is called the master drawing. A referenced drawing is visible within the master drawing and can be plotted, but it *cannot* be modified in any way. This is because the referenced drawing's database is completely separate from the database of the master drawing.

This concept is very different from a block, which becomes part of the database of the drawing it is inserted into. If the original drawing that is inserted is modified, the current drawing must also be modified to reflect the same changes. Additionally, an inserted block or drawing increases the size of the current drawing and more disk space is consumed.

An external reference, on the other hand, is only attached and not permanent. It appears in the master drawing as a single object, like a block, but it cannot be exploded. Also, the size of the master drawing is increased by only a few bytes. These bytes store the name of the external reference and its drive and directory path. Best of all, if the original external reference is modified, the changes are automatically reflected when the master drawing is opened in the AutoCAD LT drawing editor.

To more fully appreciate the value of external references, consider the sheet metal panel drawing in Figure 14-44. The panel is part of a test instrument and a subassembly drawing is required. The assembly drawing is shown in Figure 14-45. Rather than insert the panel into the assembly drawing, the panel drawing is referenced to the new assembly drawing. Thus, the panel appears in the assembly drawing as required, but is not part of the drawing's database. To remove the display of dimensions and centerlines, the appropriate layers are frozen. Next, the rotary switch, fasteners, and BNC connectors are drawn and callouts are added to complete the assembly. The finished assembly drawing takes up far less disk space than if the panel had been inserted into the assembly.

Figure 14-44.
Detail drawing of a sheet metal panel.

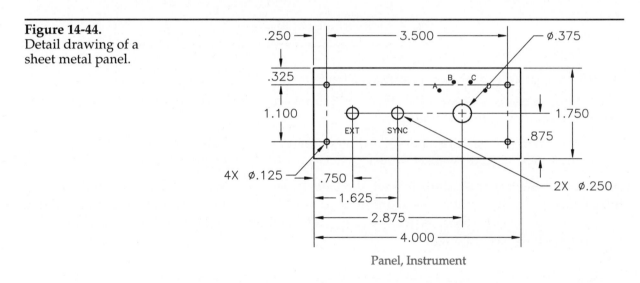

Panel, Instrument

Figure 14-45.
The panel drawing is externally referenced to the assembly drawing.

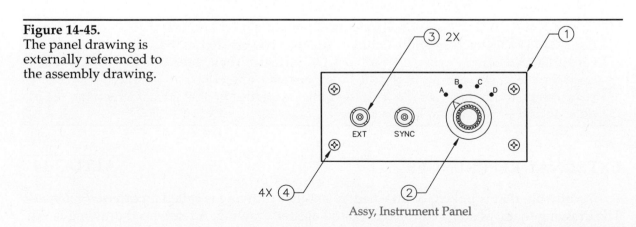

Assy, Instrument Panel

Now consider the following scenario. Later in the life cycle of the product, it is decided to add rounded corners to the panel to protect the user's fingers from injury. Fillets are applied to the object as shown in Figure 14-46. The very next time that the assembly drawing is opened, AutoCAD LT automatically reloads the external reference and the assembly drawing is updated to show the filleted edges, Figure 14-47. Automatic updating such as this can never occur when a drawing is inserted rather than referenced.

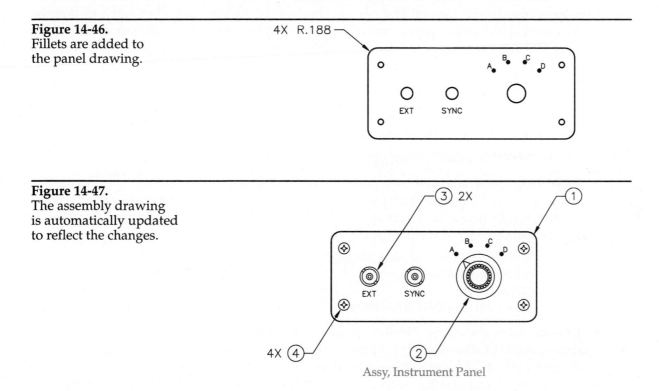

Figure 14-46.
Fillets are added to
the panel drawing.

Figure 14-47.
The assembly drawing
is automatically updated
to reflect the changes.

Assy, Instrument Panel

The XREF command

External references are called *xrefs* for short. As described below, they are linked and managed using the **XREF** command and its options:

> Command: *(type* XREF *or* XR *and press* [Enter]*)*
> ?/Bind/Detach/Path/Reload/⟨Attach⟩: *(select an option or press* [Enter]*)*

- ⟨**Attach**⟩. Press [Enter] to accept the default **Attach** option when you wish to link an external reference to your drawing. Although many external references can be linked to a master drawing, only one can be attached at a time. In the following example, the instrument panel is being referenced. If you enter a tilde (~) at the **Xref to Attach:** prompt, the **Select File to Attach** dialog box is displayed. See Figure 14-48. Select a file from the file list at the left of the dialog box, or enter the desired filename in the **File Name:** text box and click the **OK** button. After providing the filename, the command sequence starts to look like the **INSERT** command.

> Xref to Attach: **PANEL** ↵
> Attach XREF PANEL: panel
> PANEL loaded:
> Insertion point: *(locate the insertion point)*
> X scale factor ⟨1⟩/Corner/XYZ: *(enter the X scale factor or select an option)*
> Y scale factor (default=X): *(enter a different Y scale factor or accept the default)*
> Rotation angle ⟨0⟩: *(enter a rotation angle or press* [Enter]*)*
> Command:

- **?.** The **?** option lists the xref name, path, and the total number of xrefs attached to the current drawing in the AutoCAD LT text window. The following prompt is displayed:

  Xref(s) to list ⟨*⟩: *(enter a name or press* [Enter]*)*

- **Bind.** Use this option to permanently bind one or more external references to the master drawing. A bound xref becomes a block entity and must be exploded before it can be modified. Any dependent objects (blocks, layers, linetypes, text styles, and dimension styles) in the former xref become part of the master drawing and can then be accessed. The bound dependent objects are also renamed to avoid possible naming conflicts with other named objects in the master drawing. The naming convention used by AutoCAD LT is described later. The following prompt is displayed:

  Xref(s) to bind: *(enter one or more names separated by commas, and press* [Enter]*)*

- **Detach.** Use the **Detach** option to remove one or more external references from the master drawing. The following prompt is displayed:

  Xref(s) to Detach: *(enter one or more names separated by commas and press* [Enter]*)*

- **Path.** This option displays and edits the path name associated with a specified external reference. This option is used if you move an xref to a different drive and/or directory. It is also used if you rename an external reference. In the following example, a new path is entered for the PANEL xref:

  Edit path for which Xref(s): **PANEL** ↵
  Xref name: PANEL
  Old path: panel
  New path: **D:\PARTS\PANEL** ↵

- **Reload.** Xrefs are automatically reloaded each time the master drawing is opened in the AutoCAD LT drawing editor. However, you can force a reload at any time using the **Reload** option. This option is particularly useful if you are working in a networked environment and another individual is currently editing a drawing that appears as an external reference in your drawing. As soon as the changes are completed and saved to the network server by the other person, use the **Reload** option to reload the modified xref. The following prompt is displayed:

  Xref(s) to reload: *(enter one or more names separated by commas and press* [Enter]*)*

Selecting the XREF command options from a pull-down menu

If you prefer, each of the **XREF** command options can be selected from a cascading submenu by first selecting **External Reference** from the **Draw** pull-down menu. Then, select **Attach...** from the cascading submenu to display the **Select File to Attach** dialog box shown in Figure 14-48.

Figure 14-48.
The **Select File to Attach** dialog box.

Select a file —

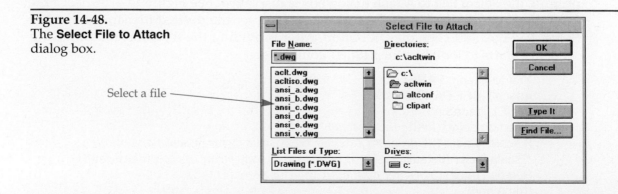

Naming conventions for referenced objects

When dependent objects such as blocks, layers, linetypes, text styles, and dimension styles are referenced to a master drawing, they are automatically renamed by AutoCAD LT. The object names are preceded by the name of the external reference. The xref name and the object name are separated by the pipe character (¦). This convention is used to avoid possible naming conflicts with other identically named objects in the master drawing. In Figure 14-49, you can see how the layers from an external reference appear in the **Layer Control** dialog box. The AutoCAD LT naming convention avoids conflict between the DIMS layer in the master drawing and the PANEL¦DIMS layer from the external reference.

Figure 14-49.
Layers from an external reference are preceded by the xref name. Xref layers are shown here highlighted in the **Layer Control** dialog box.

Externally referenced layers

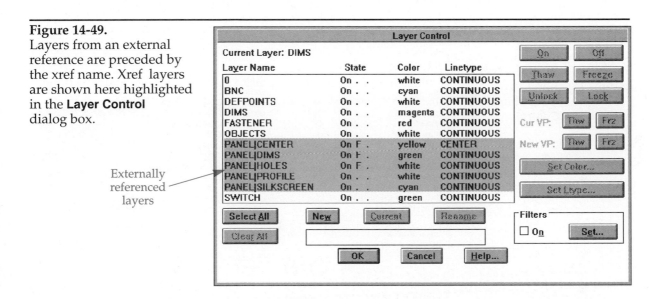

The **Bind** option of the **XREF** command permanently binds an external reference to the master drawing. All dependent objects in the former xref then become part of the master drawing. Until named objects from the xref are bound, they are not available for use in the master drawing.

Binding dependent objects individually

There may be occasions when you wish to bind only some of the named objects from an xref to the master drawing. This is accomplished using the **XBIND** command. In the example that follows, two layers from the referenced drawing are bound to the master drawing. The procedure is shown below:

```
Command: (type XBIND or XB and press [Enter])
Block/Dimstyle/LAyer/LType/Style: LA ↵
Dependent Layer name(s): PANEL¦CENTER,PANEL¦DIMS ↵
Scanning...
2 Layer(s) bound.
Command:
```

The dependent objects are automatically renamed by AutoCAD LT. As shown in Figure 14-50, the PANEL¦CENTER and PANEL¦DIMS layers become PANEL0CENTER and PANEL0DIMS, respectively. Once a named object like a layer is bound, it becomes part of the master drawing and you can do with it as you please.

If you prefer to bind dependent objects using a pull-down menu, you can do so by selecting **External Reference** and then **Bind Symbols** from the **Draw** pull-down menu. Then, select the appropriate object type from the cascading submenu.

Controlling the visibility of layers in xrefs—the VISRETAIN variable

Notice in Figure 14-49 that the layers PANEL¦CENTER, PANEL¦DIMS, and PANEL¦HOLES are frozen (F). When you wish to change the color, linetype, on/off, or freeze/thaw status of layers from an external reference, turn the system variable **VISRETAIN** (visibility retain) on as follows:

```
Command: VISRETAIN ↵
New value for VISRETAIN ⟨0⟩: 1 ↵
```

When set to the default of 0 (off), the layer status in the xref drawing takes precedence over the following master drawing settings for xref-dependent layers: color, linetype, on/off, and freeze/thaw.

Figure 14-50.
Named objects, such as layers, are renamed when bound. Two bound layers are shown here highlighted in the **Layer Control** dialog box.

Bound layers

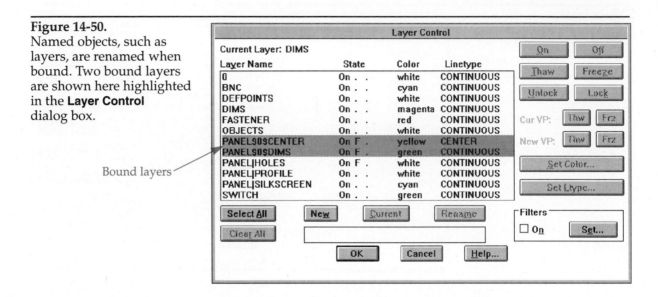

When set to 1 (on), color, linetype, on/off, and freeze/thaw settings for xref-dependent layers in the master drawing take precedence over the layer status in the xref drawing. This makes sure that any changes made to the status of xref-dependent layers in the master drawing are retained when the xref is reloaded. To increase your drawing efficiency, **VISRETAIN** should be turned on in your prototype drawing(s).

Creating an xref log file—the XREFCTL variable

AutoCAD LT can keep a record of **Attach**, **Detach**, and **Reload** operations for each drawing that contains external references. The record is in ASCII text format and is called a *log file*. A log file has the same name as the current drawing with an .XLG file extension. By default, **XREFCTL** is off and log files are not created. To have AutoCAD LT create log files, set the **XREFCTL** variable as follows:

```
Command: XREFCTL ↵
New value for XREFCTL ⟨0⟩: 1 ↵
```

The current status of the **XREFCTL** variable is stored in the ACLT.CFG file. Therefore, it is saved for each drawing session until changed.

CHAPTER TEST

Write your answers in the spaces provided.

1. What is the maximum number of characters permitted for a block name? _____

2. Identify the command that uses a dialog box to create a block. In which pull-down menu is it located? _____

3. A block is created on layer 0. What happens to it when inserted on another layer? _____
   _____

4. What is an anonymous block? Provide two examples. _____

5. Why is it helpful to create a block to fit inside a one unit square?_____
   _____

6. You are saving a block to disk. What should you enter when the filename and the block name are identical? _____

7. When using the **WBLOCK** command to compress a drawing file, what should you enter when prompted for the block name? _____

8. The **PURGE** command can be used at any time during a drawing session. (True/False)
   _____

9. Name the command that allows you to insert a block or drawing file using a dialog box. In which pull-down menu is it located? _____

10. What must you do to create a mirrored image of a block as it is inserted? _____
    _____

11. What must be done before a block can be redefined? _____
    _____

12. Identify two ways to explode a block as it is inserted. _____

13. What is the **BASE** command? Why would it be used? _____
    _____

14. Name the two commands that allow you to align a block with an entity. _____

15. What are block attributes? _____

16. What is the difference between the **Constant** and **Preset** modes? _____
    _____

17. Identify the three commands that can be used to edit attributes before they are included within a block. _____

18. Which command allows you to change an attribute definition from **Visible** to **Invisible**?
    _____

19. Name the system variable that permits you to answer attribute prompts using a dialog box. _____

20. How do the **DDATTE** and **ATTEDIT** commands differ? _____
    _____

21. Why would you use global attribute editing? _____
    _____

22. What must you do before extracting attribute information? _____

_____

23. What is CDF format? In what situation is it used? _____

24. Why must you provide a different name for the extract file than the name used by the template file? _____

25. Drawings that use external references take up less disk space than drawings that use inserted blocks. (True/False) _____

26. You have changed the display status of one or more xref layers. Which system variable should be used to store the changes? _____

27. What is the purpose of the **XREF Bind** option? _____

28. Several xrefs have been moved to a new directory on the hard drive. Which **XREF** command option must be used so that AutoCAD LT can locate the files? _____

29. You are working in a networked CAD environment. Another user has just modified and saved a drawing file that appears as an xref in your current drawing. Identify two ways to load the modified xref into your drawing. _____

_____

30. Name the system variable that controls the creation of xref log files. _____

CHAPTER PROBLEMS

1. Open the prototype drawing TITLEA from Problem 4 of Chapter 2. Define attributes for the title block information, revision block, and parts list as described in this chapter. Use the **WBLOCK** command to save the entire drawing to disk using 0,0 as the insertion base point. Repeat the procedure for prototype drawings TITLEB and TITLEC.

2. Draw and dimension the object shown below using the TITLEB prototype drawing. Create the geometric dimensioning and tolerancing symbols as blocks with attributes. Save the drawing as P14-2.

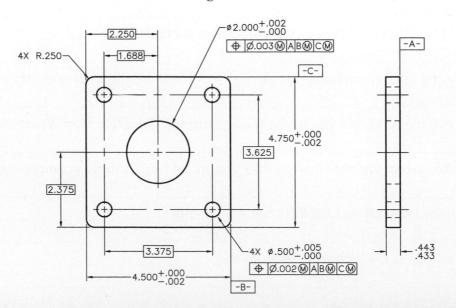

AutoCAD LT—Fundamentals and Applications

3. Draw the electrical diagram of the motor control circuit shown below using the TITLEC prototype drawing. Use blocks with attributes where appropriate. Save the drawing as P14-3.

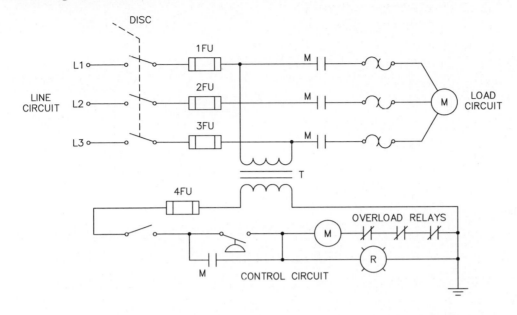

4. Using blocks with attributes, draw the schematic diagram of the plug-in card shown below using the TITLEB prototype drawing. Save the drawing as P14-4.

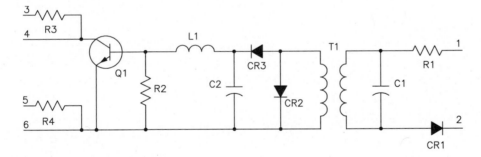

5. Draw the schematic diagram of the fine tuning indicator shown below using the TITLEB prototype drawing. Use the blocks from P14-4 where required. Save the drawing as P14-5.

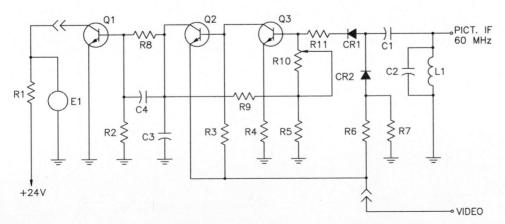

6. Draw the partial logic diagram shown below using the TITLEB prototype drawing. Use previously created blocks wherever appropriate. Save the drawing as P14-6.

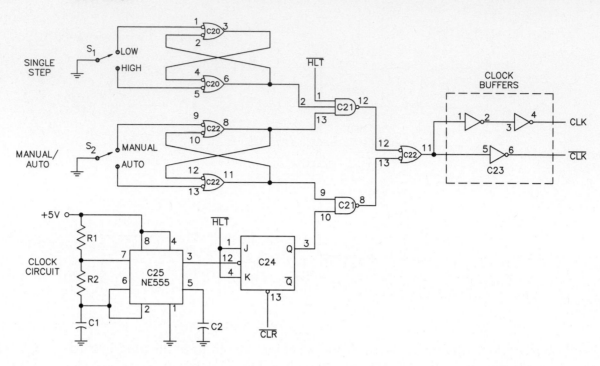

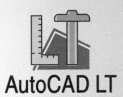

AutoCAD LT

Chapter 15

Isometric Drawing and Dimesioning

Learning objectives:

After you have completed this chapter, you will be able to:
- ○ Assign an isometric snap style and draw isometric objects.
- ○ Define and use isometric text styles.
- ○ Setup an isometric prototype drawing.
- ○ Create isometric dimensions.

Drafting is the science of fully describing three-dimensional objects using two-dimensional views. Such two-dimensional drawings are called *orthogonal*. *Pictorial* drawings use three-dimensional views to describe height, width, and depth.

An *isometric* drawing is a pictorial drawing. An object drawn isometrically has the X, Y, and Z axes spaced 120° apart, with the Z axis projected vertically. Although two-dimensional, an isometric view gives the illusion of three dimensions because several faces appear in one view. For this reason, isometric drawings are often used in technical documentation to help visualize an object. An example of a typical isometric assembly drawing appears in Figure 15-1.

This chapter describes how to draw and how to dimension isometric objects. Additionally, suggestions are provided for creating an isometric prototype drawing.

Figure 15-1.
An isometric drawing of an exploded assembly. Such drawings help to visualize objects.

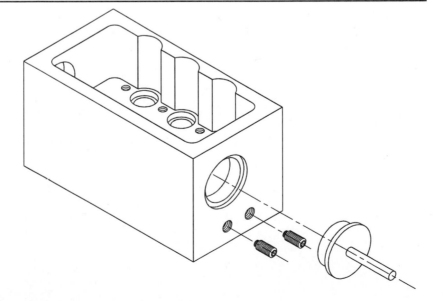

SETTING THE ISOMETRIC SNAP STYLE

When you create orthogonal drawings in AutoCAD LT, the snap style is in the default Standard mode. This mode sets the screen crosshairs in a vertical and horizontal orientation. The Standard mode also ensures that the grid and snap are aligned with the screen crosshairs.

When creating an isometric drawing, the width and depth must be drawn with lines angled 30° from the horizontal plane. All vertical measurement, or height, is drawn using 90° lines. This convention is illustrated in Figure 15-2.

Figure 15-2.
Width and depth are measured on isometric axes drawn 30° from the horizontal plane. Vertical dimensions are drawn using 90° lines.

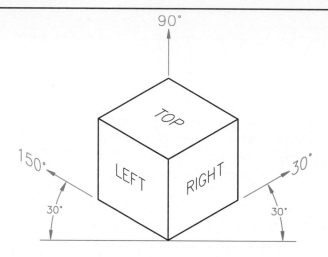

The **SNAP** command is used to toggle the snap style from Standard to Isometric and to align the grid and snap with the isometric axes. The procedure is as follows:

Command: *(type* SNAP *or* SN *and press* [Enter]*)*
Snap spacing or ON/OFF/Rotate/Style ⟨*current*⟩: **S** ↵
Standard/Isometric ⟨S⟩: **I** ↵
Vertical spacing ⟨*current*⟩: **.25** ↵
Command:

The Isometric snap style can also be set using a dialog box by clicking the **Drawing Aids** button in the toolbox or selecting **Drawing Aids...** from the **Settings** pull-down menu. See Figure 15-3. Either action displays the **Drawing Aids** dialog box, shown in Figure 15-4.

Figure 15-3.
To set the Isometric snap style using a dialog box, select **Drawing Aids...** from the **Settings** pull-down menu.

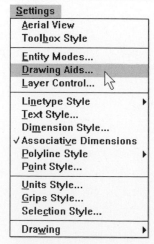

Figure 15-4.
The Isometric snap style is enabled from the **Drawing Aids** dialog box.

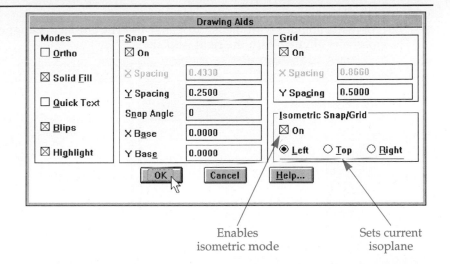

Enables isometric mode

Sets current isoplane

Click the check box labeled **On** at the lower right of the dialog box to enable the Isometric snap style. Set the snap and grid vertical spacing using the **Y Spacing** text boxes. Since horizontal grid and snap spacing is not used in isometric mode, the **X Spacing** text boxes are grayed out and unavailable. The **On** check boxes must be enabled for the snap and grid to be activated.

PROFESSIONAL TIP

Ortho mode is extremely helpful when constructing isometric drawings. If you are using the **Drawing Aids** dialog box to set up isometric mode, be sure to also enable the **Ortho** check box at the top left of the dialog box. It is also quite helpful to have coordinates in the coordinate display box using polar (distance⟨angle⟩ coordinates rather than cartesian (XY) coordinates. Keep in mind, however, that the coordinate display box is available only when you draw lines or other entity types that prompt for more than one point. You may recall from Chapter 3 that the coordinate display box can be toggled on and off, and from cartesian to polar coordinates using the [F6] function key or the [Ctrl]+[D] control key combination. You can also toggle the coordinate display states by simply clicking anywhere inside the box with your mouse. Any one of these methods may be used to cycle through the coordinate dislay states or you can use the COORDS system variable to set the polar coordinates as follows:

Command: **COORDS** ↵
New valuefor COORDS⟨*current*⟩: ↵

The coordinate display box will then switch to polar coordinaes when you perform a drawing command.

Toggling the Cursor Orientation

It is easier to draw an isometric shape if the angles of the crosshairs align with the isometric axes. The isometric cursor positions are called *isoplanes*. The crosshair positions for the three isoplane modes are shown in Figure 15-5.

When the Isometric snap style is first enabled, AutoCAD LT defaults to the left isoplane. You can toggle between the three isoplanes by pressing [F5] or [Ctrl]+[E]. As the isoplane modes are toggled, their states are displayed on the command line for reference as follows:

Command: ⟨Isoplane Left⟩ ⟨Isoplane Top⟩ ⟨Isoplane Right⟩

Figure 15-5.
A—The crosshairs aligned with the left isoplane. B—The crosshairs aligned with the top isoplane.
C—The crosshairs aligned with the right isoplane.

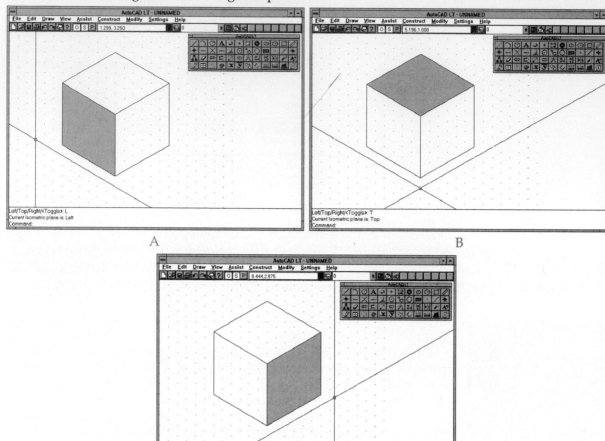

A   B

C

The desired isoplane can also be selected by picking the **Left**, **Top**, or **Right** option buttons in the **Drawing Aids** dialog box.

Another method to toggle the cursor orientation is with the **ISOPLANE** command:

Command: **ISOPLANE** ↵
Left/Top/Right/⟨Toggle⟩: ↵

Press [Enter] to toggle the isoplane to the next position. Rather than repeatedly pressing the [Enter] key, you can specify the desired isoplane by entering the first letter of the isoplane:

Left/Top/Right/⟨Toggle⟩: **T** ↵
Current Isometric plane is: Top

PROFESSIONAL TIP

Although using function key [F5] or the [Ctrl]+[E] key combination is a more efficient means to toggle the isoplane while inside another command, the **ISOPLANE** command can be used transparently to accomplish the same purpose, **'ISOPLANE**.

When the isometric snap style is in effect, the crosshairs are normally in one of the three isoplanes. When a multiple selection set method (such as Window or Crossing) is used, the crosshair orientation reverts to the horizontal and vertical positions. At the completion of the command, the crosshairs automatically resume the isoplane orientation.

EXERCISE 15-1

❑ Begin a new drawing.
❑ Set the grid spacing to .5.
❑ Set the snap style to Isometric and set the vertical spacing to .25.
❑ Draw the object shown using the dimensions given.
❑ Activate **Ortho** mode and change the coordinate display to aid in the construction of the object. Toggle the isoplane orientation as required.
❑ Save the drawing as EX15-1.

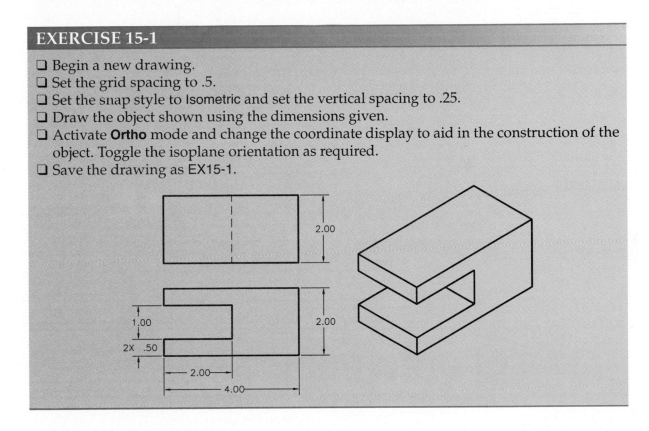

DRAWING ISOCIRCLES

Circles appear as ellipses in isometric mode, as shown in Figure 15-6. A true isometric ellipse is rotated 35°16′ about its major axis. Whenever the Isometric snap style is enabled, AutoCAD LT adds an additional option called **Isocircle** to the **ELLIPSE** command.

An *isocircle* is a true isometric ellipse and can be specified by either its radius or diameter. To create an isocircle, pick the **Ellipse** button in the toolbox or select **Ellipse** from the **Draw** pull-down menu, Figure 15-7.

> Command: *(type* ELLIPSE *or* EL *and press* [Enter])
> 〈Axis endpoint 1〉/Center/Isocircle: **I** ↵
> Center of circle: *(pick a point)*
> 〈Circle radius〉/Diameter: *(enter a radius value or type* D *for diameter)*
> Command:

After locating a center point, the isocircle appears on screen in the current isoplane. Press [F5] or [Ctrl]+[E] to toggle the correct isoplane. Remember, the **Isocircle** option is only available when the Isometric snap style is enabled.

Figure 15-6.
Isometric ellipses are drawn using the **Isocircle** option of the **ELLIPSE** command. Note the orientation of the crosshair cursor.

Figure 15-7.
Select **Ellipse** from the **Draw** pull-down menu to issue the **ELLIPSE** command.

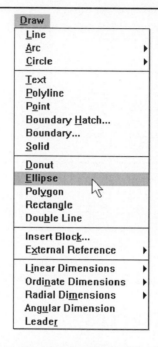

EXERCISE 15-2

❏ Open EX15-1 if it is not still on your screen.
❏ Make the modifications shown using the **Isocircle** option of the **ELLIPSE** command.
❏ Use the **TRIM** command to obtain the fully radiused feature.
❏ Save the drawing as EX15-2.

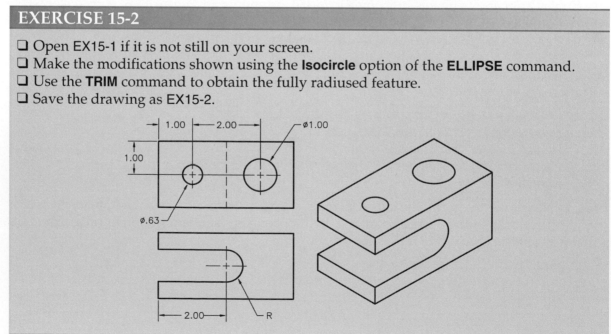

CREATING ISOMETRIC TEXT

The appearance of isometric drawings is improved through the use of isometric text. Before creating isometric text, you must first create two isometric text styles using the **STYLE** command. In the example shown in Figure 15-8, two styles are used to label each isoplane. These styles are named ISOM-F (forward) and ISOM-B (backward).

The ISOM-F style has an obliquing angle of positive 30° so that the text leans forward. The ISOM-B style has a negative 30° obliquing angle so the text leans backward. The obliquing angles of the two styles are shown in comparison with that of the Standard text style. Each style is assigned the roman simplex font (ROMANS.SHX), but any font can be used for isometric text styles.

The isometric text should be aligned with the corresponding isoplane. This is accomplished by using the proper text style and setting the text rotation angle as required. In the examples shown in Figure 15-8, the rotation angle is shown below the text style name for each isoplane and orientation.

To create an isometric text style, do the following:

Command: *(type* STYLE *or* ST *and press* [Enter]*)*
Text style name (or ?) ⟨STANDARD⟩: **ISOM-F** ↵
New style.

Figure 15-8.
Examples of isometric text.

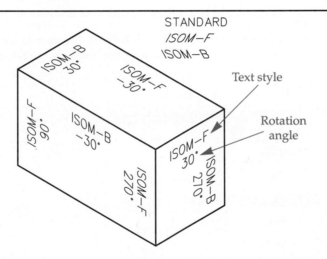

When the **Select Font File** dialog box appears, select ROMANS.SHX (or another font of your choosing) from the font file list and click the **OK** button. Continue with the procedure as follows:

Height ⟨0.0000⟩: ↵
Width factor ⟨1.0000⟩: ↵
Obliquing angle ⟨0⟩: **30** ↵
Backwards? ⟨N⟩ ↵
Upside-down? ⟨N⟩ ↵
Vertical? ⟨N⟩ ↵
ISOM-F is now the current text style.
Command:

Now press [Enter] to repeat the **STYLE** command, and create the ISOM-B text style with a negative (-30°) obliquing angle.

Before creating isometric text, you must set the appropriate style current. If you wish to set the style using a dialog box, click the current color button on the toolbar, or select **Entity Modes...** from the **Settings** pull-down menu, Figure 15-9.

Figure 15-9.
Select **Entity Modes...** from
the **Settings** pull-down
menu to open the **Entity
Creation Modes** dialog box.

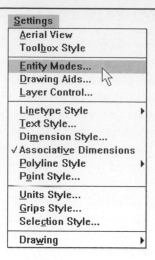

When the **Entity Creation Modes** dialog box appears, click the **Text Style...** button, as shown in Figure 15-10A. You can now select the desired style from the **Select Text Style** subdialog box, shown in Figure 15-10B. Refer to Chapter 9 if you wish to review style and text options.

Figure 15-10.
A—Clicking the **Text Style...** button in the **Entity Creation Modes** dialog box.
B—Setting the ISOM-F style current using the **Select Text Style** subdialog box.

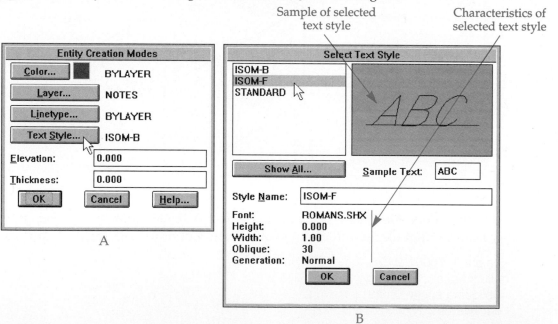

EXERCISE 15-3

❑ Draw an object similar to that shown in Figure 15-8. Use any dimensions you like.
❑ Create two isometric text styles with the Roman simplex font.
❑ Using Figure 15-8 as a guide, add text to all three isoplanes in the correct styles and with the proper rotation angles.
❑ Save the drawing as EX15-3.

ISOMETRIC PROTOTYPE DRAWING (ISOPROTO) TUTORIAL

Because isocircles comprise many small polyarc segments, it is impossible to construct a centerline through them with the dimensioning mode **CENTER** command. This tutorial enables you to create an isometric prototype drawing with isocircles with centerlines generated in each isoplane. Each isocircle is defined with a diameter of 1 unit. They are saved as individual blocks, which remain in the isometric prototype drawing. Whenever an isocircle with a centerline is required, the appropriate block can be inserted and scaled to the required diameter. This tutorial also:

- Provides you with more practice in defining text styles and creating and inserting block entities.
- Demonstrates how blocks can be utilized to streamline otherwise mundane drafting tasks.
- Illustrates the global changes made to linetypes by the **LTSCALE** system variable.

The ISOPROTO tutorial begins as follows:

▷ Start a new drawing using your PROTOA prototype drawing, Figure 15-11.

Figure 15-11.
Click the **Prototype** button and select PROTOA.DWG as your prototype drawing.

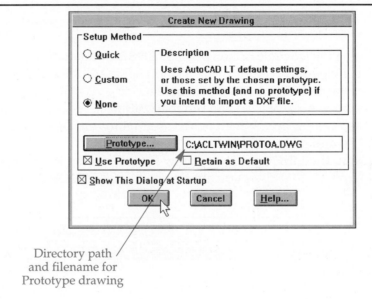

Directory path and filename for Prototype drawing

▷ Make sure that the OBJECTS layer is set current. (If you have not yet created a prototype drawing with the necessary layers and linetypes, first complete Exercise 5-4 from Chapter 5 before continuing with this procedure.)
▷ Set the grid spacing to .25.
▷ Set the snap style to Isometric and vertical snap spacing to .25.
▷ With **Ortho** mode on, and toggling the proper isoplanes, draw a 1.50 isometric cube using the **LINE** command.
▷ Toggle **Ortho** off and use the **COPY** command to copy the cube. Place the copy to the right of the original cube. Perform a **ZOOM Extents** and then a **ZOOM Scale(X)** at .8X. Your screen should appear similar to that shown in Figure 15-12.

Figure 15-12.
Two isometric cubes appear side by side.

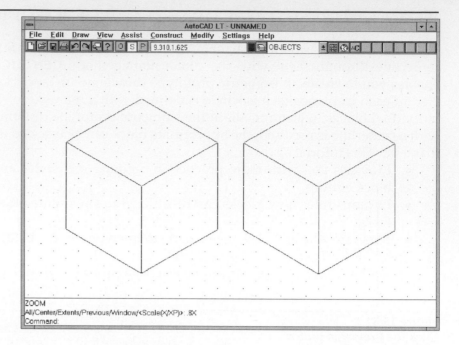

⇨ Using the **Isocircle** option of the **ELLIPSE** command, place a .5 radius (one unit diameter) isocircle in the center of each isoplane on the left cube, as shown in Figure 15-13.

⇨ Set the CENTERLINES layer current.

⇨ Set a running object snap mode to MIDpoint. (This can be set using the **Running Object Snap** dialog box, which is accessed using the **DDOSNAP** command.) Toggle the grid ([F7]) and snap ([F9]) off.

⇨ Using the **LINE** command, draw lines bisecting the surfaces of the cube, as shown in Figure 15-14. When you are finished, set the OBJECTS layer current again.

Figure 15-13.
Three one unit diameter isocircles are added to the cube surfaces.

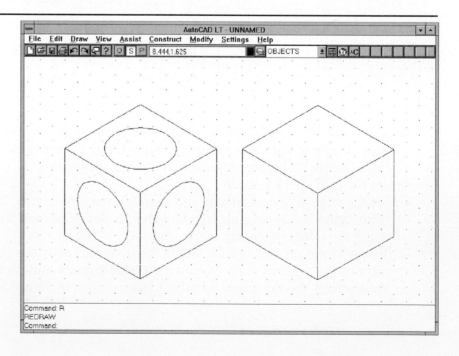

AutoCAD LT—Fundamentals and Applications

Figure 15-14.
Centerlines are constructed by connecting the midpoints of the sides of the cube.

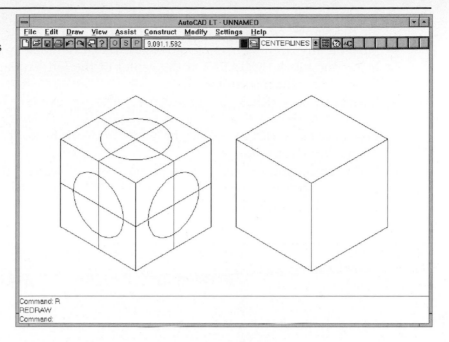

> Erase the left cube, leaving the isocircles and the centerlines.
> With the **BLOCK** command, block the left isoplane isocircle and centerline. Use a crossing box. For the insertion point, use intersection osnap and select the intersection of the centerlines. See Figure 15-15. Name the block HOLELEFT.

Figure 15-15.
Selecting the intersection of the centerlines as the insertion base point for the block.

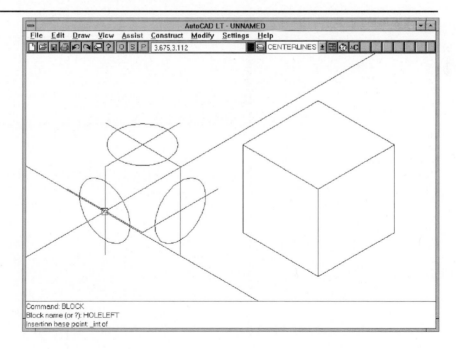

‍⬎ Repeat the block procedure for the top and right isocircles. It is not necessary to toggle the isoplanes. Name the blocks HOLETOP and HOLERGHT, respectively.

‍⬎ Turn off any running osnaps and toggle the grid and snap back on.

‍⬎ Insert the block HOLELEFT at the center of the left isoplane on the remaining cube. Enter .75 for the insertion scale.

‍⬎ Insert the block HOLETOP at the center of the top isoplane on the cube. Enter .5 for the insertion scale.

‍⬎ Insert the block HOLERGHT at the center of the right isoplane on the cube. Enter 1.125 for the insertion scale.

‍⬎ Look carefully at the centerlines of the inserted blocks, Figure 15-16. Set **LTSCALE** to .625 and observe the results. Now, set **LTSCALE** to .375 and once again note the changes, Figure 15-17.

Figure 15-16.
The inserted blocks with **LTSCALE** = 1.

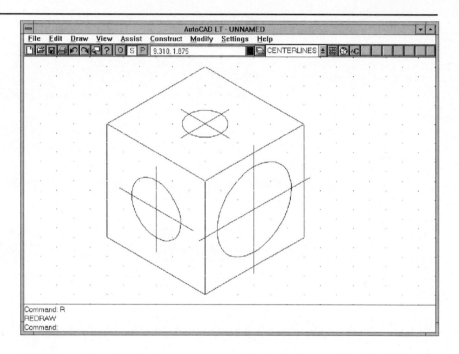

Figure 15-17.
The blocks as they appear with **LTSCALE** = .375.

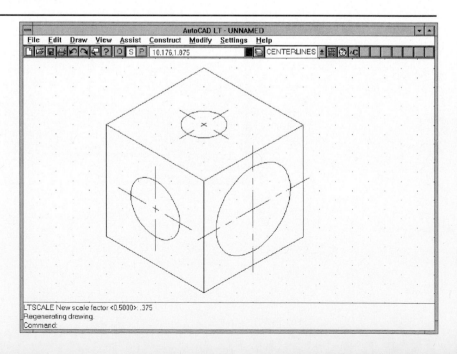

- ✑ Experiment with inserted blocks with varying scales and different **LTSCALE** values.
- ✑ When you are through experimenting, erase all displayed geometry.
- ✑ Create two isometric text styles as described earlier in this chapter. Assign the font of your choice to the styles.
- ✑ Make any dimension and system variable changes appropriate to your application. Also, add or rename drawing layers as desired.
- ✑ Finally, use the **SAVEAS** command to save the prototype drawing with the name ISOPROTO.
- ✑ Use your isometric prototype drawing whenever an isometric drawing is required. Remember that ISOPROTO can also be inserted into another drawing when needed. When prompted for the insertion point, cancel the command with [CTRL]+[C]. The isocircle blocks, isometric text styles, and the layers defined in ISOPROTO then become part of the current drawing. This insertion method is described more fully in Chapter 14.

PROFESSIONAL TIP   It is not necessary to create three separate isocircle blocks. As a quicker alternative, a single isocircle block can be rotated into the other isoplanes when it is inserted.

EXERCISE 15-4

❑ Open your TITLEA prototype drawing from the Chapter 14 drawing problems.
❑ Insert ISOPROTO into your title block. Cancel when prompted for an insertion point. Save the revised TITLEA prototype drawing.
❑ Repeat the procedure for your TITLEB and TITLEC prototype drawings.

CREATING ISOMETRIC DIMENSIONS

AutoCAD LT does not automatically create isometric dimensions. However, it is still possible to perform isometric dimensioning by editing linear dimensions.

The first step in creating an isometric dimension is to select the correct isometric text style. As an example, consider the object shown in Figure 15-18A. Two aligned dimensions and one vertical dimension have been applied to this object. The table below shows the type of linear dimension and dimension text style used for the dimensions in the illustration.

Dimension	Dimension Type	Text Style	Obliquing Angle	Rotation Angle
2.5	Aligned	ISOM-F	90°	30°
1.5	Vertical	ISOM-F	30°	30°
1.75	Aligned	ISOM-B	30°	30°

Figure 15-18.
A—Linear dimensions are applied to the object using the proper isometric text styles.
B—The **OBLIQUE** command is used to modify the angle of the extension lines.
C—The dimension text is rotated into the correct orientation using the **TROTATE** command.

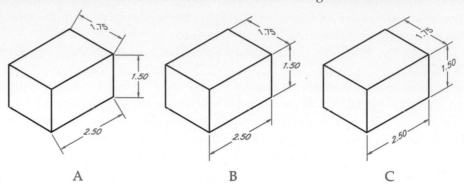

A   B   C

After creating the dimensions, an obliquing angle is applied to the extension lines. You may recall from Chapter 11 that the **OBLIQUE** command is used to change the extension line angles for existing associative dimensions. Issue the **OBLIQUE** command by selecting **Edit Dimension** from the **Modify** pull-down menu. Then select **Oblique Dimension** from the cascading submenu, Figure 15-19. Also, you can enter the following at the **Command:** prompt:

Command: *(type DIM or D and press [Enter])*
Dim: *(type OBLIQUE or OB and press [Enter])*
Select objects: *(select the 2.50 dimension)*
Select objects: ⏎
Enter obliquing angle (RETURN for none): **90** ⏎
Dim:

Figure 15-19.
The **OBLIQUE** command can be issued by first selecting **Edit Dimension** from the **Modify** pull-down menu, and then selecting **Oblique Dimension** from the cascading submenu. The **Rotate Text** menu item issues the **TROTATE** command.

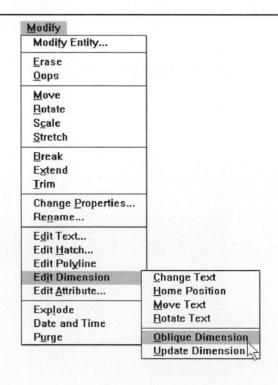

2. [...]
[...]

The **OBLIQUE** command is repeated and a 30° obliquing angle is applied to the two remaining dimensions. The results are shown in Figure 15-18B.

The final step is text rotation. The **TROTATE** dimensioning command rotates dimension text within the dimension line. Select **Rotate Text** from the **Edit Dimension** cascading submenu or enter the following at the **Dim:** prompt:

> Dim: *(type* TROTATE *or* TR *and press* [Enter]*)*
> Enter text angle: **30** ↵
> Select objects: *(select all three dimensions)*
> Select objects: ↵
> Dim:

The dimensions appear as shown in Figure 15-18C.

PROFESSIONAL TIP Applying text styles to isometric text can be confusing. Use Figure 15-8 as a reference when you create isometric text and dimensions.

EXERCISE 15-5

3. [...]

❑ Begin a new drawing using your ISOPROTO prototype drawing.
❑ Draw the object shown in Figure 15-18 on the OBJECTS layer.
❑ Set the DIMS layer current and apply dimensions as described in the preceding text.
❑ Save the drawing as EX15-5.

CHAPTER TEST

Write your answers in the spaces provided.

1. Identify the command and option to enable isometric mode. _____

    _____

2. Name the system variable that controls the state of coordinates in the coordinate display box. _____

    _____

3. What is an *isoplane*? _____

    _____

4. Identify two methods to toggle the current isoplane. _____

    _____

5. The current isoplane can be changed transparently. (True/False)_____

The TILEMODE system variable

The **TILEMODE** system variable must be set to zero (OFF) to enter paper space and create floating viewports. When **TILEMODE** is set to 1, its default setting, you are limited to model space. You can turn the **TILEMODE** variable on and off by selecting **Tile Mode** from the **View** pull-down menu, Figure 16-1. When a check mark appears next to this menu item, Tile Mode is enabled and model space is active. Tile Mode can also be turned on and off from the command line as follows:

```
Command: TILEMODE ↵
New value for TILEMODE ⟨1⟩: 0 ↵
Entering Paper space. Use MVIEW to insert Model space viewports.
```

Once paper space is entered, any model space entities disappear until you create a floating viewport. Floating viewports are created using the **MVIEW** command, which is described in a later section of this chapter.

Figure 16-1.
The **TILEMODE** system variable can be turned on and off by selecting **Tile Mode** from the **View** pull-down menu. A—The check mark indicates that Tile Mode is on and model space is enabled. B—Paper Space is active when no check mark appears next to the menu item.

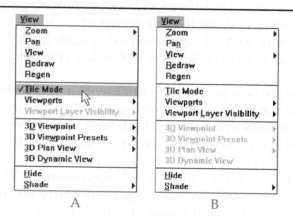

A   B

Displaying the UCS icon

Although the UCS icon is not displayed by default, it is helpful to turn the icon on when working in paper space. The icon serves as a reminder that you are working in paper space. It is activated using the **UCSICON** command:

```
Command: (type UCSICON or UI and press [Enter])
ON/OFF/All/Noorigin/ORigin ⟨OFF⟩: ON ↵
```

The **UCSICON** command can also be issued by selecting **UCS Icon** from the **Assist** pull-down menu.

When paper space is active, the model space icon, Figure 16-2A, is replaced with an icon that resembles a 30°-60° drafting triangle, Figure 16-2B.

Figure 16-2.
The UCS icon.
A—Model space activated.
B—Paper space activated.

UCS Icon
(Model space)   UCS Icon
(Paper space)

Using the Paper Space button

Once paper space is entered, the **Paper Space** button is activated, as shown in Figure 16-3. This button serves as a reminder that you are working in paper space.

After paper space is enabled and you have created a floating viewport, the **Paper Space** button can be used to toggle between paper space and model space. The equivalent commands are **PSPACE** (or **PS**) and **MSPACE** (or **MS**). If you attempt to return to model space without having at least one floating viewport on and active, AutoCAD LT displays the following error message:

> There are no active Model space viewports.

If you receive this message, simply create a viewport in paper space and then repeat the **MSPACE** command. You can return to model space without creating any floating viewports by turning Tile Mode back on.

Figure 16-3.
Once paper space is enabled, the **Paper Space** button on the toolbar can be used to toggle between paper space and model space. Observe that the UCS icon has been displayed using the **UCSICON** command.

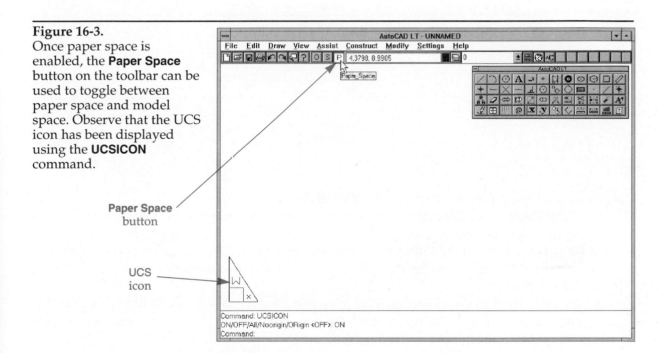

Paper Space button

UCS icon

NOTE   The ability to switch between model space and paper space using the **Paper Space** button or the **MSPACE** and **PSPACE** commands is only possible when Tile Mode is off.

The **MVIEW** (make viewport) command creates viewports in paper space. **MVIEW** is also used to turn the contents of the viewports on and off, and to perform hidden-line removal operations when plotting. Select **Viewports** from the **View** pull-down menu to start the **MVIEW** command, Figure 16-4, or enter the following at the **Command:** prompt:

    Command: **MVIEW** ↵
    ON/OFF/Hideplot/Fit/2/3/4/Restore/⟨First Point⟩: *(select an option)*

Figure 16-4.
Selecting **Viewports** from the **View** pull-down menu displays the **MVIEW** command options in a cascading submenu.

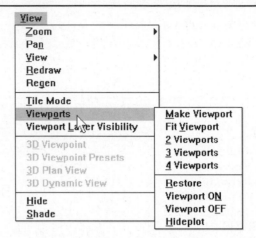

There are several options available in the **MVIEW** command:
- ⟨**First Point**⟩. The default **MVIEW** option prompts for two points that define the diagonal corners of a new floating viewport. Once the first point is specified, AutoCAD LT displays a box cursor to help you size the viewport. The viewport corners can also be specified with coordinates. The new viewport becomes the current, or active, viewport.
- **ON/OFF.** By default, newly created viewports are visible (ON). When a viewport is edited (moved or resized), its contents are regenerated. You can avoid waiting for viewports to regenerate by turning them OFF. You can also use the **OFF** option to control which viewports appear on the finished plot. The **MAXACTVP** (maximum active viewports) system variable is used to control the number of viewports that can be visible at one time. The maximum number is 16. If you turn on more than the allowable number of active viewports, the viewport will be marked ON, but its contents will not be visible until you turn another viewport off.
- **Hideplot.** This option removes hidden lines from 3D models when plotting in paper space. You are prompted to turn **Hideplot** ON or OFF and to select one or more viewports. The hidden line removal appears on the plotted output only—not the display screen. For more information on 3D models and hidden line displays, see Chapter 18 of this text.
- **Fit.** The **Fit** option creates a floating viewport that completely fills the current paper space screen display.
- **2/3/4.** These options permit you to choose two, three, or four floating viewports. After selecting the desired number and specifying how they are to be arranged, you are prompted

        Fit/⟨First point⟩:

If **Fit** is selected, the viewports are scaled to completely fill the current paper space screen display. You can also use the ⟨**First point**⟩ option to locate two points that define the diagonal corners of the screen area to fill with the new viewports.

- **2**—This option creates a horizontal or vertical (default) division between the viewports for the paper space screen area you specify.
- **3**—Divides the specified paper space screen area into three viewports with the following options:

  Horizontal/Vertical/Above/Below/Left/⟨Right⟩:

  The dominant viewport can be placed to the right (default), to the left, above, or below the other two viewports.
- **4**—Divides the specified paper space screen area into four equally sized viewports.

- **Restore.** Model space viewport configurations can be saved using the **VPORTS** command. The **Restore** option is used to translate the viewports from model space to paper space. You are prompted as follows:

  ?/Name of window configuration to insert ⟨*ACTIVE⟩:

Enter the name of a previously saved viewport configuration or use the **?** option to list all saved configurations. (If you press [Enter], the currently displayed view will be placed into a floating viewport.) If a configuration has already been restored, its name will appear as the default configuration. As with the other viewport options, you are presented with the **Fit/⟨First Point⟩:** prompt after entering the viewport name.

PROFESSIONAL TIP

A floating viewport is automatically created if you use the **Custom** setup option to begin a new drawing. The **Custom** option can also be used to insert a title block or border, as well as a date and time stamp. Refer to Chapter 2 to review drawing setup options.

Working in floating viewports

Once you have created a floating viewport, you must switch from paper space to model space to work within it. Only one floating viewport can be active at a time. The active viewport contains the crosshairs and is surrounded by a wide border. The cursor appears as an arrow in the other viewports.

The viewports are interactive; a drawing or editing command can be started in one viewport and completed in another. An inactive viewport can be made current by picking anywhere within its border with your left mouse button. You can also toggle between active and inactive viewports with [Ctrl]+[V].

NOTE

Because floating viewports can only be created in paper space, the following message appears if model space is active when the **MVIEW** command is used.

** Command not allowed unless TILEMODE is set to 0 **

EXERCISE 16-1

❑ Begin a new drawing using the **Custom** setup method.
❑ Click the **Title Block...** button in the **Custom Drawing Setup** subdialog box to display the **Title Block** subdialog box.
❑ Select **ANSI A (in)** from the list and click **OK**. Click **OK** once more to exit the **Custom Drawing Setup** dialog box.
❑ Move your cursor around the display screen. Observe that the cursor is confined within the floating viewport. Display the UCS icon using the **UCSICON** command.

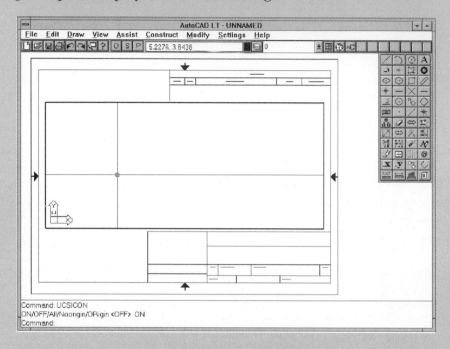

❑ Use the **PSPACE (PS)** command or pick the **Paper Space** button on the toolbar to activate paper space. Once again, display the UCS icon using the **UCSICON** command.
❑ Toggle back and forth between paper space and model space using the **Paper Space** button or the **MSPACE** and **PSPACE** commands.
❑ With model space active, try drawing a line outside of the floating viewport. What happens? Why?
❑ Save the drawing as EX16-1.

Zooming and scaling in floating viewports   ALTUG 15

Whether you are drawing microelectronic components or a shopping mall, the drawings that you create are *always* constructed at full scale. As you detail and dimension an object in a floating viewport, you can freely zoom and pan within the viewport using familiar display control commands.

When the contents of a viewport are to be dimensioned and plotted at 1:1, leave the dimension variable **DIMSCALE** at its default setting of 1 and then **ZOOM 1XP** to scale the view relative to paper space. The **XP** option of the **ZOOM** command scales the model space within a viewport relative to paper space; thus **XP** means "times paper space." To zoom the model space display relative to paper space, append an "XP" to the scale factor, as shown in the following example:

Command: *(type* ZOOM *or* Z *and press* [Enter]*)*
All/Center/Extents/Previous/Window/⟨Scale(X/XP)⟩: **.5XP** ↵

There will be instances when your drawings will be plotted at 10:1, quarter-scale, or some other scale factor. If the drawing is to be plotted at 10:1, zoom the viewport to 10XP and set **DIMSCALE**=.1. At quarter-scale, the viewport would be zoomed to .25XP and **DIMSCALE** set equal to 4. For an architectural drawing that is to be plotted at 1/4"=1', set **DIMSCALE** to 48 and zoom the viewport at 1/48XP.

Remember that drawings are always created at full scale. The viewport zoom magnification is scaled relative to paper space. Typical mechanical and architectural floating viewport scales are provided in the table below.

4=1	ZOOM 4XP
2=1	ZOOM 2XP
1=2	ZOOM .5XP
1"=2.54mm	ZOOM .3937XP
2.54mm=1"	ZOOM 2.54XP
3"=1'	ZOOM 1/4XP
3/4"=1'	ZOOM 1/16XP
1/2"=1'	ZOOM 1/24XP
3/8"=1'	ZOOM 1/32XP
1/4"=1'	ZOOM 1/48XP
1/8"=1'	ZOOM 1/96XP

You can even plot a drawing so that identical views in different viewports are scaled differently. This is useful when a detail view is to appear on the face of the drawing at a different scale.

You can verify the zoom scale factor for a floating viewport with the **LIST** command. Select the viewport border while in paper space. The text window appears and **LIST** displays the XP scale factor for the selected viewport on the line labeled Scale relative to Paper space:.

NOTE   Regardless of the scale factor set for floating viewports, title blocks used for paper space plotting are *always* inserted at full scale (1:1) and the completed drawing is plotted at full scale. Also, be sure to set your paper space limits to match the size of the paper on which you will plot.

EXERCISE 16-2

❑ Open EX16-1 if it is still not on your screen.
❑ Activate model space and insert any one of your drawing problems or exercises in the floating viewport.
❑ Enter 0,0 as the insertion point and accept the defaults for scale and rotation.
❑ Perform a **ZOOM Extents** on the inserted drawing. Now, zoom the display 1XP. Next, zoom the display .5XP. Experiment with different scale factors.
❑ Return to paper space. Try to erase one or more objects from within the floating viewport. What happens? Why?
❑ Save the drawing as EX16-2.

VIEWPORT-SPECIFIC LAYERS AND
THE VPLAYER COMMAND

You have learned from previous chapters that the **LAYER** command is used to turn layers on and off, and freeze/thaw them. These operations are global in nature and thus affect all displayed viewports. In paper space, it is possible to isolate layers and control their visibility on a *per viewport* basis with the **VPLAYER** (viewport layer) command.

With **VPLAYER**, you can see which layers are visible in a given viewport, freeze or thaw layers in one or more viewports, reset a layer to its default visibility, create a new layer that will be frozen in all viewports, and set the default visibility for layers in viewports yet to be created. As with the **MVIEW** command, the **VPLAYER** functions can only be used when Tile Mode is turned off. If you attempt to use **VPLAYER** when **TILEMODE**=1, the following error message is displayed:

** Command not allowed unless TILEMODE is set to 0 **

If you issue the **VPLAYER** command while in model space, you are temporarily returned to paper space so that you can select the viewports you wish to modify. You can invoke the **VPLAYER** command by selecting **Viewport Layer Visibility** from the **View** pull-down menu, Figure 16-5, or typing the command as follows:

Command: **VPLAYER** ↵
?/Freeze/Thaw/Reset/Newfrz/Vpvisdflt: *(select an option)*

Figure 16-5.
Selecting **Viewport Layer Visibility** from the **View** pull-down menu displays the **VPLAYER** command options in a cascading submenu.

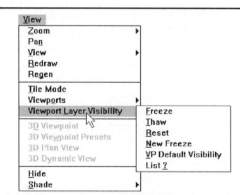

Each of the **VPLAYER** options are described below.
- **?.** This option lists the frozen layers in a viewport. If model space is active when the **?** option is invoked, you are temporarily switched to paper space for viewport selection.
- **Freeze.** You can freeze layers in viewports. After providing the layer name(s), you are prompted to select the viewports in which to freeze the selected layers.
- **Thaw.** This option thaws one or more frozen viewport layers. It will only thaw layers that have been frozen using the **Freeze** option of **VPLAYER** or **DDLMODES**. It will *not* thaw a layer that has been globally frozen with the **LAYER** command. You are prompted to provide the name(s) of the layer you wish to thaw, and to select the viewports in which to thaw them.
- **Reset.** The **Reset** option restores the default visibility setting for viewport layers. See **Vpvisdflt** on next page.
- **Newfrz.** This option permits you to create new layers that are frozen in *all* floating viewports. Whenever a viewport-specific layer is needed, it can be thawed in the appropriate viewport. The layer remains frozen in all other viewports. If a new viewport is added, the layer is frozen in it.

- **Vpvisdflt.** Using the **Freeze** and **Thaw** options of **VPLAYER** only affects *existing* floating viewports. The **Vpvisdflt** option sets the frozen or thawed default status of layers for viewports that are yet to be created. You are prompted for both the layer names and whether the layers should be frozen or thawed in any newly created viewports.

For **VPLAYER** options that request layer names, you can respond with a single name or a list of names, separated by commas. You can also use any of the AutoCAD LT selection set options, such as window or crossing, when prompted to select viewports.

PAPER SPACE TUTORIAL

In the following tutorial, you will lay out a drawing of mechanical details for a caster assembly. You will create five floating viewports using the **MVIEW** command, externally reference a different drawing in each viewport, scale each view with the **XP** option of the **ZOOM** command, and freeze layers with the **VPLAYER** command. The completed drawing appears in Figure 16-6.

Figure 16-6.
The mechanical details for a caster assembly.

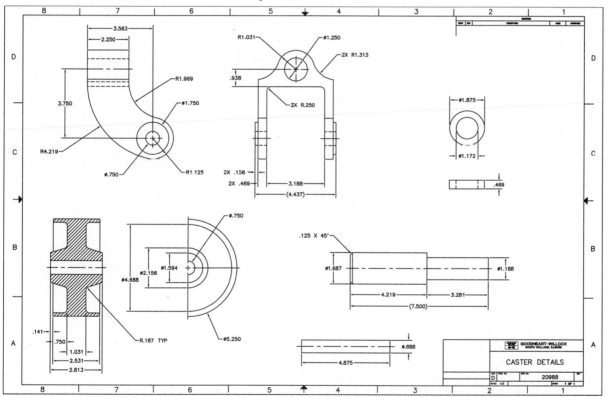

Before beginning this tutorial, draw and dimension the FRAME, WHEEL, SHAFT, COLLAR, and PIN mechanical objects shown in Figures 16-7 through 16-11. Each object is to be created as a separate drawing using the proper layers and an appropriately sized prototype drawing. Do not use title blocks for the drawings.

Figure 16-7.
The caster frame—FRAME.DWG

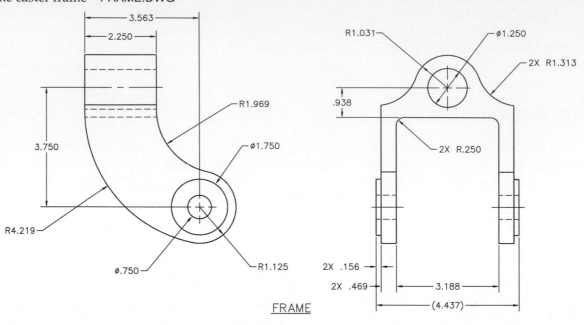

FRAME

Figure 16-8.
The caster wheel—
WHEEL.DWG

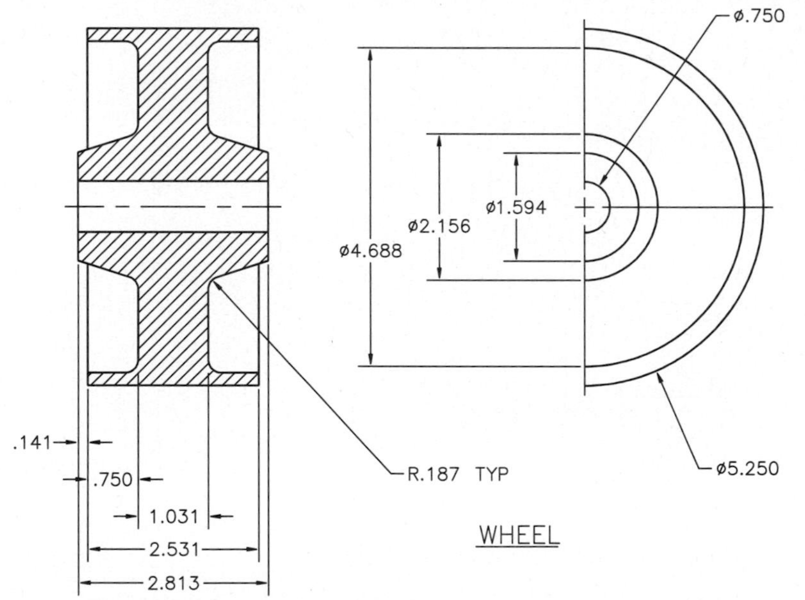

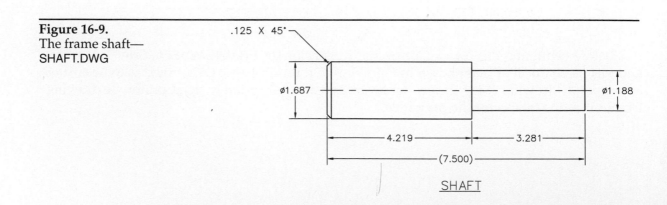

WHEEL

Figure 16-9.
The frame shaft—
SHAFT.DWG

.125 X 45°

Ø1.687

Ø1.188

4.219

3.281

(7.500)

SHAFT

Figure 16-10.
The frame collar—
COLLAR.DWG

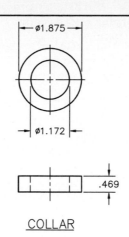

COLLAR

Figure 16-11.
The wheel pin—
PIN.DWG

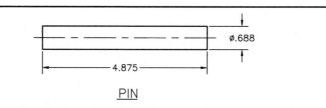

PIN

Once you have completed the five detail drawings, begin the paper space tutorial:

⇨ Begin a new drawing. Do not use one of your prototype drawings. Set **TILEMODE** to 0 (zero) to enter paper space.

> Command: **TILEMODE** ↵
> New value for TILEMODE ⟨1⟩: **0** ↵
> Entering Paper space. Use MVIEW to insert Model space viewports.
> Regenerating drawing.
> Command:

⇨ Use the **UCSICON** command to display the paper space icon.

> Command: *(type* UCSICON *or* UI *and press* [Enter])
> ON/OFF/All/Noorigin/ORigin ⟨OFF⟩: **ON** ↵
> Command:

⇨ Set the paper space limits to 0,0 and 34,22 (D-size) and then **ZOOM All**.

> Command: *(type* LIMITS *or* LM *and press* [Enter])
> Reset Paper space limits:
> ON/OFF/⟨Lower left corner⟩ ⟨0.0000,0.0000⟩: ↵
> Upper right corner ⟨12.0000,9.0000⟩: **34,22** ↵
> Command: *(type* ZOOM *or* Z *and press* [Enter])
> All/Center/Extents/Previous/Window/⟨Scale(X/XP)⟩: **A** ↵
> Command:

⇨ To ensure that viewport-specific layer status is retained, set the **VISRETAIN** variable as follows:

> Command: **VISRETAIN** ↵
> New value for VISRETAIN ⟨0⟩: **1** ↵
> Command:

⇨ Next, make the following layers.

Layer	Color
NOTES	BLUE
VIEWPORTS	MAGENTA
XREF	WHITE

Set the **VIEWPORTS** layer current. The **Layer Control** dialog box should appear as shown in Figure 16-12.

Figure 16-12.
The required layers are shown in the **Layer Control** dialog box.

Added layers

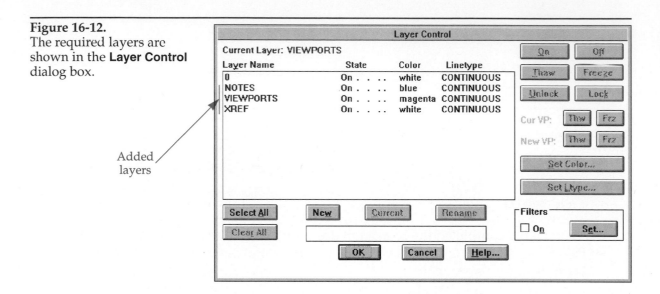

⇨ Create the first floating viewport using the **MVIEW** command:

Command: *(type* MVIEW *or* MV *and press* [Enter]*)*
ON/OFF/Hideplot/Fit/2/3/4/Restore/⟨First Point⟩: **1.5,.75** ↵
Other corner: **14,10** ↵
Regenerating drawing:
Command:

⇨ Use the **MSPACE** command to enter model space. You can also enter model space by clicking the **Paper Space** button.

Command: *(type* MSPACE *or* MS *and press* [Enter]*)*
Command:

⇨ Turn on the model space UCS icon in the viewport you just created.

Command: *(type* UCSICON *or* UI *and press* [Enter]*)*
ON/OFF/All/Noorigin/ORigin ⟨OFF⟩: **ON** ↵
Command:

Observe that the crosshairs are confined to the new viewport when model space is enabled. This is the active viewport. Your drawing should look like Figure 16-13.

Figure 16-13.
The first floating viewport is created and the UCS icon is turned on.

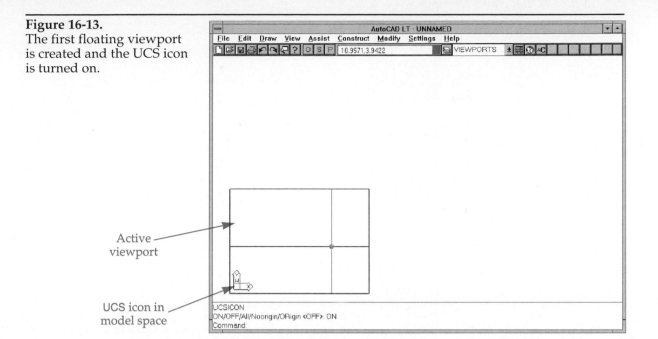

Active viewport

UCS icon in model space

⇨ Set the XREF layer current. Now, **XREF Attach** the drawing named WHEEL and insert it at 0,0 into the viewport. Accept the defaults for scale and rotation.

```
Command: (type XREF or XR and press [Enter])
?/Bind/Detach/Path/Reload/⟨Attach⟩: ↵
Xref to Attach: WHEEL ↵
Attach XREF WHEEL: wheel
WHEEL loaded:
Insertion point: 0,0 ↵
X scale factor ⟨1⟩/Corner/XYZ: ↵
Y scale factor (default=X): ↵
Rotation angle ⟨0⟩: ↵
Command:
```

⇨ Perform a **ZOOM Extents** to view the entire WHEEL drawing and then **ZOOM 1XP**. Remember that the **XP** option scales model space units relative to paper space units.

```
Command: (type ZOOM or Z and press [Enter])
All/Center/Extents/Previous/Window/⟨Scale(X/XP)⟩: E ↵
Regenerating drawing.
Command: ↵
ZOOM
All/Center/Extents/Previous/Window/⟨Scale(X/XP)⟩: 1XP ↵
Command:
```

Your drawing should now appear as shown in Figure 16-14.

Figure 16-14.
The WHEEL is externally referenced in the first viewport.

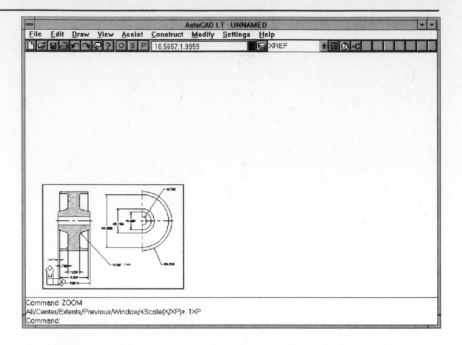

⇨ You will now use the **VPLAYER** command to control the visibility of the layers in the WHEEL drawing for each subsequently created viewport. Use the **Vpvisdflt** option and a wildcard character (*) to specify all layer names that begin with WHEEL.

> Command: *(type* VPLAYER *or* VL *and press* [Enter]*)*
> ?/Freeze/Thaw/Reset/Newfrz/Vpvisdflt: **V** ↵
> Layer name(s) to change default viewport visibility: **WHEEL*** ↵
> Change default viewport visibility to Frozen/⟨Thawed⟩: **F** ↵
> ?/Freeze/Thaw/Reset/Newfrz/Vpvisdflt: ↵
> Command:

⇨ Display the **Layer Control** dialog box and look at the layer names beginning with WHEEL. You may recall from Chapter 14 that when a drawing is referenced, the layers that come in begin with the drawing name prefixed to the layer names. The drawing name is separated from the layer name with the pipe character (|). The letter "N" appears in the last column under **State**, Figure 16-15. This indicates that each layer is frozen in any new viewports. Set the **VIEWPORTS** layer current.

Figure 16-15.
The frozen/thawed status of viewport-specific layers can be obtained or changed using the **Layer Control** dialog box. The letter "N" in the last **State** column indicates that all of the layers in the WHEEL drawing are frozen in any newly created floating viewports.

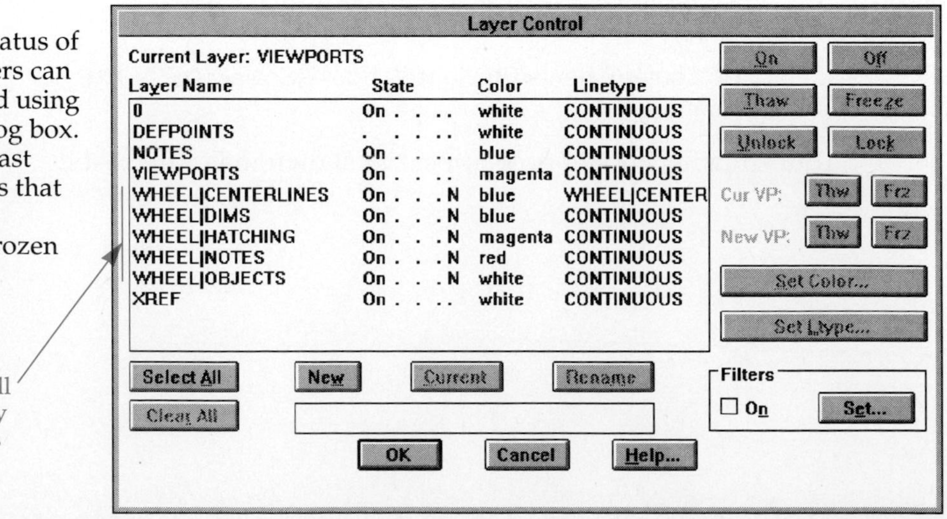

These layers will be frozen in any new viewports

⤷ Return to paper space.
⤷ Make sure that the VIEWPORTS layer is current and create another viewport with the **MVIEW** command.

> Command: *(type* MVIEW *or* MV *and press* [Enter]*)*
> ON/OFF/Hideplot/Fit/2/3/4/Restore/⟨First Point⟩: **1.5,10.25** ↵
> Other corner: **20.5,20.125** ↵
> Regenerating drawing.
> Command:

Your screen should appear as shown in Figure 16-16. Notice that the WHEEL external reference does not appear in the new viewport.

Figure 16-16.
Because they are frozen, the WHEEL layers are not displayed in the new viewport.

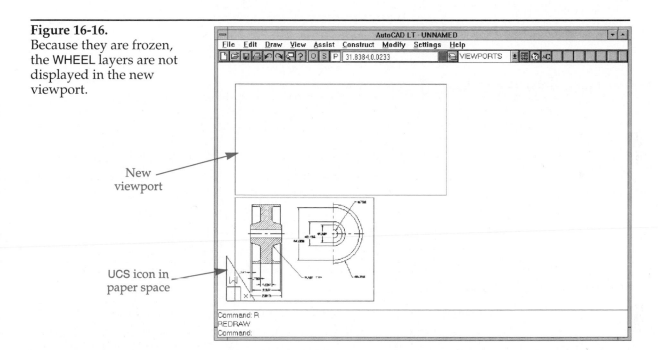

New viewport

UCS icon in paper space

⤷ Set the XREF layer current and type MSPACE (or MS) so that you can externally reference the next drawing into model space.
⤷ The upper-left viewport should be the active viewport. If it is not, either pick the viewport with your mouse or use [Ctrl]+[V] to make it the active viewport. Now, **XREF Attach** the FRAME drawing with a 0,0 insertion point. Accept the defaults for scale and rotation.

> Command: *(type* XREF *or* XR *and press* [Enter]*)*
> ?/Bind/Detach/Path/Reload/⟨Attach⟩: ↵
> Xref to Attach ⟨WHEEL⟩: **FRAME** ↵
> Attach XREF FRAME: frame
> FRAME loaded:
> Insertion point: **0,0** ↵
> X scale factor ⟨1⟩/Corner/XYZ: ↵
> Y scale factor (default=X): ↵
> Rotation angle ⟨0⟩: ↵
> Command:

⤳ Use the **PAN** command to center the drawing in the viewport and then scale the model space units to paper space units.

> Command: *(type* ZOOM *or* Z *and press* [Enter]*)*
> All/Center/Extents/Previous/Window/⟨Scale(X/XP)⟩: **1XP**↵
> Command:

If necessary, **PAN** again to position the FRAME in the viewport as shown in Figure 16-17.

Figure 16-17.
The FRAME is externally referenced into the second floating viewport. Observe that it also appears in the bottom viewport.

FRAME.DWG externally referenced into viewport

FRAME.DWG also visible in this viewport

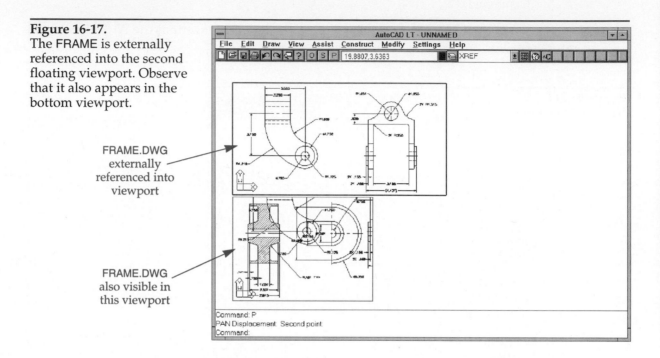

⤳ Notice that the FRAME drawing is visible in both viewports. Use the following **VPLAYER** command sequence to freeze the layer names beginning with FRAME in the lower-left viewport. Remember that the * wildcard character freezes all the layers that begin with FRAME. To select a viewport, you should pick the viewport at its border. Also, change the viewport visibility default from thawed to frozen so that the FRAME does not appear in any subsequently created viewports.

> Command: *(type* VPLAYER *or* VL *and press* [Enter]*)*
> ?/Freeze/Thaw/Reset/Newfrz/Vpvisdflt: **F** ↵
> Layer(s) to Freeze: **FRAME*** ↵
> All/Select/⟨Current⟩: **S** ↵
> Switching to Paper space.
> Select objects: *(select the lower-left viewport)*
> Select objects: ↵
> Switching to Model space.
> ?/Freeze/Thaw/Reset/Newfrz/Vpvisdflt: **V** ↵
> Layer name(s) to change default viewport visibility: **FRAME*** ↵
> Change default viewport visibility to Frozen/⟨Thawed⟩: **F** ↵
> ?/Freeze/Thaw/Reset/Newfrz/Vpvisdflt: ↵
> Command:

The **Vpvisdflt** option freezes the WHEEL and FRAME layers for all subsequent viewports. Display the **Layer Control** dialog box again and scroll through all the layers, Figure 16-18. Observe that layers beginning with WHEEL are frozen in the current (top) viewport. For these layers, the letter C (for current) appears just to the left of the

Figure 16-18.
The **Layer Control** dialog box displays the frozen/thawed status of layers in the current floating viewport.

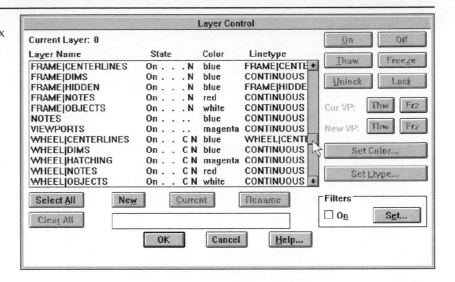

last **State** column. However, layers beginning with WHEEL and FRAME are shown frozen for any newly created viewports. For these layers, the letter N (for new) appears in the last **State** column.

⇨ Return to paper space, set the VIEWPORTS layer current, and create another viewport.

        Command: (type MVIEW or MV and press [Enter])
        ON/OFF/Hideplot/Fit/2/3/4/Restore/⟨First Point⟩: **15.5,1** ↵
        Other corner: **23.5,3.5** ↵
        Regenerating drawing.
        Command:

Your screen should appear as shown in Figure 16-19. Notice that the WHEEL and FRAME external references do not appear in the new viewport.

Figure 16-19.
A third floating viewport is created.

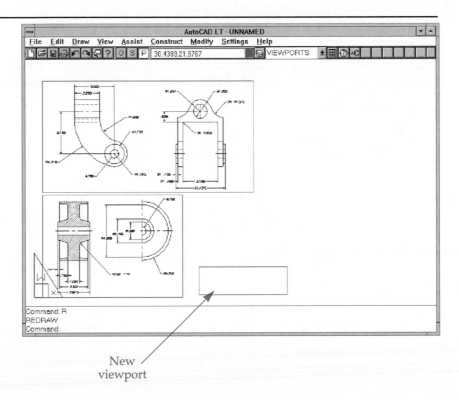

New
viewport

➪ To save regeneration time, turn off the contents of the two viewports at the left using the following command sequence.

Command: *(type MVIEW or MV and press [Enter])*
ON/OFF/Hideplot/Fit/2/3/4/Restore/⟨First Point⟩: **OFF** ↵
Select objects: *(select the two left viewports)*
Select objects: ↵
Command:

➪ Set the XREF layer current and enter model space so that you can externally reference another drawing into the new viewport.

➪ The lower-right viewport should be the active viewport. If it is not, make it so. Now, **XREF Attach** the PIN drawing with a 0,0 insertion point. Accept the defaults for scale and rotation.

Command: *(type XREF or XR and press [Enter])*
?/Bind/Detach/Path/Reload/⟨Attach⟩: ↵
Xref to Attach ⟨FRAME⟩: **PIN** ↵
Attach XREF PIN: pin
PIN loaded:
Insertion point: **0,0** ↵
X scale factor ⟨1⟩/Corner/XYZ: ↵
Y scale factor (default=X): ↵
Rotation angle ⟨0⟩: ↵
Command:

➪ Use the **PAN** command to center the PIN drawing in the viewport and then scale the model space units relative to paper space units.

Command: *(type ZOOM or Z and press [Enter])*
All/Center/Extents/Previous/Window/⟨Scale(X/XP)⟩: **1XP**↵
Command:

If necessary, **PAN** again to position the drawing in the viewport as shown in Figure 16-20.

Figure 16-20.
The contents of the two right viewports are turned off and the PIN is externally referenced and positioned in the new viewport.

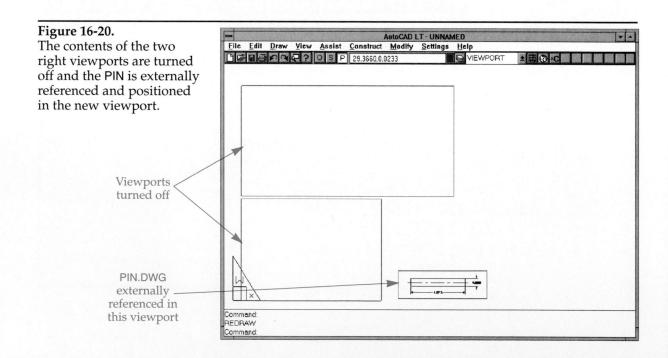

Viewports turned off

PIN.DWG externally referenced in this viewport

⇨ Now return to paper space, set the VIEWPORTS layer current, and create the last two required viewports.

Command: *(type MVIEW or MV and press [Enter])*
ON/OFF/Hideplot/Fit/2/3/4/Restore/⟨First Point⟩: **15.5,4** ↵
Other corner: **28.5,9.5** ↵
Regenerating drawing.
Command: ↵
MVIEW
ON/OFF/Hideplot/Fit/2/3/4/Restore/⟨First Point⟩: **22.5,10.25** ↵
Other corner: **28,16.75** ↵
Regenerating drawing.
Command:

Observe that the PIN external reference appears in the two new viewports, Figure 16-21. This will be remedied shortly.

Figure 16-21.
The PIN is displayed inside the two new floating viewports.

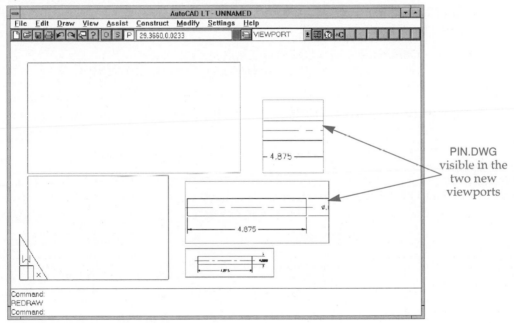

PIN.DWG visible in the two new viewports

⇨ Return to model space and set the XREF layer current.
⇨ The upper-right viewport should be the active viewport. If it is not, make it so. **XREF Attach** the COLLAR drawing with a 0,0 insertion point. Accept the defaults for scale and rotation.

Command: *(type XREF or XR and press [Enter])*
?/Bind/Detach/Path/Reload/⟨Attach⟩: ↵
Xref to Attach ⟨PIN⟩: **COLLAR** ↵
Attach XREF COLLAR: collar
COLLAR loaded:
Insertion point: **0,0** ↵
X scale factor ⟨1⟩/Corner/XYZ: ↵
Y scale factor (default=X): ↵
Rotation angle ⟨0⟩: ↵
Command:

▷ Now zoom to scale the model space units relative to paper space units.

> Command: *(type ZOOM or Z and press* [Enter]*)*
> All/Center/Extents/Previous/Window/⟨Scale(X/XP)⟩: **1XP**↵
> Command:

PAN to center the COLLAR drawing in the viewport.

▷ Activate the middle-right viewport and **XREF Attach** the SHAFT drawing with a 0,0 insertion point. Accept the defaults for scale and rotation.

> Command: *(type XREF or XR and press* [Enter]*)*
> ?/Bind/Detach/Path/Reload/⟨Attach⟩: ↵
> Xref to Attach ⟨COLLAR⟩: **SHAFT** ↵
> Attach XREF SHAFT: shaft
> SHAFT loaded:
> Insertion point: **0,0** ↵
> X scale factor ⟨1⟩/Corner/XYZ: ↵
> Y scale factor (default=X): ↵
> Rotation angle ⟨0⟩: ↵
> Command:

▷ Once again, use the **ZOOM** command to scale the model space units relative to paper space units.

> Command: *(type ZOOM or Z and press* [Enter]*)*
> All/Center/Extents/Previous/Window/⟨Scale(X/XP)⟩: **1XP**↵
> Command:

PAN to center the SHAFT drawing in the viewport. Your drawing should appear as shown in Figure 16-22.

Figure 16-22.
The COLLAR and SHAFT are externally referenced and positioned in the two remaining viewports.

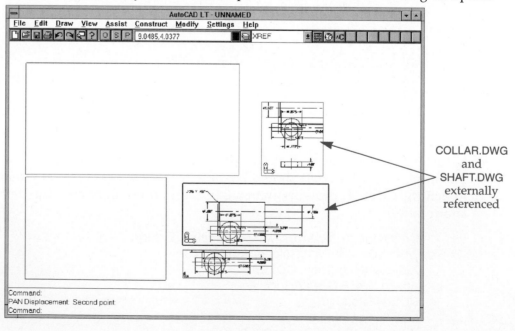

COLLAR.DWG
and
SHAFT.DWG
externally
referenced

➪ The middle-right viewport should still be active. If it is not, make it so. You will now freeze all layers beginning with PIN and COLLAR in the current viewport. Then freeze all layers beginning with PIN and SHAFT in the upper-right viewport. Finally, freeze all layers beginning with COLLAR and SHAFT in the lower-right viewport. Follow the command sequence below:

> Command: *(type* VPLAYER *or* VL *and press* [Enter]*)*
> ?/Freeze/Thaw/Reset/Newfrz/Vpvisdflt: **F** ⏎
> Layer(s) to Freeze: **PIN*,COLLAR*** ⏎
> All/Select/⟨Current⟩: *(press* [Enter] *to select the current viewport)*
> ?/Freeze/Thaw/Reset/Newfrz/Vpvisdflt: **F** ⏎
> Layer(s) to Freeze: **PIN*,SHAFT*** ⏎
> All/Select/⟨Current⟩: **S** ⏎
> Switching to Paper space.
> Select objects: *(select the upper-right viewport)*
> Select objects: ⏎
> Switching to Model space.
> ?/Freeze/Thaw/Reset/Newfrz/Vpvisdflt: **F** ⏎
> Layer(s) to Freeze: **COLLAR*,SHAFT*** ⏎
> All/Select/⟨Current⟩: **S** ⏎
> Switching to Paper space.
> Select objects: *(select the lower right viewport)*
> Select objects: ⏎
> Switching to Model space.
> ?/Freeze/Thaw/Reset/Newfrz/Vpvisdflt: ⏎
> Regenerating drawing.
> Command:

The viewports on the right are now displaying the required layers. However, the two viewports at the left need to have layers that begin with PIN, SHAFT, and COLLAR frozen.

➪ Turn on the two left viewports with the **MVIEW** command.

> Command: *(type* MVIEW *or* MV *and press* [Enter]*)*
> Switching to Paper Space.
> ON/OFF/Hideplot/Fit/2/3/4/Restore/⟨First Point⟩: **ON** ⏎
> Select objects: *(select the two left viewports)*
> Select objects: ⏎
> Regenerating drawing.
> Switching to Model space.
> Command:

➪ You will notice that the last three externally referenced drawings are visible, Figure 16-23.

Figure 16-23.
Turning on the two right viewports displays the last three externally referenced drawings.

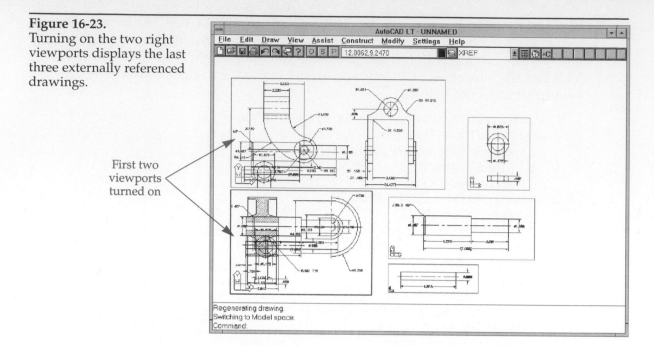

First two viewports turned on

▷ Freeze the layers of the last three externally referenced drawings.

```
Command: (type VPLAYER or VL and press [Enter])
?/Freeze/Thaw/Reset/Newfrz/Vpvisdflt: F ↵
Layer(s) to Freeze: PIN*,SHAFT*,COLLAR* ↵
All/Select/⟨Current⟩: S ↵
Switching to Paper space.
Select objects: (select the two left viewports)
Select objects: ↵
Switching to Model space.
?/Freeze/Thaw/Reset/Newfrz/Vpvisdflt: ↵
Regenerating drawing.
Command:
```

▷ Next, return to paper space and insert the ANSI_D drawing at 0,0. This drawing is supplied with AutoCAD LT and is located in the ACLTWIN directory. Accept the defaults for scale and rotation.

```
Command: (type INSERT or IN and press [Enter])
Block name (or ?): ANSI_D ↵
Insertion point: 0,0 ↵
X scale factor ⟨1⟩/Corner/XYZ: ↵
Y scale factor (default=X): ↵
Rotation angle ⟨0⟩: ↵
Command:
```

▷ Now, freeze the VIEWPORTS layer to hide the floating viewport borders. Your drawing should appear as shown in Figure 16-24.

Figure 16-24.
A D-size title block is inserted and the VIEWPORTS layer is frozen. The drawing is ready to be plotted at full scale.

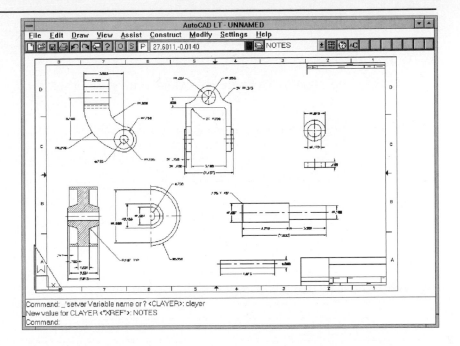

▷ Set the NOTES layer current and complete the title block information. Add any other drawing annotation as desired. The mechanical detail sheet is now complete and ready for plotting at full scale (1:1).

▷ Save the finished drawing with the name CASTER.

Summary

In the preceding tutorial, each of the detail drawings were externally referenced into the master drawing. This reduces file size and conserves disk space. The **INSERT** command can be used if xrefs are not desired.

A separate layer was created for the floating viewports. Doing so allows you to turn off or freeze your viewport borders before plotting.

Also, each of the floating viewports are scaled at 1:1 (1XP). As an experiment, try repeating this tutorial and scale the COLLAR and PIN viewports at 2XP.

The **ZOOM XP** option allows you to scale the contents of a floating viewport at any scale. This makes paper space the ideal environment to mix details with varying scales while still plotting at full scale.

Finally, remember to use model space to construct, dimension, and detail your drawings. Use paper space only to add annotation and arrange multiple views to fit on the sheet of paper on which you are plotting.

CHAPTER TEST

Write your answers in the spaces provided.

1. Identify the system variable that determines whether model space or paper space is active. _____

2. What are *tiled* viewports? What command is used to create them? _____

_____

_____

_____

3. Why is it a good idea to turn on the UCS icon when working in paper space? _____

_____

_____

4. What must be done before the **Paper Space** button can be used? _____

_____

_____

5. What is the purpose of the **MAXACTVP** system variable? What is its maximum value?

_____

_____

6. Identify the command that creates one or more floating viewports. What must be done before this command can be used? _____

_____

_____

7. Which keyboard combination is used to toggle between multiple floating viewports?

_____

8. What is the purpose of the **ZOOM XP** option and what does "XP" mean? _____

_____

_____

9. How does the **VPLAYER** command differ from the **LAYER** command? _____

_____

_____

10. What is the purpose of the **VPLAYER Vpvisdflt** option? _____

_____

_____

CHAPTER PROBLEMS

1. Begin a new drawing using the **Custom** setup method and select a C-size title block. Externally reference Problem 4 of Chapter 11 and pick a point in the middle of the floating viewport as the insertion point. Accept the defaults for scale and rotation. Use the correct **ZOOM XP** value to scale the viewport. Stretch the viewport border to reduce its size and position the transistor as shown below. Complete the title block information and add annotation as desired. Freeze the VIEWPORT layer before plotting. Save the drawing as P16-1.

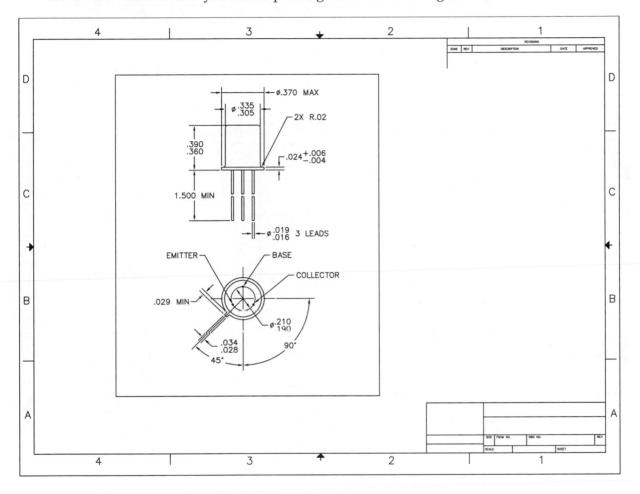

2. Once again, begin a new drawing using the **Custom** setup method and select a C-size title block. Externally reference Problem 5 of Chapter 6 at full scale into the floating viewport. Use 0,0 as the insertion point. Perform a **ZOOM Extents** and then use the correct **ZOOM XP** value to scale the viewport. Stretch the viewport border to reduce its size and position the floor plan as shown below. Complete the title block information and add annotation as desired. Freeze the VIEWPORT layer before plotting. Save the drawing as P16-2.

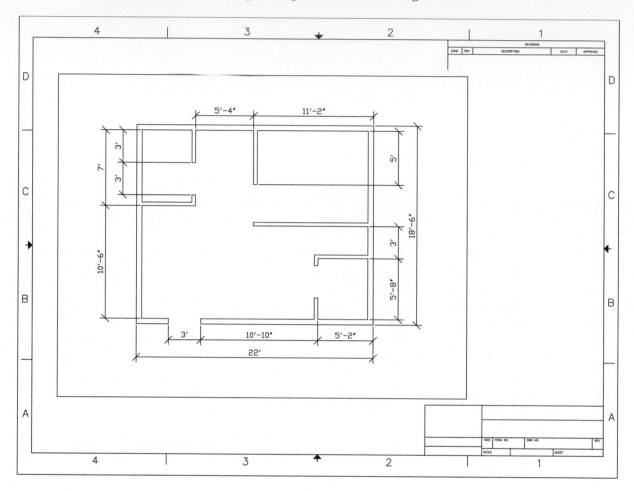

Command Aliases, Script Files, and Slide Shows

Learning objectives:

After you have completed this chapter, you will be able to:
- ❍ Edit the ACLT.PGP file to create command aliases.
- ❍ Write a script file using the Windows Notepad.
- ❍ Make and view slides of AutoCAD LT drawings and create a running slide show.
- ❍ Create a slide library using the **SLIDELIB** command.

As you become more experienced with AutoCAD LT, you will want to modify the program to suit your personal tastes and needs. *Command aliasing* allows you to define your own abbreviated command names using an ordinary text editor.

A text editor is also used in the creation of script files. A *script file* is a set of AutoCAD LT commands automatically executed in sequence. In this chapter, you will learn how to create your own command aliases and script files. You will also learn how to create slide files, slide shows, and slide libraries.

TEXT EDITORS

Text editor programs write ASCII (American Standard Code for Information Exchange) text files. The MS-DOS operating system provides two ASCII text editors: EDLIN and MS-DOS EDIT.

In the Microsoft Windows operating environment, the Windows Notepad provides a convenient method of creating text files. While Notepad is capable of performing most of the text editing tasks appropriate for AutoCAD LT, it cannot accommodate files exceeding 50K (50,000 bytes) in size.

In addition to the editors supplied with MS-DOS and Microsoft Windows, there are a wide variety of text editors available. The more powerful ASCII text editors are referred to as *programmer's editors*. Programmer's editors usually feature sophisticated search and find, cut and copy, and word wrap functions. The Norton Editor is one example of an excellent programmer's editor.

PROFESSIONAL TIP
When working in Windows, use Notepad to create or edit text files smaller than 50,000 bytes. If the file you are working with exceeds this size, use MS-DOS EDIT.

Word processors

You can also use a word processing program to create text files. The Windows Write program is included with Microsoft Windows. Like Notepad, Write can be accessed from the Accessories group window in the Program Manager. See Figure 17-1. Other Windows-compatible programs include Lotus Pro, WordPerfect, and Microsoft Word for Windows.

While word processing programs are excellent tools for producing written documentation, their capabilities exceed what is required to create text files for AutoCAD LT. However, if you use a word processor, be sure to save the file in ASCII format so that it is readable by AutoCAD LT.

Figure 17-1.
Both Notepad and Write can be accessed from the Accessories group window.

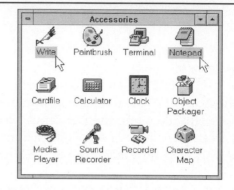

USING MS-DOS PROMPT

One of the advantages of using Microsoft Windows is the ability to have an application open in one window while working in another window. This allows you to edit a text file without exiting AutoCAD LT. Many of the text files you create will be designed and needed while running AutoCAD LT.

There are times when it is convenient to run a non-Windows application without exiting AutoCAD LT. This capability is provided with a Windows application called MS-DOS Prompt. You can access MS-DOS Prompt by returning to the Main group window in the Program Manager and double-clicking the MS-DOS Prompt icon, Figure 17-2.

After MS-DOS Prompt is selected, you are presented with messages and a prompt similar to those shown in Figure 17-3. By pressing [Alt]+[Enter], you can toggle between the full screen display and the window shown in Figure 17-3.

You can now use DOS commands or run a non-Windows application, such as EDIT. When you are ready to exit MS-DOS Prompt, simply type EXIT and press [Enter].

Figure 17-2.
MS-DOS Prompt is located in the Main group window.

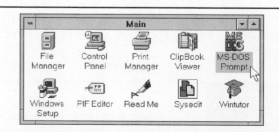

Figure 17-3.
Pressing [Alt]+[Enter] displays
the MS-DOS Prompt window.

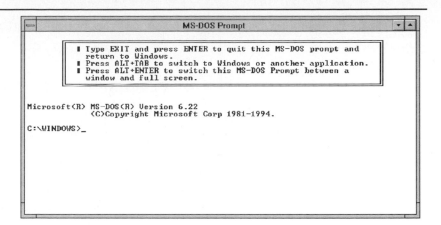

PROFESSIONAL TIP

Be sure to save your drawing before using MS-DOS Prompt. This will ensure that no work is lost in case your computer should crash while you are temporarily exited from AutoCAD LT. Keep in mind that certain DOS commands should not be used when running MS-DOS Prompt. These commands include UNDELETE and CHKDSK with the /F switch. Also, never use disk compaction and optimization programs when running Windows.

CREATING COMMAND ALIASES—THE **ACLT.PGP** FILE

As mentioned at the beginning of this chapter, you can create abbreviated command names in AutoCAD LT. Many predefined command aliases have been introduced where appropriate throughout this text. These predefined command aliases are contained in a file called ACLT.PGP (program parameters). This file is located in the \ACLTWIN directory.

When AutoCAD LT is started, the command aliases are loaded into the current drawing session. If you revise the file, you will need to restart AutoCAD LT to load the revised file.

You can display the contents of ACLT.PGP by opening the file in Notepad, Figure 17-4. Scroll down past the listing of toolbox and toolbar aliases and you will see the complete list of command aliases. A small sample is given below:

```
A,        *ARC
AA,       *AREA
AB,       *ABOUT
AD,       *ATTDEF
AE,       *ATTEDIT
AP,       *APERTURE
AR,       *ARRAY
AT,       *ATTDISP
AX,       *ATTEXT
```

You can create your own command aliases by editing the ACLT.PGP file in Notepad. You may recall that Notepad was used in Chapter 12 as a means to add a customized hatch pattern to the ACLT.PAT file. It was used again in Chapter 14 to create a template file for attribute extraction. If necessary, refer to those chapters to refresh your memory on the use of Notepad.

From the examples shown above, observe that an asterisk precedes the command name. This tells AutoCAD LT that the character string is an alias. Since each command alias uses a small amount of memory, you should keep the number of aliases to a minimum if your computer has little memory.

Figure 17-4.
The ACLT.PGP file in
the Notepad window.

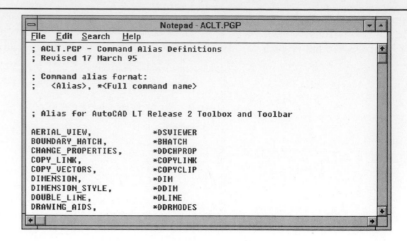

```
                          Notepad - ACLT.PGP
 File  Edit  Search  Help
 ; ACLT.PGP - Command Alias Definitions
 ; Revised 17 March 95

 ; Command alias format:
 ;   <Alias>, *<Full command name>


 ; Alias for AutoCAD LT Release 2 Toolbox and Toolbar

 AERIAL_VIEW,              *DSVIEWER
 BOUNDARY_HATCH,           *BHATCH
 CHANGE_PROPERTIES,        *DDCHPROP
 COPY_LINK,                *COPYLINK
 COPY_VECTORS,             *COPYCLIP
 DIMENSION,                *DIM
 DIMENSION_STYLE,          *DDIM
 DOUBLE_LINE,              *DLINE
 DRAWING_AIDS,             *DDRMODES
```

To add an alias for the **MEASURE** command, enter the following between the **MOVE** and **MIRROR** commands in the ACLT.PGP file:

    ME,   *MEASURE

The revised ACLT.PGP file does not take effect until AutoCAD LT is started again.

> **PROFESSIONAL TIP**
>
>
>
> Always make backup copies of text files (such as ACLT.LIN, ACLT.PAT, and ACLT.PGP) before editing them. If you corrupt one of these files through incorrect editing techniques, simply delete the file and restore the original.

EXERCISE 17-1

Obtain the permission of your instructor or supervisor before performing this exercise.
❑ Make a backup copy of ACLT.PGP.
❑ Use Notepad to add the **MEASURE** command alias as previously described.
❑ Define an alias for the **DIVIDE** command. Make sure that your new alias does not conflict with an existing one.
❑ Start AutoCAD LT and test your two new command aliases.

SCRIPT FILES

ALTUG 20

As mentioned at the beginning of this chapter, a script file is a set of AutoCAD LT commands that are automatically executed in sequence. The script file can be created with Notepad or any other ASCII text editor, but it must be given an .SCR file extension.

The example that appears below, CSETUP.SCR, can be used to begin a new C-size drawing.

LIMITS 0,0 22,17	*Sets the limits to C-size*
SNAP .5	*Sets the snap spacing to .5 units*
GRID SNAP	*Sets the grid spacing equal to the snap spacing*
ZOOM ALL	*Zooms to the new limits*
	Blank line

Although a script file can contain several commands per line, it is good practice to put one command on each line. This makes the file easier to *debug* if the script does not run correctly. For this same reason, try to avoid using command aliases and single-letter command options.

When creating a script file, you can use lowercase or uppercase letters. However, be sure to put a space between the command and its option, as shown in the example. Just as you must press [Enter] after entering a command, you must also press [Enter] after typing each line of the script file. The blank line at the end of the script file is interpreted as an [Enter] and ensures that the **ZOOM** command is executed. If you wish to add comments to your script file, you can do so by placing a semicolon (;) at the start of the line. These lines are ignored when the script file is run.

CAUTION

Commands that use dialog boxes will not work in a script file. If the script file is to open or close files, be sure to set the **FILEDIA** system variable equal to 0 to disable the file dialog boxes. If you are automating plotting procedures, turn the **CMDDIA** system variable off. This variable controls the display of the **Plot Configuration** dialog box. See Chapter 13 for more information about plotting.

Running the script file

Once the script file is complete, it is run within AutoCAD LT using the **SCRIPT** command. Select **Run Script...** from the **File** pull-down menu, Figure 17-5, or enter the following at the **Command:** prompt:

Command: *(type* SCRIPT *or* SR *and press* [Enter]*)*

The **Select Script File** dialog box is then displayed. In the example shown in Figure 17-6, the CSETUP.SCR file is selected from the file list at the left. Click the **OK** button to exit the dialog box and the script file is executed one line at a time. Each of the commands in the script file appear in the command line area as the file is run.

Figure 17-5.
The **SCRIPT** command is started by selecting **Run Script...** from the **File** pull-down menu.

Figure 17-6.
The **Select Script File** dialog box.

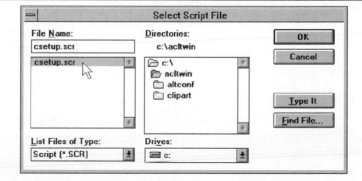

Script commands

The following commands are used in script files. With the exception of the **RSCRIPT** command, each can be invoked transparently by preceding the command with an apostrophe (**'TEXTSCR,** for example).

- **DELAY.** Delays the execution of the next script command for a specified amount of time, measured in milliseconds. Example: DELAY 2000 (about two seconds). The longest delay allowed is 32767, which is slightly less than 33 seconds.
- **RESUME.** Resumes an interrupted script.
- **RSCRIPT.** Repeats a script from its beginning.
- **TEXTSCR.** Flips to the text window
- **GRAPHSCR.** Flips to the graphics window

You can pause a script file by pressing the [Backspace] key. Type RESUME at the **Command:** prompt to start the script file where it left off. To restart the script file from its beginning, use the **RSCRIPT** command instead. Click the **Cancel** button on the toolbar or press [Ctrl]+[C] to cancel a running script file.

EXERCISE 17-2

❑ Use Notepad to write a script file named MYSCRIPT.SCR. The script file should do the following:
  ❑ Set the current color to green.
  ❑ Construct a hexagon (six-sided polygon) at coordinates 6,4 with a radius of 2 units.
  ❑ Change the current color to cyan.
  ❑ Draw a circle with a radius of 1.5 units centered on the hexagon.
❑ Start AutoCAD LT and use the **SCRIPT** command to run MYSCRIPT.SCR.
❑ If the script file does not run correctly or stops before completion, use Notepad to correct it. Run the script file again until it works.
❑ Save the drawing as EX17-2.

SLIDE FILES AND SLIDE SHOWS

ALTUG 20

A *slide file* is a raster image of the graphics window display. It is not a drawing itself; it is only a picture, or "snapshot," of the current drawing. It cannot be edited or plotted.

After a slide file has been made, it can be viewed in any drawing. A continuous (running) slide show can be viewed by displaying multiple slide files in sequence. Slide shows are useful for product demonstrations and design proposals.

Making a slide—the MSLIDE command

The first step in creating a slide is to open the drawing containing the entities to be included in the slide. Layers that are turned off or frozen and portions of the drawing that are not displayed are not included in the slide. Adjust the screen display as required so that the display shows exactly what you want included in the slide.

When you are ready to create the slide, select **Import/Export** from the **File** pull-down menu, and then select **Make Slide...** from the cascading submenu. See Figure 17-7. Or, you can enter the following at the **Command:** prompt:

Command: *(type* MSLIDE *or* ML *and press* [Enter]*)*

The **Create Slide File** dialog box is then displayed. See Figure 17-8. Slides are automatically given the file extension .SLD. Also, the slide file name defaults to the current drawing name. If you wish to enter a different name, do so by entering the new name in the **File Name:** text box.

When you are finished, click the **OK** button. The slide file is created and the **Command:** prompt reappears.

Figure 17-7.
The **MSLIDE** command is issued by first selecting **Import/Export** from the **File** pull-down menu, and then selecting **Make Slide** from the cascading submenu.

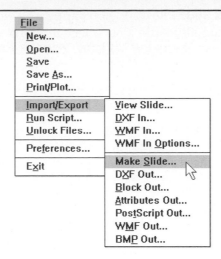

Figure 17-8.
The **Create Slide File** dialog box. Unless otherwise specified, the slide file name defaults to the current drawing name.

Name of slide file

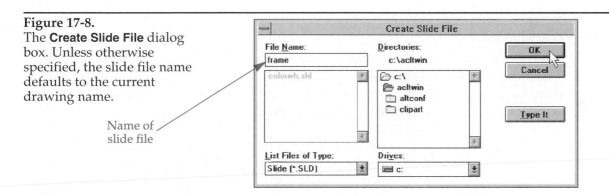

The **MSLIDE** command makes a slide file from the current viewport only if you are working in model space. In paper space, **MSLIDE** makes a slide file of the entire paper space display, including all floating viewports and their contents.

Viewing a slide—the VSLIDE command

Once you have created a slide, it can be viewed by selecting **Import/Export** from the **File** pull-down menu, and then selecting **View Slide...** from the cascading submenu. See Figure 17-9. You can also enter the following at the **Command:** prompt:

Command: *(type* VSLIDE *or* VS *and press* [Enter])

Figure 17-9.
The **VSLIDE** command is issued by first selecting **Import/Export** from the **File** pull-down menu, and then selecting **View Slide** from the cascading submenu.

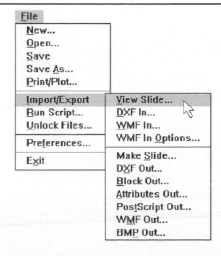

When the **Select Slide File** dialog box appears, select a slide file from the file list at the left. See Figure 17-10. The slide file you select remains displayed until one of the following commands are entered: **REDRAW**, **REGEN**, **ZOOM**, or **PAN**.

Figure 17-10.
A slide file is selected for viewing using the **Select Slide File** dialog box.

Name of slide file to be viewed

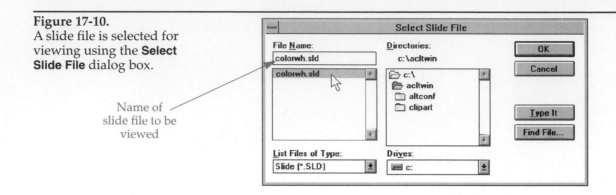

Making a slide show

A slide show can be viewed by creating a script file that displays multiple slide files in sequence. The speed at which slide files are displayed is a function of the number of disk accesses required to read the file. To expedite the process, you can preload a slide file into memory while your audience is viewing the previous slide. This is accomplished by placing an asterisk (*) before the slide file name.

An example of a typical slide show script file, DETAILS.SCR, is shown in Figure 17-11. A line-by-line explanation follows. In this example, five slides have been created from the detail drawings used in the Chapter 16 paper space tutorial. Note the use of the ***VSLIDE** and **DELAY** commands in the script.

VSLIDE FRAME	*Begin the slide show by loading the FRAME slide*
VSLIDE *WHEEL	*Preload the WHEEL slide*
DELAY 3000	*Let the audience view the FRAME slide*
VSLIDE	*Display the WHEEL slide*
VSLIDE *SHAFT	*Preload the SHAFT slide*
DELAY 3000	*Let the audience view the WHEEL slide*
VSLIDE	*Display the SHAFT slide*
VSLIDE *COLLAR	*Preload the COLLAR slide*
DELAY 3000	*Let the audience view the SHAFT slide*
VSLIDE	*Display the COLLAR slide*
VSLIDE *PIN	*Preload the PIN slide*
DELAY 3000	*Let the audience view the COLLAR slide*
VSLIDE	*Display the PIN slide*
DELAY 3000	*Let the audience view the PIN slide*
RSCRIPT	*Repeat the slide show until canceled with a [Ctrl]+[C]*

PROFESSIONAL TIP

When using slide files on disks, be sure to include the disk drive letter and path in front of the slide file name, such as A:FRAME.SLD. Each **VSLIDE** command in the script file must include the correct path.

Figure 17-11.
The DETAILS.SCR script file displayed in the Notepad window.

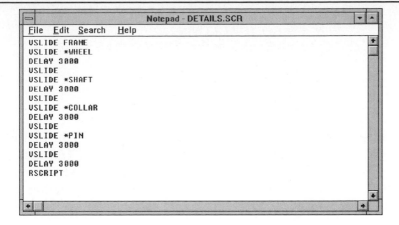

```
Notepad - DETAILS.SCR
File  Edit  Search  Help
VSLIDE FRAME
VSLIDE *WHEEL
DELAY 3000
VSLIDE
VSLIDE *SHAFT
DELAY 3000
VSLIDE
VSLIDE *COLLAR
DELAY 3000
VSLIDE
VSLIDE *PIN
DELAY 3000
VSLIDE
DELAY 3000
RSCRIPT
```

Viewing the slide show

After completing the script file, the slide show can be viewed. The **SCRIPT** command opens the **Select Script File** dialog box. Select the script file and the show begins.

EXERCISE 17-3

❑ Use the **MSLIDE** command to create slide files of the five detail drawings from the Chapter 16 paper space tutorial. If you did not complete the tutorial, select five other drawings of your choice.
❑ With Notepad, create the script file DETAILS.SCR as described above. Be sure to press [Enter] after the **RSCRIPT** command to ensure that the script file is repeated. Place the script file and the slide files in the \ACLTWIN directory.
❑ Use the **SCRIPT** command to run the slide show.
❑ Edit the script file and experiment with different delay times.

Creating a slide library—the SLIDELIB utility program

You can create a library of slide files using the SLIDELIB.EXE utility program, which is supplied with AutoCAD LT. The library is saved with a name of your choice and is automatically given a .SLB file extension.

Before you create the slide library, you must first create a list of the slides to appear in the library. Since the slide list must be saved with a .TXT file extension, use an ASCII text editor, such as Notepad or MS-DOS EDIT.

A list of the caster details used in the previous script file example can be entered in a file called DETAILS.TXT. The list would appear in the text editor as follows:

```
FRAME.SLD
WHEEL.SLD
SHAFT.SLD
COLLAR.SLD
PIN.SLD
```

After completing the slide list file, use the **SLIDELIB** command to make the slide library. The SLIDELIB.EXE program is located in the \ACLTWIN directory. Be sure to place the DETAILS.TXT file in the same directory so that SLIDELIB can find it to create the slide library. Since the slide list represents the detail drawings required for a caster assembly, an appropriate slide library name would be CASTER.SLB.

The SLIDELIB utility must be executed at the DOS prompt, so it cannot be used within AutoCAD LT. However, it can be used from an MS-DOS Prompt window.

Enter the following to switch to the AutoCAD LT directory and create the slide library:

C:\WINDOWS⟩ **CD \ACLTWIN** ↵
C:\ACLTWIN⟩ **SLIDELIB CASTER** ⟨ **DETAILS.TXT** ↵
SLIDELIB 1.2 (3/8/89)
(C) Copyright 1987-89 Autodesk, Inc.
    All Rights Reserved
C:\ACLTWIN⟩ **EXIT** ↵

In the example above, the less-than sign (⟨) instructs the SLIDELIB utility to take its input from the DETAILS.TXT slide list to create a file called CASTER.SLB.

To display a slide from a slide library, use the **VSLIDE** command. When the **Select Slide File** dialog box appears, click the **Type It** button. The dialog box disappears and the following prompt is displayed at the **Command:** prompt:

Slide file:

Enter the library file name and the slide file name using this format:

LIBRARY NAME(SLIDE NAME)

As an example, enter the following to display the WHEEL slide from the CASTER slide library:

Slide file: **CASTER(WHEEL)** ↵

Updating the slide library

It is possible that slides will be added or deleted from a slide list over a period of time. The slide library is not automatically updated, however. You must revise the slide list file and then recreate the slide library.

Using the slide library to make a slide show

It is more efficient to create a slide show from a slide library because there is no need to preload slides. Compare the following script file, which uses a slide library, with the previous example:

```
VSLIDE CASTER(FRAME)
DELAY 2000
VSLIDE CASTER(WHEEL)
DELAY 2000
VSLIDE CASTER(SHAFT)
DELAY 2000
VSLIDE CASTER(COLLAR)
DELAY 2000
VSLIDE CASTER(PIN)
DELAY 2000
RSCRIPT
```

Since slides do not have to be preloaded, delay times can be shortened. The **RSCRIPT** command repeats the slide show until canceled. Use the **REDRAW** command if you want to run the show once and then clear the screen and replace the previous display.

CHAPTER TEST

Write your answers in the spaces provided.

1. What is the purpose of a script file? _____ _____

    _____

    _____

2. Which file contains the AutoCAD LT command aliases? _____

3. If you use a word-processing program to create a script file, in what format must the file be saved? _____

4. What is the maximum file size (in bytes) that can be handled by the Windows Notepad?

    _____

5. Which Program Manager group window features MS-DOS Prompt? _____

6. New command aliases can be used immediately after the ACLT.PGP file is edited. (True/False) _____

7. All DOS commands and program utilities can be executed from MS-DOS Prompt. (True/False) _____

8. What must you do to place a comment in a script file? _____

    _____

9. Dialog boxes can be used with a script file. (True/False) _____

10. What is the purpose of the **RSCRIPT** command in a script file? _____

    _____

    _____

11. Which key should you press to interrupt a running script? _____

12. Identify the two commands used to create and view slide files. _____

    _____

13. A slide file cannot be edited. (True/False) _____

14. Identify the utility program that creates a slide library. Where is this program located?

    _____

    _____

15. List all the required steps to view a slide named DESK contained in a slide library named OFFICE. _____

    _____

    _____

CHAPTER PROBLEMS

1. Write a script file called P17-1.SCR that does the following:

   A. Sets the limits to A-size and zooms to the new limits.

   B. Sets the grid spacing to 1 unit and the snap spacing to .5 units.

   C. Changes the current color to blue.

   D. Draws a 6 × 4 rectangle with the first corner of the rectangle at 3,2.

   E. Sets the current color to red.

   F. Uses the **TEXT** command to create the character string THE END in the middle of the rectangle with a text height of .75 units.

2. Create a group of slides that are related to your professional discipline or field of interest. The slides could feature electronic components, such as resistors, capacitors, and diodes. An architectural collection could include doors, windows, and bath fixtures. As you create the drawings for the slides, label each drawing with descriptive text. When the slide files are created, write a slide list. Use the SLIDELIB utility to produce a slide library and create a script file to run the slide show. Name the script file P17-2.SCR.

Learning objectives:

After you have completed this chapter, you will be able to:

○ Select and use the **UCSICON** command.
○ Identify the various model space UCS icon representations and match them with the viewing angles they depict.
○ Apply the **VPOINT** command to obtain 3D views.
○ Describe and set both elevation and thickness.
○ Remove hidden lines and shade 3D objects.
○ Create and save multiple viewports in model space.
○ Define and apply user-defined coordinate systems.
○ Control and alter 3D viewing aspects with **DVIEW**.

Although AutoCAD LT is primarily a two-dimensional (2D) design drafting tool, it can also be used to construct simple three-dimensional (3D) objects. This chapter describes the commands used to obtain 3D viewing angles and construct 3D geometry. Display control functions applicable to 3D models are also introduced.

THINKING IN THREE DIMENSIONS

ALTUG 11

Creating 3D geometry is not very different from creating 2D geometry. The 3D point entry methods in AutoCAD LT use the *Cartesian* coordinate system that you are already familiar with. With this system, all X, Y, and Z values are related to the drawing origin. The origin is usually at the very lower left of the drawing screen, and is where X = 0, Y = 0, and Z = 0. Point distances are measured along the horizontal X axis and the vertical Y axis. Positive X values are to the right (east) and positive Y values are to the top (north). The Z axis is perpendicular to the screen. Positive Z values come out of the screen toward you, while negative Z values go into the screen away from you. The three axes form perpendicular planes.

THE WORLD COORDINATE SYSTEM VS.
THE USER COORDINATE SYSTEM

The coordinate system described above is fixed in 3D space and cannot be moved or altered. Because it is universal, AutoCAD LT refers to it as the *World Coordinate System (WCS)*. Whenever a new drawing file is created in AutoCAD LT, the graphics window defaults to a single viewport that corresponds to the WCS. In this view, the user is looking down the positive Z axis onto the XY plane. This viewing angle is referred to as the *plan view*, or *plan to the WCS*. All coordinates are measured along the X and Y axes relative to the 0, 0, 0 drawing origin at the lower left of the screen. An alternative to the WCS is the *User Coordinate System (UCS)*. With the UCS, a user can redefine the location of the origin and the direction of the XYZ axes. While the vast majority of the 2D drawings you have created using this text have been in the World Coordinate System, several UCS options were introduced in previous chapters as a way to help construct 2D auxiliary views and perform ordinate dimensioning operations. The UCS is absolutely essential for 3D geometry construction and will be discussed more fully later in this chapter.

THE MODEL SPACE UCS ICON

ALTUG 5

Before you begin working in 3D model space, it is a good idea to turn on the UCS icon. The UCS icon is a small graphical marker at the lower left of the screen that displays the origin and the viewing plane of the current UCS in model space. The icon is shown in Figure 18-1. In its default representation, the X, Y, and Z axes of the UCS icon are positioned 90° relative to one another, with the Z axis perpendicular to the XY plane and along the line of sight. You will notice a box drawn at the vertices of the X and Y axes. The box indicates that the viewpoint is from the positive Z direction. Therefore, the viewing angle is from a position above the XY plane looking down. Also notice the small W just above the box. The W indicates that the World Coordinate System is active.

Figure 18-1.
The model space UCS icon. The W above the box indicates that the World Coordinate System is active.

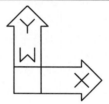

Turning on the UCS icon

You can turn the UCS icon on and off using the **UCSICON** command. This command can be issued by selecting **UCS Icon** from the **Assist** pull-down menu. You can also enter the following at the **Command:** prompt:

> Command: *(type* UCSICON *or* UI *and press* [Enter]*)*
> ON/OFF/All/Noorigin/ORigin ⟨OFF⟩: **ON** ↵
> Command:

Since it is very helpful to display the UCS icon at the origin of the current UCS, repeat the **UCSICON** command and use the **ORigin** option.

> Command: *(type* UCSICON *or* UI *and press* [Enter]*)*
> ON/OFF/All/Noorigin/ORigin ⟨ON⟩: **OR** ↵
> Command:

Each of the **UCSICON** command options are described as follows:
- **ON.** Displays the UCS icon.
- **OFF.** Turns off the icon display. This is the default setting.
- **All.** Shows changes to the icon display in all viewports.
- **Noorigin.** The icon is displayed at the lower left of the viewport, regardless of the current UCS definition.
- **Origin.** The icon is displayed at the origin (0,0,0) of the current UCS. If the origin of the current UCS is off the screen viewing area, the icon is displayed at the lower-left corner of the graphics window.

The **All** option is actually a modifier to the other **UCSICON** command options. It tells AutoCAD LT to display any changes made to the UCS icon in *all* model space viewports. When **All** is selected, the **UCSICON** command option line is redisplayed and you can then select the desired display option for all viewports. For example, suppose you want to display the UCS icon at the origin of the current UCS in four different viewports. The command sequence is as follows:

```
Command: (type UCSICON or UI and press [Enter])
ON/OFF/All/Noorigin/ORigin ⟨ON⟩: A ↵
ON/OFF/All/Noorigin/ORigin ⟨ON⟩: OR ↵
Command:
```

Other UCS icon representations

As you begin working in 3D, you will learn that the UCS icon can assume several different forms, Figure 18-2. Each of these representations has a specific meaning for the 3D user. When the icon is displayed with a plus symbol (+), the icon is located at the origin of the current UCS. When a box appears in the icon, the viewing angle is from the positive Z direction, or *above* the current UCS. When no box is displayed on the icon, the viewing angle is from the negative Z direction, or *below* the current UCS. The icon assumes the appearance of a cube in perspective whenever the **Distance** option of the **DVIEW** command is enabled. The **DVIEW** command is discussed at the end of this chapter. Finally, the icon appears as a box with a "broken pencil" if the viewing angle is perpendicular to the XY plane of the current UCS. While these different forms may at first be hard to understand, they will soon become quite familiar.

Figure 18-2.
UCS icon display examples.

A—The icon is located at the origin of the current UCS.

B—The icon is set to **NOORIGIN**.

C—The UCS is being viewed from below.

D—Perspective viewing is on.

E—The "broken pencil" representation indicates that the XY plane of the current UCS is perpendicular to the viewing plane.

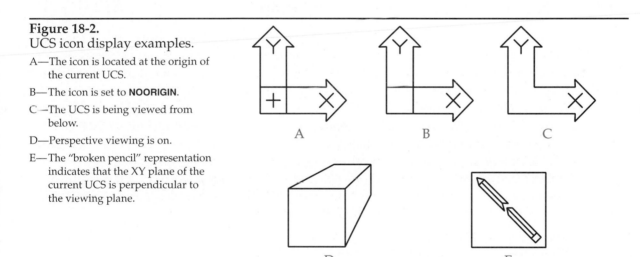

THE RIGHT-HAND RULE

The *right-hand rule* of 3D is a graphic representation of the positive coordinate directions used by most 3D CAD systems. The UCS in AutoCAD LT is based on this simple concept of visualization that requires nothing more than the thumb, index finger, and middle finger on your right hand. Try positioning your hand as illustrated in Figure 18-3. With your right hand open in front of you, extend your thumb straight out to the right, and your index finger straight up. Keep your last two fingers curled into your palm and extend your middle finger straight towards you.

Now imagine that your thumb is the positive X axis, your index finger is the positive Y axis, and your middle finger is the positive Z axis. Think of your palm as being the 0,0,0 drawing origin. Like the UCS icon, the three axes formed by your thumb and first two fingers are 90° mutually perpendicular.

Figure 18-3.
Try positioning your hand like this to understand the relationship of the X, Y, and Z axes.

The greatest advantage of the UCS is the ability to rotate the coordinate axes to any orientation desired. You can use the right-hand rule to visualize how the UCS can be rotated about any one of the three axis lines. To rotate the X axis, for example, keep your thumb stationary and turn your hand toward or away from you. To visualize Y axis rotation, keep your index finger pointed straight up and turn your hand to the left or right. Rotation about the Z axis can be envisioned by keeping your middle finger pointed toward you and rotating your entire arm to the left or right.

OBTAINING A 3D VIEWPOINT WITH VPOINT   ALTUG 11

New drawing files opened in AutoCAD LT default to a single viewport where the UCS and WCS are the same, and the viewing angle is plan to the WCS. This view orientation suits 2D drawing methods quite nicely, but 3D objects are more easily visualized and constructed when viewed from an angle.

Several techniques exist for obtaining 3D views in AutoCAD LT, but perhaps the most common method is through the use of the **VPOINT** (viewpoint) command. With **VPOINT**, a user can specify the direction that an object will be viewed from. The object itself remains fixed in 3D space. Only the line of sight changes. In other words, the *view* rotates, not the object.

The **VPOINT** command can be issued by selecting **3D Viewpoint** from the **View** pull-down menu. A cascading submenu appears offering three **VPOINT** command options **Axis**, **Rotate**, and **Vector**. On the command line, enter the following:

Command: *(type* VPOINT *or* VP *and press* [Enter]*)*
Rotate/⟨View point⟩ ⟨0.0000,0.0000,1.0000⟩: *(Select an option)*

Observe that **VPOINT** offers two options on the command line for view rotation. The default option, labeled **Vector** in the cascading submenu, allows you to rotate the view with XYZ coordinates. However, these coordinates are *not* distance coordinates, but direction (vector) coordinates. The default values shown above in the angle brackets describe a plan view, and are interpreted as follows:

- The X value is zero. Therefore, the viewing angle is *not* along the X axis.
- The Y value is also zero. Therefore, the viewing angle is *not* along the Y axis.
- The Z value is positive. A positive Z value extends out of the screen towards the viewer. Therefore, the viewing angle is along the positive Z axis above the XY plane.

You may be confused by the Z coordinate having a numeric value equal to 1. A Z value equal to 1 does *not* mean that the viewing angle is located one unit above the object being viewed. In reality, the XYZ values used by **VPOINT** are not units of measurement at all, but *directional* units. Thus, entering the values 0,0,2 or 0,0,10 produce exactly the same plan view as 0,0,1.

The VPOINT Rotate option

The **VPOINT Rotate** option allows you to define a 3D view by specifying two angles. The first angular value specified rotates the view (not the object) in the XY plane, Figure 18-4. The second angular value rotates the view away from the XY plane, Figure 18-5. The procedure for the **Rotate** option looks like this:

Command: *(type* VPOINT *or* VP *and press* [Enter])
Rotate/⟨View point⟩ ⟨0.0000,0.0000,1.0000⟩: **R** ↵
Enter angle in XY plane from X axis ⟨*current angle*⟩: *(enter an angle)*
Enter angle from XY plane ⟨*current angle*⟩: *(enter an angle)*
Regenerating drawing.
Command:

Figure 18-4.
VPOINT rotation in the XY plane is performed about the Z axis.

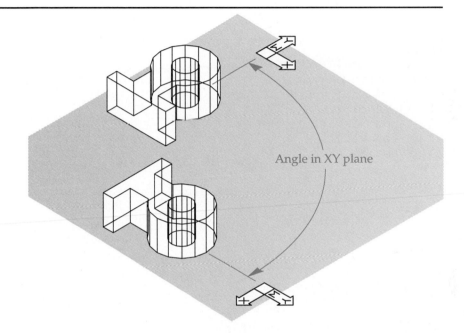

Figure 18-5.
VPOINT rotation from the XY plane is performed about the X axis.

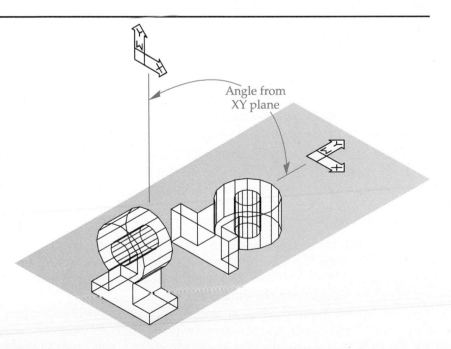

Refer to Figure 18-6 to visualize the direction of rotation in the XY plane. Starting at the upper left viewport and moving in a clockwise direction, the XY plane is rotated 45°, 135°, 225°, and finally 315°. From the right-hand rule, you will see that all rotation in the XY plane is done about the Z axis.

On the other hand, angles measured *from* the XY plane are rotated about the X axis. Using the right-hand rule, rotate your hand *away* from you so that your thumb, index finger, and palm are in a horizontal position (parallel to the floor), and your middle finger (the Z axis) is pointed straight up. In this orientation, the XY plane is considered to be at 0°. Slowly return your hand once more into a vertical position so that your middle finger is once again pointed toward you. You can now see that rotation from the XY plane is performed about the X axis (your thumb). Since the direction of rotation is positive, the angle from the XY plane is now 90°. Continue rotating your hand so that your index finger, the Y axis, is pointed straight at you. In this orientation, the angle from the XY plane is at 180°.

Figure 18-6.
View orientation by rotation in the XY plane. Clockwise from the upper left viewport:
XY rotation = 45°,
XY rotation = 135°,
XY rotation = 225°,
XY rotation = 315°.

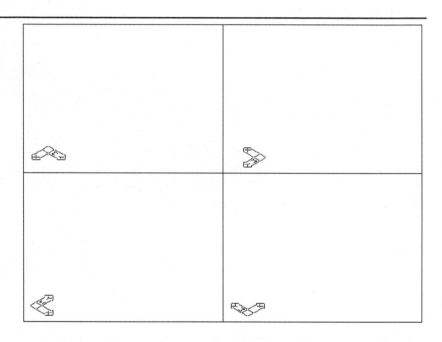

Obtaining an isometric viewing angle

Refer to Figure 18-6. The UCS icon in each of the rotated views represents a rotation angle of 35°16′ (isometric angle) from the XY plane. The following table lists the equivalent XYZ vector coordinates for the viewing angles illustrated. The viewing angles can also be quickly obtained by selecting **3D Viewpoint Presets** from the **View** pull-down menu. The four ISO view options in the cascading submenu correspond to the viewing angles as shown below:

Angle in XY plane + Angle from XY plane = XYZ vector coordinates

45°	35°16′	1,1,1	**Iso View NE**
135°	35°16′	–1,1,1	**Iso View NW**
225°	35°16′	–1,–1,1	**Iso View SW**
315°	35°16′	1,–1,1	**Iso View SE**

From the table above, you can see that four different isometric viewing angles can be obtained by entering the appropriate XYZ coordinates using the default vector option of the **VPOINT** command. You can also use the **Rotate** option to obtain the same viewing angles by rotating the views with the values shown both *in* the XY plane and *from* the XY plane. If you use the second method, you can enter 35°16′ on the command line by typing in the value like this: 35d16′. However, the simplest way to obtain an isometric viewing angle is to use one of the four ISO view options that appear in the **3D Viewpoint Presets** cascading submenu.

The VPOINT compass and tripod axes

Another quick and easy way to define a 3D viewing angle is with the **VPOINT** "axes and compass." The axes method can be selected by picking **Axes** from the **3D Viewpoint** cascading submenu, or by simply pressing [Enter] at the **VPOINT** command prompt. Whichever method is used, the axes tripod and compass appears in the graphics window as shown in Figure 18-7. The compass display at the upper right of the screen represents the north and south poles and the equator. For this reason, you may sometimes hear the compass referred to as the "globe icon."

The very center of the compass represents the north pole, the small circle represents the equator, and the large circle represents the south pole. The normal full screen crosshair cursor changes to a very small crosshair, as shown within the compass. By positioning the tiny crosshair within one of the compass quadrants and picking with your left mouse button, a 3D view is created. Any one of the four inner, or north pole, quadrants place the viewing angle *above* the XY plane, looking down on the object. The four outer, or south pole, quadrants place the viewing angle *below* the XY plane, so the object is viewed from below.

Notice that the compass is bisected along both the horizontal and vertical axes. Positioning the tiny crosshairs *below* the horizontal axis places the viewer in front of the object. Positioning the crosshairs *above* the horizontal axis places the viewer behind the object. In a similar fashion, the vertical axis controls the viewing angle from the left or right. By positioning the crosshairs to the *left* of the vertical axis, the object is viewed from the left side. Positioning the crosshairs to the *right*, views the object from the right side. A top, or plan, view can be obtained by setting the **Snap** mode on and placing the tiny crosshairs at the precise intersection of the horizontal and vertical axes. Just to the left and below the compass are located the tripod axes. The motion of the tripod axes follows the right-hand rule. See Figure 18-8. As you move your mouse about the compass, the tripod axes revolve to reflect the view orientation.

Figure 18-7.
The **VPOINT** compass and tripod axes display.

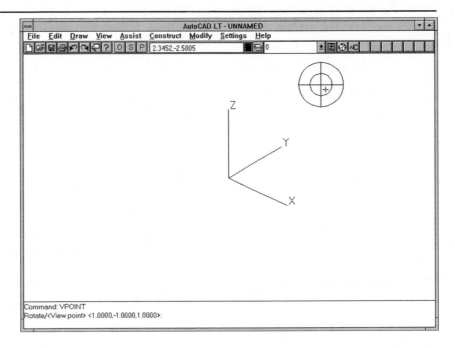

Figure 18-8.
The motion of the **VPOINT** tripod axes conforms to the right-hand rule.

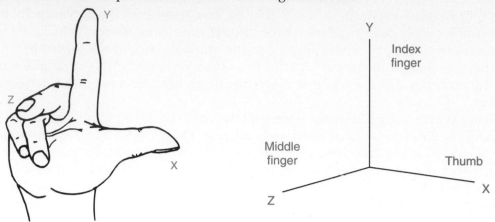

Saving the 3D view

It is always a good idea to save the view so that you can easily return to it at any time without reissuing the **VPOINT** command. Views, whether 2D or 3D, are saved with names using the **VIEW** command introduced in Chapter 4. As with other named objects in AutoCAD LT, a view name can be up to 31 characters in length, but no spaces or punctuation marks are permitted.

Remember that you can save as many views as needed. You can restore or delete them as necessary. Since sometimes you may forget the names of saved views, they can be listed for quick reference. This option is particularly handy when you find yourself working with a drawing file that was created some time ago, or with a file created by another user.

Each of the **VIEW** command options appear in a cascading submenu by selecting **View** from the **View** pull-down menu. The **VIEW** command can also be accessed at the **Command:** prompt. The options are described below:

> Command: *(type* VIEW *or* V *and press* [Enter]*)*
> ?/Delete/Restore/Save/Window: *(Select an option)*

- **?.** Lists all saved views in the AutoCAD LT text window. An M (model space), or a P (paper space) will appear next to each view name in the list. The M or P indicates the space in which the view was defined.
- **Delete.** Removes one or more defined views. Multiple view names must be separated by commas.
- **Restore.** Displays a saved view in the current viewport.
- **Save.** Names and saves the current viewport display. However, *no warning* is issued if a view is saved with the same name of an existing view.
- **Window.** Allows you to define a view with two diagonal points. The view is named and saved, but not displayed until the **Restore** option is used.

FINDING THE WAY HOME WITH THE PLAN COMMAND ┃ ALTUG 11

While working with 3D views, you may often find it useful to return to the default WCS plan view. This is particularly true when you find yourself "lost in 3D space" and need some familiar viewing angle to reorient yourself. Should you inadvertently create an unwanted or disorienting 3D view, you can use the **UNDO** command to restore the previous view point. You can also return to the previous view point using **ZOOM Previous**. This is possible because AutoCAD LT remembers the ten previous screen zooms and/or views. Zooming back to a previous 3D view point is a handy feature you are likely to use often. However, it is not a very useful method of returning to a plan view, unless your last view was a plan view. A very quick and easy way to restore a view plan to the WCS is by selecting **3D Plan View** from the **View** pull-down menu, and then selecting **World UCS** from the cascading submenu.

It is often necessary to create or restore a view that is *not* plan to the WCS, but plan to the current UCS or a previously defined UCS. These options are also located in the **3D Plan View** cascading submenu. On the command line, the **PLAN** sequence appears as follows:

> Command: *(type* PLAN *or* PV *and press* [Enter]*)*
> ⟨Current UCS⟩/Ucs/World: *(Select an option or accept the default)*

- ⟨**Current UCS**⟩. The default **PLAN** option creates or restores a view that is plan (X = 0, Y = 0, Z = 1) to the current UCS. If no UCS has yet been defined, this option restores the plan view of the WCS because the UCS is then equal to the WCS.
- **Ucs.** Creates or restores the plan view of a previously defined UCS.
- **World.** Restores the plan view of the WCS.

ELEVATION AND THICKNESS ⬛ ALTUG 11

Every entity created in AutoCAD LT, whether it is 2D or 3D, has a Z value. The *elevation* of an entity is the Z value of the XY plane that it was constructed on. By default, the base XY plane is zero. Thus, all entities created in AutoCAD LT have zero elevation. A positive elevation creates entities *above* the base XY plane, while a negative elevation creates entities *below* the XY plane. Therefore, elevation is simply an entity's height above or below the plane of construction. This is illustrated by the three circles shown in Figure 18-9. The three circles each have the same diameter, and each is located on the same X and Y center. However, the middle circle has a default base elevation of zero. The circle at the top has an elevation of 4, which places it 4 units *above* the middle circle. The circle at the bottom has an elevation of –4, which places it 4 units *below* the middle circle.

Changing the system base elevation, or Z value, is done with the **ELEV** command as follows:

> Command: *(type* ELEV *or* EV *and press* [Enter]*)*
> New current elevation ⟨0.0000⟩: *(enter a positive or negative value)*

After specifying a value for elevation, you are then prompted to enter a thickness value.

> New current thickness ⟨0.0000⟩: *(enter a positive or negative value)*
> Command:

Figure 18-9.
Elevation is the height, or depth, of an entity above or below the base XY plane.

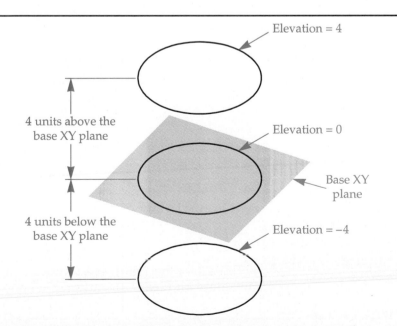

4 units above the base XY plane

4 units below the base XY plane

Elevation = 4

Elevation = 0

Base XY plane

Elevation = –4

Thickness is a property of an entity, just as color, layer, and linetype are. Entities with thickness are often called *extrusions*. A thickness value sets the distance that a 2D object is "extruded" above or below its elevation. A positive value extrudes along the positive Z axis and a negative value extrudes along the negative Z axis. This is illustrated by the three circles shown in Figure 18-10. As you can see, an entity with zero thickness is strictly two-dimensional. Also from the illustration, notice the lines connecting the two circles with thickness. These lines are called *tessalation lines*. AutoCAD LT creates them automatically along the curved surfaces of an extrusion to help you visualize its location and curvature.

Figure 18-10.
Thickness values set the distance that 2D objects are extruded above or below their elevation.

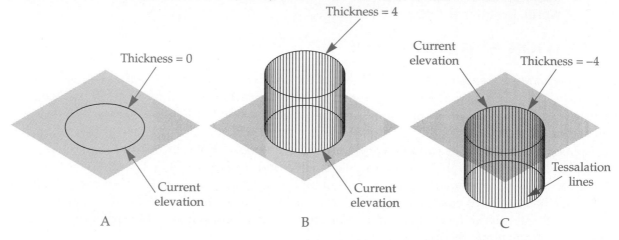

Thickness = 0   Thickness = 4   Current elevation   Thickness = –4   Tessalation lines

Current elevation   Current elevation

A   B   C

Setting elevation and thickness using a dialog box

As an alternative to the command line, the **Entity Creation Modes** dialog box can also be used to set elevation and thickness. To display the dialog box, type DDEMODES at the **Command:** prompt or select **Entity Modes...** from the **Settings** pull-down menu. You can also pick the **Current Color** button on the toolbar to quickly display the dialog box. Use the appropriate text boxes to change the values as required, Figure 18-11.

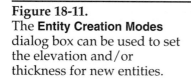

Figure 18-11.
The **Entity Creation Modes** dialog box can be used to set the elevation and/or thickness for new entities.

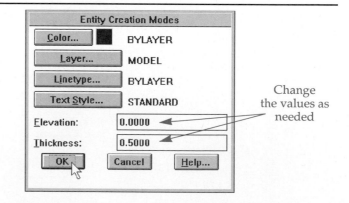

Change the values as needed

PROFESSIONAL TIP   The **ELEV** command sets the elevation and thickness for new entities. Use the **THICKNESS** system variable if you wish to set thickness only and leave elevation unchanged for new objects.

Changing the thickness of existing entities

As previously mentioned, thickness is a property of AutoCAD LT entities. As with other entity properties, it can be modified or added to existing entities using the **CHPROP** or **DDCHPROP** commands. On the command line, the sequence is as follows:

Command: *(type* CHPROP *or* CR *and press* [Enter]*)*
Select objects: *(select one or more entities with thickness to change)*
Change what property (Color/LAyer/LType/Thickness)? **T** ↵
New thickness ⟨*current*⟩: *(enter a positive or negative value and press* [Enter]*)*
Change what property (Color/LAyer/LType/Thickness)? ↵
Command:

If you wish to use **DDCHPROP**, type DDCHPROP at the **Command:** prompt or select **Change Properties...** from the **Modify** pull-down menu. The **Thickness:** text box in the **Change Properties** dialog box is used to modify the thickness of selected entities, Figure 18-12.

Figure 18-12.
The **Change Properties**
dialog box is used to modify
the thickness of existing
objects.

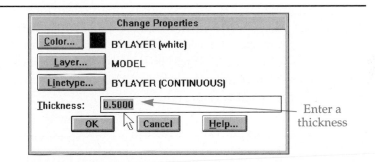

Enter a
thickness

EXERCISE 18-1

❏ Use the following procedure to create a 3D model of the object shown below.
❏ Begin a new drawing and turn on the UCS icon.
❏ Leave the elevation set at 0 but set the thickness to .375.
❏ Draw a 4 × 2 rectangle using the **RECTANG** command. Fillet the four corners in one operation using the **FILLET Polyline** option.
❏ Set the elevation to .375 and change the thickness to .25.
❏ Create the circle and the six-sided polygon at the dimensions given.
❏ Using **DDCHPROP**, change the thickness of the circle to .625.
❏ Use the **VPOINT** command to obtain a 3D viewing angle of the model. Once you have a view to your liking, save it with the name 3DVIEW using the **VIEW** command.
❏ Return to the plan view using the **PLAN** command.
❏ Save the model as EX18-1.

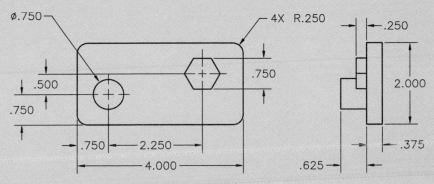

THE HIDE COMMAND

The type of 3D geometric construction that can be created in AutoCAD LT is called *wireframe modeling*. In a wireframe, all edges of an object are shown as lines. Arc, circle, and spline entities are used to define curved features. The resulting model assumes the appearance of a frame constructed out of wire, or a "wireframe." Unfortunately, all of the lines that would normally be hidden are clearly visible. Consequently, interpreting the image is often difficult.

AutoCAD LT has a way to remove, or suppress, hidden lines from view. This is done with the **HIDE** command. While this command is quite useful, it has several significant limitations. For wireframe displays, **HIDE** only evaluates circles, wide polylines, and solids. Line, polyline, and circle entities extruded with assigned thickness are also evaluated. These entities behave like opaque surfaces, hiding other entities behind them. Refer to Figure 18-13 to see the results of **HIDE** on the wireframe model constructed in Exercise 18-1. The normal display of the model is shown in the left viewport, while the hidden-line display appears in the right viewport. Since circles are treated as opaque surfaces, only the portion of the model behind the hole is hidden. Also notice that extruded objects (entities with thickness) appear open at the top, such as the extruded rectangle and polygon. After using **HIDE**, you can redraw the screen without losing the hidden-line display. However, any operation that requires a screen regeneration will restore the original display. You can also manually restore the original display using the **REGEN** command.

Figure 18-13.
The results of **HIDE** on the wireframe model from Exercise 18-1. The normal display of the model is shown in the left viewport, while the hidden-line display appears in the right viewport.

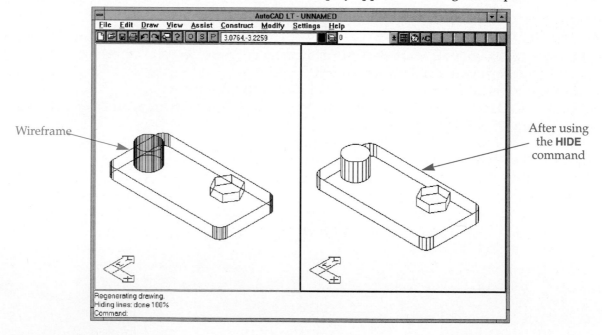

A few warnings about HIDE

Be aware that the **HIDE** command will only work in the current viewport. It also can be a very compute-intensive operation. Therefore, **HIDE** can be quite time-consuming on very large models or on slower computers. Also, layers that are turned off may still obscure other features. Even though the layers are invisible, they are *still evaluated* during a **HIDE** operation. Frozen layers, however, are *not* evaluated by **HIDE**. To improve system performance, freeze any unnecessary layers since frozen layers are not evaluated during a **HIDE** operation. Finally, hidden-line displays can only be plotted by picking the **Hide Lines** check box in the **Additional Parameters** section of the **Plot Configuration** dialog box. See Chapter 13 for more information about printing and plotting.

PROFESSIONAL TIP

Once hidden lines have been suppressed with **HIDE**, they remain suppressed until the screen is regenerated. To save a hidden-line display, use the **MSLIDE** command to make a slide of the current screen. Whenever the hidden-line display is required, simply restore it with the **VSLIDE** command.

OBTAINING A SHADED IMAGE WITH THE SHADE COMMAND

ALTUG 11

Once an object is extruded, it can be shaded with the **SHADE** command. *Shading* is another way of removing lines that are not normally hidden from view in a wireframe display. The **SHADE** command can be entered at the keyboard or issued by selecting **Shade** from the **View** pull-down menu. When using the pull-down menu, several shading options appear in a cascading submenu. These options are covered in the next section.

The speed of a shading operation is largely dependent on available physical RAM and on the area of the screen taken up by the model. Therefore, shading in a smaller viewport is faster. A shading operation in progress can be canceled with a [Ctrl]+[C]. Once an object is shaded, the operation cannot be reversed with the **UNDO** command. To return to the original display, the **REGEN** command must be used. Also, you cannot select or plot entities in a shaded image.

The SHADEDGE system variable

Several kinds of shaded renderings can be performed with **SHADE**. This depends on the number of colors available and on the current values of the **SHADEDGE** and **SHADEDIF** system variables. **SHADEDGE** determines what kind of shaded rendering will be produced by specifying how faces and edges are displayed. The **SHADEDIF** variable is covered in the next section.

You can quickly set the **SHADEDGE** variable and perform a shade in one operation by selecting from one of the options in the **Shade** cascading submenu in the **View** pull-down menu. Each of the menu options are described as follows:

- **256 Color.** This option requires a 256-color display. All faces are shaded with diffuse light, but edges are not highlighted. Selecting this option sets **SHADEDGE** = 0.
- **256 Color Edge Highlight.** This option also requires a 256-color display. All faces are shaded with diffuse light, and edges are highlighted with the screen background color. Selecting this option sets **SHADEDGE** = 1.
- **16 Color Hidden Line.** Performs a simulated hidden-line rendering and works with any display regardless of the number of available colors. Selecting this option sets **SHADEDGE** = 2.

- **16 Color Filled.** Faces are not shaded with diffuse light, but are filled in their original color (flat shading). This is the default **SHADEDGE** setting if the **SHADE** command is entered from the keyboard, and works with any number of colors. Selecting this option sets **SHADEDGE** = 3.

The model from Exercise 18-1 is shown in Figure 18-14 shaded with each of the four **SHADEDGE** settings. Compare the hidden line display in the lower right viewport with that shown in Figure 18-13.

Figure 18-14.
The model from Exercise 18-1 is shaded with the four **SHADEDGE** settings. Clockwise from the upper left viewport: **SHADEDGE** = 0, **SHADEDGE** = 1, **SHADEDGE** = 2, **SHADEDGE** = 3.

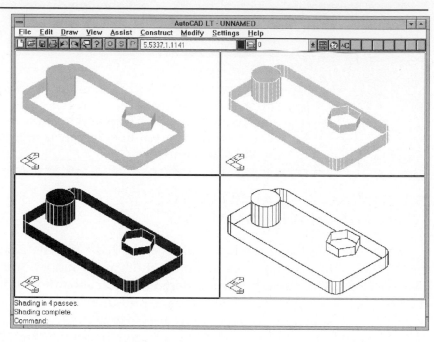

The **SHADEDIF** system variable

AutoCAD LT calculates shading based on only one light source. When **SHADEDGE** is set to zero or 1, the image is shaded based on the angle the faces form with the viewing direction. The diffuse reflection and ambient light in the shaded image are controlled with the **SHADEDIF** system variable. **SHADEDIF** can be set to any value between zero and 100. By default it is set to 70. This means that 70% of the light is diffuse reflection from the light source, and 30% is ambient light. Increasing the value of **SHADEDIF** increases diffuse lighting, thereby adding more reflectivity and contrast to an image. Observe that **SHADEDIF** has no effect when **SHADEDGE** is set to 2 (hidden), or 3 (filled). You can change the value of **SHADEDIF** by selecting **Shade Diffuse** from the **Shade** cascading submenu.

PROFESSIONAL TIP

In the event that you find yourself seated in front of an unfamiliar CAD workstation, (such as at a new job site or in a classroom environment), you can easily determine if the graphics card is capable of only 16 colors or 256 colors by selecting the **Current Color** button on the toolbar. When the **Entity Creation Modes** dialog box appears, click the **Color...** button. This action displays the **Select Color** subdialog box showing all the colors available for the *current screen resolution* on that particular machine. If there are more than 16 colors listed, the card can support 256 colors. Most computers now support *at least* 256 colors.

SETTING UP MULTIPLE VIEWS WITH THE VPORTS COMMAND

ALTUG 8

You may recall from Chapter 4 that the **VPORTS** command allows you to divide the model space display screen into a maximum of 16 multiple viewing windows, or viewports. Several typical viewport configurations are shown in Figure 18-15. The viewports are adjacent to one another with no gaps in between. This is called *tiled*. Each viewport can display a different view of your 3D model and you can pan or zoom independently in each viewport. The **REDRAW** and **REGEN** commands affect *all* displayed viewports.

Only one viewport can be active at any one time. The active viewport is surrounded by a wider border, and the screen crosshair cursor is only displayed within that viewport. For the other displayed viewports, the cursor appears as the Windows arrow cursor. All viewports are interactive. This means that a drawing or editing command can be started in one viewport and completed in another.

To make a viewport current, simply pick anywhere within its border. You can also use the [Ctrl]+[V] keyboard combination to cycle through multiple viewports, making each one current in succession. When plotting multiple viewports, only the current viewport is plotted, however.

You also may recall from Chapter 4 that a multiple viewport configuration can be saved with a name and then restored, listed, or deleted. Single viewports can be returned to at any time, and more than one configuration can be saved. Like view names, viewport configuration names can be up to 31 characters in length and the same naming restrictions apply. Also, an inactive viewport can be joined to an active viewport providing that the resulting viewport forms a rectangle. The newly joined viewport inherits all aspects of the dominant viewport that it is joined to, such as **LIMITS**, **GRID**, and **SNAP** settings.

By default, the **VPORTS** command divides the screen into three viewports with the *dominant viewport* (active viewport) to the right and the two inactive viewports arranged in a vertical orientation to the left. The **VPORTS** command can be issued by selecting **Viewports** from the **View** pull-down menu, or entered at the keyboard as shown below:

Command: (*type* VPORTS *or* VW *and press* [Enter])
Save/Restore/Delete/Join/SIngle/?/2/⟨3⟩/4: (*Select an option*)

- **Save.** Saves a defined viewport configuration with a name. The configuration name cannot exceed 31 characters.
- **Restore.** Redisplays a saved viewport configuration.
- **Delete.** Deletes a saved viewport configuration.
- **Join.** Combines two adjacent viewports into one viewport, providing the new viewport forms a rectangle.
- **SIngle.** Disables multiple viewports and displays the current viewport as a single view.
- **?.** Lists any or all saved viewport configurations in the AutoCAD LT text window.
- **2.** Divides the current viewport into two viewports. You can choose between a horizontal or vertical division.
- **3.** Divides the current viewport into three viewports. The dominant viewport can be placed to the right (the default), to the left, or above the other two viewports.
- **4.** Divides the current viewport into four equally sized viewports.

Figure 18-15.
Typical model space viewport configurations obtained with the **VPORTS** command.

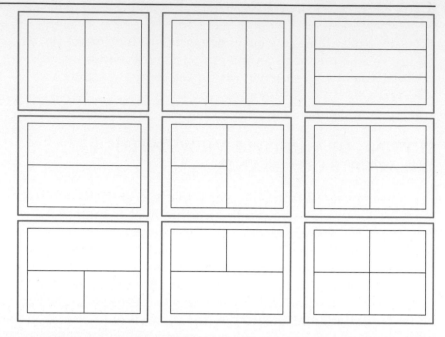

THE USER COORDINATE SYSTEM (UCS)   ALTUG 11

The World Coordinate System (WCS) in AutoCAD LT is fixed in 3D space and cannot be modified. However, with the **UCS** command you can create your own *User Coordinate System.* A UCS can be defined by:

- Specifying a new origin for 0,0,0.
- Selecting a new XY plane or Z axis direction.
- Copying the 3D orientation of an existing entity.
- Rotating the current UCS around its X, Y, or Z axes.
- Aligning a new UCS with the current viewing direction.

Like views and viewport configurations, a UCS can be saved with a name and then restored, listed, deleted, or renamed. Any number of coordinate systems can be defined in a drawing, but only one can be current at any given time.

Elevation and the UCS

Earlier in this chapter, you learned that changing the elevation can be quite handy for 3D construction. Unfortunately, you may often forget the current system elevation and entities will be inadvertently generated above or below the plane that you intended. However, creating a UCS permits you to define a construction plane at any *height,* at any *angle,* and at any *orientation.* Since the origin of a UCS can be placed at any height, you really do not need to be concerned with Z values at all. Geometry is generated in the XYZ plane defined by the UCS using familiar absolute, relative, or polar coordinates. The UCS icon serves as a marker for the current construction plane when displayed at the origin of the current UCS, so you are far less likely to construct geometry with incorrect Z values.

In Figure 18-16A, the two circles have the same 2.500 diameter, and each is located on the same X and Y center. However, the bottom circle has a default base elevation of zero. The circle at the top has an elevation of 4, placing it 4 units *above* the bottom circle. In Figure 18-16B, two circles with the same diameters and X and Y centers are shown. Both of the bottom circles were created in exactly the same way. However, for the top circle in Figure 18-16B, a UCS was defined with its origin 4 units up from the Z axis and the circle generated with the UCS in effect, rather than setting the system elevation. Note the appearance of the UCS icon. The cross at the juncture of the X and Y axes indicates that the icon is at the origin of the current UCS. Also, observe that the W has disappeared from the icon. Once a UCS is created, the World Coordinate System is no longer in effect.

Figure 18-16.
A—An entity created with elevation. B—An entity created with a UCS.

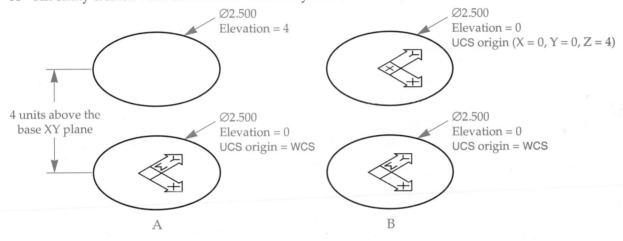

The UCS command options

Each of the **UCS** command options can be selected from a cascading submenu by first selecting **Set UCS** from the **Assist** pull-down menu, or by clicking the **Set UCS** button. The **Set UCS** button does not appear in the toolbox or on the toolbar by default. The **UCS** command can also be entered at the **Command:** prompt as follows:

> Command: **UCS** ↵
> Origin/ZAxis/3point/Entity/View/X/Y/Z/Prev/Restore/Save/Del/?/⟨World⟩:

- **Origin.** Defines a UCS by shifting the origin of the current UCS to a new location. The direction of the X, Y, and Z axes remain unchanged.
- **Zaxis.** Establishes a UCS with two points. The first point specifies the UCS origin. The second point determines the direction for the positive Z axis.
- **3point.** Defines a UCS by specifying first its origin, then a point on the positive X axis, and finally a point on the positive Y axis.
- **Entity.** Creates a UCS with the same extrusion direction (positive Z axis) as a selected entity. The orientation of the X and Y axes is determined by the type of entity selected.
- **View.** Establishes a UCS with the XY plane parallel to the screen, but leaves the origin unchanged.
- **X.** Creates a UCS by rotating the current UCS about its X axis.
- **Y.** Creates a UCS by rotating the current UCS about its Y axis.
- **Z.** Creates a UCS by rotating the current UCS about its Z axis.
- **Prev.** Restores the previous UCS. Similar to the way **ZOOM Previous** remembers the last ten zooms/views, AutoCAD LT remembers the previous ten coordinate systems.
- **Restore.** Restores a saved UCS so that it becomes the current UCS. Responding with a ? allows you to list any or all defined coordinate systems.

- **Save.** Names and saves the current coordinate system. UCS names can be up to 31 characters in length, but must conform to standard AutoCAD LT naming convention. Responding with a ? allows you to list any or all defined coordinate systems.
- **Del.** Deletes a saved UCS. More than one UCS can be deleted by separating the UCS names with commas. Responding with a ? allows you to list any or all defined coordinate systems.
- **?.** Lists the name, origin, and XYZ axes for each UCS you specify. Responding with the wildcard asterisk character lists all coordinate systems. If the current UCS is unnamed, it is listed as *NO NAME* or *WORLD*, depending on whether it is the same as the WCS.
- ⟨**World**⟩. The default option to the UCS command, **World** restores the WCS.

PROFESSIONAL TIP

It is a good idea to save a UCS once created. Saving a UCS is easier and faster than defining a new one, and it can always be renamed or deleted later.

Using the **UCS Control** dialog box

A UCS can be set current, listed, renamed, or deleted using the **UCS Control** dialog box. To display this dialog box, type DDUCS at the **Command:** prompt or select **Named UCS...** from the **Assist** pull-down menu. The **UCS Control** dialog box lists all UCS's—named or unnamed, Figure 18-17. The **UCS Names** field always displays *WORLD* for the World Coordinate System. If a previous UCS has been defined but remains nameless, the entry *PREVIOUS* is displayed. If the current UCS has not yet been named, then *NO NAME* appears in one of the name fields.

Figure 18-17.
Selecting a saved UCS from the **UCS Control** dialog box.

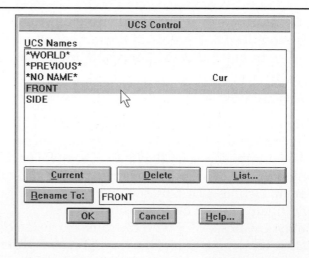

Using the **UCS Orientation** dialog box

You can use the **UCS Orientation** dialog box to select from nine preset UCS configurations. To do so, enter the DDUCSP at the **Command:** prompt or select **Preset UCS...** from the **Assist** pull-down menu. This dialog box lets you select a new UCS that is created at right angles to either the current UCS or the WCS, Figure 18-18. Specify your choice by clicking the appropriate option button. Also, you can restore the WCS or previous UCS, or set the UCS to the current view. This performs the same function as the **View** option of the **UCS** command.

Figure 18-18.
Nine preset UCS
configurations are available
in the **UCS Orientation**
dialog box.

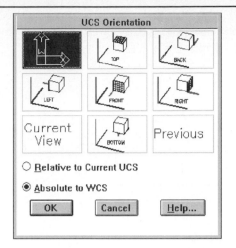

> **NOTE**
>
> The **Named UCS** and the **Preset UCS** buttons (shown in the margin on the previous page) are not on the toolbar or toolbox by default. They can be easily added. See Chapter 19 in this text.

3D MODELING METHODOLOGY

Despite the diverse geometry reflected in engineering and architecture, nearly all objects have one very important similarity—a common profile. Any object usually has at least one feature that reflects a profile that is duplicated either at its top, bottom, sides, or anywhere in between. For example, a circle might represent a hole or a polygonal feature might represent a hex head. The key to successful 3D modeling is to first identify the common profile for the object you wish to model. Once you have identified the profile, create a new UCS if necessary and construct the profile using ordinary AutoCAD LT drawing commands. When the profile is complete, copy it along the Z axis at the required dimension, and connect the two profiles using lines or polylines.

For example, the common profile of the object in Figure 18-19A is shown in 18-19B. Refer to Figure 18-20 as you follow the procedure listed below:

1. Obtain a 3D viewing angle.
2. Rotate the UCS 90° about the X axis to help with the construction of the common profile. Save the UCS with a name such as FRONT.
3. Create the closed profile with line or polyline entities as shown at A.
4. Next, copy the profile along the Z axis as required at B. You can copy along the positive or negative axis, however the negative axis is used in this example.
5. At C, connect the two profiles using line or polyline entities. A running **Endpoint** osnap and the **MULTIPLE** command modifier would be helpful here.
6. Return to the WCS or rotate the UCS –90° about the X axis. Move the UCS origin to the top corner of the object as shown at D. Save the UCS with a name such as TOP.
7. Draw the two circles at the top of the object. Copy them along the negative Z axis as required to show the hole bottoms. Connect the coaxial circles by their quadrants. Connections at all four quadrants is unnecessary—two quadrants are sufficient.
8. Use the **UCS 3point** option to create the UCS shown at E. Save it with a name such as AUXILIARY or SLANTED and create the counterbore feature using two circles with different Z values.

The 3D wireframe model is complete, Figure 18-20F.

Figure 18-19.
A—Nearly every object has a common profile. Can you identify the common profile of this object?
B—The profile is shown here highlighted.

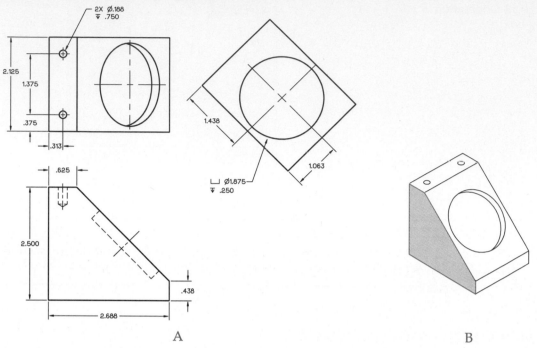

A

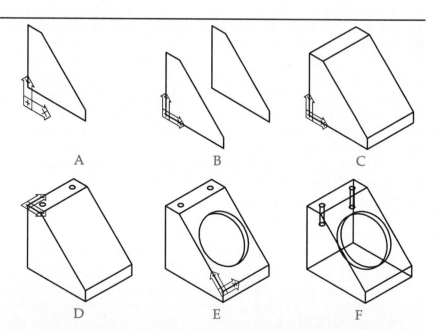

B

Figure 18-20.
A–E—The sequence of steps to construct the 3D wireframe model.
F—The completed 3D wireframe model.

A

B

C

D

E

F

PROFESSIONAL TIP

Create and save a UCS for each plane of your 3D model that represents an orthographic view (top, front, side). When organizing multiple viewport configurations in an orthographic fashion, simply activate the desired viewport and set the view plan to the named UCS that represents that view.

AutoCAD LT—Fundamentals and Applications

❑ Begin a new drawing. Obtain a 3D view with the viewpoint coordinates 1, –1, 1.

❑ Create and set current a layer called MODEL. Assign the color cyan (4) to the new layer.

❑ Turn the UCS icon on and model the object shown below in the MODEL layer using the three coordinate systems illustrated.

❑ As an aid, rotate the UCS 90° about the X axis and save the UCS with the name FRONT before creating any geometry.

❑ With the FRONT UCS active, construct the L-shaped profile of the bracket. Copy it along the negative Z axis at the correct dimension. Connect the two profiles with lines.

❑ Next, rotate the UCS 90° about the Y axis and save the new UCS with the name SIDE. Construct the radiused feature and the .750 diameter hole with the SIDE UCS active. Copy the entities along the positive Z axis as required and connect them at their quadrants as shown.

❑ Finally, restore the WCS and construct the .500 diameter hole. Once again, copy the circle along the positive Z axis as required and connect the two circles at the quadrant points as shown.

❑ Create a four-viewport configuration using **VPORTS**. Save the configuration with the name ORTHOGRAPHIC.

❑ Activate the upper left viewport and use the **PLAN** command to set the view plan to the WCS.

❑ Activate the lower left viewport and set the view plan to the FRONT UCS.

❑ Activate the lower right viewport and set the view plan to the SIDE UCS.

❑ Zoom and pan in each viewport as required to arrange the views orthographically.

❑ Save the 3D model as EX18-4.

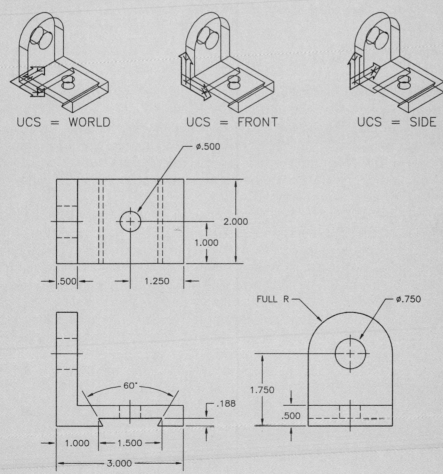

UCS = WORLD   UCS = FRONT   UCS = SIDE

Ø.500

2.000

1.000

.500   1.250

FULL R   Ø.750

60°

.188

1.750

.500

1.000   1.500

3.000

THE UCSFOLLOW VARIABLE

As you begin modeling in 3D, you will probably find it convenient to do most of your work in an oblique, or 3D view. This is easily accomplished by creating UCS's that correspond to each construction plane of your model. Creating the entire model in this fashion does have some drawbacks, however.

You may have noticed that the wireframe representation of a 3D model can sometimes play tricks on your eyes. The model seems to reverse its orientation at times or "flip" on you. Because a 3D model is a true three-dimensional object, and a computer display screen is two-dimensional, things are not always what they seem to be. Therefore, it is a good idea to build your model in two vertical (or horizontal) viewports. One viewport can be a 3D view, and the other an orthographic view. As you construct geometry with a UCS in the oblique view, the orthographic view can be set parallel, or plan to the current UCS to serve as a guide. This will verify the correct location of features on the XYZ axes. Having a plan view also enables you to better visualize the shape and orientation of the object under construction.

Earlier in this chapter, you learned how the **PLAN** command can set a view plan to the current UCS, a different UCS, or to the WCS. For multiple viewport configurations, the **UCSFOLLOW** variable allows you to do this automatically. In the two-viewport configuration suggested above, **UCSFOLLOW** can be turned on in one of the viewports. Then, whenever a UCS is created or restored in the 3D viewport, the other viewport automatically displays a view plan to the changed UCS. The **UCSFOLLOW** variable can be turned on or off as follows:

Command: **UCSFOLLOW** ↵
New value for UCSFOLLOW⟨0⟩: *(type* 0 *to turn it off or* 1 *to turn it on and press* [Enter]*)*

The **UCSFOLLOW** variable is off by default. Enter a 1 to turn it on. Just as each viewport can have individual settings for **GRID**, **SNAP**, and **LIMITS**, so can each viewport have a different setting for **UCSFOLLOW**.

DYNAMIC VIEWING WITH DVIEW

ALTUG 11

So far you have learned that a 3D view can be obtained with the **VPOINT** command and its various options. Remember though, that **VPOINT** only changes the viewing angle to the object and not the orientation of the object or its distance from the viewer. The **DVIEW** (dynamic view) command is a far more powerful and flexible way of manipulating a 3D model. Several of the **DVIEW** options provide you with a horizontal slider bar where values can be set. As you change the view with the slider bar, 3D objects move dynamically providing greater control of every aspect of the display.

An analogy can be made with **DVIEW** and photography. With **DVIEW**, the location of the viewer's eyes is the *camera* and the 3D model is the *target*. Because these two points form the line of sight and each can be adjusted to any angle, the user can control both the orientation and the distance that an object is viewed from—just as a camera can be equipped with a wide-angle or telephoto lens to alter distance. The distance from the camera to the target can also be adjusted to produce a "vanishing point" perspective display, what **DVIEW** calls *distance*. The camera can also be rotated around the line of sight to produce a different tilt, or *twist* angle. With **DVIEW**, you can also eliminate, or *clip*, the front or back planes of an object to reveal (or hide) certain features. Should you create an unsatisfactory display, **DVIEW** includes an **Undo** option to restore the previous view. Finally, a hidden-line display can also be obtained from within **DVIEW**, if thickness has been applied to the model.

DVIEW selection set and command options

The **DVIEW** command can be issued by selecting **3D Dynamic View** from the **V̲iew** pull-down menu, or by entering the following at the **Command:** prompt:

Command: *(type* DVIEW *or* DV *and press* [Enter]*)*
Select objects:

When **DVIEW** is used, the **Select objects:** prompt appears. All selection set options are valid. However, since the position of the selected objects is constantly updated on-screen, large selection sets can quickly use up system resources. Therefore, select only a few objects. Once these objects are displayed to your satisfaction, simply exit the **DVIEW** command and the rest of the entities will match the new view orientation.

*** Switching to the WCS ***
CAmera/TArget/Distance/POints/PAn/Zoom/TWist/CLip/Hide/Off/Undo/⟨eXit⟩:

Each of the **DVIEW** command options are described as follows:
- **CAmera.** This option works similarly to the **VPOINT Rotate** option. Select the angle from the camera to the target both *from* the XY plane, and *in* the XY plane (around the Z axis).
- **TArget.** Similar to the **CAmera** option, except the angle is determined from the target to the camera. In other words, the target moves and not the camera.
- **Distance.** This option sets the distance from the camera to the target and turns perspective viewing on. When perspective viewing is on, the UCS icon is displayed as a cube seen in perspective, and only a subset of AutoCAD LT commands are active.
- **POints.** With this option, you select both the target and the camera.
- **PAn.** Permits dynamic panning of the view.
- **Zoom.** Permits dynamic zooming of the view. If perspective viewing is on, the focal length of the camera can be adjusted. The default focal length is 50mm. Increasing the focal length zooms like a telephoto lens, decreasing the focal length produces a wide-angle lens effect. When perspective viewing is off, the zoom option works similarly to the **Center** option of the **ZOOM** command.
- **TWist.** Rotates the camera's viewing angle around the target. The target remains fixed in 3D space.
- **CLip.** Sets the front or back clipping planes. To turn clipping off, select the **Eye** option to **CLip**.
- **Hide.** Produces a hidden-line display of the **DVIEW** selection set.
- **Off.** Turns perspective viewing off.
- **Undo.** Reverses the last **DVIEW** option.
- **eXit.** Exits the **DVIEW** command, regenerates the display to reflect the new view, and restores the UCS, if one was in effect.

Using the DVIEWBLK

DVIEWBLK is a predefined block entity that is an easy way of setting a desired view orientation. This block appears as a house in a wireframe representation with an open door, a window, and a chimney. See Figure 18-21. Although a very simple object, it can be quite useful for manipulating a view to your liking. To use the **DVIEWBLK**, simply press [Enter] when prompted to select objects in the **DVIEW** command.

If no 3D view has yet been created, the house will display plan to the WCS. Select any of the **DVIEW** options to orient the house as you want your 3D model to be. When **DVIEW** is exited, your model will display the same view characteristics that were assigned to the house.

Figure 18-21.
The **DVIEWBLK** house.

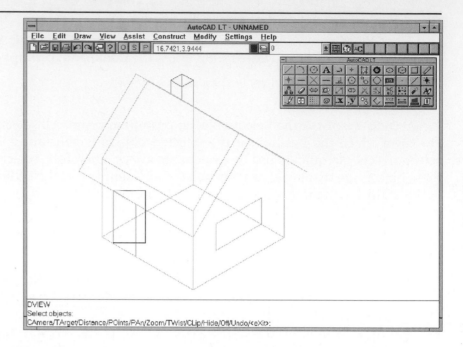

The WORLDVIEW system variable

By default, dynamic viewing angles are based on the WCS. Therefore, if a UCS is current when **DVIEW** is invoked, the display is temporarily switched to the WCS and you are informed of this. Once the **DVIEW** operation is ended, the display is switched back to the previous UCS automatically. The system variable **WORLDVIEW** (default setting = 1) switches to the WCS in **DVIEW**. In most cases, this convention eliminates much of the disorientation that might otherwise arise by viewing the model through some unfamiliar viewing angle. To perform dynamic viewing with the angles set by the current UCS, set the **WORLDVIEW** system variable equal to 0 (off).

EXERCISE 18-5

❏ Begin a new drawing.
❏ Issue the **DVIEW** command and at the **Select objects:** prompt, press [Enter].
❏ Using the **CAmera** option, rotate the house 45° from the XY plane and –45° in the XY plane.
❏ Use the **DVIEW Zoom** and **PAn** options to change the display.
❏ Rotate the camera about the ∠ axis with a **TWist** angle of 120°
❏ Experiment with the **POints** option. Pick a corner of the window as the target and the top of the door as the camera. Be sure to use the appropriate osnap modes.
❏ Create a perspective view with the **Distance** option and **Hide** it.
❏ Turn perspective viewing off, and try **CLipping** first the front plane, and then the back plane. Use the **Undo** option if you are not satsfied with the display.
❏ Exit **DVIEW** and do not save the drawing.

Write your answers in the spaces provided.

1. Which command controls the display and origin of the UCS icon? List the options to this command and the function that each performs._____

    _____

    _____

    _____

2. The UCS icon is displayed on-screen as a "broken pencil." What does this representation mean? _____

3. Describe the right-hand rule. What is its purpose? _____

    _____

    _____

    _____

4. What is a plan view?_____

    _____

5. List three methods for obtaining a 3D view with the **VPOINT** command. _____

    _____

    _____

6. What do the **VPOINT** coordinates 1,–1,1 represent? Are these distance or direction coordinates? _____

7. What does the compass icon represent? _____

8. What is the purpose of the **VIEW** command? Why is it useful for 3D work? _____

    _____

9. What are tessalation lines?_____

    _____

10. What is meant by elevation? _____

11. What is thickness and how is it used? _____

12. How do the system variables **SHADEDIF** and **SHADEDGE** affect a shaded display? _____

    _____

    _____

13. How many viewports can be displayed with the **VPORTS** command? How many can be plotted? _____

14. What is the UCS? How does it differ from the World Coordinate System?_____

    _____

    _____

15. What does the plus sign at the juncture of the UCS icon X and Y axes represent? _____

    _____

16. The UCS icon is displayed with no box at the juncture of the X and Y axes. From which direction is the XY plane being viewed? _____

17. Does the direction of the X and Y axes change when using the **UCS** command **Origin** option? (Yes/No)_____

18. Why should you save a defined UCS? _____

19. How do you arrange multiple viewports in an orthographic representation? _____

20. How can a view be automatically made plan to the current UCS? _____

21. Describe the difference between the **CAmera** and **TArget** options of **DVIEW**. How are they similar? _____

22. Which **DVIEW** command option allows you to create a perspective view? _____

23. List the advantages of **DVIEW** over the **VPOINT** command. _____

24. What purpose does the **DVIEWBLK** serve? _____

25. Is dynamic viewing performed in the WCS or the UCS? Why? _____

CHAPTER PROBLEMS

Mechanical Drafting

1. Model the object shown in Figure 18-19A. Set up three viewports with the dominant viewport to the right. Display the top view of the object in the upper-left viewport and the front view of the object in the lower-left viewport. Display a 3D view in the dominant viewport at the right. Save the model as P18-1.

Mechanical Drafting

2. Model the CLAMP BLOCK from Problem 1 of Chapter 15. Set up three viewports with the dominant viewport above. Save the configuration with the name 3VIEWS. Display the top view of the object in the lower-left viewport and the side view in the lower-right viewport. Display a 3D view in the top viewport. Save the model as P18-2.

Mechanical Drafting

3. Model the STARTING CATCH from Problem 2 of Chapter 15. Set up four viewports and save the configuration with the name 4VIEWS. Display the top view of the object in the upper-left viewport, the front view in the lower-left viewport, and the side view in the lower-right viewport. Display a 3D view in the upper-right viewport. Save the model as P18-3.

AutoCAD LT

Chapter 19

Customizing the AutoCAD LT Environment

Learning objectives

After completing this chapter, you will be able to:

- ○ Interpret and modify the ACLT.INI file.
- ○ Enable and disable file locking.
- ○ Select between English and Metric measurement.
- ○ Perform automatic drawing saves at specified time intervals.
- ○ Assign colors and fonts to the text and graphics windows.
- ○ Specify the search path for support directories and the placement of temporary files.
- ○ Resize and reposition the text and graphics windows.
- ○ Customize toolbar and toolbox buttons.
- ○ Modify program item properties.

AutoCAD LT has a variety of options to customize the user interface and working environment. These customization options allow you to configure the software to suit personal preferences or satisfy organizational requirements. This chapter explores options that include defining colors for the individual window elements, assigning fonts to both the graphics window and text window, and customizing the toolbar and toolbox buttons.

THE ACLT.INI FILE

ALTUG 18

Microsoft Windows uses *initialization files* containing information that defines your Windows environment. Both Windows and Windows-based applications, like AutoCAD LT, use the information stored in these files to configure the working environment to meet your hardware needs and personal preferences. There are two standard Windows initialization (.INI) files. The WIN.INI file primarily contains settings that Windows maintains to customize the environment according to your preferences. The SYSTEM.INI file primarily contains settings that customize Windows to meet the hardware needs of your computer and any attached peripheral devices.

When AutoCAD LT is first installed on your computer, the installation setup program adds the file ACLT.INI to the \ACLTWIN directory. This file contains the environment and configuration information needed by AutoCAD LT each time you start a new drawing session. If AutoCAD LT cannot find the ACLT.INI file, it creates one. When you customize AutoCAD LT, your changes are automatically saved in the ACLT.INI so that they will be in effect each time you launch AutoCAD LT. As with other initialization files, ACLT.INI is in ASCII format and is very compact. This makes the file quite easy to edit using Notepad or another ASCII text editor, Figure 19-1.

Figure 19-1.
The ACLT.INI file can be edited with Windows Notepad.

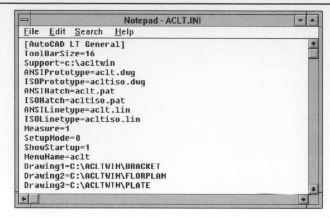

```
Notepad - ACLT.INI
File  Edit  Search  Help
[AutoCAD LT General]
ToolBarSize=16
Support=c:\acltwin
ANSIPrototype=aclt.dwg
ISOPrototype=acltiso.dwg
ANSIHatch=aclt.pat
ISOHatch=acltiso.pat
ANSILinetype=aclt.lin
ISOLinetype=acltiso.lin
Measure=1
SetupMode=0
ShowStartup=1
MenuName=aclt
Drawing1=C:\ACLTWIN\BRACKET
Drawing2=C:\ACLTWIN\FLORPLAN
Drawing3=C:\ACLTWIN\PLATE
```

CAUTION

!

Be sure to check with your instructor or supervisor before modifying any of the Microsoft Windows or AutoCAD LT initialization files.

SETTING PREFERENCES

ALTUG 2

The available options for customizing the AutoCAD LT user interface and working environment are found in the **Preferences** dialog box, Figure 19-2. This dialog box is accessed by selecting **Preferences...** from the **File** pull-down menu or by clicking the **Preferences** button. The **Preferences** button does not appear on the toolbar or in the toolbox by default, but may easily be added. Toolbar and toolbox customization procedures are covered later in this chapter. The **Preferences** dialog box can also be displayed by entering the following on the command line:

Command: *(type* PREFERENCES *or* PF *and press* [Enter]*)*

Each of the areas and options of the **Preferences** dialog box are described in the following sections.

Figure 19-2.
Customize the AutoCAD LT working environment using the **Preferences** dialog box.

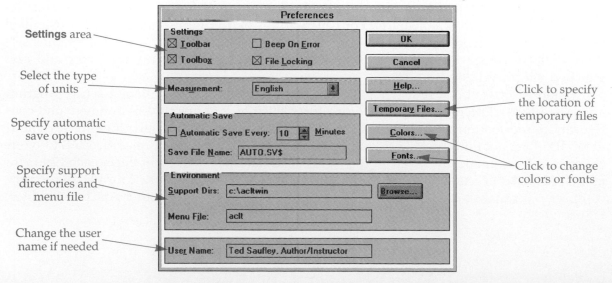

Settings area

Select the type of units

Specify automatic save options

Specify support directories and menu file

Change the user name if needed

Click to specify the location of temporary files

Click to change colors or fonts

AutoCAD LT—Fundamentals and Applications

The Settings check boxes

The four check boxes that appear at the top of the dialog box in the **Settings** area perform the following functions:

- **Toolbar**. An "X" in this check box indicates that the toolbar is on. It is on by default.
- **Toolbox**. An "X" in this check box indicates that the toolbox is on. It is on by default.
- **Beep on Error**. Activate this check box if you wish to hear a beep when you enter an unknown command or attempt to perform a function that is not permitted. The beep is off by default.
- **File Locking**. This option is useful in a networked computer environment. It is enabled by default. This prevents more than one user from updating a drawing file at the same time. Attempting to do so displays an alert message in a dialog box similar to that shown in Figure 19-3. If you do not work in a networked environment, you can improve system performance by disabling file locking.

Figure 19-3.
AutoCAD LT alerts you with a dialog box message if you attempt to open a locked file.

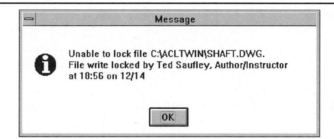

Using English or Metric measurements

The **Measurement** section in the **Preferences** dialog box features a drop-down list that allows you to choose between the default English or Metric measurements. If you select Metric measurements, AutoCAD LT uses the ACLTISO.DWG prototype drawing instead of the ACLT.DWG prototype. The ACLTISO.LIN linetype library file and the ACLTISO.PAT hatch pattern file are also substituted. The measurement changes take effect the next time new drawings, linetypes, and hatch patterns are loaded.

The Automatic Save section

You may recall from Chapter 2 that AutoCAD LT has a system variable called **SAVETIME** that can be set to save your work automatically at regular time intervals. You can set this variable from the command line or from the **Automatic Save** section within the **Preferences** dialog box. Use the up and down arrows to set the desired time interval (in minutes). Then, click the **Automatic Save Every:** check box to activate your new setting. When this feature is enabled, AutoCAD LT saves your drawing with the name AUTO.SV$. You can use the **Save File Name:** text box to specify a different name, but you cannot change the file extension.

Specifying support file directories

The **Environment** section near the bottom of the **Preferences** dialog box is where you specify the path AutoCAD LT searches to find support files. Support files include text fonts, menus, blocks to insert, linetypes, and hatch patterns. The \ACLTWIN directory is the default support directory created during installation. You can use the **Support Dirs:** text box to specify the path to any directory or subdirectory that contain support files.

For example, suppose you store all of the blocks you typically use in a directory named \BLOCKS on the C: drive. Unless this directory name is placed in the support files search path, AutoCAD LT will not be able to find your blocks when you attempt to insert them. You can add this directory to the existing search path in two ways. The first method is to type in the following directly after the C:\ACLTWIN entry in the **Support Dirs:** text box:

;C:\BLOCKS

Do not forget to use a semicolon to separate the new directory entry from any that may already exist.

The second method is easier. Simply click the **Browse...** button to the right of the **Support Dirs:** text box. The **Edit Path** subdialog box is then displayed, Figure 19-4. Select the C: drive from the **Drives:** drop-down list, and then select the \BLOCKS directory from the **Directories:** list. The path C:\BLOCKS is then displayed in the **Path:** text box at the top of the subdialog box. Click the **Add** button to add C:\BLOCKS to the **Search Path:** list shown at the right of this subdialog box. When you are done, click the **Close** button and you are returned to the **Preferences** dialog box.

Figure 19-4.
Adding a support directory to the search path using the **Edit Path** subdialog box.

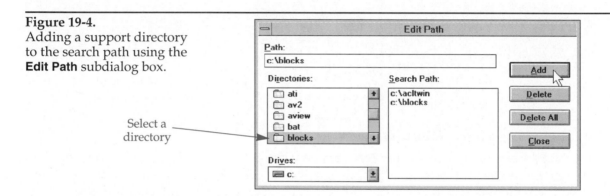

Select a directory

Specifying an alternate menu file

The default menu file used by AutoCAD LT is called ACLT.MNU. If you wish to use a custom menu file, enter the menu name in the **Menu File:** text box. Only one menu file can be active at a time. See Chapter 20 for information on how to create a custom menu.

Specifying a different user name

The **User Name:** text box at the bottom of the **Preferences** dialog box displays the user name that was specified during installation. The user name is stored in the ACLT.INI file and is used when the **REVDATE** command is issued. You may recall from Chapter 2 that the **REVDATE** command adds a date and time stamp and inserts the user name into a drawing. Use the **User Name:** text box to change the name if more than one person works on the drawing.

Placement of temporary files

AutoCAD LT creates several temporary files as it is running. These files are placed in the \ACLTWIN directory by default. When you exit AutoCAD LT, the temporary files are automatically deleted. If you wish to specify a different directory for the placement of these files, click the **Temporary Files...** button in the **Preferences** dialog box. When the **Temporary Files** subdialog box appears, deactivate the **Use Drawing Directory** check box. Enter the desired directory name in the **Directory:** text box, Figure 19-5.

If you are unsure as to which directory to specify, click the **Browse** button to display the **Edit Directory** subdialog box. Select a directory from the **Directories:** list at the left of the subdialog box and click the **Change** button to add it to the search path.

Figure 19-5.
Using the **Temporary Files** subdialog box to specify a different directory for the placement of temporary files.

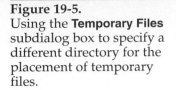

Deactivate to specify a directory

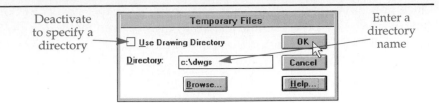

Enter a directory name

Changing the graphics and text window colors

By customizing the AutoCAD LT colors, you can add your own personal touch and make it stand out from other active Windows applications. To change colors, click the **Colors...** button at the right of the **Preferences** dialog box. The **AutoCAD LT Window Colors** subdialog box is then displayed. See Figure 19-6.

The **Window Element:** drop-down list located at the upper right of the subdialog box allows you to change individual color elements of both the graphics and text windows. These color elements include: the colors of the graphics and command line areas, the text window background, the text in the graphics window or text window, and the full-screen crosshairs. To customize the AutoCAD LT colors, do the following:

1. Click the **Colors...** button in the **Preferences** dialog box. The **AutoCAD LT Window Colors** subdialog box appears. If you have a monochrome display monitor, the **Monochrome Vectors** box is checked. If you have a gray-scale display monitor and are experiencing problems displaying elements of AutoCAD LT, try checking this box.
2. Click an area in the graphics or text window samples at the left of the dialog box, or select the element to change from the **Window Element:** drop-down list.
3. Pick the color you want from the available colors displayed in the **Basic Colors:** section. The sample window is updated to reflect your change. The color also appears in the swatch at the bottom. You can modify the selected color by using the horizontal slider controls labeled **R:**, **G:**, and **B:** to change the red, green, and blue components of the color. You can also type a number between 0 and 255 in the respective text box.
4. You can customize the AutoCAD LT windows to match the system colors defined in the Windows Control Panel. To do so, click the **System Colors** button just below the RGB horizontal slider controls. Refer to the *Microsoft Windows User's Guide* for more information about the Windows Control Panel.

Figure 19-6.
The **AutoCAD LT Window Colors** subdialog box.

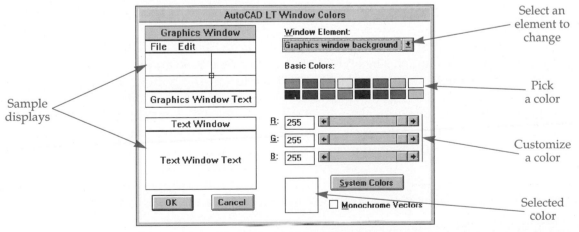

Sample displays

Select an element to change

Pick a color

Customize a color

Selected color

Once you have made your color selections, click the **OK** button in the **AutoCAD LT Window Colors** subdialog box. Then, click **OK** in the **Preferences** dialog box to apply your changes. If you modified the colors for the text window, press function key [F2] or select **Te_x_t Window** from the **Edit** pull-down menu to see the changes.

Changing the graphics and text window fonts

You can also change the font used on the toolbar, command line area, and text window. The font you select has no affect on the text in your drawings, nor is the font used in the AutoCAD LT dialog boxes. To change the font, do the following:

1. Click the **Fonts...** button in the **Preferences** dialog box. The **Fonts** subdialog box appears, Figure 19-7.

   Notice the two buttons at the lower left of the dialog box in the AutoCAD LT Window section. Click either the **Graphics** button to modify the graphics window font or the **Text** button to modify the text window font.

   Also notice that the default font used by AutoCAD LT for the graphics window is MS Sans Serif. The style is Regular (not bold or italic) and its size is 10 points. You can keep this font if you like and just change the font style and size.

Figure 19-7.
The **Fonts** subdialog box sets font types, styles, and sizes used by the AutoCAD LT graphics and text windows.

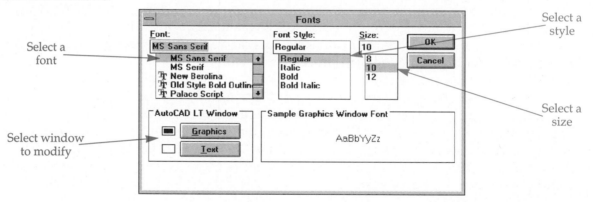

2. To select a different font, select the new font from the **Font:** drop-down list at the upper left of the dialog box. This file list displays each of the fonts installed in the \WINDOWS\SYSTEM subdirectory. If you have any third-party fonts like TrueType or Adobe®, they also appear in this list.

   In the example shown in Figure 19-8, the Lucida Handwriting TrueType font is selected from the drop-down list. The style is changed to Bold Italic and the size is changed to 12 points. The **Sample Graphics Window Font** section at the bottom of the dialog box displays a sample of the selected font as it will appear in the graphics window. If you are selecting a font for use in the text window, this box is labeled **Sample Text Window Font**.

3. Once you have selected the desired font, font style, and size for the graphics and/or text windows, click the **OK** button to assign the new fonts. Click **Cancel** to keep the previous font.

The **Preferences** dialog box is then redisplayed. If you want to apply your font changes, click **OK** to exit the **Preferences** dialog box. You can also click **Cancel** to return to the previous font.

Figure 19-8.
The Lucida Handwriting TrueType font is set current from the **Font:** drop-down list. The **Font Style:** and **Size:** are also changed.

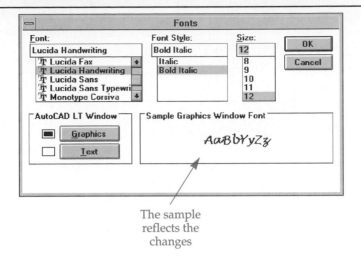

The sample reflects the changes

PROFESSIONAL TIP

    A drawing regeneration is automatically performed whenever changes are made to the colors or fonts used in the AutoCAD LT graphics and/or text windows. To speed regeneration time and improve system performance, customize the environment *before* creating any entities.

EXERCISE 19-1

❐ Start Windows.
❐ Make a backup copy of the ACLT.INI file. Keep the backup in a separate directory or on a floppy disk.
❐ Load AutoCAD LT.
❐ Use the **Preferences** dialog box to change the color elements and fonts of both the graphics and text windows to your personal liking.
❐ Exit AutoCAD LT to save the changes.

POSITIONING THE **AUTOCAD LT** GRAPHICS AND TEXT WINDOWS

    Perhaps the greatest advantage of Windows is the ability to have several applications displayed in separate windows simultaneously. It is then a simple matter to click anywhere within an open window and activate the application within it.

    The first time AutoCAD LT is loaded after the initial software installation, the graphics window fills the entire display screen. The text window is hidden behind the graphics window. It is only brought to the front when you press function key [F2], or select **Text Window** from the **Edit** pull-down menu. You can scale and position both the graphics and text windows so that each window is readily displayed. However, this is best done on a 17″ or larger monitor with a resolution of at least 800 × 600.

    Look at the screen arrangement shown in Figure 19-9. The graphics window has been positioned down and to the left of the text window. With this window orientation, activate the text window by clicking anywhere within its border with your left mouse button. The text window is then brought to the front, but a portion of the graphics window is still visible. When you want to return to the graphics window, simply click anywhere within its displayed border. Also notice the position of the floating toolbox. It has been relocated off the graphics window so that it obscures very little of the active drawing area.

Figure 19-9.
The graphics and text windows can be sized and positioned as desired. Notice that the floating toolbox can be moved away from the drawing area.

Active window

Inactive window

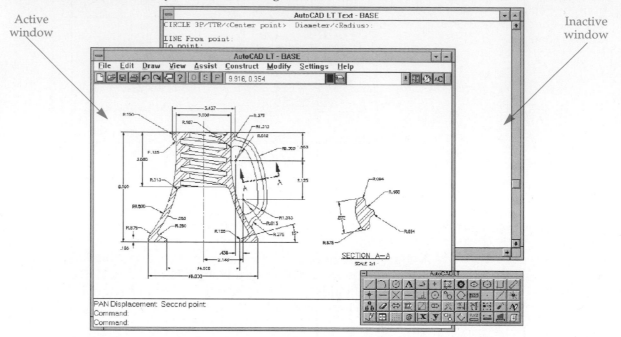

You can reposition an AutoCAD LT window by clicking within the title bar at the top of the window. Hold down the left mouse button, drag the window to the desired location, and release the mouse button. Once you have placed the graphics and text windows where you want them, return to the **Preferences** dialog box and click the **OK** button. Now, the windows will remain at the defined locations for all subsequent AutoCAD LT sessions until you relocate them.

SIZING THE **AUTOCAD LT** GRAPHICS AND TEXT WINDOWS

Resizing a window is as easy as moving its location. To stretch or shrink a window along its vertical axis, simply click and hold at the top or bottom border of the window. The mouse pointer then assumes the shape of a double arrow, Figure 19-10A. Drag the border to the desired size and release the mouse button. To stretch or shrink a window along its horizontal axis, click and hold at the left or right border of the window. The mouse pointer again assumes the shape of a double arrow. Drag the border to the desired size and release the mouse button. To stretch or shrink a window along both axes at the same time, click and hold at one of the four corners of the window. The mouse pointer changes to the double arrow, Figure 19-10B. Drag the corner to the desired position and release the mouse button.

Figure 19-10.
A—Stretching the top or bottom border adjusts the vertical size of a window. The right or left border can be similarly stretched to adjust the horizontal size of a window. B—A window can be resized along both axes simultaneously by stretching one of the window corners.

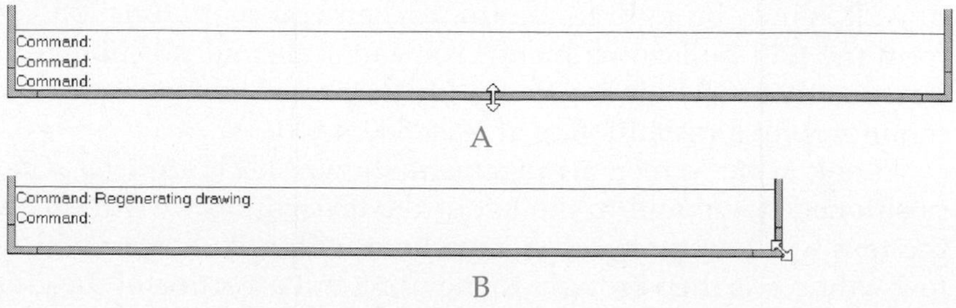

Command:
Command:
Command:

A

Command: Regenerating drawing.
Command:

B

AutoCAD LT—Fundamentals and Applications

To help select a window border, you may find it easier to increase the width of the window border. To do so, return to Program Manager and open the Main group window. Double-click on the Control Panel icon, then double-click on the Desktop icon. The Desktop dialog box appears. The Sizing Grid section at the lower left contains the Border Width drop-down list, Figure 19-11. Select a higher number from this list to increase the width of the border and a lower number to decrease the width. The border width is measured in pixels.

The AutoCAD LT graphics and text windows can also be reduced to icons. You can make an open window an icon by selecting Minimize from the control menu at the upper left of the window, or by _____ on (the down arrow) at the upper right of the window.

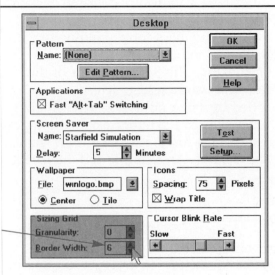

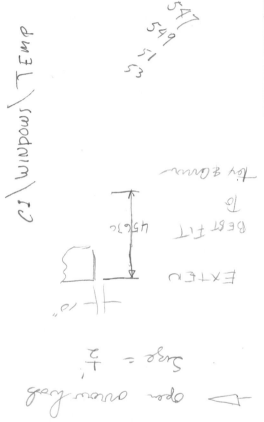

FILE   **ALTUG 18**

the sizes and positions of the AutoCAD LT graphics and
lescribed, you can also change these values by directly
make a backup copy of ACLT.INI before editing this file.
window appear in ACLT.INI under the section titled
nple and interpretation of this section appears below.

```
[AutoCAD LT Graphics Window]
WindowState=5
Font=MS Sans Serif 10 400 0
ToolBar=1
WindowPosition=Left 0, Top 0, Right 800, Bottom 600
GraphicsBackground=0 0 0
TextBackground=128 0 0
TextForeground=255 255 255
XhairPickboxEtc=128 128 128
```

- **WindowState.** This variable determines whether the graphics window is maximized, reduced to an icon, or is in a normal resizable state. The WindowState values are: 3 (maximized), 5 (normal resizable), or 6 (icon).
- **Font.** The current graphics window font is described by the four fields of this variable. The four fields are: font name, font size in points, font weight (400 = regular, 700 = bold), and italic (1 = italic, 0 = nonitalic).
- **ToolBar.** This variable is set to 1 by default. This means that the toolbar is enabled. It is disabled if set to 0.

- **WindowPosition.** This variable specifies the size and position of the graphics window in pixels. The values indicate the distance from the upper-left corner of the screen to the left, top, right, and bottom of the graphics window. In the example on the previous page, the window is 800×600 and the upper-left corner of the window starts in the upper-left corner of the screen.
- **GraphicsBackground.** This sets the color of the graphics window background. The color is specified by three numbers corresponding to red, green, and blue (RGB) values. The values 0 0 0 indicate a black background.
- **TextBackground.** This sets the background color of the command line area. The color is specified by three numbers corresponding to red, green, and blue (RGB) values. The values 128 0 0 indicate a dark red background.
- **TextForeground.** This sets the color of the text on the command line. The color is specified by three numbers corresponding to red, green, and blue (RGB) values. The values 255 255 255 indicate white text.
- **XhairPickboxEtc.** This sets the color of the crosshair cursor, pick box, aperture, and UCS icon. This variable also determines the color used for dragged images. The color is specified by three numbers corresponding to red, green, and blue (RGB) values. The values 128 128 128 indicate a medium-gray color.

The current values for the text window appear in ACLT.INI under the section titled [AutoCAD LT Text Window]. An example and interpretation of this section appears below.

```
[AutoCAD LT Text Window]
Visible=1
Font=Courier 11 400 0
Background=0 0 128
Foreground=255 255 0
WindowPosition=Left 7, Top 27, Right 793, Bottom 593
```

- **Visible.** Is set to 1 if the text window is visible. The default of 0 means that the text window is not visible.
- **Font.** The current text window font is described by the four fields of this variable. The four fields are: font name, font size in points, font weight (400 = regular, 700 = bold), and italic (1 = italic, 0 = nonitalic). The interpretation is the same as for the graphics window font.
- **Background.** This sets the text window background color. The color is specified by three numbers corresponding to red, green, and blue (RGB) values. The values 0 0 128 indicate a blue background.
- **Foreground.** This sets the color of the text in the text window. The color is specified by three numbers corresponding to red, green, and blue (RGB) values. The values 255 255 0 indicate yellow text.
- **WindowPosition.** This variable specifies the size and position of the text window in pixels. The values indicate the distance from the upper-left corner of the screen to the left, top, right, and bottom of the text window. The interpretation is the same as for the graphics window size and position.

PROFESSIONAL TIP

Although ACLT.INI can easily be modified with Notepad or any other ASCII text editor, it is far easier to make changes and update the file using the **Preferences** dialog box. Regardless of the method you choose, always make a backup copy of ACLT.INI before customizing the AutoCAD LT environment.

CUSTOMIZING THE TOOLBAR

ALTUG 19

You can customize the toolbar along the top of the graphics window. However, several of the toolbar components are preset and cannot be changed. These preset components include the **Current Color**, **Ortho**, **Snap**, and **Paper Space** buttons. The remainder of the buttons can all be customized.

The number of visible buttons on the toolbar depends on the current size of the graphics window, the screen resolution of your display monitor, and the current size assigned to the AutoCAD LT icon buttons. A maximum of 26 buttons can appear in the toolbar in addition to the four preset buttons. If the graphics window is sized too small, or at lower screen resolutions, some buttons will disappear.

Customization of the toolbar is a remarkably simple task. Place your mouse pointer over the button that you would like to modify and click the right mouse button. The **Toolbar Button Customization** dialog box appears, Figure 19-12.

In Figure 19-12, the **Zoom** button has been selected. This is toolbar button 7. The title bar at the top of the dialog box reflects this number. Also notice that the **ZOOM** command appears highlighted in the **Select Image** list box and the **Zoom** button icon image appears near the middle of the dialog box. By selecting a different command from the **Select Image** list box, the **Zoom** button can be replaced with a different command and icon.

It is also possible to modify the behavior of an existing toolbar button using this dialog box. For example, you can modify the **Zoom** button to perform a **ZOOM Center** operation by changing the command string in the **AutoCAD LT Command:** text box as follows:

'_ZOOM C

Figure 19-12.
The **Toolbar Button Customization** dialog box is used to customize toolbar buttons. The number of the selected button is displayed in the title bar.

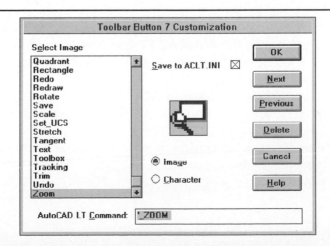

Be sure to put a space after the letter C. The space is interpreted as [Enter] (↵). Each of the elements of the **Toolbar Button Customization** dialog box are described as follows:

- **Save to ACLT.INI.** Click this check box to save your toolbar button changes to the ACLT.INI file. Although this check box is on by default, it is recommended that you turn it off before you modify any of the toolbar buttons. Once you are satisfied with your modifications, then turn it back on.
- **Image.** This option button displays a bitmap icon image when a command is selected from the **Select Image** list box. Right-clicking any of the predefined toolbar buttons automatically enables this option button. For your convenience, each of the AutoCAD LT command icons are reproduced on the inside cover of this text.
- **Character.** Right-clicking any of the blank toolbar buttons automatically enables this option button. When enabled, the **Select Image** list box is retitled **Select Character** and the letters A through Z then appear in the list box instead of command names. You can then select *one* letter to represent a command or command macro. More about this capability later in this section.
- **OK.** Click **OK** when you are finished with your toolbar button modifications. If the **Save to ACLT.INI** check box is not checked, the changes you make affect the current drawing session only.
- **Next.** Clicking this button moves to the next programmable button in the toolbar.
- **Previous.** Clicking this button moves to the previous programmable button in the toolbar.
- **Delete.** This button deletes the definition shown in the **AutoCAD LT Command:** text box for the currently selected toolbar button.
- **Cancel.** Cancels any modifications to the currently selected toolbar button and exits the **Toolbar Button Customization** dialog box.

The **Character** option button lets you assign a single character (A - Z) to an AutoCAD LT command or command macro. A *command macro* is a character string containing up to 255 uppercase or lowercase characters that can perform one or more AutoCAD LT commands with the click of a single toolbar button. As an example, consider the following command macro character string:

LIMITS 0,0 22,17 Z A SNAP .5 GRID S

Each of the spaces in the character string above are interpreted by AutoCAD LT as [Enter] (↵). Therefore, this command macro performs the following functions:

- Sets the AutoCAD LT drawing limits to 22,17 for a C-size drawing.
- Performs a **ZOOM All** to zoom to the new screen limits.
- Sets the **Snap** spacing to .5 units.
- Sets the **Grid** spacing to match the snap spacing.

To assign such a command macro, do the following:

1. Right-click one of the unassigned buttons on the toolbar.
2. When the **Toolbar Button Customization** dialog box appears, enter the command string shown above in the **AutoCAD LT Command:** text box.
3. Select a letter, such as S for Setup, from the **Select Character** list box to assign it to the selected toolbar button.
4. If desired, click the **Save to ACLT.INI** button to permanently save your new command macro. The button command string is then stored in the [AutoCAD LT General] section at the beginning of the ACLT.INI file.
5. Finally, click the **OK** button to exit the **Toolbar Button Customization** dialog box.

Now, whenever the **S** toolbar button is clicked, AutoCAD LT automatically performs the drawing setup functions described above.

As a further example, consider the **Toolbar Button Customization** dialog box shown in Figure 19-13. You can see the character string DIM ANG is entered in the **AutoCAD LT Command:** text box and that the letter A has been selected from the **Select Character** list box. Now, when the **Toolbar Button Customization** dialog box is exited and the **A** toolbar button is clicked, AutoCAD LT enters dimensioning mode and executes the **ANGULAR** dimensioning command.

The toolbar buttons shown in Figure 19-14 provide further examples of toolbar customization. Notice that the **ERASE** and **DDMODIFY** commands have been assigned to speed entity modification. Also, the letters L (Last), P (Previous), E (Extents), A (Add), and R (Remove) have been assigned to facilitate command option choices. If one of these five buttons were clicked at the **Command:** prompt, which AutoCAD LT command would be executed?

Figure 19-13.
Specialized command macros can be assigned to toolbar buttons using the **Toolbar Button Customization** dialog box.

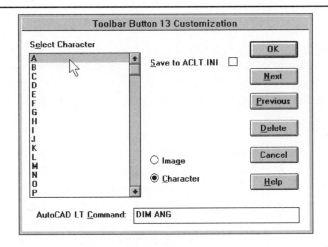

Figure 19-14.
A sample customized toolbar.

EXERCISE 19-3

❑ Make a backup copy of the ACLT.INI file before proceeding with this exercise.
❑ Customize the toolbar buttons to resemble those illustrated in Figure 19-14. Do not save the changes to the ACLT.INI file.
❑ Spend a few moments experimenting with the new toolbar configuration.
❑ Once you feel comfortable with the customization procedure, customize the toolbar to your personal liking.
❑ If you wish to make your changes available for all new drawings, do so by clicking the **Save to ACLT.INI** check box in the **Toolbar Button Customization** dialog box.

CUSTOMIZING THE TOOLBOX   ALTUG 19

You can also customize the AutoCAD LT toolbox. As with the toolbar, you can change the command assigned to a button so that it executes an entirely different command, or assign a command string (up to 255 characters) macro to a selected button. The toolbox is customized in the same way as the toolbar. Locate your mouse pointer over the toolbox button that you want to change and right-click. The **Toolbox Customization** dialog box appears, Figure 19-15.

Figure 19-15.
The **Toolbox Customization** dialog box is used to customize and insert toolbox buttons. Command macros can also be assigned to toolbox buttons, and the width of the toolbox can be specified.

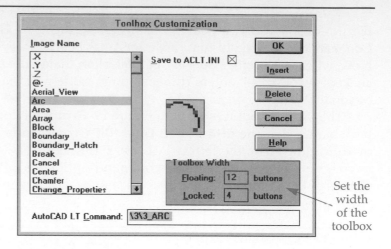

Set the width of the toolbox

In Figure 19-15, the **Arc** button was right-clicked to open the dialog box. Therefore, the **ARC** command is highlighted in the **Image Name** list box and the **ARC** command icon image is displayed in the middle of the dialog box. Look closely at the command string that appears in the **AutoCAD LT Command:** text box. It reads as follows:

\3\3_ARC

The string \3 performs a **CANCEL** command. Therefore, if you are in the middle of a command, such as the **LINE** command, and click the **Arc** button, the command is automatically canceled and the **ARC** command is executed. Notice that \3 appears twice. This performs two **CANCEL** commands. When you are in dimensioning mode, the first \3 cancels the dimensioning command in progress and the second \3 exits dimensioning mode.

If you want to replace the **Arc** button with a different one, scroll through the **Image Name** list box to find the command you wish to use. Once the new command is selected from the list, the command name appears in the **AutoCAD LT Command:** text box and the command icon image is displayed in the middle of the dialog box. Place \3 or \3\3 before the command string if you want the new button to automatically cancel a command in progress. To make the new definition available to all new drawings, activate the **Save to ACLT.INI** check box. The new button definition is then stored in the [AutoCAD LT ToolBox] section of the ACLT.INI file. When you are finished, click the **OK** button to exit the **Toolbox Customization** dialog box. If you change your mind, click the **Cancel** button to cancel any modifications to the selected button.

Inserting a new button

By default, there are 48 buttons defined in the floating toolbox, Figure 19-16A. However, the toolbox can contain a maximum of 60 buttons, Figure 19-16B. When a new button is added, it is always inserted to the left of an existing button. To insert a new button, do the following:
1. Right-click a toolbox button. Remember that the new button is inserted to the left of the button you select.
2. Select the command you wish to insert from the **Image Name** list box. For your convenience, each of the AutoCAD LT command icons are reproduced on the inside cover of this text.
3. Modify the command string in the **AutoCAD LT Command:** text box if desired.
4. Click the **Insert** button.
5. Activate the **Save to ACLT.INI** check box if you want to make your change available to all new drawings. Click **OK** to exit the **Toolbox Customization** dialog box.

The new button appears in the toolbox to the left of the selected button.

Figure 19-16.
A—The default floating toolbox contains 12 buttons across and 4 buttons down for a total of 48 buttons. B—This customized floating toolbox contains 4 buttons across and 15 buttons down for a total of 60 buttons.

A

B

If you later decide to remove the button assignment, right-click the button in the toolbox. When the **Toolbox Customization** dialog box appears, verify that the button you wish to remove is highlighted. Then, click the **Delete** button. The button is deleted and the **Toolbox Customization** dialog box closes.

The power and flexibility offered through toolbar and toolbox customization cannot be overstated. By carefully and thoughtfully designing command macros for AutoCAD LT buttons, you can increase your productivity many times over.

PROFESSIONAL TIP

Button customization can be used in a variety of ways. As an example, the prototype drawing created in Chapter 5 contains four layers named OBJECTS, DIMS, HATCHING, and NOTES. You can modify the toolbar and toolbox buttons to automatically set the appropriate layer current before creating any entities. Consider the following command macro examples:

    CLAYER OBJECTS LINE
    CLAYER DIMS DIM HOR
    CLAYER HATCHING BHATCH
    CLAYER NOTES DTEXT

Be sure to press the spacebar after each command string. The space is interpreted as an [Enter]. Add the character string \3 at the start of the command macro if you wish to cancel a command in progress. Add the string \3\3 to cancel a command in dimensioning mode.

Changing the shape of the toolbox

Refer to the **Toolbox Customization** dialog box shown in Figure 19-15 and locate the **Toolbox Width** section at the lower right. This section contains two text boxes that allow you to change the shape of both the floating and locked toolbox. You may recall from Chapter 1 that the **Toolbox** button on the toolbar is used to change the physical status of the toolbox. Remember that successive clicks of the toolbox button toggles the toolbox through the following four states:

- Locked to the upper-left corner of the graphics window.
- Hidden.
- Locked to the upper-right corner of the graphics window.
- Floating (the default state).

The two text boxes in the **Toolbox Customization** dialog box are described as follows:

- **Floating.** This is used to specify the number of buttons across (wide) for a floating toolbox. The default setting is 12, as shown in Figure 19-16A. A setting of 24 produces 24 buttons across.
- **Locked.** This is used to specify the number of buttons in each row for a locked toolbox. The default setting is 2. Figure 19-17 shows the toolbox in various locked states.

Figure 19-17.
A comparison of the toolbox in various locked states. A—The locked toolbox in its default configuration. B—The locked toolbox configured for 16 rows of buttons. C—The locked toolbox configured for 6 rows of buttons.

B

A

C

NOTE

The bitmapped images that appear in the toolbox and toolbar, as well as in the toolbar and toolbox customization dialog boxes, are defined in two dynamic link library (.DLL) files named ACLTTB16.DLL and ACLTTB32.DLL. Do not delete, rename, or move these files from the \ACLTWIN directory or you will lose your bitmap icons.

EXERCISE 19-4

❏ Make a backup copy of the ACLT.INI file.
❏ Customize the toolbox buttons to resemble those illustrated in Figure 19-16B. Do not save the changes to the ACLT.INI file.
❏ Experiment with the new toolbox configuration. Try several floating and locked toolbox configurations.
❏ Once you feel comfortable with the customization procedure, customize the toolbox to your personal liking.
❏ If you want to make your changes available to all new drawings, click the **Save to ACLT.INI** check box in the **Toolbox Customization** dialog box.

Changing the size of the toolbar and toolbox buttons

Each of the buttons in the toolbar and the toolbox are by default 16 × 16 pixels. You can change the size of the buttons from 4 to 32 pixels. To control the size of the buttons, you must change the value of the **TOOLBARSIZE** variable in the [AutoCAD LT General] section of the ACLT.INI file, as shown below:

[AutoCAD LT General]
ToolBarSize=16 *(enter a value between 4 and 32, 16 is the default)*

It is also possible to change this variable using the **SETENV** (set environment) command as follows:

Command: **SETENV** ⏎
Variable name: **TOOLBARSIZE** ⏎
Value ⟨16⟩: *(enter the number of pixels between 4 and 32)*
Command:

The new button sizes will take effect the next time you start AutoCAD LT. Note that the **TOOLBARSIZE** variable controls the size of both the toolbar and toolbox buttons. Their sizes cannot be set independently. While more buttons appear in the toolbar when a smaller size is used, the buttons become more difficult to see, Figure 19-18A. A larger size makes the buttons easier to see, but fewer buttons can be displayed in the toolbar when the button size is increased, Figure 19-18B. Additionally, the increased size of the toolbox takes up valuable drawing area.

Figure 19-18.
A—The toolbar and toolbox buttons sized at 12 pixels. B—The toolbar and toolbox buttons sized at 32 pixels. The larger size of the toolbox will cover more of the drawing area.

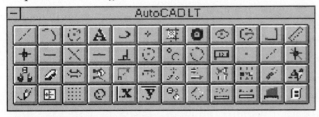

A

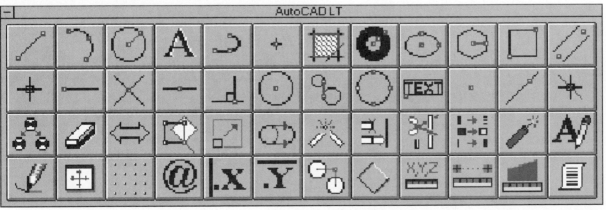

B

Set the **TOOLBARSIZE** variable to a higher value if you have a large monitor configured for 1024 × 768 or greater screen resolution. Use a lower value if you have a small monitor configured for 640 × 480 resolution. Experiment with different values to determine which button size suits your display configuration and personal preferences.

CHANGING PROGRAM PROPERTIES

The AutoCAD LT installation program automatically creates the AutoCAD LT group window and program item icon. You can modify the program item's properties if you like. These properties include such things as the description for the item, the working directory where any files that AutoCAD LT creates (or needs) are stored, defining a shortcut key to start AutoCAD LT, and choosing the icon that AutoCAD LT uses to represent the application.

To modify the AutoCAD LT program properties, first return to Program Manager and open the AutoCAD LT program group. Click on the AutoCAD LT program icon to highlight it. Next, select Properties... from the File pull-down menu or press the [Alt]+[Enter] key combination. The Program Item Properties dialog box appears, Figure 19-19. The various elements of this dialog box are described below:

- **Description:**. This is used to enter a description that uniquely identifies the application. The text description becomes the label that appears under the program icon. In Figure 19-19, the description is changed to AutoCAD LT.
- **Command Line:**. This is used to enter the name of the executable program and its path. If you change the drive or directory that contains the AutoCAD LT executables, be sure to edit this line accordingly. You will also need to reconfigure AutoCAD LT. This is because the entire path to the drivers is saved in the ACLT.CFG file.
- **Working Directory:**. This text box specifies the name of directory where the AutoCAD LT program files are located. The directory specified in this text box becomes the current directory when AutoCAD LT is running and any newly created files are placed here.
- **Shortcut Key:**. Microsoft Windows provides a special feature called an *application shortcut key*. This feature allows you to launch AutoCAD LT with a key combination that you defined. As long as you are in Program Manager, you can quickly start AutoCAD LT by using a shortcut key. Assigning a shortcut key for AutoCAD LT is described later in this section.
- **Run Minimized.** When this check box is selected, AutoCAD LT is reduced to an icon when it starts. It is recommended that you leave this box unchecked.

When you are finished making your changes, click the OK button to exit the Program Item Properties dialog box. Any changes you make take effect immediately without restarting Windows.

Figure 19-19.
The Program Item Properties dialog box is used to change the label and/or icon, and to modify the command line. A shortcut key can also be defined.

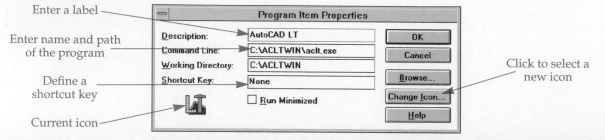

Changing the AutoCAD LT program item icon

The Program Item Properties dialog box also allows you to change the program item icon used in the program group window. To change the program item icon, do the following:

1. Click the Change Icon... button at the right of the Program Item Properties dialog box.
2. The Change Icon subdialog box appears. See Figure 19-20.
3. There are four icons to choose from. These are the icons that come with AutoCAD LT. Select the icon you wish to use and click the OK button to exit the Change Icon subdialog box. If you want to select an icon from a different location, click the Browse... button.

The new icon appears at the lower left of the Program Item Properties dialog box. When you click OK to close this dialog box, the icon appears in the program group window.

Figure 19-20.
The Change Icon subdialog box allows you to select a new icon. Four icons come with AutoCAD LT. If you want to select an icon from a different location, click the Browse... button.

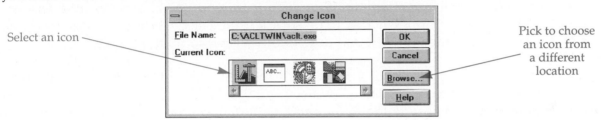

Select an icon

Pick to choose an icon from a different location

Defining a shortcut key

You can assign a shortcut key to start an application when you are in the Program Manager. You can use any letter, number, or special character on your keyboard for a shortcut key. Since AutoCAD LT does not use the [F3], [F11], and [F12] function keys, one of these would make a good choice. Whichever key you choose, Windows automatically adds a [Ctrl]+[Alt] in front of it. To assign a shortcut key for starting AutoCAD LT, do the following:

1. Open the Program Item Properties dialog box as previously described.
2. Click anywhere in the Shortcut Key: text box. The flashing vertical cursor appears at the end of the word None.
3. Now, press the key you want to assign, such as [F12].
4. The character string [Ctrl]+[Alt]+[F12] appears in the text box. See Figure 19-21.
5. Click OK to exit the Program Item Properties dialog box.

You must restart Windows to activate your new shortcut key.

Now, no matter which Windows-based application is running, you can start AutoCAD LT with the keyboard combination [Ctrl]+[Alt]+[F12] after returning to Program Manager. Refer to the *Microsoft Windows User's Guide* for more information regarding shortcut keys.

Figure 19-21.
Defining a shortcut key in
the Program Item Properties
dialog box.

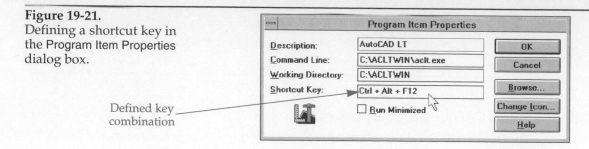

Defined key
combination

Creating an alternate AutoCAD LT configuration

It is possible to create different configurations of AutoCAD LT. For example, one configuration might have a black graphics background and use large toolbar buttons, while another might have a white graphics background and use small toolbar buttons. Each configuration requires a separate ACLT.INI and ACLT.CFG file. By default, these two files reside in the \ACLTWIN directory.

To create different configurations, first make a new directory and copy the new .INI and .CFG files into it. In the example that follows, the new directory is named \ACLTWIN\ALTCONF (alternate configuration).

By default, each configuration uses the same program icon. Refer to Figure 19-22. Notice that three separate program item icons appear in this group window and each icon is labeled differently. To create an additional program item icon, you must first copy the original AutoCAD LT icon in the group window. To do so, select the AutoCAD LT icon, hold down the left mouse button and the [Ctrl] key, and drag to the desired location in the group window. Release the mouse button and a copy appears.

Once you have copied the icon, click on it to highlight the icon. Then, press [Alt]+[Enter] to open the Program Item Properties dialog box. See Figure 19-23. Specify the location of the separate configuration directory in the **Command Line:** text box. You must add the /C switch before the path. This makes AutoCAD LT look for the configuration files in the directory designated by the switch. The line is added immediately after the line \ACLTWIN\ACLT.EXE. In the example shown in Figure 19-23, the entire line is as follows:

C:\ACLTWIN\ACLT.EXE /C C:\ACLTWIN\ALTCONF

Figure 19-22.
Three separate AutoCAD LT
configurations have been
created and assigned to
three separate icons. Notice
that each has a different
icon and label.

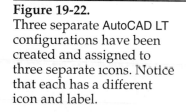

Copied program icons

Figure 19-23.
The /C switch in the
Command Line: text box
specifies the alternate
configuration directory.

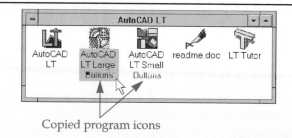

New icon label

New icon

Modified
command line

Naturally, substitute the correct drive letter and directory name if different from that shown above.

After you have added the /C switch, click the Change Icon... button to select a different icon, as described earlier in this chapter. Then, edit the label in the Description: text box. Enter a descriptive label, such as AutoCAD LT Large Buttons. When you are finished, click the OK button to exit the Program Item Properties dialog box.

Now, when you starts AutoCAD LT by clicking the new icon, the alternate configuration is loaded. You can modify the toolbar, toolbox, and all other aspects of the AutoCAD LT graphics and text windows as described in this chapter. When you change your user environment in the alternate session, the modifications are automatically saved to the ACLT.INI file in the alternate configuration directory.

NOTE   Refer to the *Microsoft Windows User's Guide* for more information about editing and deleting program item properties.

CHAPTER TEST

Write your answers in the spaces provided.

1. What is the purpose of the ACLT.INI file? _____

2. List two methods to access the **Preferences** dialog box. _____

3. Fonts assigned in the **Fonts** subdialog box can be used in an AutoCAD LT drawing. (True/False) _____

4. What is the purpose of file locking? _____

   _____

5. AutoCAD LT resides in the C:\ACLTWIN directory on your workstation. You have created two subdirectories under \ACLTWIN named \PROJECTS and \SYMBOLS. Suppose you want to store your drawings in the \PROJECTS subdirectory and your blocks in the \SYMBOLS subdirectory. What should you enter in the **Support Dirs:** text box so that these directories are added to the search path? _____

6. How do you increase the width of a window border? _____

   _____

7. Interpret the following values in the graphics window section of the ACLT.INI file:

   [AutoCAD LT Graphics Window]

   A. WindowState=6_____

   B. Font=Century Schoolbook 12 700 1 _____

   C. ToolBar=1 _____

   D. GraphicsBackground=255 255 255 _____

8. What is the maximum number of characters that can be used in a toolbar button command macro? _____

9. How is a space in a macro command string interpreted by AutoCAD LT?_____

10. What function does the /3 character string perform?_____

11. In addition to the three preset buttons, what is the maximum number of buttons that can appear in the toolbar? _____

12. Enter the required macro command string to perform the following functions. Show each space in the character string in this format: ⟨space⟩

    A. Draw a 6 × 4 rectangle with the lower left corner at 0,0.

    B. Simultaneously fillet all four corners with a .75 radius.

    C. Redraw the screen.

    _____

    _____

    _____

13. What is the maximum number of buttons that can appear in the toolbox? _____

14. Name the variable that controls the size of both toolbar and toolbox buttons. _____

15. The size of toolbar and toolbox buttons is mutually exclusive. (True/False) _____

16. What is the purpose of the application shortcut key? _____

    _____

17. Which two files must be copied to a separate directory before creating an alternate AutoCAD LT configuration? _____

CHAPTER PROBLEMS

General

1. Create an alternate configuration for AutoCAD LT dedicated to dimensioning. Use the following instructions to complete this problem.

    A. Assign a different program icon to the dimensioning configuration.

    B. Change the program icon label to read: AutoCAD LT Dimensioning

    C. Define a shortcut key for the configuration.

    D. Modify the toolbar to include the following command buttons:

        BHATCH

        DIM

    E. Add *one* command macro button to the toolbar that turns on **DIMTIX**, sets **DIMZIN** = 4, and sets **DIMCEN** to a negative value.

    F. Add *one* command macro button to the toolbar that turns on tolerancing, and sets the plus tolerance to .005 and the negative tolerance to .002.

    G. Add command macro buttons to the toolbox that perform horizontal, vertical, angular, diameter, radial, baseline, and continue dimensioning.

    H. Add three additional command macro buttons that draw a center mark, create a leader, and update an existing dimension.

    I. Print the contents of the modified ACLT.INI file.

Chapter 20

AutoCAD LT

Introduction to Menu Customization

Learning objectives:
After you have completed this chapter, you will be able to:

○ Interpret the various sections of the ACLT.MNU file.
○ Assign a menu macro to one or more mouse buttons.
○ Modify and create pull-down menus and cascading submenus.
○ Define menu accelerator and mnemonic shortcut keys.
○ Create icon menus using slides and the **SLIDELIB** program.

In Chapter 19, you learned how the AutoCAD LT working environment can be customized to suit personal preferences. It is also possible to customize the AutoCAD LT menus. You can modify the standard menus, rearrange their order on the menu bar, or create an entirely new menu system to suit your personal tastes. You can also assign command string macros to mouse buttons and create icon menus to facilitate block insertion. By mastering the fundamentals of menu customization, you can increase your productivity, knowledge, and enjoyment of AutoCAD LT. This chapter provides a brief introduction to customizing menus. For a complete description of menu customization, refer to Chapter 22 of *AutoCAD LT User's Guide*.

MENU FILES

ALTUG 22

A menu file is written in ASCII format and has a .MNU file extension. The default menu system used by AutoCAD LT is defined in the external file ACLT.MNU which is located in the \ACLTWIN directory. You may choose to customize the ACLT.MNU file, or create an entirely new one. However, be sure to make a backup copy before customizing ACLT.MNU. You can then restore the original menu file if the customized version becomes corrupted.

A better alternative would be to make a copy of the existing menu file and give the copy a different name like MYMENU.MNU. This method preserves the integrity of the original ACLT.MNU and allows you to freely edit the new menu file to suit your needs.

Specifying a different menu file

Before a menu file can be used, it must be compiled to make it machine-readable, or *executable*. The executable menu file has a .MNX file extension. AutoCAD LT performs this task automatically whenever a different menu file is specified. To specify a new menu file, select **Preferences...** from the **File** pull-down menu to display the **Preferences** dialog box. See Figure 20-1. Enter the new menu file name in the **Menu File:** text box located in the **Environment** section near the bottom of the dialog box. In the example shown, the name MYMENU is entered in the text box. It is not necessary to append the .MNU file extension. Click **OK** to exit the **Preferences** dialog box. The dialog box is closed and the following message is displayed on the command line:

    Compiling menu C:\ACLTWIN\MYMENU.mnu...

Figure 20-1.
Specifying a new menu file in the **Environment** section of the **Preferences** dialog box.

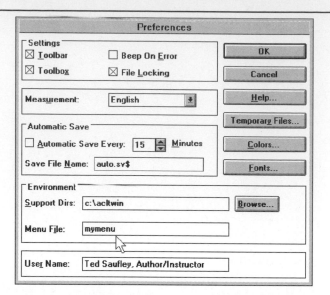

Once the menu has been compiled into the .MNX version, it is automatically loaded and ready for use.

NOTE   If you make any further modifications to the menu file, it is automatically recompiled the next time you start AutoCAD LT. If you wish to remain in AutoCAD LT as you edit the menu file, use File Manager to first delete the .MNX file that represents the previous compiled version. Then, return to AutoCAD LT and reenter the file name in the **Preferences** dialog box to recompile the menu.

MENU STRUCTURE AND SECTIONS

Before continuing, it would be a good idea to spend a few moments studying the ACLT.MNU file. Remember that the file is in ASCII format and may easily be printed. Having a printout makes interpretation and modification of the file much simpler. You can load ACLT.MNU into the Windows Notepad, Figure 20-2, or any other text editor you care to use.

Figure 20-2.
The ACLT.MNU file as it appears in the Windows Notepad.

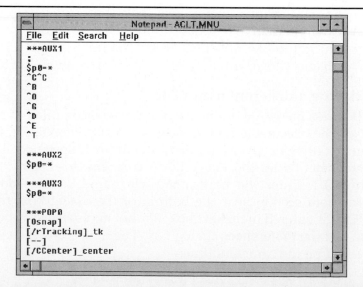

As you study the menu file, observe that it is divided into sections that relate to specific menu areas or types. The menu sections are identified by menu labels. The sections and the types of menus they represent are as follows:

- ***AUXn.** These sections are for customized mouse button functions (where *n* is a number from 1 to 4). The button menu and key/button sequences are defined below. However, keep in mind that the Windows driver used with your mouse takes precedence over the key/button sequences shown.
    - **AUX1**—Simple button pick
    - **AUX2**—[Shift] + [*button pick*]
    - **AUX3**—[Ctrl] + [*button pick*]
    - **AUX4**—[Ctrl] + [Shift] + [*button pick*]
- ***POPn.** These sections define the pull-down and cursor menus (where *n* is a number from 0 to 16). The section labeled ***POP0 defines the cursor menu. The remaining sections, ***POP1 through ***POP8, define the **File** through **Settings** pull-down menus, respectively. The **Help** pull-down menu is not defined in ACLT.MNU and thus cannot be modified. The cursor menu, plus its cascading submenus, can have a total of 499 menu items. The pull-down menus, plus their cascading submenus, may have a total of 999 menu items. However, the maximum number of menu items that can be displayed is determined by the current screen resolution.
- ***ICON.** This section describes an image tile menu. Only one image tile menu is predefined in AutoCAD LT. It can be seen in the **Select Text Font** dialog box. This dialog box is opened by selecting **Text Style...** from the **Settings** pull-down menu.

Interpreting the button (AUXn) menus

As mentioned previously, the AUXn sections of the menu file control the buttons on your mouse. However, you can not reassign the pick button of your mouse. Take a look at the ***AUX1 section of the menu file shown below.

```
***AUX1
;
$p0=*
^C^C
^B
^O
^G
^D
^E
^T
```

Because the pick button of your mouse cannot be reassigned, the first line after the section label AUX1 represents the next button on your mouse. This line consists of a single semicolon (;) that is interpreted as a carriage return. This is why clicking button 2 on your mouse (usually the rightmost button) is the same as pressing the [Enter] key on your keyboard.

The additional lines in the AUX1 section are for mouse devices that feature multiple buttons. Clicking button 3 displays the cursor menu, button 4 toggles Snap mode, button 5 toggles Ortho mode, and so on. Can you interpret the functions of the remaining lines?

PROFESSIONAL TIP

Apart from [Ctrl]+[T] that performs no function, each of the other control functions are listed in Chapter 1 of this text.

The menu section labeled ***AUX2 is used when you press the [Shift] key and click the right mouse button simultaneously. This action displays the pop-up cursor menu.

```
***AUX2
$p0=*
```

The line $p0=* is interpreted as follows:

- **$.** Loads a menu area.
- **p0.** Identifies the POP*n* menu area. Remember that POP0 defines the cursor menu.
- **=*.** Displays what is currently loaded to the specified menu area.

If you were to edit the ***AUX2 section to read $p3=*, which menu would be displayed in place of the cursor menu?

The menu section labeled ***AUX3 is used when you press the [Ctrl] key and click the right mouse button simultaneously. By default, this button assignment also enables the cursor menu. However, keep in mind that you can assign menu macros to the mouse buttons. A *menu macro* is a character string that can perform one or more AutoCAD LT commands. Consider the following menu macro:

```
***AUX3
grid .5 snap .25 limits 0,0 17,11 zoom all
```

From this example, the grid, snap, and limits are set and a **ZOOM All** operation is performed whenever the [Ctrl] key is pressed and the right mouse button is clicked simultaneously. If a menu macro does not fit on one line, it may be continued to the next line by entering a plus sign (+) as the last character of the line to be continued.

Finally, remember that you may add a fourth section, ***AUX4, so that a specialized function is performed when you press both the [Shift] and [Ctrl] keys simultaneously as you click the right mouse button.

EXERCISE 20-1

❑ Before beginning this exercise, make a backup copy of the ACLT.MNU file.
❑ Edit the ***AUX3 menu section to add a menu macro that performs the following operations:
   ❑ Sets the limits to a C-size drawing (22 × 17).
   ❑ Sets the grid spacing to 1 unit and the snap spacing to .5 units.
   ❑ Performs a **ZOOM All**.
   ❑ Turns on **Ortho** mode.
   ❑ Turns off the grid, snap, and coordinate display.
   ❑ Turns on the UCS icon.
❑ Remember to use the plus sign (+) if your macro does not fit on one line.
❑ Save the revised menu file with the name EX20-1.MNU.
❑ Begin a new drawing. Load the revised menu as described in the preceding text. If there is an error in the menu file, you will receive an alert message from AutoCAD LT as the file is compiling. Should this occur, exit AutoCAD LT and check the menu file for errors.
❑ After correcting any errors, restart AutoCAD LT and reload the corrected menu file.
❑ Test your new button assignment. Do not save the drawing when you are finished.

AutoCAD LT—Fundamentals and Applications

Interpreting the cursor and pull-down menus

As you study the ACLT.MNU file, locate the ***POP0 heading just below the ***AUX*n* sections. The ***POP0 section defines the cursor menu used for quick access to tracking, object snap modes, and point filters. Both the cursor menu and its definition in ACLT.MNU appear in Figure 20-3. Notice that the words enclosed in brackets ([ ]) appear in the on-screen cursor menu. The brackets are used to enclose labels for all of the ***POP*n* menu sections. Each label can be up to 14 characters long.

Figure 20-3.
The cursor menu as it appears on the screen (left) and how it is defined in the menu file (right).

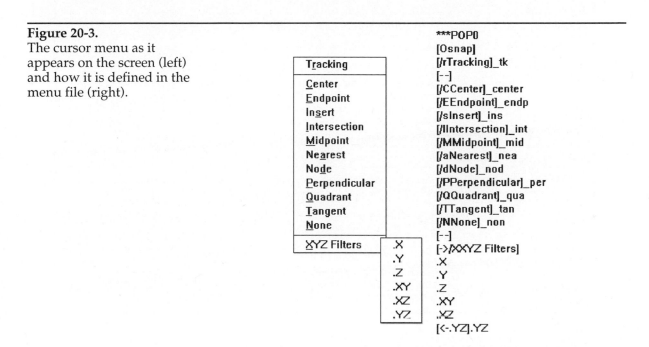

```
***POP0
[Osnap]
[/rTracking]_tk
[--]
[/CCenter]_center
[/EEndpoint]_endp
[/sInsert]_ins
[/IIntersection]_int
[/MMidpoint]_mid
[/aNearest]_nea
[/dNode]_nod
[/PPerpendicular]_per
[/QQuadrant]_qua
[/TTangent]_tan
[/NNone]_non
[--]
[->/XXYZ Filters]
.X
.Y
.Z
.XY
.XZ
[<-.YZ].YZ
```

Observe that a line separates the **Tracking** menu item from the **Center** item. Separator lines are specified by enclosing two hyphens in brackets [−−].

Note also that the first character of the label within the brackets is preceded by a forward slash [/]. The character preceded by a slash in a cursor or pull-down menu label defines the keyboard accelerator shortcut key combination used to enable that menu. To illustrate further, locate the ***POP1 section just below ***POP0 in the menu file. The ***POP1 section defines the **File** pull-down menu on the menu bar. Observe that the title of the **File** pull-down menu is defined as **[/FFile]** in ACLT.MNU; thus the **File** menu can be accessed by pressing [Alt]+[F].

Remember also that once a pull-down menu is displayed, a menu item within it may be selected using a single mnemonic character key. The mnemonic keys defined for the **New** and **Open** commands in the **File** pull-down menu appear in ACLT.MNU as **[/NNew]** and **[/OOpen]**. Therefore, these menu items are enabled with the single keys [N] and [O], respectively.

Special label characters

The following chart shows characters that perform a special function when included in a cursor or pull-down menu label.

Character	Description
[label]	Identifies the menu item as it appears in the menu.
[--]	As previously mentioned, two hyphens enclosed in brackets draw a separator line between menu items.
[-〈 label]	Identifies the beginning of a cascading submenu.
[〈 -label]	Identifies the end of a cascading submenu.
[〈-〈-label]	Indicates that this is the last item in a submenu which is itself also a submenu. A menu that features one or more submenus is called a *parent* menu. As an example, consider the menu hierarchy illustrated in Figure 20-4. The **Draw** pull-down menu is the parent of the **External References** cascading submenu that in turn is the parent of the **Bind Symbols** cascading submenu. Note the use of the 〈-〈- characters at the beginning of the **Text Style** menu item to terminate the parent menu.
***	Identifies the beginning of a menu section.
^C^C	A single ^C cancels most commands. However, ^C^C is required to return to the **Command:** prompt from a dimensioning command.
/c	Specifies the accelerator or mnemonic key in a pull-down or cursor menu label. The *c* shown here represents any character.
[~label]	The tilde character makes a menu item unavailable. Any characters following the tilde appear grayed-out.
[!.label]	An exclamation point and a period mark a menu item with a checkmark. An example can be seen with the **Tile Mode** item in the **View** pull-down menu.

Figure 20-4.
An example of parent menus and cascading submenus. Note the use of the 〈-〈- characters to terminate the parent menu.

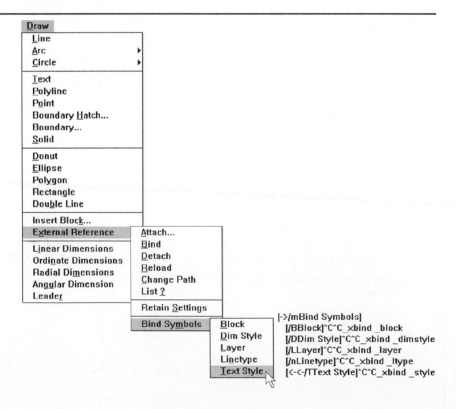

CREATING A NEW PULL-DOWN MENU TUTORIAL

In the following tutorial, you will create a new menu system that features an additional pull-down menu labeled **Custom**. The new menu is to be inserted between the existing **Settings** and **Help** pull-down menus. See Figure 20-5.

Figure 20-5.
The new **Custom** pull-down menu is located between the **Settings** and **Help** pull-down menus.

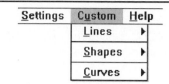

The menu contains three items labeled **Lines**, **Shapes**, and **Curves**. Each of these items features a cascading submenu with additional drawing commands as shown in Figure 20-6. Observe from Figure 20-7 that the **Arc**, **Circle**, and **Ellipse** items also feature cascading submenus. Begin the tutorial as follows:

➪ Make a copy of the ACLT.MNU file. Name the copy MYMENU.MNU.

➪ Use Notepad or your own ASCII text editor to edit MYMENU.MNU.

➪ Scroll down through MYMENU.MNU until you find the section labeled ***icon. It is located after the last line of the ***POP8 pull-down menu.

➪ Move the cursor to the line before the ***icon section and begin inserting there. Be sure to leave a blank line between pull-down menus.

➪ Next, enter the following lines listed on the next page. Although indentations are shown for greater readability and consistency with the remainder of the menu file, they are not necessary and may be omitted.

Figure 20-6.
Each of the menu items displays a cascading submenu.

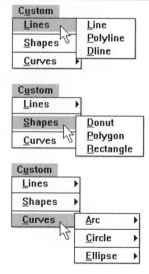

```
***POP9
[/uCustom]
[–⟩/LLines]
    [/iLine]^C^C_line
    [/PPolyline]^C^C_pline
    [⟨–/DDline]^C^C_dline
[——]
[–⟩/SShapes]
    [/DDonut]^C^C_donut
    [/PPolygon]^C^C_polygon
    [⟨–/RRectangle]^C^C_rectang
[——]
[–⟩/CCurves]
[–⟩/AArc]
    [/EStart, Center, End]^C^C_arc \_c
    [/AStart, Center, Angle]^C^C_arc \_c \_a
    [/dStart, End, Angle]^C^C_arc \_e
    [/SCenter, Start, End]^C^C_arc _c \\
    [/nCenter, Start, Angle]^C^C_arc _c \\_a
    [⟨–/33 Point]^C^C_arc \\
    [——]
[–⟩/CCircle]
    [/RCenter, Radius]^C^C_circle
    [/DCenter, Diameter]^C^C_circle \_d
    [/TTan, Tan, Radius]^C^C_circle _ttr
    [⟨–/33 Point]^C^C_circle _3p
    [——]
[–⟩/EEllipse]
    [/AAxis Endpoints]^C^C_ellipse
    [⟨–⟨–/CCenter]^C^C_ellipse _c
```

⤷ Be sure to leave a blank line between the last line you entered and the line labeled ***icon. Save MYMENU.MNU.

Figure 20-7.
The **Arc**, **Circle**, and **Ellipse** menu items each feature their own cascading submenus.

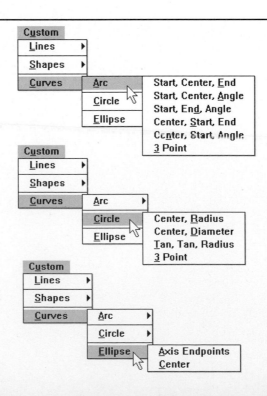

➮ Start AutoCAD LT. Add the new menu name MYMENU to the **Preferences** dialog box as described at the beginning of this chapter.

➮ If there is an error in the new menu file, you will receive an alert message from AutoCAD LT as the file is compiling. Should this occur, exit AutoCAD LT and check the menu file for any open brackets or illegal characters.

➮ After correcting any errors, restart AutoCAD LT and add the new menu name MYMENU to the **Preferences** dialog box as described at the beginning of this chapter.

➮ Try using the new **Custom** menu.

IMAGE TILE MENUS

As mentioned earlier in this chapter, the section at the end of the menu file labeled ***icon describes an image tile menu. An example of an image tile menu can be seen in the **Select Text Font** dialog box. See Figure 20-8. Observe from the illustration that image tile menus use a dialog box to display slides in groups of 20. If there are more than 20 slides in the menu, the **Next** and **Previous** buttons are used to leaf through additional menu pages.

Figure 20-8.
The **Select Text Font** dialog box is an example of an image tile menu.

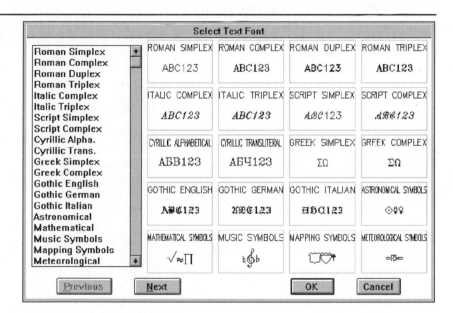

Image tile menus are particularly useful for displaying and selecting block symbols for insertion. The following sections describe how to prepare slides and add an image tile menu representing electronic schematic symbols to AutoCAD LT.

Preparing slides for image tile menus

In Chapter 17, you learned how to create slides using the **MSLIDE** command. You can greatly improve the appearance of your image tile menus by adhering to the following guidelines as you make your slides:

1. Keep the slides simple. Complex slides slow the display of the image tile menu.
2. Before making a slide, perform a **ZOOM Extents** to fill the screen with the graphic image. Use the **PAN** command to center the image on the screen.
3. Solid filled areas are not displayed in image tiles. If you are using solids, wide polylines, arrowheads, or donuts in your slides, turn off **FILLMODE** to see how the slide will appear in the image tile. Make any required modifications before making the slide.

Sizing the slide accurately

AutoCAD LT displays image tiles with an aspect ratio of 1.5 to 1 (1.5 units wide by 1 unit high). You can assure the correct proportions for your image tiles by doing the following:

1. Begin a new drawing.
2. Turn off TILEMODE to enter paper space. You may do so by selecting **Tile Mode** from the **View** pull-down menu.
3. Issue the **MVIEW** command by first selecting **Viewports** from the **View** pull-down menu and then selecting **Make Viewports** from the cascading submenu.
4. Enter the coordinates 0,0 for the first corner of the viewport and 3,2 for the other corner.
5. Enter MSPACE or MS to enter model space.
6. Construct the desired graphics symbol in the viewport. If the symbol already exists on disk, insert it into the viewport using the **INSERT** command. When complete, perform a **ZOOM Extents** to fill the viewport. Pan as necessary to center the image.
7. Use the **MSLIDE** command to make the slide.

NOTE   If necessary, refer to Chapter 16 to review **Tile Mode** and paper space commands.

Organizing the slides

Once the necessary slides are created, you can create a slide library using the SLIDELIB.EXE utility program introduced in Chapter 17. Before you create the slide library, use Notepad or another ASCII text editor to create a list of the slides to appear in the library.

In the following example, a list of slide files representing electronic components for schematic diagrams is prepared and saved with the name ELECSYM.TXT. The list might appear in the text editor as follows:

```
cap
diode
resistor
xsistor
inductor
lamp
switch
battery
```

After completing and saving the slide list file, use the **SLIDELIB** command to make the slide library. Since the **SLIDELIB** program is located in the \ACLTWIN directory, place the ELECSYM.TXT file in the same directory so that **SLIDELIB** can find it to create the slide library.

Remember that the **SLIDELIB** utility must be executed at the DOS prompt and cannot be used inside AutoCAD LT. If you are already in Windows, use the MS-DOS Prompt application covered in Chapter 17 to switch to the DOS prompt. Next, enter the following to switch to the AutoCAD LT directory and create the slide library:

```
C:\WINDOWS⟩ CD \ACLTWIN ⏎
C:\ACLTWIN⟩ SLIDELIB ELECSYM ⟨ ELECSYM.TXT ⏎
SLIDELIB 1.2 (3/8/89)
(C) Copyright 1987-89 Autodesk, Inc.
       All Rights Reserved
C:\ACLTWIN⟩ EXIT ⏎
```

In the example above, the slide library is given the same name as the list of slide files. When complete, the slide library resides on disk with the name ELECSYM.SLB. Remember that you may use any names you choose when creating slide libraries and slide lists providing the file names conform to DOS naming conventions.

Creating an image tile menu

Now that the slide library is created, the menu file may be edited. First, page down to the section labeled ***icon and make your entries similar to the examples shown below:

```
***icon
**ELECSYM
[Insert Electronic Component]
[elecsym(cap,Capacitor)]^C^Cinsert cap
[elecsym(Diode)]^C^Cinsert diode
[elecsym(Resistor)]^C^Cinsert resistor
[elecsym(xsistor,Transistor)]^C^Cinsert xsistor
[elecsym(Inductor)]^C^Cinsert inductor
[elecsym(Battery)]^C^Cinsert battery
[elecsym(Lamp)]^C^Cinsert lamp
[elecsym(Switch)]^C^Cinsert switch
```

The label **Insert Electronic Component** will appear in the title bar of the new image tile menu dialog box. Now study the syntax of the next line just below the label. The string [elecsym(cap,Capacitor)] instructs AutoCAD LT to locate the cap slide file in the elecsym slide library.

Note the addition of the word Capacitor after the cap, character string. By adding an additional field after the slide name, you can specify any name you choose in the image tile menus. This is particularly useful when a component name like capacitor or transistor exceeds 8 characters and cannot be used for the slide file name.

The next character string in the field, ^C^Cinsert cap, performs two cancel operations and inserts the block named cap into the drawing. Remember that two cancels are required to return to the **Command:** prompt from a dimensioning command.

Adding the image tile menu to the pull-down menus

Before you can view the new image tile menu, you must add a menu selection that displays it on the screen. A logical place to put the menu selection would be in the **Draw** or **Construct** pull-down menus. The following line is added to the **Draw** pull-down menu (***POP3) between the **Insert Block...** and the **External Reference** menu items:

```
[Electronic Components...]$I=elecsym $I=*
```

The label **Electronic Components...** appears as a new menu item in the **Draw** pull-down menu. See Figure 20-9. Note the addition of the ellipsis (...) to denote that this item opens a dialog box.

The next part of the entry, $I=elecsym, calls the new electronic component image tile menu. The last part of the entry, $I=*, displays the image tile menu and makes the items within it selectable.

The completed image tile menu is shown in Figure 20-10. Because image tiles cannot display solid filled areas, note the appearance of the diode and transistor symbols.

Figure 20-9.
The new image tile menu item is added to the **Draw** pull-down menu.

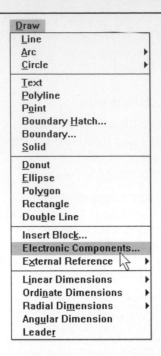

Figure 20-10.
The new **Insert Electronic Components** dialog box displays the image tiles.

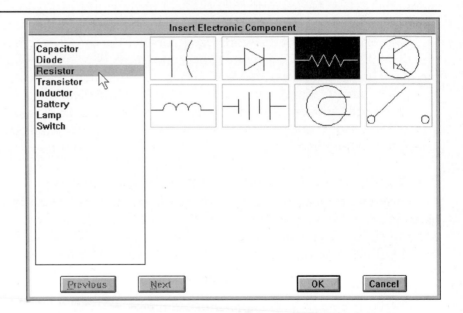

CHAPTER TEST

Write your answers in the spaces provided.

1. What is a .MNX file? _____

   _____

2. Name the file that contains the default AutoCAD LT menu system. _____

   _____

3. Why is it a good idea to make a backup copy of the original menu file? _____

   _____

   _____

4. Identify the required steps to specify a different menu file. _____

   _____

   _____

   _____

5. Which section of the menu file is used to customize mouse buttons? _____

   _____

6. The pick button on the mouse may be reassigned. (True/False) _____

7. Which section of the menu file is used to modify or add pull-down menus? _____

   _____

8. Excluding the **Help** menu, what is the maximum number of pull-down menus that may appear on the menu bar? _____

   _____

9. What character is used to continue a menu macro on another line? _____

   _____

10. What character is used in a menu label to define a keyboard accelerator key? _____

    _____

11. What characters must be entered to place a separator line between menu items? _____

    _____

12. Which section of the menu file is used to add image tile menus? _____

    _____

13. How many slides may be displayed on one page of an image tile menu? _____

    _____

14. Solid areas cannot be displayed in an image tile. (True/False) _____

15. What aspect ratio is used to display an image tile? _____

    _____

CHAPTER PROBLEMS

General

1. Create a new pull-down menu named **Special**. The new menu should include the following drawing and editing commands:

Line	Move
Arc	Copy
Circle	Stretch
Polyline	Trim
Dline	Extend
Polygon	Chamfer
Rectangle	Fillet
Dtext	Erase

Use cascading submenus as desired. Include a separator line between the drawing and editing commands, and specify appropriate accelerator and mnemonic shortcut keys.

General

2. Create a group of slides of block symbols that are pertinent to your professional discipline or field of interest. As an example, the slides might feature mechanical fasteners such as nuts, washers, bolts, etc. An architectural collection of slides would include blocks of doors, windows, receptacles, and so forth. Create a minimum of four slides and be sure to size the blocks as described in this chapter. When the slide files are created, write a slide list and use the **SLIDELIB** utility to produce a slide library. Edit the menu file and add your slides to the ***icon section. Add a new menu item called **My Symbols...** at the very bottom of the **Construct** pull-down menu.

Chapter 21

Using the Windows File Manager

AutoCAD LT

Learning objectives:

After completing this chapter, you will be able to:
- ○ Identify the various elements of File Manager.
- ○ Start applications and print drawing files from File Manager.
- ○ Drag and drop AutoCAD LT-related files into the AutoCAD LT graphics window.
- ○ Move, copy, delete, undelete, and rename files on floppy and hard disks.
- ○ Create and manage directories and subdirectories.
- ○ Format, label, and copy floppy disks.

Prudent file and disk management is very important to every computer user. This is particularly true in the case of AutoCAD LT. The loss of a large or complex drawing file through carelessness or negligence is a painful experience. Losing an entire directory of drawing files can be devastating. A variety of suggestions and procedures for managing AutoCAD LT-related files have been offered throughout the preceding chapters of this text.

This chapter introduces an excellent method of file and disk maintenance using the Microsoft Windows File Manager. With File Manager, you can perform a variety of file-manipulation tasks with remarkable ease and assurance. This powerful tool also enables you to create, delete, undelete, rename, and move entire directories. You can also use File Manager to quickly and easily format, label, and copy floppy disks. In addition, File Manager can be used to open a drawing file and start AutoCAD LT in one simple operation. The "drag and drop" capability of File Manager is also explored as a means of inserting drawing and text files into the AutoCAD LT drawing editor, as well as printing or plotting a drawing with the Windows Print Manager. For a complete description of File Manager, refer to the *Microsoft Windows User's Guide*.

INTRODUCTION TO FILE MANAGER

To launch File Manager, open the Main group window in the Program Manager and double-click the File Manager icon. You can also click the File Manager icon just once and then press [Enter].

NOTE   The examples illustrated in this chapter reflect the File Manager used by Microsoft Windows for Workgroups. If you are using Windows 3.1, your screen display may appear slightly different. However, the functions described in this chapter are identical in the two versions.

Elements of the File Manager directory window

When you use File Manager, all of your work is performed in a *directory window*. A directory window is a graphic representation of the directory structure of your disk, and each of the files and directories it contains. When you first start File Manager, the directory window displays the contents of the current drive. The directory window is divided in half with a *split bar*. The left section of the directory window displays the *directory tree*, and the right section lists the contents of the current directory. You can drag the split bar to the left or to the right to display more or less of the contents in each side of the directory window. Place your cursor on the split bar until it changes to a small vertical bar. Hold down your pick button and then drag the vertical bar to the left or right. Release the button when you get to the desired location.

The directory window for the ACLTWIN directory is shown in Figure 21-1. You can see that ACLTWIN is highlighted in the directory tree and is the current directory. This is confirmed by the directory path shown in the title bar of the File Manager window and by the ACLTWIN *directory icon* which appears as an open folder in the directory tree. The subdirectories within the ACLTWIN directory branch below and form a tree structure. Each of these subdirectories is connected with a vertical line to the directory one level above them. If the directory tree structure is not visible, double-click the directory icon.

At the right of the directory window is a contents list of the subdirectories and files which reside in ACLTWIN. Each subdirectory in this list is also represented with a directory icon. A *file icon* indicating the file type appears next to each filename. There are icons to represent program files like .EXE and .BAT files, document files like .TXT and .WRI files, and other types of files.

Figure 21-1.
The File Manager directory window lists directories and subdirectories on the left side of the window, and the contents of the current directory to the right.

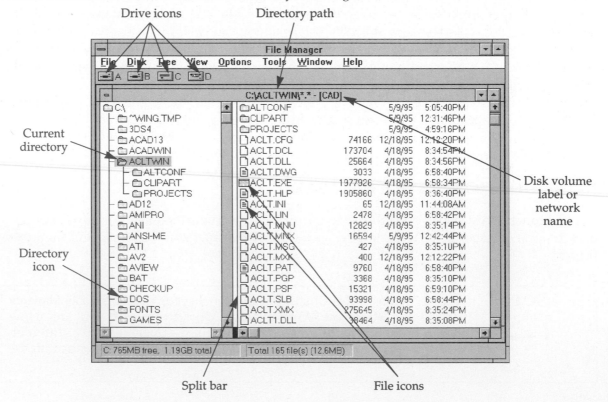

AutoCAD LT—Fundamentals and Applications

You must first select a file or directory in the File Manager directory window before you can work with it. When you want to select a file or directory, place the arrow cursor of your mouse over the desired file or directory icon and click. You can also place your cursor over the name of the desired file or directory and click. More than one file or directory can be selected by pressing and holding the [Ctrl] or the [Shift] key as you click with your left mouse button. The item(s) you select is then highlighted and you can proceed with the desired operation. More information about file and directory selection appears later in this chapter.

Drive icons which represent each of the drives on your computer are located at the upper left of the directory window. A drive letter follows each icon. You can see that the floppy disk drives—A: and B:—are represented with a different icon than that used for the hard disk—C:. You can easily change to one of the available drives with a simple click on the desired drive icon. If you have a CD-ROM device, or if you are connected to a network, appropriate icons are displayed for these drives as well. The name of the current open directory and volume label of the current drive is located just above the file list. In this example, the volume label [CAD] is shown. If no label is assigned, only the current directory name appears in this area. If you are connected to a network, and the network drive is selected, then the network name is displayed instead of the volume label.

Appearing just below the directory window title bar are the names of the eight File Manager pull-down menus. These menu names are: File, Disk, Tree, View, Options, Tools, Window, and Help. Many of the commands located in these menus are explored later in this chapter.

Finally, as with all Microsoft Windows applications, the File Manager window may be moved, resized, closed, and *iconified* at any time.

LAUNCHING APPLICATIONS WITH FILE MANAGER

Many of the files that appear in the File Manager directory window are associated with application programs. By double-clicking on the file icon, or on the filename itself, you can load the file and simultaneously start the application with which it is associated. Consider the portion of the directory window shown in Figure 21-2. Double-clicking on the drawing file CAM.DWG highlights the filename in the directory window. The Windows "hourglass" is then displayed as AutoCAD LT is loaded and opens the CAM drawing in the drawing editor.

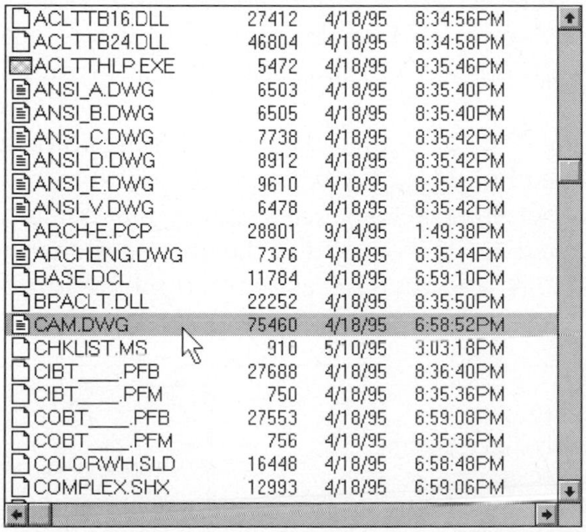

Figure 21-2.
Double-clicking a .DWG file icon, or the filename itself, from the File Manager directory starts AutoCAD LT and loads the selected file into the drawing editor at the same time.

ACLTTB16.DLL	27412	4/18/95	8:34:56PM
ACLTTB24.DLL	46804	4/18/95	8:34:58PM
ACLTTHLP.EXE	5472	4/18/95	8:35:46PM
ANSI_A.DWG	6503	4/18/95	8:35:40PM
ANSI_B.DWG	6505	4/18/95	8:35:40PM
ANSI_C.DWG	7738	4/18/95	8:35:42PM
ANSI_D.DWG	8912	4/18/95	8:35:42PM
ANSI_E.DWG	9610	4/18/95	8:35:42PM
ANSI_V.DWG	6478	4/18/95	8:35:42PM
ARCH-E.PCP	28801	9/14/95	1:49:38PM
ARCHENG.DWG	7376	4/18/95	8:35:44PM
BASE.DCL	11784	4/18/95	6:59:10PM
BPACLT.DLL	22252	4/18/95	8:35:50PM
CAM.DWG	75460	4/18/95	6:58:52PM
CHKLIST.MS	910	5/10/95	3:03:18PM
CIBT____.PFB	27688	4/18/95	8:36:40PM
CIBT____.PFM	750	4/18/95	8:35:36PM
COBT____.PFB	27553	4/18/95	6:59:08PM
COBT____.PFM	756	4/18/95	8:35:36PM
COLORWH.SLD	16448	4/18/95	6:58:48PM
COMPLEX.SHX	12993	4/18/95	6:59:06PM

Drag and drop operations with File Manager

The Windows File Manager can also be used to dynamically "drag-and-drop" file icons into the AutoCAD LT graphics window. This powerful capability allows you to insert drawing files as blocks, insert text files as dynamic text, print a drawing, and import DXF and PostScript files. Drag and drop can also be used to load menu, font, linetype, script, and slide files. A file selected for drag and drop operations with AutoCAD LT must have one of the following file extensions:

.DWG	.DXF	.EPS	.LIN	.SLD
.MNU	.MNX	.SCR	.SHX	.TXT

The following table lists the different kinds of drag and drop operations that can be used in AutoCAD LT. Also listed are the required filename extensions, the related AutoCAD LT commands, and the chapters in this text where additional command information can be found.

OPERATION	FILE EXTENSION	RELATED COMMAND	RELATED CHAPTER
Load a linetype file	.LIN	**LINETYPE**	Chapter 5
Load a text file	.TXT	**DTEXT**	Chapter 9
Load a font file	.SHX	**STYLE**	Chapter 9
Print a drawing	.DWG	**PLOT**	Chapter 13
Insert a drawing file	.DWG	**INSERT**	Chapter 14
Load a slide file	.SLD	**VSLIDE**	Chapter 17
Run a script file	.SCR	**SCRIPT**	Chapter 17
Load a menu file	.MNU	**MENU**	Chapter 20
Import a DXF file	.DXF	**DXFIN**	Chapter 22

Dragging and dropping a text file

In Chapter 14, you learned that AutoCAD LT entities, like text, may be saved to disk with the **WBLOCK** command and inserted into a drawing file at any time. A text file created with a text editor outside of AutoCAD LT may also be inserted into a drawing file using File Manager drag and drop. As an example, consider the NOTES.TXT text file shown in the Windows Notepad. See Figure 21-3. To drag this text file into AutoCAD LT, do the following:

1. Start both AutoCAD LT and File Manager. Arrange the display windows so that both are visible.
2. Issue the **DTEXT** command. Select the start point and justification for the text, and respond to the text height and rotation angle prompts. Stop when the **Text:** prompt appears.
3. Now, open the File Manager directory that contains the text file you want.
4. Drag the text file icon next to the desired filename into the AutoCAD LT graphics window, Figure 21-4, and then release the left mouse button.

Figure 21-3.
External text files with a .TXT extension (like this one shown in Notepad) can be dragged and dropped into the graphics window. Remember to save your text file prior to dragging it.

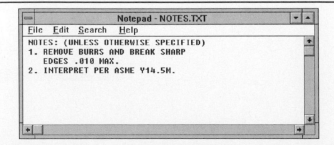

Figure 21-4.
After issuing the **DTEXT** command and answering the prompts for text height and rotation, the text file icon is "dragged" into the AutoCAD LT graphics window.

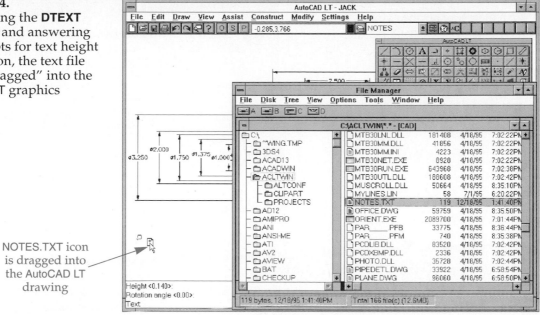

NOTES.TXT icon is dragged into the AutoCAD LT drawing

5. After the text appears in the graphics window, the **Text:** prompt remains displayed. At this point, you may enter additional text or press [Enter] to end the **DTEXT** command. The text is inserted in the current text style and on the current layer. See Figure 21-5.

External text files can be created with Notepad, MS-DOS EDIT, or your own ASCII text editor. Remember that the text file must have a .TXT extension. Without this extension, a text file has no association with an application. If you attempt to drag and drop a text file without a .TXT extension, AutoCAD LT displays the alert box shown in Figure 21-6A. Remember also that dragging and dropping text files works only with the **DTEXT** command, and not the **TEXT** command. If you attempt to drag and drop a text file when using the **TEXT** command, AutoCAD LT informs you accordingly with the alert box shown in Figure 21-6B.

Figure 21-5.
The external text is inserted in the current text style, layer, and color.

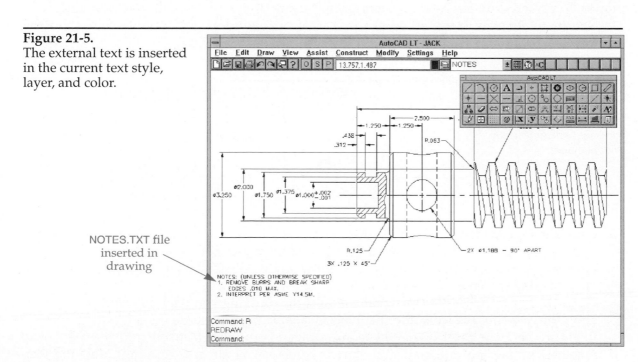

NOTES.TXT file inserted in drawing

Figure 21-6.
A—An alert box notifies you that no association exists for a text file without a .TXT extension. B—AutoCAD LT displays this alert box message when you attempt to drag and drop a text file using the **TEXT** command instead of **DTEXT**.

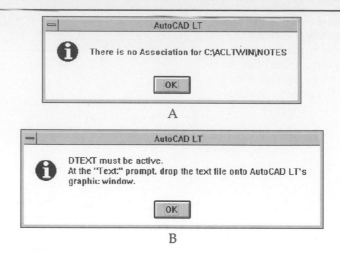

A

B

Using drag and drop to print a drawing

Drag and drop may also be used to print an AutoCAD LT drawing file by dragging the drawing file icon directly to the Windows Print Manager. AutoCAD LT need not be loaded beforehand—dragging and dropping a drawing file icon into Print Manager automatically starts the program. The drawing file icon you select is inserted into the drawing editor using the **FILEOPEN** command. This command allows you to open a file without using a dialog box, regardless of the setting of the **FILEDIA** system variable. Once the drawing appears in the graphics window, the **Plot Configuration** dialog box is displayed. You can then modify the printing parameters as required and print the drawing.

If AutoCAD LT is already running when you use drag and drop to print a drawing, an alert box appears on the display screen. You can then save or discard any changes made to the current drawing before the drawing to be printed is opened in the drawing editor.

This drag and drop operation may be used when the Windows system printer is the desired output device, but is not valid if you want to plot a drawing on a pen plotter or electrostatic plotter. To print a drawing on the system printer using drag and drop, do the following:

1. Return to Program Manager, open the Main group window and double-click the Print Manager program item icon to launch Print Manager, Figure 21-7.

Figure 21-7.
Double-click the Print Manager icon in the **Main** group window to open Print Manager.

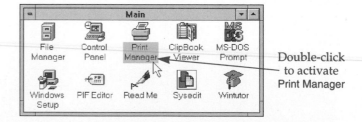

Double-click
to activate
Print Manager

2. Once the Print Manager window is displayed, click the Minimize button (the down arrow at the upper right of the window) to iconify Print Manager. See Figure 21-8.
3. Launch File Manager and arrange the window so that the Print Manager icon is visible on your display screen.
4. Open the File Manager directory that contains the drawing you wish to print.
5. Drag the drawing file icon onto the Print Manager icon and release the left mouse button. In Figure 21-9, the SHAFT.DWG file icon is dragged onto Print Manager.
6. AutoCAD LT is then automatically started (unless it is already running), and the Plot Configuration dialog box is presented. See Figure 21-10.
7. Make any desired changes to the printing configuration and click OK to begin printing.

Figure 21-8.
Click the Minimize button
(the down arrow) at the
upper right of the Print
Manager window to reduce
Print Manager to an icon.

Click to reduce Print
Manager to an icon

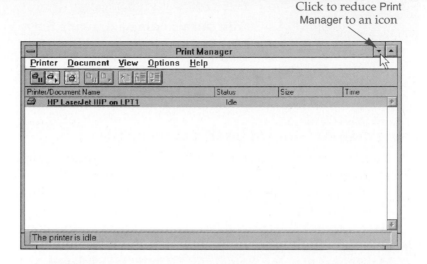

Figure 21-9.
Drag the file icon of the
drawing to be printed to
the Print Manager icon and
release the left mouse
button.

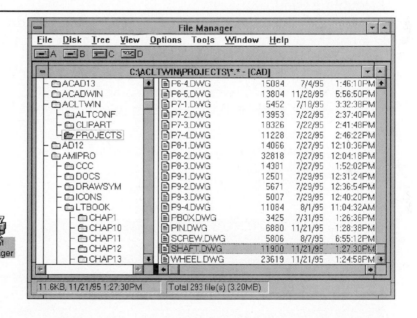

Figure 21-10.
AutoCAD LT is loaded
automatically and the
Plot Configuration dialog
box is displayed.

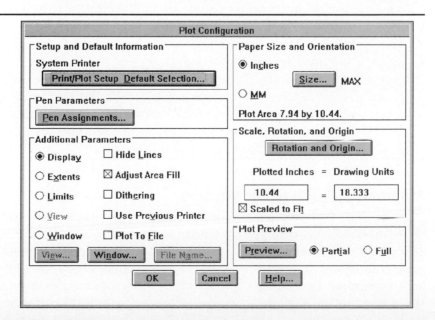

Using drag and drop to insert a drawing file

Drag and drop can also be used to insert any drawing into the current drawing session. This method is very similar to the **INSERT** command discussed in Chapter 14. Like **INSERT**, the drawing that you drag and drop becomes a block. Therefore, be sure to explode it after insertion if necessary.

1. Start both AutoCAD LT and File Manager. Once again, arrange the display windows so that both are visible.
2. Make sure that the **Command:** prompt is displayed at the bottom of the AutoCAD LT graphics window.
3. Now, open the File Manager directory that contains the drawing file that you want to insert.
4. Drag the drawing file icon next to the filename into the AutoCAD LT graphics window and then release the left mouse button.
5. The **INSERT** command is echoed in the AutoCAD LT command line area. Answer the prompts for the drawing insertion point, scale, and rotation angle.
6. If necessary, explode the inserted drawing as follows:

> Command: *(type* EXPLODE *or* X *and press* [Enter]*)*
> Select objects: *(type* LAST *or* L *and press* [Enter]*)*
> Select objects: ↵
> Command:

EXERCISE 21-1

❑ Start Windows and launch File Manager.
❑ Open the \ACLTWIN directory and double-click a drawing file icon to load AutoCAD LT.
❑ Arrange the open display windows to resemble those shown in Figure 21-4.
❑ Using the method previously described, drag a drawing file icon into the AutoCAD LT graphics window. Answer the prompts for insertion point, scale, and rotation angle. Then, explode the inserted drawing.
❑ Use Notepad to create a simple text file like that shown in Figure 21-3. Make the notes specific to your particular application. Be sure to save the drawing using a .TXT extension.
❑ Activate the AutoCAD LT graphics window and issue the **DTEXT** command. Pick a start point for the text, and accept the default text height and rotation angle values.
❑ Drag the text file you created with Notepad into the graphics window.
❑ If you are connected to a printer, try using drag and drop to print a drawing file with Print Manager as described earlier in this chapter.

Automatic StartUp of File Manager

The drag and drop capabilities of File Manager make it an excellent companion application for AutoCAD LT. As such, you may want to have File Manager open and readily accessible whenever you are working with AutoCAD LT. Having both programs start together automatically is quite convenient, and is very simple to accomplish. When Microsoft Windows is first installed on a computer, the Windows installation program creates a group window named StartUp as shown in Figure 21-11A. As you can see from the illustration, the Windows installation

Figure 21-11.
A—The StartUp group window is empty when Microsoft Windows is first installed. B—AutoCAD LT, File Manager, and Notepad program item icons are copied to the StartUp group window.

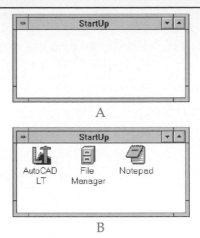

A

B

program initially creates an empty group window. However, if you move or copy a program item icon into the StartUp window, the application(s) represented by the program item icon is started automatically whenever Windows is loaded.

As an example, consider the StartUp group window shown in Figure 21-11B. This window contains the program item icons for three applications—AutoCAD LT, File Manager, and Notepad. This is a reasonable selection of applications because these three programs work so well together. Now whenever Microsoft Windows is started, the three items in the StartUp group window are automatically loaded and displayed simultaneously on the Windows desktop. See Figure 21-12.

Figure 21-12.
Each of the applications represented by program item icons in the StartUp window are loaded automatically when Windows is started. Reposition and resize each display window to your personal liking and save the new window settings for future sessions.

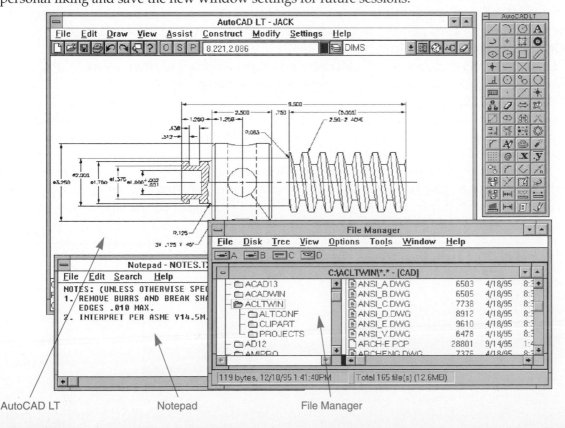

AutoCAD LT   Notepad   File Manager

You can set up a StartUp group window using the following procedure:

1. Return to Program Manager and open the StartUp, AutoCAD LT, Main, and Accessories group windows so that the program item icons are clearly visible, Figure 21-13.

Figure 21-13.
The StartUp, Main, AutoCAD LT, and Accessories group windows are each opened in Program Manager. Each window is positioned so that the program item icons are clearly visible.

StartUp group window prior to adding applications

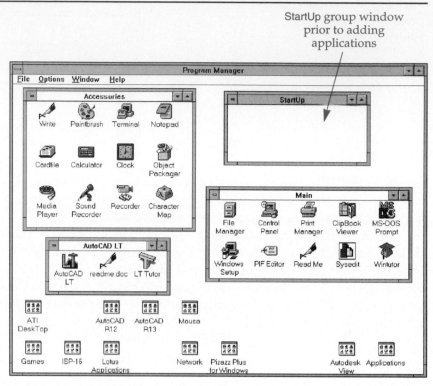

2. Drag and drop the AutoCAD LT program item icon from the AutoCAD LT group window into the StartUp group window. You may want to make a copy of the program item icon before dragging it, however. To do so, click the program item icon and hold down the [Ctrl] key as you drag the icon into the StartUp group window.
3. Repeat the procedure for the File Manager and Notepad program item icons.
4. Resize the StartUp group window to your personal liking.
5. Now, exit Windows and then restart it.

Each of the programs in the StartUp window are automatically loaded after Windows starts up. Once each application is opened, you may wish to position and resize each of the display windows to your satisfaction.

When you have the File Manager directory window sized and positioned satisfactorily, select Save Settings on Exit from the Options pull-down menu of the File Manager. See Figure 21-14. The new size and position of File Manager is now stored for future sessions.

Figure 21-14.
The File Manager Options pull-down menu. Select Save Settings on Exit to maintain the File Manager appearance for future sessions.

Additional startup considerations

If you desire, you can choose to have an application load automatically at Windows start up, but be reduced to an icon to conserve desktop workspace. When you want to use the application, simply double-click the icon on the desktop to open the minimized application.

As an example, suppose you use Notepad on a frequent basis, but do not want the Notepad display window opened on screen after Windows is started. Return to Program Manager, open the StartUp group window, and click the Notepad program item icon to highlight it. Now, select Properties... from the File pull-down menu in Program Manager (or press [Alt]+[Enter]) to display the Program Item Properties dialog box. Activate the Run Minimized check box, Figure 21-15, and then click OK to exit the dialog box. The next time Windows is started, the Notepad minimized icon will appear at the bottom of the screen. Simply double-click the minimized icon when you want to work with Notepad.

Figure 21-15.
Activating the Run Minimized check box in the Program Item Properties dialog box starts an application as a minimized icon.

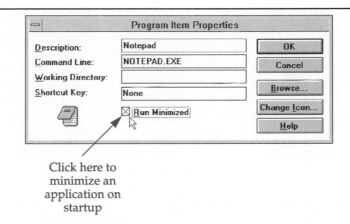

Click here to
minimize an
application on
startup

In addition, keep in mind that every open application in Windows will take memory and free system resources (FSRs) away from AutoCAD LT. For this reason, use some discretion when adding program item icons to the StartUp window. If you notice some degradation in AutoCAD LT performance, you can monitor your available system resources by returning to Program Manager and selecting About Program Manager... from the Help pull-down menu. This action displays the About Program Manager dialog box shown in Figure 21-16. Free memory and system resources are displayed at the bottom of this dialog box. If 30% or less is reported free for System Resources, you should close some of your applications and/or add additional memory to your computer.

Figure 21-16.
Free memory and system resources can be monitored in the About Program Manager dialog box.

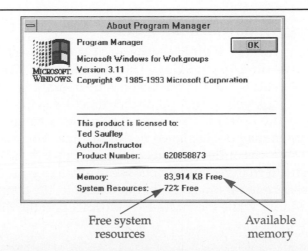

Free system
resources

Available
memory

EXERCISE 21-2

- ❑ Check with your instructor or supervisor before performing this exercise. Create a StartUp window using the techniques described in the preceding text. Be sure to include AutoCAD LT and File Manager in the StartUp window.
- ❑ Use some discretion when adding program item icons to the window. Remember that each open application requires additional memory, regardless of whether it is minimized or not.
- ❑ When you are satisfied with your StartUp configuration, resize and position the windows to your personal taste.
- ❑ Return to Program Manager and check the amount of free systems resources displayed in the About Program Manager dialog box.

WORKING WITH FILES AND DIRECTORIES

Managing files and directories is a simple task with File Manager. You can move, copy, delete, undelete, and rename files and entire directories quickly and easily. The commands that perform these functions are located in the File pull-down menu of the File Manager. This menu is shown in Figure 21-17. You will note that, like the pull-down menus in AutoCAD LT, several of the menu items are followed by an ellipsis (...). This indicates that a dialog box is associated with the menu command. In addition, there are keyboard shortcuts associated with several of the commands. The keyboard shortcuts are displayed to the right of the menu items.

Figure 21-17.
The File pull-down menu of the File Manager provides file-management functions.

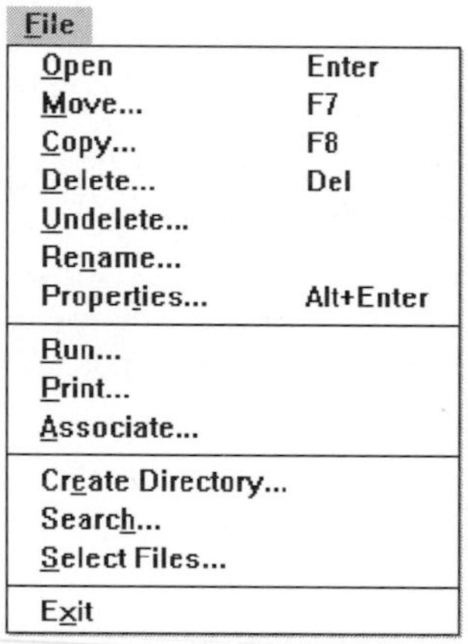
File
Open Enter
Move... F7
Copy... F8
Delete... Del
Undelete...
Rename...
Properties... Alt+Enter
Run...
Print...
Associate...
Create Directory...
Search...
Select Files...
Exit

Directory window display options

When working with File Manager, it is often useful to display more than one directory listing in the directory window. This simplifies moving files between drives and directories, and allows you to see the results of your operations. In Figure 21-18, the contents of the A: drive are displayed at the top of the directory window, and the \ACLTWIN directory listing appears at the bottom. This type of window arrangement is called a ***tiled*** display. Two or more listings may be displayed in this fashion. You can drag the split bar left or right to display more or less of the contents of the directory window.

As an alternative, you can choose to arrange your directory windows in a ***cascading*** display as shown in Figure 21-19. In this example, the contents of \ACLTWIN are displayed in the active window, while the inactive windows report the directory listings for the A: and B: drives.

Figure 21-18.
Multiple directory and drive listings can be arranged in a tiled display.

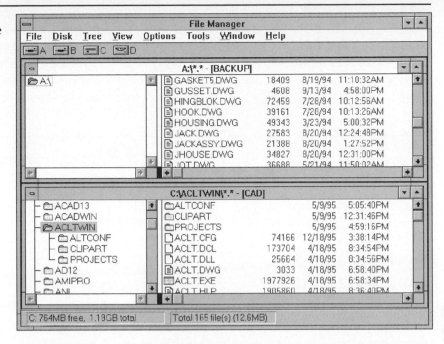

Figure 21-19.
Multiple directory and drive listings arranged in a cascading display.

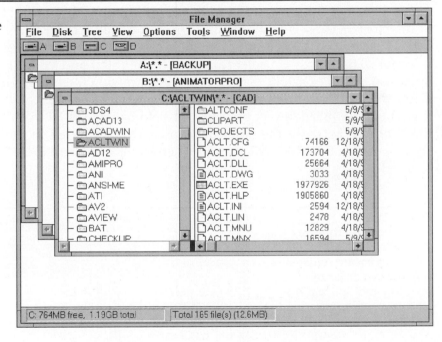

Use the <u>N</u>ew Window menu option when you want to open a new directory window. This option is located in the <u>W</u>indow pull-down menu of the File Manager. See Figure 21-20. You can also open a new window by double-clicking one of the drive icons at the upper left of the File Manager display window, Figure 21-1. Once a new directory window is opened, arrange the windows in a tiled or cascading display for easier viewing. The cascade and tiling options are also located in the <u>W</u>indow pull-down menu of the File Manager. See Figure 21-20.

Figure 21-20.
The <u>W</u>indow pull-down
menu of the File Manager
provides a means of
changing the window
display.

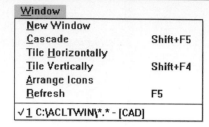

Selecting files and directories

Before you can work with a file or directory, it must first be selected. As mentioned at the beginning of this chapter, simply place the arrow cursor of your mouse over the desired file or directory icon and click to select the file or directory. You can also place your cursor over just the name of the desired file or directory and click. If you want to select more than one file or directory in consecutive sequence, press and hold the [Shift] key as you click with your left mouse button. In Windows terminology, selecting more than one item is called *extending a selection*. The items you select are then highlighted and you can proceed with the desired operation. As an example, consider the three drawing files shown highlighted in Figure 21-21. These three drawing files are selected in consecutive sequence by first clicking the PIN.DWG file. Then, the [Shift] key is pressed and held as the SHAFT.DWG file is clicked. Any file (or files) located between the two selections is then included in the selection. In the example shown, the file SCREW.DWG is located between the PIN and SHAFT drawings and is therefore selected.

Figure 21-21.
Three drawing files from the
\ACLTWIN\PROJECTS
subdirectory are selected in
consecutive order by
pressing and holding the
[Shift] key while selecting the
first and last file.

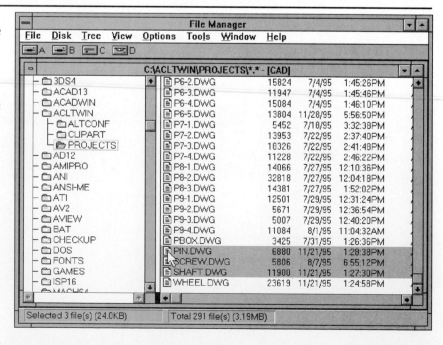

There will be occasions when you want to extend a selection, but you do not want the files selected in a consecutive fashion. You can easily select files out of sequence by pressing and holding the [Ctrl] key as you make your selections. This method is shown in Figure 21-22.

If you should inadvertently select a file or directory, and would like to cancel your selection, press and hold the [Ctrl] key as you click the highlighted item(s). The highlighting is removed and the selection is canceled.

Figure 21-22.
Three drawing files from the \ACLTWIN\PROJECTS subdirectory are selected out of sequence by pressing and holding the [Ctrl] key during file selection.

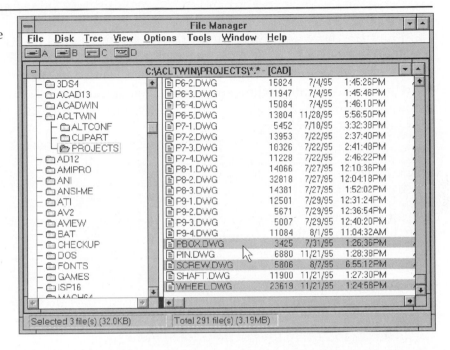

NOTE

When file and directory operations are performed, File Manager displays a dialog box prompting you to confirm the operation. Although not recommended, you can reduce or entirely eliminate the confirmation message prompting using the Confirmation dialog box shown in Figure 21-23. To access this dialog box, select Confirmation… from the Options pull-down menu of the File Manager. See Figure 21-14.

Figure 21-23.
The Confirmation dialog box is used to set confirmation prompting for file and disk operations.

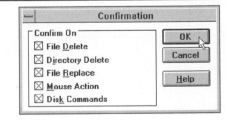

Moving and copying files

You can easily move and copy files between directories and drives by dragging the file icons with your mouse. It is also a simple matter to move or copy an entire directory. Before moving or copying files or directories, however, it is a good idea to display both the *source* (where you are moving or copying from) and *destination* (where you are moving or copying to) directories or drives in separate display windows. This is essential if you are using your mouse for these operations.

As an alternative to using your mouse, you can use the Move... and Copy... commands in the File pull-down menu of the File Manager. To move a file from one directory or drive to another, do the following:

1. Open the directory window that contains the file you wish to move. Click the file to be moved.

2. Now, select Move... from the File pull-down menu.

3. The Move dialog box then appears. See Figure 21-24. The file name you selected is displayed in the From: text box and the current directory name appears at the top of the dialog box. This is the source directory.

4. Enter the drive and directory for the file destination in the To: text box. In the example shown, the file CAM.DWG is being moved from the \ACLTWIN directory drive to the PROJECTS directory (also on the C: drive).

5. Click the OK button when you are finished entering the destination path name.

Remember that moving a file physically removes it from its source location and relocates it to a different destination.

Figure 21-24.
The Move dialog box displays the current directory, the name of the file to be moved, and the destination.

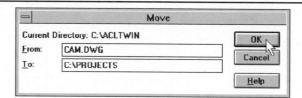

To copy a file from one directory or drive to another, do the following:

1. Open the directory window that contains the file you wish to copy. Click the file to be copied.

2. Select Copy... from the File pull-down menu.

3. The Copy dialog box then appears, Figure 21-25. The file name you selected is displayed in the From: text box and the current directory name appears at the top of the dialog box. This is the source directory.

4. Enter the drive and directory for the file destination in the To: text box. In the example shown, the file PROTOA.DWG is being copied from the \ACLTWIN directory on the C: drive to the A: drive.

5. Click the OK button when you are finished entering the destination directory name or drive letter.

Keep in mind that several files may be selected for moving or copying. When you extend your file selection, each selected file name appears in the From: text box in the Move and Copy dialog boxes.

Figure 21-25.
The Copy dialog box identifies the name of the current directory, the name of the file to be copied, and the destination.

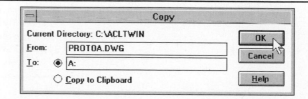

PROFESSIONAL TIP

Keep a formatted floppy disk in your machine while working with AutoCAD LT. Whenever you save one of your drawing files to the hard disk, activate the File Manager window and use the Copy command to copy the saved drawing to your floppy as a backup file.

Deleting files and directories

You can use File Manager to delete individual files or entire directories. When you delete a directory, all files and subdirectories within that directory are also deleted. As with all delete operations, slow down and think carefully before deleting any files or directories. File recovery and undelete utilities cannot always recover a deleted file. To delete a file, do the following:

1. Open the directory window that contains the file or directory you wish to delete. Click the file or directory name to be deleted.
2. Now, press the [Delete] key on your keyboard or select <u>D</u>elete... from the <u>F</u>ile pull-down menu.. The Delete dialog box appears and the file or directory name you selected is displayed in the De<u>l</u>ete: text box. Click OK to complete the operation.
3. If you like, you can enter a different file or directory name in the De<u>l</u>ete: text box. You can also use the "*" wildcard character. In the example shown in Figure 21-26, this wildcard is used to delete all of the .BAK drawing backup files in the \ACLTWIN directory.

Figure 21-26.
The Delete dialog box. If you have the File <u>D</u>elete or Directory Delete check box marked in the Confirmation dialog box, you will then be asked to confirm your deletion.

Delete
Current Directory: C:\ACLTWIN
Delete: C:\ACLTWIN*.BAK
OK   Cancel   Help

Undeleting a file

When a file or directory is deleted, its data may still be on the disk. If you wish to retrieve a deleted file or directory, do the following:

1. Open the directory window that contains the file or directory that has been deleted.
2. Select <u>U</u>ndelete... from the <u>F</u>ile pull-down menu.
3. The Microsoft Undelete dialog box appears on screen and displays a list of deleted files and directories. Select the file or directory that you wish to undelete from the file list.
4. Click the <u>U</u>ndelete button at the upper left of the dialog box.
5. The Enter First Character subdialog box is then displayed and prompts you to enter the first letter of the file or directory that was deleted. Enter the required character and click the OK button. You can enter any character, but try to use the first letter of the deleted file as you remember it.
6. A message is displayed if the deleted data is successfully recovered. Select E<u>x</u>it from the <u>F</u>ile pull-down menu to close the Microsoft Undelete dialog box.

CAUTION

It is quite possible for a deleted file's data to be overwritten during other file operations. For this reason, you should undelete files and directories as soon as possible for the best chance of recovering all your data.

Renaming a file

Renaming files or directories is also easily accomplished with File Manager. To rename a file or directory, do the following:

1. Open the directory window that contains the file or directory you wish to rename. Click the file or directory to be renamed.
2. Select Re<u>n</u>ame... from the <u>F</u>ile pull-down menu.

3. The Rename dialog box then appears. See Figure 21-27. The file or directory name you selected is displayed in the From: text box.
4. Enter the desired new file or directory name in the To: text box. In the example shown, the file ANSI_A.DWG is renamed to TITLEA.DWG.
5. Click the OK button when you have finished entering the new file or directory name.

Figure 21-27.
The Rename dialog box. The current file name is displayed in the top text box and the new name is entered in the bottom text box.

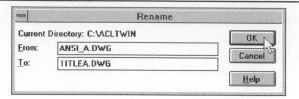

PROFESSIONAL TIP

If you rename a drawing file that has been externally referenced (**XREF**) into another drawing, AutoCAD LT will not be able to resolve the **XREF** the next time the drawing containing the external reference is opened in the drawing editor. To fix the problem, use the **XREF** command **Reload** option and reload the renamed drawing. In addition, if you rename a directory that contains an **XREF**, AutoCAD LT also will not be able to resolve the **XREF** the next time the drawing containing the external reference is opened. This is because the directory path name to the **XREF** is now different. This is easily remedied using the **XREF** command **Path** option. See Chapter 14 for detailed information about the **XREF** command and its options.

Creating a new directory

Organizing the files on your hard disk is a very important aspect of computer system maintenance. For the AutoCAD LT user, it is often desirable to keep block symbols, hatch patterns, font files, etc. in separate subdirectories. Once you have created a new directory, you can move and copy files and subdirectories to it from other locations on your hard disk. Creating directories is a simple task with File Manager. Remember, however, that the same naming conventions used for file names apply to directory names, as well. To create a directory, do the following:
1. Arrange the File Manager directory window so that the directory tree is clearly visible at the left of the directory window.
2. Click the directory icon or name in which you want the new subdirectory to appear.
3. Now, select Create Directory... from the File pull-down menu.
4. The Create Directory dialog box then appears, Figure 21-28. The current directory name is displayed at the top of the dialog box.
5. Enter the desired new directory name in the Name: text box. In the example shown, a new subdirectory named BLOCKS is created under the \ACLTWIN directory.
6. If you want to create the directory somewhere other than in the current directory, you must type in the full path to the new directory in the Name: text box.
7. Click the OK button when you are finished entering the new directory name.

Figure 21-28.
The Create Directory dialog box.

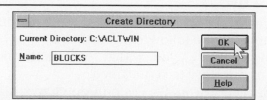

Searching for files

There will be occasions when you cannot remember the location of a file or directory on your hard disk. AutoCAD LT provides a means of locating files and directories using the Find File function. This capability is discussed in Chapter 2. However, a similar function can be performed with the Search command in File Manager. This command searches for files and directories on all, or part, of the current drive. You can search for a single file, or you can use wildcards to search for a group of files. Once the files are found, they are listed in the Search Results window. As an example, suppose you want to search for all the .DWG files in all the subdirectories located under the \ACLTWIN directory. Do the following:

1. Arrange the File Manager directory window so that the directory tree is clearly visible at the left of the directory window.
2. Select the \ACLTWIN directory from which to start the search.
3. Now, select Search... from the File pull-down menu.
4. The Search dialog box then appears, Figure 21-29. To search for all drawing files for example, enter *.DWG in the Search For: text box.

Figure 21-29.
The Search dialog box. In this example, all .DWG files in the C:\ACLTWIN directory and all of its subdirectories will be found.

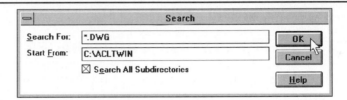

5. The current directory name appears in the Start From: text box. If you want to start the search from a different directory, type the desired directory name in this text box.
6. Observe that the Search All Subdirectories check box is activated. File Manager automatically searches all of the subdirectories located under the directory name specified in the Start From: text box. If you want to limit the search to the current directory only, deactivate this check box.
7. Click the OK button when you are ready to begin the search. To cancel the search, press the [Esc] key.
8. When the search is complete, File Manager displays the Search Results window listing each of the files found. See Figure 21-30. Files may be selected from this window to perform such tasks as copying, deleting, moving, and printing. To close the Search Results window, double-click the Control-menu icon at the upper left of the window.

Figure 21-30.
The Search Results window displays each of the files found.

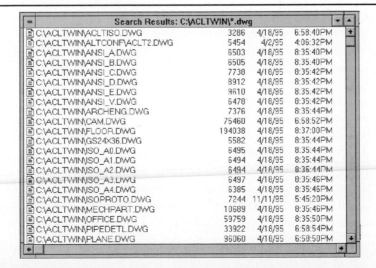

EXERCISE 21-3

❑ Insert one of your disks in the A: drive and open a new directory window for the drive.
❑ Arrange the directory windows in a tiled display with the contents of the A: drive displayed in the top window and the contents of the C:\ACLTWIN directory displayed in the bottom window.
❑ Activate the A: drive window so that it is current.
❑ Make a directory on the A: drive called DWGS, and another directory called BLOCKS.
❑ Make two subdirectories in the DWGS directory called PROBLEMS and XERCISES.
❑ Make two subdirectories in the BLOCKS directory called MECH and ARCH.
❑ Now, rename the two subdirectories to ELEC and CIVIL.
❑ Copy a group of drawing files from the hard disk to one of the subdirectories under either DWGS or BLOCKS. Be sure to open a directory window for the subdirectory before copying the files. Extend your selection of drawing files as described in this chapter.
❑ Check the directory window to verify that the files were copied correctly. Now, delete the subdirectory and all the files it contains.
❑ Delete all the directories created in this exercise.

DISK OPERATIONS USING FILE MANAGER

A variety of disk operations may also be performed with File Manager. These operations include formatting, labeling, and copying disks. Each of these functions is located in the Disk pull-down menu of the File Manager. See Figure 21-31.

Figure 21-31.
The Disk pull-down menu of the File Manager provides access to disk-related functions.

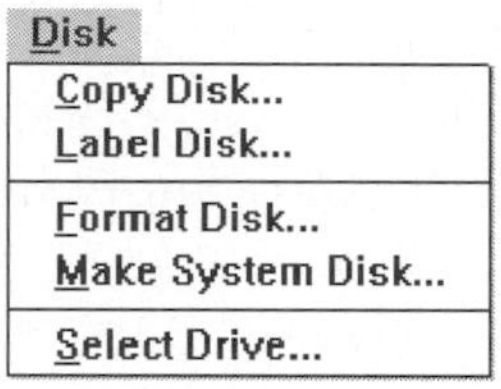

```
Disk
  Copy Disk...
  Label Disk...

  Format Disk...
  Make System Disk...

  Select Drive...
```

Formatting a floppy disk

Whenever you use unformatted floppy disks, you must first format them before they can accept data. The formatting process prepares a floppy disk so that information can then be copied to it. Formatting and labeling a disk is another procedure made simple by File Manager. If the disk you intend to format has previously been used, File Manager detects this and informs you accordingly before it removes existing data from the disk. To format a floppy disk, do the following:

1. Insert a floppy disk in the appropriate disk drive.
2. Select Format Disk... from the Disk pull-down menu.
3. The Format Disk dialog box then appears. See Figure 21-32. Specify the drive letter in the Disk In: text box or use the drop-down list to the right of the text box to select the desired drive.
4. Specify the disk capacity of the disk to be formatted in the Capacity: text box, or use the drop-down list to the right of the text box to select the correct capacity.
5. If you want to provide a volume label for the disk, enter the desired label name in the Label: text box. A *volume label* is an identifying name for the disk and is the first item displayed in a directory listing of a disk. If you choose to provide a volume label, the label name may not exceed eleven characters, and spaces are not permitted.

Figure 21-32.
The Format Disk dialog box. In this example, the disk in Drive B: will be formatted and a HATCHPATS label will be applied to the disk.

6. In the example shown in Figure 21-32, a 1.44 MB floppy is to be formatted in the B: drive. This disk will be used to store custom hatch patterns and the label HATCHPATS is entered in the Label: text box.

7. Once you have specified the appropriate drive, disk capacity, and entered a label (if desired), click the OK button to begin formatting the disk. If the Disk Commands check box is marked in the Confirmation dialog box, Figure 21-23, you will be asked whether you are sure you want to format the disk. Click Yes to proceed.

8. When the formatting is complete, another dialog box appears and asks you if you want to format another disk. Click Yes or No as required.

Observe that the Options section of the Format Disk dialog box contains two check boxes. These check boxes perform the following functions:

- **Make System Disk.** This option allows you to include MS-DOS operating system files on the disk you are formatting. These files include two hidden files and the COMMAND.COM file. Such a disk is called a *system disk* and may be used to boot up your computer. This option would not normally be used if you are formatting a floppy disk solely for backup purposes.

- **Quick Format.** When File Manager formats a floppy disk, it checks for any bad sectors which are unusable portions of the floppy disk. If you are reformatting a previously used floppy disk and are reasonably certain that it contains no bad sectors, you can speed up the formatting process by checking the Quick Format check box. Doing so speeds up the formatting process because the disk will not be scanned for bad sectors.

PROFESSIONAL TIP

Always use caution when formatting a disk. Remember that in addition to preparing a new disk, formatting will erase any existing data on a previously formatted disk. Unless you are running MS-DOS Version 5 or higher, or have a disk-recovery utility program, you *cannot* recover information on a disk that is accidentally formatted.

Labeling a disk

If you forget to label a disk when formatting, or if you decide to change an existing disk label, you can assign or change a volume label for both floppy and hard disks using File Manager. The procedure is as follows:

1. If you are labeling a floppy disk, insert it in the appropriate floppy disk drive.

2. Select the drive icon at the upper left of the directory window for the disk you want to label. As an alternative, you can pick Select Drive... from the Disk pull-down menu, Figure 21-31, and specify the desired drive from a dialog box.

3. Now, select Label Disk from the Disk pull-down menu.

4. The Label Disk dialog box then appears, Figure 21-33. Enter the new label in the Label: text box. Remember that the label name may not exceed eleven characters and spaces are not permitted. In the example shown, the label BACKUP is entered in the text box.

Figure 21-33.
The Label Disk dialog box.

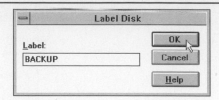

5. Click the OK button when you are finished.

Copying a disk

Throughout this text you have been advised to always make a backup copy of your AutoCAD LT drawings or related files on floppy disks. It is also a good idea to have a second backup of your original backup in the event that the original floppy disk becomes damaged. You can easily copy the contents of one floppy disk to another using File Manager. To copy a floppy disk, do the following:

1. Insert the source floppy disk in the drive you want to copy from and insert the destination floppy disk in the drive you want to copy to. The destination disk is often referred to as the *target disk*. If you only have one disk drive, insert the source disk in the drive.
2. Select the drive icon for the source disk at the upper left of the File Manager directory window.

Figure 21-34.
The Copy Disk dialog box. This function is commonly used for backing up floppy disks.

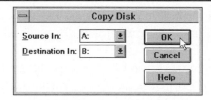

3. Now, select Copy Disk... from the Disk pull-down menu. If your computer has two floppy disk drives, the Copy Disk dialog box appears. See Figure 21-34.
4. If you have not already selected the source disk drive icon, you can specify the drive letter using the drop-down list to the right of the Source In: text box. In the example shown, drive A: is the source disk.
5. Select the letter of the destination drive from the drop-down list to the right of the Destination In: text box. In this example, the destination disk is in the B: drive. Click the OK button when you are finished.
6. The contents of drive A are then copied to drive B.

CAUTION

There is no need to spend time formatting a floppy disk before making a disk copy, since the Copy Disk command not only copies, it erases! This is because the destination disk is formatted before any copying is done. Therefore, be certain your destination disk is not one that already has files on it; unless, of course, you want to delete all the files on that disk.

- ❑ Insert one of your floppy disks containing drawing problems in the A: drive.
- ❑ Use the Label Disk command and name the floppy disk PROBLEMS.
- ❑ Copy a drawing file from the floppy to the \ACLTWIN directory on the hard disk.
- ❑ Use the Search command to list only .DWG files in the \ACLTWIN directory to verify that the file was copied.
- ❑ Change the name of the file you previously copied to \ACLTWIN to TEMP.BAK.
- ❑ Now, use the Search command to list only .BAK files in the \ACLTWIN directory to verify that the file was renamed.
- ❑ Delete TEMP.BAK from the hard disk.
- ❑ Use the Copy Disk command to make a backup copy of one of your floppy disks.

NOTE

This chapter has introduced you to only a subset of the features within File Manager. Make a point of becoming familiar with all of the functions offered by this useful tool. By making File Manager an integral part of your daily work, you can greatly increase your productivity and your knowledge of the Microsoft Windows operating environment.

CHAPTER TEST

Write your answers in the spaces provided.

1. What is a directory window? _____

_____

_____

2. How do you select more than one file or directory in consecutive order from the directory window? _____

_____

_____

3. How do you select more than one file or directory out of sequence from the directory window? _____

_____

_____

4. Once a file or directory is selected, how do you cancel your selection? _____

_____

5. Which AutoCAD LT command must be used when dragging and dropping an external text file—**TEXT** or **DTEXT**? _____

6. You can use drag and drop to plot a drawing on a pen plotter. (True/False) _____

7. What is the purpose of the directory window split bar? _____

_____

8. What action should be performed after dragging and dropping a drawing file into the AutoCAD LT graphics window? _____

---

9. Why should you not place too many program items in the StartUp window with AutoCAD LT?

_____

_____

10. How do you monitor available system resources in Microsoft Windows? _____

_____

_____

11. You would like to place a drawing file from the \ACLTWIN directory on one of your floppies, and then remove the drawing from the hard disk. Which File Manager command accomplishes this in one operation? _____

12. When you delete a directory, all the files and subdirectories within it are also deleted. (True/False) _____

13. Which File Manager command is used to assign a name to a previously formatted disk?

_____

14. You must first format a disk before using the Copy Disk command. (True/False)_____

15. Why should you exercise caution when using the Copy Disk command?_____

_____

CHAPTER PROBLEMS

General

1. This problem involves making new subdirectories and copying drawing files to them using File Manager.
   A. Make a subdirectory under the \ACLTWIN directory named STUDENT.
   B. Make the STUDENT subdirectory current.
   C. Copy all of your drawing problem files starting with the letter P from one floppy disk to the new subdirectory.
   D. Use the Search command and list all files with a .BAK file extension in the STUDENT subdirectory.
   E. Delete all files with a .BAK extension from the STUDENT subdirectory.
   F. Make another subdirectory under \ACLTWIN named EXER.
   G. Make the EXER subdirectory current.
   H. Copy all of your drawing exercise files starting with EX* from one floppy disk to the new EXER subdirectory.
   I. Open a separate directory window for each of your two new subdirectories. Display the directory windows in a tiled fashion.

General

2. If you have not yet completed Exercise 21-2 from this chapter, do so before continuing with this problem. Once the exercise is completed, open the Accessories group window and add the Cardfile program item icon to the StartUp window. The Cardfile can be used as a drawing and block manager for AutoCAD LT. This capability is described in Chapter 22.

General

3. Format four floppy disks using File Manager. Label the disks with the following names: PROBLEMS, PROBSBACKUP, XERCISES, and XERSBACKUP. Use the floppy disks to store the drawing problems and exercises presented in this text. Format additional floppy disks if required.

AutoCAD LT

Advanced AutoCAD LT Features and OLE

Learning objectives:

After completing this chapter, you will be able to:

- ❍ Identify and use advanced clipboard text and graphics options.
- ❍ Import and export Windows metafiles.
- ❍ Copy and reference AutoCAD LT drawing data to other Windows applications using Object Linking and Embedding (OLE).
- ❍ Describe the differences between linking and embedding.
- ❍ Create a drawing file manager using Windows Cardfile.
- ❍ Import and export Drawing Interchange Format files.

Working in the Microsoft Windows graphical user environment offers several distinct features to AutoCAD LT users. With Windows, AutoCAD LT text and drawing entities may be copied in bitmap (raster) or metafile (vector) format to the Windows Clipboard and pasted into other Windows-based applications. Additionally, drawing entities and even entire drawings may be linked to other applications such as a word-processing program or the Windows Cardfile. This chapter introduces you to these unique features that include: advanced clipboard support, importing and exporting metafiles and .DXF files, and Object Linking and Embedding (OLE).

ADVANCED CLIPBOARD SUPPORT

The Windows Clipboard is one of the applications included with Microsoft Windows. It is located in the Program Manager Main group window. See Figure 22-1. Think of Clipboard as a temporary storage area, or buffer, for textual and/or graphical information that lets you copy entities within a drawing, from one drawing to another, or from a drawing to another Windows application and vice-versa. Once an image is copied into the Clipboard, it may then be pasted into another Windows application such as a desktop publishing, graphics presentation, or word-processing program. The information that is copied into the Clipboard remains there until it is replaced with another piece of information, deleted from the Clipboard, or Microsoft Windows is exited. If you choose to save the contents of the Clipboard, the file is saved with a .CLP file extension. Additionally, graphical entities created in metafile format with other software applications can be copied to the Clipboard and imported into an AutoCAD LT drawing and freely edited.

Figure 22-1.
The Windows Clipboard
program item icon is located
in the Main group window.

COPYING BITMAP IMAGES TO THE CLIPBOARD

ALTUG 9

An AutoCAD LT graphics window image can be copied to the Clipboard in Windows bitmap format and then pasted into another Windows application. The bitmap image is in raster format and requires a fixed amount of memory regardless of its size or complexity, but it displays very quickly. Keep in mind, though, that a clipped image is an exact replica of what currently appears on screen. Therefore, if you are operating at a low screen resolution such as 640 × 480, the clipped image will be at that same resolution. This is often referred to as *WYSIWYG*, or *What You See Is What You Get*. Also, be aware that bitmap images are not scaleable and become somewhat *blocky* when scaled up or down. Therefore, a scaled bitmap image results in a poor image when printed. This can be a major drawback should you scale a bitmap image after pasting it into a word-processing, graphics presentation, or desktop publishing document.

AutoCAD LT graphics window images are clipped and copied to the Clipboard using the **COPYIMAGE** command. You can access this command by selecting **Copy Image** from the **Edit** pull-down menu, shown in Figure 22-2, or enter the command from the keyboard as follows:

Command: *(type* **COPYIMAGE** *or* **CI** *and press* [Enter]*)*
Select an area of the screen: *(Locate two diagonal points to define a windowed area)*
Command:

The full screen crosshairs change to a cross-shaped cursor as shown in the schematic diagram illustrated in Figure 22-3. You may recognize this diagram as drawing problem P14-4 from Chapter 14. Move the cursor and click on the first corner of the area you want to capture. Then, move the cursor diagonally to the second corner of the area you want to capture, and click once again to copy the windowed image to the Clipboard.

Figure 22-2.
Selecting **Copy Image** from
the **Edit** pull-down menu
issues the **COPYIMAGE**
command.

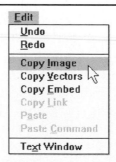

Figure 22-3.
The full screen crosshairs are replaced with a cross-shaped cursor when using the **COPYIMAGE** command. Pick a starting point with the cursor and drag diagonally to locate and pick a second point.

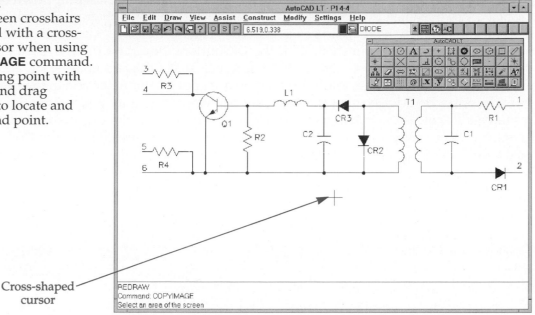

Cross-shaped cursor

Keep in mind that the **COPYIMAGE** command does not limit you to selecting AutoCAD LT entities only. You may also capture any part of the toolbar, toolbox, and command line area. However, the menu bar and title bar at the top of the graphics window cannot be captured.

Viewing and saving the Clipboard contents

Once an image is clipped, it may be viewed by returning to Program Manager, opening the Main group window, and double-clicking the Clipboard icon to launch Clipboard Viewer. Notice in Figure 22-4 that portions of the toolbar and toolbox are included in the Clipboard image. Although bitmap images created with the **COPYIMAGE** command require little memory to display, they are quite large if saved to disk as .CLP files. Keep this in mind if you plan on saving your Clipboard images on a regular basis.

Figure 22-4.
The clipped portion of the AutoCAD LT graphics window as it appears in Clipboard Viewer.

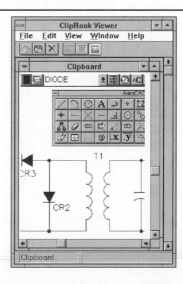

To save the contents of the Clipboard, select Save As... from the File pull-down menu in the Clipboard Viewer. When the Save As dialog box appears, shown in Figure 22-5, select the drive and directory where the file is to be stored. Now, enter the desired file name in the File Name: text box. When you are finished, click the OK button. Observe from the Save File as Type: drop-down list at the lower left of the dialog box that Clipboard images are automatically saved with a .CLP file extension. Therefore, do not append this extension to the file name you provide. Also, be advised that the Clipboard contents do require a small portion of system resources. To conserve system memory, clear the contents of the Clipboard when the copied image has been saved or is no longer needed. To delete the image from the Clipboard, select Delete from the Edit pull-down menu in the Clipboard Viewer. When the Clear Clipboard dialog box appears, click the Yes button to confirm the delete operation. See Figure 22-6.

Figure 22-5.
The Save As dialog box in Clipboard saves Clipboard images as .CLP files.

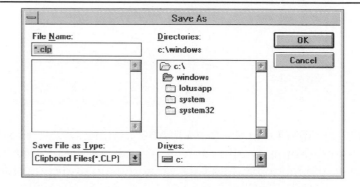

Figure 22-6.
Deleting the contents of the Clipboard displays the Clear Clipboard dialog box.

Improving the quality of the copied image

You can improve the quality of clipped AutoCAD LT images by adhering to the following guidelines:

- If the UCS icon is on, turn it off using the **UCSICON** command if you do not want it to appear in the copied image.
- If you plan on pasting your AutoCAD LT image into a black and white document, set the background color of the AutoCAD LT graphics window to white before you clip the image. Also, change the color of all the drawing entities to black. Both of these operations may be quickly performed by selecting **Preferences** from the **File** pull-down menu. When the **Preferences** dialog box appears, click the **Colors...** button to access the **AutoCAD LT Window Colors** subdialog box. Select **Graphics** window background from the **Window Element:** drop-down list at the top right of the subdialog box, and then click the color white from the **Basic Colors:** color choices below the drop-down list. To change the color of all on-screen entities to black, activate the **Monochrome Vectors** check box at the lower right of the subdialog box and then click **OK**. When the **Preferences** dialog box reappears, click **OK** once more to exit. See Chapter 19 for more information about the **Preferences** dialog box.

Pasting the **Clipboard** contents

You can paste the contents of the Clipboard, or a saved .CLP file, into other Windows-based programs at any time. However, be sure the application that you want to paste information into accepts the bitmap format created by the **COPYIMAGE** command. Most, but not all, Windows applications do accept bitmap images. To paste the contents of the Clipboard into another Windows application, do the following:

1. If necessary, use the Clipboard Viewer as previously described to verify that the AutoCAD LT image you want to paste is in the Clipboard.
2. Start the application to which you will paste.
3. Locate the insertion point where you want the pasted Clipboard contents to appear.
4. Select Paste from the application's pull-down Edit menu and the contents of the Clipboard appear in the new application.
5. Once the image is pasted, it can then be moved and resized as necessary.

NOTE   Images clipped in AutoCAD LT with the **COPYIMAGE** command are in bitmap format and *cannot* be pasted back into AutoCAD LT.

The Paintbrush program supplied with Microsoft Windows is an excellent example of an application that can accept bitmap images from AutoCAD LT. Paintbrush is located in the Accessories group window and can be used to create very simple, or very elaborate, color images. The Edit pull-down menu from Paintbrush is illustrated in Figure 22-7. Observe that whenever information exists in the Clipboard, the Paste command in a Windows-based program is not grayed-out, or dimmed. See Figure 22-7A. If the Clipboard is empty, or contains data which the application cannot paste, then the Paste command is grayed-out. See Figure 22-7B.

Figure 22-7.
A—When there are contents in the Clipboard, the Paste command is not grayed-out. B—The Paste command is grayed-out when the Clipboard is empty. This Edit pull-down menu is from Windows Paintbrush.

Edit	
Undo	Ctrl+Z
Cut	Ctrl+X
Copy	Ctrl+C
Paste	Ctrl+V
Copy To...	
Paste From...	

A

Edit	
Undo	Ctrl+Z
Cut	Ctrl+X
Copy	Ctrl+C
Paste	Ctrl+V
Copy To...	
Paste From...	

B

Clipping the entire **AutoCAD LT** graphics window   ALTUG 17

You can also clip and save the entire graphics window, including the title and menu bars, to a file in *Device-Independent Bitmap* format using the **SAVEDIB** command. This command can be accessed by first selecting **Import/Export** from the **File** pull-down menu and then selecting **BMP Out...** from the cascading submenu. See Figure 22-8. You may also type the command as follows:

Command: **SAVEDIB** ↵

Although the **SAVEDIB** command is similar to **COPYIMAGE**, it differs in two ways. Since **SAVEDIB** captures the entire graphics window, including the toolbar and toolbox and the command area, you are not asked to select a portion of the graphics window. Also, **SAVEDIB** does not clip and save to the Clipboard. Instead, it creates and saves a separate bitmap file to disk.

Figure 22-8.
Issue the **SAVEDIB** command by first selecting **Import/Export** from the **File** pull-down menu and then selecting **BMP Out...** from the cascading submenu.

Consider once more the drawing problem P14-4 shown in Figure 22-9. Once the **SAVEDIB** command is issued, the **Save DIB** dialog box is displayed. See Figure 22-10. Note that the device-independent bitmap file is saved under the same name as the current drawing, but with a .BMP file extension as evidenced by the **List Files of Type:** drop-down list at the lower left of the dialog box. If you choose, you may enter a different file name in the **File Name:** text box and also specify a different drive and directory where the file is to be stored.

Figure 22-9.
Every element of the AutoCAD LT graphics window, including the title and menu bars, may be captured as a bitmap file with **SAVEDIB**.

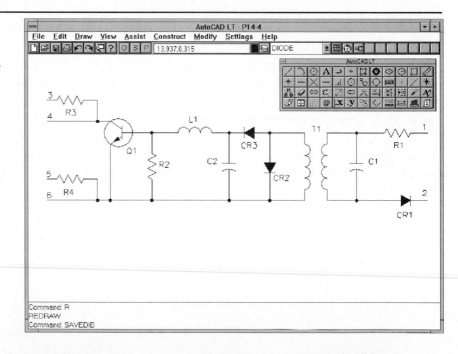

Figure 22-10.
The **Save DIB** dialog box.

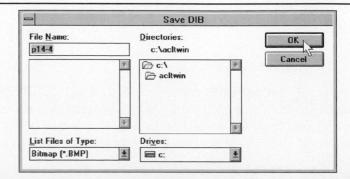

The saved file may now be pasted into any Windows-based application that supports the bitmap file format. From Figure 22-11, you can see that the entire graphics window from Figure 22-9 has been pasted into a word-processing document and that some text has been added.

Figure 22-11.
The saved device-independent bitmap file is shown pasted into a Windows Write document.

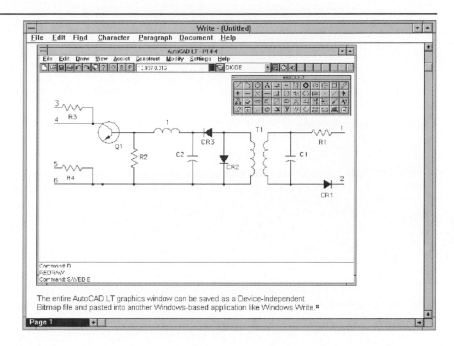

This document was created using Windows Write; a word-processing application included with Microsoft Windows. As with Paintbrush, you can access Windows Write in the Accessories group window. See Figure 22-12.

Figure 22-12.
The Windows Write program item icon is located in the Accessories group window.

Once you have pasted the image into Write, select Save from the File pull-down menu to save the document. If the file has not yet been saved, the Save As dialog box is displayed. See Figure 22-13. Enter a name for the document in the File Name: text box, and select the desired drive and directory in which to store the file. Note that Windows Write documents are automatically appended with a .WRI file extension and, unless otherwise specified, are stored in the \WINDOWS directory. The document shown in Figure 22-13 is being saved with the name TECHDOC. For a detailed description of Windows Write, refer to the *Microsoft Windows User's Guide.*

Figure 22-13.
The Save As dialog box in
Windows Write.

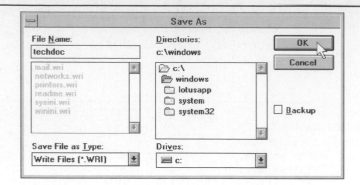

Microsoft Windows itself provides two alternative methods for capturing the screen to the Clipboard. By pressing [Alt]+[Print Scrn], the active window *only* is captured to the Clipboard. If you press just the [Print Scrn] key, all displayed windows are captured to the Clipboard. As with other Clipboard images, you then have the option to save the Clipboard contents as a .CLP file.

EXERCISE 22-1

❑ Load AutoCAD LT and open any one of your completed drawing problems or exercises into the drawing editor.
❑ Use the **COPYIMAGE** command to clip a portion of the drawing to the Windows Clipboard.
❑ Verify the contents of the Clipboard using the Clipboard Viewer window.
❑ Launch Paintbrush and paste your AutoCAD LT image. Now, return to Clipboard Viewer and delete the contents of the Clipboard.
❑ Return to AutoCAD LT and capture the entire graphics window using the **SAVEDIB** command. Save the device-independent file with the name EX22-1.BMP.
❑ Activate the Clipboard Viewer window once again. Is the new image displayed in the window? Why not?
❑ Launch Windows Write (or your own Windows-based word-processing program) and paste the EX22-1.BMP file created with SAVEDIB. If you like, add some text to the document.
❑ As an experiment, save the document and do a directory listing to check the size of the file. Compare the size of the document file with that of the original AutoCAD LT drawing.
❑ Exit the drawing session without saving.

COPYING METAFILE IMAGES TO THE CLIPBOARD | ALTUG 9 |

Because of the significant size and printing limitations of saved bitmap files, AutoCAD LT provides an alternative method for clipping images to the Clipboard. This second method is much better because AutoCAD LT then saves entities to the Clipboard in two formats; thus providing you far greater flexibility. When you paste from the Clipboard into AutoCAD LT, AutoCAD LT format is used and all relevant entity information is retained. This information includes all block references and 3D aspects. On the other hand, if you paste into another Windows application, then Windows *metafile* format is used. Metafile format entities contain screen vector information and can be pasted from the Clipboard into most other Windows applications. Unlike bitmap images, metafile images can be scaled and printed in other programs with no loss of resolution.

This alternate method of clipping AutoCAD LT entities to the Clipboard is provided using the **COPYCLIP** command. You can access this command by selecting **Copy Vectors** from the **Edit** pull-down menu. See Figure 22-14. The command sequence is as follows:

> Command: *(type* COPYCLIP *or* CC *and press* [Enter]*)*
> Select objects: *(Select the entities to be clipped)*
> Select objects: ↵
> Command:

Figure 22-14.
Selecting **Copy Vectors** from the **Edit** pull-down menu issues the **COPYCLIP** command.

 NOTE   Although the **Copy Vectors** button shown does not appear on the toolbar or in the toolbox by default, it may easily be added.

Note that all of the AutoCAD LT selection set options are valid with **COPYCLIP**. But unlike the **COPYIMAGE** command, only AutoCAD LT entities can be clipped to the Clipboard. You cannot capture any portion of the title bar, menu bar, toolbox, toolbar, or command prompt area in the copied image. In the example illustrated in Figure 22-15, the drawing notes from P12-4 are captured to the Clipboard with a crossing box.

Figure 22-15.
The **COPYCLIP** command copies selected entities to the Clipboard. All of the AutoCAD LT selection set options are valid.

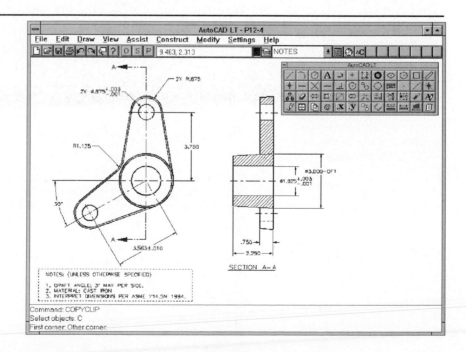

As with the **COPYIMAGE** command, you can verify the contents of the Clipboard with the Clipboard Viewer. You will observe in Figure 22-16, that the text entities captured with **COPYCLIP** appear elongated in the Clipboard Viewer. However, do not be alarmed, because the distorted appearance of the text is just the result of Clipboard adjusting the aspect ratio of the captured image to fit inside the Clipboard Viewer window. When the Clipboard contents are pasted back into AutoCAD LT, or some other Windows application, the correct aspect ratio is automatically restored.

Figure 22-16.
Entities are adjusted to fit inside the Clipboard Viewer window and therefore appear distorted.

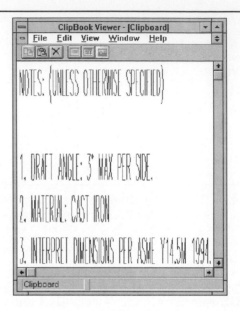

Apart from storing the vectors in the Clipboard, the **COPYCLIP** command also creates a temporary file that contains the clipped entities. By default, this file is placed in the \DOS\TEMP subdirectory, Figure 22-17. (If your computer has been configured with the TEMP subdirectory under the WINDOWS directory, than the file is placed in \WINDOWS\TEMP, instead.) Notice that AutoCAD LT uses a rather strange naming convention for the temporary file. In this example, the temporary file name is ACAD0835.DWG. The next time the **COPYCLIP**

Figure 22-17.
The **COPYCLIP** command stores copied entities in a temporary file in the \DOS\TEMP directory.

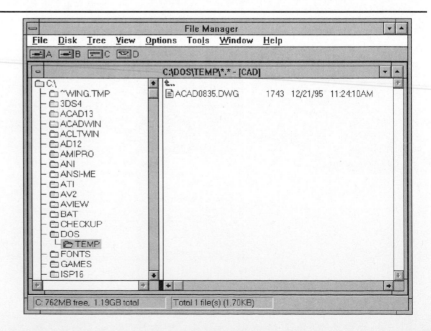

command is used, the temporary file may have a name like ACAD03DL.DWG, or something similar. Do not be concerned about the temporary file—it is automatically deleted from the hard disk once you paste the clipped vectors back into an AutoCAD LT drawing.

However, this is not the case if you paste the Clipboard contents into some other Windows application. In the example shown in Figure 22-18, the clipped AutoCAD LT text is automatically converted to metafile format when pasted into Windows Write. (This conversion occurs whenever AutoCAD LT entities are pasted into a Windows-based program other than AutoCAD LT.) In these instances, the temporary file in the \DOS\TEMP directory is not automatically deleted. If you plan on frequently using the **COPYCLIP** command to paste AutoCAD LT entities into non-AutoCAD LT applications, make a point of periodically deleting these temporary files to conserve disk space.

Figure 22-18.
Windows metafile format is used when AutoCAD LT entities are pasted into another Windows-based application such as Windows Write.

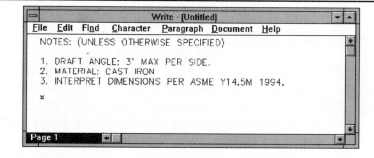

 **PROFESSIONAL TIP**

You can use **COPYCLIP** as a handy alternative to the **WBLOCK** command to quickly copy views, details, sections, and notes from one drawing to another.

Pasting the clipped vectors back into AutoCAD LT

Once AutoCAD LT entities are copied to the Clipboard using **COPYCLIP**, they may be pasted back into the current drawing, or an entirely different drawing, using the **PASTECLIP** command. You can access the **PASTECLIP** command by selecting **Paste** from the **Edit** pull-down menu, Figure 22-19, or by typing the command at the keyboard. You will note from the command sequence that follows that the **PASTECLIP** command presents you with prompts similar to those presented by the **INSERT** command. The only difference is that the required block name is automatically provided by AutoCAD LT.

Figure 22-19.
Selecting **Paste** from the **Edit** pull-down menu issues the **PASTECLIP** command.

Command: *(type* PASTECLIP *or* PC *and press* [Enter]*)*
Block name (or ?): C:\DOS\TEMP\acadxxxx.dwg
Insertion point: *(Pick an insertion point)*
X scale factor ⟨1⟩/Corner/XYZ: *(Pick a point, type a number and press* [Enter]*, select an option, or press* [Enter] *to accept the default)*
Y scale factor (default=X): *(Enter a scale factor and press* [Enter]*, or press* [Enter] *to accept the default)*
Rotation angle ⟨0⟩: *(Pick a point, enter a value and press* [Enter] *, or press* [Enter] *to accept the default)*
Command:

NOTE   Although the **Paste** button shown does not appear on the toolbar or in the toolbox by default, it may easily be added.

The Clipboard entities are then inserted as a new block entity on the current UCS. They retain the layer, color, and linetype properties that were current when they were originally created. If the entities were created on Layer 0, then they assume the properties of the receiving layer. Also, if the selection set you define with **COPYCLIP** contains one or more blocks, a nested block then results when pasted back into AutoCAD LT. Each of these conventions, therefore, are consistent with normal block creation and insertion procedures. If necessary, use the **EXPLODE** command to return the pasted block back to its original constituent entities. See Chapter 14 for complete details about the **BLOCK** and **INSERT** commands.

Refer to the illustration shown in Figure 22-20. In this example, the clipped text notes from P12-4 are pasted into an entirely new drawing session. Notice the location of the crosshair cursor relative to the notes. The cursor position reflects the insertion point for the pasted entities. You will observe that the cursor position is located some distance away from the actual text insertion point of the notes. This is because AutoCAD LT uses the origin of a drawing as the base point for entities copied with the **COPYCLIP** command. Remember that every drawing has its origin set at 0,0,0 by default. Thus, the cursor position shown in Figure 22-20 represents the 0,0,0 origin of the P12-4 drawing from which the entities were clipped.

Figure 22-20.
The prompts for the **PASTECLIP** command are the same as the **INSERT** command. The clipped enties are inserted as a block and may be scaled and rotated.

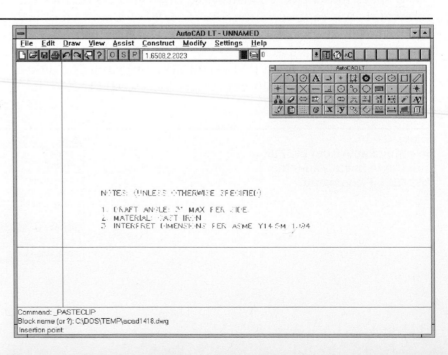

AutoCAD LT—Fundamentals and Applications

Changing the insertion point for clipped entities

You can change the insertion point for clipped entities with the **BASE** command. This is easily accomplished by performing the following steps:

1. Open the drawing that contains the entities you want to copy to the Clipboard.
2. Issue the **BASE** command by first selecting **Dra_wing** from the **Settings** pull-down menu and then selecting **Base** from the cascading submenu.
3. Use the appropriate object snap to locate the desired insertion point of the entities you wish to copy. The **INSert** object snap mode is used to pick the insertion point for the left-justified text shown in Figure 22-21.

Figure 22-21.
Using the **BASE** command to change the insertion point before copying vectors to the Clipboard.

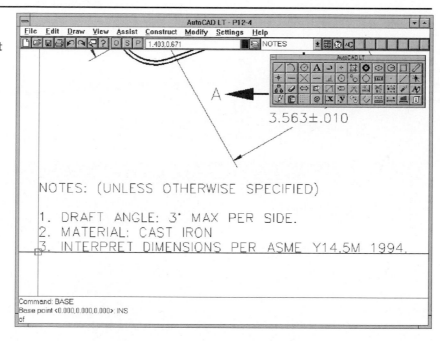

4. Issue the **COPYCLIP** command and select the entities to be copied to the Clipboard.
5. Use the **PASTECLIP** command to paste the clipped entities back into the current drawing, an existing drawing, or entirely new drawing.
6. If desired, explode the pasted entities.

The example shown in Figure 22-22 illustrates the new insertion point as the entities are pasted into a new drawing. Observe that the crosshair cursor position now represents the text insertion point defined with the **BASE** command in the previous example. Finally, do not forget to delete the contents of the Clipboard after using **PASTECLIP** to conserve system resources.

Figure 22-22.
The new insertion point for
the clipped entities reflects
the point defined with the
BASE command.

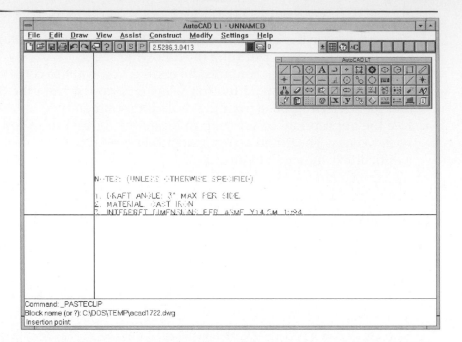

❑ Open any one of your completed drawing problems or exercises.
❑ Use the **BASE** command to change the insertion point of the drawing as described in the preceding text.
❑ Use the **COPYCLIP** command to copy the entire drawing to the Clipboard.
❑ Verify the contents of the Clipboard using the Clipboard Viewer window. Next, activate File Manager and locate the temporary file created by **COPYCLIP** in the \DOS\TEMP directory.
❑ Begin a new drawing. Use the **PASTECLIP** command to paste the contents of the Clipboard into the new drawing.
❑ Return to Clipboard Viewer and delete the contents of the Clipboard.
❑ Once again, return to the \DOS\TEMP directory in File Manager. Note that the temporary file has been deleted from the directory.
❑ Exit AutoCAD LT without saving.

PASTING TEXT INTO AUTOCAD LT   ALTUG 12

The advanced clipboard options in AutoCAD LT also permit you to import text from your Windows-based ASCII text editor or word-processing application into the AutoCAD LT graphics window. This capability is provided with the **Paste Command** option in the **Edit** pull-down menu. See Figure 22-23. To copy text to, and paste text from, the Windows Clipboard, do the following:

1. Begin a new text file using any word-processing program or text editor that supports the Windows Clipboard. The Windows Write program or Notepad text editor in the Accessories group window will suffice.
2. Type the text as required. Some typical drawing notes for a sand casting drawing are shown in Windows Write. See Figure 22-24A.
3. Select the text you want to copy so that it is highlighted, and then select Copy from the Edit pull-down menu as shown in Figure 22-24B. (If you select Cut, the text is copied to the Clipboard but is removed from the word-processing document.)
4. Now, begin a new or open an existing AutoCAD LT drawing.

Figure 22-23.
Selecting **Paste Command**
from the **Edit** pull-down
menu pastes ASCII or word-
processing text into the
AutoCAD LT graphics
window.

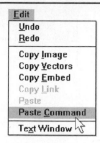

Figure 22-24.
A—Drawing notes are first
created with a word-
processing program such as
Windows Write. B—The
notes are then selected and
copied to the Clipboard.

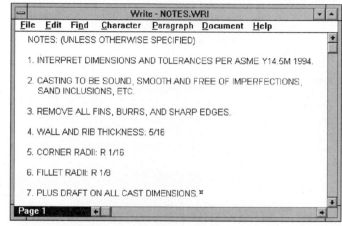

A

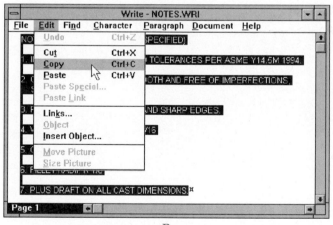

B

5. Using the **DTEXT** command, select the desired text justification and starting point, specify
   the text height and rotation angle, or accept the default values.
6. When the **Text:** prompt appears, select **Paste Command** from the **Edit** pull-down menu.
   See Figure 22-25A.

   AutoCAD LT displays the Clipboard text in the command line area and then pastes it in the
graphics window. The text is imported in the current text style, layer, and color.

CAUTION

If you created your word-processing text in a special type of font,
or in a bold face, those text characteristics are lost because the text is
converted to ASCII format before it is imported into AutoCAD LT.

Figure 22-25.
A—When the **DTEXT Text:** prompt appears, the **Paste Command** option is selected from the **Edit** pull-down menu. B—The pasted text inherits the current text style, layer, and color.

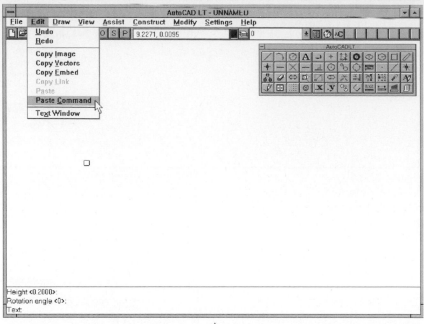

A

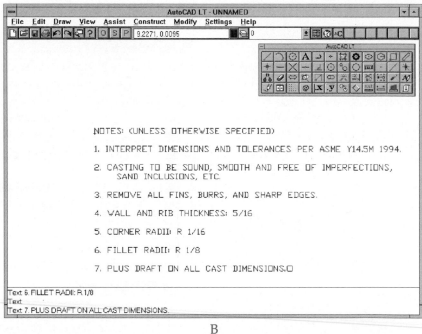

B

Observe from Figure 22-25B that the **DTEXT** command is still active after the text is imported. If you would like to add an additional line of text, press the [Enter] key. Press the [Enter] key twice to terminate the **DTEXT** command. If you need to edit the imported text to correct indentations, and so forth, you can do so quickly using the **DDEDIT** command.

PROFESSIONAL TIP

Always use the **DTEXT** command when importing multiple lines of text. To import a single line only, the **TEXT** command may be used. Remember that ASCII text files may also be imported using the *drag and drop* capability of the Windows File Manager. See Chapter 21 for detailed information on drag and drop operations.

❏ Launch Windows Write (or your own Windows-based word-processing program) and create multiple lines of text similar to those shown in Figure 22-25A. Use one of the Windows TrueType fonts to create your text.

❏ Select text and copy it to the Clipboard. If you like, save the word-processing document.

❏ Begin a new drawing and create a layer named NOTES. Assign to it a color of your choice and set the layer current.

❏ Create a new text style called EX22-3. Use ROMANS for the style font. Adjust any of the other style parameters to your personal taste.

❏ Issue the **DTEXT** command. Pick a start point and accept the defaults for text height and rotation angle.

❏ When prompted to enter text, select **Paste Command** in the **Edit** pull-down menu to insert the Clipboard text.

❏ Now, issue the **TEXT** command and repeat the paste operation. What happens? Why?

❏ Exit AutoCAD LT without saving.

IMPORTING AND EXPORTING METAFILES

ALTUG 17

AutoCAD LT provides you the option of saving all, or only a portion, of a drawing in metafile format with the **WMFOUT** command. This command is similar to the **COPYCLIP** command, except that the entities you select are written to disk as a .WMF file (Windows Metafile Format), and not copied to the Windows Clipboard. Remember that, unlike bitmaps, metafiles contain screen vector information and can be scaled and printed with no loss of resolution when imported back into AutoCAD LT or some other Windows-based application. A large number of predefined metafiles are included with AutoCAD LT. They can be located in the \ACLTWIN\CLIPART directory.

The **WMFOUT** may be issued by selecting **Import/Export**, then **WMF Out...** from the **File** pull-down menu. See Figure 22-26. The Command sequence is as follows:

Command: *(type* WMFOUT *or* WO *and press* [Enter]*)*

Figure 22-26.
Selecting **Import/Export**
from the **File** pull-down
menu displays the **WMF
In...**, **WMF In Options...**, and
WMF Out... commands in a
cascading submenu.

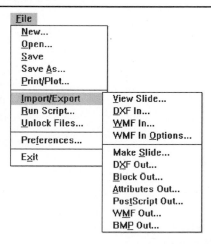

Once the command is issued, the **Export WMF** dialog box shown in Figure 22-27 is displayed. By default, the metafile is saved with the same filename as the current drawing in the \ACLTWIN directory. If you like, specify a different drive and/or directory and enter a new name in the **File Name:** text box. When you are done, click the **OK** button. The graphics window reappears and you may use any of the AutoCAD LT selection set options at the familiar **Select objects:** prompt.

Select objects: *(select the entities to be exported)*
Select objects: ↵
Command:

Figure 22-27.
The **WMFOUT** command displays the **Export WMF** dialog box.

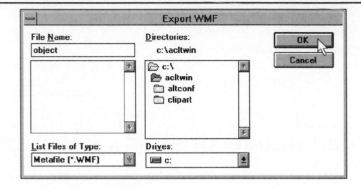

Refer now to the simple object shown in Figure 22-28. This drawing has been created with a triangular-shaped solid, wide polylines, polyarcs, and donuts with **FILLMODE** on. The drawing is then exported to a metafile named OBJECT.WMF. To import this, or any other .WMF file, use the **WMFIN** command or select **Import/Export** and then **WMF In...** from the **File** pull-down menu.

Command: *(type* WMFIN *or* WI *and press* [Enter]*)*

Figure 22-28.
This simple object drawn with a solid, wide polylines, polyarcs, and donuts is exported as a Windows metafile.

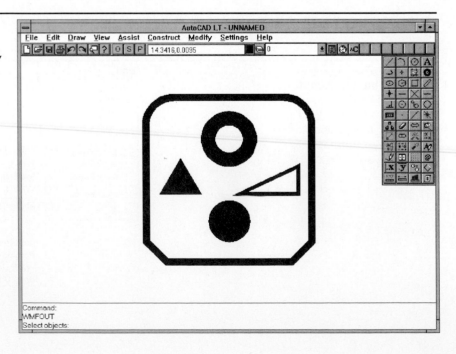

The **Import WMF** dialog box is then displayed. See Figure 22-29. Select the desired metafile to import from the file list at the left of the dialog box. The file you select is displayed in the **Preview** box at the right of the dialog box when the **Preview** check box is activated (the default setting). To turn off the **Preview** option, click the check box to remove the check mark. Once the preview is complete, click **OK** to close the dialog box and import the metafile.

Figure 22-29.
The **WFMIN** command displays the **Import WMF** dialog box. The **Preview** check box allows you to preview the metafile before importing it into your drawing.

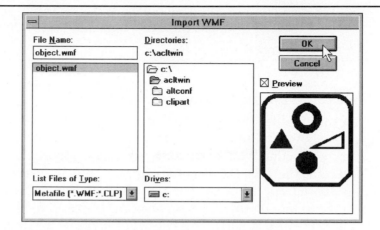

A small dialog box is then displayed on screen that features a horizontal bar that tracks the progress of AutoCAD LT as it converts the metafile to an AutoCAD LT block entity. See Figure 22-30. If you click the **Cancel** button during the conversion, nothing is imported into the current drawing.

Because the imported metafile is inserted into the current drawing as a block entity, the **WMFIN** command behaves much the same way as the **INSERT** and **PASTECLIP** commands at this point. The following prompts and options are then presented:

    _INSERT Block name (or ?): WMF0

Figure 22-30.
The horizontal bar tracks AutoCAD LT's progress in converting the metafile to a block entity.

Note from the command message above that the metafile is automatically assigned the block name WMF0 the first time you import a metafile into a drawing session. Each subsequent metafile import increments the block names as follows: WMF1, WMF2, and so on.

    Insertion point: *(pick an insertion point)*
    X scale factor ⟨1⟩/Corner/XYZ: *(pick a point, type a number and press* [Enter]*,*
        select an option, or press [Enter] *to accept the default)*
    Y scale factor (default=X): *(enter a scale factor and press* [Enter]*, or press* [Enter]
        to accept the default)
    Rotation angle ⟨0⟩: *(pick a point, enter a value and press* [Enter]*, or press* [Enter]
        to accept the default)
    Command:

The metafile is then inserted as a new block entity on the current UCS with its insertion point located at the upper left corner of the block. The imported metafile retains the layer, color, and linetype properties that were current when it was originally created. However, unlike normal block insertions, if the imported metafile was originally created on Layer 0, it *does not* inherit the color and linetype properties of the receiving layer. Also keep in mind that if a metafile contains any blocks when it is exported, those blocks are lost when imported back into AutoCAD LT. In other words, an imported metafile cannot have nested blocks.

PROFESSIONAL TIP The **BASE** command does not change the insertion point for imported metafiles. If the insertion point is critical to your application, use the **COPYCLIP** and **PASTECLIP** commands instead.

Options for importing Windows metafiles

You can modify the properties of an imported metafile using the **WMF Import Options** dialog box shown in Figure 22-31. This dialog box can be accessed with the **WMFOPTS** command or by selecting **WMF In Options...** from the **Import/Export** cascading menu.

Note that the **WMFOPTS** command can also be used with metafiles created in other Windows-based applications. The two check boxes in the **WMF Import Options** dialog box perform the following functions on AutoCAD LT-based metafiles:

- **Wire Frame (No Fills).** This check box controls whether entities such as wide polylines, polyarcs, solids, and donuts are filled or not. When the box is checked, entities are imported as wireframes; when the box is not checked, entities are imported filled.
- **Wide Lines.** If this box is checked, the lines and borders of the entities maintain their width. When the box is not checked, entity lines are imported with zero widths.

Figure 22-32 shows the effects of the two options on the imported metafile OBJECT.WMF.

Figure 22-31.
The **WMFOPTS** command displays the **WMF Import Options** dialog box.

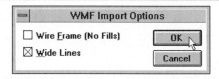

Figure 22-32.
An example of an imported metafile showing both wide lines and wire frame (no fills).

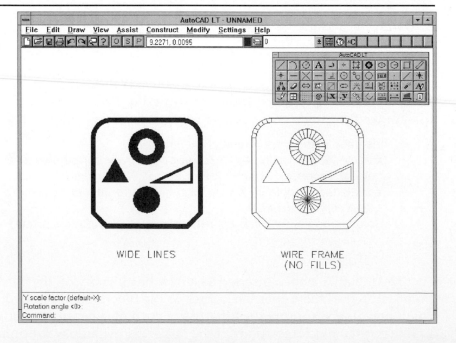

Many Windows-based drawing programs offer various pattern fills and wide line options. There are even several word-processing programs, such as Lotus' Ami Pro and Microsoft Word for Windows, that also have these drawing capabilities. If you have such a program, use it to create a drawing with these options. Then, save it in Windows metafile format and import it into AutoCAD LT. Experiment with the **WMFOPTS** command to observe the effects on the pattern fills and wide lines in your drawing.

EXERCISE 22-4

❑ Load AutoCAD LT and create a drawing similar to that shown in Figure 22-28.
❑ Save the drawing with the name EX22-4.WMF using the **WMFOUT** command.
❑ Begin a new drawing and import your saved metafile. Experiment with the options provided by the **WMFOPTS** command.
❑ Spend a few moments inserting several of the supplied metafiles located in the \ACLTWIN\CLIPART directory.
❑ Exit the drawing session without saving.

OBJECT LINKING AND EMBEDDING ALTUG 17

From the previous sections of this chapter, you have seen that the Windows Clipboard is a handy means to transfer information between various Windows-based applications. However, Microsoft Windows allows you to not only transfer, but *share* information between applications as well. This powerful capability is called *Object Linking and Embedding*, or *OLE*. OLE lets you combine data from one or more applications into one document. You can then edit the imported data using its original application. As an example, you can include an AutoCAD LT drawing in a technical document created with a word-processing program, such as Windows Write or Ami Pro. To change the drawing, you simply double-click it in the word-processing document and AutoCAD LT starts and opens that drawing. The changes you make in AutoCAD LT then appear in both the AutoCAD LT drawing and the word-processing document. When the changes occur automatically, the AutoCAD LT drawing is said to be *linked* to the document. It is also possible to not have the drawing changes automatically updated in the word-processing document. For example, there may be instances when you would rather update the document manually, or not at all. When there is no automatic updating, the AutoCAD LT drawing is said to be *embedded* in the document.

To better understand linking and embedding, you should become familiar with the following terms:
- **Object.** In OLE, an *object* is any piece of information created with a Windows-based application. A small portion, or an entire AutoCAD LT drawing, as well as a paragraph from a word-processing document are all OLE objects.
- **Source document.** The *source document* is the drawing or document from which the object originates.
- **Destination document.** The *destination document* is the document in which the object is placed (linked or embedded).
- **Server.** A *server* is an application whose objects can be linked or embedded into other applications. AutoCAD LT and Windows Paintbrush are two examples of server applications.

- **Client.** A *client* is an application that can accept linked or embedded objects. Windows Write and Cardfile are examples of client applications. Cardfile is covered in detail later in this chapter.
- **Client and Server.** Some Windows-based applications may be both a server and a client. That is, they send and accept objects. The Microsoft Excel spreadsheet program is an example of a client and server application.

Both linking and embedding let you include an AutoCAD LT drawing (the server, or source, object) in another document (the client, or destination, object) and edit the drawing in the destination document. Perhaps the easiest way to understand the concept of linking and embedding is to draw an analogy between the AutoCAD LT commands **XREF** (linking) and **INSERT** (embedding). When you use the **XREF** command, external references (Xrefs) are attached to your drawing. Should you edit the external reference, the changes are automatically reflected in the drawing in which it is referenced. This is the same concept as linking. Therefore, link a drawing if you want automatic updates to destination documents when the original drawing changes. To review the **XREF** command, refer to Chapter 14.

When you use the **INSERT** command, blocks and drawings are inserted into, and become part of, the current drawing. Thus, access to the original block or drawing need not be maintained with **INSERT**. This is the same idea behind embedding. Therefore, embed a drawing when you want to change the original drawing, but do not want the destination document updated. Also use embedding if you want to be able to edit or format the drawing in the destination document without changing the original drawing. See Chapter 14 for a complete discussion of the **INSERT** command.

Embedding an AutoCAD LT drawing

Embedding is performed in AutoCAD LT with the **COPYEMBED** command. You can access the command by selecting **Copy Embed** from the **Edit** pull-down menu. See Figure 22-33. When you issue the **COPYEMBED** command, the entities you select are first copied to the Windows Clipboard for embedding into OLE client applications. From the command syntax shown below, you can see that the familiar **Select objects:** prompt is presented. Since all of the AutoCAD LT selection set options are valid with **COPYEMBED**, you can quickly select an entire drawing with the **All** option.

Command: *(type* COPYEMBED *or* CE *and press* [Enter]*)*
Select objects: *(Select the entities to embed, or type* All *and press* [Enter]*)*
Select objects: ↵
Command:

Figure 22-33.
Selecting **Copy Embed** from the **Edit** pull-down menu issues the **COPYEMBED** command.

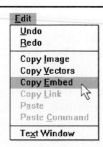

AutoCAD LT—Fundamentals and Applications

EMBEDDING A DRAWING TUTORIAL

To obtain a better understanding and appreciation of object embedding, open one of your existing drawing problems or exercises and perform the following tutorial. If you have completed drawing problem P14-4 from Chapter 14, (the plug-in card schematic diagram) use it for this example. The embedding tutorial begins as follows:

> ⬦ Load AutoCAD LT and open P14-4. Use another drawing of your choice if you have not yet completed this drawing problem.
> ⬦ Activate the Accessories group window and launch Windows Write. Arrange both windows in a display similar to that shown in Figure 22-34.

Figure 22-34.
Arrange the AutoCAD LT graphics window and the Write window so that both are visible.

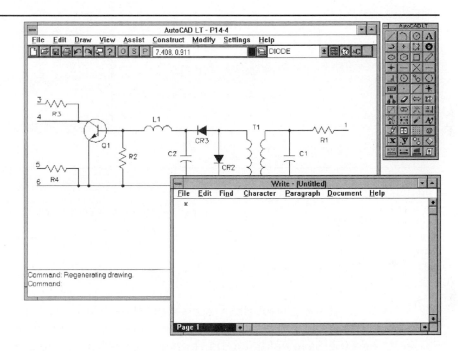

> ⬦ Ensure that the AutoCAD LT graphics window is active and issue the **COPYEMBED** command. Type ALL and press [Enter] at the **Select objects:** prompt.
> ⬦ The entire drawing is now copied to the Clipboard. If you like, you can open the Clipboard Viewer to verify the contents.
> ⬦ Now, activate the Write window. Select Paste from the Edit pull-down menu and paste the Clipboard contents into the Write document. See Figure 22-35. (It is also possible to paste the drawing into Write using the Paste Special dialog box shown in Figure 22-36. This dialog box is enabled by selecting Paste Special...from the Edit pull-down menu. You will observe that the Paste Special dialog box features two buttons labeled Paste and Paste Link. The Paste button is used to embed an object, while Paste Link is used when linking is desired. Since OLE is aware that the object in the Clipboard is to be embedded, the Paste Link button is grayed-out.)

Figure 22-35.
Selecting Paste from the Edit pull-down menu in Windows Write embeds the Clipboard contents in the Write document.

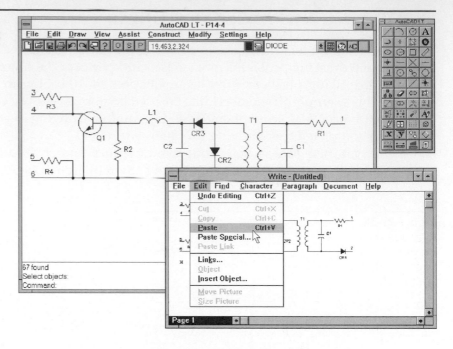

Figure 22-36.
The two buttons in the Paste Special dialog box allow you to choose between embedding or linking the source document into the destination document.

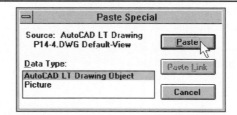

⮑ Now that the circuit drawing is embedded in the word-processing document, save the document by selecting Save from the File pull-down menu in Write.

⮑ When the Save As dialog box appears, enter the name CIRCUIT in the File Name: text box as shown in Figure 22-37. Note that Write documents are automatically saved in the \WINDOWS directory. If you like, change the drive and directory as desired. When you are finished, click the OK button. Do not exit Write.

Figure 22-37.
After embedding the drawing in Write, save the document with the name CIRCUIT.WRI in the Save As dialog box.

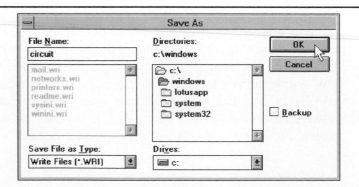

⟳ This step in the procedure is entirely optional, but you may want to try it. Windows Write provides two editing commands in the Edit pull-down menu for pasted drawings. The two commands are labeled Move Picture and Size Picture. If you like, you can move or size the circuit drawing by clicking once on it to select it. The drawing highlights and when you select the Move Picture or Size Picture commands, highlighting is turned off and a frame then surrounds the drawing. The arrow pointer also changes to a square cursor that resembles a small box within a larger box. To move the drawing, move your mouse left or right. When the drawing is placed to your satisfaction, click to set it. To size the drawing, move the square cursor to the left edge, right edge, or lower edge of the frame. Now, move your mouse in the direction you want to enlarge or reduce the drawing. Once the drawing is sized to your satisfaction, click to set it. You can cancel a move or size operation in progress with the [Esc] key.

⟳ To edit the drawing back in AutoCAD LT, first click once on the embedded drawing to highlight it. Now, select Edit AutoCAD LT Drawing Object from the Edit pull-down menu as shown in Figure 22-38. (You may notice that this menu item has been renamed. Before you pasted the drawing into Write, this menu item was labeled Object and appeared grayed-out. Refer to Figure 22-35.) As an alternative to using the Edit menu, you can also double-click on the embedded object to edit the drawing back in AutoCAD LT.

Figure 22-38.
To edit the drawing back in AutoCAD LT, select Edit AutoCAD LT Drawing Object from the Edit pull-down menu in Write.

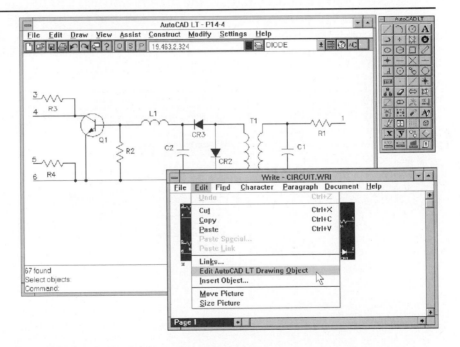

⟳ OLE now instructs AutoCAD LT to reload the embedded drawing. If you made any modifications to the drawing since you issued the **COPYEMBED** command, you are presented with a dialog box prompting you to save the changes. You may then save or discard any modifications you made. AutoCAD LT then reloads the embedded drawing using the **FILEOPEN** command. From Figure 22-39, notice the name of the reloaded drawing which appears in the prompt area. OLE creates a temporary file in the \DOS\TEMP directory with a file name such as ACAD1A6C.DWG. It is this temporary file which is reloaded into AutoCAD LT. When AutoCAD LT is exited, the temporary file is automatically deleted. Observe also that the title bar at the top of the AutoCAD LT graphics window now reads: Drawing in Client Document.

Figure 22-39.
AutoCAD LT uses the
FILEOPEN command to
reload the embedded object
into the drawing editor.
Note the temporary name
assigned by OLE to the
embedded object and the
information displayed in the
title bar of the AutoCAD LT
graphics window.

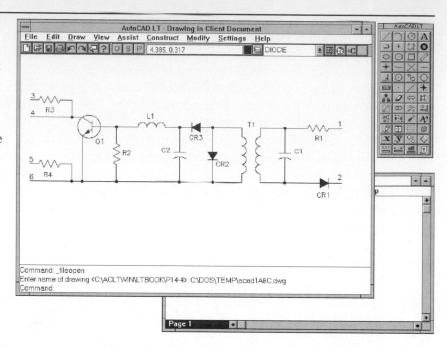

⇨ Now make some changes to the drawing in AutoCAD LT. The changes may include the
addition of notes, or the editing of colors and/or linetypes. In the example shown in
Figure 22-40, the capacitors have been modified to reflect a different representation of
capacitor symbols.

Figure 22-40.
After editing the drawing
in AutoCAD LT, select **Update
Client Document** from the
File pull-down menu to
update the Write document.

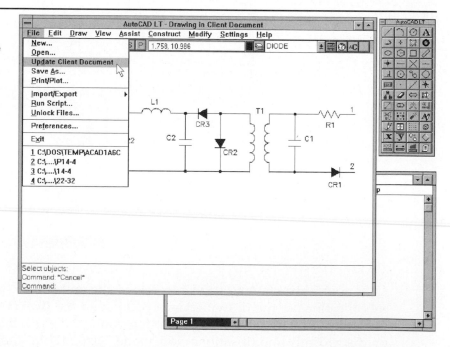

⇨ After making your changes, select **Update Client Document** from the **File** pull-down
menu. Notice that this menu item is new and replaces the former **Save** command.
After selecting this menu item, AutoCAD LT automatically issues the **QSAVE**, or **Quick
Save** command, and replaces the embedded object in Write with the updated
AutoCAD LT version.
⇨ The embedded drawing is now stored in Write—not AutoCAD LT. Exit AutoCAD LT and,
once again, save the CIRCUIT.WRI document.

⤷ When you exit Write, you are presented with the dialog box shown in Figure 22-41. This dialog box informs you that embedded objects may require updating before you close Write. Click the Yes or No buttons as appropriate.

Figure 22-41.
When you exit Write, you are informed that the embedded objects may require updating. Click Yes or No as required.

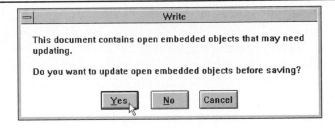

> **NOTE** Every *OLE-aware* software application will differ somewhat slightly in its required command sequence for object linking and embedding. For this reason, check the documentation of your Windows-based applications to be sure that they support OLE and to verify the precise sequence of menu commands.

Screen colors and named entities in embedded drawings

Unlike the **COPYIMAGE** command, it is not necessary to change the background color of the AutoCAD LT graphics window to white before you embed a drawing into your destination document. You may, however, want to change the color of all the drawing entities to black, because entity colors are retained in embedded drawings. Other entity properties such as layer, linetype, and thickness are also retained in embedded drawings. Additionally, any block symbols which exist in the source drawing are also retained in the destination document. However, there are several limitations regarding layers with which you should be aware.

- If any drawing layers are turned off before the **COPYEMBED** command is issued, those layers are retained and may be turned back on once the embedded drawing is reloaded back into AutoCAD LT.
- However, if any drawing layers are frozen before **COPYEMBED** is used, those layers are not retained and no longer exist once the embedded drawing is reloaded back into AutoCAD LT.

Remember also that locked layers are not selectable. If you want to embed drawing items on locked layers, be sure to unlock the layers before using **COPYEMBED**. See Chapter 5 for a complete discussion of the **LAYER** command and its options.

A few final words about embedding an AutoCAD LT drawing

There are several additional points to consider when you embed an AutoCAD LT drawing into a client document. These considerations are listed below:

- Embedded drawings are stored in the destination document and not as AutoCAD LT .DWG files. When you reload the embedded drawing back into AutoCAD LT, a copy is reloaded and not the original drawing. This is because you may have initially selected only a portion of the original drawing, (like a section view or a detail), with the **COPYEMBED** command. Therefore, AutoCAD LT cannot reload the original drawing because the embedded object may be quite different. For this same reason, the **Save** command in the **File** pull-down menu is replaced with the **Update Client Document** command to prevent you from writing over the original drawing.
- If you want to save the changes you make to a drawing after reloading the embedded object back into AutoCAD LT, use the **SAVEAS** command and save the drawing with an entirely different name.

- You cannot embed (or link) a drawing while in paper space.
- When multiple model space viewports are displayed, only the current, or active, viewport may be selected for embedding or linking.

Editing an embedded AutoCAD LT drawing

As previously mentioned, embedded drawings are stored in the destination document; they are not stored as AutoCAD LT drawing files. To edit an embedded drawing, do the following:

1. Open the destination document that contains the embedded AutoCAD LT drawing.
2. Double-click the drawing to start AutoCAD LT and open the embedded drawing. (If Windows Write is the client application, you can also click once on the drawing to highlight it and then select Edit AutoCAD LT Drawing Object from the Edit pull-down menu.)
3. Edit the drawing as required in AutoCAD LT.
4. Select **Update Client Document** from the **File** pull-down menu to update the embedded drawing in the destination document.
5. Select **Exit** from the **File** pull-down menu to return to the destination document.
6. Save the destination document in the usual manner.

Launching AutoCAD LT with OLE

One of the advantages of OLE is its ability to launch one program from within another. In other words, it is possible to start up AutoCAD LT from within Write, Microsoft Excel, or any other *OLE-aware* application. As an example, try the following:

1. Load Windows Write.
2. Select Insert Object... from the Edit pull-down menu. See Figure 22-42A.
3. The Insert Object dialog box is then displayed as shown in Figure 22-42B. This dialog box lists only those *OLE-aware* applications installed on your computer.
4. Select AutoCAD LT Drawing from the Object Type: list and click OK.
5. The familiar Windows hourglass then appears on screen as **OLE** launches AutoCAD LT.
6. Once AutoCAD LT is loaded, you have the option to open an existing drawing or start drawing in the new session. Any drawing entities you create in the new session may be embedded in Windows Write by selecting **Update Client Document** from the **File** pull-down menu.

Figure 22-42.
A—Select Insert Object... from the Edit pull-down menu in Windows Write to open the Insert Object dialog box.
B—The Insert Object dialog box displays the *OLE-aware* applications installed on your computer.

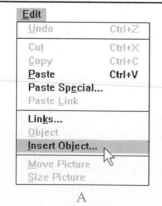
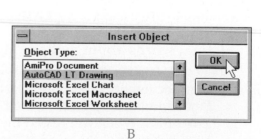

A   B

Linking an AutoCAD LT drawing

Linking is performed in AutoCAD LT with the **COPYLINK** command. You can also access the command by selecting **Copy Link** from the **Edit** pull-down menu. See Figure 22-43. Note that unlike the **COPYEMBED** command, you do not receive the familiar **Select objects:** prompt. The command sequence is as follows:

Command: *(type* COPYLINK *or* CL *and press* [Enter]*)*

Figure 22-43.
The **COPYLINK** command
may be issued by selecting
Copy Link from the **Edit**
pull-down menu.

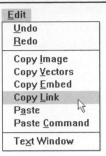

NOTE
Although the **Copy Link** button shown does not appear on the toolbar or in the toolbox by default, it may easily be added.

Instead, whatever is displayed in the graphics window is copied to the Windows Clipboard for linking into the OLE client application. Therefore, you may want to zoom in on a specific view or detail before linking. It is also a good idea to save the view with the **VIEW** command. This is because if the current view is unnamed, AutoCAD LT assigns it a name such as OLE1 when you issue the **COPYLINK** command. Each subsequent use of **COPYLINK** in the current drawing session creates additional views named OLE2, OLE3, and so on. Remember that you can rename the views later, if you like, by using the **RENAME** or **DDRENAME** commands.

Linking is an extremely powerful function. When you link entities from an AutoCAD LT drawing to another document, you create a reference or link to the source drawing. Instead of copying drawing information as embedding does, the link tells the destination document where to find the original drawing information. It is also possible to link the same drawing to several destination documents. When the source drawing is changed, you can easily update each destination document that contains a link to that drawing.

OBJECT LINKING TUTORIAL

To obtain a clearer understanding of object linking, once again load AutoCAD LT and open P14-4. Use another drawing of your choice if you have not yet completed this drawing problem. Then, activate the Accessories group window and launch Windows Write. Arrange both windows in a display similar to that previously shown in Figure 22-34. The linking tutorial begins as follows:

➪ Ensure that the AutoCAD LT graphics window is active and issue the **COPYLINK** command.

➪ The current view is now copied to the Clipboard. If you like, you can open the Clipboard Viewer to verify the contents.

➪ Issue the **VIEW** command and use the **?** option to list all views in the current drawing. Note the new view named OLE1.

➪ Now, activate the Write window. Select Paste Link from the Edit pull-down menu and link the Clipboard contents into the Write document. It is also possible to link the drawing into Write using the Paste Special dialog box previously shown in Figure 22-36. This dialog box is enabled by selecting Paste Special... from the Edit pull-down menu. Since OLE is aware that the object in the Clipboard is to be linked, the Paste Link button is no longer grayed-out.

➪ Now that the OLE1 view is linked to the word-processing document, save the document by selecting Save from the File pull-down menu in Write.

⇨ When the Save As dialog box appears, enter CIRCUIT2 in the File Name: text box. Remember to change the drive and directory if necessary. When you are finished, click the OK button, but *do not* exit Write.

⇨ To edit the view back in AutoCAD LT, reactivate the AutoCAD LT graphics window.

⇨ Now make some changes to the view in AutoCAD LT. You can link another view, or the entire drawing at this point.

⇨ After making your changes, select **Save** from the **File** pull-down menu and exit AutoCAD LT.

⇨ Now, reactivate the Write window and select Li**nks**... from the **Edit** pull-down menu. The Links dialog box is then displayed. See Figure 22-44.

Figure 22-44.
Click the **Update Now** and **OK** buttons in the **Links** dialog box to update the link between AutoCAD LT and Write.

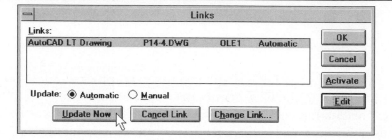

⇨ To update the document, click the Update Now button and then click OK.

⇨ The dialog box is closed and the changes you made in AutoCAD LT are immediately reflected in Write.

⇨ Save CIRCUIT2.WRI and exit Write.

The next time that you open the Write document, the Write dialog box shown in Figure 22-45 is automatically displayed. You now have the option to update the links in the destination document whether you changed the AutoCAD LT drawing or not.

Figure 22-45.
Links may be updated the next time the destination document is opened.

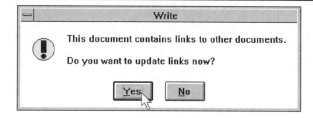

Editing a linked AutoCAD LT drawing

Remember that the destination document stores a reference or link that identifies the drawing file location. You can open a linked drawing from the destination document by double-clicking the drawing in the destination document. If the destination document is in Windows Write, you can also click once on the drawing to highlight it and then select Edit AutoCAD LT Drawing Object from the Edit pull-down menu. AutoCAD LT then starts and automatically opens the linked drawing. Now, revise the drawing or view as necessary. When you are through editing the drawing, select **Save** from the **File** pull-down menu to save the changes to the original drawing. The destination document is immediately updated.

It is also possible to edit a linked drawing without opening the destination document at all. Simply start AutoCAD LT as usual, open the linked drawing and make any necessary revisions. Be sure to save the revised drawing when you are through. As previously mentioned, the next time you open a document with a link to the revised drawing, the destination application displays a dialog box prompting you to update the link.

The power and possibilities of object linking cannot be overstated. In the following sections you will learn how one of the most overlooked Windows applications, the Windows Cardfile, can be transformed into one of the most valuable programs on your computer.

CAUTION

If you delete or rename a linked AutoCAD LT drawing, OLE will not be able to establish the link when you open the destination document. The three alert boxes illustrated in Figure 22-46 are examples of the kind of messages you receive when neither the server or client application can find the requested link. In this example, drawing P14-4 cannot be found when the Write word-processing document in which it is linked is opened.

Figure 22-46.
Take care not to delete or rename a linked file. In this example, both AutoCAD LT and Write display alert boxes when the linked source drawing cannot be found.

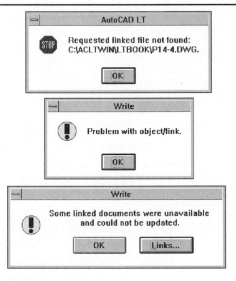

INTRODUCTION TO WINDOWS **CARDFILE**

The Windows Cardfile is located in the Accessories group window. See Figure 22-47. It is a collection of index cards that may be used to organize and manage information, which typically includes names, addresses, and phone numbers. Therefore, you can think of Cardfile as a computerized rotary card file. However, the powerful capabilities of object linking and embedding also make it possible to use Cardfile as a drawing manager.

Figure 22-47.
The Windows Cardfile program item icon is located in the Accessories group window.

When Cardfile starts up, it appears in a separate display window and contains only one index card. See Figure 22-48. Cardfile adds new index cards in the correct alphabetical order and automatically scrolls to display the new card at the front. The text in the index line can hold up to 39 characters and helps you to identify the contents of each card. You can type information on a card, duplicate the card, edit the card, and delete cards one at a time. Once you have created a set of cards to your satisfaction, the card file may be saved to disk for future use. When saved, the file extension .CRD is automatically appended to the card file.

Figure 22-48.
The Cardfile display window. Apart from organizing and managing names, addresses, and phone numbers, Cardfile may also be used as a drawing and block symbol manager.

Index line

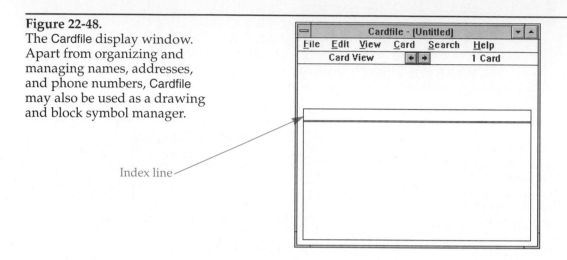

NOTE
The number of index cards you can create, and how much information may be contained in the card file, is a function of your particular computer and how much memory it has. These factors also greatly influence the speed with which Cardfile loads both files and index cards. For a complete description of Windows Cardfile, refer to the *Microsoft Windows Users's Guide*.

CREATING A DRAWING MANAGER WITH CARDFILE TUTORIAL

The following tutorial section provides you the opportunity to create and save a set of four index cards that contain linked AutoCAD LT drawings. The drawings used in this tutorial are from previous chapters and include: P9-4, P11-4, P12-3, and P14-4. If you have not yet completed these drawing problems, feel free to use four other drawing problems or exercises of your choice. The Cardfile tutorial begins as follows:

　▷ Load AutoCAD LT and open P9-4. Remember, use another drawing or exercise of your choice if you have not yet completed this drawing problem.

　▷ Activate the Accessories group window and launch Windows Cardfile. Arrange both windows in a display similar to that shown in Figure 22-49.

　▷ Activate the Cardfile window and switch to Picture mode by selecting Picture from the Edit pull-down menu. See Figure 22-50A.

　▷ Now, select Index from the Edit pull-down menu, Figure 22-50B, or press function key [F6].

　▷ The Index dialog box is displayed. Enter the description PROBLEM 4 FROM CHAPTER 9 in the Index Line: text box as shown in Figure 22-51. Remember that this index line can contain a maximum of 39 characters. Therefore, you can also enter your name, date of the drawing, etc. Click the OK button when you are finished.

Figure 22-49.
Arrange the AutoCAD LT graphics window and the Cardfile window so that both are visible and open drawing problem P9-4.

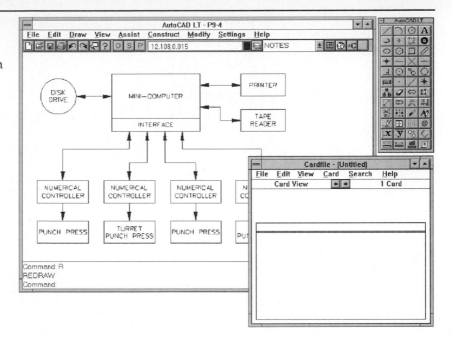

Figure 22-50.
A—Switch to Picture mode by selecting Picture from the Edit pull-down menu. B—Select Index... from the Edit pull-down menu to display and edit the index line of the first card at the front of the file.

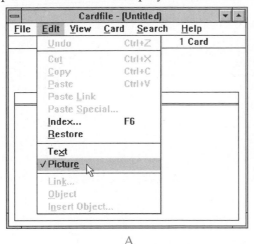
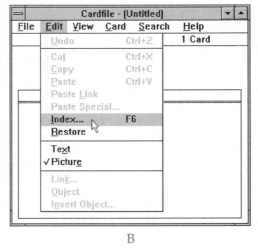

A   B

Figure 22-51.
Enter the drawing title or a description in the Index Line: text box. A maximum of 39 characters is allowed.

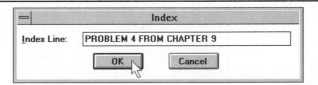

> Activate the AutoCAD LT graphics window, Figure 22-52. Issue the **COPYLINK** command to paste the drawing contents into the Clipboard.
> Return to the Cardfile window and select Paste Link from the Edit pull-down menu. See Figure 22-53. The drawing P9-4 now appears in the first index card.
> You will now add an additional card to the card file. Select Add... from the Card pull-down menu. See Figure 22-54A, or press function key [F7]. When the Add dialog box appears, enter the description PROBLEM 4 FROM CHAPTER 11 in the Add: text box as

Figure 22-52.
The **COPYLINK** command is now issued for drawing P9-4.

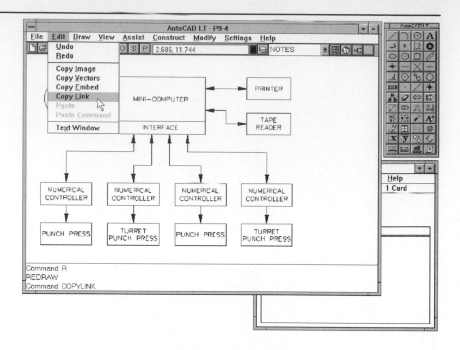

Figure 22-53.
Select **Paste Link** from the **Edit** pull-down menu to link P9-4 into the Cardfile.

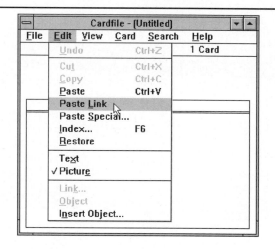

Figure 22-54.
A—Additional cards are added by selecting Add... from the Card pull-down menu.
B—A description for drawing P11-4 is entered in the Add: text box.

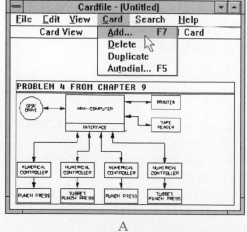

A

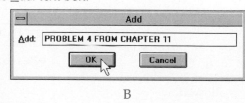

B

shown in Figure 22-54B. Feel free to enter additional information about this drawing if you like. Click the OK button when you are finished. The second index card appears at the front of the card file.

✧ Reactivate the AutoCAD LT graphics window and open drawing P11-4. Once again, use the **COPYLINK** command to copy the drawing to the Clipboard.

✧ Return to the Cardfile window to paste P11-4. This time, try using the Paste Special... option in the Edit pull-down menu. When the Paste Special dialog box appears, click the Paste Link button as shown in Figure 22-55. This function is the equivalent of selecting Paste Link from the Edit pull-down menu.

Figure 22-55.
Clicking the Paste Link button in the Paste Special dialog box is equivalent to selecting Paste Link from the Edit pull-down menu.

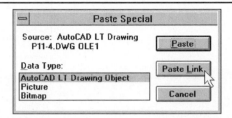

✧ The drawing problem now appears in the second index card. Your display screen should resemble that shown in Figure 22-56.

Figure 22-56.
After pasting the link, drawing P11-4 is added to the card file.

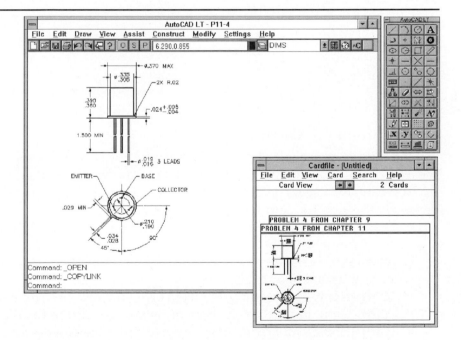

✧ Repeat the last four steps for drawing problems P12-3 and P14-4. When you are through, your card file should contain four index cards and appear as shown in Figure 22-57. This displayed format is called Card view.

✧ You can display the contents of the card file in List view by selecting List from the View pull-down menu. Note from Figure 22-58 that each card is listed alphabetically. If you double-click one of the entries, the Index dialog box is displayed and you can then edit the text in the index line. When you redisplay the card file in Card view by selecting Card from the View pull-down menu, the index card entry that you double-clicked in the list then appears at the front of the card file.

Figure 22-57.
A total of four index cards representing four AutoCAD LT drawings appear in Cardfile.

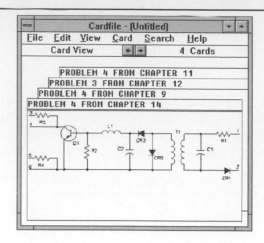

Figure 22-58.
An alphabetical list of the card file contents is obtained by selecting List from the View pull-down menu.

Moving around in Cardfile

You can change the order of the displayed cards more quickly by clicking in the index line area of each card with your mouse. The card you click is then brought to the front of the file. You can also use the left and right arrows located in the status bar to move forward and backward through the card file. If you prefer using the keyboard, use the following keys:

- **[Page Down].** Press [Page Down] to scroll forward one card in Card view or move forward one page of index lines in List view.
- **[Page Up].** Press [Page Up] to scroll backward one card in Card view and move back one page of index lines in List view.
- **[Ctrl]+[Home].** Press [Ctrl]+[Home] to bring the first card in the file to the front.
- **[Ctrl]+[End].** Press [Ctrl]+[End] to bring the last card in the file to the front.
- **[Ctrl]+[Home]+[*character key*].** Press [Ctrl]+[Home]+[*character key*] to bring a card to the front of the file. Cardfile displays the first card whose index line begins with the letter or number you press.
- **[⇦] or [⇨].** Press the [⇦] or [⇨] to scroll one card backward or forward in List view.

Saving and using the drawing manager card file

Once you have linked each of your drawings to Cardfile, save the card file to disk. If the card file has not yet been saved, the Save As dialog box is displayed. Observe that card files are saved in the \WINDOWS directory by default. Change the drive and directory as desired and enter the name DWGMGR in the File Name: text box. See Figure 22-59. Once you have saved the card file, it remains open so that you may continue working until you select Exit from the File pull-down menu.

Figure 22-59.
The card file is saved as DWGMGR using the Save As dialog box.

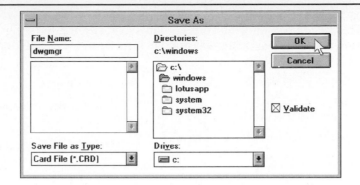

As with all linked applications, the Cardfile (the destination document) stores a reference or link that identifies the drawing file locations. You can open a linked drawing from Cardfile by first making sure that you are in Picture mode, and then double-clicking the drawing in the index card. You can also click once on the drawing to highlight it and then select Edit AutoCAD LT Drawing Object from the Edit pull-down menu as shown in Figure 22-60. AutoCAD LT then starts and automatically opens the linked drawing. Now, revise the drawing or view as necessary and then select **Save** from the AutoCAD LT **File** pull-down menu to save the changes to the drawing. The Cardfile index card is immediately updated.

Figure 22-60.
Select Edit AutoCAD LT Drawing Object from the Edit pull-down menu to launch AutoCAD LT. The drawing referenced on the front card of the card file is automatically opened in the graphics window.

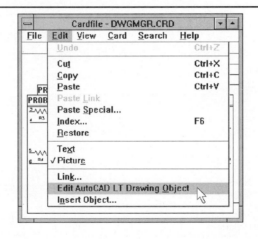

You may also edit a linked drawing without opening Cardfile at all. Simply start AutoCAD LT as usual, open the linked drawing and make any necessary revisions. Be sure to save the revised drawing when you are through. The next time you open Cardfile, the dialog box shown in Figure 22-61A prompts you to update the link so that the index card reflects the changes made to the edited drawing. This is easily accomplished using the Link dialog box shown in Figure 22-61B. You can access this dialog box by selecting Link... from the Edit pull-down menu. When the dialog box appears, click the Update Now button and the index card is updated. Click OK to exit the Link dialog box.

Figure 22-61.
A—This dialog box informs you that links may require updating when DWGMGR.CRD is opened in Cardfile. B—Click the Update Now and OK buttons in the Link dialog box to update the link between AutoCAD LT and Cardfile.

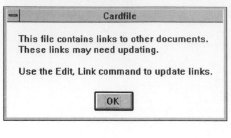

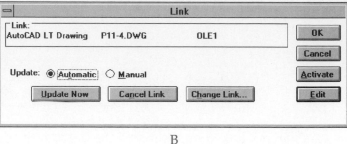

A   B

Finally, keep in mind that you can start AutoCAD LT and begin an entirely new drawing from within Cardfile as well. First, switch to Picture mode as previously described and then select Insert Object... from the Edit pull-down menu. See Figure 22-62A. The Insert New Object dialog box then appears displaying each *OLE-aware* application on your computer. Select AutoCAD LT Drawing from the Object Type: list and click OK to start AutoCAD LT. Once AutoCAD LT is loaded, you have the option to begin a new drawing session or open an existing drawing.

Figure 22-62.
A—Select Insert Object... from the Edit pull-down menu in Cardfile to open the Insert New Object dialog box. B—The Insert New Object dialog box displays the *OLE-aware* applications installed on your computer.

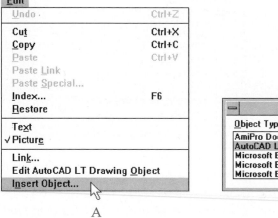

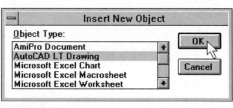

A   B

EXERCISE 22-5

❑ Object embedding can also be used productively with Cardfile. In this exercise, you will use Cardfile to create a symbol manager using the electronic component symbols from drawing problem P14-4. If you have not yet completed this drawing, use any one of your drawings that contain one or more blocks. Remember that, unlike linking, the symbols embedded within Cardfile become part of the destination document and are stored separately from AutoCAD LT.

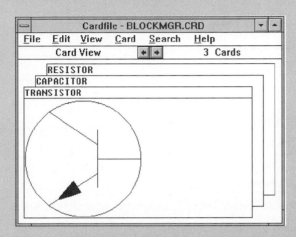

❑ Launch both Cardfile and AutoCAD LT and open drawing P14-4.
❑ Arrange and size the display windows so that both are visible on the Windows desktop.
❑ Use the **COPYEMBED** command and select the resistor block on P14-4.
❑ Create an index card in Cardfile with the description RESISTOR. Make sure that you are in Picture mode and paste (*not* Paste Link) the resistor into the card.
❑ Add a second card with the description CAPACITOR. Once again, use the **COPYEMBED** command and select the capacitor block in P14-4.
❑ Paste the capacitor into the second index card. Now, create a third index card with the description TRANSISTOR.
❑ Use **COPYEMBED** one final time to select the transistor block on P14-4. Paste the transistor into the third index card.
❑ Save the card file with the name BLOCKMGR, but do not exit Cardfile.
❑ Begin a new drawing in AutoCAD LT.
❑ Return to Cardfile and verify that you are still in Picture mode. The TRANSISTOR index card should still be at the front of the card file.
❑ Select Copy from the Edit pull-down menu to copy the transistor symbol to the Clipboard.
❑ In AutoCAD LT, use the **PASTECLIP** command to insert the transistor symbol into the graphics window. If necessary, use the **WMFOPTS** command to ensure that the arrow in the transistor symbol is pasted correctly.
❑ Repeat the procedure for the capacitor and resistor symbols.
❑ When you are finished, there should be three blocks in the new drawing—WMF0, WMF1, and WMF2.
❑ Save the drawing as EX22-5.DWG and exit AutoCAD LT.

When used together wisely, AutoCAD LT, File Manager, Notepad, Cardfile, and OLE are a powerful combination. As such, you might consider adding Cardfile to the StartUp group window so that it is launched automatically with AutoCAD LT, File Manager, and Notepad when Windows is started, Figure 22-63. For instructions on adding program item icons to the StartUp window, refer to Chapter 21 of this text.

Figure 22-63.
By adding Cardfile to the StartUp group window, Cardfile is launched automatically every time Windows is started.

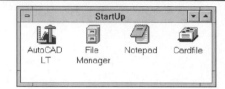

Summarizing the Clipboard options

You may find the various AutoCAD LT copy and paste options somewhat confusing until you have had some additional practice with them. Until that time, use the following summary of command options as an aid.

- **COPYIMAGE.** Copies AutoCAD LT entities, as well as the toolbar, toolbox, and command prompt area to the Clipboard in bitmap format. However, the image *cannot* be pasted back into AutoCAD LT. The command may be accessed by selecting **Copy Image** from the **Edit** pull-down menu.

- **COPYCLIP.** Copies *only* AutoCAD LT entities to the Clipboard in metafile format. No portion of the AutoCAD LT graphics window may be copied. The command may be accessed by selecting **Copy Vectors** from the **Edit** pull-down menu.

- **PASTECLIP.** Pastes a Clipboard metafile into AutoCAD LT as a block entity with the name WMF*n*. The command may be accessed by selecting **Paste** from the **Edit** pull-down menu.

- **PASTE COMMAND.** Pastes text created with an ASCII text editor or word-processing program into the graphics window as AutoCAD LT text. The text is imported in the current color, layer, and style. The command is used in conjunction with the **DTEXT** or **TEXT** commands and is accessed by selecting **Paste Command** from the **Edit** pull-down menu.

- **COPYEMBED.** Copies selected drawing entities to the Clipboard for embedding into an OLE client application. Embedded drawings are stored in the destination document and not as AutoCAD LT drawing files. The command may be accessed by selecting **Copy Embed** from the **Edit** pull-down menu.

- **COPYLINK.** Copies the currently displayed AutoCAD LT entities in the graphics window to the Clipboard for linking into an OLE client application. When the source drawing is changed in AutoCAD LT, you can easily update each destination document that contains a link to that drawing. The command may be accessed by selecting **Copy Link** from the **Edit** pull-down menu.

- **SAVEDIB.** Saves the *entire* AutoCAD LT graphics window, including the title and menu bars, to an external file in Device-Independent Bitmap format. The command may be accessed by first selecting **Import/Export** from the **File** pull-down menu and then selecting **BMP Out...** from the cascading submenu.

DRAWING INTERCHANGE FILE (DXF) FORMAT

The *Drawing Interchange File (DXF)* format was developed by Autodesk, Inc. to allow the translation of drawing files between AutoCAD LT and other CAD programs. A file in DXF format is written in standard ASCII code so that it may be read by any computer. To translate a drawing from a different CAD system into AutoCAD LT, the **DXFIN** command is used. Use the **DXFOUT** command when you wish to transfer an AutoCAD LT drawing to a different CAD program. Both the **DXFIN** and **DXFOUT** commands may be accessed from a cascading submenu by first selecting **Import/Export** from the **File** pull-down menu. See Figure 22-64.

Figure 22-64.
Selecting **Import/Export** from the **File** pull-down menu displays the **DXF In...** and **DXF Out...** commands in a cascading submenu.

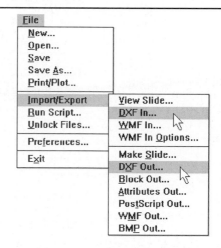

The **DXFIN** command

The **DXFIN** command is used to load a .DXF file into AutoCAD LT. To use **DXFIN**, first begin a new drawing and deactivate the **Use Prototype** check box in the **New Drawing** dialog box. Next, select the **DXFIN** command from the cascading submenu as described above, or enter the following on the command line:

Command: *(type* DXFIN *or* DN *and press* [Enter]*)*

Use the **Select DXF File** dialog box to specify the name of the file to convert. See Figure 22-65. The new drawing is discarded if AutoCAD LT detects any errors during input. Once the drawing is converted, save it as a .DWG file.

Figure 22-65.
The **DXFIN** command displays the **Select DXF File** dialog box. The selected file is then translated into AutoCAD LT format.

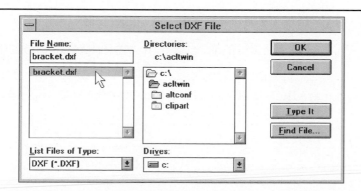

The DXFOUT command

The **DXFOUT** command creates a drawing interchange file from an AutoCAD LT drawing so that it may be used by another CAD program. Select the **DXFOUT** command from the cascading submenu as described above, or enter the following on the command line:

Command: *(type* DXFOUT *or* DX *and press* [Enter])

Specify the desired output file name in the **Create DXF File** dialog box and click the **OK** button, Figure 22-66. You then receive the following prompt:

Enter decimal places of accuracy (0 to 16)/Entities ⟨6⟩: *(type* E, *enter a value (0 to 16),*
 or press [Enter] *to accept the default)*
Command:

Figure 22-66.
Specify the output file name using the **Create DXF File** dialog box. The .DXF file extension is automatically appended to the file name.

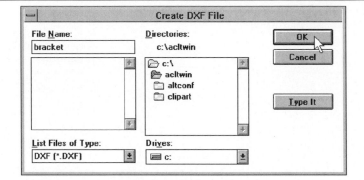

You may choose from between 0 and 16 decimal places to specify the degree of accuracy you want for numeric values. The default value of 6 should be sufficient for most applications. If you only wish to output specific entities rather than the entire drawing, use the **Entities** option. The familiar **Select objects:** prompt then appears. Select the entities you wish to translate using any of the AutoCAD LT selection set options. When you are through picking entities, you are prompted once again to specify the degree of decimal accuracy required. The file is then written to disk with a .DXF extension and is ready to be translated into another program.

CHAPTER TEST

Write your answers in the spaces provided.

1. What is the similarity between the **COPYIMAGE** and **SAVEDIB** commands? _____
   _____

2. What are the differences between **COPYIMAGE** and **SAVEDIB**?
   _____
   _____
   _____
   _____

3. Besides the **SAVEDIB** command, how else may the entire graphics window be captured?
   _____
   _____

4. How does the **COPYCLIP** command differ from the **COPYIMAGE** command? _____

_____

_____

_____

_____

_____

5. What is the name of the command used to insert copied vectors into an AutoCAD LT drawing? What type of AutoCAD LT entity is created when this command is issued? ____

_____

6. You have just pasted an AutoCAD LT image created with the **COPYCLIP** command into your word-processing program. What file format is used for the pasted image—bitmap or metafile?_____

_____

7. In which directory does AutoCAD LT store the temporary file created by **COPYCLIP**? ____

_____

8. Name the command used to change the insertion point for clipped vectors. _____

_____

9. The contents of the Clipboard are automatically deleted after pasting them into another application. (True/False) _____

10. What function does the **Edit** pull-down menu **Paste Command** option perform? _____

_____

_____

11. When importing multiple lines of word-processing text into AutoCAD LT, which command should be used —**TEXT** or **DTEXT**? _____

_____

12. How does the **WMFOUT** command differ from the **COPYCLIP** command? _____

_____

_____

13. The insertion point of an imported metafile can be specified using the **BASE** command. (True/False) _____

14. What is a source document? _____

_____

15. What is a destination document? _____

_____

16. Define a server and a client._____

_____

_____

_____

17. Which AutoCAD LT command is most similar to embedding? _____
_____

18. You have just embedded an AutoCAD LT drawing in Microsoft Word for Windows. Where is the destination document stored—Microsoft Word or AutoCAD LT? _____
_____

19. A drawing that contains a frozen layer and a layer that has been turned off is embedded into a client document. The embedded drawing is then reloaded back in AutoCAD LT. Can the layer that is turned off be turned back on? What happens to the frozen layer? _____
_____

20. Which AutoCAD LT command is most similar to linking? _____
_____

21. An AutoCAD LT drawing may be linked to only one client application. (True/False) _____
_____

23. Why should you not rename or delete a linked drawing? _____
_____

24. Once an AutoCAD LT drawing is linked, it is no longer stored as a .DWG file. (True/False)
_____
_____

25. What is the DXF format? Is a DXF file in ASCII or binary code? _____
_____
_____
_____

CHAPTER PROBLEMS

General

1. Create a card file with *embedded* block symbols appropriate to your particular application. If you do mechanical design or drafting, include symbols representing hex nuts, screws, bolts, etc. For architectural applications, include symbols for doors, windows, receptacles, etc. Save the card file as P22-1.CRD.

General

2. Create a second card file that contains *links* to each of the drawing problems completed thus far in this text. Do not include drawing exercises. Save the card file as P22-2.CRD.

Appendix A
System Requirements for AutoCAD LT

The following software and hardware is required to run AutoCAD LT for Windows 3.1 (formerly Release 2):

- MS-DOS 3.31 or later (5.0 or later is recommended).
- Windows 3.1 (or Windows for Workgroups 3.11) running in 386 Enhanced Mode.

NOTE   While AutoCAD LT runs under Windows 95 and Windows NT, be advised that these two operating systems are not officially supported for AutoCAD LT for Windows 3.1 (formerly Release 2) by Autodesk, Inc.

- 386, 486, or Pentium-based system with a math coprocessor.
- Windows-compatible video display capable of 640 × 480 screen resolution or greater.
- 3.5" 1.44MB floppy disk drive.
- CD-ROM device if you purchase the CD-ROM version of AutoCAD LT.
- Mouse or pointing device.
- 8 megabytes of RAM (16 megabytes recommended).
- 16MB of free hard-disk space to install all the AutoCAD LT files.
- Permanent swap file, two to four times the size of RAM (recommended).

Appendix B

AutoCAD LT Command Reference

The following listing contains a brief description for each of the AutoCAD LT commands. Command shortcuts are shown if applicable. An apostrophe (') at the beginning of a command name indicates a command that can be used transparently. (Transparent commands may be used while another command is running.)

Command Name	Shortcut(s)	Description
3DPOLY	–	Creates a 3D polyline using straight line segments
'ABOUT	AB	Displays information about the current version of AutoCAD LT
'APERTURE	AP	Sets the size of the object snap target box (in pixels)
ARC	A	Draws an arc
AREA	AA	Computes the area and perimeter of objects or of defined areas
ARRAY	AR	Creates multiple copies of objects in a rectangular or circular (polar) pattern
ATTDEF	AD	Creates an attribute definition
'ATTDISP	AT	Globally controls the visibility of attributes
ATTEDIT	AE	Edits attribute information independent of its block definition
ATTEXT	AX	Extracts attribute data in CDF, SDF, or DXF formats
'BASE	BA	Sets the insertion base point for the current drawing
BHATCH	–	Hatches an enclosed area with an associative hatch pattern
'BLIPMODE	BM	Controls the display of marker blips
BLOCK	B	Creates a block definition of selected objects
BMAKE	–	Creates blocks using a dialog box
BOUNDARY	–	Creates a polyline around a closed boundary
BREAK	BR	Splits an object in two or erases parts of a selected object
CHAMFER	CF	Creates bevels, or chamfers, on the edges of lines and polylines

Command Name	Shortcut(s)	Description
CHANGE	CH	Changes the properties and/or parameters of selected objects
CHPROP	CR	Changes the color, layer, linetype, and thickness of selected objects
CIRCLE	C	Draws a circle
'COLOR	CO	Sets the system color for new objects
COPY	CP	Copies objects
COPYCLIP	CC	Copies text and graphics to the Windows Clipboard
COPYEMBED	CE	Copies objects to embed in another program
COPYIMAGE	CI	Copies a selected area of the drawing in bitmap format
COPYLINK	CL	Copies the current view to the Clipboard for linking into other OLE programs
DDATTDEF	DAD	Creates an attribute definition using a dialog box
DDATTE	DE	Edits the textual attributes of a block
DDATTEXT	DAX	Extracts attribute data using a dialog box
DDCHPROP	DC	Changes the color, layer, linetype, and thickness of objects using a dialog box
DDEDIT	ED,TE	Edit text and attribute definitions using a dialog box
'DDEMODES	EM	Sets entity properties for new objects
'DDGRIPS	GR	Turns on and sets the color of grips using a dialog box
DDIM	DM	Creates and modifies dimension styles using a dialog box
DDINSERT	I	Inserts a block or drawing using a dialog box
'DDLMODES	LD	Creates and manages layers using a dialog box
DDMODIFY	–	Edits all aspects of an object using a dialog box
'DDOSNAP	OS	Sets one or more running object snap modes using a dialog box
'DDPTYPE	–	Sets the display mode and size of point objects using a dialog box
DDRENAME	DR	Uses a dialog box to rename named objects
'DDRMODES	DA	Enables the **Drawing Aids** dialog box
'DDSELECT	SL	Controls object selection modes in a dialog box
DDUCS	UC	Manages and lists defined user coordinate systems
DDUCSP	UP	Uses a dialog box to select a preset user coordinate system
'DDUNITS	DU	Sets linear and angular formats as well as the displayed precision in a dialog box
'DELAY	–	Used in script files to provide a timed pause
DIM	D	Enters dimensioning mode

Command Name	Shortcut(s)	Description
DIM1	D1	Enters dimensioning mode for one dimensioning operation only
'DIST	DI	Calculates the distance and angle between two selected points
DIVIDE	–	Places evenly spaced point markers or blocks along an object
DLINE	DL	Draws a double line using separate line and arc segments
DONUT	DO	Draws filled rings and circles
DSVIEWER	DS	Activates the **Aerial View** window
DTEXT	DT,T	Displays multiline text on screen as it is entered
DVIEW	DV	Creates parallel projection or perspective views for 3D objects
DXFIN	DN	Imports a Drawing Interchange Format (DXF) file
DXFOUT	DX	Creates a Drawing Interchange Format (DXF) file of the current drawing
'ELEV	EV	Sets the elevation and extrusion thickness for new objects
ELLIPSE	EL	Draws an ellipse
END	–	Saves the current drawing and exits AutoCAD LT
ERASE	E	Removes selected drawing objects
EXIT	–	Quits an AutoCAD LT drawing session
EXPLODE	EP,X	Returns a compound object to its component objects
EXTEND	EX	Extends an object to intersect another object
FILEOPEN	–	Opens a drawing file
'FILL	FL	Controls the filling of wide polylines, donuts, and 2D solids
FILLET	F	Draws fillets and rounds on selected objects
'GETENV	–	Displays specified variables in the ACLT.INI file
'GRAPHSCR	–	Switches from the text window to the graphics window
'GRID	G	Activates and sets the grid X and Y spacing
HATCH	H	Hatches an enclosed area with a non-associative hatch pattern
HATCHEDIT	–	Modifies an existing associative hatch pattern
'HELP	?	Activates online help
HIDE	HI	Suppresses the hidden lines in a 3D model
'ID	–	Displays the XYZ coordinates of a selected point or screen location
INSERT	IN	Places a block or drawing into the current drawing
'ISOPLANE	IS	Sets the current isometric plane

Command Name	Shortcut(s)	Description
'LAYER	LA	Creates and manages layers on the command line
'LIMITS	LM	Sets the drawing boundaries
LINE	L	Draws straight line segments
'LINETYPE	LT	Lists, creates, loads, and sets linetypes
LIST	LS	Displays database information for selected objects
LOGFILEON	–	Creates ACLT.LOG (ASCII) and begins recording the contents of the text window
LOGFILEOFF	–	Terminates the recording and closes the log file (ACLT.LOG)
'LTSCALE	LC	Globally sets the linetype scale factor
MEASURE	–	Places point markers or blocks at measured intervals along an object
MIRROR	MI	Creates a reflected image copy of selected objects
MOVE	M	Moves selected objects at a specified distance and direction
MSLIDE	ML	Creates a slide file of the current viewport
MSPACE	MS	Returns to model space from paper space
MULTIPLE	MU	Repeats the previous command until canceled
MVIEW	MV	Creates and activates floating viewports in paper space
NEW	N	Begins a new drawing
OFFSET	OF	Duplicates a single object at a distance or through a point
OOPS	OO	Reverses the last **ERASE** operation
OPEN	OP	Opens an existing drawing file
'ORTHO	OR	Constrains cursor motion to the horizontal or vertical axes
'OSNAP	O	Sets running object snaps on the command line
'PAN	P	Shifts the drawing display in the current viewport
PASTECLIP	PC	Inserts text and graphics data from the Windows Clipboard
PEDIT	PE	Edit 2D polylines and polyarcs
PLAN	PV	Displays the plan view of a user coordinate system
PLINE	PL	Draws 2D polylines and polyarcs
PLOT	PP	Plots a drawing to a printer, plotter, or file
POINT	PT	Draws a point object
POLYGON	PG	Draws an equilateral, multisided object
PREFERENCES	PF	Customizes the drawing environment using a dialog box
PSOUT	PU	Outputs an Encapsulated PostScript file

Command Name	Shortcut(s)	Description
PSPACE	PS	Returns to paper space from model space
PURGE	PR	Removes unused named objects, such as lines and blocks, from the drawing
QSAVE	–	Saves the current drawing
'QTEXT	QT	Displays each text and attribute object as a bounding box around the text object
QUIT	–	Exits an AutoCAD LT drawing session
RECTANG	RC	Creates a rectangular polyline
REDO	RE	Reverses the effects of the previous **U** or **UNDO** command
'REDRAW	R	Refreshes the display of all viewports
REGEN	RG	Regenerates (recalculates) the display in all viewports
RENAME	RN	Changes the name of named objects
'RESUME	–	Continues an interrupted script file
REVDATE	–	Inserts a revision time, date, file name, and user name into a drawing
ROTATE	RO	Rotates objects about a base point
RSCRIPT	–	Repeats a script file continuously
SAVE	SA	Saves an existing drawing with the current file name
SAVEAS	–	Saves an unnamed drawing with a name or renames the current drawing
SCALE	SC	Reduces or enlarges objects equally in the X, Y, and Z directions
'SCRIPT	SR	Executes a sequence of commands from a script file
SELECT	SE	Used to place objects in the **Previous** selection set
'SETENV	–	Changes the value of a variable in the [AutoCAD LT General] section of ACLT.INI
'SETVAR	–	Lists or changes values of system variables
SHADE	SH	Creates a flat-shaded image of a 3D model in the current viewport
'SNAP	SN	Restricts cursor movement to user-specified increments
SOLID	SO	Draws solid-filled polygons
STRETCH	S	Stretches or shrinks objects
'STYLE	ST	Creates and modifies named text styles
TEXT	TX	Creates a single line of text
'TEXTSCR	–	Switches from the graphics window to the text window
'TIME	TI	Displays time and date information of a drawing in the text window
TOOLBOX	–	Controls the position and locked/unlocked status of the toolbox

Command Name	Shortcut(s)	Description
TRIM	TR	Trims objects against the edges of other objects
U	–	Reverses the most recent operation
UCS	–	Creates and manages user coordinate systems on the command line
UCSICON	UI	Controls the visibility and origin of the UCS icon
UNDO	UN	Provides various options to reverse the effects of previous commands
'UNITS	UT	Sets linear and angular formats as well as the displayed precision
UNLOCK	UL	Unlocks one or more locked files
'VIEW	V	Saves and manages named views
VPLAYER	VL	Controls layer visibility in floating viewports
VPOINT	VP	Sets the viewing direction for 3D objects
VPORTS	VW	Divides the graphics window into multiple tiled viewports
VSLIDE	VS	Displays a slide file in the current viewport
WBLOCK	W	Writes objects to disk in a new drawing file
WMFIN	WI	Imports a Windows metafile
WMFOPTS	–	Sets options for importing metafiles
WMFOUT	WO	Saves objects in Windows metafile format
XBIND	XB	Binds dependent symbols of an xref to the current drawing
XREF	XR	Controls external references (xrefs)
'ZOOM	Z	Increases or decreases the apparent size of objects in the current viewport

Appendix C
AutoCAD LT Menu Tree

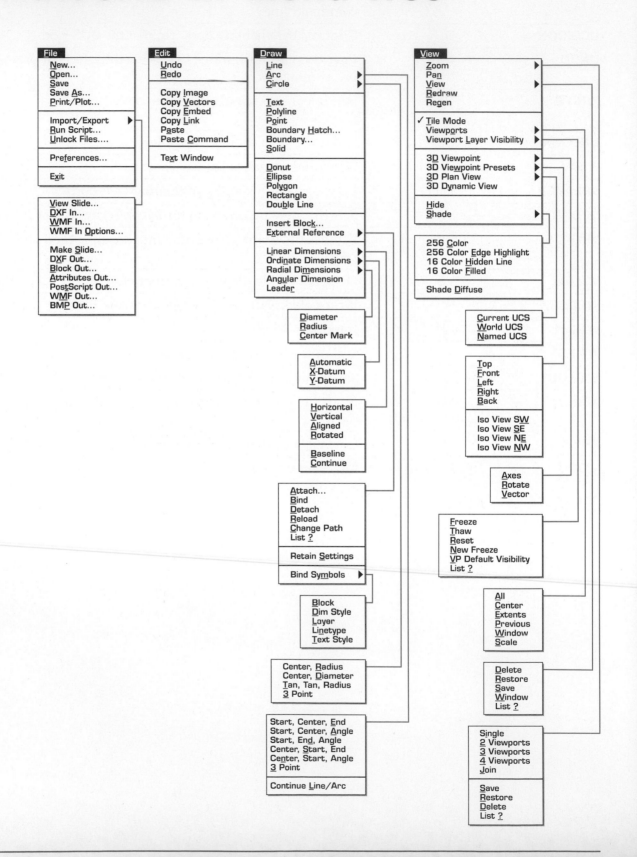

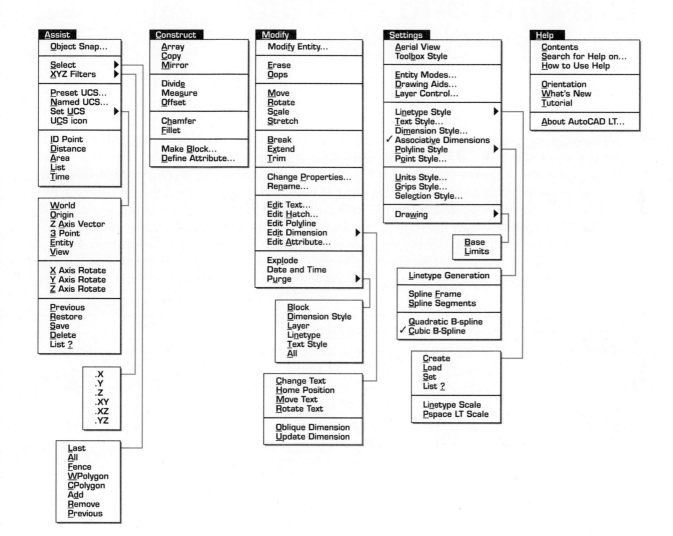

Assist
- Object Snap...
- Select ▶
- XYZ Filters ▶
- Preset UCS...
- Named UCS...
- Set UCS ▶
- UCS icon
- ID Point
- Distance
- Area
- List
- Time

- World
- Origin
- Z Axis Vector
- 3 Point
- Entity
- View
- X Axis Rotate
- Y Axis Rotate
- Z Axis Rotate
- Previous
- Restore
- Save
- Delete
- List ?

- .X
- .Y
- .Z
- .XY
- .XZ
- .YZ

- Last
- All
- Fence
- WPolygon
- CPolygon
- Add
- Remove
- Previous

Construct
- Array
- Copy
- Mirror
- Divide
- Measure
- Offset
- Chamfer
- Fillet
- Make Block...
- Define Attribute...

Modify
- Modify Entity...
- Erase
- Oops
- Move
- Rotate
- Scale
- Stretch
- Break
- Extend
- Trim
- Change Properties...
- Rename...
- Edit Text...
- Edit Hatch...
- Edit Polyline
- Edit Dimension ▶
- Edit Attribute...
- Explode
- Date and Time
- Purge ▶

- Block
- Dimension Style
- Layer
- Linetype
- Text Style
- All

- Change Text
- Home Position
- Move Text
- Rotate Text
- Oblique Dimension
- Update Dimension

Settings
- Aerial View
- Toolbox Style
- Entity Modes...
- Drawing Aids...
- Layer Control...
- Linetype Style ▶
- Text Style...
- Dimension Style...
- ✓ Associative Dimensions
- Polyline Style ▶
- Point Style...
- Units Style...
- Grips Style...
- Selection Style...
- Drawing ▶

- Base
- Limits

- Linetype Generation
- Spline Frame
- Spline Segments
- Quadratic B-spline
- ✓ Cubic B-Spline

- Create
- Load
- Set
- List ?
- Linetype Scale
- Pspace LT Scale

Help
- Contents
- Search for Help on...
- How to Use Help
- Orientation
- What's New
- Tutorial
- About AutoCAD LT...

Appendix D

AutoCAD LT Prototype Drawing and System Variable Defaults

The following listing contains the AutoCAD LT system variables that can be stored within a prototype, or any other, drawing file. The value of each of these variables is stored in the drawing file when the drawing is saved, so the values remain the same the next time the drawing is opened. Setting the values for most of these variables can be done by entering the associated command or by using the **SETVAR** command. Some variable names are derived by AutoCAD LT from the current state of the drawing, or the drawing environment, and cannot be directly set by the user. These types of variables are referred to as read-only.

The list provides a brief description of each variable and its default setting when the ACLT.DWG prototype drawing is used. Eyeglasses symbol ($\mathcal{G}$) indicates that variable is read-only.

Variable Name	Default Value	Description
ANGBASE	0	Sets the direction of the base angle 0 with respect to the current UCS
ANGDIR	0	Sets the positive angle direction from angle 0 with respect to the current UCS
ATTDIA	0	Controls whether a dialog box is used for attribute value entry
ATTMODE	1	Controls the **Attribute Display** mode
ATTREQ	1	Determines whether default attribute settings are used during insertion of blocks
AUNITS	0	Format used for angular units
AUPREC	0	Sets the decimal precision display of angular units
BACKZ	$\mathcal{G}$	Stores the back clipping plane offset from the target plane
BLIPMODE	1	Controls the visibility of marker blips
CECOLOR	"BYLAYER"	Sets the color of newly-created objects
CELTYPE	"BYLAYER"	Sets the linetype of newly-created objects
CHAMFERA	0.5000	Sets the first chamfer distance
CHAMFERB	0.5000	Sets the second chamfer distance
CIRCLERAD	0.0000	Sets the default circle radius—a 0 (zero) sets no default
CLAYER	"0"	Sets the current layer
CVPORT	2	Sets the identification number of the current viewport
DIMALT	Off	Alternate units selected
DIMALTD	2	Alternate unit decimal places

Variable Name	Default Value	Description
DIMALTF	25.4000	Alternate unit scale factor
DIMAPOST	""	Suffix for alternate text
DIMASO	On	Create associative dimensions
DIMASZ	0.1800	Arrow size
DIMBLK	""	Arrow block name
DIMBLK1	""	First arrow block name
DIMBLK2	""	Second arrow block name
DIMCEN	0.0900	Center mark size
DIMCLRD	BYBLOCK	Dimension line color
DIMCLRE	BYBLOCK	Extension line & leader color
DIMCLRT	BYBLOCK	Dimension text color
DIMDLE	0.0000	Dimension line extension
DIMDLI	0.3800	Dimension line increment for continuation
DIMEXE	0.1800	Extension above dimension line
DIMEXO	0.0625	Extension line origin offset
DIMGAP	0.0900	Gap from dimension line to text
DIMLFAC	1.0000	Linear unit scale factor
DIMLIM	Off	Generate dimension limits
DIMPOST	""	Default suffix for dimension text
DIMRND	0.0000	Rounding value
DIMSAH	Off	Separate arrow blocks
DIMSCALE	1.0000	Overall scale factor
DIMSE1	Off	Suppress the first extension line
DIMSE2	Off	Suppress the second extension line
DIMSHO	On	Update dimensions while dragging
DIMSOXD	Off	Suppress outside extension dimension
DIMSTYLE	*UNNAMED	Current dimension style (read-only)
DIMTAD	0	Place text above the dimension line
DIMTFAC	1.0000	Tolerance text height scaling factor
DIMTIH	On	Text inside extensions is horizontal
DIMTIX	Off	Place text inside extensions
DIMTM	0.0000	Minus tolerance
DIMTOFL	Off	Force line inside extension lines
DIMTOH	On	Text outside extensions is horizontal
DIMTOL	Off	Generate dimension tolerances
DIMTP	0.0000	Plus tolerance
DIMTSZ	0.0000	Tick size
DIMTVP	0.0000	Text vertical position
DIMTXT	0.1800	Text height
DIMZIN	0	Zero suppression
DWGCODEPAGE	"iso8859-1"	Set equal to **SYSCODEPAGE** when a new drawing is created
ELEVATION	0.0000	Stores the current 3D elevation relative to the current UCS

Variable Name	Default Value	Description
FILLETRAD	0.5000	Stores the current fillet radius
FILLMODE	1	Specifies whether objects are filled in
FRONTZ	∿	Stores the front clipping plane offset from the target plane
GRIDMODE	0	Toggles **GRID** on and off
GRIDUNIT	0.0000,0.0000	Specifies the X and Y grid spacing for the current viewport
HANDLES	∿	Object handles are enabled and can be accessed by applications
INSBASE	0.0000,0.0000	Insertion base point set by **BASE** command, expressed in UCS coordinates
LASTPOINT	0.0000,0.0000	Stores the last point entered, expressed in UCS coordinates
LENSLENGTH	∿	Stores the length of the lens (in millimeters) used in perspective viewing
LIMCHECK	0	Controls object creation outside the current drawing limits
LIMMAX	12.0000,9.0000	Stores upper-right drawing limits, expressed in world coordinates
LIMMIN	0.0000,0.0000	Stores lower-left drawing limits, expressed in world coordinates
LTSCALE	1.0000	Sets the global linetype scale factor
LUNITS	2	Sets the current linear units decimal places
LUPREC	4	Sets the decimal precision display of linear units
MIRRTEXT	1	Controls how **MIRROR** reflects text and dimensions
ORTHOMODE	0	Toggles **ORTHO** mode on and off
OSMODE	0	Stores the bit code of the current object snap
PDMODE	0	Sets the point object display mode
PDSIZE	0.0000	Sets the point object display size
PLINEGEN	0	Determines the linetype pattern generation around the vertices of a 2D polyline
PLINEWID	0.0000	Sets the current polyline width
QTEXTMODE	0	Toggles the quick text display mode
SHADEDGE	3	Controls the shading of edges during rendering
SHADEDIF	70	Sets ratio of diffuse reflective light to ambient light during rendering
SNAPANG	0	Sets the snap/grid rotation angle for the current viewport
SNAPBASE	0.0000,0.0000	Stores the origin point of the snap/grid in the current viewport
SNAPISOPAIR	0	Controls the isometric plane (isoplane) for the current viewport
SNAPMODE	0	Toggles **SNAP** mode on and off
SNAPSTYL	0	Sets the snap style between Standard and Isometric
SNAPUNIT	0.5000,0.5000	Sets the snap spacing for the current viewport
SPLFRAME	0	Controls the display of spline-fit polylines

Variable Name	Default Value	Description
SPLINESEGS	8	Sets the number of line segments to be generated for each spline-fit polyline
SPLINETYPE	6	Determines the type of spline curve to be generated by **PEDIT Spline**
SYSCODEPAGE	᧰	Stores the system code page specified in ACAD.XMF
TARGET	᧰	Stores location of the target point for the current viewport (in UCS coordinates)
TDCREATE	᧰	Stores the time and date when the current drawing was created
TDINDWG	᧰	Stores the total editing time for the current drawing
TDUPDATE	᧰	Stores the time and date of last drawing update/save
TDUSRTIMER	᧰	Stores user timer time elapsed
TEXTSIZE	0.2000	Sets the text height for the current style
TEXTSTYLE	"STANDARD"	Sets the current text style name
THICKNESS	0.0000	Sets the current 3D thickness
TILEMODE	1	Toggles between model space and paper space
UCSICON	0	Controls the display of the UCS icon
UCSNAME	᧰	Stores the name of the current UCS for the current space
UCSORG	᧰	Stores the origin point of the current UCS for the current space
UCSXDIR	᧰	Stores the X direction of the current UCS for the current space
UCSYDIR	᧰	Stores the Y direction of the current UCS for the current space
UNITMODE	0	Controls the unit's display format
VIEWCTR	᧰	Stores the center of view in the current viewport, expressed in UCS coordinates
VIEWDIR	᧰	Stores the viewing direction in the current viewport, expressed in UCS coordinates
VIEWMODE	᧰	Controls the **DVIEW** viewing mode for the current viewport, using bit-code
VIEWSIZE	᧰	Stores the height of view in the current viewport, expressed in drawing units
VIEWTWIST	᧰	Stores the view twist angle for the current viewport
VISRETAIN	0	Controls the visibility of layers in xref files
VSMAX	᧰	Upper-right corner of the current viewport's virtual screen
VSMIN	᧰	Lower-left corner of the current viewport's virtual screen
WORLDVIEW	1	Controls whether the UCS changes to the WCS during **DVIEW** or **VPOINT** operations

The following listing contains the AutoCAD LT system variables that are saved with the AutoCAD LT configuration file (ACLT.CFG), and not within a drawing file. Therefore, these values are identical between all drawing sessions. The default values shown here represent the values existing prior to the initial configuration of AutoCAD LT. Eyeglasses symbol (👓) indicates that variable is read-only.

Variable Name	Default Value	Description
APERTURE	10	Sets the object snap target height (in pixels)
CMDDIA	1	Controls the display of the **PLOT** and **BHATCH** command dialog boxes
FILEDIA	1	Controls the display of all dialog boxes except **PLOT** and **BHATCH**
GRIPBLOCK	0	Controls the assignment of grips within blocks
GRIPCOLOR	5	Sets the color of nonselected (warm) grips
GRIPHOT	1	Sets the color of selected (hot) grips
GRIPS	1	Toggles grips on and off
GRIPSIZE	3	Sets the size of the grip box (in pixels)
PICKADD	1	Controls the additive selection of objects
PICKAUTO	1	Controls automatic windowing at **Select objects:** prompt
PICKBOX	3	Sets the object selection target height (in pixels)
PICKDRAG	0	Controls how a selection window is drawn
PICKFIRST	1	Allows objects to be selected before a command
PLOTID	"System Printer"	Stores the current printer/plotter description
PLOTTER	0	Integer describing current printer/plotter configuration
SAVEFILE	👓	Stores the current auto-save file name
SAVETIME	120	Sets the automatic save time interval (in minutes)
TOOLTIPS	1	Toggles tooltips on and off
XREFCTL	0	Determines whether AutoCAD LT writes .XLG files (external reference log files)

This final listing shows the AutoCAD LT variables that are not saved at all. These variables revert to default values when opening an existing, or beginning a new, drawing. Many of these variables are read-only, and reference drawing or operating system-specific information. Other variables in this section are used to change standard features of AutoCAD LT and are restored to their default values in future drawing sessions to avoid unexpected results during common drawing operations. Eyeglasses symbol (👓) indicates that variable is read-only.

Variable Name	Default Value	Description
ACLTPREFIX	👓	Stores the directory path specified in the **PREFERENCES** dialog box
ACLTVER	👓	Stores the version number of AutoCAD LT
AREA	👓	Stores the last area value computed by the **AREA** or **LIST** commands
CDATE	👓	Shows date and time in calendar and clock format: YYYYMMDD.HHMMSSmsec
CMDNAMES	👓	Displays the name of the currently active command and transparent command

Variable Name	Default Value	Description
DATE	⌇	Stores the current date and time as a Julian date and fraction in a real number
DISTANCE	⌇	Stores the distance calculated by the **DIST** command
DONUTID	0.5000	Sets the inside diameter of a donut object
DONUTOD	1.0000	Sets the outside diameter of a donut object
DWGNAME	⌇	Stores the current drawing name
DWGPREFIX	⌇	Stores the drive/directory path of the current drawing
DWGTITLED	⌇	Specifies whether the current drawing has been saved
DWGWRITE	1	Toggles the read-only state when opening a drawing
EXPERT	0	Suppresses the level of warning prompts and messages
HIGHLIGHT	1	Toggles object highlighting on and off
HPANG	0	Sets the hatch pattern angle
HPDOUBLE	0	Specifies hatch pattern doubling for user-defined (U) patterns
HPNAME	"ANSI31"	Sets the default hatch pattern name. Enter a period (.) to set no default
HPSCALE	1.0000	Sets the current hatch pattern scale
HPSPACE	1.0000	Sets the hatch pattern spacing for user-defined (U) patterns
INSNAME	""	Sets the default block name for the **DDINSERT** and **INSERT** commands
LASTANGLE	⌇	Stores end angle of last arc entered, relative to the XY plane of the current UCS
MAXACTVP	16	Sets the maximum number of viewports to regenerate at one time
MENUECHO	0	Suppresses the level of menu echo prompts
MODEMACRO	""	Displays a text string on the toolbar written in the DIESEL macro language
OFFSETDIST	−1.0000	Sets the default offset distance
PERIMETER	⌇	Stores the last perimeter value computed by the **AREA** or **LIST** commands
SAVENAME	⌇	Stores the file name used during a **SAVEAS** operation

Appendix E

AutoCAD LT Hatch Pattern Descriptions

Hatch Pattern Name	Description
ANGLE	Angle steel
ANSI31	ANSI Iron, Brick, Stone masonry
ANSI32	ANSI Steel
ANSI33	ANSI Bronze, Brass, Copper
ANSI34	ANSI Plastic, Rubber
ANSI35	ANSI Fire brick, Refractory material
ANSI36	ANSI Marble, Slate, Glass
ANSI37	ANSI Lead, Zinc, Magnesium, Sound/Heat/Elec Insulation
ANSI38	ANSI Aluminum
AR-B816	8x16 Block elevation stretcher bond
AR-B816C	8x16 Block elevation stretcher bond with mortar joints
AR-B88	8x8 Block elevation stretcher bond
AR-BRELM	Standard brick elevation English bond with mortar joints
AR-BRSTD	Standard brick elevation stretcher bond
AR-CONC	Random dot and stone pattern
AR-HBONE	Standard brick herringbone pattern @ 45°
AR-PARQ1	2x12 Parquet flooring: pattern of 12x12
AR-RROOF	Roof shingle texture
AR-RSHKE	Roof wood shake texture
AR-SAND	Random dot pattern
BOX	Box steel
BRASS	Brass material
BRICK	Brick or masonry-type surface
BRSTONE	Brick and stone
CLAY	Clay material
CORK	Cork material
CROSS	A series of crosses
DASH	Dashed lines
DOLMIT	Geological rock layering
DOTS	A series of dots
EARTH	Earth or ground (subterranean)
ESCHER	Escher pattern
FLEX	Flexible material
GRASS	Grass area
GRATE	Grated area
HEX	Hexagons

Hatch Pattern Name	Description
HONEY	Honeycomb pattern
HOUND	Houndstooth check
INSUL	Insulation material
LINE	Parallel horizontal lines
MUDST	Mud and sand
NET	Horizontal/vertical grid
NET3	Network pattern 0-60-120
PLAST	Plastic material
PLASTI	Plastic material
SACNCR	Concrete
SQUARE	Small aligned squares
STARS	Star of David
STEEL	Steel material
SWAMP	Swampy area
TRANS	Heat transfer material
TRIANG	Equilateral triangles
ZIGZAG	Staircase effect

Appendix F

Drafting Standards and Related Documents

The following is a list of ANSI/ASME drafting standards or related documents. They are ANSI/ASME adopted, unless another standard developing organization, such as ANSI/NFPA, is indicated.

ABBREVIATIONS

Y1.1-1989, *Abbreviations for Use on Drawings and in Text*

CHARTS AND GRAPHS (Y15)

Y15.1M-1979 (R1993), *Illustrations for Publication and Projection*

Y15.2M-1979 (R1986), *Time-Series Charts*

Y15.3M-1979 (R1986), *Process Charts*

DIMENSIONS

B4.1-1967 (R1987), *Preferred Limits and Fits for Cylindrical Parts*

B4.2-1978 (R1994), *Preferred Metric Limits and Fits*

B4.3-1978 (R1994), *General Tolerances for Metric Dimensioned Products*

B4.4M-1981 (R1987), *Inspection of Workpieces*

B32.1-1952 (R1994), *Preferred Thickness for Uncoated, Thin, Flat Metals (Under 0.250/in.)*

B32.2-1969 (R1994), *Preferred Diameters for Round Wire-0.500 Inches and Under*

B32.3M-1984 (R1994), *Preferred Metric Sizes for Flat Metal Products*

B32.4M-1980 (R1994), *Preferred Metric Sizes for Round, Square, Rectangle, and Hexagon Metal Products*

B32.5-1977 (R1994), *Preferred Metric Sizes for Tubular Metal Products Other Than Pipe*

B32.6M-1984 (R1994), *Preferred Metric Equivalents of Inch Sizes for Tubular Metal Products Other Than Pipe*

B36.10M-1985, *Welded and Seamless Wrought Steel Pipe*

B36.19M-1985, *Stainless Steel Pipe*

DRAFTING STANDARDS

Y14.1-1980 (R1987), *Drawing Sheet Size and Format*

Y14.1M-1992, *Metric Drawing Sheet Size and Format*

Y14.2M-1992, *Line Conventions and Lettering*

Y14.3M-1992, *Multi- and Sectional-View Drawings*

Y14.4M-1989 (R1994), *Pictorial Drawings*

Y14.5M-1994, *Dimensioning and Tolerancing*

Y14.5.1-1994, *Mathematical Definition of Y14.5*

Y14.5.2, *Certification of GD&T Professionals*

Y14.6M-1978 (R1993), *Screw Thread Representation*

14.6aM-1981 (R1993), *Engineering Drawing and Related Documentation Practices (Screw Thread Representation) (Metric Supplement)*

Y14.7.1-1971 (R1993), *Gear Drawing Standards-Part 1-Spur, Helical, Double Helical, and Rack*

Y14.7.2-1978 (R1994), *Gear and Spline Drawing Standards-Part 2-Bevel and Hypoid Gears*

Y14.8M-1989 (R1993), *Castings and Forgings*

Y14.13M-1981 (R1992), *Engineering Drawing and Related Documentation Practices-Mechanical Spring Representation*

Y14.18M-1986 (R1993), *Engineering Drawings and Related Documentation Practices-Optical Parts*

Y14.24M-1989, *Types and Applications of Engineering Drawings*

14.34M-1989 (R1993), *Parts Lists, Data Lists, and Index Lists*

Y14.35M-1992, *Revision of Engineering Drawings and Associated Documents*

Y14.36-1978 (R1993), *Surface Texture Symbols*

AutoCAD LT—Fundamentals and Applications

Y14 Report 1, *Digital Representation of Physical Object Shapes*

Y14 Report 2, *Guidelines for Documenting of Computer Systems Used in Computer-Aided Preparation of Product Definition Data-User Instructions*

Y14 Report 3, *Guidelines for Documenting of Computer Systems Used in Computer-Aided Preparation of Product Definition Data-Design Requirements*

Y14 Report 4-1989, *A Structural Language Format for Basic Shape Description*

ANSI/US PRO/IPO-100-1993, *Digital Representation for Communication of Product Definition Data (Replaced ANSI Y14.26M-1981)*

GRAPHIC SYMBOLS

Y32.2-1975, *Electrical and Electronic Diagrams*

Y32.2.3-1949 (R1988), *Pipe Fittings, Valves, and Piping*

Y32.2.4-1949 (R1993), *Heating, Ventilating, and Air Conditioning*

Y32.2.6-1950 (R1993), *Heat/Power Apparatus*

Y32.4-1977 (R1987), *Plumbing Fixture Diagrams Used in Architectural and Building Construction*

Y32.7-1972 (R1987), *Railroad Maps and Profiles*

Y32.9-1972 (R1989), *Electrical Wiring and Layout Diagrams Used in Architecture and Building*

Y32.10-1967 (R1987), *Fluid Power Diagrams*

Y32.11-1961 (R1993), *Process Flow Diagrams in the Petroleum and Chemical Industries*

Y32.18-1972 (R1993), *Mechanical and Acoustical Elements as Used in Schematic Diagrams*

ANSI/AWS A2.4-91, *Symbols for Welding, Brazing, and Nondestructive Examination*

ANSI/IEEE 200-1975 (R1989), *Reference Designations for Electrical and Electronics Parts and Equipment*

ANSI/IEEE 315-1975 (R1989), *Electrical and Electronics Diagrams (Including Reference Designation Class Designation Letters)*

ANSI/IEEE 623-1976 (R1989), *Grid and Mapping Used in Cable Television Systems*

ANSI/ISA S5.1-1984 (R1992), *Instrumentation Symbols and Identification*

ANSI/NFPA 170-1991, *Public Fire Safety Symbols*

LETTER SYMBOLS

Y10.1-1972 (R1988), *Glossary of Terms Concerning Letter Symbols*

Y10.3M-1984, *Mechanics and Time-Related Phenomena*

Y10.4-1982 (R1988), *Heat and Thermodynamics*

Y10.11-1984, *Acoustics*

Y10.12-1955 (R1988), *Chemical Engineering*

Y10.17-1961 (R1988), *Greek Letters Used as Letter Symbols for Engineering Math*

Y10.18 1967 (R1977), *Illuminating Engineering*

ANSI/IEEE 260-1978 (R1992), *SI Units and Certain Other Units of Measurement*

METRIC SYSTEM

SI-1, *Orientation and Guide for Use of SI (Metric) Units*

SI-2, *SI Units in Strength of Materials*

SI-3, *SI Units in Dynamics*

SI-4, *SI Units in Thermodynamics*

SI-5, *SI Units in Fluid Mechanics*

SI-6, *SI Units in Kinematics*

SI-7, *SI Units in Heat Transfer*

SI-8, *SI Units in Vibration*

SI-9, *Metrification of Codes and Standards SI (Metric) Units*

SI-10, *Steam Charts, SI (Metric) and U.S. Customary Units*

Appendix G
Drafting Symbols

STANDARD DIMENSIONING SYMBOLS

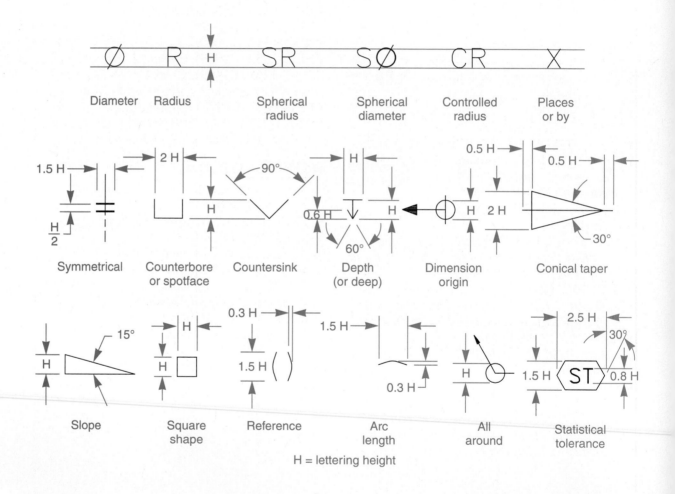

H = lettering height

GEOMETRIC DIMENSIONING AND TOLERANCING SYMBOLS, Cont.

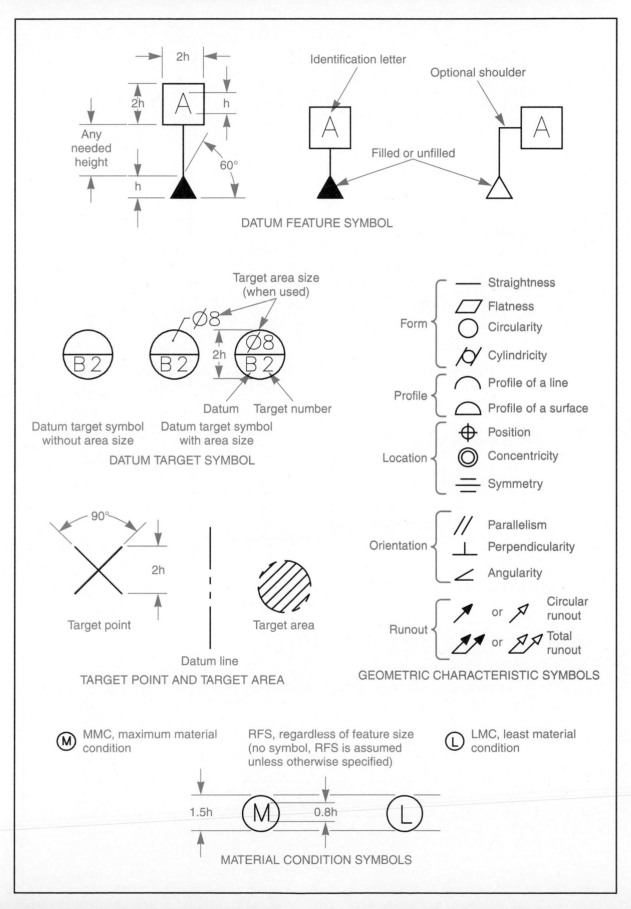

2h

2h

h

Any needed height

60°

h

DATUM FEATURE SYMBOL

Identification letter

Optional shoulder

Filled or unfilled

Target area size (when used)

Ø8

Ø8

2h

B 2

B 2

B 2

Datum   Target number

Datum target symbol without area size

Datum target symbol with area size

DATUM TARGET SYMBOL

Form
- — Straightness
- ⟋⟋ Flatness
- ◯ Circularity
- ⌭ Cylindricity

Profile
- ⌒ Profile of a line
- ⌓ Profile of a surface

Location
- ⊕ Position
- ◎ Concentricity
- ═ Symmetry

90°

2h

Target point

Datum line

Target area

TARGET POINT AND TARGET AREA

Orientation
- // Parallelism
- ⊥ Perpendicularity
- ∠ Angularity

Runout
- ↗ or ↗ Circular runout
- ↗↗ or ↗↗ Total runout

GEOMETRIC CHARACTERISTIC SYMBOLS

Ⓜ MMC, maximum material condition

RFS, regardless of feature size (no symbol, RFS is assumed unless otherwise specified)

Ⓛ LMC, least material condition

1.5h   Ⓜ   0.8h   Ⓛ

MATERIAL CONDITION SYMBOLS

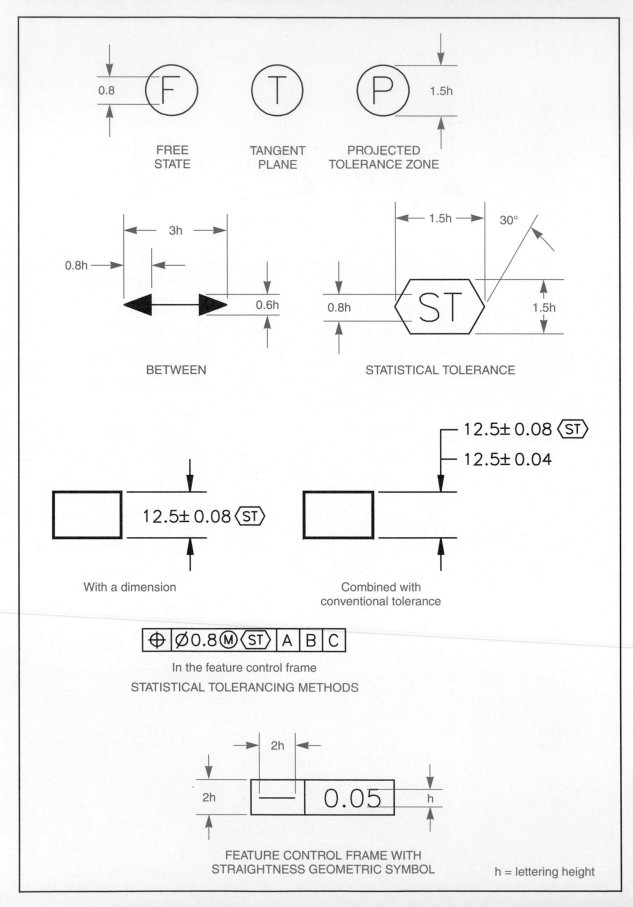

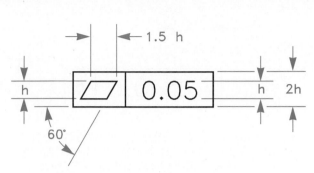

FEATURE CONTROL FRAME WITH THE FLATNESS
GEOMETRIC CHARACTERISTIC SYMBOL

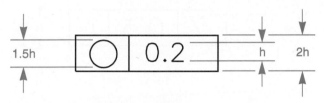

FEATURE CONTROL FRAME WITH CIRCULARITY
GEOMETRIC CHARACTERISTIC SYMBOL

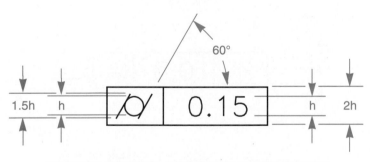

FEATURE CONTROL FRAME WITH CYLINDRICITY
GEOMETRIC CHARACTERISTIC SYMBOL

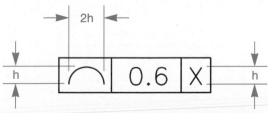

FEATURE CONTROL FRAME WITH PROFILE
OF A LINE GEOMETRIC CHARACTERISTIC
SYMBOL AND A DATUM REFERENCE

h = lettering height

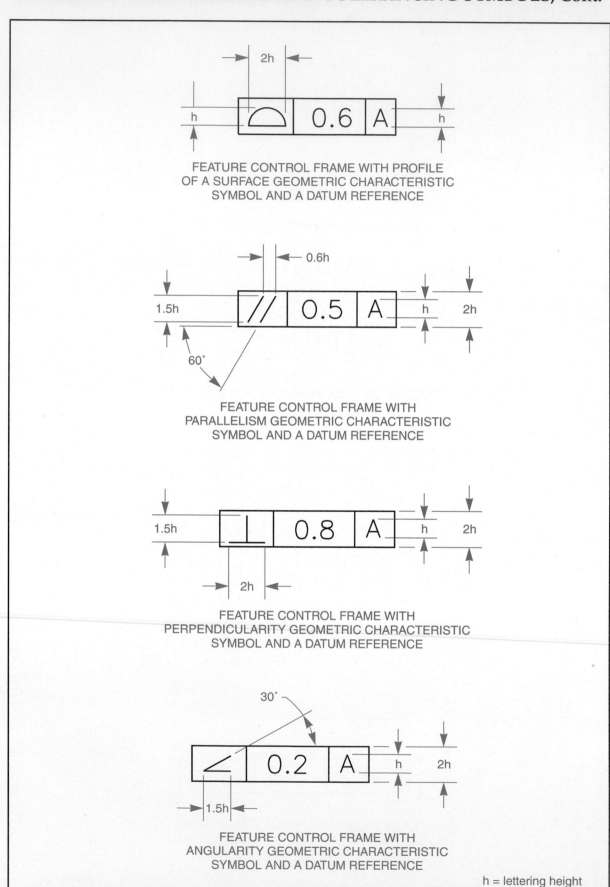

FEATURE CONTROL FRAME WITH PROFILE
OF A SURFACE GEOMETRIC CHARACTERISTIC
SYMBOL AND A DATUM REFERENCE

FEATURE CONTROL FRAME WITH
PARALLELISM GEOMETRIC CHARACTERISTIC
SYMBOL AND A DATUM REFERENCE

FEATURE CONTROL FRAME WITH
PERPENDICULARITY GEOMETRIC CHARACTERISTIC
SYMBOL AND A DATUM REFERENCE

FEATURE CONTROL FRAME WITH
ANGULARITY GEOMETRIC CHARACTERISTIC
SYMBOL AND A DATUM REFERENCE

h = lettering height

GEOMETRIC DIMENSIONING AND TOLERANCING SYMBOLS, Cont.

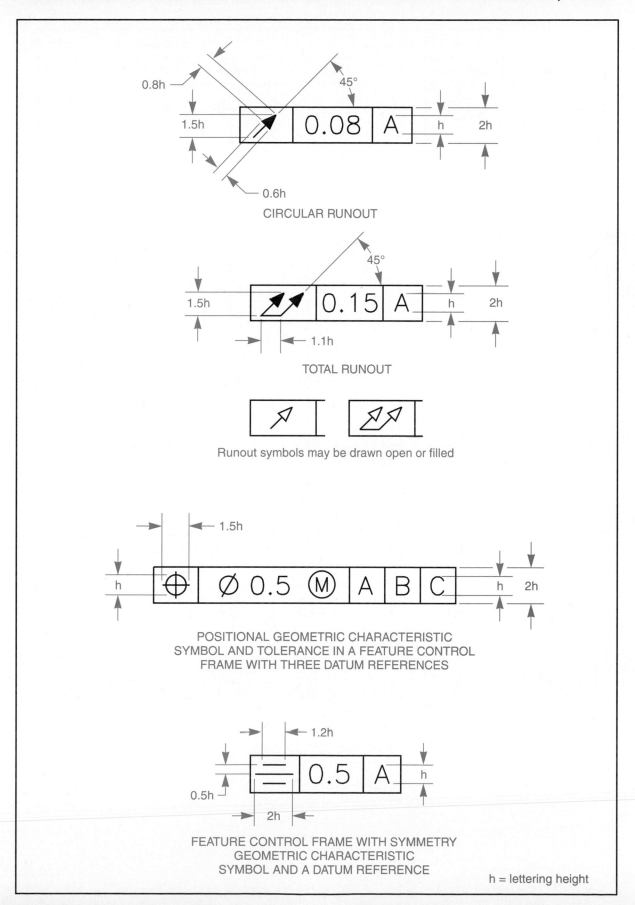

CIRCULAR RUNOUT

TOTAL RUNOUT

Runout symbols may be drawn open or filled

POSITIONAL GEOMETRIC CHARACTERISTIC
SYMBOL AND TOLERANCE IN A FEATURE CONTROL
FRAME WITH THREE DATUM REFERENCES

FEATURE CONTROL FRAME WITH SYMMETRY
GEOMETRIC CHARACTERISTIC
SYMBOL AND A DATUM REFERENCE

h = lettering height

COMMON SINGLE LINE PIPE FITTING SYMBOLS

Name	Screwed			Buttwelded		
	Left side	Front	Right side	Left side	Front	Right side
90° Elbow						
45° Elbow						
Tee						
45° Lateral						
Cross						
Cap						
Concentric Reducer						
Eccentric Reducer						
Union						
Coupling						

COMMON SYMBOLS FOR ELECTRICAL DIAGRAMS

Amplifier	Triode with directly heated cathode and envelope connection to base terminal	Fluorescent, 2-terminal lamp
Antenna, general		Incandescent lamp
Antenna, dipole	Pentode using elongated envelope	Microphone
Antenna, dipole		Receiver, earphone
Antenna, counterpoise	Twin triode using elongated envelope	Resistor, general
Battery, long line positive		
Multicell battery		Resistor, adjustable
Capacitor, general	Voltage regulator, also, glow lamp	Resistor, variable
Capacitor, variable		
Capacitor, polarized	Phototube	Transformer, general
Circuit breaker	Inductor, winding, reactor, general	
Ground		Transformer, magnetic core
Chassis ground	Magnetic core inductor	
Connectors, jack and plug	Adjustable inductor	Shielded transformer, magnetic core
Engaged connectors	Balast lamp	Auto–transformer, adjustable

COMMON ARCHITECTURAL SYMBOLS

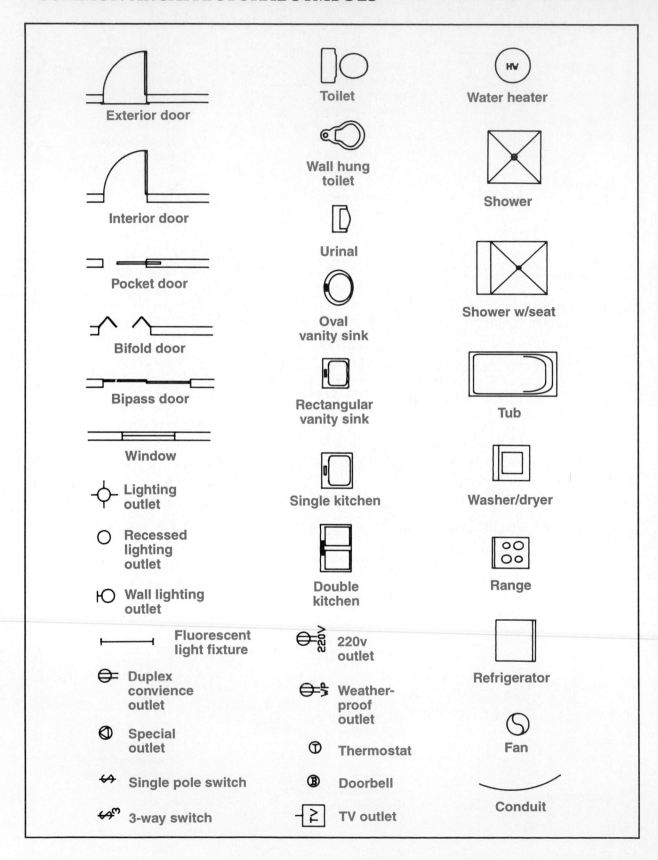

Exterior door

Interior door

Pocket door

Bifold door

Bipass door

Window

Lighting outlet

Recessed lighting outlet

Wall lighting outlet

Fluorescent light fixture

Duplex convience outlet

Special outlet

Single pole switch

3-way switch

Toilet

Wall hung toilet

Urinal

Oval vanity sink

Rectangular vanity sink

Single kitchen

Double kitchen

220v outlet

Weather-proof outlet

Thermostat

Doorbell

TV outlet

Water heater

Shower

Shower w/seat

Tub

Washer/dryer

Range

Refrigerator

Fan

Conduit

Standard Tables and Symbols

TAP DRILL SIZES FOR ISO METRIC THREADS

Nominal Size mm	Series			
	Coarse		Fine	
	Pitch mm	Tap Drill mm	Pitch mm	Tap Drill mm
1.4	0.3	1.1	–	–
1.6	0.35	1.25	–	–
2	0.4	1.6	–	–
2.5	0.45	2.05	–	–
3	0.5	2.5	–	–
4	0.7	3.3	–	–
5	0.8	4.2	–	–
6	1.0	5.0	–	–
8	1.25	6.75	1	7.0

Nominal Size mm	Series			
	Coarse		Fine	
	Pitch mm	Tap Drill mm	Pitch mm	Tap Drill mm
10	1.5	8.5	1.25	8.75
12	1.75	10.25	1.25	10.50
14	2	12.00	1.5	12.50
16	2	14.00	1.5	14.50
18	2.5	15.50	1.5	16.50
20	2.5	17.50	1.5	18.50
22	2.5	19.50	1.5	20.50
24	3	21.00	2	22.00
27	3	24.00	2	25.00

TAP DRILL SIZES UNIFIED STANDARD SCREW HEADS

Screw Thread		Tap Drill	Screw Thread		Tap Drill
Major Diameter	Threads Per Inch	Size Or Number	Major Diameter	Threads Per Inch	Size Or Number
0	80	3/64	3/8	16	5/16
				24	Q
1	64	53			
	72	53	7/16	14	U
				20	25/64
2	56	50			
	64	50	1/2	13	27/64
				20	29/64
3	48	47			
	56	45	9/16	12	31/64
				18	33/64
4	40	43			
	48	42	5/8	11	17/32
				18	37/64
5	40	38			
	44	37	3/4	10	21/32
				16	11/16
6	32	36			
	40	33	7/8	9	49/64
				14	13/16
8	32	29			
	36	29	1	8	7/8
				12	59/64
10	24	25			
	32	21	1 1/8	7	63/64
				12	1 3/64
12	24	16			
	28	14	1 1/4	7	1 7/64
				12	1 11/64
1/4	20	7			
	28	3	1 3/8	6	1 7/32
				12	1 19/64
5/16	18	F			
	24	I	1 1/2	6	1 11/32
				12	1 27/64

AutoCAD LT—Fundamentals and Applications

NUMBER AND LETTER DRILLS

Drill No.	Frac	Deci	Drill No.	Frac	Deci	Drill No.	Frac	Deci
80	—	.0135		9/64	.140	S	—	.348
79	—	.0145	28	—	.141	T	—	.358
	1/64	.0156	27	—	.144		23/64	.359
78	—	.0160	26	—	.147	U	—	.368
77	—	.0180	25	—	.150		3/8	.375
76	—	.0200	24	—	.152	V	—	.377
75	—	.0210	23	—	.154	W	—	.386
74	—	.0225		5/32	.156		25/64	.391
73	—	.0240	22	—	.157	X	—	.397
72	—	.0250	21	—	.159	Y	—	.404
71	—	.0260	20	—	.161		13/32	.406
70	—	.0280	19	—	.166	Z	—	.413
69	—	.0292	18	—	.170		27/64	.422
68	—	.0310		11/64	.172		7/16	.438
	1/32	.0313	17	—	.173		29/64	.453
67	—	.0320	16	—	.177		15/32	.469
66	—	.0330	15	—	.180		31/64	.484
65	—	.0350	14	—	.182		1/2	.500
64	—	.0360	13	—	.185		33/64	.516
63	—	.0370		3/16	.188		17/32	.531
62	—	.0380	12	—	.189		35/64	.547
61	—	.0390	11	—	.191		9/16	.562
60	—	.0400	10	—	.194		37/64	.578
59	—	.0410	9	—	.196		19/32	.594
58	—	.0420	8	—	.199		39/64	.609
57	—	.0430	7	—	.201		5/8	.625
56	—	.0465		13/64	.203		41/64	.641
	3/64	.0469	6	—	.204		21/32	.656
55	—	.0520	5	—	.206		43/64	.672
54	—	.0550	4	—	.209		11/16	.688
53	—	.0595	3	—	.213		45/64	.703
	1/16	.0625		7/32	.219		23/32	.719
52	—	.0635	2	—	.221		47/64	.734
51	—	.0670	1	—	.228		3/4	.750
50	—	.0700	A	—	.234		49/64	.766
49	—	.0730		15/64	.234		25/32	.781
48	—	.0760	B	—	.238		51/64	.797
	5/64	.0781	C	—	.242		13/16	.813
47	—	.0785	D	—	.246		53/64	.828
46	—	.0810		1/4	.250		27/32	.844
45	—	.0820	E	—	.250		55/64	.859
44	—	.0860	F	—	.257		7/8	.875
43	—	.0890	G	—	.261		57/64	.891
42	—	.0935		17/64	.266		29/32	.906
	3/32	.0938	H	—	.266		59/64	.922
41	—	.0960	I	—	.272		15/16	.938
40	—	.0980	J	—	.277		61/64	.953
39	—	.0995		9/32	.281		31/32	.969
38	—	.1015	K	—	.281		63/64	.984
37	—	.1040	L	—	.290		1	1.000
36	—	.1065	M	—	.295			
	7/64	.1094		19/64	.297			
35	—	.1100	N	—	.302			
34	—	.1110		5/16	.313			
33	—	.1130	O	—	.316			
32	—	.116	P	—	.323			
31	—	.120		21/64	.328			
	1/8	.125	Q	—	.332			
30	—	.129	R	—	.339			
29	—	.136		11/32	.344			

METRIC DRILLS

MM	DEC.	MM	DEC.	MM	DEC.	MM	DEC.
1.	.0394	3.2	.1260	6.3	.2480	9.5	.3740
1.05	.0413	3.25	.1280	6.4	.2520	9.6	.3780
1.1	.0433	3.3	.1299	6.5	.2559	9.7	.3819
1.15	.0453	3.4	.1339	6.6	.2598	9.75	.3839
1.2	.0472	3.5	.1378	6.7	.2638	9.8	.3858
1.25	.0492	3.6	.1417	6.75	.2657	9.9	.3898
1.3	.0512	3.7	.1457	6.8	.2677	10.	.3937
1.35	.0531	3.75	.1476	6.9	.2717	10.5	.4134
1.4	.0551	3.8	.1496	7.	.2756	11.	.4331
1.45	.0571	3.9	.1535	7.1	.2795	11.5	.4528
1.5	.0591	4.	.1575	7.2	.2835	12.	.4724
1.55	.0610	4.1	.1614	7.25	.2854	12.5	.4921
1.6	.0630	4.2	.1654	7.3	.2874	13.	.5118
1.65	.0650	4.25	.1673	7.4	.2913	13.5	.5315
1.7	.0669	4.3	.1693	7.5	.2953	14.	.5512
1.75	.0689	4.4	.1732	7.6	.2992	14.5	.5709
1.8	.0709	4.5	.1772	7.7	.3031	15.	.5906
1.85	.0728	4.6	.1811	7.75	.3051	15.5	.6102
1.9	.0748	4.7	.1850	7.8	.3071	16.	.6299
1.95	.0768	4.75	.1870	7.9	.3110	16.5	.6496
2.	.0787	4.8	.1890	8.	.3150	17.	.6693
2.05	.0807	4.9	.1929	8.1	.3189	17.5	.6890
2.1	.0827	5.	.1968	8.2	.3228	18.	.7087
2.15	.0846	5.1	.2008	8.25	.3248	18.5	.7283
2.2	.0866	5.2	.2047	8.3	.3268	19.	.7480
2.25	.0886	5.25	.2067	8.4	.3307	19.5	.7677
2.3	.0906	5.3	.2087	8.5	.3346	20.	.7874
2.35	.0925	5.4	.2126	8.6	.3386	20.5	.8071
2.4	.0945	5.5	.2165	8.7	.3425	21.	.8268
2.45	.0965	5.6	.2205	8.75	.3445	21.5	.8465
2.5	.0984	5.7	.2244	8.8	.3465	22.	.8661
2.6	.1024	5.75	.2264	8.9	.3504	22.5	.8858
2.7	.1063	5.8	.2283	9.	.3543	23.	.9055
2.75	.1083	5.9	.2323	9.1	.3583	23.5	.9252
2.8	.1102	6.	.2362	9.2	.3622	24.	.9449
2.9	.1142	6.1	.2402	9.25	.3642	24.5	.9646
3.	.1181	6.2	.2441	9.3	.3661	25.	.9843
3.1	.1220	6.25	.2461	9.4	.3701		

DECIMAL AND METRIC EQUIVALENTS

INCHES — FRACTIONS	DECIMALS	MILLIMETERS	INCHES — FRACTIONS	DECIMALS	MILLIMETERS
	.00394	.1	15/32	.46875	11.9063
	.00787	.2		.47244	12.00
	.01181	.3	31/64	.484375	12.3031
1/64	.015625	.3969	1/2	.5000	12.70
	.01575	.4		.51181	13.00
	.01969	.5	33/64	.515625	13.0969
	.02362	.6	17/32	.53125	13.4938
	.02756	.7	35/64	.546875	13.8907
1/32	.03125	.7938		.55118	14.00
	.0315	.8	9/16	.5625	14.2875
	.03543	.9	37/64	.578125	14.6844
	.03937	1.00		.59055	15.00
3/64	.046875	1.1906	19/32	.59375	15.0813
1/16	.0625	1.5875	39/64	.609375	15.4782
5/64	.078125	1.9844	5/8	.625	15.875
	.07874	2.00		.62992	16.00
3/32	.09375	2.3813	41/64	.640625	16.2719
7/64	.109375	2.7781	21/32	.65625	16.6688
	.11811	3.00		.66929	17.00
1/8	.125	3.175	43/64	.671875	17.0657
9/64	.140625	3.5719	11/16	.6875	17.4625
5/32	.15625	3.9688	45/64	.703125	17.8594
	.15748	4.00		.70866	18.00
11/64	.171875	4.3656	23/32	.71875	18.2563
3/16	.1875	4.7625	47/64	.734375	18.6532
	.19685	5.00		.74803	19.00
13/64	.203125	5.1594	3/4	.7500	19.05
7/32	.21875	5.5563	49/64	.765625	19.4469
15/64	.234375	5.9531	25/32	.78125	19.8438
	.23622	6.00		.7874	20.00
1/4	.2500	6.35	51/64	.796875	20.2407
17/64	.265625	6.7469	13/16	.8125	20.6375
	.27559	7.00		.82677	21.00
9/32	.28125	7.1438	53/64	.828125	21.0344
19/64	.296875	7.5406	27/32	.84375	21.4313
5/16	.3125	7.9375	55/64	.859375	21.8282
	.31496	8.00		.86614	22.00
21/64	.328125	8.3344	7/8	.875	22.225
11/32	.34375	8.7313	57/64	.890625	22.6219
	.35433	9.00		.90551	23.00
23/64	.359375	9.1281	29/32	.90625	23.0188
3/8	.375	9.525	59/64	.921875	23.4157
25/64	.390625	9.9219	15/16	.9375	23.8125
	.3937	10.00		.94488	24.00
13/32	.40625	10.3188	61/64	.953125	24.2094
27/64	.421875	10.7156	31/32	.96875	24.6063
	.43307	11.00		.98425	25.00
7/16	.4375	11.1125	63/64	.984375	25.0032
29/64	.453125	11.5094	1	1.0000	25.4001

UNIFIED STANDARD SCREW THREAD SERIES

SIZES Primary	SIZES Secondary	BASIC MAJOR DIAMETER	Series with graded pitches Coarse UNC	Fine UNF	Extra fine UNEF	4UN	6UN	8UN	12UN	16UN	20UN	28UN	32UN	SIZES
0		0.0600	—	80	—	—	—	—	—	—	—	—	—	0
	1	0.0730	64	72	—	—	—	—	—	—	—	—	—	1
2		0.0860	56	64	—	—	—	—	—	—	—	—	—	2
	3	0.0990	48	56	—	—	—	—	—	—	—	—	—	3
4		0.1120	40	48	—	—	—	—	—	—	—	—	—	4
5		0.1250	40	44	—	—	—	—	—	—	—	—	—	5
6		0.1380	32	40	—	—	—	—	—	—	—	—	UNC	6
8		0.1640	32	36	—	—	—	—	—	—	—	—	UNC	8
10		0.1900	24	32	—	—	—	—	—	—	—	—	UNF	10
	12	0.2160	24	28	32	—	—	—	—	—	—	UNF	UNEF	12
1/4		0.2500	20	28	32	—	—	—	—	—	UNC	UNF	UNEF	1/4
5/16		0.3125	18	24	32	—	—	—	—	—	20	28	UNEF	5/16
3/8		0.3750	16	24	32	—	—	—	—	UNC	20	28	UNEF	3/8
7/16		0.4375	14	20	28	—	—	—	—	16	UNF	UNEF	32	7/16
1/2		0.5000	13	20	28	—	—	—	—	16	UNF	UNEF	32	1/2
9/16		0.5625	12	18	24	—	—	—	UNC	16	20	28	32	9/16
5/8		0.6250	11	18	24	—	—	—	12	16	20	28	32	5/8
	11/16	0.6875	—	—	24	—	—	—	12	16	20	28	32	11/16
3/4		0.7500	10	16	20	—	—	—	12	UNF	UNEF	28	32	3/4
	13/16	0.8125	—	—	20	—	—	—	12	16	UNEF	28	32	13/16
7/8		0.8750	9	14	20	—	—	—	12	16	UNEF	28	32	7/8
	15/16	0.9375	—	—	20	—	—	—	12	16	UNEF	28	32	15/16
1		1.0000	8	12	20	—	—	UNC	UNF	16	UNEF	28	32	1
	1 1/16	1.0625	—	—	18	—	—	8	12	16	20	28	—	1 1/16
1 1/8		1.1250	7	12	18	—	—	8	UNF	16	20	28	—	1 1/8
	1 3/16	1.1875	—	—	18	—	—	8	12	16	20	28	—	1 3/16
1 1/4		1.2500	7	12	18	—	—	8	UNF	16	20	28	—	1 1/4
	1 5/16	1.3125	—	—	18	—	—	8	12	16	20	28	—	1 5/16
1 3/8		1.3750	6	12	18	—	UNC	8	UNF	16	20	28	—	1 3/8
	1 7/16	1.4375	—	—	18	—	6	8	12	16	20	28	—	1 7/16
1 1/2		1.5000	6	12	18	—	UNC	8	UNF	16	20	28	—	1 1/2
	1 9/16	1.5625	—	—	18	—	6	8	12	16	20	—	—	1 9/16
1 5/8		1.6250	—	—	18	—	6	8	12	16	20	—	—	1 5/8
	1 11/16	1.6875	—	—	18	—	6	8	12	16	20	—	—	1 11/16
1 3/4		1.7500	5	—	—	—	6	8	12	16	20	—	—	1 3/4
	1 13/16	1.8125	—	—	—	—	6	8	12	16	20	—	—	1 13/16
1 7/8		1.8750	—	—	—	—	6	8	12	16	20	—	—	1 7/8
	1 15/16	1.9375	—	—	—	—	6	8	12	16	20	—	—	1 15/16
2		2.0000	4 1/2	—	—	—	6	8	12	16	20	—	—	2
	2 1/8	2.1250	—	—	—	—	6	8	12	16	20	—	—	2 1/8
2 1/4		2.2500	4 1/2	—	—	—	6	8	12	16	20	—	—	2 1/4
	2 3/8	2.3750	—	—	—	—	6	8	12	16	20	—	—	2 3/8
2 1/2		2.5000	4	—	—	UNC	6	8	12	16	20	—	—	2 1/2
	2 5/8	2.6250	—	—	—	4	6	8	12	16	20	—	—	2 5/8
2 3/4		2.7500	4	—	—	UNC	6	8	12	16	20	—	—	2 3/4
	2 7/8	2.8750	—	—	—	4	6	8	12	16	20	—	—	2 7/8
3		3.0000	4	—	—	UNC	6	8	12	16	20	—	—	3
	3 1/8	3.1250	—	—	—	4	6	8	12	16	—	—	—	3 1/8
3 1/4		3.2500	4	—	—	UNC	6	8	12	16	—	—	—	3 1/4
	3 3/8	3.3750	—	—	—	4	6	8	12	16	—	—	—	3 3/8
3 1/2		3.5000	4	—	—	UNC	6	8	12	16	—	—	—	3 1/2
	3 5/8	3.6250	—	—	—	4	6	8	12	16	—	—	—	3 5/8
3 3/4		3.7500	4	—	—	UNC	6	8	12	16	—	—	—	3 3/4
	3 7/8	3.8750	—	—	—	4	6	8	12	16	—	—	—	3 7/8
4		4.0000	4	—	—	UNC	6	8	12	16	—	—	—	4
	4 1/8	4.1250	—	—	—	4	6	8	12	16	—	—	—	4 1/8
4 1/4		4.2500	—	—	—	4	6	8	12	16	—	—	—	4 1/4
	4 3/8	4.3750	—	—	—	4	6	8	12	16	—	—	—	4 3/8
4 1/2		4.5000	—	—	—	4	6	8	12	16	—	—	—	4 1/2
	4 5/8	4.6250	—	—	—	4	6	8	12	16	—	—	—	4 5/8
4 3/4		4.7500	—	—	—	4	6	8	12	16	—	—	—	4 3/4
	4 7/8	4.8750	—	—	—	4	6	8	12	—	—	—	—	4 7/8
5		5.0000	—	—	—	4	6	8	12	16	—	—	—	5
	5 1/8	5.1250	—	—	—	4	6	8	12	16	—	—	—	5 1/8
5 1/4		5.2500	—	—	—	4	6	8	12	16	—	—	—	5 1/4
	5 3/8	5.3750	—	—	—	4	6	8	12	16	—	—	—	5 3/8
5 1/2		5.5000	—	—	—	4	6	8	12	16	—	—	—	5 1/2
	5 5/8	5.6250	—	—	—	4	6	8	12	16	—	—	—	5 5/8
5 3/4		5.7500	—	—	—	4	6	8	12	16	—	—	—	5 3/4
	5 7/8	5.8750	—	—	—	4	6	8	12	16	—	—	—	5 7/8
6		6.0000	—	—	—	4	6	8	12	16	—	—	—	6

ISO METRIC SCREW THREAD STANDARD SERIES

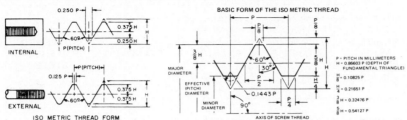

Nominal Size Diam. (mm)			Pitches (mm)														Nominal Size Diam. (mm)
Column a			Series With Graded Pitches		Series With Constant Pitches												
1	2	3	Coarse	Fine	6	4	3	2	1.5	1.25	1	0.75	0.5	0.35	0.25	0.2	
0.25			0.075	—	—	—	—	—	—	—	—	—	—	—	—	—	0.25
0.3			0.08	—	—	—	—	—	—	—	—	—	—	—	—	—	0.3
		0.35	0.09	—	—	—	—	—	—	—	—	—	—	—	—	—	0.35
0.4			0.1	—	—	—	—	—	—	—	—	—	—	—	—	—	0.4
	0.45		0.1	—	—	—	—	—	—	—	—	—	—	—	—	—	0.45
0.5			0.125	—	—	—	—	—	—	—	—	—	—	—	—	—	0.5
	0.55		0.125	—	—	—	—	—	—	—	—	—	—	—	—	—	0.55
0.6			0.15	—	—	—	—	—	—	—	—	—	—	—	—	—	0.6
	0.7		0.175	—	—	—	—	—	—	—	—	—	—	—	—	—	0.7
0.8			0.2	—	—	—	—	—	—	—	—	—	—	—	—	—	0.8
	0.9		0.225	—	—	—	—	—	—	—	—	—	—	—	—	—	0.9
1			0.25	—	—	—	—	—	—	—	—	—	—	—	—	0.2	1
	1.1		0.25	—	—	—	—	—	—	—	—	—	—	—	—	0.2	1.1
1.2			0.25	—	—	—	—	—	—	—	—	—	—	—	—	0.2	1.2
	1.4		0.3	—	—	—	—	—	—	—	—	—	—	—	—	0.2	1.4
1.6			0.35	—	—	—	—	—	—	—	—	—	—	—	—	0.2	1.6
	1.8		0.35	—	—	—	—	—	—	—	—	—	—	—	—	0.2	1.8
2			0.4	—	—	—	—	—	—	—	—	—	—	—	0.25	—	2
	2.2		0.45	—	—	—	—	—	—	—	—	—	—	—	0.25	—	2.2
2.5			0.45	—	—	—	—	—	—	—	—	—	—	0.35	—	—	2.5
3			0.5	—	—	—	—	—	—	—	—	—	—	0.35	—	—	3
	3.5		0.6	—	—	—	—	—	—	—	—	—	—	0.35	—	—	3.5
4			0.7	—	—	—	—	—	—	—	—	—	0.5	—	—	—	4
	4.5		0.75	—	—	—	—	—	—	—	—	—	0.5	—	—	—	4.5
5			0.8	—	—	—	—	—	—	—	—	—	0.5	—	—	—	5
		5.5	—	—	—	—	—	—	—	—	—	—	0.5	—	—	—	5.5
6			1	—	—	—	—	—	—	—	—	0.75	—	—	—	—	6
		7	1	—	—	—	—	—	—	—	—	0.75	—	—	—	—	7
8			1.25	1	—	—	—	—	—	—	1	0.75	—	—	—	—	8
		9	1.25	1	—	—	—	—	—	—	1	0.75	—	—	—	—	9
10			1.5	1.25	—	—	—	—	—	1.25	1	0.75	—	—	—	—	10
		11	1.5	—	—	—	—	—	—	—	1	0.75	—	—	—	—	11
12			1.75	1.25	—	—	—	—	1.5	1.25	1	—	—	—	—	—	12
	14		2	1.5	—	—	—	—	1.5	1.25 b	1	—	—	—	—	—	14
		15	—	—	—	—	—	—	1.5	—	1	—	—	—	—	—	15
16			2	1.5	—	—	—	—	1.5	—	1	—	—	—	—	—	16
		17	—	—	—	—	—	—	1.5	—	1	—	—	—	—	—	17
	18		2.5	1.5	—	—	—	2	1.5	—	1	—	—	—	—	—	18
20			2.5	1.5	—	—	—	2	1.5	—	1	—	—	—	—	—	20
	22		2.5	1.5	—	—	—	2	1.5	—	1	—	—	—	—	—	22
24			3	2	—	—	—	2	1.5	—	1	—	—	—	—	—	24
		25	—	—	—	—	—	2	1.5	—	1	—	—	—	—	—	25
		26	—	—	—	—	—	—	1.5	—	1	—	—	—	—	—	26
	27		3	2	—	—	—	2	1.5	—	1	—	—	—	—	—	27
		28	—	—	—	—	—	2	1.5	—	1	—	—	—	—	—	28
30			3.5	2	—	—	(3)	2	1.5	—	1	—	—	—	—	—	30
		32	—	—	—	—	—	2	1.5	—	—	—	—	—	—	—	32
	33		3.5	2	—	—	(3)	2	1.5	—	—	—	—	—	—	—	33
		35 c	—	—	—	—	—	—	1.5	—	—	—	—	—	—	—	35 c
36			4	3	—	—	—	2	1.5	—	—	—	—	—	—	—	36
		38	—	—	—	—	—	—	1.5	—	—	—	—	—	—	—	38
	39		4	3	—	—	—	2	1.5	—	—	—	—	—	—	—	39
		40	—	—	—	—	3	2	1.5	—	—	—	—	—	—	—	40
42			4.5	3	—	4	3	2	1.5	—	—	—	—	—	—	—	42
	45		4.5	3	—	4	3	2	1.5	—	—	—	—	—	—	—	45

a Thread diameter should be selected from columns 1, 2 or 3; with preference being given in that order.
b Pitch 1.25 mm in combination with diameter 14 mm has been included for spark plug applications.
c Diameter 35 mm has been included for bearing locknut applications.
The use of pitches shown in parentheses should be avoided wherever possible.
The pitches enclosed in the bold frame, together with the corresponding nominal diameters in Columns 1 and 2, are those combinations which have been established by ISO Recommendations as a selected "coarse" and "fine" series for commercial fasteners. Sizes 0.25 mm through 1.4 mm are covered in ISO Recommendation R 68 and, except for the 0.25 mm size, in AN Standard ANSI B1.10.   (ANSI)

SHEET METAL AND WIRE GAGE DESIGNATION

GAGE NO.	AMERICAN OR BROWN & SHARPE'S A.W.G. OR B. & S.	BIRMING-HAM OR STUBS WIRE B.W.G.	WASHBURN & MOEN OR AMERICAN S.W.G.	UNITED STATES STANDARD	MANU-FACTURERS' STANDARD FOR SHEET STEEL	GAGE NO.
0000000	- - - -	- - - -	.4900	.500	- - - -	0000000
000000	.5800	- - - -	.4615	.469	- - - -	000000
00000	.5165	- - - -	.4305	.438	- - - -	00000
0000	.4600	.454	.3938	.406	- - - -	0000
000	.4096	.425	.3625	.375	- - - -	000
00	.3648	.380	.3310	.344	- - - -	00
0	.3249	.340	.3065	.312	- - - -	0
1	.2893	.300	.2830	.281	- - - -	1
2	.2576	.284	.2625	.266	- - - -	2
3	.2294	.259	.2437	.250	.2391	3
4	.2043	.238	.2253	.234	.2242	4
5	.1819	.220	.2070	.219	.2092	5
6	.1620	.203	.1920	.203	.1943	6
7	.1443	.180	.1770	.188	.1793	7
8	.1285	.165	.1620	.172	.1644	8
9	.1144	.148	.1483	.156	.1495	9
10	.1019	.134	.1350	.141	.1345	10
11	.0907	.120	.1205	.125	.1196	11
12	.0808	.109	.1055	.109	.1046	12
13	.0720	.095	.0915	.0938	.0897	13
14	.0642	.083	.0800	.0781	.0747	14
15	.0571	.072	.0720	.0703	.0673	15
16	.0508	.065	.0625	.0625	.0598	16
17	.0453	.058	.0540	.0562	.0538	17
18	.0403	.049	.0475	.0500	.0478	18
19	.0359	.042	.0410	.0438	.0418	19
20	.0320	.035	.0348	.0375	.0359	20
21	.0285	.032	.0317	.0344	.0329	21
22	.0253	.028	.0286	.0312	.0299	22
23	.0226	.025	.0258	.0281	.0269	23
24	.0201	.022	.0230	.0250	.0239	24
25	.0179	.020	.0204	.0219	.0209	25
26	.0159	.018	.0181	.0188	.0179	26
27	.0142	.016	.0173	.0172	.0164	27
28	.0126	.014	.0162	.0156	.0149	28
29	.0113	.013	.0150	.0141	.0135	29
30	.0100	.012	.0140	.0125	.0120	30
31	.0089	.010	.0132	.0109	.0105	31
32	.0080	.009	.0128	.0102	.0097	32
33	.0071	.008	.0118	.00938	.0090	33
34	.0063	.007	.0104	.00859	.0082	34
35	.0056	.005	.0095	.00781	.0075	35
36	.0050	.004	.0090	.00703	.0067	36
37	.0045	- - - -	.0085	.00624	.0064	37
38	.0040	- - - -	.0080	.00625	.0060	38
39	.0035	- - - -	.0075	- - - - -	- - - -	39
40	.0031	- - - -	.0070	- - - - -	- - - -	40
41	.0028	- - - -	.0066	- - - - -	- - - -	41
42	.0025	- - - -	.0062	- - - - -	- - - -	42
43	.0022	- - - -	.0060	- - - - -	- - - -	43
44	.0020	- - - -	.0058	- - - - -	- - - -	44
45	.0018	- - - -	.0055	- - - - -	- - - -	45
46	.0016	- - - -	.0052	- - - - -	- - - -	46
47	.0014	- - - -	.0050	- - - - -	- - - -	47
48	.0012	- - - -	.0048	- - - - -	- - - -	48

GEOMETRIC DIMENSIONING AND TOLERANCING SYMBOLS

SYMBOL FOR:	ANSI Y14.5M	ASME Y14.5M	ISO
STRAIGHTNESS	—	—	—
FLATNESS	▱	▱	▱
CIRCULARITY	○	○	○
CYLINDRICITY	⌭	⌭	⌭
PROFILE OF A LINE	⌒	⌒	⌒
PROFILE OF A SURFACE	⌓	⌓	⌓
ALL AROUND	⟲	⟲	⟲ (proposed)
ANGULARITY	∠	∠	∠
PERPENDICULARITY	⊥	⊥	⊥
PARALLELISM	//	//	//
POSITION	⊕	⊕	⊕
CONCENTRICITY	◎	◎	◎
SYMMETRY	NONE	=	=
CIRCULAR RUNOUT	*↗	*↗	↗
TOTAL RUNOUT	*↗↗	*↗↗	↗↗
AT MAXIMUM MATERIAL CONDITION	Ⓜ	Ⓜ	Ⓜ
AT LEAST MATERIAL CONDITION	Ⓛ	Ⓛ	Ⓛ
REGARDLESS OF FEATURE SIZE	Ⓢ	NONE	NONE
PROJECTED TOLERANCE ZONE	Ⓟ	Ⓟ	Ⓟ
TANGENT PLANE	Ⓣ	Ⓣ	NONE
FREE STATE	Ⓕ	Ⓕ	Ⓕ
DIAMETER	∅	∅	∅
BASIC DIMENSION	50	50	50
REFERENCE DIMENSION	(50)	(50)	(50)
DATUM FEATURE	−A−	*⟁Ⓐ	*⟁ or *⟁Ⓐ
DIMENSION ORIGIN	⊕→	⊕→	⊕→
FEATURE CONTROL FRAME	⊕ ∅ 0.5 Ⓜ A B C	⊕ ∅ 0.5 Ⓜ A B C	⊕ ∅ 0.5 Ⓜ A B C
CONICAL TAPER	▷	▷	▷
SLOPE	◁	◁	◁
COUNTERBORE/SPOTFACE	⌴	⌴	NONE
COUNTERSINK	⌵	⌵	NONE
DEPTH/DEEP	↧	↧	NONE
SQUARE	□	□	□
DIMENSION NOT TO SCALE	15	15	15
NUMBER OF TIMES/PLACES	8X	8X	8X
ARC LENGTH	⌒105⌒	⌒105⌒	⌒105⌒
RADIUS	R	R	R
SPHERICAL RADIUS	SR	SR	SR
SPHERICAL DIAMETER	S∅	S∅	S∅
CONTROLLED RADIUS	NONE	CR	NONE
BETWEEN	NONE	*↔	NONE
STATISTICAL TOLERANCE	NONE	⟨ST⟩	NONE
DATUM TARGET	∅6/A1	∅6/A1 or ∅6/A1	∅6/A1 or ∅6/A1
TARGET POINT	✕	✕	✕

* MAY BE FILLED OR NOT FILLED

Appendix I
CD-ROM Contents

When working with AutoCAD LT (or any other CAD program for that matter), an effort should be made to be as productive as possible within the capabilities and limitations of the program. This CD-ROM contains a variety of "tools" that can be used to enhance your productivity efforts. In addition, demos of several programs that can enhance your productivity and maximize your efforts are included on the disc.

The CD-ROM is organized into separate directories, each containing a README.TXT file that describes the installation and use of the program(s) in that particular directory. (You can access the README.TXT files from Windows 3.x Notepad.) The following list indicates the names of the directories and provides a brief description of the contents of each:

Directory	Description
ARCHNOTE	Contains typical architectural notes and symbols, which can be incorporated into drawings. Also includes an architectural font.
BONUS	Includes a variety of sample drawings that were created with AutoCAD and AutoCAD LT.
CADSYM	Contains a demonstration program, which includes electrical and fluid power symbols.
CREATCAD	Provides several different fonts.
MNU&BUTT	Includes a compilation of buttons, toolbars, and menus found in AutoCAD LT.
MNU_UTIL	Includes several subdirectories, which contain a variety of AutoCAD LT menu enhancements.
PROTOTYP	Provides several prototype drawing files, which can be used to expedite drawing setup for A-size through E-size drawings.
TITLBLOC	Contains a variety of title blocks and borders for A-size through E-size drawings.
RXHIGHLI	Includes a working version of a "redlining" program and several sample drawings from manufacturers.
VIACAD1	Contains over 70 electrical symbols, which can be used in the development of electrical/electronic schematics.
VIACAD2	Includes a self-paced demo of a program used to create printed circuit board (PCB) artwork.
VIADEV	Contains a self-running demo, which shows how the process of electrical controls can be automated.

The Goodheart-Willcox Company, Inc., and the author make no warranty or representation whatsoever, either expressed or implied, with respect to any of the software or applications described or referred to herein, their quality, performance, merchantability, or fitness, for a particular purpose.

Further, The Goodheart-Willcox Company, Inc., and the author specifically disclaim any liability whatsoever for direct, indirect, special, incidental, or consequential damages arising out of the use or inability to use the software of applications described or referred to herein.

C

P

Pan button, 108, 109
PAN command, 103, 108, 109, 116, 492, 494, 496, 510, 571
Paper Size subdialog box, 406, 407
Paper space, *44, 477*
Paper Space,
    button, 551
    tutorial, 485–499
PASTE command, 640
PASTECLIP command, 611, 613, 619, 640
PDMODE, 212, 213
PDSIZE, 212
PEDIT command, 295–304, 394, 426
Pen assignments, 403, 404
Pen Assignments subdialog box, 403, 404
Pen Parameters area, 403
PICKADD system variable, 95
PICKAUTO system variable, 90, 95
Pickbox, *85*, 86
PICKBOX command, 85, 95
PICKDRAG system variable, 95
PICKFIRST system variable, 90, 94
PLAN command, 536
PLINE command, 32, 172, 174–177 , 376
PLINEGEN system variable, 303
PLINEWID system variable, 182
PLOT command, 20, 399–411, 413
Plot Configuration dialog box, 20, 399, 400, 403–410, 412, 527, 582
Plot parameters,
    saving and reusing, 402
Plot Preview dialog box, 409
Plot scale,
    setting, 408, 409
Plotting a drawing, 399–414
    exporting in postscript format, 413
    PLOT command, 399–411
    plotting to a raster file, 411, 412
POINT command, 196, 210
Point filters 202–205
    using point filters, 202, 203
    using X and Y point filters to project
        views and view features, 203–205
Point style and size,
    setting in dialog box, 210–212
Point Style dialog box, 211
Points, 210–213
Polar array,
    creating, 292, 293
Polar coordinate system, *81*

Polar coordinates, 81, 82
Polyarc options, 175, 176
Polygon,
    drawing by center and radius, 180
    drawing by specifying length of edge, 180
Polygon button, 179
POLYGON command, 179
POLYGON edge option, 180
Polyline button, 172
POLYLINE command, 231, 295
Polyline editing, 295–304
Polyline option, 184, 187
Polyline tutorial, 174
PostScript, *252*
Postscript format,
    exporting, 413
Precision: drop-down list, 45
Preferences, 542–547
Preferences dialog box, 61, 542–546, 548, 563, 571, 604
Preview options,
    Full, 409
    Partial, 409
Print Setup dialog box, 401, 405
Print/Plot button, 20, 399
Program group, *15*
Program Item Properties dialog box elements, 558
Program Manager,
    starting AutoCAD LT, 16–19
PS command, 479
PSOUT command, 413
PSPACE command, 479
Pull-down menu tutorial,
    creating new, 569–571
PURGE command, 150, 421, 429
    compressing drawing, 421, 422

Q

QSAVE command, 626
QTEXT command, 249, 250
QUAdrant object snap mode, 204
QUAdrant osnap, 199
Quick Drawing Setup subdialog box, 40–43
Quit button, 34

R

Radial dimensions, 347–351
    diameter dimensions, 348–350

drawing center marks and centerlines, 347, 348

radius dimensions, 350, 351

RADIUS command, 348, 350, 351

Radius dimensions, 350, 351

Random access memory (RAM), *15*

Raster file, *411*

plotting to , 411, 412

Ray casting, *384*

Ray detection, island detection, 384

Real Time button, 113

RECRIPT command, 508

RECTANG command, 178, 203

Rectangle button, 178

Rectangles, drawing, 178, 179

Rectangular array,

creating, 290–294

polar array, 292–294

Redo button, 21, 97

REDO command, 96–98

Redraw button, 110

Reference options, 309

Referenced, *418*

RENAME command, 120, 147, 260, 629

Rename dialog box, 119, 146

RESCRIPT command, 512

RESTORE command, 369

RESUME command, 508

REVDATE command, 51, 544

Right option, 168, 245, 362

Right-hand rule, 517, 518

RN command, 120

ROMANS command, 254

ROTATE command, 276, 278, 309

ROTATE Reference option, 278

Rotate Text from **Edit Dimension** cascading submenu, 362

ROTATED command, 325, 329

Rotated dimensions, 329

Rotating around reference point, 277

Rotating objects,

modifying the drawing, 276–279

rotating around reference point, 277

using **Reference** option, 277–279

Rotating using **Reference** option, 277–279

Rotation option, 163, 164

Round, *185*

Rounds,

and fillets, 185–187

RSCRIPT command, 508

Rubberband, *71*

Running object snap, *199*–201

S

Save button, 20

SAVE command, 369

SAVE command **?** option, 369

Save DIB dialog box, 606

Save Drawing As dialog box, 20, 24, 60, 66

Save to File subdialog box, 402

Save toolbar button, 60

SAVEAS command, 59, 60, 63, 471, 627

Saved view,

renaming, 119, 120

SAVEDIB command, 605, 640

SAVETIME system variable, 61, 543

Scale and Colors subdialog box, 323, 324

SCALE command, 279, 280, 309

Scale XP option, 108

Scale, Rotation, and Origin area, 408

Scaling,

accuracy, 69, 70

Scaling objects, 279–281

scaling entire drawing, 280, 281

using **Reference** option, 280

with known scale factor, 279, 280

Screen colors and named entities in embedded drawings, 627

SCRIPT command, 507, 511

Script commands, 508

Script file, *503*

Script files, 506–508

running script file, 507

script commands, 508

Scroll bars, 24

Search,

using, 31, 32

Search path, building, 65

Select Color subdialog box, 129, 130, 143, 148, 150, 324

Select Drawing File dialog box, 422, 424

Select DXF File dialog box, 641

Select File to Attach dialog box, 451, 452

Select Font File dialog box, 465

Select Initial View option, 63, 119

Select Linetype File dialog box, 131, 136

Select Script File dialog box, 507, 511, 512

Select Slide File dialog box, 510

Select Template File dialog box, 449

Select Text Font dialog box, 255, 571

Selection set, *84*

options, 86–94

Selections Modes, 94

Set UCS button, 531